T0271053

The Economics of Urban Transportation

This new edition of the seminal textbook *The Economics of Urban Transportation* incorporates the latest research affecting the design, implementation, pricing, and control of transport systems in towns and cities. The book offers an economic framework for understanding the societal impacts and policy implications of many factors including congestion, traffic safety, climate change, air quality, COVID-19, and newly important developments such as ride-hailing services, electric vehicles, and autonomous vehicles.

Rigorous in approach and making use of real-world data and econometric techniques, the third edition features a new chapter on the special challenges of managing the energy that powers transportation systems. It provides fully updated coverage of well-known topics and a rigorous treatment of new ones.

All of the basic topics needed to apply economics to urban transportation are included:

- Forecasting demand for transportation services under various conditions;
- Measuring costs, including those incurred by users and incorporating two new tools to describe congestion in dense urban areas;
- Setting prices under practical constraints;
- Evaluating infrastructure investments;
- Understanding how private and public sectors interact to provide services.

Written by three of the field's leading researchers, *The Economics of Urban Transportation* is essential reading for students, researchers, and practicing professionals in transportation economics, planning, engineering, or related disciplines. With a focus on workable models that can be adapted to future needs, it provides tools for a rapidly changing world.

Kenneth A. Small is Professor Emeritus of Economics at the University of California at Irvine, USA.

Erik T. Verhoef is Professor of Spatial Economics at VU Amsterdam, the Netherlands.

Robin Lindsey is Professor in the Operations and Logistics Division at the Sauder School of Business, University of British Columbia, Canada.

The Economics of Urban Transportation

Third Edition

Kenneth A. Small, Erik T. Verhoef, and Robin Lindsey

Routledge
Taylor & Francis Group

LONDON AND NEW YORK

Designed cover image: Getty Images

Third edition published 2024
by Routledge
4 Park Square, Milton Park, Abingdon, Oxon, OX14 4RN

and by Routledge
605 Third Avenue, New York, NY 10158

Routledge is an imprint of the Taylor & Francis Group, an informa business

© 2024 Kenneth A. Small, Erik T. Verhoef and Robin Lindsey

The right of Kenneth A. Small, Erik T. Verhoef, and Robin Lindsey to be identified as authors of this work has been asserted in accordance with sections 77 and 78 of the Copyright, Designs and Patents Act 1988.

All rights reserved. No part of this book may be reprinted or reproduced or utilised in any form or by any electronic, mechanical, or other means, now known or hereafter invented, including photocopying and recording, or in any information storage or retrieval system, without permission in writing from the publishers.

Trademark notice: Product or corporate names may be trademarks or registered trademarks, and are used only for identification and explanation without intent to infringe.

First edition published by Routledge 1992
Second edition published by Routledge 2007

British Library Cataloguing-in-Publication Data
A catalogue record for this book is available from the British Library

Library of Congress Cataloging-in-Publication Data
Names: Small, Kenneth A., author. | Verhoef, E. T., author. |
Lindsey, Robin, 1955– author.
Title: The economics of urban transportation / Kenneth A. Small,
Erik T. Verhoef and Robin Lindsey.
Description: Third edition. | Abingdon, Oxon; New York, NY: Routledge, 2024. |
Includes bibliographical references and index.
Identifiers: LCCN 2023055755 | ISBN 9781032706696 (hardback) |
ISBN 9781138069053 (paperback) | ISBN 9781315157375 (ebook)
Subjects: LCSH: Urban transportation. | Urban transportation—Research. |
Transportation, Automotive.
Classification: LCC HE305 .S585 2024 | DDC 388.4—dc23/eng/20240221
LC record available at https://lccn.loc.gov/2023055755

ISBN: 978-1-032-70669-6 (hbk)
ISBN: 978-1-138-06905-3 (pbk)
ISBN: 978-1-315-15737-5 (ebk)

DOI: 10.4324/9781315157375

Typeset in Times New Roman
by codeMantra

This book is dedicated to the memory of Richard Arnott

Contents

Acknowledgments

We are indebted to Joshua Linn, Eric Miller, David Ory, Ian Parry, James Sallee, and Kenneth Train for comments and advice on draft portions of this third edition. In addition, we thank the many people who have provided suggestions and answered questions related to earlier editions of this book. They include Alex Anas, Richard Arnott, John Bates, David Brownstone, Xuehao Chu, Bruno De Borger, André de Palma, John Dodgson, Gordon J. Fielding, Stephenie Frederick, Marc Gaudry, Stephen Glaister, Amihai Glazer, David Hensher, Sergio Jara-Díaz, Marvin Kraus, Charles Lave, Herbert Mohring, Juan de Dios Ortúzar, Ian Parry, Stef Proost, Seiji Steimetz, Kenneth Train, Kurt Van Dender, and Clifford Winston. We also are grateful for assistance in editing to Sandra Binnendijk, Amanda Lindsey, and Lynn Long. Of course, none of these people share responsibility for any deficiencies.

We want especially to honor the contributions of Richard Arnott, who commissioned the original 1992 edition as editor of the Regional and Urban Economics section of the series, *Fundamentals of Pure and Applied Economics*. Richard was an exemplary colleague, critic, and friend of us as well as many others in the economics profession, not to mention his own extensive and path-breaking contributions to the fields of urban economics, transportation economics, and public finance. We dedicate this book to his memory.

Selected symbols and abbreviations

Symbol	Meaning
$A(t)$	Cumulative queue-entries
a	Exponent in Cobb–Douglas utility function of goods and leisure; Parameter in BPR congestion function
ac	Average cost
B	Total benefits (willingness to pay including actual payments)
$B(q)$	Benefit function: marginal willingness to pay (function of outputs)
$B(t)$	Cumulative queue-exits (function of clock time)
b	Parameter (exponent) in BPR congestion function
C	Total cost
$\tilde{C}$	Long-run cost (when distinction with short-run is relevant)
C_B	Cost to bus agency
C_g	Congestion-related part of total cost, including capacity cost
$\tilde{C}_g$	Congestion-related part of long-run total cost, including capacity cost
C_W	Cost of waiting time to bus passengers
CRF	Capital recovery factor (annual)
c	Short-run average variable cost (SRAVC)
c_0	SRAVC on an uncongested road
c_{00}	SRAVC on an uncongested road exclusive of the value of free-flow travel time
c_1-c_5	Other cost parameters (definition may vary with context)
c_b, c_p	Cost per vehicle-mile of base and peak bus service, respectively
c_{bpr}, c_{bot}	Short-hand (derived) cost parameters in analytical long-run highway cost analysis
c_g	Congestion-related part of SRAVC
$\bar{c}_g$	Time-averaged equilibrium SRAVC in dynamic models
c_l	SRAVC on link l of a network
c_S, c_T	Parts of congestion-related SRAVC attributable to schedule delay and travel time (*i.e.*, queuing delay), respectively
$\bar{c}_S, \bar{c}_T$	Parts of congestion-related time-averaged SRAVC attributable to schedule delay and travel time (*i.e.*, queuing delay), respectively
cdf	Cumulative distribution function
D	Density of vehicle traffic
D^i	Alternative-specific dummy variable for alternative i
D_j	Jam density

(*Continued*)

Symbol	Meaning
DL	Dummy variable equal to 1 for late arrival, 0 otherwise
D_m	Density consistent with maximum flow
d	Inverse demand function, giving generalized price as a function of quantity of travel (in highway cost analysis); Average passenger trip length (in transit cost analysis)
d_{jn}	Choice variable ($=1$ if decision-maker n chooses alternative j)
d_m	Inverse demand function for market m (defined by an origin–destination pair)
E	Fuel efficiency
e, exp	Exponential function
F	Fuel consumption
$F(t)$	Cumulative desired queue-exits
G	Function for generating GEV models of discrete-choice
GEV	Generalized extreme value
H	Number of time periods per weekday
h	Time period
I_r	Inclusive value for alternative group r
iid	Identically and independently distributed
J	Number of dependent variables (aggregate models) or alternatives (disaggregate models)
J_a	Delay parameter in Akçelik's travel time function
J_r	Number of alternatives in alternative group r
K	Capital cost (present value)
K_0	Fixed part of capital cost
K_1	Coefficient of capacity in variable part of capital cost
L	Leisure (in disaggregate demand analysis); Length of a road or trip (in cost analysis)
log	Natural logarithm
M	Motor vehicle ownership (in demand analysis); Motor vehicle usage (in energy tax analysis)
MB_K	Marginal benefit of capacity expansion
mc	Marginal cost
mec	Marginal external cost
$mecc$	Marginal external congestion cost
N	Total number of people a bus can pick up and drop off along its entire route, equal to bus capacity times length of route divided by average passenger trip length (in bus cost analysis); Number of vehicles in queue (in highway congestion analysis)
n	Bus capacity
P	Price vector of other goods (in aggregate demand analysis); Choice probability (in disaggregate demand analysis); Inflow period (in duration dependent congestion functions)
PV	Present value
p	Price of a good, or generalized price of travel to user
Q	Total number of travelers ($=qV_a$ or qV_d when V_a or V_d are constant)

(Continued)

Symbol	Meaning
q	Output (in general cost analysis);
	Bus passenger volume (in bus cost analysis);
	Duration of period of desired queue entries $= t_{p'} - t_p$ (in highway queuing analysis)
$\mathbf{q}$	Vector of durations of different time periods
R	Revenue
r	Interest rate
S	Speed
S_D	Schedule delay $(=t' - t_d)$
SDE	Schedule delay early
SDL	Schedule delay late
S_f	Free-flow speed
S_m	Speed consistent with maximum flow
s	Returns to scale: ratio of average to marginal cost
s_K	Returns to scale in producing highway capacity
s_n	Vector of socioeconomic or other characteristics of decision-maker n
T	Time (or vector of times) spent in activities;
	Travel Time (usually in-vehicle) if used as scalar without sub- or super-scripts
T^0	Out-of-vehicle travel time
T_0	Free-flow travel time
T_D	Queuing-delay portion of travel time
T_f	Free-flow travel time
t_i^k	kth travel time component on ith mode
T_w	Time spent at work (in value-of-time analysis)
t	Time of day (in queueing analysis)
t'	Time of queue exit
t_d	Desired time of queue exit (in queuing analysis);
	Departure time (in VOR analysis)
$t_p, t_{p'}$	Beginning and end of desired period of queue-exits
$t_q, t_{q'}$	Beginning and end of actual period of queue-exits
t^*	Time for which actual and desired queue-exit times coincide
$\tilde{t}$	Queue-entry time leading to maximum queuing delay
U	Utility function
V	Indirect utility function (in travel demand analysis);
	Volume (flow) of vehicle traffic (vehicles per hour) (in highway cost analysis);
	Frequency of transit service (vehicles per hour) (in transit cost analysis)
$\mathbf{V}$	Vector of vehicle flows in different time periods
V_a	Rate (volume) of actual entries to queue (vehicles per hour)
V_b	Rate (volume) of actual exits from bottleneck (vehicles per hour)
V_d	Rate (volume) of desired exits from bottleneck (vehicles per hour)
V_h	Volume (flow) of vehicle traffic during time period h
V_i	Rate (volume) of entries to road or area
V_o	Rate (volume) of exits from road or area
V_K	Capacity of highway or bottleneck (vehicles per hour)
$V_l (V_r)$	Flow of traffic on link l (route r) of a network

(Continued)

Symbol	Meaning
v_T	Value of time (usually in-vehicle time)
W	Welfare measure (usually consumer surplus);
	Aggregate waiting time (in transit cost analysis)
w	Wage rate (in travel demand analysis);
	Input price vector (in general cost function analysis);
	Width of a road (in speed–flow functions)
X	Vector of other goods or a single generalized consumption good
x	Consumption good or vector of goods (in demand analysis);
	Input vector (in general cost function analysis)
	Physical location (in congestion analysis)
x_n	Fixed input in short-run cost function (in cost analysis);
	Location of nth vehicle (in car-following model)
Y	Unearned income
y	Total income (in aggregate demand analysis);
	Generalized argument for function G generating GEV models (in disaggregate demand analysis)
Z	Characteristics of travel choices and travelers
z	Independent variables for travel demand models
α	Lagged adjustment parameter (in lagged adjustment analysis);
	Value of travel time (in highway cost analysis)
α_i	Alternative-specific constant for alternative i in discrete-choice indirect utility function
β	Parameter vector in demand function (in travel demand analysis);
	Shadow price of schedule delay early (in highway cost analysis);
	Dilution factor to convert mileage-based external costs to fuel-based external costs (in optimal fuel tax analysis)
γ	Shadow price of schedule delay late
γ_i	Coefficient of an independent variable interacted with an alternative-specific constant for alternative i in discrete-choice utility function
δ	$\beta\gamma/(\beta+\gamma)$ (in highway cost analysis);
	Reaction time (in car-following models)
δ_{lr}	Dummy variable indicating route-link incidence (=1 if link l is part of route r)
δ_{rm}	Dummy variable indicating route-market incidence (=1 if route r can serve market m)
ε	Error term
ε_h	Elasticity of demand in period h
ε_i	Stochastic term for alternative i in discrete-choice indirect utility function
Θ	Meta-parameters describing densities of random parameters
θ	Parameter vector (in general cost function analysis);
	Fixed cost of arriving late (in highway cost analysis)
Λ	Lagrangian function
λ	Lagrange multiplier;
	Marginal utility of income
μ	Scale parameter for probability density function (in discrete-choice analysis);
	Lagrange multiplier (in value-of-time analysis)

(*Continued*)

Symbol	Meaning
Π	Profit
π	Annual rate of inflation
ρ	Parameter of GEV functions (in discrete-choice analysis); Capital recovery factor divided by number of weekdays per year (converts capital cost to an ongoing daily cost) (in cost analysis)
σ	Standard deviation (in statistical estimates); Parameter of GEV function ($=1-\rho$) (in travel demand analysis); Fraction of travelers exiting queue prior to t^* (in highway cost analysis)
τ	Congestion fee ($ per vehicle-mile or per passage; depending on context)
τ_L, τ_M, τ_F	Tax rates on labor, vehicle usage, and fuel
Φ	Cumulative normal distribution function
ϕ	Normal probability density function
ψ	Lagrange multiplier
ω	Weight on a representative individual when aggregating

1 Introduction

At the heart of all economic activity are interactions. People trade labor, ideas, and other services for cash, and cash for goods and services; firms trade technology, expertise, financial capacity, intermediate goods, administrative functions, and many other things with each other, with individuals, and with governments. All these transactions require communications. Most also require transportation of goods or people – to work, shopping, tourist sites, meeting locations – either directly for the transaction itself or indirectly to build trust to make the transaction viable. Thus, transportation is central to economic activity.

Cities exist when there are special advantages to carrying out economic activities in proximity. These advantages are often called "economies of agglomeration," because costs are lower when certain groups of activities locate close to each other. The primary reason for economies of agglomeration is that, despite low communication costs, transportation costs are still significant and proximity reduces them. A corollary is that anything that reduces transportation costs within an urban area increases the extent to which its activities are easily linked to each other, thus taking further advantage of agglomeration economies. In a world of many competing urban centers, those with more efficient transportation systems have an advantage.

While well-functioning transportation systems are needed for contemporary societies to flourish, transportation also brings significant societal challenges. Concerns about pollution, energy use, safety, noise, land use, and congestion, to name just a few, have been prominent for decades and are only growing over time. Naturally, many of these concerns are larger where people and firms concentrate in space, as in the urban agglomerations just mentioned. The eventual functioning and outcomes of transportation systems are the combined results of complex interrelated interactions between many individuals and firms, for which spatial and temporal variations are often pronounced. The complexity of transportation systems is further magnified because interactions typically take place in networks, and because many different behavioral margins are at stake – including spatial decisions, mobility behavior, and technology choice. Thus, policymaking and the research needed to support it are challenging.

The study of transportation involves researchers trained in many disciplines, including engineering, economics, geography, planning, psychology, business, and regional science. Regardless of its disciplinary origin, transportation research has become increasingly sophisticated in its use of economics. This trend has brought a solid practical footing to policy analysis, by showing how the ideas and goals generated within various analytical frameworks can be reconciled with actual traveler behavior and with actual resource constraints.

This book reviews the contributions that economics can make to the analysis of urban transportation. It concentrates mainly, but not exclusively, on industrialized nations – although many of the principles are equally applicable to other places. This is especially true in light of the

DOI: 10.4324/9781315157375-1

ubiquitous rise in travel by private automobiles throughout the world. Because of the predominance of road transportation, we place heavy, though certainly not exclusive, emphasis on it in developing formal models.

1.1   The scope of urban transportation economics

The boundaries of transportation economics are neither well defined nor static. Nevertheless, readers are entitled to know what principles we use to limit the scope of our treatment. Aside from the inevitable one that we try to write about what we know best, the following observations are guidelines.

Being a branch of economics, transportation economics focuses on private and public decisions under conditions of scarcity, on resource allocation, and on how the interactions among independent agents bring about a self-consistent outcome. It draws from and interacts closely with transportation engineering, urban planning, management, public administration, and other disciplines; but it has a somewhat different emphasis. While engineering emphasizes facility design and implementation, economics emphasizes behavioral principles and resource allocation. The disciplines of management, public administration, and urban planning are concerned with creating workable transportation policies, for example by studying decision processes and organizational structures; an important role of economics is to inform these disciplines about the complex ways in which transportation policies exert their influence. Economics is especially well suited to predicting the ultimate results of behavioral shifts among interacting economic actors in response to policy implementations or exogenous events. It can also identify trade-offs between efficiency and other goals.

These orientations toward the subject give transportation economics certain characteristics that are evident in this book. Transportation economics tends to focus on models that illustrate concepts, as opposed to those whose output is the actual design of facilities or regulations. Hence, its models are usually at a coarse rather than a fine geographical scale, lending themselves to "sketch planning" of the broad features of a transportation system.

Analysis often proceeds by defining a demand structure and a supply structure for a set of goods or services, and then searching for an outcome that is consistent with both structures. This is a standard microeconomic approach, although the nature of transportation creates ambiguities in the boundary between demand and supply: For example, is the time required for a trip part of the cost, or is it better viewed as an attribute affecting demand? Either viewpoint is valid, so long as demand and cost are consistently defined as is done in Chapters 2 and 3. Their interconnection is made explicit in the discussion of travelers' valuations of time and other trip characteristics, especially in Section 2.7.

Demand and supply structures are complex, involving many types of people, modes, locations, and times. For this reason, finding a consistent solution – an equilibrium, in economics parlance – requires considerable analytical sophistication. A pioneering study by Beckmann *et al.* (1956) showed how to do this for arbitrary transportation networks, given certain assumptions. In the presence of increasing returns to scale and lack of efficient pricing (conditions which, as we shall see, often characterize urban transportation), this equilibrium may differ in drastic and surprising ways from a configuration satisfying optimality conditions. In other words, what happens when people make decisions out of self-interest is not necessarily what they would choose collectively and cooperatively. A common thread throughout this book is that transportation economics should provide the tools to understand and quantify such differences and to design policies that address them.

Three important types of policies to consider are pricing, investment, and industrial organization – the latter including regulations contingent on the form of organization. Analyses of pricing and investment have long been hallmarks of urban transportation economics, and they are given full treatment in Chapters 4 and 5. Industrial organization has likewise been of great concern, as can be seen from the serpentine course of political approaches to urban transportation throughout the world. These approaches continue to highlight questions of oligopolistic markets, regulation, and private versus public provision of services. Chapter 6 considers a number of these questions.

Transportation is a voracious consumer of energy, an aspect given great prominence by the issues of unreliable energy supplies and associated environmental costs, especially climate change. Chapter 7 – new to this edition of the book – considers the special policy challenges posed by managing the energy that powers transportation systems.

Transportation also affects the nature of the urban area itself. When the widespread availability of the automobile lowered transportation costs, it led to much less dense urban development patterns, a legacy that even now makes it harder to provide nonautomotive forms of transportation. The study of such phenomena is clearly germane to transportation policy. To analyze them fully requires complementary disciplines, such as urban geography, urban economics, and regional science, that seek to explain the shape of urban development. Important as this is, it is too ambitious for this book, and we limit ourselves to a brief summary in Section 2.1.6.

Modern economics pays a great deal of attention to information – its provision, acquisition, and especially its effects on behavior in situations of uncertainty. Transportation economics is no exception, and such analyses are important for dealing with current technological frontiers as well as pressing policy issues. We provide an introduction to the analysis of information in Section 3.4.5 and show both there and in Section 4.2.4 how its ideas are applied.

Economics is also becoming more explicit about the implications of simplifying assumptions that underlie any formal analysis – including those typical of economics, such as rational decision-making, full information, and equilibrium. Some models and empirical analyses we consider incorporate departures from such conventional assumptions – for example, attitudes and misperceptions in travel behavior (Sections 2.5 and 2.7.3), choices under limited information (Section 3.4.5), and disequilibrium behavior (Section 3.4.6). We consider some implications of simplifying human behavior, in both analysis and policy formation, in our treatment of travel demand (Section 2.2), and in our assessment of future research questions (Chapter 8).

1.2   The scope of this book

The aim of this book is to provide a self-contained introduction to major research themes in contemporary transportation economics. We have chosen to explore certain topics in great detail, in order to illustrate how the analysis can be put to practical use; others, we explore more briefly. In all cases, extensive citations provide the reader with opportunities to expand on any particular theme. Thus, we aim to make the book suitable both as an initial textbook for students with a good technical background, and as a reference work for practicing researchers and professionals.

Certain topics are especially salient at the time any book is written. In our case, the world's attention was recently consumed with the effects of the COVID-19 pandemic that struck in force in 2020. The pandemic has had strong impacts on transportation patterns, which are of uncertain permanence. Because we are most interested in providing tools for the long term, we refrain from taking strong positions on the many questions that are still up in the air. Rather, we illustrate the research issues they generate through some examples, and we attempt to extract lessons that are likely to be durable. For example, at the time of writing it is widely believed that some of the work that moved to virtual formats will remain that way, whether from home or from newly configured office environments. If so, it will greatly affect the use of central-city office buildings, hence commuting patterns and urban form. Forecasting such changes so soon after a huge global shock is hazardous, but the set of tools developed here is what is needed to evaluate the possible scenarios.

Analytically, a pandemic shares several features with congestion and environmental externalities – topics treated extensively here – as is argued, for example, by Ashworth *et al.* (2022). The pandemic also provides opportunities to take advantage of natural experiments to estimate other quantities – for example, we show in Section 2.8.6 how the brief lack of traffic congestion due to travel restrictions in early 2020 has been used to identify the desired arrival times of commuters.

Above all, we attempt to show how to construct a set of workable models that can be adapted, refined, and combined in subsequent research, however technology and economies evolve. In the sections on highway congestion, for example, the models presented incorporate critical features such as queuing, trip scheduling, peak shifting, and reliability, all of which are needed to describe evolving futures. These phenomena especially affect the design of congestion-relief policies, and methodological and computational advances continue to make analysis of such phenomena more tractable. It is our hope that such models will provide a common language for researchers, facilitating comparisons among theoretical innovations and among empirical applications.

Despite the importance of formal models, we believe economics is most valuable when grounded in a realistic quantitative understanding of the phenomena under study. Abstract modeling may be useful for developing concepts; but only when the equations are combined with data do they become part of a comprehensive toolkit. At the same time, data alone, without a theoretical framework, provide incomplete and possibly misleading answers. The upcoming chapters thus provide not only conceptual modeling, but quantitative data and estimates as well, thereby illustrating how to apply models concretely and giving a feel for actual magnitudes found in various situations. To cite just two examples: In Chapter 3, we develop estimates of the full marginal and average costs of travel by car in typical big-city commuting corridors in the United States; and in Chapter 5, we report on others' estimates of total costs and benefits of a large high-speed rail investment in Spain. Of course, results from these examples need not necessarily carry over to other situations.

Many new topics have emerged or gained more prominence in the 17 years since the publication of the previous edition of this book. We have already mentioned the role of energy, to which we now devote an entire chapter. We can mention here a few others that we now treat. The advent of ride-sourcing and other digitally based services affects travel demand modeling (Section 2.1.5), cost analysis, and analysis of regulatory policy (Section 6.3.6). Autonomous vehicles are considered throughout the book, taking account of their impacts on driving patterns, cost, congestion, pricing, and regulatory policy (Sections 2.1.5, 3.5.2, 4.3.5, and 6.3.6). We discuss electric cars and their effects (Section 3.5.3). Two new tools for analyzing congestion in dense urban areas, namely the Macroscopic Fundamental Diagram and "bathtub" models, are now described (Section 3.3.3). The increased availability of very large datasets – so-called "big data" – is altering economic analysis in important ways (Section 2.8). Our treatment of congestion-reduction policies now includes monetary rewards and tradeable permits (Section 4.2.5); it also includes additional political considerations, such as public acceptability and the choices made by competing governments (Section 4.6). This is just a sampling of new areas of policy and/or research that we consider.

Needless to say, new topics and further progress on current topics will continue to emerge. Our concluding chapter provides a preview of some developments that we expect to be prominent. We are confident that the approaches to analysis provided here will serve as a good basis for such future progress.

References

Ashworth, Madison, Todd L. Cherry, David Finnoff, Stephen C. Newbold, Jason F. Shogren, and Linda Thunström (2022), "COVID-19 research and policy analysis: Contributions from environmental economists," *Review of Environmental Economics and Policy* 16(1): 153-167.

Beckmann, Martin J., C. Bartlett McGuire and Christopher B. Winsten (1956) *Studies in the Economics of Transportation*, New Haven, CT: Yale University Press.

2 Travel demand

Managing transportation facilities requires a great deal of knowledge about how travelers will use them. In order to build them, forecasts are needed of how much travel they will attract. In order to price and operate them efficiently, an understanding is needed of how users respond to prices and to service characteristics. In order to evaluate whether a project is worthwhile at all, a measure is needed of the benefits it produces. All these requirements are in the province of travel-demand analysis.

The demand for travel takes place in a multidimensional setting. The traditional sequential framework, formerly used by most metropolitan transportation planning agencies, considers four choice dimensions: trip generation (the total number of trips originating from an area); trip distribution (the locations of the trips' destinations); modal choice (the means of travel, such as car, bus, train, bicycle, or walking); and trip assignment (the exact route used). These terms are still used, but usually within a more complex framework that includes feedback among these dimensions. More recently, researchers have paid greater attention to other dimensions of choice, such as residential and job location, automobile ownership, the time of day at which trips are taken, parking locations, scheduling of activities for which travel is undertaken, and intra-household decision processes.

These multiple decisions are often envisioned as a sequence, typically starting with residential and job locations, then vehicle ownership, and then other aspects. This sequence is in decreasing order of the time span over which the decision can be easily changed. However, it does not imply a sequential decision procedure whereby one decision is made without regard to its implications for later decisions. Rather, each decision is affected by others and as such can be fully understood only as part of a simultaneous choice process. A given study may isolate just a few of these decisions for tractability; it is then all the more important to remember, when interpreting results, that other decisions are lurking in the background.

Furthermore, travel is a derived demand, usually undertaken not for its own sake but rather to facilitate a spatially varied set of activities such as work, recreation, shopping, and home life. This observation links the study of travel demand to studies of labor supply, consumption patterns, logistics, urban development, household formation, and household activities. It also calls attention to the common practice of linking together several trip purposes into one integrated itinerary or *tour*, a process known as *trip chaining*.

The chapter begins (Section 2.1) by asking what can be learned from aggregate data about travel and how conventional economic demand theory is applied to such data. It then moves on to disaggregate models (Section 2.2), also known as "behavioral" because they depict individual decision-making explicitly. Section 2.3 presents examples of models explaining some key travel choices: mode, time of day, and route. More specialized topics are then discussed (Section 2.4). Next, Sections 2.5 and 2.6 analyze attitudes, perceptions, and activity patterns, while Section 2.7

DOI: 10.4324/9781315157375-2

considers travelers' willingness to pay for (*i.e.*, valuation of) travel characteristics including travel-time savings, reliability, and comfort; these values are derived from travel-demand analysis and are of special interest to policy, as will become clear in later chapters. Finally, Section 2.8 considers new sources of "big data" which greatly enlarge the scope of empirical possibilities.

We mostly discuss passenger transportation, in part because more data are available in this area than for freight. Studies of the demand for urban freight transportation tend to use similar methods.[1]

2.1 Aggregate approaches and trends

The most obvious approach to measuring demand functions has a long history in economic analysis. The demand for some portion of the travel market is explained as a function of variables that describe the product and/or its consumers. For example, total transit demand in a city might be related to the amounts of residential and industrial development, the average transit fare, the costs of alternative modes, some simple measures of service quality, and average income. In this section, we present the basics of formulating such models, make use of them to review the demands for motorization and for public transit, and discuss some societal and technological trends with significant implications for urban travel demand.

2.1.1 Aggregate demand models

We begin with a simple mathematical function $f(\cdot)$ of a vector Z of values of all the relevant characteristics of the good and its potential consumers. Since behavior cannot be predicted precisely, an "error term" is added to represent behavior that, to the researcher at least, appears random. Thus, the quantity of travel desired, under conditions represented by Z, is:

$$x = f\left(Z\right) + \varepsilon \tag{2.1}$$

where ε is a random error term. Data on x and Z can be used to estimate the function f and the probability distribution function of ε.

While it is possible to estimate this model imposing few or no prior assumptions about the nature of these functions, most often one or both are *specified* to be a particular functional form, with parameters to be determined empirically. For example, f might be specified as a general quadratic function:

$$f(Z) = \beta_0 + \sum_k \beta_{1k} Z_k + \sum_k \beta_{2k} Z_k^2 + \sum_k \sum_{l \neq k} \beta_{3kl} Z_k Z_l \tag{2.2}$$

where Z_k and Z_l are characteristics included in vector Z, and the β parameters are to be estimated.[2] This is an example of an equation that is *linear in parameters*. To see why, define variables $z_0 \equiv 1$, $z_{1k} = Z_k$, $z_{2k} = (Z_k)^2$, and $z_{3kl} = Z_k Z_l$ (for all values of k and of $l \neq k$). Combining all the variables $\{z_0, z_{1k}, z_{2k}, z_{3kl}\}$ into a single vector z and all the corresponding parameters into a single vector β, we can write (2.1) as:

$$x = \beta' z + \varepsilon \tag{2.3}$$

where the prime on β indicates transposition (changing it from a column vector to a row vector); thus, $\beta' z$ is the inner product between β and z.

Equation (2.3) is known as a *regression* of *x* on *z*. When it is linear in β, as in this example, one can very easily estimate the unknown parameters. Even a very complex relationship between *x* and *Z* can often be represented as a linear regression. The most common way of estimating the unknown parameters in (2.3) is *ordinary least squares* (OLS), in which the value of β is found that minimizes the sum of squared residuals for a set of observations labeled $n = 1, \ldots, N$:

$$\hat{\beta} = \underset{\beta}{\arg\min} \sum_{n=1}^{N} (x_n - \beta' z_n)^2$$

where now we have indexed each observed data point (x_n, z_n) by its observation label *n*. OLS has particularly nice properties when the random error ε has the bell-shaped distribution known as the normal distribution. However, it is quite possible to estimate regression models with nonlinear functional forms or with other error distributions.

The nonrandom part of the demand equation (2.1) is sometimes based on a theory of consumer choice by a utility-maximizing representative consumer. Such a theory is not necessary in order to specify and estimate a demand function, and in fact is restrictive because groups of people acting rationally do not necessarily behave like a single person acting rationally. But such a theory may help by suggesting likely functional forms for *f* and it is useful for interpreting the results, especially for welfare analysis (*i.e.*, for calculating whether, and by how much, people are made better off by a particular change). The most common such theory postulates that a consumer (or each member of a group of consumers) maximizes a *utility function*, $u(x, X)$; this function expresses preferences over the quantities of the good *x* under consideration and of other goods represented by the vector *X*. The consumer is limited by a budget constraint, expressed in terms of the price *p* of good *x* and a price vector *P* consisting of prices of all the other goods. Consumption is then mathematically determined as a solution to the following constrained maximization problem:

$$\underset{x,X}{\operatorname{Max}} u(x, X) \quad \text{subject to:} \quad px + P'X = y \tag{2.4}$$

where *y* is income and again the prime on *P* transposes it so that *P'X* is an inner product, expressing the cost of consuming all the goods in vector *X*. Denoting the solution to (2.4) by vector (x^*, X^*), we note that it depends on prices and income:

$$\begin{aligned} x^* &= x^*(p, P, y) \\ X^* &= X^*(p, P, y) \end{aligned} \tag{2.5}$$

Thus, if we knew, or were willing to postulate, a form for the function *u*, and if we could solve the maximization problem, we would know the form of the demand function (2.1) except for its random term.

The demand functions (2.5), when derived in this way, can be used to define other useful concepts. For example, by substituting (2.5) into the utility function we see how much utility can be achieved with a given set of prices and income. The result is known as the *indirect utility function*, often written as *V*:

$$V(p, P, y) = u\left[x^*(p, P, y), X^*(p, P, y)\right]$$

If *V* is differentiable, basic microeconomic theory stipulates that it obeys *Roy's identity*:

$$x^* = -\frac{\partial V / \partial p}{\partial V / \partial y} \tag{2.6}$$

where it is understood that all quantities in (2.6) depend on p, P, and y. We will make use of the indirect utility function and Roy's identity when we discuss disaggregate demand analysis in Section 2.2. For simplicity, our notation for demand functions will omit the asterisks in (2.5) and (2.6).

The demand functions (2.5) were defined as resulting from an individual consumer's optimization. An aggregate demand function can be derived by summing over individuals the quantities demanded. The resulting aggregate demand function may look as if it could have resulted from optimization by a single "representative" consumer. However, this can be true only under a very restrictive condition: namely, that the individuals' indirect utility functions obey a particular type of separability between prices and income known as the *Gorman form*. This means that the indirect utility for an individual n with income y_n must be in the form

$$V_n(p, P, y) = a_n(p, P) + b(p, P) \cdot y_n$$

for some functions $a_n(\cdot)$ and $b(\cdot)$ (Varian 1992, p. 154). Note that the function $b(\cdot)$ cannot vary across consumers. This condition is satisfied for some utility functions commonly used for theoretical analysis, but it is not satisfied for most demand functions used in empirical work. Instead, aggregate studies more often specify an empirically plausible aggregate demand function and then use well-known welfare concepts such as consumer surplus to measure, even if only approximately, the gains and losses associated with policy changes.

In travel-demand analysis, the dependent variable (the one to be explained) often is limited in range, making ordinary regression analysis inappropriate. An example is the discrete choice between modes. For this reason, travel-demand researchers have contributed importantly to the development of techniques – discussed later in this chapter – that are appropriate for such data. Here, we describe one such technique that is applicable to aggregate data.

Suppose the dependent variable of a model can logically take a continuum of values but only within a certain range. For example, if the dependent variable x is the modal share of public transit, it must lie between zero and one. If one or both of these limits are reached in the observed data, we can explain the observations using a single- or double-censored tobit model, which explicitly accounts for this.[3] If neither limit is reached, an alternative is to explain a logistic transformation of x, rather than x itself:

$$\log\left(\frac{x}{1-x}\right) = \beta'z + \varepsilon \tag{2.7}$$

Equivalently,

$$x = \frac{\exp(\beta'z + \varepsilon)}{1 + \exp(\beta'z + \varepsilon)} \tag{2.8}$$

A simple extension of equation (2.8) works if there are several dependent variables x_i representing market shares, for example, of various modes of travel, ensuring that they are positive and sum to one:

$$x_i = \frac{\exp(\beta'z_i + \varepsilon_i)}{\sum_{j=1}^{J} \exp(\beta'z_j + \varepsilon_j)} \tag{2.9}$$

where J is the number of products. Equations (2.8) and (2.9) describe the *aggregate logit model* for one or more dependent variables.[4]

One can estimate demand equations from aggregate cross-sectional or time-series data or a combination, known as *cross-sectional time series*. Studies using pure time series need to account for dynamic features such as autocorrelation (correlation in error terms for times that are near each other).

Studies using cross-sectional time series need similarly to account for the fact that the error terms for observations from the same location at different points in time cannot plausibly be assumed to be independent; neglecting this will result in an unnecessary loss of efficiency and an overstatement of the precision of the estimates, and may also bias the estimates. At least three approaches are available, each with a cost. One is to "first difference" all variables, so that the variable explained describes *changes* in some quantity rather than the quantity itself; this effectively reduces the number of time periods by one in terms of available data points. A second is to estimate a "fixed-effects" model, in which a separate constant is estimated for every location; this adds $N - 1$ new coefficients to be estimated (assuming one constant would be estimated in any case). A third is a "random-effects" model, in which a separate random error term is specified that varies only by location (not time), usually with an assumed normal distribution; this specification adds only one parameter to be estimated (the standard deviation of the new error term) and so is especially useful where only a few time periods are available. Statistical tests are available to determine whether the more restrictive random-effects model is justified relative to the fixed-effects model.

A few authors have suggested bypassing economic demand models, relying instead on intriguing regularities in the per capita or per household expenditure of time on travel, arguing that there is a universal law of a constant time budget. However, most scholars have concluded that the regularities can be explained by more conventional models, that the regularities are only approximations, and that violations of them occur as predicted by economic theory (Schafer 2000). For example, Kockelman (2001) rejects the hypothesis of fixed travel-time budgets using data from the San Francisco Bay Area. She finds rather that total time spent traveling declines as nearby activities are made more accessible, and increases as distant activities are made more accessible. Moreover, even if the travel-time budget were constant, demand analysis would be required to know how this time budget is allocated over travel options – a knowledge that is essential to transportation policy.

In the rest of this section, we first illustrate aggregate models by reviewing results for overall use of motor vehicles and for demand for public transit. We then consider several factors which, in the near future, may significantly disrupt established trends in aggregate travel.

2.1.2   *Example: demand for motorization*

A good example of a nonlinear demand function, with very practical application, is the analysis of motorization rates in 45 nations by Dargay *et al.* (2007). The authors seek to explain aggregate motor vehicle ownership per capita, using annual data for these nations for up to 43 years (1960–2002). Assembling such data for such disparate time periods and geographies greatly restricts the possible explanatory variables, and the authors use just four: income, income growth, population density, and urbanization. They specify a highly nonlinear function to account for a tendency of motorization to rise rapidly with income to a certain point, but then to approach an asymptotic level which the authors call "saturation." The saturation level can vary across countries as a function of population density and urbanization.

In addition, the authors assume that adjustment to changed incomes does not occur immediately, but with a time lag. To implement this idea, they specify a very simple and useful dynamic process known as *partial adjustment*. It assumes that there is an unobservable target level of vehicle ownership that responds immediately to annual changes in explanatory variables; but that actual ownership changes only gradually toward the target. Specifically, the gap between the target and previous year's ridership is closed by a fraction $1 - \alpha$ in a given year. This formulation makes the regression equation quite easy to formulate, simply by including a one-year lagged dependent variable in the explanatory equation.

The target motorization rate in country i in year t is specified to take the following form:

$$M_{it}^{*} = \gamma' X_{it} \tag{2.10}$$

where X_{it} is a vector of just three variables: population density, urbanization, and a particular nonlinear function of income described below. (Population density and urbanization are truncated from below at the values for the United States, as a protection against undue influence of outliers or data errors.) Actual motorization adjusts to the target as follows:

$$M_{it} = M_{i,t-1} + (1-\alpha)\left(M_{it}^{*} - M_{i,t-1} \right) + u_{it} \tag{2.11}$$

where u_{it} is a stochastic term and parameter α may be interpreted as measuring inertia. Inserting (2.10) into (2.11), we have an estimating equation that is linear in four explanatory variables: the three that are part of X plus the lagged dependent variable:

$$M_{it} = \alpha M_{i,t-1} + (1-\alpha)\gamma' X_{it} + u_{it} \equiv \alpha M_{i,t-1} + \beta' X_{it} + u_{it} \tag{2.12}$$

Estimating this equation yields estimates of the inertia parameter α and short-run response parameter vector $\beta \equiv (1 - \alpha)\gamma$. The parameter vector γ in (2.10) is thus simply $(1 - \alpha)^{-1}$ times this short-run response vector. Furthermore, by iterating this equation for all past times back to $-\infty$, it can be seen that the expected value of M would become asymptotically equal to the target value M^{*} if all variables remained constant for infinitely many past periods. Therefore, γ gives the long-run response to variables X, and we see that long-run elasticities with respect to X variables are equal to $(1 - \alpha)^{-1}$ times the corresponding short-run elasticities. This setup is extremely useful for policy analysis, and it has many applications in economics – two of which are discussed later in this book (Sections 2.1.3 and 7.1).

Dargay *et al.* (2007) add two unusual features to the standard partial adjustment model. First, one of their "variables" in vector X (we denote it as X^3) is actually a nonlinear function of income Y (measured as per capita gross national product) with additional parameters to be estimated:

$$X_{it}^{3} = \exp\left(ae^{b_i Y_{it}} \right) \tag{2.13}$$

This function allows the relationship between income and motorization, a main interest of the study, to take a flexible shape with a steep rise at moderate incomes and a leveling off at high incomes. Its nonlinearity requires the use of nonlinear least squares to estimate parameters. The estimation of these additional parameters is facilitated by the fact that their dataset includes as many as 43 years for a given country.[5]

The second novel feature is that the speed of adjustment $(1-\alpha)$ is assumed to differ depending on whether income is rising or falling from the previous year. Formally, this means the parameter α is replaced by $(\alpha^{+} D^{+} + \alpha^{-} D^{-})$, where D^{+} and D^{-} are dummy variables for whether income in the year t is higher or lower than the previous year. The difference between estimated values for α^+ and α^- can be tested for statistical significance to see whether such asymmetry really does exist. Dargay *et al.* find indeed that there is a modest difference, with more inertia when income is falling than when it is rising.

The results of estimation show that all countries tend toward a saturation level for automobile ownership per capita, varying from 508 (per thousand) for China to 852 for the least dense and least urbanized countries. Long-run elasticities are 10–12 times as large as short-run elasticities, due to high inertia even for rising incomes. The long-run income elasticities, calculated from (2.10) and (2.13), vary strongly with per capita income, peaking at 2.1 and very gradually falling to zero for higher income levels. The peak elasticity comes at an annual income that varies by country, from a low of $4,000 to a high of $9,600, all in 1995 US$ calculated at purchasing power parity. Motorization reaches 99% of its saturation level at per capita incomes ranging from $19,000 to $46,000. These results imply that rapid future growth of motorization is quite likely in low- and middle-income countries, but only slow growth is anticipated in high-income countries.

2.1.3   Example: demand for public transit

Much urban public transportation policy depends on the financial viability of public transportation, or "transit" for short. This in turn depends crucially on its ridership under various conditions. Studies of transit ridership are especially important for predicting the response to expanded service offerings, forecasting implications of societal changes, and exploring policies regarding fare and service quality.

Such studies may be part of a larger attempt to explain urban transportation choices, in which case they normally make use of disaggregate demand models as explained in later sections of this chapter. However, the most direct approach is to observe aggregate transit ridership by country, city, or zone and to estimate regression equations explaining such ridership as a function of socioeconomic and service variables. In order to compensate for not explicitly modeling mode choice, key characteristics of other modes are often included as variables – especially fuel prices as a proxy for the cost of automobile use.

2.1.3.1   Income and price elasticities

Litman (2023a) reviews this literature and concludes that the transit fare elasticities (in absolute value) are most commonly found to be in the range 0.2–0.5 in the short run and 0.6–0.9 in the long run (five to ten years). They are twice as high for off-peak travel as for peak travel, and higher for bus than for train travel. Service elasticities (*i.e.*, elasticity of transit ridership with respect to some measured quality of service) tend to be higher, depending on how service is measured.

The distinction between short- and long-run elasticities is important. It is exemplified by a study of bus usage in India, estimated on cross-sectional time-series data giving aggregate bus travel in each of 22 large Indian states (Deb and Filippini 2013). The authors estimate both static and dynamic models, the latter using the partial adjustment framework described in the previous subsection.[6] The dynamic model fits quite well when estimated with their preferred method, implying long-run elasticities about 40% larger in value than the short-run elasticities.[7] Their resulting estimated elasticities are shown in Table 2.1 (adapted from their Table 4). The very small income elasticities probably reflect the low levels of income and car ownership in India.

Table 2.1 Estimated demand elasticities for bus transit in India

Type of elasticity	Short run	Long run
Price	−0.38	−0.52
Income	−0.03	−0.04
Service quality	−0.68	−0.96

Source: Adapted from Deb and Filippini (2013, Table 4). Reprinted with permission from *Journal of Transport Economics and Policy.*

2.1.3.2   *Aggregate results*

The demand for transit depends greatly on spatial patterns. Mostly this is dealt with in transportation research by constructing detailed models of mode choice for specific origins and destinations. However, one study considers it from a more aggregate point of view, revealing an important fact: Demand for transit is much greater for travelers who have a highly congested highway as an alternative (Anderson 2014). As will be mentioned in later chapters, this has major implications for the prediction of congestion relief from transit investments, and therefore for the evaluation of those investments.

Whatever the model, the most important variables for actually forecasting levels of transit ridership are almost always those reflecting trip generation: that is, the basic pool of potential trips that people want to take by whatever means is available. These usually reflect two things: population and employment. These are commonly represented by specifying the explanatory function $f(Z)$ in demand system (2.1) to be proportional to total population and to total employment of a city or urban area. A more elaborate variation would be some type of "gravity" model where population refers to a specific neighborhood, and employment is a weighted average of jobs located throughout the relevant region, with weights inversely related to the distance of these jobs from the neighborhood in question. (If the weight is proportional to the inverse square of distance, it resembles Newton's law of gravity, hence the model's name.) When it comes to forecasts of future transit ridership, the forecasts for population and employment are quite possibly the most important source of uncertainty, so in practice it pays to put a lot of effort into getting these right.

This last point is exemplified to an extreme by the experience of the COVID-19 pandemic starting in 2020. Employment was severely restricted by regulations aimed at curtailing the spread of the associated virus; at the same time, remote work substituted for commuting across vast portions of employment categories. This raises the very important question of how long these changes in employment and commuting patterns will persist.

The pandemic has inspired much new research and speculation into the underlying determinants of job location and the role of personal interactions in workplaces. As one example, Barrero *et al.* (2021) estimate, based on employer interviews and employee surveys, that working from home is likely to increase productivity by nearly 5%, and to lower post-pandemic commuting frequencies for all American workers by several percentage points – more so for urban workers. On the other hand, there is some evidence from a study of Microsoft employees that people working from home interact closely with a narrower slice of their colleagues than in-office workers; if this is found to inhibit innovation, as seems possible, the trend might be reversed (Longqi Yang *et al.* 2021). Of course, teleworking technology will be continually upgraded – for example, by using game software to create virtual reality experiences – with unknown implications.

The reason this is important for transportation is that work from home has significant implications for patterns in road congestion, parking availability, and transit operational design. It will be years before researchers can measure the pandemic's full impacts on travel, and this is an area where continual change can be expected.

2.1.3.3 *Public transit and bicycles in a digital world*

While transit patronage briefly surged during the Great Recession of 2007–2009, it has subsequently leveled off or fallen in nearly all of the developed world (The Economist 2018). Some of this reversal may be caused by service cutbacks resulting from fiscal distress, and some is just a continuation of long-term trends since the mid-twentieth century. Some of the reversal, however, may be due to competition from services using new technologies, especially ride-sourcing services; and there is good reason to suspect that declines in ridership will be accentuated should autonomous vehicles (AVs) become more widely used (see Section 2.1.5).

Transit also competes with bicycles and, more recently, electric scooters, whose attractiveness has been enhanced by new business models (the "sharing economy") and by newer technologies such as lighter-weight electric bicycles and dockless locking through digital apps. The same digital technologies that have facilitated short-term car rentals have thus spread to two-wheeled vehicles, making them more serious competitors to transit. Just as with ride-sourcing, much depends on how the new technologies are regulated.

One ameliorating factor for transit is that two-wheeled vehicles, like ride-sourcing, can serve as complements to transit by connecting the end points of trips with transit stops – the so-called "last mile problem." Thus, it is possible that two-wheeled vehicles will reshape public transit, possibly undercutting it in medium-density urban neighborhoods but helping it in suburbs. As for big city centers, it is hard to imagine any system, even autonomous cars, achieving the capacity needed to move large numbers of commuters in and out, making it likely that governments will continue to subsidize radial mass transit services.[8] Growing concerns over energy use from transportation make this even more likely, as urban mass transit typically involves considerably less use of energy per passenger-mile.

Some travel-demand models include "active modes," that is, bicycling and walking, usually as a single available travel mode. As new bicycle rental and parking arrangements develop, thus changing the characteristics of the non-motorized modes, it becomes important to reestimate such models. It is also becoming important to better understand motor-assisted scooters and bicycles as distinct modes, especially in light of the challenges they pose for regulation and their tendency to expand rapidly when permitted. We discuss them further in Chapters 5 and 6.

2.1.4 *Driving patterns of young adults*

Many observers have noted evidence of widespread decline in car ownership and use among young adults, including declines in the numbers of young adults having a driver's license and having access to a car. Such declines, or at least a leveling after many years of growth, have been observed for the majority of developed countries since 2000 and for some even earlier.

Kuhnimhof *et al.* (2012) document these trends thoroughly for the United States, Japan, and four countries in Western Europe. Data are based mainly on national travel surveys in which people detail their travel for a single day, or occasionally for several days. In all of these countries, the proportion of young adults (usually ages 18–29) who have a driver's license either fell or remained roughly constant between the mid-1990s and the first decade of the twenty-first century. The change is primarily among men, thereby narrowing the gap between men's and women's rates of licensure. Furthermore, the modal share of car for travel by this age group has declined since around year 2000 in five of the six countries; and apparently so has vehicle-kilometers traveled (VKT), although in two cases the surveys are too far apart in time to be sure. Delbosc and Currie (2013) measure similar changes for a wider sample of 14 developed countries, finding a decline in youth licensure in nine of them.[9]

There are many potential explanations. Leard *et al.* (2019) divide these into two categories: (i) traditional demographic and economic variables, such as income and fuel prices, and (ii) changes in "driving habits," which they define as any deviations from what can be explained by category (i). While most of these changes in driving habits are presumed to lower automobile ownership and use, some are offsetting: For example, Kuhnimhof *et al.* observe that older people are healthier and driving more.

Regarding category (i), the years 2000–2010 witnessed a nearly unprecedented worldwide economic slowdown and a sharp though volatile increase in fuel prices. These factors apply to all age groups, but perhaps more strongly to young adults who are more prone to unemployment and have less discretionary income. And indeed, income and fuel prices can explain much of the observed trends: For example, Bastian *et al.* (2016) demonstrate that a time-series model with just two variables, per capita GDP and real gasoline price, can track actual aggregate VKT quite well for several developed nations, even with a very simple model lacking any dynamic features.[10] A more extensive empirical study by Knittel and Murphy (2019) finds that controlling for such factors explains most or all of the observed differences between generations in vehicle ownership and use.

Regarding category (ii), several factors might cause changes in driving habits that could, in principle, mark a structural shift in demand for automobility. Young adults are spending more years in school, getting married later, and moving to cities. They express stronger sympathies with environmental principles and are quicker to adopt electronic technologies that facilitate travel without vehicle ownership (see the next subsection). At this point in time, it is uncertain how strongly such factors influence amount of automobile use.

Equally important is the possibility that the changes in driving habits are not exogenous, but rather are driven by long-lasting impacts of economic variables: especially the lingering negative effects of the 2007–2009 recession on the economic well-being of the generation known as millennials (sometimes defined as those born between 1982 and 2004). That recession severely cramped the ability of this cohort to purchase homes and, in many cases, even to start new households (Kotkin 2017). Thus, the changes in driving habits might be long-lasting for this cohort, but not necessarily occur for later cohorts. Similarly, an economic event that affects habit formation at a critical time can have long-lasting effects. For example, people in the United States who were 15–18 years old during the oil price shock of 1979 are observed to drive less 20 years later, perhaps because they curtailed car use just when they would typically be learning to drive (Severen and van Benthem 2022).

2.1.5 Impacts of digital automotive technologies

Technology-based innovations in vehicle design and usage are upending the way people, especially younger people, use cars. How can travel-demand analysis account for them? Here we discuss three such innovations: internet- and smartphone-based modes of short-term car rentals ("carsharing"); smartphone-based ride services ("ride-sourcing"); and AVs.

The first two innovations allow people to combine owning a personal vehicle with offering a commercial service (*i.e.*, a taxi-like ride service or a car rental). However, early experience suggests that such hybrid operations tend quickly to migrate to ones that are mostly commercial,

with providers making a serious commitment to their occupation and making vehicle investments in a business-like manner. The idea that such services are part of a "sharing economy" has
proven useful to commercial innovators for avoiding regulation, but is not helpful for analysis.

For this reason, we treat these first two innovations as commercial, despite our adoption of
the conventional name "carsharing" for the first. The third innovation, driverless cars, will affect
both commercial and personal use.

2.1.5.1   Carsharing

The expected immediate effect of carsharing is to reduce vehicle ownership; this in turn affects
subsequent choices regarding trip-making, destinations, and modes. Indeed, early experience
suggests that people who use carsharing have significantly lower car ownership, at least in
dense urban neighborhoods (Clewlow and Mishra 2017). It seems plausible that this is a causal
relationship, although more research is needed to rule out self-selection by which people who
already prefer not to own a car are the ones who choose carsharing.

It remains to be seen whether this immediate effect leads to other behaviors often associated
with low automobile ownership. In particular, the effect on transit ridership is ambiguous: Will
transit use be reduced due to its substitutability with car rentals? Or will it be enhanced due to
its substitutability with car ownership?

Related past experience suggests that automobile travel does sometimes respond opportun-
istically to new possibilities, despite the fact that its long-run demand function is usually measured as being somewhat inelastic. For example, reductions in congestion are at least partly
offset by "induced demand," as discussed in Section 5.1.3, some of which involves new automobile trips. As another example, telecommuting has been found to increase the use of cars
that are released from commuting duties for other trip purposes. Similarly, widespread use of
telecommunications in offices has created new business opportunities that have in turn led to
new vehicle uses, rather than strictly substituting for vehicle travel. Even new transit service has
sometimes resulted in an increase rather than a decrease in automobile traffic, due to stimulating
new development.

2.1.5.2   Ride-sourcing

We use the term "ride-sourcing" to describe ride services based on two-sided digital platforms
which match drivers with passengers, typically using smartphones.[11] These services began with
commercial innovations by several well-known companies including Uber, Didi, and Lyft. Experience is reviewed by Clewlow and Mishra (2017) and Hall *et al.* (2018).

Just as for carsharing, there is great interest in how ride-sourcing affects car ownership and
use of public transit (Hörcher and Tirachini 2021). The same analytical issue as for carsharing,
regarding offsetting substitutions, is at play: People who ride-hail may do so as a direct substitute for public transit, but may also reduce car ownership and thus may substitute public transit
for some of the trips they would otherwise have taken by private car. In addition, ride-sourcing
can, like cycling, be a direct complement to public transit if it solves the so-called "first-mile
problem" or "last-mile problem": that is, if it is a viable access mode permitting use of transit
for a trip whose end points would otherwise not be conveniently served. Thus, there are at least
three effects, some offsetting, and theory alone does not predict which will dominate: This is
ultimately an empirical matter.

The empirical evidence is in fact mixed. Reviewing it and adding their own study from seven
US metropolitan areas, Clewlow and Mishra (2017) find very modest impacts of ride-sourcing:

some reduction in use of bus and light rail, a slight increase in use of heavy rail, and a slight increase in amount of walking. This suggests that ride-sourcing is a substitute for transit on city streets, but a complement to longer and faster transit modes. (These findings are based on comparison of frequencies of reported travel, not on statistical estimation.) Hall *et al.* (2018) similarly find heterogeneous effects of ride-sourcing on public transit use, with complementarity on average and for larger cities.

Clewlow and Mishra find evidence of only a slight effect of ride-sourcing on vehicle ownership, perhaps because American residential patterns are so heavily suburban. They do find some reduction in use of owned personal vehicles by people choosing ride-sourcing services; but they cannot determine whether this offsets the travel of the ride-sourcing vehicles themselves.

Given the heavy use of ride-sourcing for short trips, its most probable net impact seems to be more car travel, unless ride-sourcing services are very successful in promoting ride-sharing. This qualification calls attention to the question of how successful commercial offerings of shared ride-sourcing will be, a topic to which we return in Section 6.3.5.

2.1.5.3 *Autonomous vehicles*

The advent of driverless cars, buses, and trucks on highways raises fascinating questions about its impacts on travel behavior, land use, and economic activity. It would be speculative to predict how quickly AVs will achieve significant market penetration, or what their net effects will be.[12] Indeed, even posing such a question requires distinguishing among many degrees of automation that have been identified, ranging from routine assistance to drivers (*e.g.*, lane-drift warnings, automatic braking), through modest automation with driver present, to full automation without a driver.[13] What we can say with confidence is that any transportation researcher needs to be prepared with analytical tools, and to be attuned to recognize unexpected innovations and counterintuitive impacts.

Perhaps the most pressing open question is the impact on amount of vehicle travel. AVs could have enormous effects on congestion, highway and transit investment needs, business strategies, and various public policies. Some observers focus on the ability of autonomous cars to smooth traffic flow and facilitate ride-sharing. Based on these properties, traffic simulations of Lisbon and Helsinki suggest the potential for big reductions in congestion, and also in total vehicle travel if ride-sharing is widespread.[14] But at least two factors work in the opposite direction.

First, as travel by single-occupancy vehicles becomes cheaper and easier, people will probably make new and/or longer trips. In this way, congestion may increase or arise in new places, and the long-time tendency toward low-density "sprawled" cities may be enhanced. Indeed, the consensus of most studies is that personally owned autonomous cars will be driven much more than comparable ordinary cars. Nevertheless, some observers, such as Winston and Karpilow (2020), believe that the reduced capacity requirements for handling AVs will more than offset induced travel, causing congestion to decrease.

Second, travelers to downtown areas may conserve on expensive parking spaces by sending their vehicles autonomously to outlying parking lots or back home, thereby adding a new trip to the vehicle's itinerary. Depending on where such lots are located, this could create congestion in entirely new areas or directions. It could also greatly affect land use, perhaps making urban downtowns more dense and nearby areas less dense – depending in part on city planning, zoning, and parking policies.[15]

Another possibility is that AVs will make carpool formation easier by easing the logistical requirements for people to share rides. Ostrovsky and Schwarz (2018) point out several such factors. Autonomous cars could begin and end a trip anywhere, with no constraint that the same person (the driver) occupy the car at both ends. They could add flexibility, making it feasible to adjust routes or identities of people sharing rides to accommodate schedule changes. Single-purpose carpooling vehicles could be designed for privacy and convenience of passengers who are not a family unit.

We consider broader implications of AVs in Chapters 3 and 6. Here we consider how the advent of AVs will require new or revised techniques in travel-demand analysis.

One such technique is stated preference (SP) surveys (discussed in Section 2.2.4), whereby subjects can be queried about their responses to services or situations that do not yet exist. An example is Haboucha *et al.* (2017), who measure the effects of socioeconomic variables and attitudes on the adoption of AVs. Indeed, greater use of SP surveys is a general response that can be expected to the rapid pace of new technologies and new business applications in all areas of economic life, which by their nature cannot easily be assessed by current experience.

The use of SP questions to elicit preferences is limited by the ability of respondents to know what potential new services will be like, and how they might rearrange their lives in response. There is growing awareness on the part of researchers that SP questions need to be accompanied by substantial presentations of context to assist in this process. As more surveys are conducted online, it is becoming feasible to provide detailed graphical and/or dynamic depictions of the services in question. We may see more use of driving simulators in laboratory settings, in order to better understand users' responses to new technologies and services. Harb *et al.* (2018) even created a sort of real-life laboratory experiment, by hiring on-call chauffeurs to give experimental subjects the chance to explore their own travel behavior when freed from driving duties. The authors find that much additional travel occurred – including more and longer trips, trips exclusively for children, and trips for errands with no family member in the car.[16]

In addition to specifically assessing preferences for new travel services, SP studies offer the chance to explore people's reactions to new factors or to factors whose importance is growing. Examples include cyber security, new forms of insurance, and ethical dilemmas such as how autonomous cars should be programmed to react in emergencies.

Meanwhile, the data generated by digital technologies offer dramatically expanded opportunities to analyze actual behavior. Already researchers are able to use cell phone records to analyze travel, congestion, real-time routing decisions, and much more (*e.g.*, Janzen *et al.* 2018). AVs will generate even larger datasets, covering not only amounts and timing of travel by the vehicle's passengers, but also detailed information about the behavior of those passengers and of drivers of nearby vehicles. Some facets of such data are considered in Section 2.8.

AVs will greatly affect two fundamental components of urban transportation analysis: value of time (VOT) and the options for parking. With increasing intra-vehicle amenities, the VOT (see Sections 2.2.3 and 2.7) is expected to decline for vehicle occupants, especially for (former) drivers who no longer have to concentrate on driving. Simulated driving in laboratory experiments offers one way to study this question, by asking study subjects about their trade-offs in such situations. Simulation models suggest that VOT reductions of a size expected for AVs can increase vehicle travel by large amounts, up to 59% in simulations of the Chicago area (Auld *et al.* 2017). At the same time, the reduced VOT may induce departure time adjustments that lead to longer travel time delays, nullifying at least part of the cost savings that a lower VOT could potentially bring (Van den Berg and Verhoef 2016).

Finally, consider the effects on parking policy, a topic considered further in Section 3.5.3. Regulation and pricing of parking are often viewed as the best politically available substitutes for congestion pricing to improve traffic conditions. Typical policy recommendations take the form of restricting the quantity and/or increasing the price of parking spaces near major destinations served by automobile trips. But autonomous cars would further weaken the link between the congestion-causing trip and use of parking spaces near the trip destination. This creates a strong incentive for city officials to regulate the secondary locations of parking to which such trips can send their vehicles.

2.1.6 Transportation and land use

Transportation is defined with respect to particular locations. Naturally, the ways the land at those locations is used – the types and densities of buildings occupying them and the activities that occur there – are among the most important factors influencing travel decisions. This is a consequence of travel demand being (mainly) a derived demand, as described in the introduction to this chapter. Furthermore, transportation facilities have significant effects on land use. Thus, the two-way interrelationship is important analytically and, because transportation and land use both have significant spillover effects on quality of life, it fuels contentious policy debates.

This often complex, reciprocal interrelationship has long been recognized. It has been an impediment to empirically estimating demand models because the two-way causation makes the land uses themselves – often a starting point for travel demand – endogenous. This has led to econometric innovations to account for endogeneity, typically through instrumental variables as described in Sections 2.4.4 and 2.4.5. Roughly speaking, the variable feared to be endogenous (land use) is replaced, in the equation explaining travel, by a predicted version formed by regressing the land-use variable on exogenous variables in the system, including the instrumental variables. Examples of an instrumental variable might be the age of the city, or a measure of its density several decades earlier.

Just accounting for two-way causality can lead to surprising paradoxes. For example, expanding highways to relieve congestion may attract development that undermines the intended effect. This is just one of many examples of "induced demand," discussed in Chapter 5. An even more surprising example is that expanding mass transit can exacerbate highway congestion: This occurs if it induces development that, even if predominantly transit-oriented, still generates many automobile trips. For example, the Bay Area Rapid Transit system in San Francisco is credited with causing Walnut Creek, an outlying station, to develop into a major center of office employment – to which 95% of commuting trips took place by automobile (Cervero and Wu 1996, Table 5).

But to understand the two-way causation better, the formation of land uses and land-use densities should really be modeled directly. Attempts to do so go back at least to Von Thünen's (1826) model of agricultural land use, which in turn inspired the classic and widely used Alonso–Muth–Mills model of a monocentric city.[17] These models capture the reciprocal relation between transport and land use in highly stylized settings. In the simplest of them, economic agents compete for parcels of land that differ in desirability only in their proximity to a single point of greatest economic interest, often identified as the central business district (CBD). The result is a spatial equilibrium in which land rent or price declines steadily from the CBD to the outer edge of the city. In this way, the extra transport cost required at more outlying locations is compensated for by their lower land rent. This in turn determines how land will be used and hence which equilibrium transport flows will originate at which distance.

Even in the simplest analytical settings, such spatial equilibria already describe endogenous, mutually consistent, and spatially differentiated variables including land values, land-use density, and transport demands. The basic spatial pattern, in which land values are highest closest to the center, is further reinforced by substitution between land and other inputs such as buildings. The ratio of those other inputs to land then increases toward the center, which one may visualize by imagining the skyline of the city. Thus, the model is extremely important in understanding the economic pressures for different types and densities of land development in different parts of an urban area.

These types of insights remain highly relevant even though actual cities are far from monocentric. First, most cities today still have a dominant downtown area. Second, spatial economic equilibrium patterns and mechanisms identified with a monocentric model often remain relevant around individual (sub-)centers, including a dominant downtown area, in polycentric urban areas. And third, the model explains key spatial patterns in other markets of interest, for example real-estate development and the markets for labor, for housing, and for goods characterized by agglomeration forces (as discussed in Section 5.2.5). With such a potentially complex system of interacting markets, maintaining spatial simplicity is helpful to keep analyses manageable and focused on general relationships as opposed to specific spatial idiosyncrasies.

The classic monocentric model has been extended in many directions. These include polycentric structures and models based on zone-based computable general equilibrium approaches.[18] For example, Anas and Liu (2007) describe a model that seeks to combine a detailed picture of economic decision-making with computational tractability. The model's land-use portion keeps track of product prices, wages, housing rents, and stocks of buildings, allowing for dynamic decision-making and accounting for the durability of decisions about buildings. The model's transportation portion contains the usual components of a complete travel model as described earlier in Section 2.1, including equilibration of route choices on networks representing available roads and transit lines.[19] Other extensions of the monocentric framework, which focus on consumer preferences for product variety, stem from the analysis of international trade (Krugman *et al.* 1995) and are sometimes called the New Economic Geography. Extensions may furthermore consider explicit network structures, the durability of transport facilities, durability of buildings, and spatial inhomogeneities stemming from natural conditions such as mountains, rivers, and coastlines. Among the many insights produced is the likelihood that even a long-run equilibrium depends crucially on initial conditions and on idiosyncratic occurrences such as floods and economic initiatives taken by historical individuals. Transportation costs are an important component of all spatial economic models; hence, all such models have their own specific implications for the analysis of transport demand. An important question is: When is it worthwhile to incorporate an explicit spatial model in order to better understand transport demand?

We would argue that the answer is: whenever the analysis concerns matters of long-run importance in light of large-scale changes to the transportation system. It is this combination that makes the induced adjustments in a city's or a region's spatial structure especially significant, because then short-run and long-run demand functions not only differ, but do so in a manner that varies over space. Many transport policy interventions fall into this category, especially large transport infrastructure investments and spatially differentiated pricing schemes such as cordon pricing. Examples include an analysis of cordon pricing by Anas and Hiramatsu (2013), and also an analysis of the Japanese high-speed rail network (Koster *et al.* 2022). The latter paper shows that because of this phenomenon, some newly connected cities suffer negative effects on employment; this accords with findings of before-and-after studies in several other locations as reviewed by Koster *et al.*[20]

Another case where explicit modeling of the interactions between transport demand and the spatial economy becomes crucial is when other markets are not functioning perfectly efficiently. In that case, welfare assessment of interventions in transport could go far awry if it ignores indirect effects in these other markets. For example, such interactions can be important in urban labor markets (Tikoudis *et al.* 2015) and where land-use regulations are present (Zhang and Kockelman 2016; Anas 2020). These topics will be explored further in Sections 4.2.6, 5.2.4, and 5.2.5.

2.2   Disaggregate models: methods

A more common approach to travel demand is *disaggregate* or *behavioral* demand modeling. Made possible by microdata describing individual people, households, or firms, this approach explains behavior directly at the level of decision-making units. Disaggregate models are more statistically efficient than aggregate models when microdata are available, and are based on a more satisfactory microeconomic theory of demand, a feature that is particularly useful when applying welfare economics. Often, such models in transportation analyze choices among discrete rather than continuous alternatives; hence, they are called *discrete-choice models*.[21]

2.2.1   Basic discrete-choice models

The most widely used theoretical foundation for discrete-choice models is the additive random utility model of McFadden (1974). Suppose a decision-maker n facing discrete alternatives $j = 1,..., J$ chooses the one that maximizes utility as given by

$$U_{jn} = V(z_{jn}, s_n; \beta) + \varepsilon_{jn} \tag{2.14}$$

where $V(\cdot)$ is a function known as the *systematic utility*, z_{jn} is a vector of attributes of the alternatives as they apply to this particular decision-maker, s_n is a vector of the decision-maker's characteristics (effectively allowing different utility structures for different groups of decision-makers), β is a vector of unknown parameters, and ε_{jn} is an unobservable component of utility which captures idiosyncratic preferences. U_{jn} and $V(\cdot)$ are known as *conditional indirect utility* functions: They are conditional on choice j and, like the indirect utility function of standard consumer theory, may depend on income and prices and thus implicitly incorporate a budget constraint. The budget constraint is not explicitly modeled for most discrete-choice models, as these typically pertain to a consumption decision that will not exhaust the consumer's full budget – as it does in classic consumer choice models that study the allocation of total income over alternative goods.

The choice is predicted only probabilistically because the measured variables do not include everything relevant to the decision. This fact is represented by the random terms ε_{jn}. Once a functional form for V is specified, the model becomes complete by specifying a joint cumulative distribution function (cdf) for the J random variables $\{\varepsilon_j\}$, of which the values $\{\varepsilon_{jn}\}$ are realizations of the corresponding stochastic process. Denoting this cdf by $F(\varepsilon_1,..., \varepsilon_J)$ and denoting $V(z_{jn}, s_n; \beta)$ by V_{jn}, the choice probability for alternative i is then given by the following probability:

$$
\begin{aligned}
P_{in} &= Pr\left[U_{in} > U_{jn} \text{ for all } j \neq i \right] \\
&= Pr\left[\varepsilon_j < V_{in} - V_{jn} + \varepsilon_i \text{ for all } j \neq i \right] \\
&= \int_{-\infty}^{\infty} F_i(V_{in} - V_{1n} + \varepsilon_i,..., V_{in} - V_{Jn} + \varepsilon_i) d\varepsilon_i
\end{aligned}
\tag{2.15}
$$

where F_i is the partial derivative of F with respect to its ith argument.[22]

Equation (2.15) is often infeasible to compute analytically, because the cdf is often a multidimensional integral of a specified probability density function. Two particular types of cdf have been investigated.

The first is the multivariate normal distribution, in which case (2.15) is known as the *multinomial probit model* with general covariance structure. However, neither F nor F_i for the multivariate normal distribution can be expressed in closed form; rather, F_i is a $(J-1)$-dimensional integral of the normal density function, and computation of (2.15) involves complex approximations that are often computationally intractable. The equation is simpler if the random terms are identically and independently distributed (iid), each with the univariate normal distribution; F is then the product of J univariate normal cdfs, and we have the *iid probit model*. For example, in the iid probit model for binary choice $(J=2)$, (2.15) becomes

$$P_{1n} = \Phi\left(\frac{V_{1n} - V_{2n}}{\sigma}\right) \tag{2.16}$$

where Φ is the cumulative standard normal distribution function (a one-dimensional integral) and σ is the standard deviation of $\varepsilon_{1n} - \varepsilon_{2n}$. In equation (2.16), σ cannot be distinguished empirically from the scale of utility, which is arbitrary; for example, doubling σ has the same effect as halving both V_1 and V_2. Hence, it is conventional to normalize by setting $\sigma = 1$.

The second type is the *logit model* (also known as multinomial logit or conditional logit). It arises when the J random terms are iid with the *extreme-value distribution*, sometimes called the Gumbel, Weibull, or double-exponential distribution. This distribution is defined by

$$\Pr\left[\varepsilon_j < x\right] = \exp(-e^{-\mu x}) \tag{2.17}$$

for all real numbers x, where μ is a *scale parameter*.[23] For logit, a common convention is to normalize by setting $\mu = 1$, which allows utility parameters in V to be uniquely determined. With this normalization, McFadden (1974) shows that the resulting probabilities calculated from (2.15) have the logit form:

$$P_{in} = \frac{\exp(V_{in})}{\sum_{j=1}^{J} \exp(V_{jn})} \tag{2.18}$$

This formula has the celebrated and restrictive property of *independence from irrelevant alternatives*: the odds ratio (P_{in}/P_{jn}) between any pair of alternatives depends only on those alternatives' utilities V_{in} and V_{jn} (as the denominators in (2.18) will be the same for all i), hence not on the utilities for any other alternatives. This property implies, for example, that adding a new alternative k (equivalent to increasing its systematic utility V_{kn} from $-\infty$ to some finite value) will not affect the relative proportions of people using previously existing alternatives. It also implies that for a given alternative k, the cross-elasticities $\partial \log P_{jn}/\partial \log V_{kn}$ are identical for all $j \neq k$: hence, if the attractiveness of alternative k is increased, the probabilities of all the other alternatives $j \neq k$ will be reduced by identical percentages. This feature is often referred to as the "red bus/blue bus phenomenon" identified by McFadden (1974): when starting with a binary choice between a car versus a red bus for a certain trip, modeling the impacts of the addition of a blue bus as a third alternative according to (2.18) implies that by assumption, that third alternative reduces the probabilities of taking the red bus and the car by the same proportion. One would, however, expect the blue bus to be a closer substitute to the red bus than to the car, a feature that can be accounted for in the so-called generalized extreme value (GEV) models discussed in Section 2.4.1. These properties apply only to a group of consumers with a common value for V_{in}; they do not apply to heterogeneous populations.

The binary form of (2.18), that is, the form with $J = 2$, can be written as:

$$P_{1n} = \frac{1}{1 + \exp[-(V_{1n} - V_{2n})]}$$

If graphed as a function of $(V_{1n} - V_{2n})$, this equation looks very similar to the graph of (2.16).

It is really the iid assumption – identically and independently distributed error terms – that is restrictive, whether or not it implies independence of irrelevant alternatives. Hence, there is no basis for the widespread belief that iid probit is more general than logit. In fact, the logit and iid probit models have been found empirically to give virtually identical results when normalized comparably (Horowitz 1980).[24] Furthermore, both probit and logit may be generalized by defining non-iid distributions. In the probit case, this means computing the multivariate normal distribution, as already noted,[25] whereas in the logit case, it can take a number of forms to be discussed in Section 2.4.1.

As for the functional form of V, by far the most common is linear in unknown parameters β. More general forms, such as Box–Cox and Box–Tukey transformations, have also been used. Just as with regression analysis, V can be linear in *parameters* while still nonlinear in *variables*, just by specifying new variables equal to nonlinear functions of the original ones. For example, consider the systematic utility in (2.14) of alternative i, for a traveler n with wage w_n facing travel costs c_{in} and times T_{in}. It could be specified as:

$$V_{in}(c_{in}, T_{in}, w_n; \beta) = \beta_1 \cdot (c_{in} / w_n) + \beta_2 T_{in} + \beta_3 T_{in}^2 \tag{2.19}$$

This is nonlinear in travel time and in wage rate. If we redefine z_{in} as the vector of all variables and combinations of variables included in the model,[26] then the linear-in-parameters specification is simply written as

$$V_{in} = \beta' z_{in} \tag{2.20}$$

where β' is the transpose of column vector β. Suitably complex variables z usually can fit the data just as well as functions that are nonlinear in parameters. We provide an example in Section 2.3.1.

The additive random utility model is by no means the only way to formulate models of discrete choice. Other error structures are possible, such as a multiplicative random term (Fosgerau and Bierlaire 2009). Other interpretations are also possible: for example, randomness in behavior may occur due to mistakes (Mattsson and Weibull 2000), or more generally to rational response to the cost of acquiring information (Matějka and McKay 2015). An intriguing finding of this latter approach is that even when the model leads to logit probabilities, it no longer implies the "independence from irrelevant alternatives" property of logit. Both interpretations would, however, affect welfare analysis based on the model: when the random term reflects idiosyncratic preferences, it should be accounted for in welfare analysis (see also Section 2.2.5 below); when it reflects mistakes, this no longer makes sense. Choices may also be made in the absence of any consistent utility function, thereby constituting a lapse from "economically rational" behavior; in that case, discrete-choice analysis will sometimes need to account for such a lapse (McFadden 1999).

2.2.2   Estimation

For a given model, data on actual choices, along with traits z_{jn}, can be used to estimate the unknown parameter vector β in (2.14) or (2.20) and to carry out statistical tests of the specification (*i.e.*, tests of whether the assumed functional form of V and the assumed error distribution are valid). Parameters are usually estimated by maximizing the log-likelihood function:

$$L(\beta) = \sum_{n=1}^{N} \sum_{i=1}^{J} d_{in} \log P_{in}(\beta) \tag{2.21}$$

where N is the sample size. In this equation, d_{in} is the choice variable, defined as 1 if decision-maker n chooses alternative i and as 0 otherwise, while $P_{in}(\beta)$ is the choice probability. Not only does maximizing this function give us the *maximum-likelihood estimates* of parameters, often written as $\hat{\beta}$; the derivatives of L also provide information about the statistical uncertainty in $\hat{\beta}$, usually summarized as its *variance–covariance matrix*, denoted Var($\hat{\beta}$). The diagonal elements of this matrix give the variances (*i.e.*, the squares of the standard deviations) of the individual parameter estimates, while the off-diagonal elements give the covariances between pairs of parameter estimates. This information is crucial to knowing how firm we can be in making quantitative statements about the true parameters based on the particular dataset used.

A correction to (2.21) is available for choice-based samples (*i.e.*, those in which the sampling frequencies depend on the choices made). Choice-based samples often are available for practical reasons, such as the convenience of conducting a mode choice survey at train stations and bus stops. The correction simply multiplies each term in the second summation by the inverse of the sampling probability for that sample member (Manski and Lerman 1977). This correction does not, however, make the most efficient possible use of the information on aggregate mode shares; Imbens and Lancaster (1994) show how to incorporate aggregate information to improve efficiency.

It is sometimes possible to specify disaggregate demand functions and estimate them solely using aggregate market shares. Bresnahan *et al.* (1997) provide a particularly clear exposition. Basically, they use an extension of the idea, described earlier in connection with regression analysis, of minimizing the sum of squared residuals. Recall that a residual is the discrepancy between an observed quantity (such as amount of a good consumed) and the quantity predicted by the model at any particular set of parameters; it is those parameters that are adjusted to minimize the sum of squared residuals. Bresnahan *et al.* generalize this sum of squared residuals to a quadratic form in the vector of residuals, a common procedure in econometric models. The innovation, derived from Berry (1994), is in constructing the residuals themselves, one for each alternative j; they are formed as the differences between the indirect utility V_j calculated from the discrete-choice model (at a trial set of parameter values) and the indirect utility δ_j that is implied by its observed market share.[27]

A major attraction of multinomial logit is the computational simplicity of its log-likelihood function, due to taking the logarithm of the numerator in equation (2.18). With V linear in β, the logit log-likelihood function is globally concave in β, so finding a local maximum assures finding the global maximum. Fast computer routines to do this are widely available. In contrast, computing the log-likelihood function for multinomial probit with J alternatives entails computing, for each member of the sample, the $(J - 1)$-dimensional integral implicit in equation (2.15). This has generally proven difficult for J larger than 3 or 4, despite the development of computational-intensive simulation methods (Train 2009).

It is possible that the likelihood function is unbounded in one or more of the coefficients, making it impossible to maximize. This happens if a variable is included that is a perfect predictor of choice within the sample. For example, suppose one is predicting car ownership (yes or no) and wants to include among variables s_n in (2.14) a dummy variable for high income.

If it happens that within the sample everyone with high income owns a car, and no one else does, the likelihood function increases without limit in the coefficient of this dummy variable. The problem is that income does too good a job as an explanatory variable: within this dataset, the model exuberantly declares high income to make the alternative of owning a car infinitely desirable. Of course, we know that this is not true, and that a larger sample would contain counterexamples. Given the sample we have, we might solve the problem by re-specifying the model with differently defined income groups (*e.g.*, three levels of income) or alternatives (*e.g.*, owning zero, one, or two or more cars). Alternatively, we could postulate a *linear probability model*, in which probability rather than utility is a linear function of coefficients (Caudill 1988); while theoretically such a model leads to less efficient coefficient estimates and biased standard-error estimates, in practice it often performs well and is very convenient computationally – an advantage especially in situations where the model is part of a larger suite of computations requiring iteration.

2.2.3   Interpreting coefficient estimates

Often, one needs a way to interpret the magnitudes of estimated coefficients, remembering that utility contains an arbitrary normalization. One helpful fact is that for multinomial logit, a change in $\beta'z_{in}$ in (2.20) by an amount of ± 1 increases or decreases the relative odds of alternative i, compared to each other alternative, by a factor $\exp(1) = 2.72$. Thus, a quick gauge of the behavioral significance of any particular variable can be obtained by considering the size of typical variations in that variable, multiplied by its relevant coefficient. If the result is on the order of 1.0 or larger, such variations have large effects on the relative odds.

The parameter vector may contain *alternative-specific constants*, denoted here by α_i, for one or more alternatives i. We can then modify (2.20) to:

$$V_{in} = \alpha_i + \beta'z_{in} \tag{2.22}$$

Since only utility differences matter, at least one of the alternative-specific constants α_i must be normalized, usually to zero: that alternative then serves as a *base alternative* for comparisons. The constant α_i may be interpreted as the average utility of the unobserved characteristics of the ith alternative, relative to the base alternative. In a sense, specifying these constants is admitting the inadequacy of variables z_{in} to explain choice; hence, the constants' estimated values are especially likely to reflect circumstances of a particular sample rather than universal behavior. The use of alternative-specific constants also makes it impossible to forecast the result of adding a new alternative, unless there is some basis for deducing what its alternative-specific constant would be.

Equation (2.22) is really a special case of (2.20), in which one or more of the variables z are *alternative-specific dummy variables* D^k, defined by $D^k_j = 1$ if $j = k$ and 0 otherwise (for each $j = 1,..., J$). (Such a variable does not depend on n.) In this notation, parameter α_i in (2.22) is viewed as the coefficient of variable D^i. Such dummy variables can also be interacted with (*i.e.*, multiplied by) any other explanatory variable, making it possible for that explanatory variable to affect utility in a different way for each alternative. As already described, z can be redefined to include all such variables and interactions, thus allowing (2.20) still to represent the linear-in-parameters specification.

The most economically meaningful quantities obtained from estimating a discrete-choice model are often ratios of coefficients, which represent marginal rates of substitution – that is, the rates at which two variables can be traded against each other without changing utility. By interacting the variables of interest with socioeconomic characteristics or with alternative-dummy variables, these ratios can be specified quite flexibly so as to vary in a manner thought to be *a priori* plausible. A particularly important example is the marginal rate of substitution between time and money in the conditional indirect utility function, often called the *value of travel-time savings* (VTTS), or *value of time* (VOT) for short. It represents the monetary value that the traveler places on time savings, and is very important in evaluating the benefits of transportation improvements. For example, the VOT in the utility function (2.19) is

$$(v_T)_{in} \equiv -\left(\frac{dc_{in}}{dT_{in}}\right)_{V_{in}} \equiv \frac{\partial V_{in}/\partial T_{in}}{\partial V_{in}/\partial c_{in}} = \left(\frac{\beta_2 + 2\beta_3 T_{in}}{\beta_1}\right) \cdot w_n \tag{2.23}$$

which varies across individuals since it depends on w_n and T_{in}.

An example of this type of specification is the "naïve" mode choice model reported by McFadden *et al.* (1977, pp. 121–123), explaining choice among four modes with an estimated specification:

$$V = -0.0412 \cdot c / w - 0.0201 \cdot T - 0.0531 \cdot T^o - 0.89 \cdot D^1 - 1.78 \cdot D^3 - 2.15 \cdot D^4 \tag{2.24}$$
$$(0.0054) \quad\;\; (0.0072) \quad (0.0070) \quad\;\; (0.26) \quad\;\; (0.24) \quad\;\; (0.25)$$

where estimated standard errors are below the coefficients. Note that this is a simplification of (2.19), with $\beta_3 = 0$, except that here travel time is broken into two components: in-vehicle time T and out-of-vehicle time (waiting and walking for transit access) T^o. Adapting (2.23), we see that the VOT for each of these two components is assumed proportional to the post-tax wage rate, the proportionality constant being the ratio of the corresponding time-coefficient to the coefficient of c/w. Hence, the values of in-vehicle and out-of-vehicle time are 49% and 129% of the after-tax wage, respectively.

We emphasize that VOT as defined here is a marginal concept, being the ratio of two derivatives: namely, the marginal values of time gains and income. It is thus a measure, per unit of time, that applies to small time savings. For a larger time saving, say from T_{in}^1 to T_{in}^2, the total value to travelers would be the integral of (2.23), which in this example can be computed analytically:

$$\int_{T_{in}^1}^{T_{in}^2} (v_T)_{in} \, dT = \left(\frac{\beta_2 + 2\beta_3 \bar{T}}{\beta_1}\right) \cdot w_n \cdot \Delta T$$

where $\bar{T} = (T_{in}^1 + T_{in}^2)/2$ and $\Delta T = T_{in}^2 - T_{in}^1$. Thus, in this example, the value of a finite time saving is computed as the time saving multiplied by the marginal VOT, with the latter evaluated at the average trip time before and after the change.

As a more complex example, suppose we extend equation (2.19) by adding alternative-specific dummies, both separately (with coefficients α_i) and interacted with travel time (with coefficients γ_i):

$$V_{in} = \alpha_i + \beta_1 \cdot (c_{in} / w_n) + \beta_2 T_{in} + \beta_3 T_{in}^2 + \gamma_i T_{in} \tag{2.25}$$

where one of the α_i and one of the γ_i are normalized to zero.[28] This yields the following VOT, applicable when individual n chooses alternative i:

$$(v_T)_{in} = \left(\frac{\beta_2 + 2\beta_3 T_{in} + \gamma_i}{\beta_1} \right) \cdot w_n \tag{2.26}$$

Now the VOT varies across modes, even if they have identical travel times, due to the presence of γ_i. This is a common specification to capture the possibility that time spent in some modes is more onerous than in others. There is a danger in this, however: What appears to be variation in VOT across modes may just reflect selection bias because people who have high values of time, for reasons we cannot observe, will tend to self-select onto the faster modes. This possibility can be modeled explicitly using a random coefficient model, described in Section 2.4.2.[29]

Confidence bounds for a ratio of coefficients, or for more complex functions of coefficients, can be estimated by standard approximations for transformations of normal variates. Daly *et al.* (2012) discuss several methods.[30]

Sometimes there is interest in elasticities of probabilities with respect to a variable. These are especially simple in the logit model, for which the own- and cross-elasticities with respect to a continuous variable z^k are:

$$\eta_{ii} \equiv \frac{\partial P_i}{\partial z_i^k} \frac{z_i^k}{P_i} = \beta^k z_i^k (1 - P_i); \quad \eta_{ij} \equiv \frac{\partial P_i}{\partial z_j^k} \frac{z_j^k}{P_i} = -\beta^k z_j^k P_j \tag{2.27}$$

2.2.4   *Data*

Some of the most important explanatory variables for travel-demand modeling are determined endogenously within a larger model, of which the demand model is just one component. A common example is the use of travel times for explaining travel on roads: travel times depend on congestion, which depends on the amount of travel. Thus, the application of a travel-demand model may require a process of *equilibration*, in which a solution is sought to a set of simultaneous relationships. The classic formulation of such supply–demand equilibration is by Beckmann, McGuire, and Winsten (1956).

The possible endogeneity of travel characteristics is also a barrier to obtaining valid statistical estimates of demand parameters. With aggregate data, the issues are identical to those arising in simultaneous equations throughout economics, and solutions are similar: typically, instrumental variables, as treated in any econometrics textbook. True endogeneity is less likely when using disaggregate data, because a single observation is unlikely to influence characteristics of the travel environment. But disaggregate demand analysis, like all statistical work, is subject to a different problem which has essentially identical statistical properties as endogeneity: namely, the well-known "omitted variable bias" that arises when a variable not included in the model affects demand directly and also affects another explanatory variable that *is* included. In the jargon of econometrics, the problem arises when the omitted variable is correlated with the error term in the equation. The techniques for removing endogeneity bias also work to remove omitted variable bias.

Aside from endogeneity, just measuring the values of independent variables, which typically vary by alternative, is more difficult than it may first appear. How does one know the attributes that a traveler would have encountered on an alternative that was not in fact used?

One possibility is to use objective estimates, such as the *engineering values* produced by network models of the transportation system. Another is to use *reported values* obtained directly from survey respondents. Each is subject to limitations.

Engineering values of travel attributes are often inaccurate and expensive to compute. Something as simple as the travel time on a particular highway segment at a particular time of day is difficult to ascertain; measuring the day-to-day variability of that travel time (a variable in many models) is even more difficult.[31]

Reported values measure people's perceptions of travel conditions. These perceptions do not necessarily reflect the conditions as objectively measured, which are usually needed to apply the model to practical questions. Furthermore, model estimation may be biased because people are especially unclear about alternatives they do not choose, and may exaggerate their relative disadvantages (Vreeswijk *et al.* 2014) – another type of endogeneity bias. A perverse side effect of such endogeneity bias is that the estimated model may appear to fit very well.

Ideally, a model could be formulated in which perceived attributes and actual choice are jointly determined, each influencing the other and both influenced by objective attributes and personal characteristics. McFadden (1999) discusses such approaches. This type of model most faithfully replicates the actual decision process, but may not be worth the extra complexity unless there is inherent interest in perception formation – for example to inform marketing strategies. For purposes of transportation planning, the main concern is the relationship between objective values and actual choices; a model limited to this relationship may be interpreted as the reduced form of a more complex model including perceptions, and so may be theoretically valid even if perceptions differ from objective values.

In light of these consideration, the most fruitful expenditure of research effort is usually on finding ways to measure objective values as accurately as possible. An alternative method, in a large sample, is to assign values for a given alternative according to averages reported by people in the sample in similar circumstances who use that alternative. This limits endogeneity bias by using an identical procedure to assign values to chosen and unchosen alternatives, although it might not work if users are more uncertain about the attributes of some alternatives than about others.

The types of data described thus far are used for *revealed preference* (RP) studies, which attempt to explain choices actually made. Another approach is to use SP data, based on responses to hypothetical situations as described in Section 2.1.5.3. In that case, the dependent variable is a hypothetical choice, and the independent (explanatory) variables are hypothetical attributes chosen by the researcher. SP data permit more control over the ranges of and correlations among the independent variables through an appropriate experimental design.[32] With computer-aided or online surveys, the questions posed can be adapted to information about the respondent as it is collected. Another advantage of SP surveys is that they can elicit information about potential travel options that do not exist at the time of the survey.

A disadvantage, however, is the inherent uncertainty as to how accurately SP data describe what people do in real situations. Researchers have worked to design survey procedures and statistical adjustments to prevent or compensate for such inaccuracy (*e.g.*, Fifer *et al.* 2014).

It is possible to combine RP and SP data in a single estimation procedure in order to take advantage of the strengths of each.[33] As long as observations are independent of each other, the log-likelihood functions simply add. To account for differences in the nature of RP and SP data, it is recommended to estimate certain parameters separately in the two portions of the data: Typically these include alternative-specific constants, the scale factors μ for the two parts of the sample (see next subsection), and behavioral coefficients of special interest.

Discrete-choice modeling of travel demand has mostly taken advantage of data from large and expensive transportation surveys. Deaton (1985) shows that it can also be used with household expenditure surveys, which are often conducted for other purposes and are frequently available in developing nations. Today, researchers are increasingly able to take advantage of large datasets created using digital technologies, a topic we discuss in Section 2.8.

2.2.5 *Randomness, scale of utility, and measures of benefit*

The variance of the random utility term in equation (2.14) reflects, among other things, randomness in individual behavior and heterogeneity among observationally identical individuals. Hence, it plays a key role in determining how sensitive travel behavior is to changes in observable quantities such as price, service quality, and demographic traits. Little randomness implies a nearly deterministic model, one in which behavior suddenly changes at some crucial switching point (*e.g.*, when transit service becomes as fast as a car). Conversely, if there is a lot of randomness, behavior changes only gradually as the values of independent variables are varied.

However, when the variance of the random component is normalized, the overall extent of randomness becomes represented not by the random term but by the inverse of the scale of the systematic utility function. For example, in the logit model (2.18), suppose systematic utility is linear in parameter vector β as in (2.20). If all the elements of β are small in magnitude, the corresponding variables have little effect on probabilities so choices are dominated by randomness. If the elements of β are large, most of the variation in choice behavior is explained by variation in observable variables.

Randomness in individual behavior can also be viewed as producing variety, or *entropy*, in aggregate behavior. Indeed, it can be measured by the entropy-like quantity $-\Sigma_n \Sigma_j P_{jn} \log P_{jn}$, which is larger when the choice probability is divided evenly among the alternatives. Anderson *et al.* (1988) show that the aggregate logit model can be derived by maximizing a utility function for a representative traveler that includes an entropy term subject to a consistency constraint on aggregate choice shares. Thus, entropy is a link between aggregate and disaggregate models: at the aggregate level we can say the system tends to favor entropy or, equivalently, that a representative consumer craves variety, whereas at the disaggregate level we represent the same phenomenon as randomness in utility.

It is often useful to have a measure of the overall desirability of the choice set being offered to a decision-maker (*e.g.*, a consumer or traveler). Such a measure must account both for the utility of the individual choices being offered and for the variety of choices offered. The value of variety is directly related to randomness because both arise from unobserved idiosyncrasies in preferences. If choice were deterministic (*i.e.*, determined solely by the ranking of systematic utility V_{in} across alternatives i), the decision-maker would care only about the traits of the best alternative; improving or offering inferior alternatives would have no value. But with random utilities, there is some chance that an alternative with a low value of V_{in} will nevertheless be chosen; so it is desirable for such an alternative to be offered and to be made as attractive as possible. A natural measure of the desirability of choice set J is the expected maximum utility of that set, which for the logit model has the form:

$$E \max_j (V_j + \varepsilon_j) = \mu^{-1} \cdot \log \sum_{j=1}^{J} \exp(\mu V_j) + \gamma \tag{2.28}$$

where $\gamma = 0.5772$ is Euler's constant (it accounts for the nonzero mean of the error terms ε_j in the standard normalization). Here we have retained the scale parameter μ from (2.17), rather than normalizing it, to make clear how randomness affects expected utility. When the amount of randomness is small (large μ), the summation on the right-hand side of (2.28) is dominated by its largest term (its index will be denoted by j^*); expected utility is then approximately $\mu^{-1} \cdot \log[\exp(\mu V_{j^*})] = V_{j^*}$, the utility of the dominating alternative. When randomness dominates (small μ), all terms contribute more or less equally; denoting their average utility by V, expected utility is then approximately $\mu^{-1} \cdot \log[J \cdot \exp(\mu V)] = V + \mu^{-1} \cdot \log(J)$. This is the average utility plus a term reflecting the desirability of having many choices. Because of this formula, sometimes an explanatory variable defined as $\log(J_i)$ is added to a model explaining choice among various composite alternatives i each consisting of J_i separate elemental alternatives.

Naturally enough, expected utility is directly related to measures of consumer welfare. Small and Rosen (1981) show that provided price is included among the variables in V_{jn}, changes in aggregate consumers' surplus (the area to the left of the demand curve and above the current price)[34] are appropriate measures of consumer welfare even when the demand function is generated by a set of individuals making discrete choices. Consider a set of ω_n observationally identical individuals characterized by systematic utilities V_{jn}. Changes in their consumers' surplus are proportional to changes in this expected maximum utility. The proportionality constant is ω_n divided by λ_n, the marginal utility of income for a consumer in this group. Thus, a useful welfare measure for such a set of individuals, with systematic utilities $\{V_{jn}\}$ estimated using the normalization $\mu = 1$, is:

$$W_n = \frac{\omega_n}{\lambda_n} \log \sum_{j=1}^{J} \exp(V_{jn}) \tag{2.29}$$

a formula also derived by Williams (1977). This is identical to expected maximum utility (2.28), except that here we omit Euler's constant γ since it is cancelled out when making welfare comparisons.

Because portions of the utility V_i that are common to all alternatives cannot be estimated from the choice model, λ_n is not estimated directly in a discrete choice estimation. However, if a price or cost variable c is included in the specification, λ_n can be determined from Roy's identity (2.6):

$$\lambda_n = -\frac{1}{x_{jn}} \cdot \frac{\partial V_{jn}}{\partial c_{jn}} \tag{2.30}$$

where x_{jn} is consumption of good j conditional on choosing it among the discrete alternatives.[35] For a single choice among discrete alternatives (*i.e.*, a single *choice occasion*), we have $x_{jn} = 1$, so that λ_n is simply the coefficient of the monetary attribute c_{jn} if that attribute is included in V_j linearly and without interactions. For multiple choice occasions, and ignoring discounting within the period in which the choice occasions occur, welfare then becomes the sum of the values computed for each of the choice occasions. When such multiple choice occasions occur over a well-defined time period, such as a year, and involve identical objective conditions as measured by $\{V_{jn}\}$, then this way of computing welfare for that time period leads to the same result as what is obtained from (2.29) with x_{jn} in (2.30) set equal to the number of choice occasions over that time period. In the case of commuting mode choice, for example, x_{jn} is then just the individual's number of work trips per year, and we will find the same annual welfare independently of whether we multiply the welfare for one choice situation with the number of choices made, or adjust the marginal utility of income by substituting that number x_{jn} in (2.30).

Expression (2.30) is valid provided that its right-hand side is independent of j; when it is not, tractable approximations are available (Chattopadhyay 2001).

There is an important condition for the validity of (2.29), which is that any *income effects* in the response of transportation demand be small – that will ensure that λ_n does not differ significantly between two situations that are being compared in a welfare analysis. (This condition is likely to be met for transportation analysis, because the fraction of income spent on any one transportation activity is usually small.) The reason for this caveat is that changes in transportation costs or service quality not only influence choice directly, as explained by the choice model, but also influence it indirectly through the overall effect on the traveler's standard of living. For example, suppose the price of gasoline rises by 50%, and gasoline accounts for 2% of total expenditures by a particular group of people. The price increase makes activities that use gasoline somewhat less attractive than before and so tilts consumers toward choosing fewer of them. (They might travel less, or they might buy smaller cars with fewer energy-consuming options.) This is sometimes expressed by defining a *compensated price elasticity*: the responsiveness to price that would occur if incomes were supplemented so as to leave people just as well off as before. But presuming they are not so compensated, the price increase makes them worse off by reducing their discretionary income for other consumption. As a first-order approximation, in the above example people would behave as though they had 1% less discretionary income (50% of 2%). If gasoline is a *normal* good – one whose consumption increases with income – then this indirect effect also reduces gasoline consumption, by an amount proportional to the product of the income elasticity of gasoline and the fraction of income spent on gasoline. This indirect effect is called an *income effect*.[36]

2.2.6 Aggregation and forecasting

Once a disaggregate travel-demand model is estimated, this raises the question of how to predict aggregate quantities such as total transit ridership or total travel flows between zones.

The most straightforward and common method is *sample enumeration*. A sample of consumers is drawn, each assumed to represent a subpopulation with identical observable characteristics. (The estimation sample itself may satisfy this criterion and hence be usable as an enumeration sample.) Each individual's choice probabilities, computed using the estimated parameters, predict the shares of that subpopulation choosing the various alternatives. These predictions can then simply be added, weighting each sample member according to the corresponding subpopulation size – just as we did using weight ω_n when computing welfare changes in (2.29). Standard deviations of forecast values can be estimated by Monte Carlo simulation methods.

The effects of a policy can be simulated by determining how it changes the values of independent variables for each sample member, and recomputing the predicted probabilities accordingly. Doing so requires that these variables be explicitly included in the model. For example, to simulate the effect of better schedule coordination at transfer points on a transit system, the model must include a variable such as waiting time at a transfer point. Such a specification is called *policy-sensitive*; the ability to examine complex policies by computing their effects on an enumeration sample is one of the major advantages of disaggregate models.

A naïve calculation based on a representative individual might give a quite misleading forecast of policy sensitivity. For example, suppose the choice between travel by automobile or bus (alternatives 1 and 2) is determined by a logit model with utilities given by equation (2.19) with $\beta_3 = 0$. Then the probability of choosing bus travel is:

$$P_{2n} = \frac{1}{1 + \exp[(\beta_1 / w_n) \cdot (c_{1n} - c_{2n}) + \beta_2 \cdot (T_{1n} - T_{2n})]} \tag{2.31}$$

Suppose everyone's bus fare is c_2 and everyone's wage is w. Then

$$\frac{\partial P_{2n}}{\partial c_2} = (\beta_1 / w) \cdot P_{2n} \cdot (1 - P_{2n}) \tag{2.32}$$

Now suppose instead that half the population has conditions favorable to bus travel, such that $P_{2n} = 0.9$, whereas the other half has $P_{2n} = 0.1$. Aggregate bus share is then 0.5. Applying (2.32) to each half of the population, we see that the rate of change of aggregate bus share with respect to fare is $(\beta_1/w)[\frac{1}{2}(0.1)(0.9) + \frac{1}{2}(0.1)(0.9)] = 0.09(\beta_1/w)$. But if we were to apply (2.32) as though there were a single representative traveler with $P_2 = 0.5$, we would get $(\beta_1/w)(0.5)(0.5) = 0.25(\beta_1/w)$, nearly three times the true value. Again, the existence of variety reduces the actual sensitivity to changes in independent variables, in this case because there are only a few travelers (those with extreme values of $\varepsilon_{1n} - \varepsilon_{2n}$) who have a close enough decision to be affected.

2.2.7 Specification

Like most applied statistical work, travel-demand analysis requires balancing completeness against tractability. A model that includes every relevant influence on behavior may require too much data to estimate with adequate precision, or it may be too complex to serve as a practical guide to policy analysis. A related problem is that the statistical properties of the model, such as standard errors of estimated coefficients, are valid only when the model's basic assumptions are known in advance to be correct. But in practice, the researcher usually chooses a model's specification (*i.e.,* its functional form and set of included variables) using guidance from the same data as those from which its parameters are estimated.

A good way to handle both problems is to base empirical models on an explicit behavioral theory. Rather than trying out dozens of specifications to see what fits, relationships that are predicted by a plausible theory are preferred. For example, a specification like (2.19) would be chosen if there is good theoretical reason to think the VOT is closely related to the wage rate – a question explored later in this chapter.

Bayesian methods offer a more formal approach to using prior information or judgments when specifying empirical models. Instead of all-or-nothing decisions about model structure, they allow one to explicitly describe prior uncertainty and to calculate the manner in which prior beliefs need to be modified in light of the data. Such methods have been developed for parameter estimation in discrete-choice models (Train 2009, Chap. 12) and for selection among competing model specifications (Berger and Pericchi 2001).

One of the goals of disaggregate travel-demand modeling is to describe behavioral tendencies that are reasonably general. This would enable a model estimated in one time and place to be used for another time and place. The progress toward this goal of *transferability* has been disappointing, but some limited success has been achieved: The alternative-specific constants and the scale of the utility function are often found to be different in a new location, while relative values of most other coefficients tend to be the same. Thus, adjustments can be made relatively inexpensively by using limited data collection in a new location or even by adjusting alternative-specific constants to match known aggregate choice shares (Koppelman and Rose 1985). The adjustment procedure is sometimes called calibration, and requires an iterative algorithm for matching the choice shares predicted by the model to observed shares.[37]

2.2.8   Ordered and rank-ordered models

Sometimes there is a natural ordering to the alternatives that can be exploited to guide specification. For example, suppose a researcher wants to explain a household's choice among owning no vehicle, one vehicle, or two or more vehicles. They might postulate a single index of propensity to own many vehicles, determined in part by observable variables like household size and employment status.

In such a case, an *ordered response model* might be assumed. In this model, the choice is determined by the size of an unobservable "latent variable" $y^*_n = \beta'z_n + \varepsilon_n$, with choice j occurring if this latent variable falls in a particular interval $\left[\mu_{j-1}, \mu_j\right]$ of the real line, where $\mu_0 = -\infty$ and $\mu_J = \infty$. The interval boundaries $\mu_1, ..., \mu_{J-1}$ are estimated along with β, except that one of them can be normalized arbitrarily if $\beta'z_n$ contains a constant term. The probability of choosing alternative j is then

$$P_{jn} = \Pr[\mu_{j-1} < \beta'z_n + \varepsilon_n < \mu_j] = F(\mu_j - \beta'z_n) - F(\mu_{j-1} - \beta'z_n) \tag{2.33}$$

where $F(\cdot)$ is the cdf assumed for ε_n. In the *ordered probit model* $F(\cdot)$ is standard normal, while in the *ordered logit model* it is logistic, that is, $F(x) = [1 + \exp(-x)]^{-1}$. Note that all the variables in this model are characteristics of individuals, not of the alternatives. Thus, if the latter information is available, this model does not take advantage of it.

In some cases, the alternatives are integers indicating the number of times a particular event occurs. An example would be the number of trips per month by a given household to a particular destination. For such cases, a set of models based on Poisson and negative binomial regressions is available (Washington *et al.* 2010, Chap. 10).

Sometimes information is available not only on the most preferred alternative, but on the individual's ranking of other alternatives. In that case, "choices" for numerous situations are effectively observed. Efficient use can be made of such data through the *rank-ordered logit model*.[38] If a complete ranking of J alternatives is obtained, the probability formula is a product of J logit probability formulas, one for each ranked alternative, giving the probability of choosing that alternative from the set of itself and all lower-ranked alternatives. The researcher may want to ignore the stated ordering among some low-ranked alternatives, or alternatively to estimate a separate scale factor for those choices, to allow for the possibility that a survey respondent pays less attention when answering questions about alternatives of little interest.

2.3   Disaggregate models: examples

Discrete-choice models have been estimated for nearly every conceivable travel decision, forming a body of research that cannot possibly be reviewed here. In practice, these models are typically linked into large simultaneous systems requiring extensive computer simulation. Many planning organizations maintain such a suite of models and constantly update and adapt them as needed.

In this section, we present three very modest disaggregate models, each chosen for its compact representation of a behavioral factor that is central to urban transportation policy as analyzed in later chapters.

2.3.1   *Mode choice*

A study by Fox *et al.* (2014) of mode and destination choice for work trips in the Toronto–Hamilton area of Canada provides an example of a simple mode choice model. The authors analyze survey data from four different years, of which we focus on their results from 74,993 commuters in 2006. We describe just the mode choice component, whose logit probabilities are modeled as conditional on destination. We focus on the simplest of several specifications estimated.

Commuters are assumed to choose among four modes: auto driver (AD), auto passenger (AP), local transit (LT), and walking (WK). Systematic utility is linear in parameters with 12 explanatory variables and hence 12 coefficients to be estimated. The variables are defined in Table 2.2, or equivalently as the terms within the square brackets in the following specification:

$$
\begin{aligned}
V = {}& \beta_1 \big[c \big] + \beta_2 \big[\log c \big] \\
& + \beta_3 \big[D_A T_A \big] + \beta_4 \big[D_{LT} T_{LT}^{veh} \big] + \beta_5 \big[D_{LT} T_{LT}^{wait} \big] + \beta_6 \big[D_{LT} T_{LT}^{walk} \big] \\
& + \beta_7 \big[D_{AP} d_{AP} \big] + \beta_8 \big[D_{WK} d_{WK} \big] \\
& + \beta_9 \big[D_{AP} \big] + \beta_{10} \big[D_{LT} \big] + \beta_{11} \big[D_{LT} CBDdest \big] + \beta_{12} \big[D_{WK} \big]
\end{aligned}
\tag{2.34}
$$

where D_{AD}, D_{AP}, D_{LT}, and D_{WK} are alternative-specific dummy variables for each of the four modes; $D_A \equiv D_{AD} + D_{AP}$ is an indicator for either auto mode; T_A and T_{LT}^{veh} are in-vehicle times for auto and transit; superscripts *wait* and *walk* refer to expected waiting time and walking time to access transit; d is distance by the indicated mode; and *CBDdest* is a dummy variable for trips with a destination in the CBD of Toronto or Hamilton. We have omitted the alternative subscripts for simplicity. The variables in (2.34) appear in the same order as in Table 2.2; each separate line in the equation corresponds to a separate section of the table.

We note several features of this specification. Utility is declining and convex as a function of cost c, provided β_1 and β_2 are negative, indicating that cost is disliked at the margin but less so for more costly trips. The cost variable is *generic* (*i.e.*, its coefficient is not mode-specific).[39] The variable "auto time" is generic in the limited sense of applying to both auto modes. The time required for a transit trip is disaggregated into three components, to allow for different marginal disutilities of each. Distance is assumed a relevant source of disutility for auto passengers and walking – perhaps reflecting disadvantages of being isolated far from home without a vehicle. Costs, times, and distances are engineering values extracted from "skims" of coded highway and transit networks, which are the results of an algorithm calculating the best path, one for each mode, from each origin to each destination.

Finally, three pure alternative-specific dummy variables are provided to capture unmeasured advantages and disadvantages. Since only utility differences affect choice, one alternative (chosen arbitrarily to be auto passenger) has no alternative-specific dummy. In addition, the dummy for local transit is interacted with a dummy for destinations in the CBD, in order to allow for the possibility that transit has advantages for trips to the CBD even after accounting for the measured levels of service. For example, a transit trip to the CBD provides greater flexibility of rerouting due to unexpected circumstances, and it might involve a monthly fare pass that is useful for within-CBD trips during the workday.

The estimated coefficients suggest that time in a car and time waiting for transit have greater disutility than time in a transit vehicle. As is common, waiting time is found to have marginal

Table 2.2 Variables and coefficient estimates: mode choice, home–work trips, Toronto–Hamilton area, 2006

Dependent variable: Mode chosen

AD = auto driver; AP = auto passenger; LT = local transit; WK = walk

Explanatory variable	Applicable modes	Coefficient	t-Statistic[a]
Cost variables[b]			
Cost	All	−0.0015	−16.1
Log cost	All	−0.242	−20.8
Travel-time variables[c]			
Auto time	AD, AP	−0.039	−38.3
Transit in-vehicle time	LT	−0.023	−35.5
Transit wait time	LT	−0.061	−31.4
Transit walk time	LT	−0.029	−20.8
Trip distance variables[d]			
Distance by car	AP	−0.030	−35.0
Distance by walking	WK	−0.624	−52.3
Mode constants and			
destination indicator[e]			
AP	AP	−3.459	−49.3
LT	LT	0.224	4.7
LT * CBD dest.	LT	0.945	22.8
WK	WK	0.049	0.6
Implied values of time (C\$/hr)			
Auto		8.63	
Transit in-vehicle		5.09	
Transit waiting		13.51	
Transit walking		6.42	

[a]   The *t*-statistic is the ratio of the estimated coefficient and its estimated standard error.
[b]   Cost is in Canadian cents per trip.
[c]   Time is in min/trip.
[d]   Distance is in km/trip.
[e]   These are dummy variables, taking on values 0 or 1.

Source: Adapted from Fox et al. (2014, Table 14, last column, plus authors' calculations). Reprinted with permission.

disutility two to three times as high as in-vehicle time; many other studies find a similar penalty for walking time. These relative values often vary from study to study, probably because they depend greatly on the conditions in which waiting or walking occurs.

The VOT, defined by the ratio following the second equality sign in (2.23), is a function of cost, because cost enters the utility function nonlinearly and hence its marginal utility (the denominator of that ratio) is not a constant. We have calculated the four values of time defined by the model for one particular value of trip cost, namely C\$2.[40] VOT is commonly expected to vary also with income or wage rate, as for example in (2.19), but the needed variables to measure that variation were unavailable in this study.

The estimated mode constants show that, relative to auto driver, there is significant disutility to being an auto passenger, perhaps due to dependence on someone else's schedule. All else being equal, there is a moderate positive utility (0.224) for transit relative to auto driver for trips outside the CBD, and a large positive utility (0.224+0.945) for such trips to the CBD.

The constant for walking is very small and not statistically distinguishable from zero according to its t-statistic, suggesting that desirability of walking relative to other modes is adequately captured by the other variables in the model.[41]

More complete models typically aim to directly measure some of the preferences that are captured indirectly here through the alternative-specific constants. For example, some studies include a dummy variable indicating if a transfer was necessary, or a count variable denoting how many transfers were necessary, for the trip being explained. The resulting "transfer penalty" is often expressed as the equivalent number of minutes of in-vehicle time. Currie (2005) compares results of ten such studies, finding that the average transfer penalty ranges from 8 minutes for transfers between subway lines to 22 minutes for transfers between bus lines.

2.3.2   *Trip-scheduling choice*

One of the key decisions affecting congestion is the timing or scheduling of work trips. There is now a substantial body of empirical work on this subject, reviewed by Thorhauge *et al.* (2016).

Although the scheduling decision is inherently continuous, it is often modeled as a discrete choice among time intervals. There are two reasons for this: Survey responses are rounded off to a few even numbers, and disaggregate models can easily portray the complex manner in which travel time varies across possible schedules.[42] Small (1982) estimates the choice among 12 possible 5-minute intervals for work arrival time, using a set of auto commuters from the San Francisco Bay Area who report an official work start time. The dataset includes characteristics of the workers and a network-based engineering calculation of the travel time that each worker would encounter at each arrival time. Commuters are assumed to have full information and so can choose arrival time with certainty.

The utility specification postulates a linear penalty for arriving early, on the assumption that time spent before work is relatively unproductive, and an empirically larger linear penalty for arriving late. This basic approach forms the starting point for many subsequent studies of the timing of work trips. To write this mathematically, define *schedule delay*, S_D, as the difference (in minutes, rounded to nearest 5 minutes) between a given arrival time and the official work start time. Define "Schedule Delay Late" $SDL = \text{Max}\{S_D, 0\}$ and "Schedule Delay Early" $SDE = \text{Max}\{-S_D, 0\}$. Define a "late dummy," DL, equal to one for the on-time and late alternatives, zero otherwise. Define T as the travel time (in minutes) encountered, which varies by alternative due to congestion.

The estimated utility function, with estimated standard errors in parentheses, is:[43]

$$V = -0.106 \cdot T - 0.065 \cdot SDE - 0.254 \cdot SDL - 0.58 \cdot DL$$
$$(0.038) \quad (0.007) \qquad (0.030) \qquad (0.21) \tag{2.35}$$

For simplicity, we exclude two variables used by Small to represent a tendency of respondents to round off answers to the nearest 10 or 15 minutes. More complex models are also estimated, in which the various penalties are nonlinear or depend upon such factors as the worker's family status, occupation, car occupancy, and stated work-hour flexibility.

Figure 2.1 shows the portion of utility function (2.35) that is a function of schedule delay, divided by the coefficient of travel time. The marginal rates of substitution (ratios of coefficients) indicate that the commuter is willing to suffer an extra 0.61 minutes of congestion to reduce the amount of early arrival by 1 minute, and 2.40 minutes of congestion to reduce late

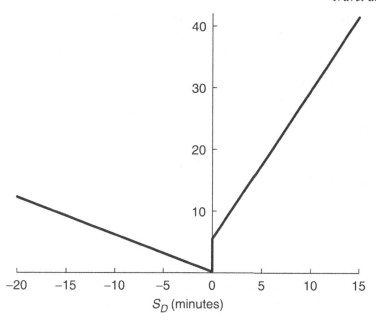

Figure 2.1 Disutility of schedule delay in units of equivalent minutes of travel delay.

arrival by 1 minute, plus an extra 5.47 minutes of congestion to avoid any of the just-on-time or late alternatives. These turn out to be key parameters in models, to be presented in the next chapter, which describe equilibrium when congestion occurs in the form of queuing behind a bottleneck. They also can be used to formulate models of travelers' responses to infrequent transit service and to network unreliability, as described in Section 2.7.

The alternatives in the choice model just described have a natural ordering in terms of chronological time; so why is the ordered response model not used? The reasons are that the ordered response model cannot take advantage of information that varies by alternative, such as travel time, as already noted; and that no plausible combination of variables would exert a monotonic influence on the time of day chosen. There is a different model, described in Section 2.4.1, that can account for this ordering: It has been used to estimate this same utility function (Small 1987).

Often, it is impractical to model trip timing in this much detail. Instead, one may define a few time periods, such as peak and off-peak, and treat them as composite alternatives. An example of this approach is Hess *et al.* (2007). At the other extreme, especially fine-grained data may permit estimation of the more general model of Tseng and Verhoef (2008) and Fosgerau and Engelson (2011), following an approach originally suggested by Vickrey (1973). Here, utility (2.35) is derived as the difference between utility of time spent at the destination versus time spent at the origin. If those utilities are assumed time-varying, they imply a time-varying value of travel time as well as a more nuanced analysis of scheduling choice. For example, Börjesson *et al.* (2012) distinguish between patterns where the marginal utilities of time spent at different locations vary over time in a linear or stepwise fashion. Buchholz *et al.* (2022) use this approach to analyze data from a Prague ride-sourcing system called Liftago, in which several providers submit bids – the price and pickup time – to serve a specific ride request. The traveler then often faces a trade-off between price and waiting time at the origin. Under certain conditions, these data identify not only the value of waiting time but also the underlying values of time spent at the origin and the destination, and how those values vary by time of day, location, and individual.

Scheduling constraints are likely to be more flexible for long-run than for short-run decisions, while the value of travel-time savings are likely to be higher if these savings are anticipated rather than come as a surprise. Peer *et al.* (2015) model these aspects and find confirming empirical evidence from behavior of travelers faced with an experimental peak-load pricing program in the Netherlands.

2.3.3   Route choice and reliability of travel

Lam and Small (2001) analyze data from commuters with an option of paying to travel in a set of express lanes on a very congested freeway, State Route 91 (SR91), in southern California. The express-lane toll depends on time of day and on car occupancy, both of which differ across respondents. Travel time also varies by time of day – fortunately in a manner not too highly correlated with the toll. The authors construct a measure of the unreliability of travel time by obtaining data on travel times across many different days, all at the same time of day. Specifically, they use the median (*i.e.*, 50th percentile) travel time across days as a measure of travel time, and the difference between 90th and 50th percentile travel times (also across days) as a pragmatic summary measure of unreliability. This latter choice is based on the idea, supported by the results of trip-scheduling models, that people are more averse to unexpected late arrivals than to unexpected early arrivals. (More on this in Section 2.7.4.)

The model explains a pair of related decisions: (a) whether to acquire an electronic toll-collection transponder (required for use of the express lanes) and (b) which lanes to take on the day in question. A natural way to view these decisions is as a hierarchical set, with transponder choice governed by the potential benefits of express-lane travel and other factors. As we will see in the next section, a model known as "nested logit" has been developed precisely for this type of situation, and indeed Lam and Small estimate such a model. However, they obtain virtually identical results with a simpler "joint logit" model with three choice alternatives: (1) no transponder, (2) have a transponder but travel in the free lanes, and (3) have a transponder and travel in the express lanes.

Selected results are described in Table 2.3. Here, $D^{tag} \equiv D^2 + D^3$ is a composite of alternative-specific dummy variables for those choices involving a transponder, or "toll tag"; its negative coefficient presumably reflects the hassle and cost of obtaining one. Getting a transponder is apparently more attractive to people with high annual incomes (*Inc*, in \$1,000s per year) and less attractive to those speaking a foreign language (dummy variable *Lang*). The statistical insignificance of the coefficient of D^3, an alternative-specific dummy for using the toll lanes, suggests that the most important explanatory factors are included explicitly in the model – although its large standard deviation leaves this conclusion uncertain.

The coefficients on per-person cost c, median travel time T, and unreliability R can be used to compute dollar values of time and reliability. Here, we focus on two aspects of the resulting valuations. First, reliability is highly valued, with a coefficient of similar magnitude as that of travel time (recall that both variables are measured in units of time). Second, men seem to care less about reliability than women; their value is only 53% as high according to the point

Table 2.3 Selected estimated coefficients of route-choice model

Variables	Estimated coefficient		
	Symbol	Coefficient	Standard error
Alternatives requiring a transponder ("toll tag"):			
Alt.-specific dummy	D^{tag}	−0.862	0.411
Income ($1,000s/year)	$D^{\text{tag}} \cdot \text{Inc}$	0.0239	0.0058
Speaks foreign language at home	$D^{\text{tag}} \cdot \text{Lang}$	−0.766	0.412
Alternative requires payment of toll	D^3	−0.789	0.853
Cost per person ($/trip)	C	−0.357	0.138
Travel time, median (min/trip)	T	−0.109	0.056
Unreliability (90th–50th percentile travel time)	R	−0.159	0.048
Unreliability × male dummy	$\text{Male} \cdot R$	0.074	0.046

Source: Listing of selected coefficients from Lam and Small (2001, Table 11, Model 4b); with adjustments per Lam and Small, p. 234 and Table 11 (note *a*). Reprinted with permission from Elsevier.

estimates,[44] although the difference (*i.e.*, the coefficient of *Male·R*) is not quite statistically significant even at a 10% significance level.

This provides a good opportunity to consider how to select the list of variables to include in a travel-demand model. In this case, the model is specified to yield a constant VOT and a constant *value of reliability* (VOR), to be defined shortly. Although theory suggests that these values might vary by income or other factors, the authors report that including such variations (through interaction with variables *T* and *R*) mostly resulted in imprecise and ambiguous results. However, the authors did find that those same factors strongly affect the alternative-specific constants, via several interactions – only three of which are reported here. The alternative-specific constant D^3 is included to control for unmeasured factors that could affect the actual decision to pay for the express lanes.

The variable *Male·R* is included, despite its statistical insignificance, because several studies of this particular toll facility have found women more likely to use the express lanes than men – experimentation showed that this formulation fits better than a simple interaction variable *Male* $\cdot D^3$. Wondering whether this gender difference could be due to differing responsibility for children, the authors tried a variable equal to *R* multiplied by a dummy for women with children; it was unsuccessful.[45]

Using these results, we can define a useful quantity: the *generalized price* of a particular type of travel.[46] The idea is that if a traveler considers money price and other aspects of travel, such as time and reliability, in fixed proportions, it may be analytically useful to combine them into a single index denominated in money. The generalized price *p* for females would be defined in this case as

$$p = c + \frac{0.109}{0.357}T + \frac{0.159}{0.357}R \qquad (2.36)$$

with males similar except a smaller coefficient on *R*. The first ratio of coefficients in (2.36) is just the VOT defined earlier, and the second is the VOR. The generalized price could also incorporate more than one component of travel time, as in (2.24).

The scheduling variables of (2.35) used by Small (1982) could also be included in a generalized price. His study includes no cost variable; but it does include travel time, whose coefficient could be converted to money using external evidence on VOT. For example, suppose one be-lieves that the VOT measured in (2.36), namely $0.109/0.357 \equiv \$0.305/\text{min.}$, is also appropriate for the population from which (2.35) was estimated. Then the results in (2.35) could be com-bined to define a generalized price as:

$$p = c + 0.305 \cdot \left[T + \frac{0.065}{0.106} SDE + \frac{0.254}{0.106} SDL + \frac{0.58}{0.106} DL \right] \tag{2.37}$$

Chapter 3 will show that a generalized price of this form, except excluding DL, has been used extensively in "bottleneck models" to analyze equilibria with travelers individually choosing their trip schedules in response to time-varying congestion.

2.4   Advanced discrete-choice modeling

2.4.1   *Generalized extreme value models*

It is often implausible to assume that the additive random utility components ε_j are independ-ent, especially if important variables are omitted from the model's specification. This will make either logit or iid probit predict poorly.

A simple example illustrates this: mode choice among automobile, bus transit, and rail tran-sit. The two public-transit modes have many unmeasured attributes in common, such as lack of privacy, occasional crowding, dependence on a schedule, waiting time at a stop, and walk-ing time to and from stops. Suppose a traveler initially has available only auto ($j = 1$) and bus ($j = 2$), with equal systematic utilities V_j so that the choice probabilities are each one-half. Now suppose we want to predict the effects of adding a rail service ($j = 3$) with measurable char-acteristics identical to those for bus. The iid models would predict that all three modes would then have choice probabilities of one-third. In reality, the probability of choosing auto would most likely remain near one-half while the two transit modes divide the rest of the probability between them. The argument is even stronger if we imagine that the newly added mode is not rail, but simply a bus of a different color: This is the famous "red bus/blue bus" example already referred to above in Section 2.2.1.

This kind of situation calls for relaxing the iid assumption on the distributions of error terms of the various alternatives. The probit model generalizes naturally to non-iid joint distributions, as already noted, by allowing the distribution function in (2.15) to be multivariate normal. It must be remembered that not all the elements of this matrix can be distinguished (*identified*, in econometric terminology) because, as already noted, it is only the ($J - 1$) utility *differences* that affect behavior.[47]

The logit model generalizes in a comparable manner, as shown by McFadden (1978, 1981). The distribution function is postulated to be *generalized extreme value* (GEV), given by

$$F(\varepsilon_1, \dots, \varepsilon_J) = \exp\left[-G(e^{-\varepsilon_1}, \dots, e^{-\varepsilon_J}) \right]$$

where G is any continuous function that is increasing in its arguments and that satisfies certain technical conditions. With this distribution, the choice probabilities are of the form

$$P_i = \frac{e^{V_i} \cdot G_i(e^{V_1}, \dots, e^{V_J})}{G(e^{V_1}, \dots, e^{V_J})} \tag{2.38}$$

where G_i is the *i*th partial derivative of G. (The technical conditions assure that these probabilities add to one.) The expected maximum utility is

$$E \max_j (V_j + \varepsilon_j) = \log G(e^{V_1}, \dots, e^{V_J}) + \gamma \tag{2.39}$$

where (again) γ is Euler's constant.[48] Logit is the special case $G(y_1, \dots, y_J) = y_1 + \dots + y_J$.

The best known GEV model, other than logit itself, is *nested logit*. It is also called *structured logit* or *tree logit* and was first developed by Ben-Akiva (1974). In this model, certain groups of alternatives are postulated to have correlated random terms. This is accomplished by grouping the corresponding alternatives within function G in a manner we can illustrate using the auto–bus–rail example, with auto the first alternative:

$$G(y_1, y_2, y_3) = y_1 + (y_2^{1/\rho} + y_3^{1/\rho})^\rho \tag{2.40}$$

In this equation, ρ is a parameter between 0 and 1 that indicates the degree of dissimilarity between bus and rail; more precisely, $1-\rho^2$ is the correlation between ε_1 and ε_2 (Daganzo and Kusnic 1993). The choice probability for this example, computed from (2.38), may be written:

$$P_i = P\left(B_{r(i)}\right) \times P\left(i \mid B_{r(i)}\right) \tag{2.41}$$

$$P(B_r) = \frac{\exp(\rho \cdot I_r)}{\displaystyle\sum_{s=1}^{2} \exp(\rho \cdot I_s)} \tag{2.42}$$

$$P(i \mid B_r) = \frac{\exp(V_i / \rho)}{\displaystyle\sum_{j \in B_r} \exp(V_j / \rho)} \tag{2.43}$$

where $B_1 = \{1\}$ and $B_2 = \{2, 3\}$ are a partition of the choice set into groups; $r(i)$ indexes the group containing alternative i; and I_r denotes the *inclusive value* of set B_r, defined as the logarithm of the denominator of (2.43):

$$I_r = \log \sum_{j \in B_r} \exp(V_j / \rho) \tag{2.44}$$

When $\rho = 1$ in this model, ε_2 and ε_3 are independent and we have the logit model. As $\rho \downarrow 0$, ε_2 and ε_3 become perfectly correlated and we have an extreme form of the "red bus/blue bus" example, described earlier, in which auto is pitted against the better (as measured by V_i) of the two transit alternatives; in this case, $\rho I_1 = V_1$ and $\rho I_2 \to \max\{V_2, V_3\}$.

The model just described can be generalized to any partition $\{B_r, r = 1, \dots, R\}$ of alternatives, and each group B_r can have its own parameter ρ_r in equations (2.40)–(2.44), leading to the form:

$$G(y_i, \dots, y_J) = \sum_r \left(\sum_{j \in B_r} y_j^{1/\rho_r}\right)^{\rho_r} \tag{2.45}$$

This is the general two-level nested logit model. It has choice probabilities (2.41)–(2.44), except that the index s in the denominator of (2.42) now runs from 1 to R. Like logit, it can also be derived from an entropy formulation (Brice 1989). The groups B_r can themselves be grouped, and those groupings further grouped, and so on, giving rise to even more general "tree structures" of three or more levels. Such models are quite common in practical applications.

As in the logit model, the inclusive value is a summary measure of the overall desirability (expected maximum utility) of the relevant group of alternatives. For example, in a destination-choice model, the inclusive value of a set of shopping destinations, with travel times and costs measured from a given origin, can serve as a measure of accessibility of that origin to shopping (Ben-Akiva and Lerman 1979). This fact gives the "upper-level" probability (2.42) a natural interpretation as a choice among groups, taking the logit form with I_r playing the role of the independent variable and ρ_r its coefficient. Consistent with this interpretation, the welfare measure that generalizes (2.29) to a representative individual following the two-level nested logit model is, from (2.39), (2.44), and (2.45):

$$W = \frac{\omega}{\lambda} \log \sum_r \exp(\rho_r \cdot I_r) \tag{2.46}$$

where again λ is the marginal utility of income and Euler's constant γ is omitted since welfare is a relative, not absolute, measure.

In nested logit, $\{B_r\}$ is an exhaustive partition of the choice set into mutually exclusive subsets. Therefore, equation (2.43) is a true conditional probability, and the model can be estimated sequentially: first estimate parameter vector (β/ρ) from (2.43), then use it to form the inclusive values (2.44), and finally estimate ρ from (2.42). Each estimation step uses an ordinary logit log-likelihood function, so it can be carried out with a logit algorithm. However, this sequential method is not statistically efficient, nor does it produce consistent estimates of the standard errors of the coefficients. Several studies show that maximum-likelihood estimation, although computationally more difficult, gives more accurate results.[49]

Most other GEV models that have been studied generalize (2.45) by not requiring the subsets B_r to be mutually exclusive. The *ordered GEV model* of Small (1987) defines subsets, each encompassing two or more alternatives, that lie close to each other on some ordering.[50] Chu (1981) and Koppelman and Wen (2000) define a model known as *paired combinatorial logit*, in which the subsets B_r include all possible pairs of alternatives – giving it generality comparable to that of multinomial probit with a general covariance structure. Even more general, but still based on nests of alternatives, is the *cross-nested logit model* of Vovsha (1997), in which all possible subsets B_r are permitted and in which a given alternative can be assigned weights representing degrees to which it is allocated to each of the subsets that include it.

GEV models are often difficult to estimate because of the highly nonlinear manner in which ρ_r enters the equation for choice probabilities. When the true model is GEV but differs only moderately from logit, a reasonable approximation can be estimated using two steps of a standard logit estimation routine, a procedure that appears to be more stable numerically than maximum-likelihood estimation (Small 1994).

A different direction for generalizing the GEV model is to maintain independence between error terms while allowing each error term to have a unique variance. This is the *heteroscedastic extreme value model* of Bhat (1995). Its probabilities cannot be written in closed form and so require numerical integration.

Yet another direction for generalizing GEV is to assume continuous rather than discrete choice alternatives – not to be confused with models described later (Section 2.4.3) that combine a discrete choice with a related continuous choice. This is accomplished by first dividing the continuous response variable into intervals, then defining a GEV model on the resulting discrete alternatives, and finally taking the limit as the number of intervals becomes infinite. Starting with logit yields the *continuous logit model*, which has been known since the 1970s. Starting with cross-nested logit yields the *continuous cross-nested logit model* of Lemp et al. (2010); its probabilities resemble (2.41)–(2.44), but with subset definitions appropriately generalized and summations replaced by integrals. While computationally complex, the model yields plausible results for departure time choice on a sample of work-related tours.[51]

2.4.2   Random parameters and mixed logit

In the random utility model of (2.14)–(2.15), randomness in individual behavior is represented as an additive error term in the utility function. Other parameters are deterministic: that is, the only variation in them is due to observed variables. Thus, for example, the VOT defined by (2.19) varies with observed travel time and wage rate, but otherwise is the same for everyone – an example of *observed heterogeneity*.

Experience has shown, however, that parameters of critical interest to transportation policy vary among individuals for reasons that we do not observe – a phenomenon called *unobserved heterogeneity*. Such reasons could include unobserved socioeconomic characteristics, personality, special features of the travel environment, and data errors. In order to account for such variation, a parameter in the logit model can be allowed to vary randomly across individuals by specifying a distribution, such as normal with unknown mean and variance, for the parameter in question. The overall probability is then determined by embedding the integral in (2.15) within another integral over the density function of that distribution.

Such models are now tractable because the outer integration (over the distribution defining random parameters) can be performed using simulation methods based on random draws, while taking advantage of the fact that the inner integration (that over the distribution of additive errors ε_{jn}) can yield the closed-form logit formula (2.18) if those errors are assumed iid extreme value. The model is called *mixed logit* because the combined error structure has a distribution that is a mixture of the extreme value distribution with the posited distribution of the random parameters.

Its mathematical formulation is as follows. Using the logit formulation of (2.18) and (2.20), the choice probability conditional on random parameters is

$$P_{in|\beta} = \frac{\exp(\beta' z_{in})}{\sum_j \exp(\beta' z_{jn})} \tag{2.47}$$

Let $f(\beta|\Theta)$ denote the density function defining the distribution of random parameters, which depends on some unknown "meta-parameters" Θ (such as means and variances of elements in random parameter vector β). The unconditional choice probability is then the multidimensional integral:

$$P_{in} = \int P_{in|\beta} \cdot f(\beta|\Theta) d\beta \tag{2.48}$$

Integration by simulation consists of taking R random draws β^r, $r = 1, ..., R$, from distribution $f(\beta \mid \Theta)$, given some trial value of Θ; calculating $P_{in\mid\beta}$ each time; and averaging over the resulting values:

$$P_{in}^{sim} = (1/R) \sum_{r=1}^{R} P_{in\mid\beta}^r \tag{2.49}$$

The likelihood function defined by these simulated probabilities can then be maximized with respect to Θ. Under reasonable conditions, this procedure yields statistically consistent estimates of the meta-parameters Θ as well as the utility parameter β. Details are provided by Train (2009).[52]

Brownstone and Train (1999) demonstrate how the mixed logit model can be shaped to capture anticipated patterns by specifying which parameters are random and what form their distribution takes – in particular, whether some of them are correlated with each other.[53] In brief, the utility parameters posited to vary randomly can include coefficients of certain combinations of alternative-specific constants, giving those constants a correlation pattern representing common features of the corresponding alternatives, for which people may have idiosyncratic preferences. This is very similar to the rationale for nested logit.

Thus, mixed logit can be used not only to specify unobserved randomness in the coefficients of certain variables, but also to mimic the correlation patterns for which the GEV model was developed. Even more complicated error structures can be accommodated within this framework; for example, one designating repeated observations from a given individual (Small *et al.* 2005) or spatial correlation related to geographical location (Bhat and Guo 2004). Indeed, McFadden and Train (2000) show that mixed logit can closely approximate virtually any choice model based on random utility.

Like any random term, the random parameters in mixed logit are partly a reflection of our inability to include all relevant explanatory factors in an empirical model. The more such factors are included, the less important will be unobserved heterogeneity.

The mixing idea can be applied to any choice model, not just logit, leading to a class called *mixture models* (Walker and Ben-Akiva 2011). It happens that the very first description of a multinomial probit model was also formulated as a mixture model (Hausman and Wise 1978), causing some commentators to mistakenly think that the probit family of models is more general than the GEV family. Usually it is harder to estimate random-parameters multinomial probit than mixed logit, because it is necessary to simulate not only the explicit integral in (2.48) but also the integral for computing a multinormal variate, which is part of the definition of the conditional choice probability $P_{in\mid\beta}$ and, unlike for GEV, has no closed form.

2.4.3   *Combined discrete and continuous choice*

In many situations, the choice among discrete alternatives is made simultaneously with some related continuous quantity. For example, a household's automobile ownership decision is closely intertwined with its choice of how much to drive. Thus, an econometric model to explain usage, conditional on ownership, is subject to *sample selection bias* (Heckman 1979). A variety of methods are available to remove this bias.[54]

The essence of the problem can be illustrated within an example of binary choice: that of owning a new or used automobile, denoted $j = 1$ or 2. Each type of car has a fixed measurable quality level Q_j that we can assume is higher for new cars: $Q_1 > Q_2$. For example, Q could be a measure of safety features, or simply an alternative-specific dummy variable equal to 1 for a new car. Suppose that the decision of how much to drive, x, depends on car quality Q, income Y, and other explanatory variables X as follows:

$$x = \beta_X X + \beta_Q Q + \beta_Y Y + u \tag{2.50}$$

where u is a random error term. For simplicity, we have omitted the subscript n denoting the individual. Car quality is determined by the choice variable d_1 (equal to 1 if a new car is chosen):

$$Q = d_1 Q_1 + (1 - d_1) Q_2 \tag{2.51}$$

Substituting (2.51) into (2.50) makes explicit the dependence of the usage decision (x) on the ownership decision (d_1).

Suppose also that the ownership decision depends on some set of observable variables Z, which might include Y, some elements of X, and/or the quality difference ($Q_1 - Q_2$):

$$\begin{aligned} &d_1 = 1 \text{ if } U_1 > U_2, \ 0 \text{ otherwise} \\ &U_1 - U_2 = \beta_Z' Z + \varepsilon \end{aligned} \tag{2.52}$$

This equation defines a binary probit model if ε is assumed normal, and binary logit if ε is assumed logistic.

Selection bias is present if u and ε are correlated. This is likely because unobservable factors may affect both usage and the relative desirability of a new car. An example of such a factor is how much this individual likes listening to a high-quality car stereo. If u is correlated with ε, it is also correlated with the car-type indicator d_1, via (2.52), and therefore with car quality Q, via (2.51). This biases the estimated coefficients in (2.50), especially β_Q, if the correlation is ignored.

If we can find an exogenous proxy for Q, we can solve the problem by using it instead of Q in estimating (2.50). This can be accomplished using the following two-step procedure proposed by Heckman (1979).

Step 1 consists of estimating the discrete-choice model (2.52). Its explanatory variables include ($Q_1 - Q_2$), an exogenous objective measure. From the estimated coefficient vector $\hat{\beta}_Z$, we can compute a predicted probability $\hat{P}_1$ of choosing a new car; for example, $\hat{P}_1 = \Phi(\hat{\beta}_Z' Z)$ if the model is probit or $\hat{P}_1 \equiv \left[1 + \exp(-\hat{\beta}_Z' Z) \right]^{-1}$ if the model is logit.

Step 2 consists of estimating a variant of (2.50) that is purged of endogeneity. There are two alternative strategies for doing this:

Step 2 Version (a): replace Q by an exogenous predictor $\hat{Q}$. We look for an unbiased estimate of Q that does not use the observed ownership choice, d_1, as does (2.51). There are at least three possibilities, which are Methods II, I, and III, respectively, of Train (1986, p. 90):

(i) Compute $\hat{Q}$ as $E(Q) \equiv \hat{P}_1 \cdot Q_1 + (1 - \hat{P}_1) \cdot Q_2$.
(ii) Compute $\hat{Q}$ as the predicted value from an auxiliary regression of observed Q on all the exogenous variables of the system, namely X, Y, and Z. (This method does not actually require that Step 1 be carried out.)
(iii) Compute $\hat{Q}$ from an auxiliary regression as in (ii), but adding as an additional variable the value of $E(Q)$ calculated as in (i). This procedure is more statistically efficient than either (i) or (ii) because it incorporates data on actual choices (via the process for computing $\hat{P}_1$) as well as on variables X, Y, and Z.

Method (iii) is probably the best choice in most cases, although like (ii) it requires the exact functional form of the auxiliary regression to be arbitrarily specified.

Step 2 Version (b): add a "correction term" to (2.50) so that the remaining error is independent of u. One way to look at selection bias is that observed Q is conditional on the individual's ownership decision. Therefore, (2.50) would be appropriate if it could be transformed into an equation describing usage *conditional on* ownership. This can be done by making its error term conditional on ownership. If u is assumed to be normal, as is usual, the required transformation is accomplished by subtracting the conditional expectation of a normal variable, given its link to ownership via (2.52), from u; the remaining error term is independent of Q and so (2.50) is purged of selectivity bias. Equivalently, that conditional expectation is added as a "selectivity correction term" to the equation itself, so that the error u that remains is no longer correlated with ε. This technique is the most common implementation of Heckman (1979) in general econometric practice. An example in transportation is West's (2004) model of automobile type choice and amount of use.

The conditional expectation just mentioned can be computed explicitly for binary probit and logit models.[55] We write the result as a term γC to be added to (2.50), where γ is a parameter to be estimated and C is a "correction variable" computed from the results of Step 1. The correction variable is included in an ordinary regression as though it were a real variable, and its coefficient is an estimate of γ. The estimated value of γ will be proportional to the correlation between u and ε, which we denote by ρ. It is this correlation that causes the problem, so we can test for selection bias by testing whether γ is different from zero. The other coefficients in the model are now estimated without bias.

Table 2.4 gives formulas for the correction variable $C = d_1C_1 + (1 - d_1)C_2$; it also shows how parameter γ is related to correlation ρ. In this table, $\phi(\cdot)$ denotes the probability density function of a standard normal random variable, σ_u is the standard deviation of u, and $\hat{P}_2 = 1 - \hat{P}_1$. We note that some authors use an opposite sign convention to ours.

This procedure adds correction γC_1 for those individuals in the sample who chose a new car and γC_2 for the others. Note that in each row, C_1 is positive and C_2 is negative. Thus, if ρ is positive, indicating that people choosing new cars are likely to drive more for unobserved reasons, the adjustment γC is positive for those individuals who choose new cars and negative for those who choose used cars – exactly the pattern we want for γC to replace the part of error term u that is correlated with Q. (Sometimes, data are lacking on people making choice $j = 2$, in which

Table 2.4 Selectivity correction terms $\gamma \cdot (d_1C_1 + d_2C_2)$ for regression model of vehicle usage

Model	Correction variable		Coefficient
	C_1	C_2	γ
Probit	$\dfrac{\phi\left(\hat{\beta}_z'z\right)}{\hat{P}_1}$	$-\dfrac{\phi\left(\hat{\beta}_z'z\right)}{\hat{P}_2}$	$\rho\sigma_u$
Logit	$-\left[\dfrac{\hat{P}_2 \ln \hat{P}_2}{1-\hat{P}_2} + \ln \hat{P}_1\right]$	$\left[\dfrac{\hat{P}_1 \ln \hat{P}_1}{1-\hat{P}_1} + \ln \hat{P}_2\right]$	$\left(\sqrt{6}/\pi\right)\cdot\rho\sigma_u$

case the correction factor is simply C_1 and the usage equation is estimated on just the subsample of new car owners.)

Some authors prefer to follow Dubin and McFadden (1984) and specify an explicit utility function whose maximization leads to simultaneous equations for a discrete and a related continuous choice. The main advantage of doing so is that it facilitates welfare analysis, since the researcher can explicitly simulate effects of changes in relevant economic factors on utility. The main disadvantage is that, as noted earlier (Section 2.1), the form of a demand function is severely constrained by deriving it from a representative consumer, and generally there is no empirical support for such restrictions.

This disadvantage can be mitigated by adding random parameters to the discrete-discontinuous model. Bento *et al.* (2009) illustrate this approach with a comprehensive model of vehicle ownership and use. Simplifying their model, the conditional indirect utility function for a household owning and using vehicle type j is specified as:

$$U_j = \gamma' z_j - \lambda^{-1} \exp\left[-\lambda\left(y - r_j\right)\right] - \beta_j^{-1} \exp\left(\alpha_j + \beta_j p_j\right) + \mu \varepsilon_j \tag{2.53}$$

where z_j is a vector of vehicle characteristics interacted with household characteristics; y is household income scaled by number of adults; r_j is the annual fixed ownership cost of vehicle j; p_j is the per-mile operating cost of vehicle j; μ is a utility scale parameter; and ε_j is a random variable with the extreme-value distribution (conventionally normalized). Parameters γ, λ, and $\{\alpha_j, \beta_j\}_{j=1,\ldots,p}$ are allowed to depend both on observable household characteristics and on random terms with specified distributions. Applying Roy's identity to (2.53) yields the demand for vehicle-miles x, conditional on choice of vehicle j:

$$\log x_j \equiv -\log \frac{\partial V_j / \partial p_j}{\partial V_j / \partial y} = \alpha_j + \beta_j p_j + \lambda \cdot \left(y - r_j\right) \tag{2.54}$$

This equation conveniently expresses the logarithm of vehicle usage as a linear function of per-mile operating cost and of income net of annual fixed cost. It implicitly contains an additive error term consisting of the part of α_j that is random.[56] The choice of automobile type j obeys the logit probability formula, (2.18), with each indirect utility V_j replaced by $(U_j - \mu \varepsilon_j)/\mu$ from (2.53). (Note we have suppressed the household indicator n.)

It is characteristic of many complex econometric models that adding an extreme-value error term results in convenient logit-like equations conditional on other parameters or endogenous variables. Such formulations do not eliminate the need to deal with endogeneity; but they make it easier because the randomness associated with ε_j does not need to be integrated explicitly, as doing so results in a closed-form logit-like term in the likelihood function.

2.4.4 *Panel data*

The ability to accurately estimate parameters of a demand model can be greatly increased if observations from individual respondents are collected repeatedly over time. The set of respondents is called a *panel*, and the information on them is called *panel data* or *longitudinal data*.[57]

The methods described earlier for aggregate cross-sectional time series are applicable in this case. The key issue is that the error term can be expected to be correlated across all the choices made by a given individual, and perhaps also across the choices made by different individuals in a given time period. The general representation is to identify both the individual n and the time period t for which a choice among alternatives j is observed. Adapting (2.14), utility is then written as:

$$U_{j,n,t} = V(z_{j,n,t}, s_{n,t}; \beta) + u_{j,n,t} \tag{2.55}$$

where the error term has been renamed u as a reminder that it is no longer expected to be independent across all observations. A convenient special case of (2.55) is when u is divided into individual-specific and time-specific error terms plus a random term that is truly independent across all observations:

$$U_{j,n,t} = V(z_{j,n,t}, s_{n,t}; \beta) + \phi_{j,n} + \eta_{j,t} + \varepsilon_{j,n,t} \tag{2.56}$$

The terms $\phi_{j,n}$ and $\eta_{j,t}$ in (2.56) may be viewed as constants that capture, respectively, unmeasured preferences by individual n for alternative j, and unmeasured preferences for alternative j that are common at time t. Given data for enough different time periods, it may be possible to estimate all the possible "fixed effects" $\phi_{j,n}$, in which case (2.56) is called a *fixed-effects model*.[58] Alternatively, $\phi_{j,n}$ may be specified as the coefficient of an alternative-specific dummy variable, the coefficient varying randomly across individuals according to some specified distribution whose parameters will be estimated; we then have a *random-effects model*. The latter is a special case of the former, and its validity is typically tested using an application of Hausman (1978). One must remember, however, that the test is asymptotic, and judgment is required as to whether a fixed-effects model "overfits" the data by including implausible variations in parameters. Similarly, it may be possible to estimate all the possible constants $\eta_{j,t}$, in which case the model is said to include *time effects*.

The very last error term, $\varepsilon_{j,n,t}$ in (2.56), is assumed iid. Its assumed distribution determines the type of panel model that is estimated (*e.g.*, logit if $\varepsilon_{i,n,t}$ is extreme-value distributed).

The availability of panel data offers both opportunities and dangers. The opportunities involve learning about dynamic behavior, which can be done by explicitly modeling how time enters the utility function and/or the error component $\eta_{j,t}$ in (2.56). For example, it is possible to specify lagged variables to explore the role of habit, learning, or shaping of preferences on choice. As another example, Cherchi *et al.* (2017) decompose $\eta_{j,t}$ into a component representing specific days and another representing specific weeks in a six-week panel dataset from Karlsruhe, Germany, discovering that most of the unexplained variability in behavior is across specific days of the week (*e.g.*, Monday versus Tuesday) rather than across weeks. Cirillo and Xu (2011) review dynamic discrete-choice models more generally.

The dangers of panel data are the usual ones from time series: serial correlation in errors, the interpretation of lagged variables, and especially the effect that dynamic processes have on estimates of standard deviations of coefficients. As always in dynamic models, one must be aware of the difficulty of distinguishing between state dependent behavior (*i.e.*, choices that depend on past choice) and unobserved heterogeneity. These topics are covered in Wooldridge (2010) and Greene (2018).

Another issue arising in panel models is sample attrition. Over time, some respondents will be lost from the sample, and for reasons not necessarily independent of the behavior being investigated. One way to overcome the resulting endogeneity bias is to create an explicit model of what causes an individual to leave the sample, and to estimate it simultaneously with the choice model. This topic is treated very generally by Semykina and Wooldridge (2013) and specifically for travel demand by Brownstone and Chu (1997).

2.4.5   *Endogenous prices and external information*

We have already mentioned the endogeneity bias that can be introduced by including an explanatory variable that is not independent of what is being explained. A prime example is a variable measuring price. Due to sorting in markets, the observed price in an individual transaction may reflect individual consumer traits such as a taste for stylish cars. If those consumer traits are not observed and also directly affect demand, this sorting will have created omitted variable bias. Equivalently, the observed transaction prices may be viewed as endogenous, creating endogeneity bias.

The automobile-type choice model of Train and Winston (2007) provides an enlightening example of dealing with this problem. Train and Winston seek to explain individual consumers' choices among 200 different makes and models of cars. Naturally, they want to include the price of the car as a variable. The trouble is that manufacturers' pricing decisions take account of the car's quality, including some aspects of quality that the investigators are unable to measure. If some makes and models have higher unmeasured quality than others, and their prices reflect this, it can appear as though consumers are drawn to high prices whereas they are really drawn to high unobserved quality.

One solution to endogeneity would be to include a full set of alternative-specific dummy variables. This works if alternatives are defined finely enough that each has a single price applicable to all customers, because then the alternative-specific coefficients account for any attributes that vary only across the observed alternatives. The trouble is that in that case, it would not be possible to include price itself as a variable – nor any other explanatory variable that fails to vary across individuals.[59] If the observed price of a given alternative does vary across individuals, we are back to the same problem of endogeneity unless we are sure each alternative always offers the same set of attributes.

A solution to this problem is available, and it has other advantages as well. The key is to estimate a full set of alternative-specific constants and then regress them on price and other variables that vary only by alternative. Estimating the constants need not be done in a single econometric step, but can take advantage of information outside the estimation sample, as described below.

Even without endogeneity, such a regression reveals important information about what characteristics people value. If endogeneity is present, we can eliminate the resulting bias by using an *instrumental-variables estimator*, mentioned briefly in Section 2.2.4, for the regression.[60] An instrumental variable in this example is one that does a good job of predicting price, but is independent of unmeasured quality attributes that might be correlated with price. The estimator then effectively replaces "price" in the regression equation by its predicted value, based on all exogenous variables in the model including the instrumental variables. The procedure is econometrically consistent only in a linear regression, which is why it cannot be applied directly to the discrete-choice model itself.

The full Train–Winston procedure, then, looks like this. The systematic utility component of conditional indirect utility (2.14) is decomposed into two parts, one varying across consumers and the other not, so that:

$$U_{jn} = \beta_n' z_{jn} + (\gamma' x_j + \xi_j) + \varepsilon_{jn} \qquad (2.57)$$

where z_{jn} and x_j are vectors of explanatory variables (the former incorporating any socioeconomic variables s_n by interacting them with alternative-specific constants). The first part of this decomposition, $\beta_n' z_{jn}$, has exactly the same meaning as in the mixed logit model of (2.47), although we now notate explicitly, using subscript n, that β varies across consumers. The second part, which we write as

$$\delta_j \equiv \gamma' x_j + \xi_j \tag{2.58}$$

varies only across products; it varies due to both observed attributes x_j (including price) and unobserved attributes ξ_j. (In equation (2.14), the observed attributes x_j were included among variables z_{jn}, but here they are distinguished separately.) If γ is of no interest, (2.58) can be substituted into (2.57) so that δ_j serves as a simple alternative-specific constant.

If the values δ_j can somehow be inferred, we can view (2.58) as a regression of them on characteristics of alternatives, with ξ_j playing the role of an error term. The number of observations in this regression is just the number of alternatives J; so hopefully, there are a lot of them! Also, we still have to face the endogeneity of price and perhaps of other variables in vector x.

There are at least two situations that greatly enhance the ability to estimate the alternative-specific constants δ_j. The first is if external information on aggregate choice shares s_j is available. Such external information is more informative than computing shares from the estimated probabilities, because it accounts for consumers who are not part of our sample. Given such information, the model can be estimated iteratively as follows. Start with a guess (or an estimate from a previous iteration) of constants $\{\delta_j^{old}\}$. Estimate the distribution of parameter vector β across consumers using the mixed-logit estimator with utility (2.57), holding the part in parentheses constant at value δ_j^{old}. Compute predicted choice shares $\hat{s}_j$ by aggregating the mixed-logit probabilities (2.47) over the estimation sample (weighted if the sample is not random). Finally, update δ_j according to the *contraction mapping* described in a note to Section 2.2.7:

$$\delta_j^{new} = \delta_j^{old} + \log(s_j) - \log(\hat{s}_j)$$

These steps are iterated until they converge to values $\{\delta_j\}$ that cause the model to most closely predict the actual market shares.[61] Finally, the desired behavioral parameter vector γ is estimated by regressing the resulting values $\{\delta_j\}$ on x_j according to (2.58), using instrumental variables to control for endogeneity of price and any other endogenous variables.

What sort of variable would make a good instrument for price? Its value for a given make/model of automobile needs to be correlated with that make/model's price, but not with its unmeasured characteristics. Berry (1994) proposed that a good instrument can be constructed from measured characteristics of *other* makes and models. This is because automobile prices are presumed to be determined in an oligopoly setting, in which each firm sets product prices while taking account of all the other products in the market; hence, price is influenced by the instrumental variable, as required. Furthermore, because there are many other makes and models, it is reasonable to assume that a broad index of those characteristics is not significantly influenced by the price of the make/model under consideration, thus meeting the other requirement for an instrument.[62]

A second situation can aid in estimating the critically important regression (2.58): when observations are available at distinct time periods or across separate markets – just as in panel data. This is because the discrete-choice model (2.57) can include a constant δ_{jt} for each product j in each time period (or separate market) t, which expands the number of constants that can be estimated. Nevo (2000) shows how the entire system, including parameters of the distribution of ξ_j, can then be rewritten as a logit model containing complex arrays of parameters. Its likelihood function can, in principle, be formulated from the joint probabilities of observed individual choices and/or observed aggregate market shares, given all the other information that is known and accounting for possible correlation of alternative-specific preferences ξ_{jt}, the error term in the expanded version of regression (2.58), across time periods or separate markets.

The Train–Winston study and our exposition here are examples of a general approach most famously formulated by Berry *et al.* (1995), hereafter BLP. Nevo (2000) provides a comprehensive yet accessible exposition. The BLP procedure is widely used in the field of industrial organization, especially for analyzing data where product variety plays a key role.[63]

Our discussion of endogenous prices and instrumental variables is just one example of a much broader issue in econometrics, often called *identification*. A parameter is identified if there is variation in the data that permits its estimation – at a minimum, a purely mathematical condition, but in practice a conceptual one: Does the experimental situation contain enough independent variation in the quantities that determine all its parameters? In this sense, a model may exhibit various degrees of identification (*e.g.*, unidentified, barely identified, well identified). Researchers may disagree because they have different beliefs about the independence of the data-generating processes – for example, how closely a given market resembles one with perfect competition. When a parameter is endogenous or inadequately identified in normal situations, one might look for a special situation that creates exogenous variation. For example, in the study of transit demand by Anderson (2014), mentioned in Section 2.1.3, the likelihood that congestion is endogenous with respect to transit demand is dealt with by making use of a transit strike, which produced exogenous variation in highway travel and hence in congestion.

2.4.6 *Automobile ownership and use*

The studies reviewed in the previous subsection are part of a venerable literature explaining consumer purchases of new automobiles. Often, a given study has a specific purpose. For example, Train and Winston (2007) examine causes for the decline in market share of automobiles by US manufacturers over the previous decade, finding that it could be largely explained by changes in the measurable traits of vehicles offered – with no need to appeal to preferences biased toward or against imports. Most such studies use disaggregate data, in part to more easily control for product heterogeneity and the associated biases due to endogeneity of the price variable, as discussed earlier.

Some studies account for the fact that automobile choice is inherently dynamic because it results in a long-lived asset with high transaction costs for buying or selling, and because consumers develop habits and preferences that influence future decisions. Hensher and Le Plastrier (1985) show one way in which these dynamics can be modeled rigorously. In each decision period (one year), a household is assumed to assess the desired size and composition of its fleet of vehicles, using a nested-logit utility function, and then to make a choice influenced by both this desired vehicle portfolio and its current portfolio. The latter, of course, has characteristics that are affected by past decisions, creating a recursive decision process. The process is estimated using a retrospective survey of current and past automobile transactions and other variables, thus providing the rough equivalent of a panel survey. Base models of fleet holdings (size and composition) are estimated from information about respondents' holdings at the earliest time reported; adjustment models are then estimated for subsequent transactions, including variables that capture brand loyalty or other types of inertia.

Mohammadian and Miller (2003) take the transaction itself, rather than current holdings, as the dependent variable. This approach is theoretically equivalent, but makes the dynamic dependence more transparent. The model postulates a nested structure of a household's transaction options, which are: (1) do nothing; (2) reduce holdings by disposing of a vehicle, which leads to a nested sub-choice of which vehicle to retire (if there is more than one); (3) increase holdings by adding a vehicle, leading to two subsequent nests for choosing type of vehicle and, below that, its vintage (new or used); or finally (4) trade one vehicle for another, leading to three subsequent nests: which vehicle to retire and what type and vintage to buy. Dynamics are represented by letting a transaction depend not only on levels of explanatory variables (such as income, household size, and existing fleet size) but also on one-year *changes* in selected variables. In the interest of parsimony, the authors assume that previous transactions affect current ones through a single variable, defined as an exponentially weighted average of past transaction decisions; this is then a variant of the partial adjustment model described in Section 2.1.2. The model is estimated on a retrospective survey, including up to nine years of previous transactions. The variables capturing dynamics are found to have strong explanatory power.

Mannering and Winston (1985) use Dubin-McFadden (1984) as a starting point to consider the simultaneous decisions of: (1) how many vehicles a household will own; (2) what specific makes and models will be chosen; and (3) how much their vehicles will be used. They accomplish this using data from a 30-month panel survey of US households. Vehicle type and number of vehicles owned are interrelated through a standard nested-logit setup and estimated in separate steps, with log-sums from type choice entering as a variable in the choice of number of vehicles. Their results show strong brand loyalty and a high implicit discount rate for fuel costs, a topic discussed further in Section 7.1.3.

Berry *et al.* (2004) also find strong brand loyalty, using a dataset of recent purchases of cars from General Motors. Their paper is an application of the BLP procedure, mentioned earlier, to disaggregate data. One innovation consists of making use of survey respondents' statements of what their second-best choice would have been if the vehicle they actually chose had not been available; this is a form of *ranked* choice, mentioned earlier (Section 2.2.8).

A number of studies focus on measuring price and income elasticities for specific products or classes of products, as these are useful in applied economic analysis. As we will see in Chapter 7, one of the most pertinent for policy is the "market price elasticity" of new light-duty vehicles, that is, the elasticity describing the aggregate demand function for new vehicles. Most such studies work within the discrete choice framework we have described, often framing non-purchase as one of the discrete options. An important aspect of this choice is the substitutability between used vehicles and new vehicles. Leard (2022) measures this elasticity by combining actual sales data for many automobile makes and models with a consumer survey in which respondents provided their second-best choice (as in Berry *et al.* 2004 as just discussed). Leard's model predicts, for any make and model, how a price increase would divert potential purchasers to other makes and models and, crucially, to used vehicles. His estimate of the aggregate long-run price elasticity is 0.34, roughly one-third the size that many earlier studies obtained using more restricted models.[64] Leard goes on to show that this has substantial implications for the net benefit of proposed changes in fuel efficiency regulations.

A different approach to transactions of consumer durables over time is to view the holding of such an asset to be a process whose *duration* can be modeled as a function of explanatory variables. This can be done by estimating the *hazard rate*, here the probability per unit time of making a specified change in the household vehicle stock, as a function of explanatory variables. Yamamoto *et al.* (1999) illustrate this approach and review several other such studies.

An alternative to statistical estimation of complex consumer choices is simulation using a calibrated model. This has several advantages: It can be more detailed than would be practical for statistical estimation; it can utilize prior information from a variety of earlier studies; and subsequent use of the model can incorporate subsequent empirical information about parameters. An example in the arena of motor vehicle purchase is that by Oak Ridge National Laboratory, carried out by David Greene and colleagues (ORNL 2012). They construct a detailed nested-logit model that is calibrated to reproduce own-price elasticities, drawn from the literature, and shares of vehicle makes and models, as actually observed in the market. A model such as this has the potential to trace and understand complex paths of adjustments to a proposed policy change such as fuel efficiency standards, but it would be virtually impossible to fully estimate statistically on any available dataset.

2.5 Attitudes, perceptions, and latent variables

Demand studies for many products, including travel, have often found that variables measuring consumer attitudes provide significant explanatory power and may improve the precision and/ or plausibility of other explanatory relationships. For example, Popuri *et al.* (2011) enhance the explanatory variables in the demand for public transit in Chicago by compiling replies to 23 attitudinal questions. These replies are aggregated using factor analysis, which uses correlations among the 23 primary variables to define six factors explaining most of the variation, namely: (1) aversion to stress; (2) desire for privacy and comfort; (3) desire for flexibility; (4) tolerance for walking and waiting; (5) attitude toward social importance of public transportation; and (6) perceived safety of a transit trip. The authors then fit binary logit models to explain commuting mode choice, using conventional time and cost variables as well as socioeconomic indicators. They do this first without and then with the attitudinal factors included.

Including these six factors substantially improves the model fit, as well as the statistical significance and plausibility of the coefficient of in-vehicle travel time. This suggests that correlation of attitudes with travel time may sometimes hide the effects of the latter.

However, the importance of attitudinal factors is easy to exaggerate, because attitudes are often endogenous to the purchase decision. In the study just mentioned, the factor with strongest explanatory power is #5 in the above list, which is especially likely to involve self-justification of the choice made by the user. Endogeneity bias can be overcome by explicitly modeling both the travel decision and the formation of attitudes, using variables related to attitudes but more likely to be exogenous. Examples include socioeconomic characteristics that might otherwise be thought unimportant, locational characteristics (although these may also be endogenous), or other behaviors not directly related to the choice under consideration. Such issues are explored for general economic demand theory by McFadden (2014) and specifically for travel demand by papers summarized by Newman and Chorus (2015).

Attitudes can be viewed as *latent variables*, mentioned earlier (Section 2.2.8). Latent variables are unobservable but can be inferred from behavior; Morikawa *et al.* (2002) provide a thorough exposition and an application explaining choice of mode for intercity travel in the Netherlands. The idea is that one observes indicators that are directly influenced by the latent variables – for example, answers to the attitudinal questions of Popuri *et al.* (2011), or observations of behavior related to attitudes, such as recycling or ownership of electric cars (as indicators of environmental preferences). Morikawa *et al.* estimate their model in two steps: The first uses standard software for *structural equations*, which allow flexible specification and testing for directions of causality; the second uses maximum likelihood on the discrete choice observations, in which fitted values of the latent variables from Step 1 appear as additional explanatory variables.[65] Johansson *et al.* (2006) apply the same kind of framework to explain mode choice for long urban commutes in Sweden, incorporating both types of latent-variables indicators.

Attitudes may be strongly influenced by social interactions, creating yet another avenue to explain them simultaneously with travel choices. Kamargianni *et al.* (2011) consider how such models can be formulated and estimated, taking advantage of data from teenagers in the

Republic of Cyprus that measure attitudes toward walking. The study reveals that teenagers' attitudes are interrelated with those of their parents and, potentially, those of their peers.

A particular kind of latent variable is membership in one of a postulated class of decision-makers, known as a *latent class*. Thus, for example, a population of individuals choosing among urban residential locations might be postulated to come from two types, "yuppies" and "families," which respond similarly to price and amenities but differently to space and proximity to the city center. Vij and Walker (2016) provide a good review.[66]

Closely related to attitudes is people's limited ability to carry out cognitive processing. It is well known that people use simplifying rules to process an overabundance of information or of choices; attitudes may influence these rules. Some travel-demand models consider this process explicitly. For example, the model might posit that a decision-maker first choose a subset among all the alternatives available to consider more carefully, then gather further information, and finally choose among the alternatives in this subset according to a utility-maximizing process. The subset of considered choices (sometimes called simply a "choice set") might be updated iteratively for recurring choices such as daily trip patterns, since the recurrence provides opportunities to learn about new options. Such a modeling approach is more natural using an agent-based model such as described in the next section (Vovsha 2017).

2.6   Activity patterns, trip chaining, and agent-based modeling

A more fundamental approach to the demand for travel is to explain the entire structure of decision-making about activities: which ones to undertake, where to do them, and how transportation connects them. The challenges of implementing this common-sense idea are daunting. Pinjari and Bhat (2011) provide an excellent summary of research progress and results of such *activity-based travel models* (ABMs).

This research typically focuses on a *tour* – a connected sequence of trips – as the fundamental unit about which decisions are made, and on *time*, often represented continuously, as the domain for scheduling decisions that connect activities. The trips in a single tour are said to form a *trip chain*. The emphasis on time connects this topic to the trip-scheduling literature discussed earlier (Section 2.3.2); indeed, some of the early advances focus on the interrelationship of activities with trip scheduling, for example the simultaneous choices of scheduling and activity duration (Vovsha and Bradley 2004).

Activity research depends crucially on advances in data collection, computing power, and statistical methods. Advances in data collection include multiday diaries, permitting analysis of activity patterns that vary from day to day or whose purpose is realized over multiday cycles (*e.g.*, shopping). Both computing power and theoretical advances in statistics facilitate computation of statistical distributions through simulation, described earlier in connection with mixing models (Section 2.4.2), thereby permitting econometric estimation of complex models and forecasts of the results of multiple interacting decision processes.

The process of simulating individual choices can be taken a step further by basing the entire travel model on a set of artificially simulated agents, each of whom follows the statistical distribution(s) that are identified by the model and, in addition, interacts with the environment according to prescribed behavioral rules. These rules may include explicit interactions with other agents – for example intra-household decisions about vehicle use, or inter-household decisions about carpools. This type of simulation defines *agent-based travel models*.

An example illustrates how these modeling strategies are connected. Roorda *et al.* (2009) describe an agent-based travel model called the Travel Activity Scheduler for Household Agents. In this model, individual decision-makers are simulated as they consider possible activities, arrange them according to the purposes they facilitate, and create schedules consistent with time constraints. The schedules of household members are then reconciled for internal consistency, to accommodate vehicle constraints (given a household vehicle fleet) and desired simultaneous activities such as having meals together. The vehicle constraints are resolved by minimizing the potential utility loss for household members who might have to use a different mode. This process measures the aggregate utility gain from adding a vehicle to the household's fleet, which in turn is used to create variables explaining vehicle transactions (buy, sell, or hold) in the model of Mohammadian and Miller (2003), described earlier (Section 2.4.6). The activity model is thus nested underneath the vehicle transaction model in a larger integrated system.

Activity-based models are especially helpful in analyzing policies that affect the generation, chaining, or timing of trips – for example, travel-demand management policies aimed at using behavioral incentives to reduce car traffic. Thus, for example, Shiftan and Auhrbier (2002) find that a policy to encourage telecommuting eliminates some long-distance work trips, but creates some new short tours as people substitute special-purpose trips for work-related trip chains. This result is consistent with studies suggesting that telecommuting complements, rather than substitutes for, travel in aggregate (*e.g.*, Choo *et al.* 2005).

The agent-based framework permits several further advances (Vovsha 2017). Individual agents can be modeled as forming plans and learning from experience (*e.g.*, Auld and Mohammadian 2012), leading to forecasts of the dynamic transition path to new patterns after a change. Individuals can adapt certain behavioral parameters in real time – for example, the VOT can rise if they are delayed *en route* to work. Individuals can negotiate within a household, a process susceptible to empirical research. They can learn from the experience of others through social networks or spatially based networks of friends. The agent-based framework also facilitates dynamic traffic assignment, in which speeds on a congested highway network are computed within a simulation at each point in time, responding to tentative route choices made by the model's agents at previous times.

Activity-based models were formerly the province of academia, but are now well established as the basis for applied transportation planning in many cities and metropolitan areas. For example, the Metropolitan Transportation Commission in the San Francisco region replaced its trip-based planning model by an activity-based model in 2011, finding the new model better at analyzing phenomena such as changing duration of the peak travel periods. The model is documented in a thorough yet exceptionally clear report for the Commission's 2040 transportation plan (MTC and ABAG 2017).

2.7   Values of time, reliability, and crowding

Among the most important quantities inferred from travel-demand studies are the monetary values that people place on improvements in specific trip characteristics. These are primary inputs to analyses used throughout transportation research and policy. Here, we focus on three such values that are of special importance, including two already introduced earlier in this chapter.

The first, the *VOT*, is by far the most widely used. The second, the *VOR*, is increasingly important as economic activity depends more and more on flexibility and logistics.[67] The third, the *cost of crowding*, is used especially to determine public transit schedules and to appraise investment in transit vehicles; as we will see, it is highly relevant also in modeling how demand for public transport plummeted during the COVID-19 pandemic.

These quantities account for a large portion of the benefits (positive or negative) of changes in the urban transportation environment. Analysts are generally not satisfied with capturing these benefits only implicitly, as part of consumer surplus – as, for example, in equation (2.29).

If possible, it is preferable to separate them explicitly in order to illuminate the nature of the changes being considered. In this section, we consider theories behind consumers' responses to time and reliability, and we review our empirical knowledge about all three quantities.

2.7.1   Value of time: theory

The most natural definition of VOT is in terms of compensating variation (Varian 1992). The value of saving a given amount and type of travel time by a particular person is the amount that person could pay, after receiving the saving, and be just as well off as before. This amount, divided by the time saving, is that person's average VOT saved for that particular change. Aggregating over a class of people yields the *average VOT* for those people in that situation. The limit of this average value, as the time saving shrinks to zero, is the marginal value of time savings, or just *VOT*.

Because aggregate travel patterns are in a constant state of flux, a particular event such as a new transit line may trigger a chain of complex reactions, differing across travelers. But here we are interested in the average benefits or costs of an identifiable group of travelers after they have settled into the new circumstances.

The VOT for a given trip may depend on many aspects of the trip-maker and of the trip itself. To name just a few: trip purpose (*e.g.*, work or recreation), demographic and socioeconomic characteristics, time of day, amenities available during travel, and trip duration. Most often, these are accounted for by using theoretical reasoning to postulate a functional form for how VOT varies, as in (2.23), and producing that result by interacting relevant variables with cost or time in a travel model, as in (2.19).

A useful theoretical framework builds on that of Becker (1965), in which utility is maximized subject to a time constraint. Becker's theory has been extended in many directions; here, we present ideas developed mainly by Oort (1969) and DeSerpa (1971), adapting the exposition of MVA Consultancy *et al.* (1987).

Let utility U depend on goods consumption G, time T_w spent at work, and times T_k spent in other activities k (including travel). The price of goods can be normalized to one. Utility is maximized subject to several constraints. First, the budget constraint requires that expenditures on goods and any activities undertaken are no greater than total income $(Y+wT_w)$, where Y is unearned income and w is the net wage rate after labor taxes. Second, a time constraint requires that time spent on all activities be within total time available, $\bar{T}$. Finally, undertaking any activity k has cost c_k and requires minimum time $\bar{T}_k$ (both of which could be zero). We let δ_k be a dummy variable for whether activity k is undertaken.

Within these constraints, the consumer decides how much to consume, how much to work, which activities (including travel) to undertake, and how much time to spend on them. The mathematical problem can be solved by maximizing the following Lagrangian function with respect to G, T_w, $\{\delta_k\}$, and $\{T_k\}$:

$$\Lambda = U(G,T_w,\{T_k\}) + \lambda \cdot \left[Y + wT_w - G - \sum_k \delta_k c_k \right]$$

$$+ \mu \cdot \left[\bar{T} - T_w - \sum_k T_k \right] + \sum_k \phi_k \delta_k \cdot \left[T_k - \bar{T}_k \right]$$

(2.59)

where λ, μ, and $\{\phi_k\}$ are Lagrange multipliers that indicate how tightly each of the corresponding constraints limits utility. The first-order condition for maximizing (2.59) with respect to work time T_w is

$$U_{Tw} + \lambda \cdot \left[w + T_w \cdot (dw / dT_w)\right] - \mu = 0 \qquad (2.60)$$

while that for activity time T_k (for any activity that is undertaken at all) is

$$U_{Tk} - \mu + \phi_k = 0 \qquad (2.61)$$

where subscripts on U indicate partial derivatives. We have allowed for a nonlinear compensation schedule by letting w depend on T_w.

We can denote the value of utility at the solution to this maximization problem by V, the indirect utility function; it depends on Y, $\bar{T}$, the wage schedule $w(T_w)$, activity costs $\{c_k\}$, and minimum activity times $\{\bar{T}_k\}$. From the properties of Lagrange multipliers, the rate at which indirect utility increases as the kth minimum-time constraint is relaxed is given by its Lagrange multiplier, ϕ_k; the rate at which it increases with respect to unearned income is λ. Hence, the marginal VOT for the kth activity that is undertaken (*i.e.*, for which $\delta_k = 1$) is the ratio of these quantities:

$$v_T^k \equiv \left(\frac{\partial Y}{\partial \bar{T}_k}\right)_V \equiv -\frac{\partial V / \partial \bar{T}_k}{\partial V / \partial Y} = -\frac{\partial \Lambda / \partial \bar{T}_k}{\partial \Lambda / \partial Y} = \frac{\phi_k}{\lambda} \qquad (2.62)$$

Those activities for which the minimum-time constraint is not binding (*i.e.*, those for which $\phi_k = 0$) are called *pure leisure activities* by DeSerpa (1971).

Substituting (2.61) into (2.62), and then using (2.60) to eliminate μ, provides a decomposition of VOT:

$$v_T^k = \frac{\mu}{\lambda} - \frac{U_{Tk}}{\lambda} = w + T_w \cdot \frac{dw}{dT_w} + \frac{U_{Tw}}{\lambda} - \frac{U_{Tk}}{\lambda} \qquad (2.63)$$

Applying this to the travel activity, we see from the first equality that the VOT is the opportunity cost of time that could be used for work, μ/λ, less the value of the marginal utility of time spent in travel, U_{Tk}/λ. The opportunity cost μ/λ is both pecuniary (the first two terms after the last equality) and nonpecuniary (the third term). The nonpecuniary portion is positive or negative depending on whether work is enjoyable or onerous.

This opportunity cost μ/λ is sometimes called *the value of time as a resource*, because it tells us how much utility could be raised at the margin if the total time constraint could be relaxed. It is also called the *value of leisure* because, as is seen by setting $\phi_k = 0$ in (2.61), it is the monetized marginal utility of spending time in a pure leisure activity.

Most of the theoretical literature assumes that the wage rate is fixed, in which case $dw/dT_w = 0$ and so equation (2.63) gives the result noted by Oort (1969): The VOT exceeds the wage rate if time spent at work is enjoyed relative to that spent traveling, and falls short of it in the opposite case. This is a fundamental insight into how the VOT, even for nonwork trips, depends on conditions of a person's job (or other means of earning a livelihood).

How do we measure these quantities empirically? For the travel activity, variables c_k and $\bar{T}_k$ are simply a trip's cost and travel time. We see from (2.59) and the properties of the Lagrangian function that λ equals $(-\partial V/\partial c_k)$, the negative of the coefficient of cost in a discrete-choice model. (This is just an application of Roy's identity (2.30), assuming one trip per time period.) If time and cost are entered solely as non-interacted variables, we have the simple intuitive relationship that VOT is the ratio of coefficients of time and cost. If they are interacted with other variables, the result is more complex, but still has the same intuition.

Actually, (2.63) suggests an empirical modeling strategy that does interact cost and/or time with variables believed to be related to compensation and work enjoyment. Suppose, for example, we believe that the marginal utility of work relative to travel, $(U_{Tw} - U_{Tk})$, is negative and proportional to the wage rate. Suppose further that the wage rate is fixed, so the second term in the last equality of (2.63) disappears. Then (2.63) implies that the VOT is a fixed fraction of the wage rate, as for example with specification (2.19) with $\beta_3 = 0$. Alternatively, we might think that work enjoyment varies nonlinearly with the observed wage rate: (2.63) then implies that VOT is a nonlinear function of the wage rate, which could suggest specifying utility as (2.19) with a nonzero term β_3.

As another example of a potential interaction variable, our theory suggests that VOT will be higher for people who routinely take long trips – this is because the total time constraint will then bind more tightly, causing μ, the Lagrange multiplier of that constraint, to rise. To capture this possibility, we might interact the time variable with some measure of trip length. We will see that empirical evidence supports this hypothesis. A potential pitfall with such an approach, however, is that the causation between commute length and VOT may go in both directions, making commute length endogenous and thus problematic as an explanatory variable.

Extensions

Human behavior is complex, and many additional factors affect how people allocate their time. No analytical model can account for all of them, but we can mention several interesting extensions to the theory just presented.

First, consider work-hour constraints. People cannot always change the amount of time they spend at work, perhaps because they are locked into a particular job with fixed hours. To some extent this is handled by allowing w to depend on T_w; but we could also consider a stricter constraint that T_w be fixed, say at $\bar{T}_w$. This adds a term $\phi_w \cdot [T_w - \bar{T}_w]$ to (2.59), where ϕ_w is another Lagrange multiplier whose sign indicates whether this person would prefer to work fewer ($\phi_w > 0$) or more ($\phi_w < 0$) hours. This modification adds a term ϕ_w/λ to the VOT as given by (2.63), thus raising or lowering the VOT depending on the sign of ϕ_w. Indeed, MVA Consultancy *et al.* (1987, pp. 149–50) find that people who are required to work extra hours at short notice have 15%–20% higher values of travel time than other workers, suggesting that such a model may apply to them.

Second, consider the time constraint inside the second set of square brackets in (2.59). The implied ability to reallocate time among activities is most plausible in a long-run decision. In the short run, time lost or saved in travel may not affect time spent on other activities, which would tend to lower its perceived value. This differential between long- and short-run values of time is confirmed in an RP setting by Peer *et al.* (2015) and in an SP experiment by Peer and Börjesson (2018).

Next, consider the situation where the amount of time devoted to consuming goods is proportional to the amount of goods – as occurs, for example, when the "good" consists of watching a movie. For simplicity, let us label this as activity 0 and consider it a generalized leisure activity, whose consumption time is proportional to all goods consumption G. Then the term $\phi_0 \cdot [T_0 - \bar{T}_0]$ in (2.59) must be changed to $\phi_0 \cdot [T_0 - \ell G]$, where ℓ is the unit time requirement for consumption. The constraint is binding if $\phi_0 > 0$. While this modification does not alter the formulas derived for VOT, it does change the meaning of λ (Jara-Díaz 2003): It no longer equals U_G, the marginal utility of consumption, but rather $U_G - \phi_0\ell$. Since λ appears in the denominator of expressions for VOT, this change would tend to raise the VOT. The interpretation is that consumers are pressed for time in all their activities because of the time needed for ordinary consumption. The richer people are, the more goods they consume so the tighter their time constraint – they become the "harried leisure class" of Linder (1970). This phenomenon has been verified empirically in Australia, Germany, Korea, and the United States (Hamermesh and Lee 2007).

Jara-Díaz *et al.* (2008) show that the extension just mentioned makes it possible to measure the value of leisure as a separate component of (2.63), provided one observes a leisure good requiring both time and monetary expenditure. They do so using data from three separate cities in Chile, Germany, and Switzerland.

Now, suppose that working more hours requires spending more time commuting. This would be the case, for example, if it requires a secondary worker entering the work force or a part-time worker increasing the number of days worked. De Borger and Van Dender (2003) extend the theory to show that this would decrease the VOT. The intuition is that the effective hourly wage rate (*i.e.*, the wage rate net of commuting cost) is reduced.

What if that commuting time, or any travel time, is stressful? For example, what if drivers must exert effort to remain safe in the face of congested traffic? Equation (2.63) tells us that anything making the travel activity onerous (hence U_{tk} less positive or more negative) will raise the value of travel time, consistent with the widely observed finding that VOT is higher during congestion. But it is more complex if we consider that safety also has a value, which accounts for some of the stress. Thus, VOT will be higher when safety is more highly valued. Alternatively, we might choose to analyze choices about time and safety simultaneously, deriving separate values for the two motivations; the measured VOT will then not reflect this safety component, as indeed is shown by Steimetz (2008) and further discussed in Section 3.4.

This last point offers a reminder to pay attention to what is implicitly being held constant in the utility function in the course of any empirical measurement. This will determine whether the measured behavioral quantity value does or does not incorporate effects of a related decision.

Currently, there is strong interest in the effects of in-vehicle technology on travel behavior, including VOT. Simple intuition and equation (2.63) both suggest that VOT will become smaller if travel becomes more enjoyable, due, for example, to better in-vehicle entertainment, or if it becomes more productive, due, for example, to Wi-Fi connections in a bus or train. Fosgerau (2019) offers a simple extension of the theory developed here to quantify these effects, decomposing travel time into components including time spent at leisure and time spent working, along with explicit productivities for each. A general property of the model is that the net wage rate w becomes multiplied by $(1 - \alpha)$, where α is the relative productivity of time spent at work or leisure while traveling.

Other extensions to the theory of VOT include those showing how it depends on tax rates (Forsyth 1980) and on time of day (Tseng and Verhoef 2008; Buchholz *et al.* 2022). The latter variation is closely connected to the VOR, as we will see soon.

In addition, there is a long tradition of modeling the VOT used in business travel, usually by decomposing expected sources of time value into some version of the "Hensher equation," which accounts for productivity of time while traveling, proportions of travel time that are diverted from regular work and leisure, and implications for employer's profits (Hensher 1977). Typically, the resulting VOT is considerably higher than for other trip purposes. Kato (2013) and Batley (2015) provide thorough reviews.

2.7.2   *Value of reliability: theory*

It is amply documented that uncertainty in travel time, which may result from congestion or poor adherence to transit schedules, is a major perceived cost of travel. How can this aversion to unreliability be captured in a theoretical model?

One approach, adapting Noland and Small (1995), is to begin with the model of trip-scheduling choice of the form presented in equation (2.35). Dividing utility by minus the marginal utility of income, this model can be written in terms of trip cost, in a conventional notation that we will use extensively in the next chapter:

$$C(t_d, T_r) = \alpha \cdot T + \beta \cdot SDE + \gamma \cdot SDL + \theta \cdot DL \tag{2.64}$$

where $\alpha = v_T/60$ is the per-minute value of travel time (if v_T is expressed in an hourly measure), β and γ are per-minute costs of early and late arrival, and θ is a fixed cost of arriving late. Travel time T is disaggregated into a free-flow value T_f that represents the lowest possible travel time for this particular trip, plus a random (unpredictable) component of travel time, $T_r \geq 0$. Since T_f is simply a given for the traveler, we use the functional notation $C(t_d, T_r)$ to focus attention on two variables: departure time t_d and stochastic delay T_r. Specifically, our objective is to measure the increase in expected cost C due to the dispersion in T_r, given that t_d is subject to choice by the traveler. Letting $C*$ denote this expected cost after the user chooses t_d optimally, we have:

$$C^* = \underset{t_d}{\text{Min}} \, E\left[C(t_d, T_r)\right] = \underset{t_d}{\text{Min}}\left[\alpha \cdot E(T) + \beta \cdot E(SDE) + \gamma \cdot E(SDL) + \theta \cdot P_L\right] \tag{2.65}$$

where E denotes an expected value taken over the distribution of T_r, conditional on t_d, and where $P_L \equiv E(DL)$ is the probability of being late, again conditional on t_d. This equation can form the basis for specifying the reliability term in a model such as described in Section 2.3.3. It captures the effect of travel time uncertainty upon expected schedule delay costs, but may omit other reasons why uncertainty could cause disutility.

To focus just on reliability, we shall ignore the dynamics of congestion for now by assuming that T_f and $E(T)$ are independent of departure time, causing the term involving α in (2.65) to be constant. To find the optimal departure time, then, we need to differentiate the other three terms with respect to t_d and set the sum to zero. Let $f(T_r)$ be the probability density function for T_r and let t^* be the preferred arrival time at the destination. The next-to-last term in the square brackets of (2.65) can then be written as:

$$\gamma \cdot E(SDL) = \gamma \cdot E(t_d + T_r - \tilde{t} \mid T_r > \tilde{t} - t_d)$$

$$= \gamma \cdot \int_{\tilde{t} - t_d}^{\infty} (t_d + T_r - \tilde{t}) \cdot f(T_r) dT_r$$

where $\tilde{t} = t^* - T_f$ is the time at which the traveler would depart if T_r were equal to zero with certainty. Differentiating this term and evaluating at the optimal departure time t_d^* yields:

$$\frac{d}{dt_d} \gamma \cdot E(SDL) = \gamma \cdot \int_{\tilde{t} - t_d^*}^{\infty} \left[\frac{d}{dt_d}(t_d + T_r - \tilde{t}) \cdot f(T_r)\right] dT_r = \gamma P_L^*$$

where P_L^* is the probability of being late given the optimal departure time. Similarly, differentiating the term involving β in (2.65) yields $-\beta \cdot \left(1 - P_L^*\right)$. Finally, differentiating the last term yields

θf^0, where $f^0 \equiv f(\tilde{t} - t_d^*)$, is the probability density at the point where the traveler is neither early nor late. What these three derivatives tell us is that departing later will lower the expected cost of early arrival (involving β) but raise the expected costs of late arrival (involving γ and θ). Combining all three derivatives and setting them equal to zero gives the first-order condition for optimal departure time:

$$P_L^* = \frac{\beta - \theta f^0}{\beta + \gamma} \tag{2.66}$$

In the special case $\theta = 0$, equation (2.66) yields the rule $P_L^* = \beta / (\beta + \gamma)$.

Equation (2.66) gives an implicit equation for the optimal departure time. It can be regarded as a rule for setting a buffer to allow for occasional delays, a buffer whose size balances the aversions to early and late arrival. The greater is the cost of being early (β) relative to that of being late (γ), the less buffer one will choose and so one will be late more often. Furthermore, when the distribution of T_r is dispersed, the time buffer required by (2.66) is large, and expected cost is also large because the early and late arrivals that occur are of greater magnitude.

The values of the optimal departure time and associated minimized travel cost implied by equations (2.66) and (2.65) can be calculated explicitly for some special cases of the probability distribution of T_r, for example uniform and exponential (Noland and Small 1995). In the case of a uniform distribution with range b, (2.66) becomes simply:

$$P_L^* = \frac{\beta - (\theta / b)}{\beta + \gamma}$$

The value of C^* in this case is given by Noland and Small (1995); if $\theta = 0$, it is equal to the cost of expected travel time, $\alpha \cdot E(T)$, plus the following cost of unreliability:

$$v_R \cdot R = \left(\frac{\beta \gamma}{\beta + \gamma} \right) \cdot \frac{b}{2} \tag{2.67}$$

The quantity in parenthesis is a composite measure of the unit costs of scheduling mismatch, which plays a central role in the cost functions considered in the next chapter. Thus, (2.67) indicates that reliability cost derives from the combination of scheduling mismatches (the term in parentheses) and dispersion in travel time ($b/2$). If unreliability R is defined as half the possible range of travel times, then the corresponding VOR, v_R, is just the term in parenthesis in (2.67).

More generally, the last two terms in (2.65) are potentially important if γ and θ are large relative to β, conditions that are in fact true according to the empirical findings described in Section 2.3.2. Because they contain $E(SDL)$ and P_L, these terms depend especially on the shape of the distribution of T_r in its upper ranges, which governs the likelihood that T_r takes a high enough value to make the traveler late. Thus, the expected cost of unreliability depends especially on this part of the distribution (its "upper tail"). This idea, using just the effect of the γ term (*i.e.*, assuming $\theta = 0$), is made precise by Fosgerau and Karlström (2011). They derive reliability cost as

$$(v_R) \cdot [R] = (\beta + \gamma) \cdot [\Omega_\psi \sigma] \tag{2.68}$$

where σ is the standard deviation of the distribution and Ω_ψ is a measure of its shape; the latter is a composite measure of all the percentiles of F exceeding $\psi \equiv \gamma / (\beta + \gamma)$. Their formula applies to any well-behaved distribution function F.[68]

The scheduling preferences behind this theory, sometimes called $\alpha - \beta - \gamma$ preferences when θ is taken to be zero, can be generalized and derived from a more basic theory by assuming that travelers have time-varying flow-of-utility levels for spending time at the origin (*e.g.*, home for a commute trip) and the destination (*e.g.*, work). Typically, the former may be expected to be highest early in the morning and then to decline, while the latter would be low before normal work hours and higher during hours when a person is expected at work. Given a fixed travel time, choosing departure time to maximize the sum of such utilities leads to a well-defined value of travel time that is higher for longer trips – as is in fact found empirically. Furthermore, making travel time stochastic leads to an even stronger aversion to travel-time dispersion. This model, sometimes referred to as the $H - W$ formulation, is summarized by Small (2012, p. 7).[69]

Interestingly, the same considerations that cause VOR to be positive also provide one way to look at the value of waiting time for users of a scheduled service, such as public transit. If travelers arrive randomly at a transit stop and vehicles arrive at a steady rate with headway b, the travelers' average cost of scheduling inconvenience is exactly the same as equation (2.67).[70] Since their average waiting time is $b/2$, this implies a waiting-time cost premium of $\beta\gamma/(\beta + \gamma)$, in addition to the cost α of the lost time itself. Given typical empirical values assumed for parameter ratios β/α and γ/α in (2.65), this premium adds about 50% to the VOT.[71] The assumption of random arrivals is reasonable for short headways; for longer headways, a timetable may be used instead, which changes the calculation. Fosgerau (2009) derives some simple formulas, based on $\alpha - \beta - \gamma$ preferences, that incorporate the decision of whether or not to consult a timetable.

Reliability is most often thought of as a property of road systems, but it applies to public transit as well. If the transit headway is uncertain, or the vehicle might be too full to accommodate another passenger, the derivation of reliability cost for transit becomes very complicated (*e.g.*, Bates *et al.* 2001).

Not all travel time variability implies unreliability. For instance, travelers can be expected to be aware of travel time variations due to predictable variations over time of day, between weekdays, over (holiday) seasons, and weather conditions if known sufficiently far in advance. For empirical work on travel time unreliability and its valuation, it is therefore important to make this distinction between variability and unreliability. Also, above we have defined unreliability with respect to information possessed by the traveler: Its cost arises from having to plan a trip without full information about what the travel time will actually be. This implies there is value to providing such information, so it is no surprise that much technological development is focused on exactly that topic. It is not straightforward, however, to determine whether providing information creates social as well as private value. This is because people will adjust their schedules to the available information and this will change the pattern of congestion, perhaps for the worse. The problem becomes even more complex if information is provided *en route* so that people make departure decisions anticipating that they will learn more about the trip as it progresses, and perhaps will adjust their route or even their mode. Not only that, but people can choose how much costly information to acquire and how much attention to pay to it. Such issues, explored in Section 3.5.2, provide a rich source of research into properties of equilibria.[72]

2.7.3   *Empirical results: values of time and crowding*

Research has generated an enormous literature on empirical estimates of values of time and reliability, including several reviews and meta-analyses of these literatures.[73]

Small (2012) suggests that 50% of the gross wage rate is a typical average value of automobile travel time, based especially on earlier meta-analyses in which values obtained by many studies are analyzed statistically. Indeed, values close to this are often adopted by transportation agencies as official guidance and are generally supported by the more recent meta-analyses discussed further below. These values seem to apply across many countries.[74]

VOT would be expected to rise with income. Indeed, there is considerable evidence that it does, but less than proportionally. Thus, expressing it as a fraction of the wage rate, as we have just done, is only an approximation. The easiest way to summarize this evidence is as an elasticity of VOT with respect to per capita gross domestic product. Abrantes and Wardman (2011) find this elasticity to be 0.9 using meta-analysis of studies based mainly on time series; but they and others find it smaller (around 0.5–0.7) using cross-sections.[75]

Abrantes and Wardman's (2011) meta-analysis is especially useful for discerning how various trip attributes affect the VOT. For example, commuting trips have 12% higher VOT than others, and business trips more than twice as high as others. Even larger differences are found in recent studies of the UK and the Netherlands (ITF 2019, p. 22). There are also considerable differences across modes, with bus riders having a lower than average value and rail riders a higher than average value – possibly due to self-selection by speed. Longer trips are found to have a higher VOT, as suggested earlier.[76]

Most importantly, walking and waiting time are valued much more highly than in-vehicle time – a universal finding conventionally summarized as 2.0–2.5 times as high. Abrantes and Wardman, however, observe smaller multipliers than this in most of the studies they review. There is considerable dispersion in the reported estimates of these relative valuations, especially in the relative value of waiting time. This is probably because conditions under which travelers wait for a transit vehicle vary greatly. Aversion to waiting time is analyzed by Psarros *et al.* (2011), who find that many factors can alter individuals' perceived waiting time relative to objective measures.

SP data often yield considerably smaller values of in-vehicle time than RP data. Brownstone and Small (2005) take advantage of three datasets, all from "high-occupancy toll (HOT) lane" facilities in southern California, that obtained RP and SP data from comparable populations, in some cases from the same individuals. They find that SP-based measurements of VOT are one-third to one-half the corresponding RP-based measurements.[77] A similar, though smaller, difference is found by Abrantes and Wardman (2011), but they find a difference in the opposite direction for walking and waiting time: SP measures of those valuations are 40% higher than RP measures (p. 12).

One possible explanation for SP–RP differences in measured VOT is that people overestimate the actual time savings from the toll roads, by roughly a factor of two according to surveys on the corridors studied by Brownstone and Small. Thus, when answering SP survey questions, they may indicate a per-minute willingness to pay for *perceived* time savings that is lower than their willingness to pay for *actual* time savings.[78] To be used in policy analysis, where actual travel times are typically observed and/or modeled, VOT needs to correspond to these actual travel times (*i.e.*, to the RP measure).

Another reason for divergence may stem from the distinction between short-run and long-run valuations of travel-time savings, mentioned earlier. Particularly when an SP questionnaire asks the respondent to consider a specific recent trip and then make choices between specified variations of that trip, the respondent may be inclined to take a short-run perspective, imagining time gains of a more incidental nature (that would not, for example, justify adaptations of daily routines). RP studies, in contrast, may capture decisions taken by agents with a long-run perspective.

VOT is usually measured from travel behavior, such as mode or route choice. But the theory does not preclude inferring it from other behavioral decisions. For example, estimates have been made based on labor-market search, price differences for similar commodities across space, and measures of subjective well-being.

There is much interest in just how strongly the availability of communications technology in cars and transit vehicles, used either for entertainment or work, affects travel behavior. As noted earlier, by making time spent traveling less onerous, the availability of technology should reduce VOT; it could also affect mode choice. Indeed, both effects are confirmed empirically.[79] The implications could be dramatic for urban travel patterns and obviously have implications for both public and private investments in in-vehicle technology.

With so many likely sources of heterogeneity in VOT and other behavioral parameters, we cannot expect to capture all of them through explanatory variables in demand models. Therefore, it has become routine to also measure variation from unobserved sources in the disutility of time and reliability, using mixture models such as mixed logit (Hensher 2001). Small *et al.* (2005) illustrate how this can be done while combining RP and SP data, and how summary measures of observable and unobservable heterogeneity can be computed. Fosgerau (2006) provides an important warning, however: he shows that a researcher can manipulate the extreme right tail of the distribution of uncertain travel times through the particular scenarios presented to SP survey respondents; and that resulting estimates are then quite sensitive to the distribution assumed.[80]

Fosgerau (2006) and Koster and Koster (2015) demonstrate how heterogeneity can be estimated semi-parametrically, thus bypassing the need to impose a functional form for it. However, one must beware of over-fitting: In a Monte Carlo study, Cherchi *et al.* (2009) find that even though semi-parametric models usually have a better goodness of fit, they perform worse than parametric models at computing user benefits for non-marginal changes in travel conditions. Yet another approach, taken by Buchholz *et al.* (2022), is to measure values of time at the level of a single trip; by observing repeated trips by the same individual, they can thus infer heterogeneity across people, locations, and times of day. Indeed, Börjesson *et al.* (2013) find that much unobserved heterogeneity is across different trips taken by the same individual.

Cost of crowding

The value of time spent in transit vehicles is affected by amenities other than entertainment or communication technologies. Comfortable seats and surroundings are obvious ones. Particularly important is the degree of crowding, and since this is endogenous, it considerably complicates analyses of transit equilibria. For this reason, considerable research effort has gone into measuring how passengers react to crowding, usually specified as an influence on their VOT. Estimates of such costs of crowding are available from many parts of the world.[81]

Most such estimates are from SP data, due to the complexity of measuring the crowding encountered by real passengers. Many different questionnaire formats have been tried, including verbal descriptions and diagrams showing standing passengers. Yet there is still doubt about how accurately survey respondents perceive such questions, with some evidence that SP-based studies tend to overestimate the effects of crowding on traveler choice.

Hörcher *et al.* (2017) provide a purely RP estimate of train crowding along routes available to passengers in Hong Kong. They combine real-time data on fare collection and on vehicle locations, along with best-path simulations to estimate the route taken by passengers, to construct measures of actual crowding encountered by travelers whose trips they observe. These measures are used to construct two variables: one measuring the probability of having to stand, and the other the number of standing passengers per square meter of floor space. Both variables are found to be highly significant in an otherwise simple route-choice model, with coefficients implying crowding premia on VOT of 26% for a standing passenger (*i.e.*, VOT is 26% greater standing than sitting) and 12% for each standing passenger per square meter. Thus, the crowding premium relative to time seated is 38% for standing in relatively uncrowded conditions (one person/m^2), and 86% for standing in the most crowded conditions they measure for an entire trip (five people/m^2.)[82]

These premia measured for Hong Kong are somewhat lower than typically found by SP studies – for example, Li and Hensher (2011, Table 3) report multipliers of 57%–152% for standing 15 minutes or more in an Australian study.[83] One study that combines SP and RP data, by Kroes *et al.* (2014) for Paris, also suggests tentatively that SP respondents overestimate their valuation of crowding. Wardman and Murphy (2015), using SP/RP observations from four English cities, find that there are significant preferences for various configurations of seating layout as well as for lower seat occupancy.

The crowding premium is important for many analyses of transit operations, from optimal fare to investment in frequency to design of transit vehicles, especially the amounts of space devoted to seated versus standing passengers. We address these issues in later chapters.

The COVID-19 pandemic has given transit crowding an entirely new dimension of significance – and a new analytical tool to analyze crowding in a context of disease transmission. Rødseth *et al.* (2021) show how a standard crowding analysis, based on physical passenger density within a vehicle, can be combined with models of disease transmission that incorporate factors including the proportion of population infected, inherent disease transmissibility (an epidemiological parameter much discussed for COVID-19), duration of proximity to infected individuals, and health costs of getting the disease. Anyone infected during the ride incurs not only a cost themselves, but passes the disease on to others, again based on well-measured epidemiological parameters. A rider, not knowing if they are infected at the start of a trip, considers their own risk of becoming infected as part of average cost. In addition, they impose a marginal external cost by potentially infecting others, due to being unknowingly infected – either at the start of the trip due to some previous exposure, or by its end due to exposure during the trip itself. As part of this calculation, the authors estimate a relationship between train occupancy and total number of secondary infections. The COVID-19 pandemic provided the dramatic changes in infection rates and transit ridership that made such estimates possible. With the great interest in studying COVID-19, and taking advantage of the resulting leap in knowledge of disease transmission, we expect this kind of analysis to be applied further to help understand the public health implications of public transit.

2.7.4   Empirical results: value of reliability

We now turn to empirical research on VOR. Most of it has been based on SP data, for at least two reasons: It is difficult to measure unreliability in actual situations, and unreliability tends to be correlated with travel time itself. However, a few studies have used RP data. One key development is to measure unreliability as a property of the upper percentiles of the distribution of travel times, as suggested by the theory discussed earlier. It turns out that such a measure is less correlated with travel time than is a symmetric measure like standard deviation (Small *et al.* 2005). This is because the upper-percentile travel times (*i.e.*, travel times that occur only rarely) tend to arise from incidents such as crashes or stalled vehicles. The occurrence of such incidents is closely correlated with congestion, but the delays they cause are less so because the effects of the incident persist long after it occurs.

Li *et al.* (2010) review SP studies of car travel that define unreliability in various ways, suggesting that the results are affected by how unreliability is presented to survey respondents. Tseng *et al.* (2009) interview people to test their ability to understand different presentation methods. Together, these two studies suggest that verbal presentations of a set of equally likely travel times works best, at least when the travel-time distributions are relatively smooth. An example of such verbal presentation is to specify an equal chance of arriving at any of five different times. For highly skewed distributions or for particular trip purposes, such as travel to an airport, an alternative option is to specify the probability of being late. Results of VOR studies are often summarized in terms of the *reliability ratio*, defined as VOR/VOT. A review by ITF (2019, p. 19) finds results mostly consistent with an earlier review by Bates *et al.* (2001), concluding that VOR/VOT is between 0.8 and 1.3 when unreliability is measured as a standard deviation of travel times.

Other studies have adopted the unreliability measure of Small *et al.* (2005), namely the difference between the 90th and 50th percentile of the travel-time distribution across days, with similar results. Small *et al.* find that this measure fits their data well, and they rationalize it based on the presumption that travelers are more averse to unexpected delays than to unexpected rapid speeds, even after accounting for the time savings.

A study by Brent and Gross (2017), based on data from a HOT lane in the Seattle area, finds a much higher reliability ratio, namely 3.3 (based on the same percentile-based reliability measure just mentioned). Brent and Gross analyze a pseudo-panel of HOT-lane counts at many separate entry points and at 5-minute intervals over most of the day. They pay special attention to autocorrelation (*i.e.*, unobserved influences on HOT lane usage that persist across 5-minute intervals) and, less importantly as it turns out, to the endogeneity of the dynamic toll-setting algorithm with respect to number of high-occupancy vehicles. These controls make a big difference, as without them they obtain a positive effect of price – also observed in some other studies (see Brownstone and Small 2005) and interpreted as travelers using the price as a signal of worse-than-usual congestion. Plausibly, Brent and Gross find the reliability ratio is much greater in the direction toward major employment centers (11.7) than in the opposite direction (0.7). Their high reliability ratio may result from their low value for VOT ($6.20/hr), which we suspect is underestimated.[84]

Given that travel time and unreliability are positively correlated, estimates of VOT that do not control for reliability are likely to be higher than those that do. In addition, Bento *et al.* (2024) argue that much of what is commonly measured as VOT is actually a "value of urgency," which can be interpreted as a form of reliability: namely, the ability to opt mid-trip for a faster route, in order to compensate for unexpected delays earlier in the trip. Their measurements are based on a dynamically priced HOT lane in Los Angeles that permits users to enter or exit at frequent intervals, being charged accordingly.

The reliability ratio should not be confused with the question of whether travelers value reliability more or less than travel time. First, VOR depends on what reliability measure is used; but more importantly, their relative importance is also governed by the amounts of time and reliability, however measured, that a traveler encounters. Using data from the HOT lane on State Route 91 in the Los Angeles region, Brownstone and Small (2005) find that roughly one-third of the advantage of the HOT lane to the average traveler is due to its higher reliability, and the rest to travel-time savings. Brent and Gross (2017) find on a different facility that two-thirds of the advantage is due to reliability. This advantage of a HOT lane arises primarily from the differences in both time and reliability between uncongested and congested travel. Thus, in Section 3.4.9, we use the average of these two values, that is, 50%, for the ratio of typical reliability costs to travel-time costs of congestion.

Turning to freight transportation, it is clear that values of both time and reliability are important, but empirical evidence is sparse. Most studies use SP methodology. Decisions on freight shipments are complex due to interacting parties (shippers, forwarders, carriers, receiving customers) and a multiplicity of commodities and types of receiving businesses. This leads to a wide dispersion in methodology and results. Literature reviews of VOT studies can be found in de Jong (2007), Goenaga and Contillo (2018), and de Jong *et al.* (2014). The latter study also reviews studies of VOR, as do Shams *et al.* (2017). Shams *et al.* provide a small meta-analysis of 13 studies, which suggests that results are sensitive especially to treatment of unobserved heterogeneity, as well as specifics of survey design.

2.8 Big data

Much of our knowledge of travel-demand behavior comes from surveys of travelers, which are subject to the inaccuracies of ordinary people's statements about their preferences or behavior. Such inaccuracy affects virtually all survey evidence, not just travel demand; and it may be getting worse as people are deluged by survey requests from commercial, political, and philanthropic institutions. Meyer *et al.* (2015) describe this situation as a crisis for survey research.

One way to address such limitations is to take information directly from electronic records of consumer behavior. This has a long-standing parallel in research using administrative records, for example records of government agencies administering social programs or those collecting taxes. Since the late 1990s, many new large-scale datasets, often known as *big data*, have become available to transportation researchers. Sources include traffic cameras, smartphones, and providers of transportation services such as ride-sourcing and bicycle sharing. In the future, AVs and other new technologies are likely to produce more such data.

The advent of big data was brought about by the confluence of several factors: enhanced technologies for data collection and transmission, decreasing costs of data storage, dramatic increases in computing power, and wide availability of analytical software for processing large datasets.[85] These factors have led to new analytical methods, specialized data analytics companies, and new research outlets.

In this section, we review the benefits and challenges brought by the availability of big data.

2.8.1 *What are big data?*

Definitions of big data vary widely. Two important criteria are volume and velocity. *Volume* refers to the quantity of data, measured in gigabytes or even higher units. V*elocity* is defined by the rate at which data are generated or collected, which may be periodically, intermittently, or continuously. One practical definition is that the datasets are too large or complex to be stored or processed conveniently using a personal computer with easily available software (Griffin *et al.* 2020). Another is "any data generated by sensors, vehicles, videos and the Internet of Things" (ITF 2019, p.10). Other criteria often discussed, such as variety and ability to visualize, are potential characteristics of any dataset, big or small.

2.8.2 *Sources of big data*

Large datasets in transportation may be collected for a specific purpose, such as traffic counting or toll collection; or they may arise as a by-product of other purposes, such as mobile phone communications or social media. We can distinguish several types of sources.

2.8.2.1 *Point sources*

Point-source data are collected at a given location, for example to record vehicle flows or collect payments. Technologies include conventional ones: traffic cameras, gate counters, inductance loops, microwave radar, infrared detectors, and electronic toll collection. These technologies typically provide precise and stable information, but are costly to deploy and maintain (Wang *et al.* 2015). There are also newer technologies: LiDAR (light detection and ranging) and sensors that measure speed, noise, and traffic flow (Selod and Soumahoro 2020). Bicycle sharing systems have become a major source of point data, with the rollout of so-called third-generation bicycle sharing system technology.

2.8.2.2   *Journey data*

Data describing full journeys have traditionally been collected from household surveys, but some new sources are now available. Bicycle sharing systems have released data on bicycle journeys that include origin and destination and undocking and docking times, from which one can infer route choices. Journey data can either augment or validate point data. For example, point data from a bicycle sharing system may indicate the number of bicycles at a station, whereas journey data will reveal how many departed from the station and how many returned.[86]

2.8.2.3   *GPS and mobile networks*

Data from the Global Positioning System (GPS) are used for many purposes such as measuring traffic congestion, measuring bus service on-time performance, and analyzing travel behavior by mode of transport (Shen and Stopher 2014). Many of these data are from smartphones.

Mobile telephone network operators collect call detail records for customer billing purposes, which can be used to infer trips and paths – a technology well developed in crime detection.

2.8.2.4   *Social media and crowdsourcing*

Social networks, user forums, and other social media have become important sources of real-time big data on transportation. In addition, there are specialized social networks that ask members explicitly to provide data about their travel.[87] There are also commercial operations that enlist travelers to provide travel data. For example, INRIX collects driving times from smartphones in order to provide travelers with traffic updates and routing advice, and to compile statistics as in its collaboration with the Texas A&M Transportation Institute for reports on congestion trends (Schrank *et al.* 2019). Similarly, Waze gathers information submitted by users on traffic conditions, incidents, and so on, in order to make recommendations to users.

Such data sources are sometimes called *crowdsourcing* when they are provided voluntarily by large numbers of ordinary people. See Nelson *et al.* (2020) for discussion.

2.8.2.5   *Digital maps*

Digital maps provide travel and spatial information by combining data on transportation networks, typically using a geographic information system (GIS), with other sources including high-resolution street imagery and GPS location data from travelers.[88]

2.8.2.6   *Public transit operators*

Automatic collection of transit fares using smart cards or smartphones generates big data that can be used to study passenger travel behavior. The operators are often interested in predicting the effects of changes in fares, schedules, and other dimensions of service quality (*e.g.*, Lovrić *et al.* 2016).

2.8.2.7 Administrative databases

Dedicated administrative databases continue to be useful sources. An example is an initiative by the US Federal Highway Administration to create two complementary databases designed to enhance road safety.[89] One is the *Roadway Information Database*, containing geospatial data on roadway characteristics, railroad crossings, traffic volumes, crash histories, and so forth. The *Naturalistic Driving Study* adds to this roadway information additional data it collects on speed, acceleration, etc. from individual vehicles; the object is to study how driver behavior and the roadway environment together contribute to crash risks.

2.8.3 Advantages of big data

One clear advantage of big data for research is that their high volume and velocity make it possible to include more explanatory variables and more flexible functional relationships, while maintaining sufficient degrees of freedom, than would otherwise be possible. Standard statistical inference methods can then be applied even if the environment is changing rapidly (Milne and Watling 2019). Big data can also be used to facilitate conventional surveys, for example using data on actual journeys to partially prefill travel diaries that people are asked to provide (ITF 2021b). Another use is to fill gaps in information that transportation agencies collect infrequently, if at all, such as on bicycling and pedestrian flows (Griffin *et al.* 2020).

Just as with conventional data (Section 2.2.4), big data from various sources can be combined for econometric analysis in order to take advantage of the sources' relative strengths.

High-velocity real-time data can facilitate management of congestion and incidents. As already noted, they can support real-time traffic forecasting: sometimes called *nowcasting*. Continuously collected data can be used to study travel behavior throughout the day, thus expanding the scope of most traditional data collection. Pervasive location data can be used to better define the shape and size of the traffic analysis zones used in more conventional analysis. High spatial and temporal resolutions may allow more accurate calculation of accessibility for use in conventional modeling – especially important for modeling use of public transit and active transport modes, whose accessibility can vary substantially across short distances and over time (Benenson *et al.* 2017).

2.8.4 Limitations and challenges

The use of big data has a number of limitations, posing challenges. New approaches are required to collect, store, and manage it, while new skills are needed to analyze it. Data collected for other purposes typically need to be converted into a form useful for transportation research (Griffin *et al.* 2020). As already noted, data sources may differ in format, spatial resolution, and temporal resolution, making them difficult to combine. Technological standards would help in this respect, but also might impede innovation (ITF 2021b).

Big data, like any other data, are susceptible to inaccuracies and measurement errors. For example, GPS signals can be lost while traveling between tall buildings, at the start of a trip while the device is finding signals, and while switching back to working mode after a long stop. The spatial resolution of mobile-phone data is limited by the reach of individual cellular towers, whose coverage can range up to 10 km in radius (ITF 2021b). Thus, mobile phones in close proximity may be hard to distinguish. And mobile phones or SIM cards do not always correspond one-to-one with people, since a person may use multiple phones or share a phone with someone else. Furthermore, high volume and velocity are not an advantage for understanding very rare events (Vovsha 2020), which may require special-purpose data collection.

A pervasive problem is sampling bias when data collection is limited to people using a particular service or technology. For example, usable mobile network data are generated by people who use cellular phones, perhaps only those who subscribe to a particular carrier, and in most cases only those who opt to allow location sharing. Similarly, data from navigation systems are restricted to those vehicles that are equipped with them, which tend to be newer and more expensive vehicles. Use of social media tends to be concentrated in certain socioeconomic groups, especially in the case of specialized media such as those for recreational cyclists and runners; and social media are often used intermittently. Metadata that provide information on how, when, and/or where data are collected may help to alleviate sampling bias, just as for conventional data, although metadata may also be circumscribed by privacy restrictions.

Other limitations include frequent lack of information on trip purpose, car ownership, and socioeconomic characteristics; and data longevity, which can be impaired by technological evolution, changes in the legal environment, and software obsolescence. These problems may be exacerbated when the owners and users of big data are not part of the same organization. Milne and Watling (2019) provide further discussion.

Big data are amenable to analysis using machine learning methods, which can be both a strength and a weakness.[90] These methods are powerful, especially for filling in missing variables based on predictions using other variables. However, they are also atheoretical: being designed to find correlations rather than to explain causation, they are prone to finding spurious correlation (in the sense that the correlations identified could also appear in randomly generated data).[91] Furthermore, they typically cannot separately identify the influence of variables such as travel time, reliability, and crowding that may be central to policy concerns – we give some examples in Section 2.8.6. Since understanding causation is paramount for most research purposes, analysis still needs to be guided by theory no matter how large the dataset is.

Finally, the same problems of selection and endogeneity that beset classical statistical testing also apply here. Indeed, these problems can be exacerbated by the fine-grained spatial nature of big data: For example, self-sorting of individuals making location choices is more prevalent among small than large geographical areas (Glaeser *et al.* 2018).

2.8.5   *Practical applications*

In this section, we offer some examples that illustrate uses of big data for practical purposes.

2.8.5.1   *Travel information*

An obvious use, already mentioned, is to provide travelers with detailed, up-to-date information on trip options and travel conditions.[92] Private crowdsourcing services provide route guidance by identifying quickest routes and giving users step-by-step directions on how to reach a destination. The quality of service is generally better in dense urban areas where the volume of users (and information providers) is high. Rio de Janeiro was the first city to convey comprehensive travel information by collecting and combining real-time data from Waze, the public transportation app Moovit, and various sensors and cameras. The city of Rio de Janeiro conveys information about weather, traffic signal malfunctions, disasters, and other travel condition anomalies.[93] The city of Tokyo, in collaboration with the private sector, provides real-time information on shortest and least-congested routes (Selod and Soumahoro 2020). Chicago provides transit users with estimated departure and arrival times, and also compiles weekly updates on bus crowding (created as part of its COVID-19 response).[94]

2.8.5.2   *Accessibility information*

Big data are used to provide information on accessibility of locations for use by planners, analysts, and potential residents. For example, Walk Score measures the walkability of an address, as well as its bicycle friendliness and transit accessibility, using data from Google, OpenStreet-Map, and other sources, while Windermere Real Estate employs INRIX data to calculate drive times from a given location by time of day, to enable users to identify convenient residential or workplace locations for their situation.[95]

2.8.5.3   *Planning and operations*

Transit operators have long used smart card data to improve routes and timetables (Pelletier *et al.* 2011). If boarding and alighting locations are both recorded, distance-based fares can be implemented. With sufficient data on users, individual travel packages could potentially be offered as envisaged with Mobility as a Service (see Section 6.3.6). More generally, the high velocity of big data enables planners to experiment with new services and policy changes, in the knowledge that the changes can be quickly evaluated and aborted if called for (Milne and Watling 2019).

2.8.5.4   *Performance measurement and service enhancement*

Smart card data can be used to measure transit service quality using metrics such as schedule adherence, average boarding times, total vehicle-kilometers, and total person-kilometers. This permits an agency to assess its own performance or that of private-sector transit operators, perhaps including such metrics in contracts with such operators (see Section 6.3.3).

Similar logic is employed in the ride-sourcing industry. For example, UberX uses customer ratings to assess its drivers. There is tentative evidence that this is effective: Athey *et al.* (2019) obtain telemetric data from on-board sensors (*e.g.*, data on acceleration, braking, and phone handling) to compare driver performance for drivers of UberX with those for UberTaxi (which does not similarly collect customer ratings), finding that UberX drivers perform better. Some of this effect, however, could be due to self-selection of better drivers into services that monitor their performance in this way.

2.8.6   *Use of big data for research*

Applications of big data in transportation research are now numerous. We provide a few examples.

2.8.6.1   *Transit user preferences*

We noted earlier that automated fare collection data can be useful for estimating effects of conventional economic variables, such as fare changes. For example, Halvorsen *et al.* (2016) and Lovrić *et al.* (2016) assess the effects on ridership of off-peak discount fares in Hong Kong and free travel in Singapore, respectively. Sometimes other aspects of ride quality can be measured by combining big data with conventional data describing vehicle ownership, network configuration, public transport timetables, and so forth (ITF 2021b). For example, as described in Section 2.7.3, Hörcher *et al.* (2017) use automated fare collection and vehicle location data to measure train crowding, and thus are able to derive RP estimates of the cost of crowding. As another example, acceleration and deceleration can be measured with smartphones, enabling some inferences about ride quality.

2.8.6.2   Mode choice

GPS devices can provide a wealth of data on trip trajectories, but they miss some important trip characteristics such as travel mode, trip purpose, and vehicle occupancy. In some cases, machine learning is helpful and reasonably accurate in classifying travel mode (Hagenauer and Helbich 2017). This is more difficult in dense urban areas: Streets and transit lines run close to each other, and bicycle trips can be difficult to distinguish from other modes.

2.8.6.3   Toll lane choice

In Section 2.3.3, we note research using survey data to study lane-choice decisions on managed lanes, that is, reserved expressway lanes offering a faster trip by paying a toll. One might hope to increase the sample size for such studies using GPS data. Ashraf *et al.* (2021) study the Katy Freeway in Houston, Texas, where roadside antennas make it possible to identify which lane a given vehicle is using. Their data were sampled from observations of multiple trips by over 3 million unique transponder IDs, taken over a 30-month period. Unlike results from many surveys, these data indicate remarkable stability in choices: Over 80% of unique transponder IDs were never observed on the toll lanes, while nearly 5% used them all the time.

   Ashraf *et al.* also investigate the ability of machine learning methods to predict which lane will be chosen on a given trip. They find that such methods outperform logit models. Yet, as they note, the machine learning techniques do not identify the independent influence of predictors such as toll and travel time on the choices that are made, and hence do not measure such basic quantities as monetary values of travel time and reliability.

2.8.6.4   Trip-timing preferences

As explained in Section 2.3.2, trip-timing decisions are often modeled as a trade-off between schedule delay costs (the costs of arriving earlier or later than desired) and travel time. Kim and Moon (2022) estimate these preferences for a large sample of commuters, focusing especially on the distribution across commuters of ideal arrival time. They accomplish this by first obtaining individual information on trip origins, destinations, and chosen arrival times (from the 2012 California Household Travel Survey), and then estimating travel-time profiles (*i.e.*, the travel time faced by an individual commuter at alternative times of day). The latter step involves querying Google Maps, over roughly 18 months in 2020–2021, for each origin–destination pair as defined by the zip codes reported by the 2012 travelers. The authors take steps to verify stability of conditions across the decade separating these two steps.

   They then estimate preferred arrival times for each commuter in the 2012 sample in three steps. (1) First, they equate the preferred arrival time for each commuter whose trip is within a single zip code, with the actual arrival time reported by this commuter (assuming such a commuter need not adjust arrival time due to time-varying congestion). (2) Next, using machine learning, they develop a predictive model of how these preferred arrival times depend on characteristics reported in the travel survey. (3) Finally, they use this predictive model to infer preferred arrival times for all commuters. This procedure reveals that preferred arrival times are quite widely dispersed. The travel-time profiles are also quite flat, much more so than would be expected from simply graphing aggregate speeds over time. Both of these observations support the findings of Hall (forthcoming), who argues that in fact most commuters are infra-marginal, in contrast to the assumptions of equilibrium models (see Section 3.4.3).

   The authors use these results to estimate consumers' utility functions over arrival times. Their estimates indicate that commuters are willing to incur about 2 additional minutes of schedule delay in order to reduce travel time by 1 minute. For the trip-timing model (2.64), this implies marginal rates of substitution for early arrival (β / α) and late arrival (γ / α) of about 0.5. The estimated ratio β / α is similar to that in Small (1982) and later studies, but the estimated γ / α is much smaller. Due to the size of their dataset, they also are able to get quite precise estimates of nonlinearities in the utility functions.

2.8.6.5   *Other applications*

Big data have been used in many other travel-demand applications. For example, Yang and Gonzales (2014) model taxi demand in New York City as a function of location, time of day, and other factors. They combine a database of 147 million taxi trips with information on transit service from Google transit feed and from demographic, socioeconomic, and employment data. Gonzalez-Navarro *et al.* (2021) use proprietary Uber data to further investigate whether ride-sourcing is a substitute or complement for public transit, adding further detail on the heterogeneity of such effects found by Hall *et al.* (2018) using market data (as noted in Section 6.3.6).

We mention here two applications not related to travel demand, but rather to traffic congestion. One, by Mangrum and Molnar (2020), estimates street-specific speed–density relationships (see Section 3.3) in northern Manhattan. They note the simultaneity problem due to density and speed being jointly determined by travel demand and road network capacity (the latter responding to speed through policy decisions). They overcome this problem by exploiting a policy change in 2013 that authorized a new class of taxi to operate, thus serving as a demand shock. Their strategy includes collecting 1.3 billion taxi-trip records, along with observations of traffic densities using aerial orthoimagery (*i.e.*, aerial photography corrected for the visual distortions caused by variations in elevation). Using the trip time and density measurements, both at reasonably fine geographical resolution, they are able to estimate the point relationship between speed and density. They call this the "congestion elasticity," finding it to be quite large. They go on to estimate the marginal congestion externality of a commuting trip, a key variable in much cost and policy analysis (see especially Sections 3.3 and 4.1).

Another congestion-related application is the study by Pasidis (2019) of how accidents affect congestion. This question also poses an identification problem, since congestion can affect accident frequency. The author overcomes this challenge by using a comprehensive database of highway traffic and injury accidents in the UK, in order to compare speeds on days with and without accidents, specific to highway segment, time of day, and day of the week.

2.8.6.6   *Summary*

Big data can reveal empirical relationships that may be missed using traditional methods and traditional data. As illustrated here, they may be combined with other data sources that provide complementary information.

2.9   Conclusions

All tractable approaches to travel-demand analysis are based on greatly simplified portrayals of behavior. This is necessary because the variety of purposes and available choices make travel behavior very complex. As a result, distinct or even mutually contradictory analytical approaches may each provide useful information for particular circumstances. The sophisticated planner or analyst will want to understand several different approaches. This includes deciding whether or not interactions between transportation and urban form are important enough, in the particular context being investigated, to require explicit modeling.

How well do transportation professionals perform at actually predicting the demand for particular facilities? The record is mixed, and research has found that, in practice, many traffic forecasts have been subject not only to imprecision, which is to be expected, but to serious biases and even intentional deception – presumably in order to favor projects in which parties have a professional or financial interest (Flyvbjerg *et al.* 2005). We take up this topic in Chapter 5, where we also address similar biases is estimating the costs of investment projects.

Among the many features exhibited by travel-demand analysis, we have highlighted three: the values of time, schedule delays, reliability and crowding. Each can be defined rigorously from an appropriate demand model. While the value of time has always been recognized as central to almost all policy investigations, the other three have become increasingly important in urban contexts as urban transportation systems have become more complex and varied.

The advent of huge data sources is transforming research in transportation, as it is in just about every other field of study. It opens many avenues for constructive research, as well as pitfalls that, we hope, can be avoided by applying a thorough knowledge of the underlying principles determining travel behavior.

Notes

1 On freight demand, see Feo-Valero *et al.* (2011), Chow *et al.* (2010) and de Jong *et al.* (2014).
2 If the variables Z_k in (2.2) are replaced by their natural logarithms, and the mean values of these logarithms subtracted, then (2.2) becomes the *translog* functional form:

$$f(Z) = \beta_0 + \sum_k \beta_{1k}\tilde{Z}_k + \sum_k \beta_{2k}\tilde{Z}_k^2 + \sum_k \sum_{l \neq k} \beta_{3kl}\tilde{Z}_k\tilde{Z}_l, \text{ where } \tilde{Z}_k \equiv (\log Z_k - \overline{\log Z_k}) \text{ and the bar indi-}$$

cates a sample average. This function is widely used in cost analysis, as described in Chapter 3.
3 The single-censored tobit model postulates a "latent" (unobserved) variable x^* that is explained by an ordinary regression equation like $x^* = \beta'z + \varepsilon$, and an observed variable $x = \max\{x^*, 0\}$. The idea is that we observe x^* except when it is outside the range of observability (below zero in this example); in that case we observe only that it fell outside the range. See any econometrics text. The double-censored tobit model is similar except now $x = 0$ if $x^* < 0$, $x = x^*$ if $0 \leq x^* \leq 1$, and $x = 1$ if $x^* > 1$.
4 Equation (2.8) is a special case of (2.9) in which $J = 2$ and we define $x = x_1$, $z = z_1 - z_2$, and $\varepsilon = \varepsilon_1 - \varepsilon_2$; the interpretation is that option 1 is to take the mode in question, while option 2 represents all other alternatives including not traveling.
5 We have changed their notation to one more similar to the rest of this book. Our parameters a, b, α, β^1, β^2, and β^3 correspond to their parameters α, β, θ, λ, φ, and $\lambda\gamma$.
6 However, estimation is more complex in this case because the authors want to control for possible endogeneity of the fare and level of service (*i.e.*, the possibility that average fare and aggregate service provision responded to the ridership level during the same year).
7 This statement is based on calculating the ratio of long- to short-run elasticities as $(1-\alpha)^{-1}$, as described in Section 2.1.2, where α is the estimated coefficient of the lagged dependent variable. We use $\alpha = 0.294$ from the last column of their Table 3. The long-run elasticities reported by the authors are slightly different due to their accounting for statistical probability distributions of estimated coefficients. We have rounded all reported elasticities to two decimal places.
8 For useful insights on the future of public transit, see Volinski (2018) and Currie (2018).
9 For an excellent review, see Goodwin and Van Dender (2013). The phrase "peak car" in their title refers to the hypothesis that aggregate car use has already peaked or will soon do so
10 Their estimated equations are based on country-specific annual time series 1980–2015 (or −2013 in some cases). One drawback is that their estimation uses the same years they want to explain, especially those since 2004. Wadud and Baierl (2017) note that this biases the experiment in favor of the result found, and provide alternate results estimated on samples ending in 2003; their implications, however, are ambiguous (see Bastian *et al.* 2017).

11 This mode is sometimes called "ride-sharing," but we reserve that term for situations when multiple passengers travel together in a small vehicle. It is also called "ride-hailing," but unlike with taxis, ride-sourcing vehicles cannot be hailed visually from the street. We adopt the terminological distinctions advocated by ITF (2021a, pp. 48–49).

12 Daziano *et al.* (2017) estimate willingness to pay for automated vehicles, and Zmud (2016) assesses their consumer acceptability. Thorough assessments of prospects for market penetration and the ensuing effects include those by Fagnant and Kockelman (2015), Mudge *et al.* (2018), and Winston and Karpilow (2020). The US National Highway Traffic Safety Administration suggests that commercial market penetration of partially automated operations (*e.g.*, lane-keeping assistance, self-parking) will take place in a 2016–2025 time frame, and fully driverless vehicles after 2025 (as cited by Mudge *et al.* 2018, Table 4). Regional Plan Association (2017, p. 16) suggests that autonomous vehicles will enter the market for selected services in 2022–2027, and autonomous trucks will become widespread in 2027–2040.

13 The Society of Automotive Engineers has defined five distinct phases of automation covering this range. See SAE (2021).

14 ITF (2015b, 2017).

15 For a discussion, see Zakharenko (2016); for quantitative simulation, see Millard-Ball (2019).

16 Other insights from interviews with these subjects include: (i) some made trips when they would not want to drive due to night conditions, fatigue, age, or desire to drink alcohol; (ii) the effect on walking trips was mixed, decreasing for some and increasing for others.

17 Alonso (1964), Mills (1967), and Muth (1969). Textbook treatments include Fujita (1989) and O'Sullivan (2019). Duranton *et al.* (2015) provides a comprehensive handbook.

18 For polycentric structures, see, for example, Fujita *et al.* (1997), McMillen (2001), and McMillen and Smith (2003). For studies using computable general equilibrium, see Ahlfeldt *et al.* (2015). Acheampong and Silva (2015) review one branch of this literature, known as land use transport interaction (LUTI) models.

19 Safirova *et al.* (2006) combine the same underlying land-use model with a different transportation model, known as START, for policy analysis for the Washington, DC area. Waddell (2002) describes a model known as UrbanSim, and also reviews older models and modeling strategies specifically designed for the needs of transportation agencies.

20 Specifically, the new rail lines depressed the growth of newly connected cities that are intermediate in location between larger connected cities. Bröcker and Mercenier (2011) discuss the use of computable general equilibrium models more generally in transport policy analysis.

21 Train (2009) and Hensher *et al.* (2015) provide book-length treatments.

22 The derivation of (2.15) follows McFadden (1974, p. 108). The quantity $F_i(\cdot)d\varepsilon_i$ in the last line is, by the properties of distribution functions, the joint probability that the inequalities of the previous line hold and that the ith random term lies in the interval $[\varepsilon_i + d\varepsilon_i]$; its integral over all possible values of ε_i is thus the desired probability.

23 See Swait and Louviere (1993). Some authors, such as Train (2009), define the scale of the logit model to be μ^{-1} instead of μ.

24 Comparable normalization is accomplished by dividing the logit coefficients by $\pi/\sqrt{3}$ in order to give the utilities the same standard deviations in the two models. In both models, the choice probabilities depend on $(\beta/\sigma_\varepsilon)$, where σ_ε^2 is the variance of each of the random terms ε_{in}. In the case of probit, the variance of $\varepsilon_{1n} - \varepsilon_{2n}$, which is $2\sigma_\varepsilon^2$, is set to one by the conventional normalization; hence, $\sigma_\varepsilon^{PROBIT} = 1/\sqrt{2}$. In the case of logit, the normalization $\mu = 1$ in equation (2.17) implies that ε_{in} has standard deviation $\sigma_\varepsilon^{LOGIT} = \pi/\sqrt{6}$. Hence, to make logit and iid probit comparable, the logit coefficients must be divided by $\sigma_\varepsilon^{LOGIT}/\sigma_\varepsilon^{PROBIT} = \pi/\sqrt{3} = 1.814$.

25 By a historical accident, the generalization of binary to multivariate probit was made simultaneously with another generalization, namely random parameters β (Hausman and Wise 1978). This second generalization is the same as that leading in the logit family of models to mixed logit or mixed GEV (Section 2.4.2).

26 In this example, z_{in} is a vector with three components: c_{in}/w_n, T_{in}, and T_{in}^2.

27 The indirect utilities δ_j implied by observed market shares are determined (again for a given set of trial parameters) by solving the equation for probabilities, for example, (2.18), for V_j as a function of probabilities P_i ($i = 1, \ldots, J$); the solution is interpreted as giving δ_j (the empirical analog of V_j) in terms of

observed market shares (the empirical analogs of P_j). The fact that (2.18) can be solved for V_j is due to a property peculiar to the logit model: If a full set of alternative-specific constants is included, the predicted choice shares for each of the alternatives can be made exactly equal to the observed shares in the sample by setting parameter β to its maximum-likelihood estimate. Bresnahan *et al.* assume that the discrete-choice model contains no variables describing characteristics of consumers, which enables us to omit subscript n from indirect utility.

28 The variable T_{in} itself is a generic variable, having the same meaning (time) for each alternative i to which it is applied. This is the case for the terms in (2.25) with coefficients β_2 and β_3. But including it with an alternative-specific coefficient γ_i, as in the last term in (2.25), is the same as interacting it with an alternative dummy variable D^i as in (2.24) and as described in the text following (2.22).

29 One might wonder if the coefficient of cost could be alternative specific. This is possible empirically, but presents a problem conceptually because it is inconsistent with theoretical equivalence, expressed formally in eq (2.30), relating the cost coefficient of each alternative to the marginal utility of income.

30 One of the simplest is the "delta method" for the ratio of two estimated coefficients, for example, $\hat{v}_T \equiv \hat{\beta}_2 / \hat{\beta}_1$. Denote the "coefficients of variance" of $\hat{\beta}_1$, $\hat{\beta}_2$, and $\hat{v}_T$ by s_1, s_2, and s_v, respectively (*i.e.*, $s_1 = SD(\hat{\beta}_1) / \hat{\beta}_1$, etc.). Also let $s_{12} \equiv \text{Cov}(\hat{\beta}_1) / (\hat{\beta}_1\hat{\beta}_2)$ denote the fractional covariance. When these ratios are small, they are approximately related by $s_v^2 = s_1^2 + s_2^2 - 2s_{12}$.

31 For examples of measuring both quantities, see Lam and Small (2001), which is described in Section 2.3.3; also Brownstone *et al.* (2003) or Small *et al.* (2005).

32 Louviere *et al.* (2000) describe such aspects of survey design and other issues with SP data.

33 See, for example, Hensher, Louviere, and Swait (1999), Morikawa *et al.* (2002), or Small *et al.* (2005). Börjesson (2008) applies joint RP–SP estimation, along with mixed logit (see Section 2.4.2), to analysis of trip-timing data. Brownstone *et al.* (2000) discuss explicitly the way in which the two types of data complement each other in the context of automobile purchase. They find that RP data are needed to get realistic estimates of choice among different car body types and also of the model's scale factor, while SP data are critical for measuring consumer response to attributes that are not currently available in the marketplace.

34 A *demand function* describes quantity as a function of price (and perhaps other characteristics), as in (2.1). Equivalently, an *inverse demand function* describes price as a function of quantity (and perhaps other characteristics). It is conventional in economics to depict these equivalent relationships graphically as a *demand curve* by plotting them with quantity along the horizontal axis and price along the vertical axis. Consumers' surplus as defined graphically here in the text can be represented mathematically either as $\int_{p*}^{\infty} x(p)\,dp$ or $\int_0^{x*} \left[p(x) - p* \right]dx$, where $x(\cdot)$ is the demand function, $p(\cdot)$ is the inverse demand function, and $p*$ and $x*$ are the current price and quantity. (Other characteristics that are arguments of these functions are omitted for simplicity.) The second formulation can also be written as $\int_0^{x*} p(x)\,dx - p* x*$, which can be characterized as the difference between the consumer's total willingness to pay for consuming $x*$ (*i.e.*, the area under the demand curve and to the left of current quantity) and the amount actually paid.

35 If income y_n is included as an explanatory variable, one might think that $\partial V_{jn} / \partial y_n$ is a measure of λ_n. This would be incorrect because the systematic utilities V_{jn} capture only the *relative* effects of income on utility of the various alternatives, not the direct influence of income on utility of all alternatives. If price c_{jn} is *not* included as an explanatory variable, then there is no way to estimate λ_n from the model results, so welfare changes cannot be expressed in monetary terms; nevertheless, changes in (2.29) remain useful indicators of relative changes in the welfare of groups facing unchanged prices and believed to have identical values of λ_n. For example, if travel time is one of the variables, welfare changes can be computed in terms of equivalent time saved, rather than money, by substituting t_{jn} for c_{jn} in (2.30). One might then take the further step of converting the results to monetary values by multiplying by an externally estimated VOT (see Section 2.7).

36 The combined direct and indirect effects may be expressed as the total price elasticity, sometimes called the *uncompensated price elasticity* to distinguish it from the compensated elasticity. For normal

goods the price and income effects reinforce each other, so the uncompensated price elasticity is larger in magnitude than the compensated one. The relationship between the uncompensated and compensated price elasticities, ε^u and ε^c, is given by the Slutsky equation: $\varepsilon^u = \varepsilon^c - s \cdot \eta_y$, where s is the share of income spent on the good in question and η_y is its income elasticity. See Willig (1976) or any mathematical microeconomics textbook for a derivation.

37 A commonly used algorithm, sometimes known as a *contraction mapping*, adjusts the alternative-specific constants $\{a_i\}$ at each iteration by an amount $\log[s_i] - \log[\hat{s}_i (a_1,\ldots, a_J)]$, where s_i is the observed share and $\hat{s}_i(\cdot)$ is the share predicted by the model.

38 Rank-ordered logit, sometimes called "expanded logit" or "exploded logit," is analyzed by Beggs, Cardell, and Hausman (1981) and Hausman and Ruud (1987). Beggs *et al.* call it "ordered logit," but that name is now usually reserved for an ordered response model as described here.

39 Cost includes auto operating cost, parking, and transit fare. Walking is assumed to incur no cost.

40 The denominator $\partial V_{in}/\partial c_{in}$ in (2.23), at c=200 cents, is equal to $\beta_c - \beta_{log (c)} \cdot d\ln(c)/dc = -0.0015 - 0.242/200 = -0.00271$. Thus, for example, the value of auto time is $-0.039/(-0.00271) = 14.39$ cents/min × (60min/hr)/(100¢/$) = $8.63hr.

41 To interpret these constants, we need to account for the fact that according to the authors' text, the utility scale μ is different from one: specifically, $\mu < 1$ because the mode choice model is part of a larger nested logit model structure (Section 2.4.1). The authors also changed the scale in order to make comparisons across time periods in a test of transferability.

42 Continuous trip-timing models are explored by Gadda *et al.* (2009). One natural approach is to treat the interval before a trip departure as an activity with a hazard rate (*i.e.*, the conditional probability of ending per unit time) that is a function of variables of interest.

43 Small (1982, Table 2, Model 1).

44 The coefficient for women is -0.159, and that for men is $-0.159 + 0.074 = -0.085$.

45 See Small *et al.* (2005) for further discussion of this same issue in a different data set from SR91.

46 It is sometimes called *generalized cost* or *inclusive price*. Throughout this book, we will call it a "generalized price" whenever it includes components, such as fares and tolls, that are transfers between parties rather than societal costs.

47 The variance–covariance matrix of these utility differences has $(J - 1)^2$ elements and is symmetric. Hence, it has only $J(J - 1)/2$ identifiable elements, less one for utility-scale normalization.

48 Equation (2.39) is derived by Lindberg, Eriksson, and Mattsson (1995, p. 134) and demonstrated more simply by Choi and Moon (1997, p. 131).

49 See Hensher (1986) or Brownstone and Small (1989). If maximizing the log-likelihood function is numerically difficult, one can start with the sequential estimator and carry out just one step of a Newton–Raphson algorithm toward maximization; this yields a statistically efficient estimate and seems to work well in practice (Brownstone and Small 1989).

50 The ordered GEV model is extended by You-Lian Chu (2009) to allow some decision-makers to be captive to a particular time interval, which is also the idea behind the "dogit" model of Gaudry and Dagenais (1979).

51 The parameter ρ in the specification of Lemp *et al.* (2010) is the inverse of the corresponding parameter(s) in our equations (2.40)–(2.45).

52 The computational efficiency can be greatly improved by taking draws from the distribution of β that are not strictly random, but that more thoroughly cover the portions of β-space over which the distribution varies most strongly. See Train (2009, ch. 9) and Munger *et al.* (2012) for discussions.

53 Small and Verhoef (2007, Section 2.4.4) provide intuitive summaries of the Brownstone–Train paper.

54 See Washington *et al.* (2010, Chap. 15) or Mannering and Hensher (1987). More elaborate systems of equations can be handled with the very flexible tools of *structural equations modeling*, sometimes used with large data sets describing mutually related decisions. Golob (2003) provides a review.

55 Supposedly it also can be computed for logit models with more than two alternatives, but doing so is extremely complex: see Dubin and McFadden (1984).

56 Dubin and McFadden (1984) use a functional form somewhat different from (2.53), with the factor $\exp(\beta p_j)$ multiplying a linear function of income with its own error term. In their model, which lacks random parameters, an additive error term shows up in the equation for x_j, rather than that for $\log(x_j)$ as in (2.54).

57 Wooldridge (2010) provides a comprehensive treatment of panel models, while William Greene (2018) reviews them specifically for discrete-choice models.

58 Assuming no overall constant term is included, a total of $N \cdot (J - 1)$ constants $\phi_{i,n}$ can be estimated, where N is the number of individuals and J the number of alternatives; the others may be set to zero for normalization. This is because only utility *differences* across alternatives affect choice.

59 Such a variable would be perfectly collinear with the alternative-specific dummies: that is, some linear combination of them adds to zero. The separate effects of perfectly collinear variables cannot be distinguished when systematic utility is specified as linear in parameters.

60 An alternative approach, proposed by Petrin and Train (2004), is to add artificial variables to the model to absorb the part of the error term that is correlated with price, just as is done in the approach of Heckman described as "Step 2 Version (b)" in Section 2.4.3.

61 Proof of convergence is given by Berry, Levinsohn, and Pakes (1995, Appendix I). The contraction mapping adjusts the constants so that, if used with the previous iteration's estimated distribution (across n) of parameter vector β, it equates predicted with actual shares. The next iteration uses this better set of constants to improve the estimate of β, and so forth.

62 Train and Winston (2007) create four such instrumental variables. The first two are the sums of differences in measured characteristics (like horsepower) between the make/model in question and (i) all other makes/models by the same manufacturer, or (ii) all other makes/models by other manufacturers. Two additional instruments are formed the same way, but using the squares of differences in characteristics.

63 The BLP procedure is further developed for aggregate data by Bresnahan *et al.* (1997). Applications to disaggregate data include Berry, Levinsohn, and Pakes (2004) for automobiles and Goolsbee and Petrin (2004) for television reception.

64 For example, if "no purchase" is one of many choice options in a logit model of new-vehicle purchases, the logit functional form forces it to have the same high substitutability with various purchase options that they have with each other.

65 Morikawa *et al.* also provide the formal framework for constructing a likelihood function that combines RP and SP data.

66 Latent classes can be viewed as another way to incorporate heterogeneity, so it is natural to ask how this approach compares with mixed logit for that purpose. This question is analyzed by Greene and Hensher (2003).

67 Two projects in the United States survey the integration of travel-time reliability into transportation planning tools and, specifically, the computation and use in practical applications of value of reliability (National Academies of Sciences, Engineering, and Medicine 2014a,b).

68 We have factored the right-hand side of (2.68) the same way as Small (2012), so that v_R is a behavioral quantity and R is a property of the distribution of travel times. This is consistent with recommendations in some literature to measure R as some property of the upper tail of the distribution. Fosgerau and Karlström factor it a different way, so that σ alone is the measure of reliability, another common choice in the literature.

69 It is developed by Vickrey (1973), Tseng and Verhoef (2008), and Fosgerau and Engelson (2011).

70 This equivalence is pointed out by Wardman (2004, p. 364); the equation is also derived by de Palma and Lindsey (2001).

71 Assuming $\beta/\alpha = 0.6$ and $\gamma/\alpha = 2.4$, the premium is $\beta\gamma/(\beta + \gamma) = 0.48\alpha \approx 0.50\alpha$.

72 For examples, see Yang (1998), Paz and Peeta (2009), and Fosgerau and Jiang (2019).

73 For reviews, see especially Shires and de Jong (2009), Hensher (2011), Small (2012), ITF (2019), and Litman (2023b).

74 As just three examples: Commissariat Général du Plan (2001) for France, Munizaga *et al.* (2006) for Chile, and Cook *et al.* (2016) for rural Africa. Somewhat higher values have been obtained in Spain using SP data (Álvarez *et al.* 2007) and in Japan (Japan Research Institute Study Group on Road Investment Evaluation 2000).

75 Abrantes and Wardman (2011, p. 10); Hensher (2011, pp. 144–145); Shires and de Jong (2009, pp. 320–321).

76 This finding should not be confused with the idea that small time *savings* might have a smaller or even zero marginal value, which has often been proposed but has no empirical support and would be inconsistent with standard theory. Such a conclusion may seem to arise from SP data, but this is most likely due to the existence of reference points and the tendency of people to resist unfavorable departures from such reference points, as postulated by prospect theory (De Borger and Fosgerau 2008). As noted earlier, reference points are transitory and so have little bearing on the VOT needed for policy decisions.

Such results do suggest caution in using SP data (Fosgerau 2019, p. 18). The issue of small time savings is discussed thoroughly by Daly *et al.* (2014), who also advise caution in using SP data to measure VOT.

77 See their Table 1, rows 4–5, 13–14.

78 Peer *et al.* (2014) find a 50% overstatement of travel time by travelers, especially by inexperienced commuters. But their modeling suggests that, unlike in the explanation given here, some of this over-reporting does not reflect actual distortions in perception.

79 See de Jong and Kouwenhoven (2019) for VOT, and Lee *et al.* (2019) for mode choice in Seoul.

80 To address the resulting need for a guide to choosing an appropriate assumed distribution of random parameters, Fosgerau and Bierlaire (2007) provide a statistical test for such a distribution.

81 Such studies are reviewed by Li and Hensher (2011) and summarized as a meta-analysis by Wardman and Whelan (2011). Hörcher *et al.* (2017) include some newer studies in their literature review, including results for Hong Kong, the UK, Paris, Santiago (Chile), and Seoul.

82 The estimated premia are those from Model (4) of their Table 2, computed simply as the ratios of coefficients for "crowd density" or "standing probability" to that for in-vehicle time. The maximum crowding for a computed trip was $5.1/m^2$ (p. 114).

83 Calculated from their Table 3, column 1, as $8.1/14.1 = 0.57$ (for standing 15 min), and $(11.5 + 10.0)/14.1 = 1.52$ (for standing 20 min in "crush" conditions).

84 The regression measuring VOT includes a control variable defined as speed in the general-purpose lanes. This variable is the most important part of their measure of the user's expected travel-time savings. Thus, if travelers use a more complex algorithm to estimate these savings than that assumed by Brent and Gross, some of that control variable's measured effect on HOT usage might actually reflect additional VOT.

85 ITF (2015a) has a useful review, while Varian (2014) describes implications for econometric methods.

86 Gal-Tzur *et al.* (2014), Romanillos *et al.* (2016), and Venigalla *et al.* (2020) describe data from bicycle sharing systems.

87 For example, Strava Metro (https://metro.strava.com/), a social network devoted to active transportation.

88 Leading examples are Google Maps, OpenStreetMap, Citymapper, and Apple Maps.

89 https://highways.dot.gov/research/data-sets/safety-training-analysis-center/data

90 Athey and Imbens (2019) provide an overview for economists of machine learning methods.

91 For discussions see Gandomi and Haider (2015) and Calude and Longo (2017).

92 Section 3.4.5 discusses how travelers use information.

93 https://use.metropolis.org/case-studies/rio-operations-center

94 https://www.transitchicago.com/howto/trackerexplained/, https://www.transitchicago.com/coronavirus/dashboard/

95 https://www.walkscore.com/methodology.shtml; https://www.windermere.com/

References

Abrantes, Pedro A. L. and Mark R. Wardman (2011) "Meta-analysis of UK values of travel time: an update," *Transportation Research Part A: Policy and Practice* 45(1): 1–17.

Acheampong, Ransford A. and Elisabete A. Silva (2015) "Land use–transport interaction modeling: a review of the literature and future research directions," *The Journal of Transport and Land Use* 8(3): 1–28. doi:10.5198/jtlu.2015.806.

Ahlfeldt, Gabriel M., Stephen J. Redding, Daniel M. Sturm and Nikolaus Wolf (2015) "The economics of density: evidence from the Berlin Wall," *Econometrica* 83(6): 2127–2189.

Alonso, William (1964) *Location and Land Use: Toward a General Theory of Land Rent*, Cambridge: Harvard University Press. doi:10.4159/harvard.9780674730854

Álvarez, Óscar, Pedro Cantos and Leandro Garcia (2007) "The value of time and transport policies in a parallel road network," *Transport Policy* 14(5): 366–376.

Anas, Alex (2020) "The cost of congestion and the benefits of congestion pricing: a general equilibrium analysis," *Transportation Research Part B: Methodological* 136: 110–137.

Anas, Alex and Tomoru Hiramatsu (2013) "The economics of cordon tolling: general equilibrium and welfare analysis," *Economics of Transportation* 2(1): 18–37.

Anas, Alex and Yu Liu (2007) "A regional economy, land use and transportation model (RELUTRAN©): formulation, algorithm design, and testing," *Journal of Regional Science* 47: 415–455.

Anderson, Michael L. (2014) "Subways, strikes, and slowdowns: the impacts of public transit on traffic congestion," *The American Economic Review* 104(9): 2763–2796.

Anderson, Simon P., André de Palma and Jacques F. Thisse (1988) "A representative consumer theory of the logit model," *International Economic Review* 29: 461–66.

Ashraf, Sruthi, Arezoo Samimi Abianeh and Mark Burris (2021) "Predicting the use of managed lanes using machine learning," *Journal of Big Data Analytics in Transportation* 3(3): 213–227.

Athey, Susan and Guido W. Imbens (2019) "Machine learning methods that economists should know about," *Annual Review of Economics* 11: 685–725.

Auld, Joshua and Abolfazl Mohammadian (2012) "Activity planning processes in the Agent-Based Dynamic Activity Scheduling (ADAPTS) model," *Transportation Research Part A: Policy and Practice* 46(8): 1386–1403.

Auld, Joshua, Vadim Sokolov and Thomas S. Stephens (2017) "Analysis of the effects of connected-automated vehicle technologies on travel demand," *Transportation Research Record: Journal of the Transportation Research Board* 2615: 1–8.

Barrero, Jose Maria, Nicholas Bloom and Steven J. Davis (2021) "Why working from home will stick," Working paper 28731, National Bureau of Economic Research (April).

Bastian, Anne, Maria Börjesson and Jonas Eliasson (2016) "Explaining 'peak car' with economic variables," *Transportation Research Part A: Policy and Practice* 88: 236–250.

Bastian, Anne, Maria Börjesson and Jonas Eliasson (2017) "Response to Wadud and Baierl: explaining 'peak car' with economic variables: an observation," *Transportation Research Part A: Policy and Practice* 95: 386–389.

Bates, John, John Polak, Peter Jones and Andrew Cook (2001) "The valuation of reliability for personal travel," *Transportation Research Part E: Logistics and Transportation Review* 37(2–3): 191–229.

Batley, Richard (2015) "The Hensher equation: derivation, interpretation and implications for practical implementation," *Transportation* 42: 257–275.

Becker, Gary S. (1965) "A theory of the allocation of time," *Economic Journal* 75(299): 493–517.

Beckmann, Martin J., C. Bartlett McGuire and Christopher B. Winsten (1956) *Studies in the Economics of Transportation*, New Haven, CT: Yale University Press.

Beggs, S., S. Cardell and J. Hausman (1981) "Assessing the potential demand for electric cars," *Journal of Econometrics* 6: 1–19.

Ben-Akiva, Moshe (1974) "Structure of passenger travel demand models," *Transportation Research Record: Journal of the Transportation Research Board* 526: 26–42.

Ben-Akiva, Moshe and Steven R. Lerman (1979) "Disaggregate travel and mobility-choice models and measures of accessibility," in David A. Hensher and Peter R. Stopher (eds.) *Behavioural Travel Modelling*, London: Croom Helm, pp. 654–679.

Benenson, Itzhak, Eran Ben-Elia, Yodan Rofe and Amit Rosental (2017) "Estimation of urban transport accessibility at the spatial resolution of an individual traveler," in Vonu Piyushimita, Thakuriah Nebiyou and Moira Zellner (eds.) *Seeing Cities Through Big Data*, Springer, New York, pp. 331–348.

Bento, Antonio M., Lawrence H. Goulder, Mark R. Jacobsen and Roger H. von Haefen (2009) "Distributional and efficiency impacts of increased US gasoline taxes," *American Economic Review* 99(3): 667–699.

Bento, Antonio M., Kevin Roth and Andrew Waxman (2024) "Avoiding traffic congestion externalities? The value of urgency," *Journal of Political Economy Microeconomics,* forthcoming. Prepublication version: Working paper 26956, National Bureau of Economic Research (Feb.). https://www.nber.org/papers/w26956

Berger, James O. and Luis R. Pericchi (2001) "Objective Bayesian methods for model selection: introduction and comparison (with discussion)," in P. Lahiri (ed.) *Model Selection*, Institute of Mathematical Statistics Lecture Notes – Monograph Series, Vol. 38, Bethesda, MD: Institute of Mathematical Statistics, pp. 135–207.

Berry, Steven T. (1994) "Estimating discrete-choice models of product differentiation," *RAND Journal of Economics* 25(2): 242–262.

Berry, Steven T., James Levinsohn and Ariel Pakes (1995) "Automobile prices in market equilibrium," *Econometrica* 63(4): 841–890.

Berry, Steven T., James Levinsohn and Ariel Pakes (2004) "Differentiated product demand systems from a combination of micro and macro data: the new car market," *Journal of Political Economy* 112(1): 68–105.

Bhat, Chandra (1995) "A heteroscedastic extreme value model of intercity travel mode choice," *Transportation Research Part B: Methodological* 29: 471–483.

Bhat, Chandra R. and Jessica Guo (2004) "A mixed spatially correlated logit model: formulation and application to residential choice modeling," *Transportation Research Part B: Methodological* 38(2): 147–168.

Binsuwadan, Jawaher, Mark Wardman, Gerard de Jong, Richard Batley and Phill Wheat (2023) "The income elasticity of the value of travel time savings: a meta-analysis," *Transport Policy* 136: 126–136.

Börjesson, Maria (2008) "Joint RP-SP data in a mixed logit analysis of trip timing decisions," *Transportation Research Part E: Logistics and Transportation Review* 44(6): 1025–1038.

Börjesson, Maria, Elasabetta Cherchi and Michel Bierlaire (2013) "Within-individual variation in preferences: equity effects of congestion charges," *Transportation Research Record: Journal of the Transportation Research Board* 2382: 92–101.

Börjesson, Maria, Jonas Eliasson and Joel P. Franklin (2012) "Valuations of travel time variability in scheduling versus mean-variance models," *Transportation Research Part B: Methodological* 46(7): 855–873.

Brent, Daniel A. and Austin Gross (2017) "Dynamic road pricing and the value of time and reliability," *Journal of Regional Science* 58(2): 330–349.

Bresnahan, Timothy F., Scott Stern and Manuel Trajtenberg (1997) "Market segmentation and the sources of rents from innovation: personal computers in the late 1980s," *RAND Journal of Economics* 28: S17–S44.

Brice, Stéphane (1989) "Derivation of nested transport models within a mathematical programming framework," *Transportation Research Part B: Methodological* 23(1): 19–28.

Bröcker, Johannes and Jean Mercenier (2011) "General equilibrium models for transportation economics," in André de Palma *et al.* (eds.) *A Handbook of Transport Economics*, Cheltenham: Edward Elgar, pp. 21–45.

Brownstone, David, David S. Bunch and Kenneth Train (2000) "Joint mixed logit models of stated and revealed preferences for alternative-fuel vehicles," *Transportation Research Part B: Methodological* 34(5): 315–338.

Brownstone, David and Xuehao Chu (1997) "Multiply-imputed sampling weights for consistent inference with panel attrition," in Thomas F. Golob, Ryuichi Kitamura and Lyn Long (eds.) *Panels for Transportation Planning: Methods and Applications*, Amsterdam: Kluwer Academic Publishers, pp. 259–273.

Brownstone, David, Arindam Ghosh, Thomas F. Golob, Camilla Kazimi and Dirk Van Amelsfort (2003) "Drivers' willingness-to-pay to reduce travel time: evidence from the San Diego I-15 congestion pricing project," *Transportation Research Part A: Policy and Practice* 37(4): 373–387.

Brownstone, David and Kenneth A. Small (1989) "Efficient estimation of nested logit models," *Journal of Business and Economic Statistics* 7(1): 67–74.

Brownstone, David and Kenneth A. Small (2005) "Valuing time and reliability: assessing the evidence from road pricing demonstrations," *Transportation Research Part A: Policy and Practice* 39(4): 279–293.

Brownstone, David and Kenneth Train (1999) "Forecasting new product penetration with flexible substitution patterns," *Journal of Econometrics* 89: 109–129.

Buchholz, Nicholas, Laura Doval, Jakup Kastl, Filip Matejka and Tobias Salz (2022) "The value of time: evidence from auctioned cab rides," Working paper, Princeton Univ. (June). https://nbuchholz.scholar.princeton.edu/document/16

Calude, Cristian S. and Giuseppe Longo (2017) "The deluge of spurious correlations in big data," *Foundations of Science* 22: 595–612.

Caudill, Steven B. (1988) "An advantage of the linear probability model over probit or logit," *Oxford Bulletin of Economics and Statistics* 50(4): 425–427.

Cervero, Robert and Kang-Li Wu (1996) "Subcentering and commuting: evidence from the San Francisco Bay Area, 1980–1990," Working paper, Department of City and Regional Planning, University of California, Berkeley, Berkeley, CA.

Chattopadhyay, Sudip (2001) "Welfare measurement in the discrete-choice random utility model under general preference structure," unpublished manuscript, Department of Economics, San Francisco State University, San Francisco, CA.

Cherchi, Elisabetta, Cinzia Cirillo and Juan de Dios Ortúzar (2017) "Modelling correlation patterns in mode choice models estimated on multiday travel data," *Transportation Research Part A: Policy and Practice* 96: 146–153.

Cherchi, Elisabetta, Cinzia Cirillo and John W. Polak (2009) "Assessment of user benefits in presence of random taste heterogeneity: comparison of parametric and nonparametric models," *Transportation Research Record: Journal of the Transportation Research Board* 2132: 78–86.

Choi, Ki-Hong and Choon-Geol Moon (1997) "Generalized extreme value model and additively separable generator function," *Journal of Econometrics* 76(1–2): 129–140.

Choo, Sangho, Patricia L. Mokhtarian and Ilan Salomon (2005) "Does telecommuting reduce vehicle-miles traveled? An aggregate time series analysis for the U.S.," *Transportation* 32: 37–64.

Chow, Joseph Y. J., Choon Heon Yang and Amelia C. Regan (2010) "State-of-the art of freight forecast modeling: lessons learned and the road ahead," *Transportation* 37: 1011–1030.

Chu, Chausie (1981) "Structural issues and sources of bias in residential location and travel mode choice models," unpublished dissertation, Northwestern University, Evanston, IL.

Cirillo, Cinzia and Renting Xu (2011) "Dynamic discrete choice models for transportation," *Transport Reviews* 31(4): 473–494.

Clewlow, Regina R. and Gouri S. Mishra (2017) "Disruptive transportation: the adoption, utilization, and impacts of ride-hailing in the United States," Institute of Transportation Studies, University of California, Davis, Research Report UCD-ITS-RR-17-07. https://escholarship.org/uc/item/82w2z91j (accessed 20 Feb 2025).

Commissariat Général du Plan (2001) *Transports: Choix des Investissements et Coût des Nuisances* [*Transportation: Choice of Investments and the Cost of Nuisances*], Paris: Commissariat Général du Plan.

Cook, Joseph, Peter Kimuyu, Annalise G. Blum and Josephine Gatua (2016) "A simple stated preference tool for estimating the value of travel time in rural Africa," *Journal of Benefit Cost Analysis* 7(2): 221–247.

Currie, Graham (2005) "The demand performance of bus rapid transit," *Journal of Public Transportation* 8(1): 41–55.

Currie, Graham (2018) "Lies, damned lies, AVs, shared mobility, and urban transit futures," *Journal of Public Transportation* 21(1): 19–30.

Daganzo, Carlos and Michael Kusnic (1993) "Two properties of the nested logit model," *Transportation Science* 27(4): 395–400.

Daly, Andrew, Stephane Hess and Gerard de Jong (2012) "Calculating errors for measures derived from choice modelling estimates," *Transportation Research Part B: Methodological* 46(2): 333–341.

Daly, Andrew, Flavia Tsang and Charlene Rohr (2014) "The value of small time savings for non-business travel," *Journal of Transport Economics and Policy* 48(2): 205–218.

Dargay, Joyce, Dermot Gately and Martin Sommer (2007) "Vehicle ownership and income growth, worldwide: 1960–2030," *Energy Journal* 28(4): 143–170.

Daziano, Ricardo A., Mauricio Sarrias and Benjamin Leard (2017) "Are consumers willing to pay to let cars drive for them? Analyzing response to autonomous vehicle," *Transportation Research Part C: Emerging Technologies* 78: 150–164.

De Borger, Bruno and Mogens Fosgerau (2008) "The trade-off between money and travel time: a test of the theory of reference-dependent preferences," *Journal of Urban Economics* 64(1): 101–115.

De Borger, Bruno and Kurt Van Dender (2003) "Transport tax reform, commuting and endogenous values of times," *Journal of Urban Economics* 53(3): 510–30.

de Jong, Gerard (2007) "Value of freight travel-time saving," in David A. Hensher and Kenneth J. Button (eds.) *Handbook of Transport Modelling*, Vol. 1, Leeds: Emerald Group Publishing, pp. 649–663.

de Jong, Gerard and Marco Kouwenhoven (2019) "Time use and values of time and reliability in the Netherlands," Discussion paper 2019/11, International Transport Forum, OECD Publishing, Paris. https://www.oecd-ilibrary.org/transport/time-use-and-values-of-time-and-reliability-in-the-netherlands_c5f7c67f-en de Jong, Gerard, Marco Kouwenhoven, John Bates, Paul Koster, Erik T. Verhoef, Lori Tavasszy and Pim Warffemius (2014) "New SP-values of time and reliability for freight transport in the Netherlands," *Transportation Research Part E: Logistics and Transportation Review* 64: 71–87.

de Palma, André and Robin Lindsey (2001) "Optimal timetables for public transportation," *Transportation Research Part B: Methodological* 35(8): 789–813.

Deaton, Angus (1985) "The demand for personal travel in developing countries: an empirical analysis," *Transportation Research Record: Journal of the Transportation Research Board* 1037: 59–66.

Deb, Kaushik and Massimo Filippini (2013) "Public bus transport demand elasticities in India," *Journal of Transport Economics and Policy* 47(3): 419–436.

Delbosc, Alexa and Graham Currie (2013) "Causes of youth licensing decline: a synthesis of evidence," *Transport Reviews* 33(3): 271–290.

DeSerpa, Allan C. (1971) "A theory of the economics of time," *Economic Journal* 81(324): 828–846.

Dubin, Jeffrey A. and Daniel L. McFadden (1984) "An econometric analysis of residential electric appliance holdings and consumption," *Econometrica* 52(2): 345–362.

Duranton, Gilles, J. Vernon Henderson and William C. Strange (eds.) (2015) *Handbook of Regional & Urban Economics*, Vol. 5, Amsterdam: Elsevier.

Fagnant, Daniel J. and Kara M. Kockelman (2015) "Preparing a nation for autonomous vehicles: opportunities, barriers and policy recommendations," *Transportation Research Part A: Policy and Practice* 77: 167–181.

Feo-Valero, Maria, Leandro García-Menéndez and Rodrigo Garrido-Hidalgo (2011) "Valuing Freight transport time using transport demand modelling: a bibliographical review," *Transport Reviews* 31(5): 625–651.

Fifer, Simon, John Rose and Stephen Greaves (2014) "Hypothetical bias in stated choice experiments: is it a problem? And if so, how do we deal with it?" *Transportation Research Part A: Policy and Practice* 61: 164–177.

Flyvbjerg, Bent, Matte K. Skamris Holm and Søren L. Buhl (2005) "How (in)accurate are demand forecasts in public works projects? The case of transportation," *Journal of the American Planning Association* 71(2): 131–146.

Forsyth, Peter J. (1980) "The value of time in an economy with taxation," *Journal of Transportation Economics and Policy* 14(3): 337–362.

Fosgerau, Mogens (2006) "Investigating the distribution of the value of travel time savings," *Transportation Research Part B: Methodological* 40(8): 688–707.

Fosgerau, Mogens (2009) "The marginal social cost of headway for a scheduled service," *Transportation Research Part B: Methodological* 43(8–9): 813–820.

Fosgerau, Mogens (2019) "Automation and the value of time in passenger transport," Discussion paper 2019/10, International Transport Forum, Roundtable 176, OECD. https://www.itf-oecd.org/automation-and-value-time-passenger-transport (accessed 21 January 2020).

Fosgerau, Mogens and Michel Bierlaire (2007) "A practical test for the choice of mixing distribution in discrete choice models," *Transportation Research Part B: Methodological* 41(7): 784–794.

Fosgerau, Mogens and Michel Bierlaire (2009) "Discrete choice models with multiplicative error terms," *Transportation Research Part B: Methodological* 43(5): 494–505.

Fosgerau, Mogens and Gege Jiang (2019) "Travel time variability and rational inattention," *Transportation Research Part B: Methodological*: 120: 1–14.

Fosgerau, Mogens and Anders Karlstrom (2010) "The value of reliability," *Transportation Research Part B: Methodological* 44(1): 38–49.

Fosgerau, Mogens and Leonid Engelson (2011) "The value of travel time variance," *Transportation Research Part B: Methodological* 45(1): 1–8.

Fox, James, Andrew Daly, Stephane Hess and Eric Miller (2014) "Temporal transferability of models of mode-destination choice for the Greater Toronto and Hamilton Area," *Journal of Transport and Land Use* 7(2): 41–62.

Fujita, Masahisa (1989) *Urban Economic Theory: Land Use and City Size*. Cambridge, UK: Cambridge University Press.

Fujita, Masahisa, Jacques-François Thisse and Yves Zenou (1997) "On the endogenous formation of secondary employment centers in a city," *Journal of Urban Economics* 41(3): 337–357.

Gadda, Shashank, Kara M. Kockelman and Paul Damien (2009) "Continuous departure time models: a Bayesian approach," *Transportation Research Record: Journal of the Transportation Research Board* 2132: 13–24.

Gal-Tzur, Ayelet, Susan M. Grant-Muller, Tsvi Kuflik, Einat Minkov, Silvio Nocera and Itay Shoor (2014) "The potential of social media in delivering transport policy goals," *Transport Policy* 32: 115–123.

Gandomi, Amir and Murtaza Haider (2015) "Beyond the hype: big data concepts, methods, and analytics," *International Journal of Information Management* 35(2): 137–144.

Gaudry, Marc J. I. and Marcel G. Dagenais (1979) "The dogit model," *Transportation Research Part B: Methodological* 13(2): 105–111.

Glaeser, Edward L., Scott Duke Kominers, Michael Luca and Nikhil Naik (2018) "Big Data and big cities: the promises and limitations of improved measures of urban life," *Economic Inquiry* 56(1): 114–137.

Goenaga, Boris and Victor Cantillo (2018) "Willingness to pay for freight travel time savings: contrasting random utility versus random valuation," *Transportation* 47: 705–736. doi:10.1007/s11116-018-9912-5

Golob, Thomas F. (2003) "Structural equation modeling for travel behavior research," *Transportation Research Part B: Methodological* 37(1): 1–25.

Gonzalez-Navarro, Marco, Jonathan D. Hall, Harrison Wheeler and Rik Williams (2021) "Uber versus trains? Worldwide evidence from transit expansions," Working paper no. 21-11, NET Institute (September). https://papers.ssrn.com/sol3/papers.cfm?abstract_id=3959760

Goodwin, Phil B. and Kurt Van Dender (2013) "'Peak Car' — Themes and Issues," *Transport Reviews* 33(3): 243–254.

Goolsbee, Austan and Amil Petrin (2004) "The consumer gains from direct broadcast satellites and the competition with cable TV," *Econometrica* 72(2): 351–381.

Greene, William H. (2018) "Panel data models for discrete choice," in Badi H. Baltagi (ed.) *The Oxford Handbook of Panel Data*, Oxford: Oxford University Press.

Greene, William H. and David A. Hensher (2003) "A latent class model for discrete choice analysis: contrasts with mixed logit," *Transportation Research Part B: Methodological* 37(8): 681–698.

Griffin, Greg P., Megan Mulhall, Christ Simek and William W. Riggs (2020) "Mitigating bias in Big Data for transportation," *Journal of Big Data Analytics in Transportation.* doi: 10.1007/s42421-020-00013-0.

Haboucha, Chana J., Robert Ishaq and Yoram Shiftan (2017) "User preferences regarding autonomous vehicles," *Transportation Research Part C: Emerging Technologies* 78: 37–49.

Hagenauer, Julian and Marco Helbich (2017) "A comparative study of machine learning classifiers for modeling travel mode choice," *Expert Systems With Applications* 78: 273–282.

Hall, Jonathan D. (forthcoming) "Inframarginal travelers and transportation policy," *International Economic Review.* Prepublication version: https://papers.ssrn.com/sol3/papers.cfm?abstract_id=3424097

Hall, Jonathan D., Craig Palsson and Joseph Price (2018) "Is Uber a substitute or complement for public transit?," *Journal of Urban Economics* 108: 36–50.

Halvorsen, Anne, Haris N. Koutsopoulos, Stephen Lau, Tom Au and Jinhua Zhao (2016) "Reducing subway crowding analysis of an off-peak discount experiment in Hong Kong," *Transportation Research Record: Journal of the Transportation Research Board* 2544: 38–46. DOI: 10.3141/2544–05

Hamermesh, Daniel S. and Jungmin Lee (2007) "Stressed out on four continents: time crunch or yuppie kvetch?," *Review of Economics and Statistics* 89(2): 374–383.

Harb, Mustapha, Yu Xiao, Giovanni Circella, Patricia L. Mokhtarian and Joan L. Walker (2018) "Projecting travelers into a world of self-driving vehicles: estimating travel behavior implications via a naturalistic experiment," *Transportation* 45: 1671-1685, doi 10.1007/s11116-018-9937-9

Hausman, Jerry A. (1978) "Specification tests in econometrics," *Econometrica* 46(6): 1251–1271.

Hausman, Jerry A. and Paul A. Ruud (1987) "Specifying and testing econometric models for rank-ordered data," *Journal of Econometrics* 34(1–2). 83–104.

Hausman, Jerry A. and David A. Wise (1978) "A conditional probit model for qualitative choice: discrete decisions recognizing interdependence and heterogeneous preferences," *Econometrica* 46(2): 403–426.

Heckman, James J. (1979) "Sample selection bias as a specification error," *Econometrica* 47(1): 153–62.

Hensher, David A. (1977) *Value of Business Travel Time*, Oxford: Pergamon Press.

Hensher, David A. (1986) "Sequential and full information maximum likelihood estimation of a nested logit model," *Review of Economics and Statistics* 68(4): 657–667.

Hensher, David A. (2011) "Valuation of travel time savings," in André de Palma *et al.* (eds.) *A Handbook of Transport Economics*, Cheltenham: Edward Elgar, pp. 135–159.

Hensher, David A. and Vicki Le Plastrier (1985) "Towards a dynamic discrete-choice model of household automobile fleet size and composition," *Transportation Research Part B: Methodological* 19(6): 481–495.

Hensher, David A., Jordan Louviere and Joffre Swait (1999) "Combining sources of preference data," *Journal of Econometrics* 89(1–2): 197–221.

Hensher, David A., John M. Rose and William H. Greene (2015) *Applied Choice Analysis*, Cambridge, UK: Cambridge University Press.

Hess, Stephane, John W. Polak, Andrew Daly and Geoffrey Hyman (2007) "Flexible substitution patterns in models of mode and time of day choice: new evidence from the UK and the Netherlands," *Transportation* 34: 213–238.

Hörcher, Daniel, Daniel J. Graham and Richard J. Anderson (2017) "Crowding cost estimation with large scale smart card and vehicle location data," *Transportation Research Part B: Methodological* 95: 105–125.

Horowitz, Joel L. (1980) "The accuracy of the multinomial logit model as an approximation to the multinomial probit model of travel demand," *Transportation Research Part B: Methodological* 14(4): 331–341.

Imbens, Guido W. and Tony Lancaster (1994) "Combining micro and macro data in microeconometric models," *Review of Economics Studies* 61(4): 655–680.

ITF (2015a) "Big data and transport: understanding and assessing options," International Transport Forum Corporate Partnership Board Report, OECD, Paris.

ITF (2015b) "Urban mobility system upgrade: how shared self-driving cars could change city traffic," International Transport Forum Corporate Partnership Board Report, OECD, Paris.

ITF (2017) "Shared Mobility Simulations for Helsinki," International Transport Forum Case-Specific Policy Analysis Report, OECD, Paris.

ITF (2019) "Smart use of roads," Research Report. https://www.itf-oecd.org/smart-use-roads

ITF (2021a) "The Innovative Mobility Landscape: The Case of Mobility as a Service," International Transport Forum, OECD, Paris.

ITF (2021b) "Big data for travel demand modelling: summary and conclusions," ITF Roundtable Reports, No. 186, OECD, Paris. https://www.itf-oecd.org/sites/default/files/docs/big-data-travel-demand-modelling.pdf

Janzen, Maxim, Maarten Vanhoof, Zbigniew Smoreda and Kay W. Axhausen (2018) "Closer to the total? Long-distance travel of French mobile phone users," *Travel Behaviour and Society* 11: 31–42.

Japan Research Institute Study Group on Road Investment Evaluation (2000) *Guidelines for the Evaluation of Road Investment Projects*, Tokyo, Japan: Japan Research Institute.

Jara-Díaz, Sergio R. (2003) "On the goods-activities technical relations in the time allocation theory," *Transportation* 30: 245–260.

Jara-Díaz, Sergio R., Marcela A. Munizaga, Paulina Greeven, Reinaldo Guerra and Kay Axhausen (2008) "Estimating the value of leisure from a time allocation model," *Transportation Research Part B: Methodological*: 42(10): 946–957.

Johansson, Maria Vredin, Tobias Heldt and Per Johansson (2006) "The effects of attitudes and personality traits on mode choice," *Transportation Research Part A: Policy and Practice* 40(6): 507–525.

Kamargianni, Maria, Moshe Ben-Akiva and Amalia Polydoropoulou (2011) "Incorporating social interaction into hybrid choice models," *Transportation* 41: 1263–1285.

Kato, Hironori (2013) "On the value of business travel time savings: derivation of Hensher's formula," *Transportation Research Record: Journal of the Transportation Research Board* 2343: 34–42.

Kim, Jinwon and Jucheol Moon (2022) *Congestion Costs and Scheduling Preferences of Car Commuters in California: Estimates Using Big Data*, San Jose, CA: Mineta Transportation Institute Publications. doi:10.31979/mti.2022.2031

Knittel, Christopher R. and Elizabeth Murphy (2019) "Generational trends in vehicle ownership and use: are Millennials any different?" Working paper 25674, National Bureau of Economic Research (March).

Kockelman, Kara M. (2001) "A model for time- and budget-constrained activity demand analysis," *Transportation Research Part B: Methodological* 35(3): 255–269.

Koppelman, Frank S. and Geoffrey Rose (1985) "Geographic transfer of travel choice models: evaluation and procedures," in Bruce G. Hutchinson, Peter Nijkamp and Michael Batty (eds.) *Optimization and Discrete Choice in Urban Systems: Proceedings of the International Symposium on New Directions in Urban Systems Modelling*, Berlin: Springer-Verlag, pp. 272–309.

Koppelman, Frank S. and Chieh-Hua Wen (2000) "The paired combinatorial logit model: properties, estimation and application," *Transportation Research Part B: Methodological* 34(2): 75–89.

Koster, Hans R.A., Takatoshi Tabuchi, and Jacques-François Thisse (2022) "To be connected or not to be connected? The role of long-haul economies," *Journal of Economics Geography* 22(4), doi 10.1093/jeg/lbab042

Koster, Paul R. and Hans R. A. Koster (2015) "Commuters' preferences for fast and reliable travel: a semi-parametric estimation approach," *Transportation Research Part B: Methodological* 81(1): 289–301.

Kotkin, Joel (2017) "The high cost of a home is turning American millennials into the new serfs," *The Daily Beast* (February 4). https://www.thedailybeast.com/the-high-cost-of-a-home-is-turning-american-millennials-into-the-new-serfs

Kroes, Eric, Marco Kouwenhoven, Laurence Debrincat and Nicolas Pauget (2014) "Value of crowding on public transport in Île-de-France, France," *Transportation Research Record: Journal of the Transportation Research Board* 2417: 37–45.

Krugman, Paul, Richard N. Cooper and T. N. Srinivasan (1995) "Growing world trade: causes and consequences," *Brookings Papers on Economic Activity* 1995(1): 327–377.

Kuhnimhof, Tobias, Jimmy Armoogum, Ralph Buehler, Joyce Dargay, Jon Martin Denstadli and Toshiyuki Yamamoto (2012) "Men shape a downward trend in car use among young adults: evidence from six industrialized countries," *Transport Reviews* 32(6): 761–779.

Lam, Terence C. and Kenneth A. Small (2001) "The value of time and reliability: measurement from a value pricing experiment," *Transportation Research Part E: Logistics and Transportation Review* 37(2–3): 231–251.

Leard, Benjamin (2022) "Estimating consumer substitution between new and used passenger vehicles," *Journal of the Association of Environmental and Resource Economists* 9(1): 27–49.

Leard, Benjamin, Joshua Linn and Clayton Munnings (2019) "Explaining the evolution of passenger vehicle miles traveled in the United States," *Energy Journal* 40(1): 25–54. DOI 10.5547/01956574.40.1.blea.

Lee, Sungwon, Gyeng Chul Kim, Seung Kook Wu and Jieun Oh (2019) "Influence of ICT on public transport use and behaviour in Seoul," Discussion paper 2019/02, Roundtable 176, International Transport Forum, OECD. https://www.itf-oecd.org/influence-ict-public-transport-use-and-behaviour-seoul (accessed 23 January 2020).

Lemp, Jason D., Kara M. Kockelman and Paul Damien (2010) "The continuous cross-nested logit model: formulation and application for departure time choice," *Transportation Research Part B: Methodological* 44(5): 646–661.

Li, Zheng and David A. Hensher (2011) "Crowding in public transport: a review of willingness to pay evidence and its relevance in project appraisal," *Transport Policy* 18(6): 880–887.

Li, Zheng, David A. Hensher and John M. Rose (2010) "Willingness to pay for travel time reliability in passenger transport: a review and some new empirical evidence," *Transportation Research Part E: Logistics and Transportation Review* 46(3): 384–403.

Lindberg, Per Olov, E. Anders Eriksson and Lars-Göran Mattsson (1995) "Invariance of achieved utility in random utility models," *Environment and Planning A* 27: 121–142.

Linder, Steffan (1970) *The Harried Leisure Class*, New York: Columbia University Press.

Litman, Todd (2023a) *Transit Price Elasticities and Cross-Elasticities*. Victoria, BC: Victoria Transport Policy Institute. https://www.vtpi.org/tranelas.pdf (accessed 26 July 2023).

Litman, Todd (2023b) "Travel time and speed," *Transportation Cost and Benefit Analysis*, 2nd edition, Section 5.2, Victoria, BC: Victoria Transport Policy Institute. http://www.vtpi.org/tca/tca0502.pdf (accessed 26 July 2023).

Longqi Yang, David Holtz, Sonia Jaffe *et al.* (2021) "The effects of remote work on collaboration among information workers," *Nature Human Behaviour* 6: 43–54. doi:10.1038/s41562-021-01196-4

Louviere, Jordan J., David A. Hensher and Joffre D. Swait (2000) *Stated Choice Methods: Analysis and Applications*, Cambridge: Cambridge University Press.

Lovrić, Milan, Sebastian Raveau, Muhammed Adnan, Francisco C. Pereira, Kakali Basak, Harish Loganathan and Moshe Ben-Akiva (2016) "Evaluating off-peak pricing strategies in public transportation with an activity-based approach", *Transportation Research Record: Journal of the Transportation Research Board* 2544: 10–19. DOI: 10.3141/2544-02.

Mangrum, Daniel and Alejandro Molnar (2020) "The marginal congestion of a taxi in New York City," December 9. https://www.danielmangrum.com/docs/Boro_current.pdf

Mannering, Fred L. and David A. Hensher (1987) "Discrete/continuous econometric models and their application to transport analysis," *Transport Reviews* 7(3): 227–244.

Mannering, Fred L. and Clifford Winston (1985) "A dynamic empirical analysis of household vehicle ownership and utilization," *Rand Journal of Economics* 16(2): 215–236.

Manski, Charles F. and Steven R. Lerman (1977) "The estimation of choice probabilities from choice based samples," *Econometrica* 45(8): 1977–88.

Matějka, Filip and Alisdair McKay (2015) "Rational inattention to discrete choices: a new foundation for the multinomial logit model," *American Economic Review* 105(1): 272–298.

Mattsson, Lars-Göran and Jörgen W. Weibull (2000) "Probabilistic choice as a result of mistakes," Working paper No. 544, Research Institute of Industrial Economics, Royal Institute of Technology.

McFadden, Daniel (1974) "Conditional logit analysis of qualitative choice behavior," in Paul Zarembka (ed.) *Frontiers in Econometrics*, New York: Academic Press, pp. 105–142.

McFadden, Daniel (1999) "Rationality for economists?" *Journal of Risk and Uncertainty* 19(1–3): 73–105.

McFadden, Daniel (2014) "The new science of pleasure: consumer choice behavior and the measurement of well-being," in Stephane Hess and Andrew Daly (eds.) *Handbook of Choice Modelling*, Cheltenham: Edward Elgar, pp. 7–48.

McFadden, Daniel, Antti P. Talvitie and Associates (1977) "Demand model estimation and validation: urban travel demand forecasting project phase I," Report UCB-ITS-SR-77-9, Institute of Transportation Studies, University of California, Berkeley, CA.

McFadden, Daniel and Kenneth Train (2000) "Mixed MNL models for discrete response," *Journal of Applied Econometrics* 15(5): 447–470.

McMillen, Daniel P. (2001) "Nonparametric employment subcenter identification," *Journal of Urban Economics* 50: 448–473. Doi: 10.1006/juec.2001.2228

McMillen, Daniel P. and Stefani C. Smith (2003) "The number of subcenters in large urban areas," *Journal of Urban Economics* 53: 321–338. Doi: 10.1016/S0094–1190(03)00026-3

Meyer, Bruce D., Wallace K. C. Mok and James X. Sullivan (2015) "Household surveys in crisis," *Journal of Economic Perspectives* 29(4): 199–226.

Millard-Ball, Adam (2019) "The autonomous vehicle parking problem," *Transport Policy* 75: 99–108.

Mills, Edwin S. (1967) "An aggregative model of resource allocation in a metropolitan area," *American Economic Review* 57(2): 197–210.

Milne, David S. and David Watling (2019) "Big data and understanding change in the context of planning transport systems," *Journal of Transport Geography* 76: 235–244.

Mohammadian, Abolfazl and Eric J. Miller (2003) "Dynamic modeling of household automobile transactions," *Transportation Research Record: Journal of the Transportation Research Board* 1831: 98–105.

Morikawa, Taka, Moshe Ben-Akiva and Daniel McFadden (2002) "Discrete choice models incorporating revealed preferences and psychometric data," *Advances in Econometrics* 16: 29–55.

MTC and ABAG (2017) *Plan Bay Area 2040*, San Francisco: Metropolitan Transportation Commission and Association of Bay Area Governments (July). https://mtc.ca.gov/planning/long-range-planning/plan-bay-area-2040 (accessed 24 Jan. 2024).

Mudge, Richard R., Alain Kornhauser and Matt Hardison (2018) "Market framework and outlook for automated vehicle systems," Report, Society of Actuaries (November). https://www.soa.org/resources/research-reports/2018/market-framework-automated-vehicle/ (accessed 30 June 2020).

Munger, David, Pierre L'Ecuyer, Fabian Bastin, Cinzia Cirillo and Bruno Tuffin (2012) "Estimation of the mixed logit likelihood function by randomized quasi-Monte Carlo", *Transportation Research Part B: Methodological* 46(2): 305–320.

Munizaga, Marcela A., Rodrigo Correia, Sergio R. Jara-Díaz and Juan de Dios Ortúzar (2006) "Valuing time with a joint mode choice–activity model," *International Journal of Transport Economics* 33(2): 193–210.

Muth, Richard F. (1969) *Cities and Housing: The Spatial Pattern of Urban Residential Land Use*, Chicago: University of Chicago Press.

MVA Consultancy *et al.* (1987) "The value of travel time savings," A Report of Research Undertaken for the Department of Transport, Prepared by the MVA Consultancy, Institute for Transport Studies, University of Leeds and Transport Studies Unit, University of Oxford, Newbury, Berkshire, UK.

National Academies of Sciences, Engineering, and Medicine (2014a) *Incorporating Reliability Performance Measures into Operations and Planning Modeling Tools*, Washington, DC: The National Academies Press. doi:10.17226/22388.

National Academies of Sciences, Engineering, and Medicine (2014b) *Value of Travel Time Reliability in Transportation Decision Making: Proof of Concept Maryland*. Washington, DC: The National Academies Press. doi:10.17226/22280.

Nelson, Trisalyn, Colin Ferster, Karen Laberee, Daniel Fuller and Meghan Winters (2020) "Crowdsourced data for bicycling research and practice," *Transport Reviews* 41(1): 97–114.

Nevo, Aviv (2000) "A practitioner's guide to estimation of random-coefficients logit models of demand," *Journal of Economics & Management Strategy* 9(4): 513–548.

Newman, Jeffrey P. and Caspar Chorus (2015) "Attitudes and habits in highly effective travel models," *Transportation* 42: 3–5.

Nielsen, Thomas Alexander Sick and Sonja Haustein (2018) "On sceptics and enthusiasts: what are the expectations towards self-driving cars?" *Transport Policy* 66: 49–55.

Noland, Robert B. and Kenneth A. Small (1995) "Travel-time uncertainty, departure time choice, and the cost of morning commutes," *Transportation Research Record: Journal of the Transportation Research Board* 1493: 150–158.

Oort, Conrad J. (1969) "The evaluation of travelling time," *Journal of Transport Economics and Policy* 3(3): 279–286.

ORNL (2012) "Consumer vehicle choice model documentation," Report EPA-420-B-12–052, Oak Ridge National Laboratory, Oak Ridge, TN.

Ostrovsky, Michael and Michael Schwarz (2018) "Carpooling and the economics of self-driving cars," Working paper 24349, National Bureau of Economic Research.

O'Sullivan, Arthur (2019) *Urban Economics*, 9th edition, London: McGraw Hill.

Pasidis, Ilias (2019) "Congestion by accident? A two-way relationship for highways in England," *Journal of Transport Geography* 76: 301–314.

Paz, Alexander and Srinivas Peeta (2009) "Behavior-consistent real-time traffic routing under information provision," *Transportation Research Part C: Emerging Technologies* 17(6): 642–661.

Peer, Stefanie and Maria Börjesson (2018) "Temporal framing of stated preference experiments: does it affect valuations?," *Transportation Research Part A: Policy and Practice* 117: 319–333.

Peer, Stefanie, Erik T. Verhoef, Jasper Knockaert, Paul Koster and Yin-Yen Tseng (2015) "Long-run vs. short-run perspectives on consumer scheduling: evidence from a revealed-preference experiment among peak-hour road commuters," *International Economic Review* 56(1): 303–323.

Peer, Stefanie, Jasper Knockaert, Paul Koster and Erik T. Verhoef (2014) "Over-reporting vs. overreacting: commuters' perceptions of travel times," *Transportation Research Part A: Policy and Practice* 69: 476–494.

Pelletier, Marie-Pier, Martin Trépanier and Catherine Morency (2011) "Smart card data use in public transit: a literature review," *Transportation Research Part C: Emerging Technologies* 19(4): 557–568.

Petrin, Amil and Kenneth Train (2004) "Omitted product attributes in differentiated product models," Working paper, University of California. http://elsa.berkeley.edu/~train/pt42504.pdf.

Pinjari, Abdul Rawoof and Chandra R. Bhat (2011) "Activity-based travel demand analysis," in André de Palma *et al.* (eds.) *A Handbook of Transport Economics*, Cheltenham: Edward Elgar, Chpt 10, pp. 213–248.

Popuri, Yasasvi, Kimon Proussaloglou, Cemal Ayvalik, Frank Koppelman and Aimee Lee (2011) "Importance of traveler attitudes in the choice of public transportation to work: findings from the Regional Transportation Authority Attitudinal Survey," *Transportation* 38: 643–661.

Psarros, Ioannis, Konstantinos Kepaptsoglou and Matthew G. Karlaftis (2011) "An empirical investigation of passenger wait time perceptions using hazard-based duration models," *Journal of Public Transportation* 14(3): 109–122.

Regional Plan Association (2017) *New Mobility: Autonomous Vehicles and the Region*, New York: Regional Plan Association. https://rpa.org/work/reports/new-mobility

Rødseth, Kenneth Løvold, Paal Brevik Wangsness and Stef Proost (2021) "Marginal external crowding costs in the era of COVID-19: assessment and policy implications," Presented to International Transportation Economics Association Annual Conference 2021.

Romanillos, Gustavo, Martin Zaltz Austwick, Dick Ettema and Joost De Kruijf (2016) "Big Data and cycling," *Transport Reviews* 36(1): 114–133.

Roorda, Matthew J., Juan A. Carrasco and Eric J. Miller (2009) "An integrated model of vehicle transactions, activity scheduling and mode choice," *Transportation Research Part B: Methodological* 43(2): 217–229.

SAE (2021) *Recommended Practice: Taxonomy and Definitions for Terms Related to Driving Automation Systems for On-Road Motor Vehicles*, SAE J3016, updated 30 April, SAE International. https://www.sae.org/blog/sae-j3016-update (accessed 31 October 2022).

Safirova, Elena *et al.* (2006) "Congestion pricing: long-term economic and land-use effects," Discussion paper 06-37, Resources for the Future. http://rff.org/rff/Documents/RFF-DP-06-37.pdf.

Schafer, Andreas (2000) "Regularities in travel demand: an international perspective," *Journal of Transportation and Statistics* 3(3): 1–31.

Schrank, David, Bill Eisele and Tim Lomax (2019) *2019 Urban Mobility Report*, College Station, TX: Texas A&M Transportation Institute. https://mobility.tamu.edu/umr/.

Selod, Harris and Souleymane Soumahoro (2020) "Big Data in transportation: an economics perspective," Working paper 9308, World Bank Policy Research. http://documents1.worldbank.org/curated/en/144551593524811620/pdf/Big-Data-in-Transportation-An-Economics-Perspective.pdf

Semykina, Anastasia and Jeffrey M. Wooldridge (2013) "Estimation of dynamic panel data models with sample selection," *Journal of Applied Econometrics*, 28(1): 47–61.

Severen, Christopher and Arthur A. van Benthem (2022) "Formative experiences and the price of gasoline," *American Economic Journal: Applied Economics* 14(2): 256–284.

Shaheen, Susan and Adam Cohen (2019) "Shared ride services in North America: definitions, impacts, and the future of pooling," *Transport Reviews* 39(4): 427–442. DOI: 10.1080/01441647.2018.1497728

Shams, Kollol, Hamidreza Asgari and Xia Jin (2017) "Valuation of travel time reliability in freight transportation: a review and meta-analysis of stated preference studies," *Transportation Research Part A* 102: 228–243.

Shen, Li and Peter R. Stopher (2014) "Review of GPS travel survey and GPS data-processing methods," *Transport Reviews* 34(3): 316–334.

Shiftan, Yoram and John Auhrbier (2002) "The analysis of travel and emission impacts of travel demand management strategies using activity-based models," *Transportation* 29: 145–168.

Shires, Jeremy D. and Gerard C. de Jong (2009) "An international meta-analysis of values of travel time savings," *Evaluation and Program Planning* 32(4): 315–325.

Small, Kenneth A. (1982) "The scheduling of consumer activities: work trips," *American Economic Review* 72(3): 467–479.

Small, Kenneth A. (1987) "A discrete choice model for ordered alternatives," *Econometrica* 55(2): 409–424.

Small, Kenneth A. (1994) "Approximate generalized extreme value models of discrete choice," *Journal of Econometrics* 62(2): 351–382.

Small, Kenneth A. (2012) "Valuation of travel time," *Economics of Transportation* 1(1–2): 2–14.

Small, Kenneth A. and Erik T. Verhoef (2007) *The Economics of Urban Transportation*, London: Routledge.

Small, Kenneth A. and Harvey S. Rosen (1981) "Applied welfare economics with discrete choice models," *Econometrica* 49(1): 105–130.

Small, Kenneth A., Clifford Winston and Jia Yan (2005) "Uncovering the distribution of motorists' preferences for travel time and reliability," *Econometrica* 73(4): 1367–82.

Steimetz, Seiji S. C. (2008) "Defensive driving and the external costs of accidents and travel delays," *Transportation Research Part B: Methodological* 42(9): 703–724.

Swait, Joffre and Jordan Louviere (1993) "The role of the scale parameter in the estimation and comparison of multinomial logit models," *Journal of Marketing Research* 30(3): 305–314.

The Economist (2018) "Missing the bus," June 23, pp. 52–53.

Thorhauge, Mikkel, Elisabetta Cherchi and Jeppe Rich (2016) "How flexible is flexible? Accounting for the effect of rescheduling possibilities in choice of departure time for work trips," *Transportation Research Part A: Policy and Practice* 86: 177–193.

Tikoudis, Ioannis, Erik T. Verhoef and J. van Ommeren (2015) "On revenue recycling and the welfare effects of second-best congestion pricing in a monocentric city," *Journal of Urban Economics* 89: 32–47.

Train, Kenneth (1986) *Qualitative Choice Analysis: Theory, Econometrics, and an Application to Automobile Demand*, Cambridge, MA: MIT Press.

Train, Kenneth and Clifford Winston (2007) "Vehicle choice behavior and the declining market share of U.S. automakers," *International Economic Review* 48(4): 1467–1494.

Tseng, Yin-Yen and Erik T. Verhoef (2008) "Value of time by time of day: a stated-preference study," *Transportation Research Part B: Methodological* 42(7–8): 607–618.

Tseng, Yin-Yen, Erik T. Verhoef, Gerard de Jong, Marco Kouwenhoven and Toon van der Hoorn (2009) "A pilot study into the perception of unreliability of travel times using in-depth interviews," *Journal of Choice Modeling* 2(1): 8–28.

Van den Berg, Vincent A. C. and Erik T. Verhoef (2016) "Autonomous cars and dynamic bottleneck congestion: the effects on capacity, value of time and preference heterogeneity," *Transportation Research Part B: Methodological* 94: 43–60.

Varian, Hal R. (1992) *Microeconomic Analysis*, 3rd edition, New York: Norton.

Varian, Hal R. (2014) "Big data: new tricks for econometrics," *Journal of Economic Perspectives* 28(2): 3–28.

Venigalla, Mohan, Shruthi Kaviti and Thomas Brennan (2020) "Impact of bikesharing pricing policies on usage and revenue: an evaluation through curation of large datasets from revenue transactions and trips," *Journal of Big Data Analytics in Transportation* 2(1): 1–16.

Vickrey, William S. (1973) "Pricing, metering, and efficiently using transportation facilities," *Highway Research Record* 476: 36–48.

Vij, Akshay and Joan L. Walker (2016) "How, when and why integrated choice and latent variable models are latently useful," *Transportation Research Part B: Methodological* 90: 192–217.

Volinski, Joel (2018) "Reflections on the future of public transportation," *Journal of Public Transportation* 21(1): ii–vi.

Von Thünen, Johann H. (1826) Der isolirte Staat in Beziehung auf Landwirtschaft und Nationalökonomie. *Wirtschaft & Finan.*

Vovsha, Peter (1997) "The cross-nested logit model: application to mode choice in the Tel-Aviv metropolitan area," *Transportation Research Record: Journal of the Transportation Research Board* 1607: 6–15.

Vovsha, Peter (2017) "Microsimulation travel models in practice in the US and prospects for agent-based approach," in Javier Bajo *et al.* (eds.) *Highlights of Practical Applications of Cyber-Physical Multi-Agent Systems: PAAMS 2017*, Springer, Cham. doi:10.1007/978-3-319-60285-1_5.

Vovsha, Peter (2020) "Complex decision-making process underlying individual travel behavior and its reflection in applied travel models," in Edgardo Bucciarelli *et al.* (eds.) *Decision Economics: Complexity of Decisions and Decisions for Complexity*, Switzerland: Springer Nature, pp. 1–9.

Vovsha, Peter and Mark Bradley (2004) "Hybrid discrete choice departure-time and duration model for scheduling travel tours," *Transportation Research Record: Journal of the Transportation Research Board* 1894: 46–56.

Vreeswijk, Jaap, Tom Thomas, Eric Cor van Berkum and Bart van Arem (2014) "Perception bias in route choice," *Transportation* 41(6): 1305–1321.

Waddell, Paul (2002) "UrbanSim: modeling urban development for land use, transportation, and environmental planning," *Journal of the American Planning Association* 68(3): 297–314.

Wadud, Zia and Martin Baierl (2017) "Explaining 'peak car' with economic variables: a comment," *Transportation Research Part A: Policy and Practice* 95: 381–385.

Walker, Joan and Moshe Ben-Akiva (2011) "Advances in discrete choice models: mixture models," in André de Palma *et al.* (eds.) *A Handbook of Transport Economics*, Cheltenham: Edward Elgar, pp. 160–187.

Wang, Feng, Liang Hu, Dongdai Zhou, Rui Sun, Jiejun Hu and Kuo Zhao (2015) "Estimating online vacancies in real-time road-traffic monitoring with traffic sensor data stream," *Ad Hoc Networks* 35: 3–13.

Wardman, Mark (2004) "Public transport values of time," *Transport Policy* 11(4): 363–377.

Wardman, Mark and Paul Murphy (2015) "Passengers' valuations of train seating layout, position and occupancy," *Transportation Research Part A: Policy and Practice* 74: 222–238.

Wardman, Mark and Gerard Whelan (2011) "Twenty years of rail crowding valuation studies: evidence and lessons from British experience," *Transport Reviews* 31(3): 379–398.

West, Sarah E. (2004) "Distributional effects of alternative vehicle pollution control policies," *Journal of Public Economics* 88(3–4): 735–757.

Williams, Huw C. W. L. (1977) "On the formation of travel demand models and economic evaluation measures of user benefit," *Environment and Planning A* 9(3): 285–344.

Willig, Robert D. (1976) "Consumer's surplus without apology," *American Economic Review* 66(4): 589–597.

Winston, Clifford and Quentin Karpilow (2020) *Autonomous Vehicles: The Road to Economic Growth?* Washington, DC: Brookings Institution Press.

Wooldridge, Jeffrey M. (2010) *Econometric Analysis of Cross Section and Panel Data*, Cambridge, MA: MIT Press.

Yamamoto, Toshiyuki, Ryuichi Kitamura and Seiji Kimura (1999) "Competing-risks-duration model of household vehicle transactions with indicators of changes in explanatory variables," *Transportation Research Record: Journal of the Transportation Research Board* 1676: 116–123.

Yang, Ci and Eric J. Gonzales (2014) "Modeling taxi trip demand by time of day in New York City," *Transportation Research Record: Journal of the Transportation Research Board* 2429: 110–120.

Yang, Hai (1998) "Multiple equilibrium behaviors and advanced traveler information systems with endogenous market penetration," *Transportation Research Part B: Methodological* 32(3): 205–218.

You-Lian Chu (2009) "Work departure time analysis using dogit ordered generalized extreme value model," *Transportation Research Record: Journal of the Transportation Research Board* 2132(1): 42–49.

Yurtsever, Ekim, Jacob Lambert, Alexander Carballo and Kazuya Takeda (2020) "A survey of autonomous driving: common practices and emerging technologies," *IEEE Access* 8: 58443–58469, doi 10.1109/ACCESS.2020.2983149

Zakharenko, Roman (2016) "Self-driving cars will change cities," *Regional Science and Urban Economics* 61, 26–37.

Zhang, Wenjia and Kara M. Kockelman (2016) "Optimal policies in cities with congestion and agglomeration externalities: congestion tolls, labor subsidies, and place-based strategies," *Journal of Urban Economics* 95: 64–86.

Zmud, Johanna, Ipek N. Sener and Jason Wagner (2016) "Revolutionizing our roadways: consumer acceptance and travel behavior impacts of automated vehicles," Report TTI-2016-8, Texas Transportation Institute, Texas A&M University, College Station, TX. https://tti.tamu.edu/documents/TTI-2016-8.pdf

3 Costs

Having surveyed the demand for travel in the previous chapter, we now turn to its supply: that is, the conditions that determine how much travel of various types can be accomplished at what costs and prices. Just as travel demand is multi-dimensional, a full analysis of the supply of transportation involves many facets, including multiple outputs, complex price structures, dimensions of service quality, and alternative forms of industrial organization.

It is useful to separate supply analysis into different parts. The first part, the subject of this chapter, consists of describing the technologies and factor supplies faced by transportation providers, information that is usefully summarized as cost functions. Other parts, in Chapters 4–6, consist of pricing, investment, and strategic decisions; these analyses involve transportation providers' economic behavior, resulting market outcomes, and normative criteria by which policy makers might like to influence those outcomes.

Because different aspects of service quality are so important to the demand for transportation, they must also be included in any supply analysis. One way to do so is to define quality dimensions for each output. This is conceptually natural but cumbersome. Another way is to view consumers as part of the production process, as in Becker's (1965) theory of household production; the level of service quality, like any other productive input, is then determined by conditions for efficient production. This approach, adopted here, treats user-supplied inputs, such as time, as if purchased in markets at prices equal to the values that are determined from demand analysis. In doing so, it moves such user inputs from the demand side to the supply side of the analysis and embeds them directly into cost functions. Consumers thus treat, for example, their own time spent traveling as a (generalized) cost component, an approach that is not typically followed in economic analysis of other consumption decisions.

Knowledge of cost functions enables us to answer questions about the relative efficiency of various types of transportation and about the relative importance of various parts of the production process such as capital, user time, operator wages, public facilities, and even unintended spillovers to non-users. The discussion begins in the next section with basic cost concepts. Section 3.2 then surveys current knowledge of cost functions for public transit service. Sections 3.3–3.5 do the same for highway transportation, with an emphasis on private automobiles and congestion; these sections provide a variety of models of congestion and synthesize our knowledge of key quantitative parameters affecting the social cost of automobile transportation. Section 3.6 considers the complex role played by parking, and Section 3.7 reviews the role of bicycles and scooters.

3.1 The nature of cost functions

The literature on transportation cost contains much confusion that can be avoided by using standard economic concepts and terminology. Basso et al. (2011) provide a useful review of the literature on cost functions in transportation analysis.

DOI: 10.4324/9781315157375-3

3.1.1 *General definitions*

A general description of technology, allowing for multiple outputs and inputs, is the *transformation function*:

$$F(q,x;\theta) = 0 \qquad (3.1)$$

where q and x are vectors of outputs and inputs, respectively, and θ is a vector of parameters which may include service quality descriptors. (Alternatively, services of different quality may be considered different outputs in the vector q.) When there is just one output, (3.1) can be rewritten as a *production function* $q(x; \theta)$, giving q as a function of inputs and θ.

The *cost function* for a given producer gives the minimum cost C of producing output vector q, given the transformation function and the supply relations for inputs. Usually, these supply relations are assumed to consist of a fixed price vector w, so that the firm is a "price-taker" in the input markets, in which case the problem becomes minimizing input expenditures $w'x$ subject to the technology constraint (3.1). The solution, if unique, determines an optimal input vector x^*. The resulting minimum cost $w'x^*$ depends on q, w, and θ, so the cost function is written as $C(q, w;\theta)$. If input prices w do depend on the producer's input choices, and therefore cannot be treated as fixed parameters, the vector w in the cost function should be redefined to represent parameters of these more elaborate factor supply equations. It is thus important to bear in mind that the cost function reflects optimizing behavior (*i.e.*, cost-minimizing input choice) in establishing the relation between output quantity and cost.

If all such optimized input quantities are included in the vector x, including those that can be varied only over a long time period, we have the *long-run cost function*. It will be denoted $\tilde{C}$ when the distinction between the short and the long run is relevant. If instead one or more inputs are held fixed during the minimization to reflect that they cannot be optimized, a *short-run cost function* is obtained. Typically, the fixed input is a measure of capital stock, say x_n. Its fixed value $\bar{x}_n$, which cannot be optimized, becomes another argument of the resulting short-run cost function, which we may then write as $C(q, w;\theta,\bar{x}_n)$. By definition,

$$\tilde{C}(q, w;\theta) = \min_{x_n} C(q, w;\theta, x_n) \qquad (3.2)$$

A cost function may approach some positive constant C^0 as $q \to 0$. If so, C^0 is called the *fixed cost* and $C - C^0$ the *variable cost*. A short-run cost function always contains a fixed cost because it includes the carrying cost of the fixed (capital) input (*e.g.*, $w_n\bar{x}_n$); the rest of the short-run cost is called *operating cost* since it characterizes ongoing operations. But operating cost may again contain a fixed component, independent of q: for example, the cost of maintaining the air supply in a subway tunnel or of repainting an automobile stored outdoors. Furthermore, a fixed cost should not be confused with a *sunk cost*, a dynamic concept that expresses irreversibility in starting a business: for example, the cost of the marketing analysis and initial advertising campaign that might precede the introduction of a new transit service. A fixed operating cost can be eliminated by closing down the service entirely, whereas a sunk cost cannot.

This conceptual distinction between a fixed cost and a sunk cost is highly relevant when investigating to what extent new competitors might enter a given market. The entry barrier will be larger when there are high sunk costs. This, for example, makes competition in aviation different from that in rail: an aircraft, the capital costs of which are fixed, can be used for serving different markets when exiting a given market, so that these costs are not sunk; whereas many investments in rail infrastructure are too location-specific to be reallocated.

Letting C denote either a short-run or long-run cost function, a marginal cost may be defined with respect to output q_i as $mc_i = \partial C/\partial q_i$. It can be seen from (3.2) that, as follows from the envelope theorem (*e.g.*, Varian 1992), the long-run marginal cost is equal to the short-run marginal cost with $\bar{x}_n$ set to x_n^*; this implies that if capital stock is optimal, the incremental production cost is the same whether or not capital stock is allowed to vary.[1]

3.1.2   Economies of scale

Interest often centers on the degree of *scale economies*, which we express as a measure s that summarizes how fast costs rise with respect to output(s). If output q is scalar, s is defined simply as the ratio of average to marginal cost, which equals the inverse of the output elasticity of cost. So, letting $ac = C/q$ be average cost,

$$s \equiv \frac{ac}{mc} = \frac{C}{q \cdot (\partial C / \partial q)} \tag{3.3}$$

If $mc < ac$, so that ac decreases with q, we have *economies of scale* ($s > 1$). The opposite case ($s < 1$) is *diseconomies of scale*. When $s = 1$, there is a situation of neither economies nor diseconomies of scale or, more simply, *neutral scale economies*. Because a short-run cost function has a larger fixed cost than the corresponding long-run cost function, it is more likely to show scale economies.

Sometimes we want to consider cases where input prices w are functions of the amount of input that is purchased, thus indirectly of output, $w(q)$. In such cases, scale economies can be defined using the total, rather than partial, derivative in (3.3); we may then call the (total) relationship between C and q the *general-equilibrium supply function* and the corresponding scale economies *general-equilibrium scale economies*.

If all input prices w are constant, then economies (diseconomies) of scale, which are properties of cost functions, are equivalent to *increasing (decreasing) returns to scale*, which are properties of the transformation function (3.1) and the production function implied by it. (The term "returns to scale" refers to whether production rises more or less than proportionally when all inputs are increased together by the same proportion.) As a result, scale economies and returns to scale are often treated as synonymous. However, for a general-equilibrium supply function, a rising or falling supply price of a factor input can upset this relationship.

Perhaps somewhat unexpectedly, the indicator s is also a direct measure for the profitability of operations when a firm sells output q at a price equal to its marginal cost. Revenue then is

$$R = q \cdot (\partial C / \partial q) = C / s \tag{3.4}$$

Hence, revenue will exactly cover the total cost if there are neutral scale economies ($s = 1$); scale diseconomies will produce a profit, while scale economies will produce a deficit. This observation makes it clear that an analysis of scale economies has significant implications for the financial terms at which marginal cost pricing can take place, which makes it of interest in the study of regulation, competition, and public pricing – as we shall see in later chapters.

This relationship between cost coverage and economies of scale generalizes readily to many outputs, provided the degree-of-scale indicator s is redefined in a particular but natural way. Following Bailey and Friedlaender (1982), define s by the last equality in (3.3) but with the denominator replaced by $\sum_i q_i \cdot \partial C / \partial q_i$. (This version of s is a measure of *multiproduct scale economies*.) Then, (3.4) again holds under marginal cost pricing for all outputs i. In this case, s

can be related to a combination of individual product scale economies and *economies of scope*, which measure the extent to which it is cheaper to produce several products within the same firm, rather than in separate firms.

3.1.3 Definition of outputs

The definitions just given can be made operational only by simplifying the complex production processes encountered in real life. For example, a transit agency does many things, only a few of which can be measured and analytically manipulated as outputs; it draws on many resources, only a few of which find their way into formal analysis as inputs. There is no one correct set of definitions; what matters is that the definitions chosen to study a particular phenomenon facilitate understanding and prediction.

For transportation cost analysis, it is useful to consider two classes of output. One, which can be called *final* or *demand-related outputs*, measures the quantity and/or extent of trips taken. This type of output corresponds to the variables studied in travel demand analysis. A complete cost analysis would distinguish among all the various kinds of trips produced, such as trips from central London to Heathrow Airport during the afternoon rush-hour. In practice, final outputs are usually aggregated in some manner for tractability – expressed, for example, as total passenger trips, revenue passengers (the number of distinct fares paid), unlinked passenger trips (the number of passenger boardings of distinct vehicles), passenger-kilometers, vehicle-kilometers (of private vehicles), or even total revenues (a valid output measure if the fare structure is held constant in the analysis).

From the point of view of the transportation provider, however, final outputs are not under its control in the same way that, say, the number of chairs produced is under the control of a furniture manufacturer. No one would analyze a furniture manufacturer by counting as its output the number of its chairs that are occupied at any moment. Similarly, the transit firm may be more interested in the cost of producing the potential for trips – as measured, for example, by vehicle-kilometers (of transit vehicles), vehicle-hours, or seat-kilometers of service. We may consider such measures to be *intermediate outputs* because they are combined with user time to produce the final outputs; they are also called *supply-related outputs*. Intermediate outputs are sometimes bought and sold as intermediate goods – for example, when a public transit agency contracts to pay a private firm for a particular amount and type of bus service on a particular route – while the agency itself undertakes to use its marketing abilities to convert this service into actual trips taken.

Whether cost functions are measured in terms of final or intermediate outputs depends upon the purpose of the analysis. A study of the technical efficiency of firms' production would use intermediate outputs, whereas a study of the effectiveness of the firms' service offerings and marketing policies would use final outputs. Both may also be included in a multi-output analysis.

Implicit in the definition of a cost function for producing *final* outputs is a decision rule for choosing intermediate outputs. For example, determining the minimum cost of producing passenger trips along a given bus route entails finding the cost-minimizing headway (the time interval between buses). This suggests a two-step strategy for analyzing transit service. In the first step, a cost function is defined in terms of intermediate outputs such as vehicle-kilometers, vehicle-hours, and peak vehicles in service. In the second step, a model is constructed to represent the optimal choice of intermediate outputs, given the environment and final output demands. A description of this environment might include the length of a corridor, the area from which it draws patronage, densities of trip origins and destinations, and possible methods by which passengers can access the system and reach their final destinations. This two-step model makes explicit the optimization of intermediate outputs, and thereby makes it possible to analyze a firm's operating policies as well as its technical production process.

Whatever the type of outputs considered, care should be taken when aggregating them into a manageable number of empirical measures. A pragmatic way of handling multiple outputs parsimoniously in cost functions is to choose aggregate measures of output (*e.g.*, vehicle-kilometers), while allowing the function to also depend on descriptors of the operating environment (*e.g.*, traffic speeds). It is especially important to retain the distinction between expanding the *density* of output – for example, by adding more vehicle-kilometers on a given route network – and expanding the *spatial scale* of output: for example, by extending service to new suburban locations. The former often allows more intense use of equipment, thereby lowering the average cost – a form of scale economies called *economies of density*. In contrast, extending service to new locations may or may not involve scale economies: if it does, they are called *economies of size*. Many transportation industries have been found to have economies of density but not of size (Braeutigam 1999). However, some have argued that the usual forms of network aggregation defining economies of size are ambiguous and do not correspond to useful policy questions (Basso *et al.* 2011).

3.1.4   Methods of measurement

There are at least three general approaches to empirically measuring cost functions. The *accounting* approach examines the budgetary accounts of one or more enterprises, adjusts as needed to match economic concepts of opportunity cost, and then attributes specific accounts to specific outputs. The *engineering* approach builds a production function from technical descriptions of the production process and adds information about input prices. The *statistical* approach infers how cost varies with levels of output and other variables by observing the costs actually incurred in many different situations: for example, over many time periods or over a cross-section of firms. The generality of the statistical approach has been greatly enlarged by techniques, pioneered by Christensen *et al.* (1973) and Spady and Friedlaender (1978), for estimating flexible functional forms such as the trans-log function (which is quadratic in logarithms of all variables). There is considerable overlap among these three approaches, and any given study may make use of more than one.

3.1.5   External, social, and full costs

Often, some costs are borne not by the providing agency or the individual users of a given service but by other parties. Examples abound: air pollution, greenhouse gas emissions, noise, ground-water contamination, and wildlife disruption, to name a few. Such costs are called *external* because they fall on parties who are not part of the decision resulting in that cost. Those parties might be people who have themselves made similar decisions, but unless they do so as part of a collective (*e.g.*, a tour operator), it can be presumed for the most part that each person disregards such external effects when deciding on travel arrangements. External costs thus drive a wedge between the private costs, as faced by the decision-maker, and the social costs, as incurred by society at large. As will be discussed later, this wedge implies that the market will fail to produce an efficient outcome. External costs like these should not be confused with the so-called *pecuniary externalities*, which arise when one actor's market behavior affects the prevailing market prices. Pecuniary externalities are not, by themselves, a source of market failure, although other market failures such as monopoly power will, of course, affect prices.

There are other reasons why observable factor prices do not measure an input's true cost to society. Some factor prices may reflect subsidies, taxes, or regulations, and therefore may cause someone beside the factor owners to be affected by their use. Likewise, when the supplier of the input holds market power, the input's price will generally exceed the supplier's true cost. In such cases, part of the cost to the purchaser of the input is not a cost to society, but rather a transfer to someone else, and so again, there is a discrepancy between private and social costs.

Social or *full costs* are the total costs to society, including any external costs and correcting for transfers as just described. We may next define the *marginal social cost* (*msc*) of a particular travel movement (such as a vehicle-kilometer traveled by an automobile) as the derivative of social cost with respect to that movement. Most often, when studying divergences between private and social costs, the analyst is interested in external costs, rather than distorted factor pricing; the *msc* therefore includes both the marginal private cost as defined from a private cost function (excluding taxes and subsidies) and the *marginal external cost* (*mec*): that is, the effect of that movement on other parties. If consumers are atomistic price-takers and ignore their own impact on cost levels, then their perceived marginal private cost equals their average private cost. If, furthermore, the externality is fully mutual, in the sense that external costs are borne entirely by other travelers making the same kind of decision, then the average private cost must be the same as the average social cost (*ac*), so that *mec* = *msc* − *ac*. Congestion is usually modeled this way.

With a mutual externality, costs do not divide up neatly between the perpetrators and the recipients of the externality because they are the same people. Therefore, measures of the "total external cost," for example, obtained by multiplying *mec* by quantity, are not easy to interpret and, frankly, not very useful. This is especially true because many externalities are only partly mutual. For example, carbon monoxide emissions from motor vehicles tend to remain close to the highway, so their damage is borne partly by the parties producing it (drivers on that highway) and partly by third parties (pedestrians or nearby residents). As another example, motor vehicle injuries involve a complex mix of private costs, mutual external costs, and external costs borne by non-motorists. Note that for the determination of *mec*, which is relevant for the formulation of efficient (tax) policies, it is immaterial whether or not the externality is mutual: all that is relevant is whether the effect is external to the individual causing it.

Numerous studies have attempted to quantify and categorize social costs: for example, Jakob *et al.* (2006), Delucchi and McCubbin (2011), Friedrich and Quinet (2011), Litman (2016), and European Commission *et al.* (2020).

3.2 Cost functions for public transit

This section examines some of the many attempts to measure the cost of providing bus or rail transit service, following the two-step strategy described earlier. We review the first step – analyzing the cost of producing intermediate outputs – very briefly, devoting most attention to optimization models of the production of final outputs.

The first step may be accomplished in many ways. One is through accounting: for example, Abbas and Abd-Allah (1999) dissect the cost accounts of the primary transit provider in Cairo, Egypt, to allocate costs among output categories. We caution that accounting practices vary from agency to agency and do not always accurately reflect the economic costs that are the real concern of the transportation analyst. A second way is through engineering analysis, which uses detailed engineering information to construct cost functions in a "bottom-up" fashion. The classic study by Meyer *et al.* (1965) is a masterful example of engineering costing, supplemented by accounting methods. More recently, Abe (2019) supplements accounting-based estimates of taxi and bus transit costs with engineering assumptions about cost reductions due to automation, including, for example, how many driverless taxis can be managed by a single human opera-tor or by a single automated control center. A third way is statistical, in which data from many transit agencies and/or time periods are pooled, and statistical inference is used to estimate the parameters of cost functions. Statistical studies are reviewed by De Borger and Kerstens (2008).

3.2.1   Cost functions including user inputs

As already noted, travelers must supply some inputs, especially their time, as part of producing final outputs such as trips. As such time is valuable, it constitutes an important component of social cost and welfare, which should be accounted for in policy decisions. We illustrate here with public transit users, and in Sections 3.3–3.6 with users of private vehicles.

Transit users spend time accessing the system, waiting for vehicles, riding in vehicles, pos-sibly transferring between vehicles, and getting to final destinations. We begin by considering just waiting time. The consequences of including waiting time as an input to the production of trips are far-reaching; similar consequences follow from including time spent walking or transferring. Specifically, Mohring (1972) shows that when waiting-time costs are included, transit service is subject to strong economies of density in producing final outputs, even if such economies are absent for producing the intermediate outputs. This phenomenon has become known as the *Mohring effect*.

We can demonstrate this proposition with a simplified version of Mohring's model for peak-period bus transit on a single route.[2] The measure of final output, q, is the number of passengers per peak hour traveling on the route. It is produced using two inputs. First is the intermediate good V defined as vehicles passing a given bus stop per peak hour (*i.e.*, frequency), produced at unit cost c_p. (The inverse of frequency, $1/V$, is known as the headway.) Second is a user-supplied input, aggregate waiting time per peak hour W, valued at unit cost α^W. Suppose average waiting time per passenger, W/q, is equal to half the headway, $1/(2V)$; this would reflect arrivals at the stop independent of the schedule. Aggregate costs to the bus agency and to the users, respectively, are then

$$C_B = c_p V; \; C_w = \frac{\alpha^W q}{2V}$$

We choose V to minimize the sum of these costs, subject to a constraint imposed by bus capacity:

$$q \leq NV$$

where N is the total number of passengers a bus can pick up and drop off as it travels the entire route. That is, when all passengers travel the entire route, N is simply the physical capacity of the bus. Otherwise, as long as demand is spatially homogeneous, we can write $N = nL/d$, where n is the physical capacity of the bus (maximum number of passengers at any time); d is the aver-age passenger's trip length; and L is the length of the route.

Letting λ be the Lagrangian multiplier of the constraint, the first-order condition is

$$c_p - \frac{\alpha^W q}{2V^2} - N\lambda = 0$$

There are two possible solutions. If $\lambda = 0$, indicating that buses are not full, the solution is (with a star denoting optimized choices)

$$V^* = \sqrt{\frac{\alpha^W}{2c_p}} \cdot \sqrt{q}; \quad W^* = \frac{q}{2V^*} = \sqrt{\frac{c_p}{2\alpha^W}} \cdot \sqrt{q}$$

$$C_B^* = c_p \cdot V^* = \sqrt{\frac{\alpha^W \cdot c_p}{2}} \cdot \sqrt{q}; \quad C_W^* = \alpha^W \cdot W^* = \sqrt{\frac{\alpha^W \cdot c_p}{2}} \cdot \sqrt{q}$$

Two properties of this solution are worth noting. First, the optimal bus frequency V^* is proportional to the square root of the passenger density q; this is known as the "square root rule" for operating policy. Second, the cost function is also proportional to $\sqrt{q}$, which gives it economies of scale (*i.e.*, of density): specifically, $s = 2$. This implies that setting the generalized price equal to marginal cost would require a fare that is insufficient for the transit provider to cover its average cost. In fact, that fare is zero, which is the difference between the marginal cost $\partial C/\partial q$ and the value of the inputs supplied by users, C_W/q. The intuition here is simple: if buses are not full, then it costs nothing to take another passenger. In more general models, this simple rule does not hold, but the intuition remains important. Optimal fares are derived more formally in the next chapter.

If $\lambda > 0$, indicating the capacity constraint is binding, the solution is $V^* = q/N$, $W^* = q/(2 \cdot V^*)$ $= N/2$, $C_B^* = c_p \cdot q/N$, and $C_W^* = \alpha^W N/2$. Over the range of output for which this solution holds, the total cost function is linear in output and has fixed cost C_W^*. It thus again exhibits density economies, namely, $s = 1 + (C_W^*/C_B^*)$.[3] Once again, setting generalized price equal to marginal cost will not make the fare high enough for the transit provider to cover its cost: they differ by $\alpha^W \cdot N/(2q)$.[4] The fare includes the average cost (c_p/N) because now the agency has to increase its service frequency to accommodate a new passenger; but the fare is then discounted below that amount because the increased service reduces waiting costs to other passengers.

These two cases for the value of λ, then, show that there are economies of density whether or not the constraint is binding. This is because in both cases, operating cost, waiting cost, or both grow less than proportionally as output expands.

Analogous models can be constructed to show how the transit operator could respond by increasing route density instead of, or in addition to, increasing frequency along a route.[5] In this case, savings in both walking time and waiting time cause increasing returns. Because there are now two ways the agency can reduce users' costs through increased service frequency, optimal vehicle-miles offered grow more rapidly with passenger density than in the simpler model – specifically, with its two-thirds power. As vehicle-miles are expanded, half of the increased service is configured so as to reduce waiting costs and the other half to reduce walking costs.

There are many ways in which this model could be made more realistic. We could consider off-peak travel as a separate output. We could consider the width of the peak period to be variable and take into account the effect that peak broadening would have on parameter c_p. We could take into account the effect on average speed of additional passengers boarding or leaving the vehicle, thereby obtaining a positive optimal fare even when buses are not full.[6] We could allow users to consult transit time schedules when frequency is low, which somewhat lowers their waiting costs relative to assuming waiting time equal to half the headway (Fosgerau 2009). Yet another improvement would be to account for a minimum-safe-headway constraint between trains, which tends to create scale diseconomies (Coulombel and Monchambert 2023).

We could also allow bus capacity (*i.e.*, the size of individual vehicles) to be endogenous, chosen as part of overall cost minimization, and estimate optimal bus size. Doing so would recognize that greater bus capacity costs more, in both purchase price and operational costs, but also reduces the degree of crowding and the likelihood that the first bus to arrive will be too crowded to enter. Research using this approach, applied to Sweden and the UK in the 1980s, suggested that the buses used by most transit systems at that time were too large. Subsequent partial bus deregulation in the UK did in fact lead to niche services using small buses.

Models incorporating optimization along the lines discussed here are very useful for understanding the full implications of new modes or technologies, which might drastically change the service patterns chosen by transit providers. An example is the study by Tirachini and Antoniou (2020) of how autonomous buses might alter the economics of providing public transit services. Using case studies of Munich and of Santiago (Chile), they show how the cost reductions lead to more frequent optimal service by smaller vehicles, thus reducing scale economies and optimal subsidies, more so where labor costs are high.

Researchers have integrated variable bus size into more general optimization models, for example, by requiring a single vehicle fleet to service both peak and off-peak travel. In such cases, the optimal adjustment to a marginal increase in demand can become quite complex. Still, the results often follow a structure that is recognizable from the simple model developed here. For example, optimal bus frequency varies negatively with bus operating cost, as seen in the solution for V^* above; hence, if automation or some other innovation were to greatly reduce that parameter, it would become optimal to provide greater frequency. In most models, this would be done with smaller buses. We discuss such results in Chapter 4 when considering transit pricing.

The economies of density resulting from treating waiting time as a cost are a fundamental insight into transportation modes that depend on matching a set of desired trips, each at a particular time and place, to available vehicles. Besides public transit, examples include airlines and shared-ride services using shuttles, taxicabs, or ride-hailing services. In addition to creating an *a priori* case for transit subsidies, economies of density create a barrier to policies encouraging competition among transit providers.

The insight does not depend upon a literal view of waiting time but applies to any disutility created by infrequent service; for example, having to deviate from a desired arrival time or needing to consult timetables when frequencies are lower. Any such disutility can be expected to diminish with service frequency. The average user is then better off when ridership increases, provided there is no overriding negative impact on comfort. The practical consequences of this insight depend on the precise service arrangements. If intermingling of services by more than one firm causes the user to care only about the firms' combined service frequency (as occurs, *e.g.*, with airline alliances), the economies of density apply to a group of firms, and individual firms within the group confer externalities on one another. If, on the other hand, the user has to pre-commit to one firm, the economies are firm-specific.

Finally, we remark that the above economies of density occur at the time scale where service frequency is adjusted to reflect higher ridership. In the shorter run, crowding externalities in public transport may very well dominate travelers' perceptions of whether or not they benefit from additional fellow travelers. Optimization of frequency then should naturally also reflect the impacts on equilibrium crowding costs (*e.g.*, de Palma *et al.* 2017).

3.2.2   *Transit network design*

Cost minimization for public transit includes choosing an optimal network. This is a highly technical and specialized topic that we make no attempt to cover fully here.[7] However, we do point out that the existence of scale economies is highly relevant for transit networks. In this respect, they are similar to airlines, which responded by building what are widely called "hub and spoke" (HS) networks following deregulation in the 1970s and 1980s. The corresponding network structure for public transit is often called *trunk-feeder*, as contrasted with *direct service*.

The rationale is simple: there are scale economies (*i.e.*, economies of density) in grouping many passengers into a single vehicle, which can be realized only if a sufficient number of passengers are carried on a single route. As seen in the previous section, this creates a tradeoff between cost savings from using larger vehicles and the inconvenience of less frequent services. One way to make this tradeoff more favorable is to bundle passengers by operating more frequent services to and from a hub, encouraging passengers to transfer there. This can then replace some direct services between origins and destinations other than the hub. To connect N different nodes by return services (*i.e.*, services in both directions), a so-called fully connected (FC) network would require $N \cdot (N-1)/2$ such return services: from each node to $(N-1)$ other nodes, and dividing by 2 as a return service connects its nodes both as origins and as destinations. An HS network, in contrast, would require $N-1$ return trips only: between the hub and each other node. The number of connections for HS needed is then smaller for $N > 2$, and the difference increases with N due to the quadratic relation for FC versus the linear one for HS. If, therefore, bundling passengers brings economies of scale, the advantage increases with the size of the network. Many passengers may prefer a multi-leg trip through a hub to a direct (single-leg) trip with less frequent service options, provided the inconvenience cost of a transfer is not too high, frequency benefits are important, and the supplier's cost savings are passed on at least partly to passengers.

In a simple setting, all these factors are incorporated into average total cost of travel. This observation might suggest simply using the network structure that minimizes that average cost. However, other factors may also come into play. For example, Pels (2020), in reviewing the literature on HS networks, emphasizes that market power may be perversely strengthened through HS operations. Pels also notes some potentially adverse environmental consequences.

Just as airlines do, transit systems sometimes create hubs (*i.e.*, transfer stations), where many lines converge to facilitate transfers. A main "trunk" line may then be created to which many routes, which may include other modes, feed traffic (hence, the name "trunk-feeder" for this type of network). This arrangement permits more frequent service to the more outlying locations that are origins or destinations for many trips, while still allowing for fast trips for the many trips that use only the trunk line. Just as for airlines, modeling these tradeoffs involves knowing the provider's cost per route-mile in various size vehicles, users' values of in-vehicle travel time, users' values of waiting time (or of the inconvenience of infrequent schedules), and users' inconvenience cost of transfers. These factors are elegantly modeled by Gschwender *et al.* (2016), showing how the optimal structure depends on dispersion in transfer costs perceived by travelers. Fielbaum *et al.* (2016), using a stylistic city representation, find that optimally designed public transport networks tend to become more direct, with fewer transfers and hence shorter trips, when patronage increases – yet another type of scale economy in public transport.

Again similar to airlines, the cost of a transfer rises strongly if connecting service is unreliable. Furthermore, the scale economies are most easily realized if trunk service carries a high volume of people whose origin and/or destination already include one of its stops (again, just as for airlines). Most cities have experienced a decline in the proportion of suburb-to-city trips, which facilitated a particular type of HS transit service where the primary hub was downtown, making that type of network less desirable.

These factors were very much at play in two rather famous restructurings of transit service in Bogotá, Columbia, and in Santiago, Chile, described in some detail in Section 6.3.5. The complexity of these restructurings, especially in Santiago, prevents us from drawing clear conclusions about HS networks; nevertheless Muñoz *et al.* (2014) draws some valuable lessons for policy.

Trunk-feeder service can also be contrasted with transit service via an informal industry of private bus or minibus providers. Several developing nations have moved to augment an informal system with trunk service, usually in the form of bus rapid transit (BRT) as described in the next subsection (Ferro *et al.* 2015). Such restructuring typically combines a change in network with a change in the nature of the industry, and thus opens many possibilities for success, failure, and controversy.

3.2.3   *Cost comparison: express bus vs rail transit*

A recurring issue in urban transportation is the relative efficiency of bus and rail for providing public transit. Each mode, of course, has many variants, so no universal answer should be expected. The fundamental factors are that rail is very costly, especially the initial investment due to the need to lay rail lines; and that bus is more flexible due to its use of an existing street system and the ease of redesigning routes and schedules as conditions warrant. The most salient questions are as follows: (1) Can rail, with its fixed lines and relatively long access times, provide satisfactory overall origin-to-destination trip times compared to the more flexible network layouts that are possible with bus service? (2) Can express bus systems be designed to provide amenities comparable to rail transit at lower cost?

The first question is likely to involve a tradeoff between the street congestion encountered by most bus services and their ability to travel on routes that are close to many origins and destinations, often including the ability to provide no-transfer service. This tradeoff is affected by many factors. High spatial densities of population and of trip destinations favor rail, while more dispersed travel patterns, including increasingly common travel between suburban areas, are difficult for rail to serve due to longer access distances. Cities with sufficient traffic and space to provide exclusive bus and/or tram lanes can reduce the adverse impact of congestion on bus and mixed-traffic rail service. If high-speed highway lanes are available for the "line-haul" portion of bus trips (*i.e.*, mostly non-stop travel between residential areas and employment or other activity centers), total trip times may be quite low with integrated bus service, in which the same vehicle engages in rapid travel over most of the trip and low-speed access and distribution within residential and employment areas. (The same is true for tram service and occasionally for commuter rail, when the latter can feasibly make multiple stops in residential areas along with a non-stop run between them and a station at a central business district.)

The second question, about amenities as perceived by travelers, involves both the experience of entering a vehicle and the comfort of the ride. Typically, rail is superior: vehicles are larger, may have multiple large doors, and the ride is usually smoother both in terms of bumpiness and of starting and stopping in response to traffic. BRT has been developed in an attempt to overcome this amenity gap. It has many forms, often including off-vehicle fare payment (to save boarding time), priority in mixed traffic (*e.g.*, exclusive lanes and/or favorable timing at traffic signals), raised boarding platforms (to reduce need to climb steps), and enhanced waiting areas for boarders. BRT has been successfully implemented in a number of cities – most famously Curitiba, Brazil.[8]

With so many factors at play, it is no surprise that researchers reach widely varying conclusions about the relative merits of rail and bus transit. Much of the research analyzes specific instances of a change in service. For example, Kain (1997) argues that the subway system in the Atlanta region, introduced starting in 1979, was very costly and resulted in little new ridership compared to the bus systems it replaced. (The argument distinguishes between number of vehicle *boardings*, which did increase substantially, and number of *trips*, which increased much less because many previous single-vehicle trips required a transfer under the new system.) Clifton *et al.* (2014) analyze the costs and benefits to travelers of the North West Rail Link in Sydney, Australia, finding mixed results: travel times were improved for many trips to the largest activity centers but became longer to locations such as one just outside Sydney's main central business district.

An additional factor besides cost may affect the comparison of modes. There is much evidence that good transportation fosters agglomeration economies (see Chapter 1), which make urban areas more productive. Some of this evidence is specific to public transit (Hazledine *et al.* 2017, Graham and Gibbons 2019). It is likely that a major fixed investment such as a rail line or bus tunnel has more such effects than a reversible improvement in bus service because the increased overall capacity may be regarded as longer-lasting. Thus, it is more likely to promote the huge capital investments, such as skyscrapers, that make big-city business districts possible. A smaller-scale agglomeration economy is also relevant: there is a widespread belief, supported by some research, that rail stations make it possible to create "transit-oriented development" patterns nearby, in which local concentrations of high-density housing and/or commercial space yield agglomeration benefits and increase transit usage (Zamir *et al.* 2014; Boarnet *et al.* 2017). Such factors may also modify in complex ways the optimal supply and pricing rules discussed earlier (Hörcher *et al.* 2020).

3.3   Highway travel: congestion technology

The importance of the automobile in urban travel patterns has created great interest in how best to cope with the various costs that it imposes. This question can be addressed by defining and measuring cost functions for motor vehicles on highways. Doing so facilitates pricing and investment analyses, which are the central contributions of economics to public policy. For example, questions about optimal pricing or privately owned highways can be addressed by applying standard economic tools to carefully defined cost functions. The use of cost functions also makes precise what it really costs society to undertake a particular kind of trip by motor vehicle.

We therefore analyze the costs of highway travel in this and the next two sections. This section presents the pure technology of highway congestion, a subject brought squarely into transportation analysis by Beckmann *et al.* (1956). Because it is so crucial to urgent policy questions, we provide considerable detail. Section 3.4 then derives short-run cost functions (*i.e.*, those for fixed road capacity), and confronts them with demand functions to characterize short-run equilibrium. By incorporating user time directly as a cost, we make the congestion technology an integral part of the cost function. We also review empirical evidence on the magnitudes of short-run variable costs. Section 3.5 adds information about infrastructure costs in order to compute long-run cost functions.

3.3.1   *Fundamentals of congestion*

A rather general economic definition of congestion is that it occurs when the quality of service of a facility depends on the intensity of use. For transportation, important aspects of quality include expected travel time, expected arrival time, reliability, and convenience of travel.

Highway congestion arises from many causes. Vehicles form queues at traffic signals. Cars entering from side streets wait for gaps in traffic on a main highway. Cars traveling behind slower vehicles on two-lane roads must wait for gaps in oncoming traffic before passing. Consequently, many types of congestion and modeling approaches can be distinguished. One distinction is between *link* and *nodal* congestion. The former involves slowing down of traffic when the traffic density increases, independent of upstream or downstream bottlenecks; the latter refers to intersections (or, in the case of other modes, to stations, harbors, and airports). When congestion at nodes or other bottlenecks takes the form of queuing, its implications for travel times no longer depend on the flow but on the length of the queue, which thus becomes a necessary variable for analysis. Another, related, distinction is between *static* or *stationary-state* congestion versus *dynamic* congestion, the latter involving changes in traffic conditions over time and often interdependencies across different points in time. Distinctions like these are sometimes clearer within abstract models than when describing congestion in reality – which often involves mixtures of these "ideal" types.

Congestion models can furthermore be categorized along several dimensions: what facilities are considered (whether *single link*, *network*, or *area* without explicit network representation); the assumed similarities among travelers (*homogeneous* or *heterogeneous*); and the assumed mechanisms governing route choices, traffic volumes, and travel times (*deterministic* or *stochastic*). The best choice of model to use depends on the question under consideration.

We begin with what is probably the simplest case to describe, but not always yielding the most straightforward modeling insights: namely, stationary-state congestion on a uniform highway without traffic signals, used by homogeneous travelers. When many vehicles try to use the highway simultaneously, the resulting high density D (number of vehicles per unit of distance) forces them to slow down for safety reasons, thereby reducing average vehicle speed S. One way to depict congestion, then, is as a functional relationship $S(D)$. An example is shown in quadrant a of Figure 3.1, in mirror-image form in which D increases toward the left. (For expositional ease, it is shown as convex, although realistically it may well be concave.)

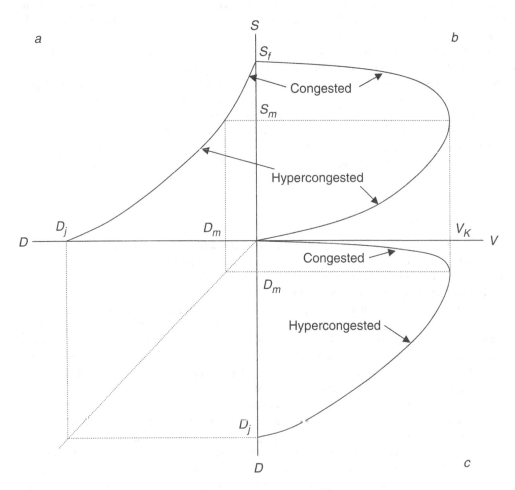

Figure 3.1 The fundamental diagram of traffic congestion in three forms.

Also of interest is traffic *flow* or *volume V*, defined as the number of vehicles passing a given point per unit time. Traffic flow is identically equal to the product of speed and density:

$$V \equiv SD \tag{3.5}$$

which is consistent with its units of measure: *e.g.* vehicles/hour = (vehicles/mile)·(miles/hour). Note that, unless stated otherwise, we normalize V and D with respect to road width (in lanes), so that "vehicles" becomes a shorthand for "vehicles/lane" in these definitions.[9]

Given identity (3.5), the congestion technology can be expressed equivalently as a functional relationship between *any* two of the variables V, D, and S. One is the *speed–flow relationship* $S(V)$ shown in quadrant *b*; it is defined over the region $V \in [0, V_K]$, where V_K is the per-lane *capacity* of the highway: the maximum flow it can carry. As seen in the figure, the relation is double-valued; we refer to the upper branch as *congested* or *normally congested* and the lower branch as *hypercongested*.[10] Hypercongestion occurs when traffic is particularly heavy and slow. As discussed in Section 3.3.2 below, it is observed empirically at individual loop detectors on individual highways, particularly when placed upstream of a bottleneck. It is also observed in studies that average such observations over links of an urban network, as is done in the Macroscopic Fundamental Diagram (MFD) models discussed in Section 3.3.3 below. The third possible relationship, that between V and D, is called by Haight (1963, pp. 69–73) the *fundamental diagram of traffic flow*; it is shown (rotated clockwise by 90°) in quadrant *c* of Figure 3.1. Haight shows that flow first rises and later falls as density increases from zero, as depicted in the diagram.

Figure 3.1 shows diagrammatically how any of these three relationships can be derived from any one of the others. (The unused quadrant, in the lower left, is simply a diagonal line to connect values of density on two adjacent axes). The figure also shows the density D_m and speed S_m that correspond to maximum flow V_K. All other feasible flow levels can result from either a congested or a hypercongested speed and density. For example, a zero flow prevails when there are no vehicles on the road ($D = 0$), allowing the free-flow speed S_f; or when density reaches the value, known as the *jam density* D_j, that reduces speed to zero – this situation is shown at the origin of quadrant *b* and at the points marked D_j in quadrants *a* and *c*.

If these variables are defined over a very small region of time and space, the relationships shown in Figure 3.1 are instantaneous and local ones. However, much of the economic literature has used the instantaneous speed–flow relationship to analyze aggregate performance of an entire highway. This is a seemingly innocuous step if it is assumed that homogeneous traffic conditions prevail along the entire highway, so that V, S, and D are single-valued over time and space. In that case, speed S can then be transformed to travel time T according to $T = L/S$, with L denoting the length of the highway. This yields an aggregate relation between traffic flow V, assumed constant over time and along the road, and travel time T for traveling that entire road. This procedure may work well for situations where conditions change only slowly over time and space, but in other situations, the instantaneous flow at any given point may be quite different from the economic demand for travel on the highway as reflected in the number of vehicles attempting to enter it. We discuss this problem more completely in Section 3.4.

3.3.2 *Empirical speed–flow relationships*

We begin with some empirical evidence concerning the fundamental diagram, and some extensions of it that have been found necessary to portray observed data.

3.3.2.1   *Instantaneous relationships*

There is uncertainty about the true shapes of the curves in Figure 3.1 in the neighborhood of maximum flow V_K and density D_m. Figure 3.2 illustrates why. Figure 3.2a plots observations of flow versus occupancy, a measure of density, for the Queen Elizabeth Way in Toronto, Canada. (Thus, it is depicting the curve in Figure 3.1c after rotation by 90°.) Although the two branches of the flow–density curve are reasonably well defined, the middle portion connecting them is obscured by scatter; and it is not clear whether the branches meet, that is, whether the relationship is continuous.

Similarly, the speed–density data plotted in Figure 3.2b, from the Santa Monica Freeway in Los Angeles, California, appear to reflect two distinct regimes. They are connected, not by a continuous curve but by a region where the relationship is only vaguely defined.

At least two explanations have been put forth for the dispersion of observations where flow is close to capacity. Both posit two distinct flow regimes, one congested and the other hypercongested. One explanation is a measurement problem: since speed, flow, and density are in practice measured over a finite span of space and time, a given observation may inadvertently average two points from the two different regimes. Another explanation is that many intermediate-density observations correspond to disequilibrium conditions during transition between the congested and hypercongested regimes (Hall *et al.* 1986). Compounding matters is that in many data sets there is a paucity of observations at flows near capacity. This is presumably due to bottlenecks upstream or downstream from the point in question. Indeed, empirical estimates of speed–flow relationships are strongly influenced by nearby bottlenecks (Hall and Hall 1990).

Despite these difficulties, many empirical estimates are reported in the literature; Hall (2002) provides a review. Some illustrative examples are described here.

Of historical interest is Greenshields' (1935) linear speed–density relationship, estimated on a two-lane, two-way road:

$$S = S_f \left(1 - D / D_j \right)$$

Applying identity (3.5) yields a parabolic speed–flow relationship. Later studies revealed that this parabolic shape is less accurate for larger highways, where instead speeds often remain constant, or nearly so, over a substantial range of flow levels.

Not surprisingly, the functional form used in the estimation may strongly affect the shape of the estimated function, even when the same data are used. As an older but still illustrative example: two separate research groups have fit speed–flow curves like that in Figure 3.1b to the same data from a four-lane section of the Capital Beltway in Washington, DC. Boardman and Lave (1977) get the following result:[11]

$$V = 2490 - 0.523 \cdot \left(S - 35.34 \right)^2$$

where V is in vehicles per hour per lane. The two solutions for S to this quadratic equation represent congestion and hypercongestion. Inman, by contrast, (1978) obtains[12]

$$V^{(2.95)} = 3.351 \cdot 10^9 - 231.4 \cdot \left(S - 7.2 \right)^{(4.06)}$$

where, for any quantity X, $X^{(a)}$ denotes the Box–Cox transformation of X, defined as $(X^a - 1)/a$. The Boardman–Lave and Inman curves are both plotted in Figure 3.3, along with the scatter of data points. It appears that the Boardman–Lave curve represents the data more faithfully; but neither curve captures well the previously mentioned tendency, obvious from the raw data, for

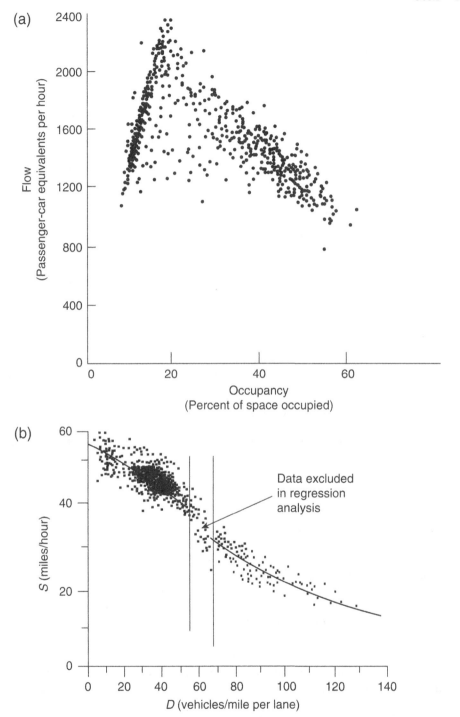

Figure 3.2 Flow–density and speed–density scatter plots. (a) Queen Elizabeth Way (Toronto). Adapted from Hall *et al.* (1986) with permission from Pergamon Journals Ltd. (b) Santa Monica Freeway (Los Angeles). Adapted from Payne (1984, *F*igure 6, p. 145). Copyright, National Academy of Sciences with permission of the Transportation Research Board.

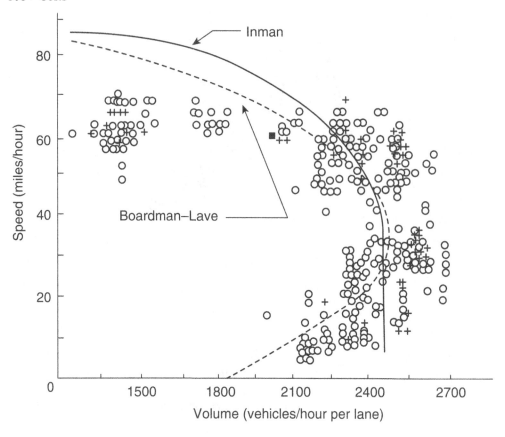

Figure 3.3 Capital Beltway, Washington, DC. Adapted from Boardman *et al.* (1977) with permission from Academic Press.

expressway speed in the region of normal congestion to remain nearly constant throughout most of the range of volume–capacity ratios.[13]

Figure 3.4 shows two more recent "official" speed–flow relations, which do account for this phenomenon: the COBA11 and Highway Capacity Manual (HCM2000) formulations in the UK and USA, respectively.[14] Both portray normal congestion, not hypercongestion, and do so with two joined segments that meet at V_B. HCM2000 joins a completely flat segment with a segment defined by a power function, maintaining a continuous derivative; whereas COBA11 joins two linear segments, making a discontinuous slope. The parameters depend on highway geometry, the share of heavy vehicles, and other factors. The more recent sixth edition of the Highway Capacity Manual (HCM2016)[15] contains yet further updated versions, which are still very similar to what is shown in our Figure 3.4: they also have the two separate segments and are parametrized depending on free-flow speed and type of road (freeways versus multilane highways). Also shown in the figure are dotted lines representing two other regimes posited by Hall *et al.* (1992): one for queue discharge within a bottleneck, the other for flow within a queue behind the bottleneck. In Section 3.4, we shall see that these regimes and their descriptions are consistent with some recent views on the hypercongested branch of the speed–flow relationship.

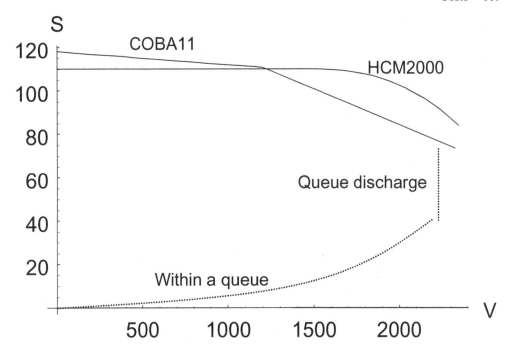

Figure 3.4 Sample speed–flow curves for US and UK government analyses. *Notes*: *S* in km/hr, *V* in veh/l/hr. HCM2000 and COBA11 curves assume an expressway with no hills, bends, or heavy vehicles. Capacities under these idealized conditions are $V_K = 2,330$ (COBA) and $V_K = 2,350$ (HCM), and the break points (V_B in note 14) are 1,200 (COBA) and 1,450 (HCM). The two COBA segments are given by $S = 118 - 0.006\ V$ for $V \le V_B$ and $S = 110.8 - (33/1,000)\ (V - V_B)$ for $V_B < V \le V_K$. The two HCM segments are given by $S = 110$ for $V \le V_B$ and $S = 110 - [(730/28)$ $((V - 1,450)/900)2.6]$ for $V_B < V \le V_K$. The two additional (dotted) segments proposed by Hall, Hurdle and Banks (1992) are hand-drawn.

3.3.2.2 *Space-averaged relationships*

The relationship holding at a single time and place is not, by itself, directly useful for economic analysis of congestion because it does not relate service quality for entire trips to the number of people attempting to travel. On real highways, queues form behind bottlenecks and traffic volumes vary over time and place, so that the (expected) time required to make a certain trip cannot be directly computed from a single local and instantaneous value for speed. One way to take such features into account is through formal network models, in which a speed–flow relationship applies to each link and users choose the resulting quickest routes (Marcotte and Nguyen 1998). Here, we discuss simpler approaches, namely, those that average over space and time to keep the relevant traffic variables single-valued.

Keeler and Small (1977) obtain a space-averaged relation, using observations on three expressways in the San Francisco Bay area to estimate quadratic functions (like Boardman and Lave 1977) relating speed and volume–capacity ratio V/V_k, each averaged over a long stretch of highway. One resulting equation is[16]

$$\frac{V}{V_K} = 0.8603 - 0.001923 \cdot (S - 45.68)^2$$

In contrast to the instantaneous speed–flow curves, Keeler and Small's averaged curves show, on the upper (congested) branch, a substantial negative slope over the entire range of average vehicle flow. This reflects the fact that as traffic is added to a real highway, non-uniformities in the highway design or in demand patterns cause minor slowdowns even when the average volume–capacity ratio is well below one.

Clearly, the exact nature of such an aggregate speed–flow relationship critically depends on the extent and nature of heterogeneity, so a function fitted for one highway is unlikely to generalize. This is all the more true for streets and arterial highways subject to congestion at signalized intersections, whose technology is entirely different from that of an unobstructed highway. Here, there are even more sources of heterogeneity including signal timing, turn lanes, intersection geometry, and on-street parking. In a study of historical interest, Smeed (1968, p. 34) reports the following relationship, attributed to Wardrop, for city streets in London:

$$\frac{V}{w} = 68 - 0.13 \cdot S^2$$

where w is width of road in feet. This relationship does not have a hypercongested branch, but rather approaches zero speed, implying infinite density, as $V \to 68w$.

For some purposes, it may be more useful to model speeds and flows over areas, rather than along a single roadway. The so-called Macroscopic Fundamental Diagram (MFD) and bathtub models to be discussed in Section 3.3.3 do exactly that, while allowing for traffic conditions that change over time – an aspect that the above formulations bypass.

3.3.2.3　*Time-averaged relationships*

The space-averaged relationships just described cannot explain what happens when demand is so high that the maximum flow capacity cannot accommodate it. In such situations, growing stocks of vehicles can be expected to accumulate somewhere, usually in the form of queuing. Travel time then depends not only on contemporaneous flow but also on past flows, through the impact on accumulated numbers of vehicles in queues. Time-averaged speed–flow functions aim to incorporate such time dependence by relating average speed over a specified period to the average vehicle inflow over that period.

Two functional forms that allow for traffic flow above capacity are in common use. The first specifies travel delay as a power function of the volume–capacity ratio:

$$T = T_f \cdot \left[1 + a \cdot (V / V_K)^b\right] \tag{3.6}$$

where T denotes travel time per mile (the inverse of speed). This function has been used in many economic models of congestion such as Vickrey (1963), with parameter b typically assumed to be between 2.5 and 5.0. With parameter values $a = 0.15$ and $b = 4$, it is known as the Bureau of Public Roads (BPR) function, used widely in US transportation planning.[17] There is also an "updated BPR function" (BPR-U), intended to approximate the speed–flow functions in the 1994 Highway Capacity Manual (a predecessor to HCM2000 and HCM2016) discussed above.[18] The potentially unlimited flow permitted by equation (3.6) might seem unrealistic at first sight; however, if the equation is used sensibly, the traffic will be limited by other factors such as total demand or upstream bottlenecks. Moreover, a time-averaged relation allows for a difference between the durations of the periods of inflow and outflow, as will become clear in the next example. If that is the case, a relatively high average inflow, over a shorter period, will result in a longer period of lower outflows as the latter are limited by various segment capacities.

An inflow V exceeding outflow capacity V_K is then by no means a physical impossibility: it merely indicates that the outflow will last for a longer period of time than the inflow and will therefore on average be lower – in particular, it is limited by overall capacity.

Nevertheless, (3.6) has the important drawback that it does not explicitly account for how long traffic exceeds capacity, if it does so. This disadvantage is remedied in a duration-dependent function derived by Small (1983) to express the average travel time over a peak period of fixed duration P, when peak-period inflow V is at a uniform rate and delay results from queuing behind a single bottleneck with a constant capacity V_K. As will be derived in more detail in Section 3.4.3, it yields a piecewise-linear relationship:

$$T = \begin{cases} T_f & \text{if } V \le V_k \\ T_f + \frac{1}{2} P \cdot (V / V_K - 1) & \text{if } V > V_k \end{cases} \qquad (3.7)$$

Both equations (3.6) and (3.7) fit surprisingly well in certain circumstances.[19] Neither accounts explicitly for yet another feature, which is that the relationship near capacity appears to be history-dependent: flow at maximum capacity (like that shown at the extreme right of the upper curves in Figure 3.4) can be maintained briefly, but small fluctuations are likely to disrupt it, making the relationship like (3.6) or (3.7) but with lower capacity. Hall (2018) cites many studies finding this effect.

Akçelik (1991) develops a travel time function that is smooth, like (3.6) and that also approaches linearity for very high flows, like (3.7). It introduces a "delay parameter" J_a that is motivated by stochastic queuing models with random arrivals. The function is

$$T = T_f + 0.25P \cdot \left[\left(\frac{V}{V_K} - 1 \right) + \sqrt{\left(\frac{V}{V_K} - 1 \right)^2 + \frac{8 J_a V / V_K}{V_K P}} \right] \qquad (3.8)$$

which has (3.7) as a special case when $J_a = 0$.[20] Akçelik's function seems to produce reasonable results when used in network models (Dowling *et al.* 1998).

Figure 3.5 compares the relationships depicted by (3.6), (3.7), and (3.8) by plotting normalized average speed (relative to S_f) versus normalized inflow (relative to V_K) for $P = 1$ hr, $V_K = 2000$ veh/hr, $J_A = 0.1$, and two different values of T_f, one corresponding to a one-mile-long road with top speed 75 mi/hr and the other to a 75-mile-long road with the same top speed. The curves labeled BPR, BPR-U, and PL represent BPR, updated BPR, and piecewise-linear functions, respectively, the latter from (3.7).

For the shorter road, the speed–flow curves derived from Small's and Akçelik's models are similar over most of the range considered but diverge for inflows near V_K. For the longer road, the two functions become graphically indistinguishable; this is because the travel delay from bottleneck queuing is unaffected by the length of the road and thus is diluted when averaging over the longer road. The BPR speed–flow functions, by contrast, do not depend on road length.

3.3.3 *Macroscopic Fundamental Diagrams*

Can formulations such as those above be generalized to a dense street network, such as the downtown of a large city? Olszewski and Suchorzewski (1987) and May *et al.* (2000) address this question using actual data from Warsaw, Poland, and simulated data from the UK, respectively. They find that in terms of averaged flow and speed on the network itself, a backward-bending

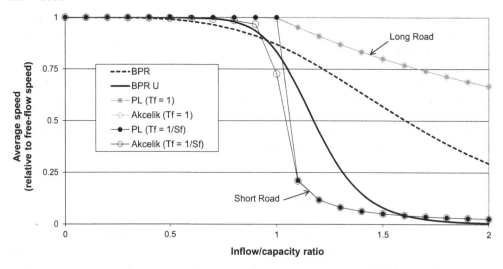

Figure 3.5 Inflow rates and travel times in time-averaged models.

speed–flow relation as depicted in Figure 3.1b still applies, suggesting the existence of hyper-congestion for the area as a whole. But if they account also for queuing times on approaches to the network, they find that trip travel times increase monotonically with demand, yielding average speeds like the curves for a "short road" in Figure 3.5. This could suggest a modeling approach for downtown areas in which flow greater than capacity creates both hypercongestion and bottleneck queuing, an approach developed by Small and Chu (2003) as discussed later.

Research into area-wide models of traffic congestion has received an enormous boost since Geroliminis and Daganzo (2008) presented strong empirical evidence of a backward-bending instantaneous area-wide relation between space-averaged density and flow in the central part of Yokohama, Japan. The relationship is stable in the sense that observations from different days and different times of day appear to represent the same underlying relation. It also has less scatter than relationships discussed earlier, for example, Figure 3.2a. They coined this relationship the *Macroscopic Fundamental Diagram* (MFD).

Figure 3.6 shows this empirical relation for Yokohama and contrasts it with similar relations found from microsimulation models for Nairobi (Gonzales *et al.* 2011) and San Francisco (Geroliminis and Daganzo 2007). All three relations have a hypercongested branch, which however appears more prominent for the simulated data than for the empirical relation.

Under the assumption of travel conditions being spatially uniform within the "reservoir" modeled at any moment in time, and using the identity $V \equiv SD$, the MFD then offers a congestion function applicable for an area-wide dynamic model of congestion. The temporal evolution of the number of vehicles in the reservoir translates into temporal variation of travel speeds. The use of a spatial average traffic density at any given moment of time, resulting in a single speed that applies throughout the area, resembles the Agnew (1976) model, discussed further in Section 3.3.4. However, an important distinction with Agnew's model is that in MFD models, there is no direction of travel, no single point of entry, and no single point of exit. Instead, inflow, internal flow, and outflow interact with each other as areawide averages, hence effectively are treated as though spatially homogeneous.

The MFD has been used to add empirical rigor to a dynamic process known as a *bathtub model*. This model was introduced by Vickrey in a widely circulated but only posthumously

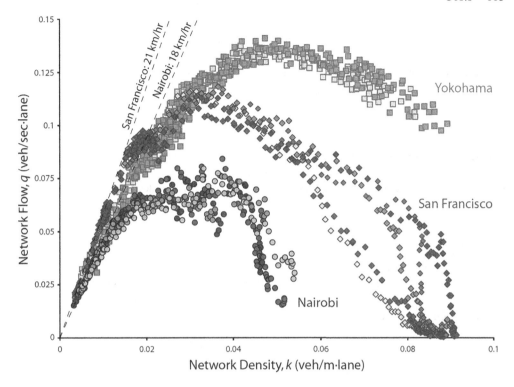

Figure 3.6 MFDs for the cities of Yokohama (empirical), San Francisco (simulated) and Nairobi (simulated). *Source*: Gonzales *et al.* (2011). MFD = Macroscopic Fundamental Diagram.

published paper (Vickrey 2019), and the model now is typically combined with the MFD.[21] The idea is that water flowing into and out of a bathtub corresponds to the in- and outflow of vehicles to an area; while the level of water in the tub at any given moment corresponds to traffic density. (The area modeled is sometimes referred to as a "reservoir.") Like water in a bathtub, traffic density can be treated as spatially homogeneous, even while its level is dynamically evolving. We will refer to these dynamic isotropic models as bathtub models and reserve the term MFD as referring exclusively to the associated area-wide fundamental diagram. We acknowledge that in the traffic engineering literature, the term (dynamic) MFD model is also often used for a bathtub model.

In its bare essence, the dynamic bathtub congestion technology for a single reservoir can be represented by the differential equation

$$\dot{D}(t) = V_i(t) - V_o(t) \tag{3.9}$$

where $D(t)$ is the number of vehicles in the reservoir at time t, the dot above it denotes a time derivative, $V_i(t)$ is the inflow rate to the reservoir, and $V_o(t)$ is the outflow rate. Because the size of the reservoir can be normalized, $D(t)$ can also denote the density of vehicles.

Two types of models have been proposed to describe the outflow: accumulation-based models and trip-based models.

3.3.3.1   Accumulation-based bathtub models

Accumulation-based bathtub models treat outflow from the reservoir as determined by the MFD function itself: instantaneous traffic conditions in the reservoir determine the instantaneous outflow through a so-called Network Exit Function $v_o(t)$ of density:

$$V_o(t) = v_o(D(t))$$

This modeling approach has a simple dynamic structure and is generally believed to perform reasonably well when traffic conditions evolve only slowly over time. However, it has the unsettling feature of being free of memory: because outflow is anonymous, the time at which a given driver leaves the reservoir bears no relationship to that driver's desired trip length. For this reason, Arnott and Buli (2018) call such models "improper" bathtub models.

3.3.3.2   Trip-based bathtub models

Trip-based bathtub models, which Arnott and Buli (2018) call "proper" bathtub models, avoid the disadvantage just mentioned by tracking the progress of individual travelers. A traveler k with a trip of length L_k who enters the reservoir at time t_i^k exits it at time t_o^k, where t_o^k is determined implicitly by the equation

$$\int_{t_i^k}^{t_o^k} S(D(z))\, dz = L_k$$

where $S(D(z))$ is the instantaneous speed of travel at time z during the trip, as determined by the MFD. The outflow rate $V_o(t)$ is then determined by the sum or integral of all travelers for whom $t_o^k = t$. The trip-based specification allows trip length to depend on the user – indeed, heterogeneous trip lengths may be required for an equilibrium to exist. Although conceptually more attractive than accumulation-based models, trip-based models are intractable analytically. Arnott and co-authors in several papers have attempted to overcome this limitation, with only partial success (Arnott 2013; Arnott *et al.* 2016, 2018).

Since the earlier contributions, a robust literature has emerged, reviewed by Mariotte *et al.* (2017) and Johari *et al.* (2021). One important extension includes the development of multi-reservoir models, which allow for spatial variation in traffic conditions (*e.g.*, Geroliminis and Daganzo 2007). Another extension admits multiple modes of travel (*e.g.*, Zheng and Geroliminis 2013).

The assumption of spatial homogeneity of traffic conditions in these models may appear to be a reasonable simplifying approximation, but it comes at a significant price: namely, the need for auxiliary assumptions in order to find an equilibrium or to verify that one exists. For example, for the improper bathtub model presented in Arnott (2013), equilibrium can exist only if trip lengths have a negative exponential distribution and travelers do not know their trip distances in advance. For a proper bathtub model such as that in Fosgerau (2015), equilibrium requires assumptions regarding heterogeneity of trip lengths and also a specific temporal sorting of travelers. For the homogeneous-preferences model, this sorting takes the form of "regular" sorting, where for any pair of travelers the one who entered earlier should also be the one exiting later. In both cases, the need for such assumptions seems closely connected with the property that the speed of each driver is determined solely by the total number of drivers in the reservoir. Thus, a driver who enters immediately reduces the speed of every other driver, regardless of when they entered and whether they are located nearby or far away. This symmetry is unrealistic, the more so the greater the spatial asymmetry of actual traffic flows. For example, if flow is predominately inbound to a city center during a morning peak, adding a car in the inbound direction will in reality have a bigger impact on congestion than adding one in the reverse direction; and the added car will have different effects on vehicles depending on how far in their trips they have already progressed.

The analyst should thus trade off the benefits of using an area-wide, isotropic model against such limitations when deciding which model to use. The analytics of bathtub models are cumbersome even with the assumption of spatial homogeneity. Single-reservoir models are particularly ill-suited for assessing link-specific policy interventions such as cordon tolls or capacity increases, since spatial asymmetries and network interactions are inherent in such situations. In contrast, MFD and bathtub models may be suitable for understanding how dynamic patterns of congestion respond to area-wide policies and other shocks with only modest spatial variation, especially when such policies or shocks vary sharply over time, and especially when it is important to track dynamic responses to changes in area-wide conditions. Examples could be generic policies that stagger working hours or that create greater flexibility to work from home.

Thus, it seems safe to predict that MFD and bathtub models will remain an important and fertile field for advances in congestion modeling in conjunction with other types of models. We now continue with other dynamic congestion models, diving deeper into matters of endogenous scheduling and dynamic equilibrium.

3.3.4 Dynamic congestion models

3.3.4.1 Queuing at a bottleneck

Although some of the time-averaged models discussed in Section 3.3.2 implicitly or explicitly incorporate queuing, they take demanded flow as given and as constant over the period of interest. A dynamic formulation with endogenous scheduling and queuing behind a bottleneck can deal better with extreme congestion and with policies to address it. The workhorse model in economics that takes this approach is Vickrey's (1969) celebrated bottleneck model, which considers dynamic equilibrium queuing at a single bottleneck.

We begin with the simple case of exogenous departure times. Let $V_a(t)$ be the flow of traffic arriving at time t at a point bottleneck of capacity V_K, or at the queue behind it if there is one. Let $V_b(t)$ be the flow exiting the bottleneck. Flows V_a and V_b are often called "arrivals" and "departures" (at and from the queue), respectively, in the queuing literature; but *vice versa* in the bottleneck congestion literature, where V_a is often referred to as "departures from home" and V_b as "arrivals at work" (both on the assumption that travel times upstream and downstream of the bottleneck are zero). To avoid confusion, we call V_a *queue-entries* and V_b *queue-exits* – even when the queue is of zero length.

Let $N(t)$ be the number of vehicles stored in the queue at time t. It is common to ignore the physical length of highway required to store them or, equivalently, to consider the queue to be "vertical" rather than horizontal. Suppose any reduction of speed from congestion other than queueing can be ignored. Then, the following kinked performance function relates queue-exits to queue-entries:

$$V_b(t) = \begin{cases} V_a(t) & \text{if } V_a(t) \leq V_K \text{ and } N(t) = 0 \\ V_K & \text{otherwise} \end{cases} \tag{3.10}$$

The number of vehicles N in the queue, if any, evolves according to the difference between inflow and outflow:

$$\dot{N}(t) = V_a(t) - V_b(t) \qquad (3.11)$$

where the dot again denotes a time derivative (possibly one-sided). This simply expresses the conservation of vehicles, similarly to (3.9).

Consider the typical case where the entry rate starts low, builds, and then decreases, always remaining finite. Let t_q be the time when $V_a(t)$ first equals capacity V_K. Then, $N(t) = 0$ for $t \leq t_q$ and has a right derivative at t_q given by $V_a(t_q) - V_K$; the queue builds, then shrinks, changing at rate $V_a(t) - V_K$ until it finally disperses at some time t_q' defined by

$$N(t_{q'}) \equiv \int_{t_q}^{t_{q'}} (V_a(t) - V_K)\, dt = 0$$

With a first-in, first-out queuing discipline, each vehicle entering the queue at time t must wait for $N(t)$ vehicles to pass through the bottleneck before it can pass through. This causes a *queuing delay* T_D which, for a driver entering the queue at t, is equal to

$$T_D(t) = \frac{N(t)}{V_K} = \int_{t_q}^{t} \left(\frac{V_a(z)}{V_K} - 1 \right) dz, \quad t_q \leq t \leq t_q' \qquad (3.12)$$

where z is a variable of integration. Because we are ignoring other sources of delays, we also refer to T_D as *travel-time delay* or simply *travel delay*.

An example, taken from Newell (1987), is shown in Figure 3.7. The two curves show cumulative queue-entries and queue-exits as functions of time, so that their slopes represent entry and exit flows V_a and V_b. When V_a exceeds V_K, a queue develops, and $N(t)$ can be found as the vertical distance between cumulative entries and exits. The queuing delay $T_D(t)$, for the driver entering the queue at t, is given by the horizontal difference between cumulative entries and exits.

Now let us reconsider the special case of a fixed peak period for input flows, with incoming traffic constant at V_a during the time interval $[t_p, t_{p'}]$ and zero outside it: that is, the case underlying the piecewise-linear time-averaged congestion function discussed in Section 3.3.2. If a queue forms, it begins at time $t_q = t_p$. The above equations then yield the following queuing delay, for $t \in [t_p, t_{p'}]$:

$$T_D(t) = \begin{cases} 0 & \text{if } V_a \leq V_K \\ [(V_a / V_K) - 1] \cdot (t - t_p) & \text{if } V_a > V_K \end{cases} \qquad (3.13)$$

The average travel delay is

$$\bar{T}_D = \frac{1}{(t_{p'} - t_p)} \int_{t_p}^{t_{p'}} T_D(t)\, dt$$

Adding a free-flow travel time T_f per unit distance for the journey yields equation (3.7) for $P = (t_{p'} - t_p)$. Note that the period of outflows lasts longer than the period of inflows P, extending from t_p to $t_p + P \cdot (V_a / V_K)$. Also note that each successive traveler suffers a longer queueing delay

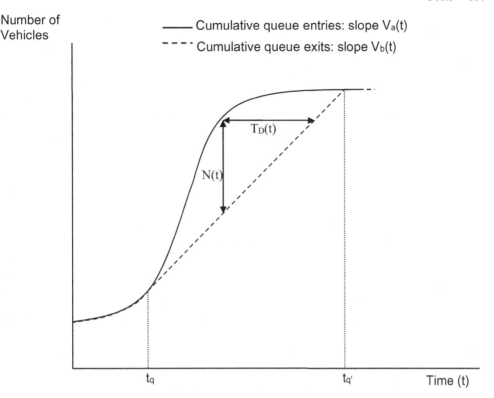

Number of
Vehicles

—— Cumulative queue entries: slope $V_a(t)$

---- Cumulative queue exits: slope $V_b(t)$

$T_D(t)$

$N(t)$

t_q $t_{q'}$ Time (t)

Figure 3.7 Deterministic queuing.

and higher trip cost than any previous traveler. (This apparent disequilibrium property will disappear when endogenous scheduling is introduced in Section 3.4.3.)

We shall refer to this congestion technology, where travel delays result exclusively from
vertical queuing at a bottleneck, as *pure* bottleneck congestion. Its consequences for equilibrium
queues and optimal pricing are considered in Section 3.4 and Chapter 4.

3.3.4.2 *Analysis of shock waves*

It is possible to undertake economic analysis of congestion using more sophisticated dynamic
models. We provide here a brief survey, based in part on Lindsey and Verhoef (2000).

A classic dynamic model is the *hydrodynamic* or *kinematic* model, developed by Lighthill
and Whitham (1955) and Richards (1956) and therefore known as the LWR model; see Daganzo (1997) for a review. It is a *continuum* model in that traffic characteristics V, D, and S are
assumed to be continuous functions of location x and time t, in a manner similar to models of
fluids (*i.e.*, liquids and gases). The model features three essential assumptions. First, a relationship $S(D)$ holds between speed and density, as shown in Figure 3.1a, also under non-stationary
conditions. Second, identity (3.5) holds everywhere, thus defining functions $V(D)$ and $V(S)$.
And third, vehicles are neither created nor destroyed along the road, resulting in the following
conservation or *continuity equation*:[22]

$$\frac{\partial V(t,x)}{\partial x} + \frac{\partial D(t,x)}{\partial t} = 0 \tag{3.14}$$

The resulting dynamics can be described in terms of *shock waves*, which are disturbances to traffic caused by traffic lights, accidents, lane reductions, or other discrete variations. Specifically, a shock wave is the moving boundary between two stationary states; that is, it is the moving point at which vehicles leave one state and enter another. Consider a discrete example, with an upstream steady state with $V_u = S_u \cdot D_u$, and a downstream steady state with $V_d = S_d \cdot D_d$. The location dividing these two states will propagate along the highway at some wave speed S_w, the value of which is to be determined. Upstream traffic catches up with the boundary at relative speed $S_u - S_w$, and hence enters the shock wave at rate $D_u \cdot (S_u - S_w)$. Similarly, downstream traffic leaves the boundary at relative speed $S_d - S_w$, and hence exits the wave at rate $D_d \cdot (S_d - S_w)$. Conservation of vehicles requires these rates to be equal, implying

$$S_w = \frac{V_u - V_d}{D_u - D_d} \tag{3.15}$$

It can be shown that a forward-moving shock wave can never travel faster than the traffic that carries it, provided the function $V(D)$ is concave and crosses the origin.[23]

Finding a solution for the LWR model is tedious when traffic inflow varies continuously over time (Newell 1988). Therefore, a number of simplified models have been formulated. Indeed, the model of pure bottleneck congestion can be regarded as one of these, in which the shock wave, defined as the back of the queue, travels at speed $S_w = 0$ (since the queue is assumed to have no spatial extent). Equivalently, according to (3.15), the queue density D_d in the pure bottleneck model is infinite.

Agnew (1977) and Mahmassani and Herman (1984) propose a simplification involving *instantaneous propagation*, by which changes in a road's inflow rate V_i immediately affect its outflow rate V_o. With N denoting the number of vehicles on a finite stretch of road, Agnew's model is summarized by the differential equation of state:

$$\dot{N} = V_i - V_o(N) \tag{3.16}$$

where the function $V_o(N)$ has the same general shape as $V(D)$ in Figure 3.1c. This model is usually interpreted as implying that density is uniform along the entire road at every instant, so that shock waves propagate at an infinite speed. This has the unrealistic implication that drivers adjust speeds in response to changes in traffic conditions (far) upstream.

Note that differential equation (3.16) is isomorphic to equation (3.9) of the MFD model. The assumption of traffic conditions that are uniform over space at all instants indeed creates strong conceptual and analytical similarities between the Agnew model, on the one hand, and bathtub or MFD models, on the other. The main difference is that the Agnew model considers a single road that all users traverse in its entirety, whereas bathtub and MFD models describe urban networks or areas and make various assumptions on the distances traveled by users.

A different simplification, by Henderson (1974) and Chu (1995), adopts the opposite assumption of *no propagation*: a vehicle's speed – assumed constant during the trip – is determined as a function only of the flow at one point in space and time. That point is either where the vehicle enters (Henderson) or where it exits (Chu) the road. This formulation therefore does not consider possible interactions between adjacent vehicles that depart at different times, despite the fact that the distance between them may be changing during the trip because they travel at different speeds. Hence, there is no propagation of shock waves.

Mun (2002) uses the LWR model to examine the total travel time for traffic entering an otherwise uniform road with a bottleneck at its exit. That is, the exit has a lower capacity than the rest of the road and therefore a different speed–density function $S(D)$. When traffic exceeds the bottleneck capacity, a "horizontal" queue builds up, which occupies an endogenous and time-varying part of the road's length at the downstream end and exits the bottleneck at a rate equal to bottleneck capacity. Mun assumes that traffic in the queue travels at the hypercongested speed, with flow equal to the bottleneck's capacity. Given an exogenous inflow rate $V_a(t)$ upstream of the bottleneck, volumes and densities can then be found both upstream of the queue and within it; (3.15) determines the rate at which the back of the queue moves, allowing one to compute the queue length at every instant of time. Total trip time is the sum of time traversing the distance to the back of the queue (at the speed determined by the speed–density function), plus the time spent in the queue itself. The model reduces to the Henderson model when inflow never exceeds the bottleneck's capacity, and to the deterministic queuing model of (3.12) – augmented by a constant free-flow travel time over the entire length of the road – when the upstream section has sufficient capacity so that its speed–flow curve can be approximated by a constant free-flow speed.

3.3.4.3 Car-following models

Another approach is to allow for continuous-time and continuous-space traffic dynamics, like LWR, but to treat traffic itself as consisting of discrete vehicles whose behavior is specified. A car-following equation stipulates how the motion of vehicle $n+1$ (the "follower") depends on the motion of vehicle n (the "leader"). The dependent variable is usually acceleration, and it depends on the distance between the leader and follower and on their speed difference, as in the General Motors model described by May (1990):

$$\ddot{x}_{n+1}(t+\delta) = \frac{a \cdot \left[\dot{x}_{n+1}(t+\delta) \right]^m}{\left[x_n(t) - x_{n+1}(t) \right]^l} \cdot \left[\dot{x}_n(t) - \dot{x}_{n+1}(t) \right] \tag{3.17}$$

where x denotes location, $\dot{x}$ is speed, $\ddot{x}$ is acceleration, δ is a reaction time, and a, l, and m are non-negative parameters.

Under stationary traffic conditions, car-following models imply a relationship between speed and density (the inverse of vehicle spacing) that is consistent with the relationships considered above. As also illustrated by Leclercq (2007), car-following and kinematic models therefore converge to the same equilibria if appropriately specified. For example, May (1990) shows that if $m = 0$ and $l = 1$, integrating (3.17) over t yields

$$\dot{x}_{n+1} = a \cdot \log(x_n - x_{n+1}) + C_0$$

with C_0 denoting a constant of integration. Equivalently,

$$S = a \cdot \log\left(D_j / D \right) \tag{3.18}$$

where speed $S \equiv \dot{x}_{n+1}$, density $D \equiv 1/(x_n - x_{n+1})$ (the inverse of vehicle spacing), and $D_j \equiv \exp(C_0/a)$ is the jam density, at which $S = 0$. This equation reproduces a speed–density relationship that was proposed by Greenberg (1959); it suffers from the disadvantage that free-flow speed is infinite which makes it problematic for analyzing light traffic conditions. Other parameter values for (3.17) have been found to correspond to other macroscopic models (Hall and Hall 1990).

Verhoef (2001, 2003) proposes a simpler car-following model which is even more obviously a dynamic extension of a steady-state model. He postulates a desired speed $S(D)$, with density D measured as the inverse of the distance from the leader. With S non-decreasing in D, the

driver adjusts in continuous time by speeding up or slowing down as desired. This model reproduces the basic behavioral assumption in the more complex model of (3.17), namely, that driver
$n+1$ accelerates when driving more slowly than driver n. Verhoef finds the model to be quite
tractable and useful for examining the stability of steady-state equilibria under conditions of
hypercongestion.

Surprisingly, economists have rarely considered the behavioral motivations behind the relationship between density and speed, which in most congestion models is treated as though it
were a physical law. But it really is a behavioral law. If high density causes traffic to slow down,
this must somehow reflect decisions by individual drivers, presumably decisions that trade off
speed against safety as proposed by Rotemberg (1985) and Steimetz (2008). Verhoef and Rouwendal (2004) show that such a model can indeed produce a locus of equilibrium outcomes in
the form of a backward-bending speed–flow relation, just like the one in Figure 3.1b. Furthermore, this economic trade-off produces an unexpected insight: economic efficiency (taking into
account drivers' own evaluations of accident costs) could be improved by inducing drivers to
simultaneously go faster than the equilibrium level. This is because an individual driver ignores
the effect of their own choice of vehicle speed on both the density and traffic speed encountered
by other drivers. These two considerations work in the same direction: for a given flow, an increase in speed implies a decrease in density, as shown by (3.5), which, in turn, reduces accident
risks for other drivers. However, the severity of accidents increases with speed, which partially
offsets this effect. We return to accident costs later in this chapter and in Chapter 7, where we
consider the implications of vehicle sizes on accident severity.

3.3.5   *Congestion modeling: a conclusion*

Our review reveals a varied menu of approaches to modeling congestion, which by no means
exhausts the list of phenomena found through other models.[24] Most economic analysis has used
just two of these: the static speed–flow curve and the dynamic deterministic bottleneck model.
Furthermore, researchers have barely begun to describe the behavior that underlies congestion
technology or to identify externalities in that behavior.

As always, researchers face a difficult tradeoff between tractability and realism. Traditionally,
economics has concentrated on tractability and engineering on realism. One of the strengths of
transportation studies is that it has often proven possible to have both, thanks to collaboration
across the two fields of study. Additional examples will be encountered later as we discuss dynamic congestion tolls and the policy implications of hypercongestion.

3.4   Highway travel: short-run costs and equilibrium

The congestion models we have described can be used to formulate cost functions for highway
travel. This section deals with short-run models, which we define as describing a highway with
fixed capacity. (Certain other types of capital, such as vehicles and parking facilities, may still
be assumed to be variable.) Section 3.5 considers long-run cost functions.

In order to simplify the exposition, we assume that everyone has the same value of time,
denoted here by α. The average cost c on a defined length of road then consists of monetary
expenses c_{00} (such as fuel consumption and maintenance), the cost of free-flow travel time $\alpha \cdot T_f$,
the cost of travel delays $\alpha \cdot (T - T_f)$, and, in some models, the cost of undesirable schedules c_s
(to be defined). The first two cost components make up the travel cost in absence of congestion,
c_0; the latter two give the congestion-related cost c_g. Thus,

$$c = c_0 + c_g = \left[c_{00} + \alpha \cdot T_f \right] + \left[\alpha \cdot \left(T - T_f \right) + c_s \right] \tag{3.19}$$

For simplicity, any dependence of money costs on congestion is ignored.

We assume that average cost c is borne entirely by the user; it is sometimes called the *generalized cost* because it indicates the monetary value of the resources supplied by an individual taking a trip. The related concept of generalized price, introduced in Section 2.3.3, adds to c any applicable tolls and taxes – which are from the conventional economic viewpoint transfers, not social costs. We denote generalized price by p.[25]

3.4.1 *Stationary-state congestion on a homogeneous road*

We begin with stationary-state congestion on a single homogeneous road with identical users. Simple as this setup may seem, the resulting model has proven capable of creating great confusion. We therefore provide a detailed discussion.

We define a stationary state as a situation where traffic flow V is constant over time and space and is equal to the rates at which trips start and end. Thus, in principle, the situation could last indefinitely. In reality, of course, traffic congestion undergoes rapid changes; stationary-state models abstract from such changes, and for this reason, their practical usefulness is limited. Their advantage is that they are relatively simple.

The key simplification is to recognize that with V constant and equal to the inflow and outflow rates, it can represent both the per-unit-of-time quantity demanded (by users) and the per-unit-of-time quantity supplied (according to the congestion technology) at a given average cost c. Following Walters (1961), the situation might be pictured as resulting from the interaction of a demand curve $V = V_d(c)$ or its inverse, $d(V)$, and a supply curve $c(V)$. When congestion is described by a speed–flow function $S(V)$ on a road of length L, and there are no scheduling costs, this supply curve takes the form

$$c = c(V) = c_{00} + \alpha \ T(V) = c_{00} + \alpha \ L / S(V) \tag{3.20}$$

So long as we stay on the normally congested portion of $S(V)$, this supply curve is rising and leads to conventional equilibrium results. We will need to keep in mind, however, that although the user is assumed to be a price-taker, and thus to perceive c as both average and marginal private cost, marginal social cost will be different from c unless $c(V)$ is constant. This is because $c(V)$ incorporates a *technological externality*: a direct technological dependence of one person's average travel cost on the travel decisions of others. The consequences of this are described in the pricing analysis of the next chapter.

When examining the hypercongested portion of $S(V)$, we run into trouble with Walters' interpretation. For one thing, the existence of hypercongestion implies that the average cost depicted by (3.20) is not single-valued – in fact, it does not fit the formal definition of a cost function, which is the *minimum* cost of producing a given output. Furthermore, when we confront it with the inverse demand function $d(V)$, as in Figure 3.8, we can get as many as three different candidate equilibria, whose properties have engendered considerable controversy (Verhoef 1999; Small and Chu 2003). The normally congested equilibrium, denoted x in the figure, resembles a standard economic market equilibrium with downward-sloping demand and upward-sloping supply. But for the two hypercongested equilibria, y and z, the "supply curve" slopes downward. Intuition warns that there is something peculiar here. How should a situation be interpreted where an increase in traffic inflow produces faster travel and thus a lower average cost? Is such a relationship really a supply curve?

Conventional stability analysis of the candidate equilibria is inconclusive: x is stable for both price and flow perturbations, y for flow perturbations only, and z for price perturbations

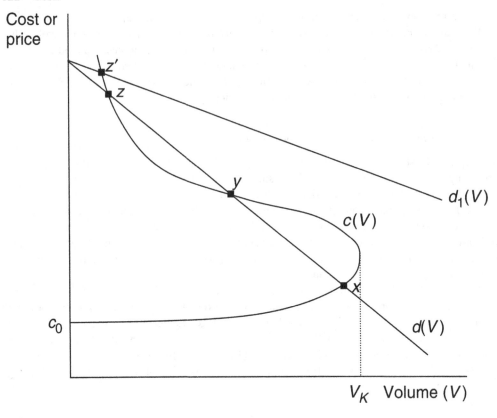

Figure 3.8 The conventional stationary-state average cost curve.

only.[26] Thus, whichever type of perturbation is taken as the criterion for stability in a conventional analysis, the model produces two candidate equilibria in the case of the demand curve shown. If we insist that an equilibrium should be stable against both types of perturbations, both hypercongested candidate equilibria would be rejected; but then we must acknowledge that for a higher demand curve like $d_1(V)$, there is no stable equilibrium.

One difficulty with conventional stability analysis is that the quantity perturbations considered involve simultaneous changes in the flow rates *into* and *along* the road, which is physically impossible. It therefore seems more appropriate to consider perturbations of the inflow rate, treating flow levels along the road as endogenous. Doing so introduces the concept of dynamic stability: can a given stationary state arise as the end state following some transitional phase initiated by a change in the inflow rate?

Verhoef (2001) examines dynamic stability using the car-following model in Section 3.3.4, allowing for vertical queuing before the entrance when inflows cannot be physically accommodated on the road. He finds that the entire hypercongested branch of the $c(V)$ curve in Figure 3.8 is dynamically unstable.[27] The locus of dynamically stable stationary states turns out to be the curve shown as $c_{stat}(k)$ in Figure 3.9; it follows the normally congested part of $c(V)$ and rises vertically once volume reaches capacity, just as with deterministic queuing. This generates a new stationary state, x', which is dynamically stable. This state involves a maximum flow on the road, a constant-length queue before its entrance with cost c_q', and rates of queue-entries and queue-exits both equal to the capacity of the road. It does not involve hypercongestion on

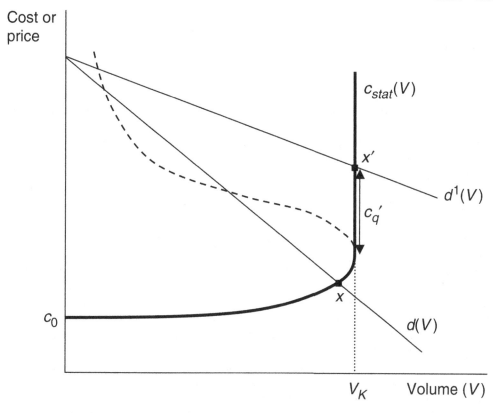

Figure 3.9 Stability of stationary-state equilibria and the stationary-state average cost function.

the single road itself. However, hypercongestion does exist within the entrance queue when it is modeled horizontally (taking up space), rather than vertically (spaceless). Verhoef (2003) shows this in a serial-links extension of the same car-following model, an extension in which drivers obey the same car-following equation but the upstream link has double the capacity of the downstream link. Provided the dynamic equilibrium lasts sufficiently long, a hypercongested queue then arises on this upstream link as a stable equilibrium phenomenon, while flow at the downstream link remains normally congested and approaches the maximum flow, as does the single road in Verhoef (2001). This result is consistent with the terminology of Figure 3.4, as well as with empirical observations by Daganzo, Cassidy and Bertini (1999) who state that "evidence suggests that downstream bottlenecks cause these transitions [to hypercongested speeds] in a predictable way" (p. 365). It also seems consistent with findings by Arnott and Inci (2010), who also find that hypercongestion can be a stable equilibrium outcome in urban traffic (corresponding to the upstream link), if there is limited parking capacity (corresponding to the downstream link).

Note that the flow rate and speed inside the queue are irrelevant to total trip time. This makes the economic properties of the model independent of the shape of the hypercongested portion of the speed–flow curve, even though traffic in the queue travels at a hypercongested speed.

Thus, when upstream queuing is possible, the true supply curve for stationary-state traffic, $c_{stat}(V)$, is rising everywhere and intersects any downward-sloping demand curve exactly once.

It has two distinct regimes, one of them vertical; but it is smooth and may sometimes be approximated by a power function like (3.6) (which we originally described as a time-averaged relationship):

$$c(V) = c_{00} + \alpha T_f \cdot \left[1 + a \cdot \left(V / V_K \right)^b \right]$$

(3.21)

There seems to be broad consensus on the empirical relevance of hypercongestion and on its likely occurrence in queued traffic upstream of bottlenecks, although McDonald *et al.* (1999) claim to observe sustained hypercongestion even in the absence of a downstream bottleneck. Our views on the dynamic instability of hypercongestion for a single, uniform-capacity road, however, are not undisputed. Indeed, alternative solutions to the questions raised by the conventional diagram of Figure 3.8 have been proposed. Else (1981), Hills (1993), and Ohta (2001) try to solve the problem by using traffic density, number of travelers on the road, or the total number of trips (not expressed per unit of time) as the relevant argument in static inverse demand and average cost functions. In our view, these non-flow-based quantities do not give a meaningful economic measure of aggregate stationary-state output. The total number of trips is not even defined until a time period for measurement is specified – in which case the measure becomes flow-based after all. As for traffic density, it is an aggregate measure of the proportion of road space occupied at a given point in time, not of the number of trips taken over an interval of time. A demand function defined over density would therefore assume that the good demanded is not the completion of trips, but rather the occupation of road space. (Try telling that to your average harried commuter!) We conclude that traffic flow is the appropriate output measure for stationary-state analyses, while the total number of trips is appropriate for time-averaged or dynamic models that specify, possibly endogenously, an applicable time period.

For dynamic network models, the possible occurrence of hypercongestion as an equilibrium phenomenon appears to be beyond dispute. It occurs, for example, where roads merge and where lanes are reduced (such as at bridges and tunnels). These are examples where heavy traffic creates attempted inflow into a link that exceeds its capacity, inevitably causing queuing upstream that would then take place under hypercongested conditions. The bathtub and MFD models discussed in Section 3.3.3 capture this by using empirical speed–flow relations that reflect such hypercongestion, and thus provide models that can, in principle, deal with such situations. However, such treatment of hypercongestion is highly stylized and reduced form in nature due to the absence of space in these models, with no consideration to the direction of traffic movements or to the locations of entry and exit points. Just as for single-link models, an important question is under what conditions can the hypercongested segment of an MFD be reached via a dynamic path of aggregate trip departures or attempted inflows? Such an analysis may well reveal that the observed hypercongestion over an area actually occurs because of spatial heterogeneity, which is assumed away in the MFD model. Whether such an inconsistency would lead to biased policy recommendations is an interesting and important question for further research.

3.4.2   *Time-averaged models*

Cost models using the time-averaged congestion functions described earlier avoid problems of hypercongestion. They can accommodate temporary inflows greater than capacity, yet are single-valued and look much like the cost function of Figure 3.9. For fixed time period P, the time-averaged inflow volume V has a simple interpretation as quantity demanded: namely, it is the number of trips divided by the constant P.

Figure 3.10 compares the cost functions derived from two different time-averaged speed–flow relationships, (3.7) and (3.8). The stationary-state average cost function $c_{stat}(V)$ of Figure 3.9 is shown for comparison. Both of the time-averaged functions become steeper for higher P; and both functions approach a vertical line at V_K as $P \to \infty$. This increasing similarity between time-averaged cost functions and the stationary-state function, as the time period becomes indefinitely large, makes intuitive sense. Yet the correspondence is imperfect in both cases: at flows below capacity, the piecewise-linear function allows for no congestion, while the Akçelik function c_{AK} may allow for too much since, for high enough values of P, it will cross the c_{stqt} curve and exhibit arbitrarily high travel times even when $V < V_K$.

Furthermore, the time-averaged static models have some inherent weaknesses. First, it is not clear how to measure P from observed traffic patterns, which fail to adhere to the assumption of a constant flow occurring only over a well-defined period.[28] Second, P is set exogenously in the model, but in reality, it will vary with traffic conditions and policies. Third, the assumed exogenous inflow rate is unlikely to be consistent with any rational demand behavior. All three problems are solved by formulating dynamic models that endogenize departure times. We turn to such models in the next subsection.

3.4.3   Dynamic models with endogenous scheduling

The dynamic congestion technologies discussed in Section 3.3 allow construction of dynamic equilibrium models, in which departure times (and therefore peak duration) are endogenous and travel delays vary continuously over time. A common assumption in such models is that travelers

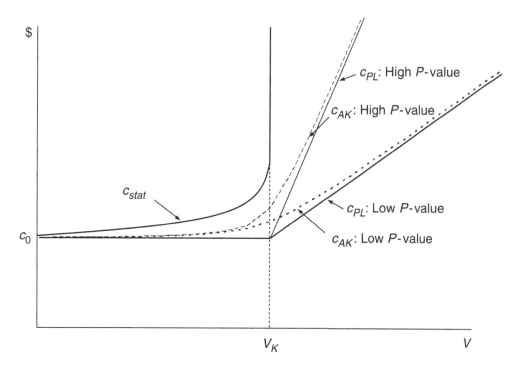

Figure 3.10 Short-run variable cost in stationary-state model (c_{stat}) and two time-averaged models: piecewise linear (c_{PL}) and Akçelik (c_{AK}).

choose an optimal schedule for their trip by trading off travel-time cost against schedule-delay cost, as in the demand model of Section 2.3.2. Average cost, as defined in (3.19), then includes a part c_S due to schedule delay. It could also include a part due to unreliability, due, for example, to incidents as in Fosgerau and Lindsey (2013).

We treat here the case where scheduling costs arise from deviations between an individual's actual and desired arrival time at work, following the notation of equation (2.64) with $\theta = 0$. (This case applies best to the morning peak period; modeling the afternoon peak would presumably require assuming a desired departure time from work – a case that has received far less analysis.) Recall that the per-minute costs of early and late arrival are β and γ, respectively. Then, the travel cost for an individual departing from home at time t is

$$c(t) = c_{00} + \alpha \cdot T(t) + c_S(t); \qquad c_S(t) = \begin{cases} \beta \cdot \big(t_d - t - T(t)\big) & \text{if } t + T(t) \leq t_d \\ \gamma \cdot \big(t + T(t) - t_d\big) & \text{if } t + T(t) > t_d \end{cases} \qquad (3.22)$$

where t_d is the desired arrival time at work and $T(t)$ the travel time incurred when departing at t. Of course, $T(t)$ and therefore $c(t)$ depend also on capacity and perhaps on past, current, or even future traffic levels (the latter possibility arising with instantaneous propagation).

We take the simplest dynamic congestion technology discussed in Section 3.3.3, namely, pure bottleneck congestion, where congestion occurs solely through vertical queuing behind a bottleneck. It is convenient to assume one traveler per vehicle. Also for convenience, and without loss of generality when there is no route choice, we set free-flow travel time T_f to zero. Then, $T(t)$ is equal to the travel delay $T_D(t)$ defined in (3.13), except that now the time t_p when congestion begins is endogenous; we denote it by t_q.

Because desired schedules are defined in terms of arrival time at work, it is convenient to focus on the time t' when a traveler exits the queue. Given that $T_f = 0$, this is also that traveler's arrival time at work. If there were no congestion, the rate at which travelers depart from the queue would be simply the distribution of desired work arrival times, which we denote by $V_d(t')$. We can now work backward to find the equilibrium queue-entry rate $V_a(t)$ (i.e., the rate of arrivals at the vertical queue) that is consistent with travelers' uncoordinated scheduling decisions. (Given zero free-flow time, $V_a(t)$ is also the rate of departures from home.)

If $V_d(t') \leq V_K$ for all t', there is no queuing or schedule delay, and the entry and exit rates are both equal to the desired rate: $V_a(t) = V_d(t') = V_b(t)$ for $t = t'$. If capacity is insufficient, however, travelers must trade off queuing delay against schedule delay in choosing their queue-entry times; in equilibrium, this implies some queue-entry time pattern $V_a(t)$, for which no traveler has an incentive to reschedule the trip. The resulting equilibrium can be quite complex.[29] However, the following special case, first analyzed by Vickrey (1969, 1973) and further elaborated by Fargier (1983), is tractable and leads to surprisingly elegant and insightful results.

Suppose, then, that $V_d(t)$ is constant at V_d during the interval $[t_p, t_{p'}]$ and zero outside that interval. Hence there is a total of $Q \equiv q \cdot V_d$ travelers when demand is inelastic, where $q = t_{p'} - t_p$ denotes how long the peak period would last if capacity were unrestricted. Assume $\beta < \alpha$, which is supported by the empirical evidence of Section 2.3.2, and which is necessary to achieve an equilibrium without mass departures at a single instant in time. (This assumption is satisfied if, as seems plausible, commuters prefer to spend early time at the workplace, rather than staying somewhat longer in their parked or cruising vehicle.) Consider the case $V_d > V_K$, so that the desired exit rate cannot be achieved and thus queuing and/or schedule delay must occur. Our analysis follows the logic and much of the notation of Arnott et al. (1990).[30]

For a commuter exiting the queue before the desired time t_p equilibrium requires that the chosen queue-entry time minimizes the combined costs for early exits in the upper line of (3.22). This requires that $T_D(t)$ change at rate $\beta/(\alpha - \beta)$ so long as anyone entering the queue at time t is exiting early. Similarly, so long as anyone entering at t is exiting late, the lower line of (3.22) must be minimized, so $T_D(t)$ must change at rate $-\gamma/(\alpha+\gamma)$.[31] The first and last commuters exiting must face a zero queue length in equilibrium because otherwise a discretely lower travel cost could be realized by departing just before t_q or after $t_{q'}$.

Comparing these equilibrium rates of change in T_D to that implied by equation (3.13), namely $[(V/V_K) - 1]$, we see that vehicles must be entering the queue at rates

$$V_a^{early} = V_K \cdot \frac{\alpha}{\alpha - \beta}; \quad V_a^{late} = V_K \cdot \frac{\alpha}{\alpha + \gamma} \qquad (3.23)$$

during the early and late parts of the peak period, respectively. Both rates are constant and positive; the first being above capacity when $0 < \beta < \alpha$, and the second being below capacity. The resulting pattern is shown in Figure 3.11, in which $N(t)$ is the number of vehicles in the queue, $\tilde{t}$ is the entry time for the commuter incurring maximum queuing delay T_{Dm}, and this commuter's exit time is

$$t^* \equiv \tilde{t} + T_D(\tilde{t}) \equiv \tilde{t} + T_{DM} \qquad (3.24)$$

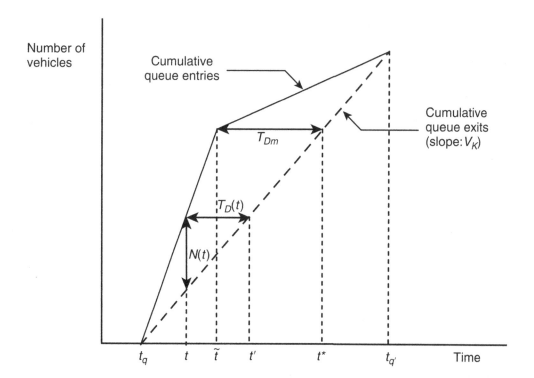

Figure 3.11 Dynamic queuing equilibrium. Adapted from Arnott *et al.* (1990) with permission from Elsevier.

Commuters with $t_d < t^*$ enter the queue before (or possibly at) $\tilde{t}$, and those with $t_d > t^*$ enter after (or possibly at) $\tilde{t}$.[32]

The exit rate is constant at V_K during the interval $[t_q, t_{q'}]$ which, in order to accommodate the total of Q vehicles, must be of duration

$$t_{q'} - t_q = Q / V_K = q \cdot V_d / V_K > q \tag{3.25}$$

This peak travel period thus encompasses but exceeds the desired peak $[t_p, t_{p'}]$, whose duration is q; congestion begins prior to the earliest desired queue-exit and lasts beyond the latest desired queue-exit. Furthermore, the duration of this interval depends inversely on V_K, showing that expanding capacity narrows the peak period – as postulated, for example, by Downs (1962).

In order to solve for the entire equilibrium configuration, define

$$\sigma = \frac{t^* - t_p}{q} = \frac{t^* - t_p}{t_{p'} - t_p} \tag{3.26}$$

as the proportion of commuters who exit the queue before t^* (equivalently, the proportion who enter the queue before $\tilde{t}$). They enter at rate V_a^{early}, so their number must be

$$\sigma \cdot Q = V_a^{early} \cdot \left(\tilde{t} - t_q \right) \tag{3.27}$$

Similarly, the proportion $(1 - \sigma)$ who enter after $\tilde{t}$ do so at rate V_a^{late}, so

$$(1 - \sigma) \cdot Q = V_a^{late} \cdot \left(t_{q'} - \tilde{t} \right) \tag{3.28}$$

Equations (3.23) through (3.28) can be solved for

$$\sigma = \gamma / (\beta + \gamma) \tag{3.29}$$

$$t_q = t_p - \sigma \cdot q \cdot \left[(V_d / V_K) - 1 \right] \tag{3.30}$$

$$t_{q'} = t_{p'} + (1 - \sigma) \cdot q \cdot \left[(V_d / V_K) - 1 \right] \tag{3.31}$$

$$t^* = t_p + \sigma \cdot q$$

$$\tilde{t} = t_p + \sigma \cdot q - T_{Dm}$$

$$T_{Dm} = \delta \cdot Q / (\alpha \cdot V_K) \tag{3.32}$$

where

$$\delta \equiv \beta \gamma / (\beta + \gamma) = \beta \sigma \tag{3.33}$$

The maximum delay (3.32) corresponds to a maximum travel delay cost $\delta \cdot Q / V_K$.

Figure 3.12 shows how costs vary as a function of exit time. Travel-delay cost per traveler, $c_T(t')$, rises linearly from zero to $\alpha \cdot T_{Dm}$ (reached at time t^*) and falls linearly back to zero. Schedule-delay cost per traveler, $c_s(t')$, falls linearly from a maximum of $\beta \cdot (t_p - t_q)$ for the earliest traveler to zero (at t^*), then rises linearly to a maximum of $\gamma \cdot (t_q' - t_p')$; computing these maxima from

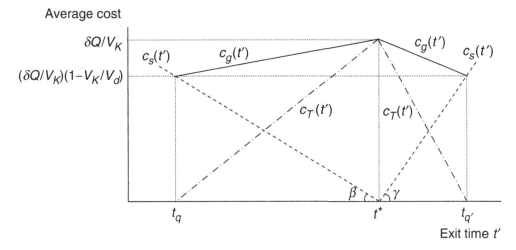

Figure 3.12 Equilibrium average costs of time delay (c_T), schedule delay (c_S), and their sum (c_g), under linear schedule delay cost functions and with a dispersion of desired queue-exit times.

(3.29)–(3.31), we find they are both equal to $(\delta \cdot Q/V_K) \cdot (1 - V_K/V_d)$. Note that their sum $c_g(t')$ need not be constant in equilibrium because each consumer has a different desired schedule t_d.[33]

From the piecewise-linear cost patterns just described, we can easily see that the time-averaged cost components, c_T and c_S, are just half their maximum values. Thus time-averaged travel delay cost per traveler is

$$\bar{c}_T = \frac{1}{2} \cdot \frac{\delta \cdot Q}{V_K} \equiv \frac{\delta \cdot q}{2} \cdot \frac{V_d}{V_K} \tag{3.34}$$

The middle expression is the same formula as that derived by Fargier (1983) and Arnott *et al.* (1990) for the special case $q = 0$. Perhaps surprisingly, it depends only on the total number of travelers Q, not on the distribution of their desired queue-exit times. Similarly, the time-averaged schedule-delay cost per traveler is

$$\bar{c}_S = \frac{1}{2} \cdot \frac{\delta \cdot Q}{V_K} \cdot \left(1 - \frac{V_K}{V_d}\right) = \frac{\delta \cdot q}{2} \cdot \left(\frac{V_d}{V_K} - 1\right) \tag{3.35}$$

This portion of congestion cost does depend on the distribution of desired exit times: for a given number of travelers $Q \equiv V_d \cdot q$, distributing the desired exit times over a shorter interval q raises V_d and thereby raises average schedule delay cost. In the extreme case when $q = 0$ while $V_d = \infty$ (with Q finite), $\bar{c}_S$ becomes equal to $\bar{c}_T$, as derived by Arnott *et al.* (1990).

Adding $\bar{c}_T$ and $\bar{c}_S$ and including the possibility of $V_d \le V_K$ with its lack of queuing, we can write the time-averaged congestion cost as

$$\bar{c}_g(V_d, q; V_k) = \begin{cases} 0 & \text{if } V_d \le V_K \\ \dfrac{\delta \cdot Q}{V_k} \cdot \left(1 - \dfrac{V_K}{2V_d}\right) \equiv \delta \cdot q \cdot \left(\dfrac{V_d}{V_K} - \dfrac{1}{2}\right) & \text{otherwise.} \end{cases} \tag{3.36}$$

Equation (3.36) is the average congestion cost, given the constraint that people are free to adjust their schedules according to their tradeoff between queuing delay and schedule delay. It should be viewed as part of a second-best aggregate cost function, in which the entry pattern $V_a(t)$ is determined suboptimally (namely, such that there is a dynamic equilibrium, rather than that costs are minimized given q and V_d). This is why it is discontinuous at $V_d = V_K$: as soon as there is any congestion, the average queuing delay (3.34) jumps from zero to $\frac{1}{2}\delta q$. As we will see in Chapter 4, a different queue-entry pattern would eliminate queuing delay and thereby reduce $\bar{c}_g$ to $\bar{c}_s$, making it the congestion cost for a first-best cost function and also making it continuous in V_d.

These costs have the remarkable feature of being independent of the value of travel time, α. So long as $\alpha > \beta$, so that the analysis applies, increasing the value of time causes no change in the duration or timing of the peak interval $[t_q, t_{q'}]$, or in the proportion of travelers who exit early; instead, it causes the queuing delay to decrease just enough to hold queuing cost constant, while schedule delay remains unchanged. This point was first noted, for a closely related model, by de Palma and Arnott (1986).

Equally remarkable is that the entire pattern of queue-entries and queue-exits shown in Figure 3.11 is unaffected by how demand Q is factored into q and V_d, so long as t^* is unchanged and V_d is greater than capacity. This again results from the perverse private incentives that cause a substantial queue to form even if V_d exceeds capacity by only a tiny amount. Spreading Q over a wider interval thus does not decrease travel-delay cost, as might be hoped; however, it *does* reduce scheduling costs because the pattern in Figure 3.11 imposes fewer costs when some people already prefer to arrive at some time other than close to t^*.

In the special case where all users are identical and have the same desired arrival time t^*, there is always congestion for any non-zero Q and (3.36) simplifies to a linear average cost function (since $V_d = \infty$):

$$\bar{c}_g(Q;V_K) = \frac{\delta \cdot Q}{V_K}. \tag{3.37}$$

Equilibrium travel cost is now constant over time. This simplification has the advantage that demand is summarized by a single quantity, Q, rather than two quantities (q and V_d) as in (3.36). It is therefore very easy to interact it with an inverse demand function to derive the equilibrium. Indeed, this is one of the advantages noted by Arnott, de Palma and Lindsey (1993): once the model is solved in this form, as a function of Q, average cost looks exactly like that of the stationary-state model (3.20) with travel delay cost proportional to Q. In what follows, we use the term *basic bottleneck model* to refer to this widely used version of the model, which features identical desired arrival times, a linear schedule delay cost function, and pure bottleneck congestion.

The bottleneck model presented above has seen an enormous intellectual offspring, reviewed in more depth by Small (2015) and Li *et al.* (2020). Extensions include heterogeneous traveler preferences (*e.g.*, Arnott *et al.* 1992, 1994; Lindsey 2004; Van den Berg and Verhoef 2011); uncertainty and stochastic travel times (*e.g.*, Fosgerau and Lindsey 2013 – see also Section 3.4.5 below); morning and evening peak behavior (*e.g.*, de Palma and Lindsey 2002); variable capacity (*e.g.*, Yang and Huang 1997, Fosgerau and Small 2013); and integration of the bottleneck model with locational decisions (Arnott 1998, Fosgerau and de Palma 2012, Gubins and Verhoef 2014). Some extensions still admit closed-form analytical solutions, while others require numerical methods to find equilibria.

The derivation of dynamic equilibrium for other dynamic congestion technologies involves roughly the same steps as for the bottleneck model. Because most dynamic congestion technologies are non-linear, the analytics become more cumbersome and typically no closed-form analytical solutions can be obtained. An exception is the zero-propagation model of Chu (1995), already mentioned in Section 3.3.4, which has closed-form analytical solutions. The infinite-propagation model of Agnew (1977) does not seem to have a closed-form solution; neither do the related bathtub and MFD models discussed before, nor continuous-time continuous-space kinematic or car-following models. Nevertheless, numerical analysis allows the analyst to compute equilibrium for calibrated versions of these models. A lesson from such exercises is that to obtain equilibrium, additional assumptions may have to be made. For example, restrictions may have to be imposed on the functional form of schedule delay cost, notably avoiding the kink implied by the conventional α–β–γ model; and heterogeneity may have to be introduced, for example in trip lengths (Fosgerau 2015; Arnott *et al.* 2016).

All these models assume that desired arrival times are sufficiently concentrated that the resulting travel-time profile is steep, so that most commuters achieve equilibrium through a tangency condition between that profile and their scheduling cost function. However, Hall (forthcoming) presents evidence that most commuters in three large US cities have sharp utility profiles and face rather flat travel time profiles, so are essentially inframarginal in their trip-timing decisions – that is, they choose the travel time that maximizes their scheduling utility regardless of how congestion varies with time at that moment. This observation reconciles some otherwise severe discrepancies between observed congestion patterns and those predicted by a bottleneck model.

Why might utility profiles be sharp relative to travel time profiles? One reason is spatial averaging, as noted by Mangrum and Molnar (2020): due to heterogeneity and self-sorting across routes, the travel-time profile faced by a traveler for an entire trip is much flatter than the profile for individual links. Another reason is the difference between short-run and long-run behavioral values of time and schedule delay, along with the endogenous choice of desired arrival times at work, as discussed by Peer *et al.* (2015) and noted in Chapter 2. Verhoef (2020) shows that the lower long-run values of schedule delay imply a dispersion of desired arrival moments that, in equilibrium, causes flatter travel time profiles when there are sufficient inframarginal travelers – many of whom can therefore arrive exactly at their desired arrival moment.

Summary

We have considered three types of models of congestion costs: stationary-state, time-averaged, and dynamic. Each type of model leads to a tractable formula for short-run variable cost under certain assumptions. Stationary-state and time-averaged models are both characterized by a rising average cost function (in one case with a vertical asymptote), so conceptual analyses are often similar for both types of models; when this is the case in later chapters, we will treat the two models jointly and refer to them as "static models." Dynamic models show how scheduling flexibility reduces or eliminates the time variation in costs that underlie time-averaged models. Dynamic models also permit internally consistent analyses of staggered and flexible work schedules, as well as of the "shifting-peak phenomenon" discussed in the next chapter. Furthermore, as seen above, a conventional static model can be derived from a dynamic model as a reduced-form relationship among time averages or cumulative quantities.

3.4.4 *Network equilibrium*

Up to this point, we have largely ignored the fact that traffic operates on a network. Accounting for this requires us to recognize that the cost of a trip depends on flows on one or more links, each of which may be serving several trip types. Furthermore, users will seek out the best routes for their trips, and the resulting cost will depend on the allocation of traffic to links that results from this process. Typically, it is assumed that the search for routes settles down rather quickly to an equilibrium characterized by each user choosing the route that minimizes cost for that particular trip. Such a situation is called a *user equilibrium* (UE) because it results from individual optimization by each user, as opposed to any collaborative procedure.[34]

To analyze such problems, we define a network structure consisting of M origin–destination pairs or "markets" (denoted $m = 1,..., M$), R routes (denoted $r = 1,..., R$), and L directed links (denoted $l = 1,..., L$). "Directed" means that a two-way roadway is represented by two links carrying traffic in opposite directions. A single origin–destination (OD) pair may be served by multiple routes; each route may comprise multiple links; and any link may be part of more than one route. As a result, traffic serving different OD pairs is likely to interact on certain links, and, of course, this affects how congestion forms. We define a set of dummy indicators $\delta_{rm} \in \{0,1\}$ to denote whether route r serves market m (in which case $\delta_{rm} = 1$), and another set δ_{lr} to denote whether link l is part of route r.

The simplest case is when all users are identical, alternative routes are perfect substitutes, and congestion on a link depends only on the flow on that link (as opposed to, say, an intersection). An appropriate concept for the UE is then *Wardrop's first principle* (Wardrop 1952): for a given OD pair, all used routes (those with positive flows) should have equal average cost, and there should be no unused routes with lower costs. So long as users take aggregate traffic conditions as given, this principle is consistent with the standard game-theoretic concept of Nash equilibrium: no user can reduce cost by unilaterally changing route. When demand for trips between an OD pair is elastic, an additional equilibrium condition is that the equalized average cost for used routes be equal to the marginal willingness to pay for trips between that origin and destination.

These conditions can be expressed mathematically in terms of route flows V_r as follows, where the first statement signifies that it applies only for every $\{m, r\}$ for which $\delta_{rm} = 1$:

$$\forall \delta_{rm} = 1 : \begin{cases} \displaystyle\sum_{l=1}^{L} \delta_h \cdot c_t(V_t) - d_m(V_m) \geq 0 \\ V_r \geq 0 \\ V_r \cdot \left[\displaystyle\sum_{l=1}^{L} \delta_h \cdot c_t(V_t) - d_m(V_m) \right] = 0 \end{cases} \tag{3.38}$$

where $V_l = \displaystyle\sum_{\rho=1}^{R} \delta_{l\rho} \cdot V_\rho$ and $V_m = \displaystyle\sum_{\rho=1}^{R} \delta_{\rho m} \cdot V_\rho$ are the link and market flows, respectively, and where ρ denotes a route. The inverse demand functions d_m are defined at the level of OD pairs, rather than having separate functions for distinct routes because of the assumed perfect substitutability: people do not care about any characteristics of routes except their costs in this simplest model. Because the specification implicitly assumes that all that matters to the traveler in choosing routes is known to the modeler, it is often referred to as a *deterministic user equilibrium* (DUE). Its natural counterpart, *stochastic user equilibrium* (SUE), arises when there is also randomness in route choice, not captured by observed attributes (Daganzo and Sheffi 1977).

A simple formulation of SUE could use the logit model discussed in Chapter 2 to predict flows – or a nested or cross-nested model accounting for correlated random terms across routes. Another approach is taken by Fosgerau *et al.* (2013), who assume that travelers dynamically decide, at the end of each link, how to proceed through the network from that point on.

The term SUE is often used in the narrow sense when randomness is due entirely to unexplained idiosyncratic differences in utility of a given route. But randomness can occur for other reasons as well, which is important to distinguish as the two sources of randomness have different policy implications. (This becomes especially important when analyzing information, as we will see in the next subsection.) To be specific, if the only randomness is in unobserved taste variations, then the random term for route selection should be accounted for in consumer surplus computations in a log-sum term or its generalization; this is because, in that case, some of the randomness benefits travelers with particular idiosyncratic tastes, as explained in Chapter 2. If, instead, the random term reflects the impacts of imperfect information, it is a measure of ignorance and thus does not produce additional utility; so consumer surplus would not then include a term of the log-sum type.

Beckmann *et al.* (1956) have shown that the equilibrium problem (3.38) can be formulated and solved as an equivalent convex optimization problem, meaning that there exists an optimization problem with (3.38) as its optimality conditions. This remains true even when direct link interactions are present, provided they are symmetric (Sheffi 1985). Such a formulation facilitates analyzing the existence and uniqueness of equilibria as well as finding them numerically. (Equilibria are typically unique in terms of link flows and OD flows, though not in terms of route flows.) The objective to be minimized in this equivalent optimization problem involves integrals of average cost functions $c_l(\cdot)$ summed over all links, minus the integrals of marginal benefits $d_m(\cdot)$ summed over all OD pairs. This objective has no meaningful economic interpretation and is best viewed as an artificial mathematical construct for computing the equilibrium conditions (3.38). The classic numerical algorithm to solve this minimization problem is that of Frank and Wolfe (1956); improved algorithms are also available (Sheffi 1985; Patriksson 2004).

Network equilibrium may sometimes lead to surprising and counterintuitive implications for public policy. A famous example is the so-called *Braess paradox* (Braess 1968): adding a new link to a congested network may cause equilibrium travel times to *increase*. Intuitively, this can happen if using a newly available route results in a lower average travel time for its users but a higher marginal contribution to congestion than using competing routes.[35] Formally, it is possible because the objective function whose minimization yields the UE conditions, described above, is different from the negative of social surplus (benefits minus costs); therefore users may use the new link even if, due to congestion, using it lowers social surplus.

Another paradox, known as the Downs-Thomson paradox, occurs in a simple two-link, two-mode network in which one mode (public transit) operates with scale economies. When the capacity of the other mode (a congestible road) is increased, the average cost of both modes can go up. This happens because users switch from transit to driving, which undermines the scale economies of transit while increasing congestion on the road. The paradox has been demonstrated under quite restrictive assumptions: total travel demand is fixed, car and transit trips are perfect substitutes, transit is not crowded, cars and transit vehicles operate on separate rights of way, the road is not tolled, and the transit operator is obliged to cover its costs from fare revenues. Zhang *et al.* (2016) show that the paradox cannot occur either if transit is operated publicly without a self-financing constraint, or if the operator is private and maximizes profit. The paradox is less likely with imperfect mode substitutability since then the generalized costs of travel on the two modes are not generally equal and the modal shift is attenuated. Transit crowding also militates against the paradox because it tends to offset the positive externality of transit usage due to scale economies.

Such paradoxes are extreme examples of *induced demand*, a common phenomenon which is simply a consequence of downward-sloping demand curves as discussed in Section 5.1.3. Yet even when *overall* demand is perfectly inelastic, so that induced demand might not be expected, these paradoxes can still occur if the demand *for a particular link or mode* is not fixed. This can be caused by endogenous route choice (producing the Braess Paradox) or endogenous mode choice (producing the Downs-Thomson Paradox). In both cases, the paradoxes occur because user prices are not set optimally. To anticipate, Chapter 4 shows that optimal pricing for a network involves link-based tolls that bridge the gap between average and marginal cost. Including these tolls in the user equilibrium conditions (3.38) would make those conditions correspond to the first-order conditions for maximizing social surplus; the paradoxes could then no longer occur.

Other advances have shown how the existence and uniqueness of a solution to Wardrop's equilibrium conditions can be guaranteed even when asymmetric link interactions are present. The conditions can be interpreted as the solution to a mathematical optimization problem known as *variational inequality* (Dafermos 1980). Doing so permits some far-reaching generalizations by means of a trick: a larger network is defined as multiple copies of the original one with certain links interacting with the corresponding links in a copy. The copies could refer to the same network at different moments in time (to model dynamics), or to different classes of traffic using the network at the same moment but causing congestion in an asymmetric way (*e.g.*, trucks hindering passenger cars but not the other way around).

Network equilibrium can alternatively be addressed through micro-simulation. Such a process is typically agent-based, meaning the simulation considers individual hypothetical travelers (or potential travelers), typically with preferences randomized according to some specified probability distribution, and traces the aggregate consequences of their behavior given rules governing their interactions. Examples include Raney *et al.* (2003), the METROPOLIS model (de Palma and Marchal 2002), and the MATSim model (Horni *et al.* 2016). It is also possible to use an agent-based model for one part of the network (*e.g.*, intersections) and a macroscopic model for another part (*e.g.*, link flow), as in de Souza *et al.* (2019).

3.4.5   The role of information

Individuals often face uncertainty about traffic conditions or other characteristics of the travel options available to them. We can identify two types. *Idiosyncratic uncertainty* exists when travel conditions and options are predictable, but individuals do not know them precisely and instead form their own perceptions. *Environmental uncertainty* exists when travel conditions vary unpredictably, for example, due to crashes, bad weather, or special traffic-attracting events. Environmental uncertainty is responsible for nonrecurring traffic congestion, which accounts for a substantial portion of congestion delays.

Information is valuable when it reduces the amount or the impact of either idiosyncratic or environmental uncertainty. For example, it can help travelers choose alternative routes in light of construction delays. Naturally, the value of information depends on such factors as its accuracy and timing. Efforts to provide travel information have grown since the early advanced traveler information systems (ATISs) of the 1970s, spurred by several factors including growing traffic congestion, increasing computer power, advances in the Global Positioning System (GPS) and in geographic information system (GIS) technologies, the advent of ride-sourcing, the widespread adoption of cellphones, and the growing availability of "big data." Reviews of information systems in transportation include Rietveld (2011), Ben-Elia and Avineri (2015), Van Essen *et al.* (2016), and ITF (2019).

Information can be descriptive or prescriptive, the latter including guidance such as recommended alternative route. Prescriptive information can be valuable by relieving individuals from the effort of making decisions, though it may not be adequate for a given situation unless it is personalized – and even then experienced travelers sometimes prefer to make their own decisions (Zhao *et al.* 2020). Generally, information technologies have progressed from broad-based descriptors to fine-grained descriptors to personalized prescriptive suggestions.

Information comes from many sources, old and new. An ATIS typically combines information from conventional sources, electronic toll collection systems, and mobile communications networks. Singapore, for example, collects probe data from vehicles equipped with on-board units used for toll collection (see Section 4.3.1). Information on traffic conditions and crashes is often collected from individual drivers via crowdsourcing sources such as Waze (www.waze.com). "Vehicular Ad Hoc Networks" are also being developed, enabling vehicles to communicate directly with each other or with roadside infrastructure, providing information in the process (Kumar *et al.* 2015).

3.4.5.1   *Decision-making with imperfect information*

Most models discussed in previous sections assume that travelers have complete knowledge of the alternatives facing them and of their own internal valuations of those characteristics. When travelers lack such knowledge, a different approach is required. Early work postulated an *error-reduction model*, in which new information reduces the variance of the error terms in individuals' utility or cost functions. However, this approach has several weaknesses: the error term reflects taste differences as well as lack of information, it may be correlated across the various links on a journey, and new information may affect more than the random components of perceptions.

Furthermore, when travel information might be inaccurate, receipt of information interacts with uncertainty in the travel itself.[36] To illustrate for a case of environmental uncertainty, suppose travel conditions are either Good, with probability $1-p$, or Bad, with probability p. The information system issues one of two messages: "Good" or "Bad". But it does so imperfectly, with quality described by an index $q \in \left[0,1\right]$ that varies with the likelihood of sending the correct message. To be specific, suppose the probabilities of each state *conditional* on each message are those shown in Table 3.1. If $q = 1$, the traveler will experience the state described by the message with probability 1; if $q = 0$, messages are worthless since the message does not alter the probabilities of good and bad days from their unconditional values, $1-p$ and p.

This modeling approach readily extends to more complex settings and can be used to rank various message systems in terms of information quality (Arnott *et al.* 1996). Such models can explore the effects of information under various assumptions about the nature of uncertainty, accuracy of information, who receives information, information that is costly to acquire, and goals of the information provider.

In what follows, we focus on imperfect and/or costly information about environmental uncertainty. Information adds a new dimension to the equilibria of stochastic models (*i.e.*, the SUE broadly defined as in the previous subsection). Namely, as travelers respond to information, they alter the pattern of congestion actually experienced. Equilibrium requires not only that users lack an incentive to change their travel given what they know, but also that they lack an incentive to change the amount of information they acquire. Because congestion is influenced by how much information travelers choose to acquire, their decisions to acquire information need not

Table 3.1 State probabilities conditional on the message

		State	
		Good	Bad
Message	"Good"	$1-(1-q)p$	$(1-q)p$
	"Bad"	$(1-q)(1-p)$	$1-(1-q)(1-p)$

be socially optimal. In fact there is the possibility of an *information paradox*, where providing information reduces aggregate welfare. Some examples will be provided in this section.

We consider three types of travel decisions: trip generation (*i.e.*, number of trips taken), route, and departure time. Here we assume travelers are fully rational.

3.4.5.2   *Endogenous trip generation*

Emmerink *et al.* (1996a) adopt a prototypical setting that has also been used in a number of later studies. Their model features one origin and one destination connected by a single link with a linear travel cost function. Travel conditions each day are either good or bad, as in the example above. In addition, there are two kinds of travelers, who obtain different kinds of information. The *informed* type learns the true state each day and chooses whether or not to travel depending on that user's travel benefit and travel cost. (Information is implicitly assumed to be descriptive, rather than prescriptive.) The *uninformed* type learns only the *probabilities* of the two states, choosing to travel if benefit exceeds *expected* cost.

With this setup, providing information (thereby increasing the proportion of travelers who are informed) creates two types of benefits. *Internal information benefits* (also called "decision-making benefits") accrue to the people who receive the information since they can make travel decisions that are better for themselves. *External information benefits* accrue to the uninformed group from the reactions of the newly informed group to receipt of information – for example, congestion on a bad day is lessened because some users learn about the bad state and forego a trip. Emmerink *et al.* show that, under these conditions, availability of information reduces expected travel costs, increases expected usage, and increases expected consumers' surplus for both types of travelers. Thus, it is Pareto improving if it costs nothing to provide.

Emmerink *et al.* (1998a) show that information continues to be Pareto-improving even if it is imperfect, under the assumption of linear demand and cost curves. But this may not be true if, for example, the demand curve is inelastic below a threshold volume of travel and elastic above it (Verhoef *et al.* 1996). Then, on good days, when information increases travel because more people know that congestion is light, elastic demand causes this increase to be large and thus results in some congestion. On bad days, when information suppresses decisions to travel, usage falls, but not by much because the inelastic portion of demand applies. Consequently, the beneficial effect of information from reducing usage (slightly) on bad days is outweighed by the adverse effect of information from increased usage on good days. This information paradox is an unlikely result if congestion formation is highly non-linear in traffic, as in the BPR function discussed earlier in this chapter; but quite plausible with other congestion functions such as some time-averaged models.

Emmerink *et al.* (1996b) consider the case when accessing information is costly, and individuals must decide whether or not to acquire it. This introduces the external effect noted above: each traveler who decides to acquire and act on information imposes costs or benefits on others, via congestion, that are ignored in the information-acquisition decision. The authors show that the resulting pattern of net social benefit is an increasing function of the market penetration rate of information. However, in other settings the marginal net benefit of information provision can turn negative at less than 100% market penetration (*e.g.*, in Yang 1999). One way to understand this is to observe that, in a congested system, it is harmful for everyone to make the same decision; thus it is optimal to preserve a bit of randomness. Naturally, this finding is relevant to public policies regarding information dissemination and promotion of information technologies.

3.4.5.3   *Route choice*

Numerous studies have investigated the effects of information provision on travelers' choice of route. Many have focused on the prototypical network with two parallel routes pioneered by Pigou (1920). Some studies assume that travel demand is fixed, while others consider endogenous trip generation.

Emmerink *et al.* (1998) extend the model in Emmerink *et al.* (1996a), described above, to two routes. Travel costs on each route can be good or bad and are statistically independent. As with the single-route model, an exogenously determined fraction of informed drivers receive perfect information, while the uninformed drivers know only the probability distributions of costs on each route. The results depend on the number of informed drivers. If there are many, both routes are needed to accommodate them, so that private costs are equalized across routes. Informed drivers then have no informational advantage over uninformed drivers; but all drivers still benefit from a more efficient route split. If, instead, there are few informed drivers, all of them take whichever route is less congested on a given day. This gives them an advantage over uninformed drivers. In that case, information is welfare-improving, provided that free-flow travel costs are state independent and equal on both routes – in other words, neither of the two routes has any inherent advantage. If this stringent condition is not satisfied, it is possible for information to be welfare-reducing.

De Palma and Picard (2006) and Engelson and Fosgerau (2020) consider the value of information within models that take scheduling uncertainty into account. These models incorporate an aversion to "risk" (*i.e.*, to uncertain travel time). This aversion may arise due to concave utility with respect to arrival time because of schedule delay cost, as in the conventional derivation of a value of reliability (VOR) in Section 2.7.2. Or it may arise because utility is explicitly specified to depend on dispersion in travel time, as postulated (though not found empirically) by Noland *et al.* (1998). Individuals furthermore may differ in their degrees of risk aversion. De Palma and Picard consider cases with two routes and with good and bad days, something like in Table 3.1 above; the effects of providing information are complex and depend on the form of the utility function. In some cases, less risk-averse drivers gain from information, while others may lose because the safe route becomes more congested.

De Palma *et al.* (2012) add costly information to the De Palma – Picard set-up. Drivers then self-select into three groups. The least risk-averse drivers abstain from buying information and take the risky route every day. The most risk-averse drivers also eschew information and take the safe route every day. Drivers with intermediate levels of risk aversion acquire information and select a route given that information. Thus, the people who benefit most are those with intermediate levels of risk aversion. Sufficiently risk-averse drivers can be worse off, and with enough highly risk-averse drivers, the information paradox can appear.

The welfare effects of information depend on many other factors, including the magnitude of fluctuations in travel conditions and correlation between routes in travel conditions.[37] Many paradoxical results can occur. Perfect information can have no effect; zero information can support the social optimum; perfect information can result in the worst possible allocation of traffic. It is difficult to say to what extent these various paradoxes reflect real situations. However, two conclusions seem warranted. First, information is more effective if free-flow costs are similar across routes; otherwise, the shorter or quicker route tends to be over-utilized and information can exacerbate the imbalance.[38] Second, information is more effective if travel conditions vary independently across routes (*e.g.*, due to crashes); for then information that induces drivers to shift from a "bad" to a "good" route tends to be beneficial to all. By contrast, if travel conditions are positively correlated across routes (*e.g.*, due to weather), driver responses to information are more likely to be harmful.

The examples reviewed here employ analytical methods that are practical only for small ("toy") networks. Various numerical models have been developed for traffic assignment on general networks with ATISs. These are reviewed by Bifulco *et al.* (2016).

3.4.5.4 *Departure time choice*

Compared to route choice, adjustment in departure time has received less attention as a traveler's possible response to information. Nearly all studies of this use the bottleneck model. Arnott *et al.* (1991) analyze the effects of pre-trip information when the capacity of the bottleneck is random and demand is fixed, finding even in that simple set-up that an information paradox is possible. Arnott *et al.* (1999) extend the analysis to elastic demand; in that case, perfect information is welfare-enhancing, but imperfect information can reduce welfare. In general, the effects of information depend on the shape of the schedule-delay cost function and on the joint probability distribution of capacity and demand. Khan and Amin (2018) consider a context where only an exogenous fraction of drivers receive information, finding that higher-quality information enhances social benefit at low levels of market penetration, but not necessarily at higher levels.

Similar to most of the literature on departure-time choice (see Sections 2.3.2 and 3.4.3), the studies mentioned here consider trips such as morning commutes for which trip-timing preferences are primarily governed by arrival time. Evening commutes deserve more attention, as they are equally numerous and occur under quite different conditions: people generally have more scheduling flexibility, trip chaining is more common, more non-work trips compete for road space, the evening peak typically lasts longer, and travel times are more variable. Perhaps for these reasons, travelers are more prone in the evening to switch routes in response to information (Chorus *et al.* 2006).

3.4.5.5 *Policy implications*

As the review in this section has shown, providing information to travelers is worthwhile only under certain conditions. Accurate and timely information is hampered by rapidly changing travel conditions, and, as we have seen, may sometimes be counter-productive due to congestion externalities. Untimely information has particular dangers, creating the so-called anticipatory route guidance problem, in which people try to guess what a possibly outdated piece of information implies for their trip. For example, providing current information to users about delay at a downstream bottleneck can lead to instability in route choice.[39] Complicating matters further, a message that induces widespread changes in behavior can alter the conditions themselves, thus invalidating the message.

Furthermore, information is useful only if people can easily access it and adapt to it. Information received *en route* can affect only a subset of travel decisions, and if it is complex, it risks creating cognitive overload and driver distraction. Furthermore, providing routing advice may discourage travelers from learning, thereby removing one of the stabilizing factors affecting traffic conditions (Chorus and Timmermans 2011).

Most studies assume that travel information is truthful in the sense that it accurately reflects what the information provider knows. However, an authority might be tempted to disseminate false information in order to guide traffic toward more socially-desirable outcomes. Apart from ethical questions, would doing so undermine credibility in the minds of potential users? Van Essen *et al.* (2020) investigate this by asking whether travelers can be motivated to follow routing advice that entails a personal sacrifice in travel time. Using RP and SP data, they find that compliance sometimes occurs if the amount of time sacrificed is small, especially if information is presented as promoting congestion relief. Thus, the framing of such messages could be important.

One strategy might be to disseminate information selectively, withholding it where it might be counter-productive (Lee and Shin 2011). However, private provision will tend to undermine such a strategy. A more effective public policy, discussed in Section 4.2.4, is to combine full and truthful information with tolling in order to better align private and social interests.

3.4.6 *Disequilibrium behavior*

Equilibrium methods for studying information and traveler behavior assume that users are fully rational. In the context of uncertainty and information, this means they are assumed to fully understand their environment – which may include predicting the behaviors of others and that they follow expected utility theory. But we know that, in a wide range of settings, people making even simple decisions under uncertainty violate expected utility theory. This is an example of behavioral economics, which we discuss in Chapters 1 and 8.[40]

Furthermore, policy makers often need to understand not only equilibrium behavior but also the transition to equilibrium following a change in the transportation environment. Such transitions often are assumed to follow simple heuristic rules: for example, Smith (1984) suggests a "proportional swap system" in which travelers faced with new conditions choose among any two routes at a rate proportional to the cost difference between them. Smith shows that route flows may converge to an equilibrium under sufficient smoothness of cost functions.

Similarly, departure-time decisions may adapt to changed conditions through heuristic rules. For example, drivers could make departure-time decisions each day on the basis of travel conditions on the previous day, using a proportional swap system to choose among departure times; congestion might then evolve in the current period assuming queuing behind a bottleneck. Guo *et al.* (2018) show that this adjustment process does *not* converge to equilibrium. Essentially, this is because the congestion externality is now asymmetric: a given traveler delays not all other travelers but only those who depart later. As a result, the adjustment process can lead to an endless cycle of overshooting and undershooting the dynamic equilibrium.

Lamotte and Geroliminis (2021) examine stability using the more general Vickrey (1973) version of the bottleneck model, in which agents derive utility at the origin and at the destination; this is the H–W model discussed in Section 2.7.2. They show that the cost function for departing at a given time is guaranteed to be monotonic (as a function of number of departures at that time) only if utility at the destination does not increase over time. But this condition is violated in the standard bottleneck model, in which utility jumps upward at the desired arrival time. This jump magnifies the cost of delay imposed by early travelers on late travelers and strengthens the tendency toward disequilibrium.

In addition to analytical methods, out-of-equilibrium behavior has been studied using agent-based models (mentioned earlier), driving simulators, surveys, and field experiments. However, these methods often are unable to describe such subtleties as learning and interactions between travelers.

An alternative approach to gaining insight about disequilibrium is via *laboratory experiments*, widely used in economics, sociology, and psychology. Experiments are relatively inexpensive to conduct, and conditions can be tightly controlled and easily modified. Dixit *et al.* (2015) review the role of laboratory experiments in transportation research. Such experiments can empirically explore the responses of individuals to changing environments perceived to depend on the responses of others making similar decisions at similar times. They are usually interpreted in terms of game theory. Such an experimental game in transportation research might involve between ten and twenty subjects, often undergraduates, who engage in repeated play for several dozen rounds spanning an hour or so, usually with some monetary reward that depends on their performance and, possibly, that of competitors. Competitive payoffs have been used to study information and congestion, among others.

Selten *et al.* (2007) present an early and influential study involving route choice on congested roads. Subjects are found to display two patterns of behavior: a direct response mode, where low payoffs in one round of play induce a behavior change, and a contrary response mode, where the opposite occurs. One explanation for the contrary response is that subjects anticipate that high payoffs would induce overreaction by attracting too many other players on the next round (Liu *et al.* 2020) – similar to what happens in the anticipatory route guidance problem mentioned earlier. Other studies have found what might be considered a third response mode, namely, inertia (Srinivasan and Mahmassani 2000; van Essen *et al.* 2016).

Several tendencies characterize the results of laboratory experimental games. In early rounds of play, subjects experiment by making different choices, whereas in later rounds they are more likely to exhibit rational choice with risk aversion (Ben-Elia and Shiftan 2010). Play usually tends toward user equilibrium as experiments progress, but fluctuations persist (Knorr *et al.* 2014). Individual behavior is quite heterogeneous (Rapoport *et al.* 2014). Subjects who switch more frequently tend to earn lower payoffs (Selten *et al.* 2007).

Another set of insights concerns the effects of information. Post-trip information about the payoffs of unchosen alternatives accelerates convergence toward equilibrium (Selten *et al.* 2007). Post-trip information also increases average payoffs (Selten *et al.* 2007). Learning takes longer when the information is less reliable (Bifulco *et al.* 2014). Information reduces variations in travel time (Lu *et al.* 2014). Finally, as we might expect, willingness to pay for information is higher when the variance of payoffs is higher, and when information is more detailed (Denant-Boèmont and Petiot 2003). More research is needed to assess how well these results accord with actual driver behavior in the field.

Laboratory experiments have limitations. First, subjects are often students who may lack driving experience. Second, it can be challenging to develop realistic scenarios that can be explained within the time limits of an experiment. Third, since experiments typically involve small numbers of subjects, agents are not atomistic in their effects on results – contrary to what seems plausible in real traffic congestion – hence subjects may attempt to influence each other in ways that would be impractical in real transportation environments. Fourth, the number of subjects is often too small to obtain statistically precise averages describing results, and it can lead to proportionally more bunching or concentration of choices than would occur with many subjects. Finally, when an information paradox occurs in an atheoretical setting, its cause can be difficult to assess.

3.4.7 Traffic accidents and economics of traffic safety

Accident costs affect such diverse policy issues as fuel taxes, drunk driving laws, fuel-efficiency standards, and provision of public transportation. Estimating these costs – and especially their external components – requires care and sophistication. This is because the burden of accident costs is shared in complex ways among drivers, passengers, their relatives and friends, other parties to accidents, insurance companies, and government agencies.

Early studies estimated tangible economic costs such as productivity loss due to injury and death, property damage, travel delay, and insurance administration. Productivity loss, however, is a poor measure of the value to an individual of avoiding a casualty or injury. A more theoretically justified measure is the individuals' willingness to pay for reducing the probability of such an event. Traffic hazards raise all drivers' risk of being hurt or killed; their willingness to pay for a reduction in that risk is the relevant measure of the cost those hazards impose. To give an example, suppose people are willing to pay $5000 each to reduce the risk of fatality from 1 per thousand to zero. The willingness to pay per unit of risk reduction is then $5000/0.001 = $5 million. Equivalently, 1000 such people would in aggregate pay $5 million and would reduce expected fatalities by one. As a shorthand, such willingness to pay is summarized as a *value of a statistical life* (VSL) of $5 million. Similarly, the magnitude of people's willingness to pay to reduce the risk of specific kinds of injuries may be expressed as the *value of a statistical injury*. The term "statistical" in these definitions distinguishes the concept from an attempt to value an "identified life" or "identified injury," that is, that of a specific known individual – a procedure that is unneeded for economic policy analysis and that would appear unethical to many people.

There is considerable empirical evidence on the magnitudes of these values, which are much larger than productivity losses. We will first discuss fatalities. Historically, most evidence came from hedonic wage studies. Such studies measure the wage premiums required by workers to accept risky jobs in competitive labor markets. This approach has the advantages that risk levels tend to be stable, and people are likely to have some knowledge of them. They have the disadvantage that it is difficult to control for working conditions that both affect job enjoyment and are correlated with risk.[41] Attempts to use other markets, such as residential smoke detectors, to infer VSL tend to founder on the impossibility of controlling for the time and disruption involved in equipment installation.

Bellavance *et al.* (2009) perform a meta-analysis of studies using hedonic wage methods to measure VSL, from nine nations. It is carefully controlled: for example, if more than one study is based on the same sample, the authors include only one; and among the multiple estimates typically reported in a given study, they rely on either the authors' or their own criteria for which estimate is most reliable, taking into account the desire that values from various studies be based on comparable methodologies. They convert estimated VSLs to US dollars (USD) for year 2000, using purchasing power parity to convert currencies and the US Consumer Price Index to adjust for the year. We have further updated to 2020 prices, finding that their 29 preferred studies have an average VSL of $9.3 million.[42] The authors are also able to explain a lot of variation as arising from different methodologies and samples. Especially notable is that those studies controlling for endogeneity of the risk variable (*e.g.*, using instrumental variables) reported much higher results for VSL than others.

Hedonic wage studies face two challenges especially. First, measures of occupational-related fatalities are notoriously inaccurate, and studies using different data sources have obtained quite different results. Second, people with high tolerance for risk may self-select into risky jobs. This second problem can sometimes be controlled for using the econometric tools now in widespread use for empirical studies in many fields of economics. Evans and Taylor (2020) address both of these problems and make recommendations for best practice.

Alberini (2019), pointing to the endogeneity problem, argues for the value of another leading methodology used to measure VSL: stated preference (SP) experiments, along similar lines to those described in Chapter 2. SP studies present subjects with hypothetical scenarios involving risk/monetary tradeoffs, thus permitting a more fine-grained analysis of how people think about mortality risk in different situations (*e.g.*, sudden versus protracted death, painful or not, how much control the person has over the activity in question). For use in transportation policy, it is helpful if the scenarios are specifically about transportation safety (Rizzi and Ortúzar 2006).

SP studies carry their own potential biases, which Alberini reviews carefully and for which she offers some remedies. One is to include debriefing questions at the end of a survey to determine how well the scenarios were understood. Another is to provide a "scope test" to ensure that stated willingness to pay increases with size of risk, as it must theoretically. (This potential inconsistency is similar to the "part-whole bias" in willingness to pay for existence value of environmental resources, reflecting confusion between a general resource and one of its components.) Generally, SP studies yield somewhat lower values for VSL.

Robinson and Hammitt (2016) review both hedonic wage and SP studies for the United States, applying strict criteria that limit analysis to only six wage studies and three SP studies. They find a central value of VSL which, updated to price and income levels for 2020, is $11.4 million (Robinson *et al.* 2021, Table ES-1).

There are also studies specifically for transportation scenarios, in which people are observed choosing (or hypothetically asked to choose) among transportation options with varying degrees of safety. (Indeed, VSL could be considered just another outcome of travel demand models, analogous to value of time or value of reliability; but in practice, it is usually estimated in studies designed for that purpose.) Andersson and Treich (2011) tabulate 31 such studies performed between 1974 and 2007, finding estimated VSL typically between $3 million and $13 million when we restate them in 2020 USD.

Much interest lies in how VSL varies with income or wealth. It is well established that the average value of statistical life or injury rises with income, as would be expected if safety is a normal good (*i.e.*, if demand for safety exhibits positive income elasticity). The income elasticity appears to be less than one, probably between 0.5 and 0.8, for wealthy nations; but much higher, perhaps 1.0–3.0, for poor ones (Hammitt and Robinson 2011).[43] This matters for transferring or comparing results across nations and for converting figures to price levels of different years. We note also that, just as with values of time (Chapter 2), VSL may vary differently across individuals within a nation or time period than across nations or time periods.

Overall, current evidence supports the widespread practice of valuing a statistical life in rich nations in the range of roughly $8 million to $14 million in 2020 prices. We use $11 million in the calculations below.

We now turn briefly to non-fatal injuries. Such injuries may be valued based on willingness to pay for risk reduction, just like value of life, supplemented by identifiable medical costs – while taking care to avoid double-counting.[44] Parry (2004) adopts estimates used by the US Federal Highway Administration for its policy analyses, which are useful because they distinguish many distinct types of accidents and categories of damage. We have updated Parry's estimates for non-fatal accidents to 2020 price levels using the average between growth in prices and growth in wages, [45] and we substitute our assumed VSL. Parry's estimates then imply that in the USA, non-fatal injuries add another 52% to the cost of fatalities in aggregate: each non-fatal injury accident is only 0.67% as costly as a fatality, but there were 77 times as many of them during the

Table 3.2 Components of social average cost of accidents

By type of cost		By type of accident	
Type	Cost ($/veh-mi)	Type	Cost ($/veh-mi)
WTP of death, injury	0.189	Fatality	0.153
Productivity	0.018	Disabling injury	0.033
Medical expenses	0.011	Other injury	0.046
Property damage	0.010	Property damage only	0.005
Legal, police, fire	0.005	Unknown	0.003
Insurance admin.	0.005		
Traffic delay	0.003		
Total	0.241	Total	0.241

Source: Computed from Parry (2004), Tables 1 and 2, with permission from Elsevier.

Note: WTP = willingness to pay (for avoidance). Costs are from 1998–2000 US data, but updated to 2020 prices (see text footnotes).

time period considered.[46] Traffic accidents with property damage only are even more numerous but less costly, adding another 4% to aggregate cost.

The results are summarized in Table 3.2. Average social cost is $0.24/veh-mi (*i.e.*, $0.15/ veh-km). The table confirms that costs are dominated by accidents involving death or injury and by the willingness to pay to avoid such outcomes. The large cost for fatalities and injuries mainly reflects a fatality rate of 0.0136 per million vehicle-miles and a disabling-injury rate of 0.1322, with assumed costs of $11 million per fatality and $137 thousand per disabling injury. Multiplying these numbers and adding them yields $0.150+0.018 = $0.168 per vehicle-mile; adding the costs of less serious injuries (which are more numerous) brings the total to the figure of $0.189 shown in the table.

How much of these costs are external to the individual user? To fully address this question would require models of driver behavior, insurance, tort and criminal law, and the effects of congestion on accident rates. To give an idea of the difficulties, consider the simple question of whether adding more vehicles to the road raises accident costs for existing drivers. If so, this would be an inter-user externality just like congestion and could be analyzed similarly. Empirical evidence suggests that more congestion causes a higher rate of accidents but that they are less severe, probably due to lower speeds.[47] The resulting effect on average accident costs is ambiguous, and for this reason, it is sometimes assumed to be zero.

Parry (2004) approaches the question heuristically, using simple rules of thumb to label various cost components as internal or external. For example, his "medium" scenario assumes that in a two-vehicle crash, half the cost incurred by occupants of each vehicle is caused by the other vehicle, hence external; this is equivalent to assuming a severity-adjusted accident elasticity with respect to traffic volume of 1.5. Costs to pedestrians and bicyclists are all external. The accident externality (social *mc* minus private *ac*) is, by these calculations, 44% as large as the average social cost – a serious impediment to efficient resource allocation. We use these values in our cost summary of Section 3.4.8.

The external cost just described assumes that all vehicles and their drivers are identical. Thus, it measures the over-incentive to drive if the external cost is not offset through other incentives. When more specific decisions are considered, such as driver behavior or vehicle choice, external costs become both more complex and more important. Two prominent issues involving such decisions are alcohol consumption and vehicle size and weight. Levitt and Porter (2001) estimate that drivers who have been drinking impose more than seven times the external accident risk of other drivers. This kind of finding is one justification for the considerable attention devoted to policies toward drunk driving.

As for vehicle size and weight, they have two very important effects on accident costs: those of the vehicle's own occupants and those of others on the road. Starting with the latter, White (2004) finds that the probability of an automobile driver or passenger being killed in a two-vehicle crash is 61% higher if the driver collides with a light truck (*i.e.*, a van, pickup truck, or sport utility vehicle) than if it collides with another car. For a pedestrian, the risk is 82% higher if hit by a light truck versus being hit by a car; for a motorcyclist the figure is 125%. White calculates that replacing a million light trucks by automobiles in the USA as of the early 2000's would have eliminated 30–81 fatalities annually. We suspect the marginal effect of a large vehicle on fatalities is even greater in developing nations, where overall accidents and fatality rates are much higher.

The incentive problem is highlighted by the fact that the larger vehicle is safer for its own occupants in a given two-car crash. To some extent this is compensated by drivers of small vehicles driving more carefully, an example of the broader phenomenon of offsetting behavior.[48] But even if drivers of small cars were to fully offset the added danger from two-car crashes, they would incur the cost of more effort in vigilance against accidents (Steimetz 2008).

Thus, there is an inter-vehicle externality, whose empirical importance is amply confirmed and refined by a substantial subsequent literature.[49] For example, it is clear that it applies not only to light trucks versus cars, but to different size cars as well. These findings suggest that the greater use of light trucks and large cars as passenger vehicles potentially imposes very large accident costs.

Yet the story is not finished: the market for vehicle purchases must also be considered. White (2004) and several subsequent authors model the results when driver behavior and vehicle markets equilibrate in the face of these safety relationships. Such modeling produces an "arms race" by which travelers choose larger cars to protect themselves against others doing the same thing. The result is a fleet of vehicles all larger than optimal, producing safety outcomes similar to those that would occur with a smaller fleet but with wasted expenditures on larger vehicles as well as the infrastructure (parking, road widths, refueling stations) to support them. The inter-vehicle externality is thus at least partly converted into wasteful spending and excess fuel use. Due to its impact on fuel use, we return to it in Chapter 7.

The externality can be addressed to some extent by public policy aimed at shifting car purchases to smaller vehicles. Many nations impose excise taxes on vehicles that help in this respect. Ironically, an opposite policy incentive arises in the forms that energy-efficiency and pollution-control regulations have taken in the USA and some other nations. These regulations are less stringent for larger vehicles – ostensibly, in case of US fuel-efficiency regulations, for safety reasons!

The inter-vehicle externality is even more dramatic in mixed traffic of automobiles and other vehicles, especially motorcycles. Tsai *et al.* (2015) find that the implied externality fee on cars, in a business center within the metropolitan area of Taipei, Taiwan, exceeds that for congestion. Lindberg (2001) finds yet another surprise: the presence of mopeds, bicycles, and pedestrians on Swedish roads slows other traffic so much that total accidents between them and cars *decrease* as their volume increases, presumably due to drivers being more cautious. If true, this implies that the inter-vehicle externality is being partly converted into a travel-time externality. By contrast, large trucks appear to increase the accident rates of cars with each other on secondary roads, presumably due to maneuvers taken by car drivers to avoid trucks (Muehlenbachs *et al.* 2021).

Insurance and legal systems can address accident externalities in various ways: for example, through tort law, criminal law, and the structure of insurance premia. White (2004) provides an illuminating analysis. Whether such arrangements provide efficient incentives depends on how they affect the marginal decisions of those potentially causing an accident, prior to its realization. This is an important reason why per-mile insurance premiums, also known as "pay-as-you-drive" schemes, have gained interest as a substitute for fixed, yearly premiums. It is probably also partly responsible for the downward trend in accident rates observed in most developed nations.

3.4.8 Environmental costs

Motor vehicles impose many kinds of environmental damage, both directly from vehicles and from roads on which they operate. Extensive study has shown two kinds to predominate quantitatively: damage to human health from air pollution, and contribution to global climate change through the greenhouse effect. The latter is considered at length in Chapter 7. Here, we take up "local" or "tropospheric" air pollution (so named to distinguish it from globally distributed gases, such as greenhouse gases, which concentrate in the upper atmosphere, *i.e.*, the stratosphere). We focus on the extent to which one can attribute monetary costs to health damage from local pollutants.

Such quantification is subject to substantial changes over time. Four reasons stand out in importance. First, as we will see, the needed quantitative factors depend on complex scientific and technical relationships, about which new research is constantly improving knowledge. Second, willingness to pay to mitigate pollution damage changes along with people's economic circumstances. Third, the actual emissions from motor vehicles change with technology and regulation. To give one dramatic example, if electric cars are widely adopted, the relevant emissions will be those from power plants, rather than internal combustion engines, which are very different in location, quantity, chemical composition, and time pattern. Fourth, vehicle emissions increase over a vehicle's lifetime, so they depend on such variable factors as vehicle-inspection policy and vehicle retirement decisions.

That said, we review here what is known about the effects of vehicles burning gasoline. Our goal is to guide the steps needed to create a quantitative estimate for any given time, location, and scenario.

Several major air pollutants in the lower atmosphere that are emitted by motor vehicles impair human health. The most important are particulate matter (PM), sulfur oxides, nitrogen oxides, volatile organic compounds (VOCs), carbon monoxide, and ozone (a product of atmospheric reactions involving other primary pollutants). To estimate their costs, a complex impact pathway must be traced: emission rates, resulting ambient air concentrations (which involve complex meteorology and atmospheric chemistry), individuals' exposure to these concentrations, resulting health damage, and the costs of that damage. The latter includes, in principle, people's willingness to pay to avoid impairment and the cost of actions they take to mitigate it. There are uncertainties in each of these steps, leading to a range of estimates. Yet there is a near consensus among researchers that the total costs are sufficiently quantifiable and important to incorporate into quantitative analyses and policy formulation.

One broad conclusion is well supported by such research: the dominant cost is mortality – more so than in the case of motor vehicle accidents. While morbidity (non-fatal disease), mitigation costs, aesthetics, and damage to natural areas are important problems, in most regions they are dwarfed by willingness to pay to reduce fatalities. This is largely because the mortality from local air pollution is very high, even in countries that have made great strides in pollution control. As a result, the VSL, discussed in the previous subsection, is especially important to cost estimates for air pollution.[50]

A second conclusion was widely held until well into the twenty-first century: that mortality is caused mostly by PM, especially fine particulates. This conclusion is now less certain due to new evidence that ozone causes significant mortality, too. We discuss these two pollutants, in turn.

Starting with particulates, the evidence for mortality is very well established (Qian *et al.* 2017). As measurement technology has improved, it has become clear that very small particles are the worst culprits because they are inhaled more deeply. Regulations have evolved accordingly: originally aimed at total PM, they now usually target particles less than 10 μm in diameter (PM_{10}), or those smaller than 2.5 μm ($PM_{2.5}$). Even the latter are now sometimes divided into finer-grained categories.

Ozone (O_3) is more complicated. It is a form of oxygen formed in the atmosphere from nitrogen oxides (NO_x), sulfur oxides, VOCs such as hydrocarbons, and a variety of short-lived intermediate reactants known as photochemical oxidants. Its effects on health are the key drivers of expensive and controversial regulations limiting emissions of these precursors, of which NO_x and VOCs are especially important to motor vehicles.

Ozone is linked to morbidity and also to short-term mortality;[51] but we are interested in long-term effects, for which the mortality evidence was weak until recently.[52] The new evidence is largely due to much greater sample sizes and improved statistical methods. We mention two relevant studies here, both measuring the effects of ozone exposure averaged over a summer season. Qian *et al.* (2017) find a strong relationship among the entire population of Medicare recipients in the United States between ozone concentrations and mortality.[53] They also find the mortality effects to be approximately linear in concentration throughout the observed ranges of pollution concentrations, once they account for an interaction between the effects of $PM_{2.5}$ and ozone; in particular, there is no threshold (in either $PM_{2.5}$ or ozone) for the onset of mortality risk.

The second study is by Deschênes *et al.* (2017), who relate summer ozone levels to mortality using an 11-year panel of US counties. They find that summer deaths from all causes respond to ozone levels (measured as maximum over an 8-hour period) with an elasticity of 0.2.[54]

Ozone may directly affect labor productivity – at least for agricultural workers, as measured by Graff Zivin and Neidell (2012). Agriculture is a small sector in advanced economies, and we do not know how much of this effect is already captured in willingness to pay to reduce sickness. Thus, it is an open question whether this adds a new dimension to ozone costs.

One might wonder, in light of the varied chemical composition of emissions from different sources, whether the adverse effects of particulates and ozone can be tied specifically to motor vehicles. A convincing affirmative answer comes from Anderson (2020), who finds a relationship between mortality and long-term exposure to busy highways in Los Angeles. Specifically, doubling the time spent downwind of a major highway over a three-year period raises mortality among older adults by 3.8%–6.5%.

Given the importance of mortality, we should note a difference in the way VSL affects air pollution and accident costs. Fatalities from air pollution typically occur many years after the time of exposure and disproportionally among elderly people. This raises two distinct analytical issues. First, because VSL is defined for an immediate fatality risk (*e.g.*, in labor-market studies), it needs to be discounted to the time at which a policy affecting future health risks is put in place. Second, a person's VSL might depend on remaining life span, suggesting it could be smaller for elderly people. This second effect, however, appears to be empirically weak or even negligible.[55]

Considerations of discounting and possible age dependence together make it reasonable to assume a lower VSL in evaluating environmental mortality than accident mortality. Our 2007 evaluation used a value that was 78% of that used for traffic accidents (Small and Verhoef 2007, p. 104), a ratio that we also adopt here.

Using these relationships to derive numerical values for the cost of vehicle air emissions involves many assumptions. The relationship to health requires assumptions about the atmospheric chemistry (how emissions relate to ambient concentrations), atmospheric transport (where in a region those concentrations occur), and exposure (how many people are breathing these concentrations). The chemistry is not straightforward, even for particulates: they consist of both solid and liquid particles, produced directly as combustion products and indirectly through atmospheric chemical reactions. (They are also produced by brakes and by the friction of tires on road surfaces.) Small and Kazimi (1995) provide a simple example of such quantification.

Several subsequent researchers use elaborate simulation models which relate emissions at specific times and places (taking into account vehicle speed and weather conditions) to ambient air concentrations, hence to ensuing exposures among the population, and thereby to subsequent health damage.[56] For example, Mayeres and Van Dender (2002) use the ExternE model, developed by the European Commission, in order to forecast pollution costs from automobile traffic in Brussels in 2005; their estimates for gasoline cars average €0.004/km and are dominated by particulate matter.[57] Delucchi and McCubbin (2011) use the Co-Benefits Risk Assessment model, developed for the US Environmental Protection Agency (EPA); their result for the average US light-duty motor vehicle in 2008 is $0.006/km. Cui and Levinson (2020) estimate emissions using the EPA-sponsored Motor Vehicle Emission Simulator, which permits detailed input assumptions specific to location, highway type, weather, fuel formulation, and vehicle age distribution; they combine this with a dispersion model, also developed by EPA, to estimate the impact on regional ambient concentrations; and finally they add estimates of population and average exposure times. This results in emissions-cost estimates by pollutant and by highway link, for the Minneapolis-St. Paul (US) urban area, which average $0.020/km for conditions prevailing in 2010.[58]

An alternative to the direct measurement of costs described above is to infer them indirectly from how they affect property values. The usual technique is to estimate a *hedonic price function*, in which a price (typically of houses or of residential rentals) varies with measurable characteristics, including measures of air quality or other environmental amenities. Aside from measurement difficulties, hedonic prices have at least two drawbacks: they measure only the value of marginal changes; and it is hard to separate the effects of the targeted environmental quantities from those of other correlated housing amenities. Bishop *et al.* (2020) provide a useful review and recommendations for how best to avoid pitfalls.

The upshot is that the environmental costs of motor vehicles are quite large in aggregate, even in countries with extensive pollution control, thereby justifying substantial expenditures on such controls. But what other types of policies does this observation support? To answer that, we need information on other costs of motor vehicle travel, to which we now turn. As will be shown, the total costs of motor vehicle travel are dominated by other components, so that air pollution is relatively small – even compared to other external costs. Consequently, simply internalizing air pollution costs on a per-kilometer basis would make little difference to people's travel decisions. By contrast, fees based on actual emissions (as opposed to vehicle-kilometers traveled), as well as direct control regulations, can and do have enormous beneficial impacts on emissions. It follows that optimal policy toward environmental externalities from automobiles would focus on specific measures to reduce the externalities, rather than general measures to reduce automobile travel.

3.4.9   *Empirical evidence on short-run variable costs*

In this section, we compile estimates of short-run average variable costs of urban automobile travel. Our purpose is to illustrate how existing research, including many far more exhaustive studies, can be used to glean the most relevant information for use in policy analysis. Such information includes the overall size of such costs in typical urban areas, the relative sizes of their constituent categories, and the factors that determine which costs are external to the user. A subsidiary purpose is to immunize the reader against some of the more extreme claims that are sometimes made by advocates of particular approaches to urban transportation policy.

In the interest of simplicity and comparability, we focus on US urban commuters. We present estimates in USD per vehicle-mile, at 2020 prices, for a medium-size car. Due to the prevalence of ample parking at US workplaces, we do not include parking search costs. We assume that trip distance and travel time are typical for a US one-way urban commute, namely, 12.2 miles and 26.0 minutes (*i.e.*, a speed of 28.15 mi/hr). We assume 30% of this travel time is due to congestion, hence that free-flow speed is 40.2 mi/hr.[59]

We distinguish between variable and fixed costs and also between private and social costs. Private average costs include, among other things, fuel taxes (a cost from the user's point of view, though socially a component of price, rather than cost) and the average costs of travel time, travel time unreliability, and accidents. Social average costs, by contrast, *exclude* taxes but *include* those costs imposed by highway users on non-users: namely, air pollution, greenhouse gas emissions, and injuries to people who are not occupants of motor vehicles. We also estimate marginal social cost, which is the incremental social cost due to one additional vehicle-mile of travel. Thus, it includes inter-user external costs, that is, the costs imposed by a given vehicle user on other vehicle users via congestion and traffic accidents. These costs are shown in Table 3.3, in which external cost is simply the difference between marginal social cost and private average cost. (Hence, external cost is here defined as net of costs paid by users.)[60]

For convenience, we divide variable costs into the two categories shown in Table 3.3: those borne directly by highway users as a group (for which private and social average costs are equal) and those borne partly by non-users. Fixed costs are treated as part of our review of capital costs in Section 3.5.4.

1   *Operating and maintenance*

The costs of fuel, maintenance, and tires are usually assumed to be proportional to distance traveled and are typically estimated from such data as fuel consumption, tire wear, maintenance experience, and prices. The American Automobile Association estimates these expenses in to be US$0.180 per mile in 2020 prices, about half of which is for fuel and oil.[61] Of this cost, $0.015 is for fuel taxes, which are a private but not a social cost.[62]

2   *Vehicle capital*

Motor vehicle ownership costs can be analyzed using standard discounting techniques for capital assets (Nash 1974). As a starting point, the combined interest and depreciation costs, averaged over the life of the car, can be approximated by multiplying the price of a new car by the capital recovery factor:[63]

$$CRF = r/(1 - \delta^T), \quad \delta = (1+r)^{-1} \tag{3.39}$$

where r is the annual interest rate and T is the lifetime in years of the capital good.

Table 3.3 Some typical short-run costs of automobile travel: US urban commuters

Type of cost	Private	Social	Social	External
	Average	Average	Marginal	
Variable costs				
Costs borne mainly by highway users in aggregate:				
(1) Operating and maintenance	0.180	0.164	0.164	−0.017
(2) Vehicle capital	0.190	0.190	0.190	0.000
(3) Travel time	0.422	0.422	0.637	0.215
(4) Schedule delay and unreliability	0.148	0.148	0.221	0.074
Costs borne substantially by non-users:				
(5) Accidents	0.141	0.241	0.284	0.143
(6) Government services	0.004	0.028	0.028	0.023
(7) Environmental costs:				
Local	0.001	0.032	0.032	0.031
Global	0.016	0.033	0.033	0.017
Total short-run variable costs	1.102	1.256	1.588	0.486
Fixed costs				
(8) Roadway	0.003	0.079		
(9) Parking	0.005	0.199		
Total fixed costs	0.008	0.278		
Total costs	1.110	1.534	1.588	

Note: All costs in US$ per vehicle-mile at 2020 prices.

In the USA the price of a new car was on average $26,690, cars were driven 12,661 miles per year, and the median lifetime was approximately 15 years.[64] Annualizing at a real interest rate of 4%, based on car loans,[65] the average ownership cost comes to $0.190 per mile, a potentially important cost component. We have ignored any taxes levied on the manufacture, sale, or ownership of the vehicle.

Vehicle capital cost varies considerably by age of the vehicle. This is determined by examining the shape of depreciation: that is, how the loss in value each year varies over the life of the vehicle. Using international data, Storchmann (2004) finds that the market price of an automobile largely follows a declining exponential pattern by age, declining on average by 31% per year in OECD countries, and by 15% per year in developing countries. It can be shown that such a depreciation pattern, in which the absolute depreciation cost is greater for a newer than an older car, implies that the value of the car to the user is also declining, presumably because of rising maintenance costs and technological obsolescence. This means that the use of a capital recovery factor, which implicitly assumes a constant value, is at best an approximation to the annualized cost averaged over all vehicles.

One reason depreciation of car price is so large during a car's early years is the "lemons penalty" that arises from asymmetric information about car quality between buyers and sellers of used cars. As famously formulated by Akerlof (1970), car owners are more likely to put their car up for sale, especially when it is nearly new, if they know it has quality defects that are not easily observed by others. Knowing this is likely, someone will buy it only at a discount. This phenomenon could destroy the used-car market altogether, except that people sell for other reasons as well – for example, death, change in family status, change of residence, or need to tap their savings, of which automobile asset value is sometimes a major component. Blundell *et al.* (2023) use this last motivation to model an equilibrium used-car market in which some cars are lemons but others are sold by people with adverse income shocks. Crucially, because dealers can offer quality guarantees when selling, the lemons penalty appears only when the dealer buys the car, not when it is sold to a consumer. The lemons penalty represents the value of the quality difference between an average used car (of the same age and observable characteristics) and one being offered for sale. Using data from Denmark on the characteristics of those people selling their cars to dealers, Blundell *et al.* estimate the lemons penalty at 12% of value for a one-year-old car, 6% for a two-year-old car, and declining quickly thereafter.

However the value of a new vehicle is determined, its *average* ownership cost does not tell us the *marginal* depreciation cost of operating it conditional on owning it. Barnes and Langworthy (2003) analyze data from the *Official Used Car Guide* of the National Association of Automobile Dealers to determine the effect of increased mileage on a given vehicle's market price. They conclude that marginal depreciation cost is 40% of the average ownership cost.

But even fixed driving costs become variable when considering policies that expand or contract the vehicle fleet. Consider two policies that increase the aggregate number of vehicle-miles traveled on commuting trips (to and from work), one by affecting commute length and the other by affecting commute mode. The first does not affect the size of the vehicle fleet, so the applicable marginal ownership cost includes only distance-related depreciation. The other causes some workers to increase their auto ownership and still others to impose inconvenience on family members by tying up the family vehicle for part of each week. In this latter case, some or all of interest and time-related depreciation cost is variable as well. In the table, we show the case where it is all variable: that is, the vehicle fleet expands proportionally to vehicle-miles.

3   *Travel time*

Our review in Section 2.7.3 suggests that a typical value of time for work trips is 50% of the gross wage, or approximately $11.88/hr for US metropolitan areas in 2020.[66] This amounts to $0.423/mi for a single-occupant automobile moving at 28.15 mi/hr. We use this figure for both average private and average social cost since this cost is borne by users as a group.

Our analysis of congestion shows that there is, in addition, an external social cost of driving in urban areas due to the contribution of a given vehicle to travel delays for others. This external cost varies greatly by time and location. Van Essen *et al.* (2019) examine the external congestion cost for various vehicles and road types for large European cities, finding that for conditions near capacity (flow-to-capacity ratio 0.8–1.0), the marginal external congestion cost of a car is 1.7 times its average congestion cost in urban areas.[67] With our assumption that 30% of the commute time is due to congestion, this implies that the external cost is $1.7 \times 0.3 = 0.51$ times the average time cost.

We omit the external time cost that congestion imposes on pedestrians, freight haulers, and transit agencies and their riders.

4   *Schedule delay and unreliability*

Based on our review in Section 2.7.4, we assume that the costs imposed by unreliability in our typical commute are 50% of the excess time costs due to congestion. We further assume this same ratio applies to the external components. Hence, in Table 3.3 we assume the average and external costs of unreliability are each half the corresponding costs of excess travel time (*i.e.*, travel time due to congestion). This excludes the cost of any schedule delay that is independent of unreliability.

5 *Accidents*

We adopt the social average cost shown in Table 3.3, as well as the methods described there to distinguish private and social external costs. By this accounting, private cost is 56%, and marginal cost is 118%, of social average cost. The resulting marginal external cost of 14.3 US cents per vehicle mile may at first sound high for readers familiar with the European Handbook of external cost of traffic, which reports a value of 1.41 €ct per passenger kilometer for dense metropolitan car traffic (European Commission, 2020; Table 125). (€ct stands for Euro cent, *i.e.*, 0.01 Euro.) The factor 10 between them can, however, be fully explained by four straightforward factors. The first is a factor 1.6 for kilometers per mile. The second is a factor 1.14 for 2020 USD per euro. The third stems from using per-vehicle versus per-passenger cost, contributing a factor 1.7 due to average vehicle occupancy (EC, 2020, Table 94). The fourth reflects the difference between assumed VSLs of $11 million for the USA vs €3 million for Europe. Thus, despite differences in population densities and vehicle fleets, US and European external effects through accidents appear to be similar.

6 *Government services*

Governments provide many services to highway users, from pavement maintenance to police patrols. We estimate the cost of these services from US disbursements of highway-user revenues for maintenance, administration, research, law enforcement, and safety.[68] Most is for highway maintenance, spent by mostly state and local governments in roughly equal portions. We arbitrarily take the private portion of these costs as those funded by taxes and fees other than on motor fuel, vehicles, property taxes, and general fund appropriations. This is a small category compared to most other costs.

7 *Environmental costs*

For local (tropospheric) air pollution, we adopt the estimate of $0.020/km by Cui and Levinson (2020) described earlier, since it is up to date, based on a detailed model, and applicable to the prototype location considered in this section. Cui and Levinson's results show that 4.5% of this cost is incurred by people in the vehicles producing the pollution, so is private; the rest is an external cost. We note that this is much larger than estimates for average air pollution costs from all cars because the number of people exposed to car emissions in a dense urban area is much greater than for emissions generally.

For global (stratospheric) air pollution, that is, climate costs, we adopt the social cost of carbon dioxide of $104 per metric ton, or $0.929 per gallon of gasoline, from Section 7.3.2. Given the 2019 US fleet average fuel efficiency of 28.3 mi/gal, noted earlier, this implies a climate cost of $0.033/mi, which we include in Table 3.3.

In the case of climate cost, there is a private cost that directly addresses this externality: the fuel tax. Its average value, converted to a mileage basis, is therefore shown in the table as a private cost.[69] Although fuel taxes are usually viewed in the USA as a means of paying for roads, from an economic perspective they contribute to addressing externalities based on fuel consumption, which primarily means climate change. As it happens, the fuel tax internalizes approximately half the climate externality in 2020, which reduces the external climate cost shown in the table (the difference between marginal social cost and average private cost) by roughly half. However, this is probably temporary because US fuel taxes typically rise only slowly over time, whereas the cost of carbon dioxide will rise steadily, as explained in Chapter 7. (We also note here that fuel taxes could help address other externalities, as discussed in detail in Chapter 7.)

Summary

The upper panel of Table 3.3 summarizes the numbers just presented for variable costs of automobile travel. These costs are very large and give some idea of the importance of policy decisions affecting use of motor vehicles. Their relative sizes highlight the importance of certain categories – especially travel time, travel scheduling, and motor vehicle accidents – in such policy decisions. Perhaps surprisingly, in light of current policy interests, environmental costs are much smaller than most other categories.

The European Commission (2020; Table 125) also reports that the cost of congestion dominates in marginal external cost estimates, at least for dense traffic.[70] What also stands out in the European numbers is the strong spatial variation of external cost estimates. Accidents are relatively less important in the EU numbers than in our US estimates, but this is mainly due to the differences in assumed VSL ($11 million vs €3 million). Congestion cost, by contrast, is larger in the EU numbers; this probably reflects the use of "dense" traffic to generate the EU numbers, compared to our broader definition of urban commuting, some of which is at low traffic density, for the US estimates.

These findings do not mean that environmental costs are small in an absolute sense. Given the 3.3 trillion vehicle-miles traveled annually in the USA even modest environmental costs per mile can imply a large total. Rather, the small relative size of environmental costs simply means that the other costs are huge. But there is another important implication: given that charging for environmental costs would make a relatively small addition to private costs of travel, it is likely that an optimal environmental policy would address these costs directly, so as to induce car use to have better environmental properties, rather than indirectly by attempting to reduce overall car travel. We already made this point for local air pollution, and it applies for climate change as well. Reducing car travel may be desirable on other grounds – for example, if the large externalities in accidents and congestion cannot otherwise be addressed or in order to promote broader goals of urban design – but it is probably not the best response to air pollution or climate change. Fortunately, environmental goals of clean air and low CO_2 emissions are amenable to direct policies, as indeed has been shown by experience even with policies that are far from ideal.

Short-run *fixed* costs at any point in time are the results of past decisions about capital structures, such as for roads and parking. Thus, we postpone completing discussion of Table 3.3 until we have reviewed knowledge about capital investments for roads, in the next section.

3.5   Highway travel: long-run costs

In order to complete the cost analysis for highway travel, we need to include the capital cost of building roads and parking facilities, converted to an annual or daily flow. Defining road cost as a function of capacity and adding it to a short-run cost function enable us to derive a long-run cost function by choosing, for each output, the size of highway that minimizes the two costs combined. This mimics the difference between short-run and long-run cost functions for firms in standard microeconomics, where in defining cost functions, at least one input (usually capital) is held fixed in the short run, whereas it is optimized (conditional on output) in the long run. Such a long-run cost function for highway travel provides a comprehensive summary of what it costs society to undertake different amounts of motor vehicle travel in a corridor. This is important, for example, in evaluating policies designed to influence the total amount of highway travel.

The long-run cost function may be derived under the assumption that capacity is continuously variable, or alternatively that it can be built only in discrete units such as lanes. In the latter case, the resulting function is not smooth, but rather is the lower envelope of several distinct short-run curves. The actual possibilities for capacity, however, are probably continuous, despite the fact that *changes* in road capacity are in practice often undertaken in discrete units. The design capacity of a lane can vary widely depending on lane width, shoulders, curves, median, exits and entrances, intersections, traffic signals, grade, drainage, sight lines, and so on. Hence it is possible to design a highway with virtually any capacity, and the question really becomes whether the cost function exhibits small or large bumps. Assuming no bumps enables the choice of optimal capacity to be formulated analytically in an illuminating manner, as illustrated in this section.

We first derive analytic long-run cost functions for some common situations. We then consider the impact of new motor-vehicle technologies. Finally, we provide some empirical evidence on capital costs, and apply it to complete Table 3.3.

3.5.1   *Analytic long-run cost functions*

As shown in Section 3.1, an analytic long-run cost function can be derived by combining a short-run cost function with information about the cost of capacity. To simplify, we begin with several assumptions. First, we assume a single uniform output, measured as vehicle trips or flow on a road of unit length. Second, we assume that capital investment serves solely to expand road capacity; we therefore ignore (for now) parking requirements as well as any auxiliary benefits of road investment such as higher free-flow speeds, lower operating costs, and greater safety.[71] Third, for our current purposes we may simply assume that capital cost is linear in capacity:

$$K(V_K) = K_0 + K_1 \cdot V_K \tag{3.40}$$

with $K_1 > 0$. Parameter K_0 denotes any fixed cost independent of capacity, such as lighting or shoulders. Fourth, interest and depreciation on capital can be written as $\rho \cdot K(V_K)$ per day, where ρ is the annual capital recovery factor divided by the number of days per year during which the travel conditions under consideration apply.

We specify the average short-run variable cost (3.19) to be a function of volume-capacity ratio V/V_K during that period:

$$c(V) = c_0 + c_g(V/V_K) \tag{3.41}$$

where $c_g(\cdot)$ describes congestion-related average user cost and $c_g(0) = 0$. Depending on the model, V may represent static flow, time-averaged flow, or desired arrival rate, each measured over a given time period of duration q; thus short-run total variable cost over that period is $qVc(V)$. Several such periods may be considered, in which case a function like (3.41) applies in each one; if so, we assume for simplicity that each has the same value of c_0.

Multiplying (3.40) by ρ and adding it to (3.41), short-run total cost may be written as

$$C(V, q; V_K) = \rho K_0 + c_0 Q + C_g(V, q; V_K) \tag{3.42}$$

where V is the flow (or vector of flows V_h, one for each time period); q is the duration (or vector of durations q_h); $Q = V'q$ is total vehicle-trips; and function $C_g(\cdot)$ includes all the parts of (3.40) and (3.41) involving V_K: namely, the last term in (3.40) plus the sum over time periods of the last term of (3.41). The first two terms of (3.42) are unaffected by capacity, so we can ignore them in deriving investment criteria. We thus focus on the tradeoff between the costs of capacity and congestion in the third, congestion-related, term. We consider two alternate congestion models: a static (stationary-state) model and the dynamic bottleneck model with endogenous scheduling.

3.5.1.1   Static congestion model

We follow here the model of Keeler and Small (1977). Suppose the typical weekday is divided into distinct periods $h = 1, \ldots, H$, each with constant flow V_h for a duration q_h. With short-run variable cost given by (3.41) in each period, the resulting congestion-related part of the long-run total cost function (cost per day) is

$$\tilde{C}_g(V, q) = \min_{V_K} C_g(V, q; V_K) = \min_{V_K} \left\{ \sum_h q_h \cdot V_h \cdot c_g(V_h / V_K) + \rho K_1 V_K \right\} \tag{3.43}$$

The first-order condition for minimization in (3.43) leads to the following investment rule:

$$\rho K_1 = -\sum_h q_h \cdot V_h \cdot \frac{\partial c_g(\cdot)}{\partial V_K} = \sum_h q_h \cdot \left(V_h / V_K \right)^2 \cdot c_g'(\cdot) \tag{3.44}$$

where c_g' denotes the derivative of c_g with respect to the ratio V_h/V_K. This rule is intuitive: the marginal capital cost of expanding the highway is equated to resulting marginal travel cost savings. Solving this for V_K as a function of the vector V and substituting into the minimand in (3.43) gives the long-run cost function, individual terms of which give the congestion cost in each time period and the capital cost. (For example, the congestion cost during a typical peak period in a big city is included in row (3) of Table 3.3; the capital cost of the highway, whose value is estimated later in this section, is depicted in row (8).) Such cost functions have been estimated empirically for many locations around the world.

It is illuminating to write the long-run cost function analytically for the special case of just one time period. Dropping the time subscripts, the total number of vehicle trips served is $Q \equiv V \cdot q$; but as discussed earlier, V and q are really distinct outputs. This is because the cost of providing for total traffic Q differs depending on whether it results from a very high volume for a short duration, or from a lower volume for a long duration, the latter being cheaper to accommodate. The failure of most literature in transportation economics to distinguish between these two outputs has limited its ability to analyze policies that affect the duration of the peak period. We illustrate here for the case where $c_g(\cdot)$ is the power function $\alpha T_f a \cdot (V/V_K)^b$ as in (3.21). Applying investment rule (3.44) enables us to solve for capacity V_K:

$$\rho K_1 = q \cdot \left(\frac{V}{V_K} \right)^2 \cdot \alpha T_f ab \cdot \left(\frac{V}{V_K} \right)^{b-1} \Rightarrow V_K^* = V \cdot \left(\frac{q \alpha T_f ab}{\rho K_1} \right)^{1/(b+1)}$$

The capacity chosen is proportional to traffic volume V, with proportionality constant depending on the duration of the congested period, the value of time, parameters of the congestion function, and capacity cost. Substituting V_K^* into the total cost function, after some calculations, the following is obtained:

$$\tilde{C}_g(V, q) = c_{bpr} \cdot V \cdot q^{1/(b+1)} \text{ with: } c_{bpr} = (\rho K_1)^{b/(b+1)} \cdot (\alpha T_f ab)^{1/(b+1)} \cdot (1 + b^{-1})$$

This shows that the congestion-related part of the long-run cost function exhibits no scale economies or diseconomies with respect to V; but it exhibits scale economies with respect to q because the same investment in capacity can accommodate more people at a given level of service if the time period is longer. This is the basis for public policies that attempt to spread traffic peaks, for example, by staggering work hours. These scale economies in q are greater the more sharply curved is the congestion function, that is, the greater is the exponent b. In the special case $b = 1$, congestion-related costs are proportional to $Vq^{1/2}$.

3.5.1.2 Dynamic congestion model with endogenous scheduling

We now consider an alternative congestion model, namely, dynamic bottleneck congestion as described earlier. We have already seen that the average variable congestion-related cost is c_g as given by (3.36), in which demand is represented by desired trip volume V_d with duration q (of desired queue-exits). This equation again conforms to the restriction in (3.41) that congestion depends on volume only through the volume-capacity ratio, in this case denoted by V_d/V_K. Thus, daily congestion-related total cost is in the form (3.43) with just one time period, but now with V_d replacing V_h, q replacing q_h, and $\bar{c}_g$ replacing c_g, where

$$\bar{c}_g(V_d / V_K) = \begin{cases} 0 & \text{if } V_d \leq V_K \\ \delta \cdot q \cdot \left(\dfrac{V_d}{V_K} - \dfrac{1}{2} \right) & \text{otherwise.} \end{cases}$$

There are two possible solution regimes. If ρK_1 is small, it will be cheaper to provide enough capacity so that no queuing occurs; that is, $V_K = V_d$. Capacity is then proportional to V_d and is independent of q. If ρK_1 is larger, it will be cheaper to allow some queuing, in which case (3.44) applies with $c'_g(\cdot) = \delta \cdot q$; this yields the investment rule $\rho K_1 = q \cdot (V_d/V_K)^2 \cdot \delta \cdot q$, whose solution is

$$V_K^* = \left(\dfrac{\delta}{\rho K_1} \right)^{1/2} \cdot V_d \cdot q$$

In this regime, optimal capacity is proportional to $Q \equiv V_d \cdot q$; the proportionality constant is greater if the composite scheduling-cost parameter δ is large or if the capacity-expansion cost ρK_1 is small.

The total congestion-related cost in the first regime is simply $\tilde{C}_g = \rho K_1 V_d$, and in the second regime, it can be written as

$$\tilde{C}_g(V_d, q) = V_d \cdot q \cdot \left(c_{bot} - \dfrac{\delta \cdot q}{2} \right) \quad \text{with}: c_{bot} = 2 \left(\rho K_1 \delta \right)^{1/2}.$$

In both regimes, total congestion-related costs show scale economies with respect to duration q: average long-run congestion-related cost $\tilde{C}_g/(V_d \cdot q)$ is equal to $\rho K_1/q$ in the first regime and $(c_{bot} - \delta \cdot q/2)$ in the second, in both cases declining with q. This is again because if demand is spread out more, it takes less capacity to keep congestion to a reasonable level.[72] Note that there are still neutral scale economies with respect to the *level* of peak demand, V_d.

Thus, if there are no scale economies or diseconomies in capital cost (*i.e.*, $K_0 = 0$), total long-run cost is proportional to the peak volume of desired trip completions but less than proportional to the duration of this demand – just as we found for the static model with congestion given by a power function. In both models, then, it is important to distinguish flow from duration in considering the properties of long-run costs.

As with the short-run function on which it is based, this long-run cost function is second-best because it is constrained by the requirement that users time their trips according to their own individual interests.

3.5.2   *Implications of autonomous vehicles*

Autonomous vehicles (AVs), such as driverless cars, will have far-ranging implications for both short-run and long-run costs of cars, trucks, and public transit. This is a rapidly evolving field of study, and here we simply try to point out some of the main features.

The most obvious is the reduced role of, or even elimination of, a driver. As noted in Chapter 2, this undoubtedly reduces the value of time of the car's (former) driver, as well as producing likely savings in operating costs. Abe (2019) suggests that private variable costs of car travel would be decreased by 11%–16%.

Another obvious feature is that congestion formation will be transformed. As we have noted, the relationships summarized in a speed–density function, or any other congestion law, derive from behavioral responses to conditions by drivers. AVs have the potential to drastically change such responses, presumably resulting in closer vehicle spacing (hence greater capacity for a given size roadway) and smoother flow. As an example of the latter, Stern *et al.* (2018) report experimental results on a circular test track in which spontaneously occurring flow instability can be reduced by adding just a few AVs to the flow; the reduction can be magnified if manufacturers optimize the AV's car-following algorithms for this purpose.

Safety and environmental costs will also be affected. For example, individual AVs are expected to be safer due to reduced driver error and to be more energy-efficient due to better control of speed fluctuations. However, as noted in Chapter 2, adoption of AVs will probably lead to an increase in total vehicle use. Thus, it is unknown whether reduced per-kilometer environmental costs will lead to reduced aggregate costs.

Many of the potential benefits of AVs will not be realized until they comprise a dominant share of traffic. An interesting question, which we do not address in detail, is whether government policy is warranted to alter the speed of transition. In a conceptual study applying the basic bottleneck model, Van den Berg and Verhoef (2016) show that a person's decision to switch from a conventional to an autonomous car can create both positive and negative external effects on other drivers: a positive effect on everyone because of a favorable impact on bottleneck capacity, but a negative effect on inframarginal users of AVs as the reduced value of time of the switching person increases equilibrium queuing delays for those who already drive AVs. This will be easier to understand after our discussion of dynamic congestion with heterogeneous preferences in Section 4.1.2: in the upper panel of Figure 4.4, AVs would be group *A*, conventional vehicles group *B*, and the negative effect occurs when a driver switches from group *B* to group *A*. This negative effect therefore basically reflects the external cost of congestion with heterogeneity.

Such external effects are already sufficient reason to suspect that unregulated diffusion may not produce a socially optimal outcome. Additional market failures may also arise. One is due to market power of suppliers of AVs. Another is the difficulty that policy makers face in trading off benefits of harmonized standards across suppliers (notably on communication between automated vehicles) against risks of technological lock-ins.

All these factors mean the balance between beneficial and harmful effects of AVs depend on the dynamic transition path toward high market penetration. We do not know what an optimal path would look like, or to what extent private markets will lead to efficient configurations. The transition will almost certainly transform the automobile industry, as emphasized by Winston and Karpilow (2020), and indeed is already doing so.

One question is to what extent it will prove viable for AVs to share roadways with conventional vehicles, especially in urban settings. Challenges are numerous (Yurtsever *et al.* 2020), and public attitudes need not match expert judgment (Nielsen and Haustein 2018). For instance, when bicyclists or pedestrians learn that AVs will always brake to avoid collisions, they may take less care or aggressively take the right of way. Some people may even find pleasure in purposely making AVs stop. Such behavior may make it difficult for AVs to obtain acceptable average speeds. There are ethical concerns about programming AVs to choose between different bad outcomes in complex traffic accident conflicts. Security threats to software raise fears. Legal questions arise regarding liability: is the car's owner, occupant, or manufacturer responsible? These and other reasons justify some skepticism about the prospects for rapid market penetration in urban areas.

3.5.2.1 *Shared autonomous cars*

It seems likely that AVs could enhance ride-sharing, and so it is no accident that some companies in the ride-sourcing business have introduced both ride-sharing services and service using driverless cars. For analysts wondering about the social effects of autonomous cars, much hinges on whether they become widely used for sharing rides.

Some possible impacts are reviewed by Shaheen and Cohen (2018). Effects on public transit use are ambiguous, for reasons already discussed; but we believe they are probably negative, perhaps even fatal to the financial viability of many existing transit services with which they compete. Indeed, ITF (2015) suggests that shared AVs might replace existing transit with "a new form of low capacity, high quality public transport" (p. 6).

It is not hard to imagine a future where shared autonomous cars replace public transit on all but high-density transit corridors. Whether this would be good or bad for overall mobility is a complex question, to which we will return in Section 6.3.6. It will depend in part on the relative degrees of scale economies of conventional public transit versus shared ride-sourcing services (both discussed earlier in this chapter).

3.5.2.2 *Autonomous buses, trucks, and air deliveries*

Driverless technology offers the possibility of greatly reducing the cost of operating trucks and buses and of increasing the capacity of highway lanes serving them. Far-reaching effects seem likely.

As for buses, exclusive bus lanes already serve as high-capacity mass transit routes. Using automation to more closely space buses on these lanes would raise their passenger-carrying capacity to levels now possible only with high-speed rail. Might this transform the provision of conventional urban transit? Furthermore, automation eliminates driver wages, the largest item in public transit costs, especially for bus transit. Could this allow transit providers to radically improve their finances, while increasing ridership through lower fares? Possibly this factor could offset the negative impact of ridership losses on finances.

As for trucks, automated driving promises to save on the most important cost element in freight shipment by road, namely (again) driver wages. Furthermore, it could be used to reduce disparities in truck speeds and spacing, thereby reducing the aggravation for people traveling in cars on the same highways. Automation of trucks might also facilitate special truck-only lanes or roads. For delivery vehicles, automation could reduce the disruption they cause to local traffic flow patterns – increasingly important as single-parcel delivery services grow in importance.[73]

3.5.3 *Electric vehicles*

Growing concerns about the environmental effects of internal combustion engines have spurred the development of vehicles with electric power trains, and the transition from fossil-fuel to electric vehicles (EVs) can be expected to affect the cost of driving. Two types of EVs can be distinguished: battery electric vehicles, powered completely by a battery, and plug-in hybrids, containing a small internal combustion engine to extend the range of the battery. Both types contain a battery that can be recharged using an external charger.

The first electric cars were produced in the 1880s, but they were supplanted by conventional vehicles until the modern EVs started to become popular after around 2010 (Jenn, 2021). This followed a decade of dissemination of hybrid-electric car, popularized by the Toyota Prius. Such cars have a dual power train, permitting simultaneous propulsion from internal combustion and electric engines; they also allow the battery to be recharged from the internal combustion engine. Hybrids lacking an external charging option remain popular and indeed may attain considerable market share, but we do not consider them here because they are essentially an elaborate way of reducing emissions and energy use of a car powered by a conventional engine.

Battery technology is rapidly advancing in terms of cost and range. Continuing innovation, learning by doing, and exploitation of scale economies are likely to yield further improvements. Yet, battery limitations are still an impediment to rapid and widespread adoption of EVs. In addition to temperature-sensitivity of driving range, battery lifetime is a constraint. Lithium-ion batteries age over time as the number of discharge–recharge cycles accumulates, and their constituent materials degrade. Fast charging, overcharging, and deep discharging reduce battery life, too.

Another concern is whether the materials used to make batteries and electric motors will continue to be available at a reasonable cost. Batteries contain lithium, cobalt, nickel, manganese, graphite, aluminum, and iron; electric motors require rare-earth elements. Demand for such materials will grow as production of EVs accelerates, as well as production of wind turbines, electronic appliances, and various defense and aerospace equipment. There are several impediments to extensive use of such materials including limited reserves, supply lags, political risks, industrial concentration, and shortages of the water needed to extract lithium (International Energy Agency 2021).

In North America, charging stations for EVs come in three types. Level 1 stations are standard electric outlets that deliver 120 V alternating current (AC). Most of these stations are installed in homes. Level 2 stations involve special chargers that use 240 V AC, available at most homes (though typically only with upgraded electrical panels) and at workplaces and public areas. Level 3 stations use 480 V direct current (DC), and deliver fast charging at rates of 250 kW or even more, applied directly to a vehicle's battery without using an AC/DC converter. Level 3 stations can charge battery electric vehicles but not plug-in hybrids.[74]

EV owners with access to home chargers do most of their recharging at home, but this is not available for everybody. Home charging is generally done in the evening, whereas public stations are used earlier in the day. The time of day when charging occurs affects the price that the owner pays, the total load on the electricity network, and the emissions generated in producing electricity.

By 2020, battery electrics accounted for well over half of new EV registrations (International Energy Agency 2021). Sales growth has been encouraged by several factors: a rapid decline in battery costs, an increase in driving range, improvements in charger technology, reductions in charging time, expansion of charging infrastructure, an increase in the number of makes and models of EVs, and growing familiarity among consumers and mechanics with the technology (Holland *et al.* 2016; Adler *et al.* 2019).

Despite these advances, several barriers to widespread adoption of EVs remain. EVs are as of 2024 still more expensive than conventional vehicles with similar capabilities. Recharging EVs takes much more time than refilling a fuel tank. Range anxiety continues to exist for consumers who drive long distances or who lack ready access to chargers. EV driving range is reduced in very cold or very hot conditions. There is uncertainty about EV reliability, battery lifetimes, maintenance costs, resale values, and the relative future prices of electricity and gasoline.

The advent of EVs raises a number of analytical and policy questions. How does driver behavior change? What are the local and global environmental effects? Is government support for EVs justified, and if so, in what form? Will substantial investments in electricity generation capacity be needed, and how will electricity prices be affected? Will and should EVs fully replace conventional vehicles, with or without government mandates? These and other questions will occupy transportation economists and other researchers for years to come. We address some of them below.

3.5.3.1 *Ownership and usage decisions*

Economists have long studied consumer preferences for alternative fuel vehicles.[75] Because experience with such fuels is lacking by definition, most empirical studies have relied on SP data. The same is true for EVs. All the demand models considered in Chapter 2 are potentially relevant. For example, aggregate forecasts may be used to study overall growth in EV ownership, or to inform investment decisions in electric generation capacity (Daina *et al.* 2017). The finer spatial and temporal resolutions of disaggregate models are needed to study such driver decisions as where and when to recharge, and how those decisions interact with time-of-day variations in electricity tariffs and power-plant emissions. Activity-based models (Section 2.6) appear well-suited for tracking travel patterns and vehicle dwell times between movements during which recharging can occur. Here, we examine possible conclusions about EVs that we can draw from our knowledge of travel demand.

First, consider vehicle ownership. Electric vehicles add some new factors affecting vehicle purchase, beyond those affecting choice among conventional vehicles. These include "hard" variables like driving range, recharging times, and density of charging infrastructure; but also "soft" variables reflecting environmental attitudes, innovativeness, social status, and other symbolic values that EVs possess in the minds of consumers (Daina *et al.* 2017). The effect of purchase price has attracted special attention due to the large price differences across vehicle technologies, locations, and times. However, purchase-price elasticities estimated specifically for EVs are likely to change because early EV adopters tend to be more affluent and often motivated by environmental preferences or love of innovative technology (Li *et al.* 2017). Muehlegger and Rapson (2021) estimate EV demand using data from a program in California that offers subsidies to low- and middle-income households to scrap old vehicles for cleaner and more fuel-efficient vehicles. They obtain quite large elasticity estimates, in the range of −3.2 to −3.4, which they attribute mainly to the relatively low incomes of households that participated in the program.

The effects of socio-economic and demographic variables are not yet well understood; studies have yielded mixed and even conflicting results (Li *et al.* 2017). Nevertheless, knowledge of EV demand has been enhanced by studying willingness to pay for different types of EV models, as well as willingness to substitute between vehicle types. Using household survey data including information on second choices (*i.e.*, the next-most-preferred alternative to the first choice), Xing *et al.* (2021) draw several conclusions. First, households living in urban areas are more inclined to purchase an EV than others, due mainly to concern about range and access to charging locations.

Second, while buyers of hybrids value fuel economy, few would consider an EV as their second choice: this reinforces the view that a hybrid-electric vehicle is largely seen as providing another fuel-efficiency technology within the category of conventional vehicles (*i.e.*, those using internal combustion engines), rather than as a different type of vehicle. Third, buyers of plug-in hybrids are more likely to have a regular hybrid than a battery electric as their second choice. Finally and importantly, the second choice for those purchasing an EV is likely to be a fuel-efficient gasoline vehicle, suggesting the fossil-fuel savings will be less than might be predicted naively.[76]

For the fast-growing vehicle sector of light trucks – that is, pickups, sport utility vehicles (SUVs), crossovers, and vans – electric versions are relatively new. Electrification for such vehicles is more expensive (due to larger batteries), but some other factors are encouraging it: benefits from lower operating costs are larger, there are economies of scale in battery size, and large vehicles command higher profit margins (International Energy Agency 2021). Indeed, electrification even of large trucks hauling inter-city cargo is proceeding apace.

High purchase costs are clearly a deterrent, particularly with future EV prices and capabilities in rapid flux. One way for automakers to reduce the up-front costs of EV ownership is to lease vehicles to consumers, which enables an automaker or dealer to absorb some of the risk of obsolescence. For example, the firm could periodically refurbish vehicles with newer or improved batteries. A lease could also allow consumers to trade in a vehicle for a new model, or to rent a larger vehicle on favorable terms when needed temporarily.[77]

Lifetime operating costs are the other big financial consideration for vehicle ownership. The costs per mile of driving an EV are generally lower than for a comparable conventional vehicle, but the difference varies widely by location, charging behavior, and equipment cost. And, of course, the fuel-cost *savings* from buying an EV also depend on future gasoline prices, which are uncertain. Furthermore, for plug-in hybrids, the cost of driving depends on the "utility factor," defined as the fraction of driving done on battery power – yet another complex consumer decision. All this makes it difficult to quantify the savings in operating cost or in greenhouse gas emissions.

EVs have other operating-cost advantages, though quantifying them has been difficult (Borlaug *et al.* 2020). Regenerative braking reduces wear and tear on brake pads and wheel discs even while improving range. Battery electric vehicles have fewer moving parts, fewer fluids, simpler and more standardized parts, and no emissions control equipment.

EVs are especially well-suited for car sharing (Axsen and Sovacool 2019), particularly in cities because trips are shorter and charging facilities more readily available. Furthermore, companies offering car sharing services can maintain a diverse fleet of vehicles so that users can switch between EVs and conventional vehicles depending on needs and desires for a given trip.

Next, we consider driver behavior. *A priori*, it is unclear whether an EV will be driven more or less than the conventional vehicle it replaces. Its lower operating cost would tend to increase usage (the rebound effect, discussed in Chapter 7); but inconvenience or anxiety about recharging might reduce it. Preliminary US evidence shows lower annual usage for EVs (Davis 2019). This finding may partly reflect households with multiple vehicles using their EVs mostly for short trips (Daramy-Williams *et al.* 2019), a practice that presumably will change if EVs become dominant. As noted in Section 7.1.4, Jeremy West *et al.* (2017) provide empirical evidence that poorer performance of EVs, from consumers' points of view, fully offset the rebound effect of a 2009 incentive program in the USA.

Range anxiety has been a major impediment to owning EVs, especially in areas with low charging-station densities and a lack of fast chargers. Dimitropoulos *et al.* (2013) carry out a meta-analysis of 33 studies on the attitudes toward driving range of individuals who lacked relevant experience. They find that willingness to pay for a one-mile increase in driving range is substantial, with a mean value of US $67 and a positive skew. US drivers express a much higher value for increased driving range than Europeans, perhaps due to longer travel distances and lower urban densities.

Even the details of driving behavior seem to differ somewhat between EVs and other vehicles. EV owners have been found to drive more slowly and smoothly and to reduce the use of auxiliary features such as air conditioning and electronic devices. These same individuals tend to adopt at least some of these same energy-saving techniques when they drive conventional vehicles.[78]

3.5.3.2 *Environmental effects*

How will electric vehicles change the nature and magnitudes of environmental effects discussed earlier? This depends on several factors, especially the amount of emissions generated in producing electricity but also environmental externalities caused by manufacturing and eventually decommissioning EVs and their batteries. Each of these components has been researched, but significant gaps in knowledge remain.

A number of studies have investigated the greenhouse gas emissions caused by operating EVs in the USA. Graff Zivin *et al.* (2014) examine 2010–2012 data on power-plant CO_2 emissions per kWh of electricity produced. We describe this result to illustrate the factors that must be considered, although emissions profiles have changed significantly since 2012 due to reduction in coal-fired generation. Graff Zivin *et al.* find that per-distance emissions by an EV were low in the west of the USA but actually exceeded those of conventional vehicles in some other regions. They also find that emissions vary appreciably by time of day, depending on which power plants are operating "on the margin." Specifically, EV emissions while charging tend to be higher during off-peak hours because more power is generated then by coal-fired units.

Holland *et al.* (2016) build on Graff Zivin *et al.* (2014) to estimate the effect of changes in electricity load for each power plant in an electrical grid. They also track how the damages due to local pollutants are exported to distant locations. The result is that the geographical pattern of EV emissions differs considerably from that of conventional cars. Furthermore, the composition of local pollutants changes: For example, the generating plants powering EVs emit less ozone but more particulates (Thielmann *et al.* 2020) than do modern internal combustion engines. Consequently, the net environmental benefits from replacing a conventional car by an EV vary substantially with location and depend on such factors as the relative health damage of ozone and particulates (discussed in Section 3.4.5). From this information, Holland *et al.* estimate that EVs produced a net environmental benefit from an individual *state's* perspective in only 32 out of 48 states, and from a *national* perspective in only 11 states. This result has no doubt changed as cleaner fuels have expanded in the power sector; but the difference between state and national perspectives is likely to remain, suggesting that environmental policies concerning EVs are best administered by the national government. The same lesson applies all the more to countries with geographically smaller provinces and regions.

Holland *et al.* (2020) reconsider these findings in light of the marked decrease in emissions from electricity generation since 2012. They conclude that, on average, EVs have become cleaner than conventional cars. This progress reflects the principle that controlling emissions at electric power plants, rather than from the tailpipes of individual vehicles, has the advantage of being able to exploit economies of scale.

Considering lifecycle emissions, including car manufacture and disposal, could change these conclusions. Manufacturing and disposing of EVs is energy-intensive, due especially to the batteries. Nevertheless, Thielmann *et al.* (2020) conclude that, under current trends, an EV produced in 2020 will emit 15%–30% fewer greenhouse gases over its lifetime than a comparable conventional vehicle. The International Energy Agency (2019) estimates a similar reduction.

3.5.4 *Empirical evidence on capital costs*

This section addresses the two most important capital costs that are fixed in the short run but variable in the long run: namely, the costs of building roads and parking spaces. In both cases, we seek to estimate the dollar value of relevant capital stock for the United States, under the same assumptions as those used for Table 3.3: including annualizing using the capital recovery factor (3.39). For average cost, we divide by the relevant usage, either vehicle-miles or daily trips. As always, the interest rate in (3.39) is crucial; we adopt a real rate of 4% per annum (the same as for vehicle capital in Table 3.3), based on the discussion of project evaluation for public investments in Section 5.2.3.

3.5.4.1 *Roads*

Capital costs of roads vary greatly with terrain – *e.g.*, flat, rolling, or mountainous – and with the degree of urbanization. Both affect such factors as the number and types of structures required (*e.g.*, bridges, overpasses, intersections, drainage facilities, retaining walls, and sound walls), ease of access to construction sites, difficulty of grading, extent of demolition, and, of course, land prices.

Scale economies with respect to capacity, s_K, may be defined analogously to equation (3.3) as the ratio of average to marginal cost of capacity. Scale economies might arise from many factors such as fixed land requirements (*e.g.*, shoulders and medians) or efficiencies of multi-lane traffic flows. Scale diseconomies could result from the increased cost of building more or bigger intersections, especially when they require complex signals or overpasses. If we generalize to a general-equilibrium supply function (with variable factor prices), as defined in Section 3.1, then scale diseconomies could also arise from a rising supply price of scarce urban land (Small 1999).

Kraus (1981) estimates the degree of scale economies on urban road networks while explicitly accounting for the costs of intersections, which he finds to have a major effect. Using UK data on costs and design standards, he estimates overall scale economies at $s = 1.19$ for a circular urban area of ten-mile radius containing a specified highway network.[79] This value is the net result of substantial scale economies in constructing individual road segments, partially offset by scale diseconomies of intersections (the latter due to the fact that their size tends to be proportional to the square of the width of the highways being connected). This offset, seen only at the network level, is ignored by many studies, which therefore may overestimate scale economies.

Altogether, the evidence supports the likelihood of mild scale economies for the overall highway network in major cities – probably larger in small cities.

What can we say about the average capital cost per vehicle-mile? The US Department of Commerce (2020) estimates the depreciated value of the entire US highway capital stock, excluding land, at $3,852 billion in 2019. We assume that 60% of this cost is attributable to passenger vehicles, based on the fraction of federal highway costs attributable to passenger vehicles in the cost allocation study by US FHWA (2000, Table 4). Annualizing at a 4% real interest rate and a 20-year average remaining life and updating to 2020 prices, this implies an annual cost of $172 billion.[80] We add 30% for the cost of urban land, based on Keeler and Small (1977, p. 9). (We augmen their figure slightly by a portion of "administration and research" disbursements.) The result is an average capital cost of $0.079/veh-mi for passenger vehicles.[81] This total is listed near the bottom of Table 3.3 as the social short-run fixed cost for roads. We estimate that just a small portion of these are privately paid fixed costs, mainly because the bulk of US highway funding is through fuel taxes, which we included as a private variable cost.[82]

3.5.4.2   Parking

Providing parking spaces is costly wherever land is expensive. As emphasized by Shoup (2005), in the USA there are three to four parking spaces for every registered vehicle in cities. If we consider just commuting trips and allow for a 20% vacancy rate of parking spaces,[83] we could assume that adding a car trip for commuting requires $1/0.8 = 1.25$ parking spaces at the workplace, plus an additional 1.0 space at the residence if the trip requires acquiring an additional vehicle. We proceed here by estimating costs for just the 1.25 spaces at the workplace.

Such costs vary widely by location and type of structure. Shoup (2018a) compiles construction-cost estimates, excluding land, made by a commercial firm for 12 large US cities in 2012. They average $33,000 or $24,000 per space for an underground or above-ground structure, respectively. With various additional assumptions,[84] the cost per representative urban space in 2020 is $24,044. Annualizing with a 40-year lifetime and 4% real interest rate and ignoring operating cost, this implies an annual fixed cost per parking space of $1,215. Assuming 250 round trips per year each of length 24.4 miles (as in Table 3.3), this yields average capital cost for parking at the workplace of $0.199/mi. It may seem anomalous that parking costs are larger than roadway costs; but this reflects our focus on an urban commuting trip, whose parking space typically has a high opportunity cost and, unlike roads, is usually not shared by any other trips.

For privately paid cost, we follow Manville (2014), who estimates that US urban commuters pay for 2.5% of workplace parking cost on average. This is lower than in many countries – yet even in the UK, Bates (2014) estimates that only 6% of parking acts are charged for.

Parking costs are clearly a significant part of the social cost of urban commuting travel and are all the more remarkable because they are fully absorbed by the vast majority of US employers, rather than being charged to the commuter.

3.5.5   Is highway travel subsidized?

Calculations such as those shown in Table 3.3 are sometimes used to debate whether automobile travel, or highway travel more broadly, is subsidized. Such debates can be confusing because "subsidy" has several different meanings, each raising different conceptual issues.

At least four such meanings, not mutually exclusive, for "subsidy" can be discerned. The first is *fiscal*: Is a particular set of government accounts in balance? Such balance might be sought as a way of facilitating public scrutiny of financial decisions in order to encourage honest and competent management. We might also care about budgetary imbalances because raising public funds to cover deficits generally has some economic cost (the so-called excess burden). These concerns are reflected in the frequent use of hypothecation, or "earmarking," of highway-based revenues to be spent only on highway-related purposes.

A second meaning is *distributional*: Does the system of highway finance benefit certain groups at the expense of others? Here, the motivation might be understanding the political economy of decision-making, or simply the desire to promote a broad trust in the fairness of the system. These concerns, as well as fiscal ones, are prominent in the highway cost allocation studies that have been done periodically at both the federal and state levels in the USA.

A third meaning involves *long-run allocation*: Does the gap, if any, between social costs and revenues from highway transportation indicate likely misallocations of investment? Some discussions, especially in the literature on privatization, appear to take the position that allocations of investment across sectors of the economy are best made in unregulated private markets, by allowing investment funds to flow out of sectors that make losses into sectors that make profits. This could be justified, for example, if the industry exhibits neutral scale economies and involves only small external costs, so that average total cost approximates long-run marginal cost. Our review suggests that this is not the case for urban transportation.

A fourth meaning is *efficiency*: Is there a discrepancy between social and private marginal cost, reflecting market failures? This question is the basis for most economic analysis of optimal pricing and investment, which is described in subsequent chapters, and in many policy documents as well. In contrast to the first three meanings of "subsidy," this one has more of a short-run focus because of the prominence of short-run marginal cost in economic pricing theory; it is also more focused on the marginal decision-making of a single user, as opposed to a policy maker who can influence many users simultaneously.

Conceptual difficulties abound. In assessing fiscal balance, which taxes should be considered to be user taxes? For example, what about the portion of a normal sales or value-added tax that falls on fuel? Or what about a specific exemption of fuel from such taxes? Similarly, which expenditures are undertaken primarily for the benefit of highway users? (This question is especially salient with expenditures that are part of broader efforts to promote public safety, such as police, emergency response, and alcohol-abuse prevention.) The same problems afflict attempts to assess distributional impacts, hence attempts to define fairness. The third and fourth meanings are somewhat more amenable to precise definitions because they can be used to address precise questions, such as what would happen if a particular suite of policies were introduced to restrain downtown road traffic; but then the most direct approach is to model the policies explicitly and forgo the step of measuring the long-run average or marginal cost of expanding road traffic.

Even in addressing efficiency, the most valuable lessons from computing social and private costs most likely come from the individual components. For example, the bottom row of Table 3.3 could be used to argue that private decision-makers are "subsidized" by US$0.424 per vehicle-mile if they choose to travel by car. This could be interpreted as measuring the distortion in the average incentive facing car users. But a more striking observation arises from disaggregating the discrepancy between short-run social marginal and private average variable costs, which is US$0.478. More than half of this discrepancy arises from the congestion externality, and most of the rest arises from inter-user externalities connected with accidents. These externalities vary greatly by circumstance. So, from an efficiency point of view, the table is most useful by pointing to congestion and accidents as two places to look for big savings from more efficient policies. Similarly, looking at long-run policies, we see that parking is supplied with an enormous subsidy, leading to oversupply of parking spaces – as we describe in the next section. So there are potentially big savings to be reaped from policies that reduce provision of parking spaces, especially if some of the fixed costs can be recovered by converting parking lots to other uses or by arranging for existing parking structures to be shared with nearby new users.

We therefore see little value in arguing over the extent of aggregate subsidies to road users but much value in examining specific cost components and how decisions affecting them are made.

3.6   The role of parking

Most research on road travel is concerned with the design or performance of vehicles while in motion, covering topics such as speed, safety, fuel consumption, and so on. Yet the average personal vehicle is driven only about one hour per day, spending the other 23 hours parked (Shoup 2005, Appendix B). Moreover, parking takes up a lot of land, as noted above – indeed its land consumption per car exceeds land consumption per person for housing (Shoup 2018a). Devoting all this space to parking is expensive, yet as we have seen, parking is frequently underpriced. This combination of high capital costs and low user fees creates serious distortions in both the supply and demand for parking. This section considers the implications for costs; Section 4.4 considers pricing policies in more detail.[85]

The availability, accessibility, and pricing of parking can influence many travel decisions: how frequently to travel and where, what type of parking to use and for how long, when to travel, what mode to use, and so on. In the long run, they also affect decisions about vehicle ownership and where to live and work. Furthermore, parking supply and usage decisions have social consequences since they affect safety, air quality, temperature (the urban heat island effect), and the operations of public transport.

Parking policies have multiple and sometimes conflicting objectives: *e.g.*, to reduce congestion and emissions, to generate revenue, to improve accessibility, to support the local economy, and to promote horizontal and vertical equity. Not surprisingly, then, it is a complicated, divisive, and politicized issue. As a result, parking policies in many countries are misguided in several ways, at least from the perspective of economic analysis. Two longstanding policies stand out. The first is pricing: many cities charge zero or only nominal fees for on-street parking; yet off-street parking is sometimes also free, especially for employees and shoppers, whereas sometimes it is quite expensive – often provided by private firms. Free on-street parking can lead to a great deal of "cruising" – that is, driving around a street network looking for a vacant parking space. This can cost drivers substantial time and contribute noticeably to local traffic levels, measured by Hampshire and Shoup (2018) to be 15% of all daytime traffic in central Stuttgart, Germany. Cruising is analyzed in detail in Section 4.4.

The second problem is minimum parking requirements. These typically oblige developers to build a minimum amount of off-street parking based on the size and type of business or other activity. Such requirements can be quite onerous and may effectively compel enough parking to satisfy even peak-period demands with free parking.[86] This is especially true in North America, where employer-provided free parking is very common. Minimum parking requirements are also prevalent in Asian cities despite their high density, mixed land use, and relatively low levels of vehicle ownership (Barter 2018).

These policies create various inefficiencies. Underpriced on-street parking encourages driving and cruising, as just noted, which contribute to traffic congestion, pollution, and other externalities, as well as discouraging the use of public transit. Overpriced garage parking further boosts drivers' incentives to search for cheaper on-street parking, causing too much cruising even while garage capacity is inefficiently underutilized. Minimum parking requirements and employer-provided free parking cause too much land to be devoted to parking relative to other uses of scarce urban space, which is an allocative inefficiency in itself and also undermines the economies of agglomeration that make cities work. These inefficiencies feed each other, as more driving creates a perceived need for more parking, in a vicious cycle similar to the phenomenon of road capacity expansion and latent demand for roads (see Section 5.1.3).

These disadvantages are increasingly being recognized, as discussed in Section 4.4. Several cities now set fees for on- and off-street parking that vary by time of day and/or by the parking space occupancy. Many cities are also relaxing or abandoning minimum parking requirements, or even replacing them with maximum requirements.[87]

3.7 Bicycles and scooters

Because of its traditionally modest share in most developed countries, and the limited range of traditional bicycles, bicycling has received only modest attention in the transportation economics literature. However, we expect that this may soon change with the higher speeds made possible by electric bikes, coupled with their environmental benefits compared to cars. This section begins by reviewing the benefits and policy challenges related to conventional bicycles. It then briefly examines recent developments with bicycle sharing systems (BSSs), electric bicycles (e-bikes), and electric scooters (e-scooters).

3.7.1 *Determinants of bicycling and modeling considerations*

As a transportation mode, bicycles differ from automobiles in several respects. Ownership and operation are far cheaper. Bicycles occupy less space, an advantage when (urban) land is scarce. Maximum achievable speeds are much lower for bicycles, except occasionally in highly congested areas. Bicycling is prohibited on some types of road but sometimes is granted dedicated rights of way. As already noted, bicycling creates fewer negative externalities, and it has some health benefits for riders – although personal safety is a concern and some people are deterred by the physical effort required.

As noted in Section 2.1.3, travel demand modeling can be improved by treating bicycling as a separate mode, due to its distinct characteristics. One such characteristic is that the value of travel time depends strongly on the circumstances and stage of a trip. For example, Börjesson and Eliasson (2012b) estimate a VOT for cycling of 16 €/hr on a street but only 10 €/hr on a separate bicycle lane. Waiting time at intersections is valued at more than double the value of time in motion; and time parking a bike is valued even more highly. Bicyclists are sensitive to many other aspects of travel conditions, sometimes summarized as measures of the overall bicycle friendliness – accounting for such features as reserved bicycle lanes, presence of on-street parking, speed limits, traffic volumes, and pavement condition. Examples include the Level of Traffic Stress index, and Bicycle Level of Service (Transportation Research Board 2016; Buehler and Dill 2016).

One limitation of these measures is that they disregard heterogeneity in individual bicycling skills and preferences. Griswold *et al.* (2018) seek to overcome this weakness by using latent class choice models (see Section 2.5) to identify groups of individuals with different preferences. They note that such segmentation can be useful to decision-makers in identifying what type of policies are most effective for attracting bicyclists on a given facility: for example, turn frequency, slope, and type of intersection control (Broach *et al.* 2012).

Bicyclists also choose routes differently than motorists. For example, Broach *et al.* (2012), using GPS data, find that cyclists often choose longer paths to avoid traffic congestion or hills. Thus, network algorithms based on travelers choosing minimum distance or minimum travel time are not well suited to analyze bicycling.

As a consequence of these characteristics of bicycling, the share of trips taken by bicycle depends on many factors not usually included in mode choice models. Examples include climate, topography, road type, availability of bicycling facilities, and public policies defining interaction between bicycles and other vehicles. These factors differ widely across countries, and even across cities within a given country. For example, public policies in Stockholm have emphasized transit investments, whereas those in Copenhagen have prioritized bicycle infrastructure (Bastian and Börjesson 2018). There are significant regional variations as well. For example, bicycling is more prevalent in Northern Europe than most other parts of the developed world; Pucher *et al.* (2010) attribute this to the prevalence in Northern Europe of limited car parking, car-free zones, use of traffic calming and speed limits to reduce car speeds, land-use plans encouraging short-distances trips, and high taxes on car ownership and use.

3.7.2 Bicycling and cost–benefit analysis

Many of the policies that influence bicycling involve public investments. Examples include creating car-free zones, traffic calming measures, dedicated bicycle facilities, signed bicycle routes, bicycle parking facilities at rail stations, and configuring trains and buses to accommodate bicycles. Some of these policies were accelerated in response to the COVID-19 pandemic (Bereitschaft and Scheller 2020), often using emergency funding.

But usually such investments must compete for scarce funds with other priorities. Thus, it is important to quantify how much they contribute to the public good. Cost–benefit analysis (CBA, reviewed in Section 5.2) is an obvious tool for such assessments. But it has rarely been used for bicycling projects and policies, for reasons analyzed by Van Wee and Börjesson (2015): some effects are difficult to estimate or to value monetarily; the effort to carry out a CBA may be excessive for small initiatives; and the agencies responsible for bicycling may lack experience with CBA. Cities often incorporate such investments into broader policy packages, making it hard to identify the effects of individual measures. Furthermore, as with all empirical relationships, it can be challenging to identify causal relationships, as discussed in Section 5.1.3; for example, parking facilities for bicycles may be intended to encourage bicycling, but they are also built in response to increased usage caused by other factors.

Most of these difficulties affect all cost-benefit analyses, and many refinements are available to deal with them. Here, we consider two aspects of bicycling that are important for CBA but especially difficult to measure: health benefits and safety.

Bicycling is generally viewed as a healthy activity due to the physical effort required. However, it is not straightforward to assess the incremental health benefits of additional bicycling (Börjesson and Eliasson 2012a). If individuals take into account their personal health effects when making their travel decisions, then their own health benefits are already accounted for in measured expected utility and thus should not be added separately (although there may be spillovers to the public within the health care system). Health benefits are probably nonlinear in the amount of bicycling undertaken by a given individual and also depend on the extent of local air pollution that individual encounters. Furthermore, if people substitute between cycling and other forms of exercise, the benefits of additional cycling may be partly offset by reductions in other activities.

Safety is perhaps the greatest downside of bicycling. Motorists are protected from injury by the weight, strength, and safety features of the vehicle they are in. Bicyclists benefit from none of these factors, and their vulnerability is increased by proximity to motorized traffic. To analyze this, researchers need data on safety outcomes (*e.g.*, fatalities) and on exposure (*e.g.*, distances or times spent cycling). But such data are not always easily available. Nevertheless, the data we have makes clear that bicycling is far more dangerous than traveling in a car. Victoria Transport Policy Institute (2019) reports fatality rates per vehicle-km for both cycling and car travel in the USA and Britain: in both countries, fatality rates for bicycles are about ten times higher than for passenger cars. In The Netherlands, traditionally a bicycle-friendly country, fatality rates are eight times as high as by car (Netherlands Institute for Road Safety Research 2023). By way of comparison, being a pedestrian is slightly less dangerous than riding a bicycle; while riding a motorcycle is far more so, by a factor of nearly four. We note that these differentials shrink if rates are measured per unit time instead of per unit distance.

In high-income countries, the situation seems to be improving: mortality rates for bicyclists have decreased since 1990 (Carvajal *et al.* 2020). One possible explanation is "safety in numbers:" bicycling becomes safer as more people engage in it. Using data from several countries, Jacobsen (2003) finds that total injuries and fatalities increase with the 0.4 power of exposure:

hence, injury and fatality *rates* decline with the 0.6 power of exposure, a type of scale economy that is external to the individual decision-maker. The most likely explanation for this finding is that drivers become more aware of bicycles when they are more numerous, for at least two reasons (Pucher *et al.* 2010; Thompson *et al.* 2019): motorists are more likely to be bicyclists themselves (hence, more aware of bicyclists' behavior and sensitive to their well-being), and drivers are deterred from crossing in front of oncoming cyclists when the latter are more numerous. This last observation implies that a policy that concentrates bicyclists on particular corridors may be effective.

3.7.3 Bicycle sharing systems

A BSS is an arrangement that permits an individual to use a bicycle without owning one. Over 3000 cities worldwide had one as of 2021 (PBSC Urban Solutions 2021). These systems serve three primary functions: as an affordable means of transportation for short trips, as a "first mile" or "last mile" connection to public transit, and simply as a way to increase bicycle mode share for social purposes.

Such sharing systems have evolved through several identifiable generations (Eren and Uz 2020; Jara-Díaz *et al.* 2022). Early systems were introduced in Amsterdam in 1965 and then Copenhagen in the 1990s, but succumbed to problems with vandalism, theft, and failure of users to return bicycles promptly if at all. These problems were due mainly to low or zero prices. Later generations, in use currently, benefit from mobile digital technologies. Third generation systems ("station-based") have kiosks or docking stations where bicycles can be locked and accessed using smartphones or smart cards. Fourth generation systems ("free-floating" or "dockless") allow bicycles to be parked anywhere within designated areas. Dockless systems are cheaper to set up than station-based ones and more convenient for users; but they are more susceptible to theft and vandalism and carelessly parked bicycles often obstruct travelers or create safety hazards. Dockless systems also lack infrastructure to recharge e-bikes. Third and fourth generation systems sometimes use volunteers and are typically financed by a combination of user fees, advertising, government subsidies, and charities.

The usage level of a BSS is largely determined by location, rules of usage, fees, topography, and weather (Eren and Uz 2020; Hossain *et al.* 2023). Usage is deterred by mandatory helmet laws and enhanced by proximity to subway stations, bus stops, bicycle lanes, and bicycle paths. Spatial and temporal variations in demand are extensive, causing imbalances that some BSS operators alleviate by relocating bicycles between areas using motorized vehicles, and occasionally by adjusting user fees (*e.g.*, by charging lower fees to users who return bicycles to uphill stations).

BSSs have scale economies for reasons similar to public transit, ride-hailing services, and conventional taxi service (see Section 3.2.1): the more usage, the more feasible it becomes to provide easy access. Larger scale also tends to smooth out fluctuations in demand, thus reducing the average waiting times to obtain or to park a bicycle. Jara-Díaz *et al.* (2022) develop a series of stylized aggregate models that nicely illustrate the scale economies of a station-based BSS. In one model, the operator chooses the rental fee, the number and spacing of stations, the number of docking sites per station, the number of bicycles per station, and the amount of bicycle repositioning. Just as with transit, scale economies have implications for public policy. A subsidy is required to balance the budget under marginal cost pricing; and if two or more operators compete in the same area, total costs will be lower if users can freely substitute among them.

Do BSSs reduce congestion and other externalities? As with public transit, their potential for doing so depends on how much the resulting demand for bicycling is diverted from cars. It also depends on how easy it is to relocate bicycles to accommodate demand patterns and on how much road capacity is used by bicycles – a relevant factor here is that a cyclist uses less space than a car driver, certainly at lower vehicle occupancies. Ultimately, the scope to reduce motorized traffic via bicycling policy is limited by bicycles' relative inability to carry goods and serve long-distance trips. A further limitation is that any reductions in auto driving may be partially offset by induced car traffic, as discussed in Section 5.1.3.

3.7.4 Electric bicycles

E-bikes are two-wheeled vehicles with a battery-powered motor that supplements, though does not fully replace, the motive power provided by the rider. E-bikes have been a popular mode of transportation in Asia since the 2000s, and they are gaining market share elsewhere. In The Netherlands, for example, the share of e-bikes in total sales of new bicycles exceeded 50% in 2022, having grown from only 30% five years earlier. Their main attractions compared to ordinary bicycles are increased speed and reduced physical exertion.

Similarly to the case of electric cars (see Section 3.5.3), e-bikes have benefited from advances in battery and motor technology, use of component modularity, and economies of scale in production. These factors have improved range and speed while also reducing manufacturing cost (Fishman and Cherry 2016). Maximum speeds are typically between 32 and 45 km/h (Reynolds 2020), while motor power ranges from 250 to 500 W and total bicycle weight from 20 to 45 kg (Bigazzi and Wong 2020).

E-bike trips can thus replace conventional bicycle trips, but they can also create new trips or displace trips by other modes. The extent of these responses has been measured in several studies. Bigazzi and Wong (2020) conduct a meta-analysis, measuring the fraction of usage diverted from various other modes: the median diversion rates are 33% from public transit, 27% from conventional bicycles, 24% from automobiles, and 10% from walking. Of course, these medians hide considerable variation, presumably reflecting differing dominant modes: in China, for example, the substitution from public transit is especially high. Bigazzi and Wong note that these percentages reflect decisions by early adopters; later adopters may exhibit different substitution patterns. They also point out that the mode-shift percentages do not necessarily reflect the amount of displaced travel from other modes because destinations, distances, and vehicle occupancy vary by mode and may be affected by a shift in modes.

E-bikes differ from conventional bicycles in their environmental, health, and safety impacts. Due to their light weight and electric power, e-bikes are only marginally less friendly than conventional bicycling and walking. Furthermore, riders of e-bikes generally exert less effort than riders of conventional bicycles but still derive health benefits from the activity. Stenner *et al.* (2020) study the impacts of e-bikes through experimental programs in Germany; most users traveled the same distance per trip as with conventional bicycles, but with e-bikes, they took more trips and spent more time riding per week. They did not change time spent on other physical activities.

The safety consequences of e-bikes are ambiguous relative to conventional bicycles (Schepers *et al.* 2018). Since they are heavier and faster than conventional bicycles, e-bikes require more time and distance to stop. They also tend to be less stable when riders are mounting and dismounting, and a fall at higher speed increases its physical impact. On the other hand, their speed difference with surrounding traffic is smaller, which could reduce crashes; although they can create hazards for pedestrians and conventional bicyclists.

Most e-bikes are powered by lithium-ion batteries, and so share the problems of materials availability with electric cars. In addition, these batteries can cause fires and even explosions during crashes and when they are recharged. We did not mention this in the case of electric cars because the main comparison mode is gasoline- or diesel-powered cars, which are subject to the same hazard. However, this property does create an additional hazard for users of e-bikes relative to conventional bicycles.

3.7.5   *Electric scooters*

E-scooters in our definition are scooters – that is, small two- or three-wheeled vehicles with the rider standing on a footboard and steering with handlebars – powered by an electric motor. In this definition, they are not to be confused with electric versions of mopeds (also, confusingly, sometimes called "scooters"), which have pedals and on which riders sit. As a light-weight means of transportation designed for short trips, e-scooters are considered a form of micromobility. They are typically used for commuting, shopping, and performing other errands in city centers, especially where driving is slow and parking is costly (Kazemzadeh *et al.* 2023), and on university campuses. Shared e-scooter systems have been available since 2017. Similar to e-bikes, e-scooters can be either substitutes or complements for other modes. They are also subject to the same problems of lithium-ion batteries.

E-scooter riders stand rather than sit as with e-bikes, but do not exert effort to propel the vehicle. Speed, acceleration, and deceleration all differ from those of e-bikes. Average trip distance is limited by a tendency for vibrations to make riding uncomfortable (Kazemzadeh and Sprei 2022). Rules and regulations on where e-scooters can be ridden and parked vary and, in many jurisdictions, are in flux as authorities evaluate the safety and other consequences of these additions to the streets and sidewalks. Most sidewalks, bicycle lanes, and other infrastructure have not been designed with e-scooters in mind, often creating conflicts with other uses.

Due to their small size, e-scooters are relatively agile; but their small wheels, the upright posture of the rider, and differences in speed with other modes compromise their safety. Detailed data on e-scooter accidents is still limited, and studies are few as of this writing (Kazemzadeh *et al.* 2023). Partly because of their novelty, the number of accidents involving e-scooters has been rising, with head and face injuries reported to be the most common.

3.8   Conclusions

Cost models may be simple or excruciatingly complex, depending on their purpose. But to be useful, they must at least be rigorous. That means carefully distinguishing what is an output, what is a parameter, and what is being held constant. By doing this, the researcher can summarize a host of information in useful ways, such as average costs, marginal costs, and economies of scale and scope. Carefully distinguishing between long-run and short-run variations and rigorously defining the associated cost functions help to clarify what costs need to be considered in particular policy decisions.

Such summary measures and their underlying components can, in turn, be used to understand significant features affecting how transportation services are, or could be, supplied. As just one example, recognizing that the time supplied by users is a necessary input into the production of trips leads to a recognition of scale economies for producing scheduled services such as public transit, which, in turn, implies that marginal cost pricing, often recommended on efficiency grounds, will produce revenue shortfalls.

Turning to congested highways, it is possible to use cost functions to understand the outcome of allowing many users to choose trip frequencies, routes, and travel schedules endogenously, in a context where their choices in aggregate determine the pattern of travel times that each of them takes as given. Even a simple static model of congestion provides a valuable insight about the inefficiencies of such situations and (as shown in the next chapter) about the possibilities of pricing to alleviate them. When applied to an artificial network of two or three competing routes, the static model shows that unexpectedly perverse results can occasionally occur from widening a highway or from adding a new highway link. When applied to a realistic network, a static model enables planners to estimate the effects of changes in transportation demand or infrastructure, so long as these changes are modest enough that the model's assumptions continue to be valid approximations.

Dynamic models provide further insights. For example, total congestion cost may be dominated by how strongly people care about their preferred schedules, rather than how much they value the time lost in delays. We have argued that further progress in refining our understanding of policies on the public agenda today will require researchers to combine economic analysis with increasingly detailed engineering models of dynamic congestion formation and evolution.

The most important components of transportation costs have been studied extensively, making it possible to compile and compare reasonable empirical estimates of them. We have done this illustratively, for urban commuting by automobile in the USA. For that case, social costs are dominated by congestion, accidents, and parking – all areas where charging users for these costs is not straightforward. Each of these three cost components appears to be larger than environmental costs, even though estimates of the latter have grown as the true threat of climate change is clarified.

Our tabulations also reveal considerable differences between marginal social costs and average private costs, suggesting the likelihood of overuse of private automobiles in urban contexts. We will have more to say about this in the next chapter, where we consider the implications of different ways to price automobile users.

Many newer technologies are rapidly changing the nature of transportation costs and promise to do so more in the future. These include electric vehicles, AVs, and various digital forms of organizing travel services including ride-sourcing, shared-ride car services, e-bikes, and e-scooters. While we have no crystal ball to predict exactly how these will shape urban transportation, there is no doubt that they will. We have offered some thoughts based on research to date and suggest that there will be much room for rigorous research to better understand this evolutionary picture.

Notes

1 This assumes capital stock is divisible; if not, the equal-marginal-cost principle holds at most output levels, but breaks down wherever an increase in output requires a discrete change in capital stock and hence long-run marginal cost is undefined.
2 We follow here Mohring (1976, pp. 145–46).
3 Derivation: $s = ac / mc = [(C_B^* + C_W^*)/ q]/[c_p / N] = (C_B^* + C_W^*)/ C_B^*$. Note however, that $s \leq 2$ in an optimum, because otherwise we would have $C_W^* > C_B^*$, implying that a marginal increase in frequency V would reduce waiting costs by more (namely by C_w/V) than it would raise the cost to the bus agency (namely by $c_p = C_B/V$) – contrary to the assumption that the agency is minimizing the sum of these costs.
4 Derivation: we want to set generalized price equal to $mc = d(C_B^* + C_W^*)/ dq = c_p /N$. But the part of that price paid in the form of user-supplied costs is $C_W^*/q = \alpha^w N/(2q)$. The fare is the difference.
5 See Jansson (1980) and Nash (1988).
6 Mohring (1972), Kraus (1991), and Jara-Díaz and Tirachini (2013) all show that this last effect can be quite important.

7 Among the considerations is whether to operate bus lines as grids, with transfers at crossing points, or as more special-purpose lines linking common origins with common destinations. Many network algorithms developed by engineers are relevant. For a full treatment, see Vuchic (2005).

8 See, for example, Hensher and Golob (2008) and Fitzsimmons (2018).

9 A more precise term than "vehicles" is "passenger-car equivalents," a measure that combines vehicles of different sizes and acceleration capabilities, each with a weight indicating its contribution to congestion.

10 Engineers sometimes call the upper branch of the speed–flow relationship "uncongested flow" and the lower branch "congested flow." In our terminology, more common in economics, "uncongested" or "free flow" refers instead to the absence of mutual hindrance; *i.e.*, where $S(V)$ is perfectly flat, such as in the limiting condition as $V \to 0$ on the upper branch in Figure 3.1. We use the terms "congested" and "normally congested" interchangeably, depending on whether an explicit distinction with "hyper-congested" is needed.

11 This is their preferred equation (20, p. 350), converted to units of vehicles per lane per hour by setting $V = 5q$.

12 This is calculated from Inman's equation (2), p. 23, with parameter estimates from the top row of his Table 1, p. 25. The units and the unreported constant X were supplied by Inman, private conversation; they are $N = V/500$, $G = S/10$, and $X = 36.488$. The Inman curve is undefined for $S < 7.2$ mi/hr, and can show no backward-bending portion unless the exponent on the right-hand side is constrained to be precisely an even integer, as it is for the special case represented by the Boardman–Lave formula.

13 This tendency is also noted by Banks (1989) for San Diego, California, and by Hall and Hall (1990) for Toronto, Canada, in both cases for short uniform stretches of highway unaffected by a bottleneck.

14 These curves were drawn by us using information provided by UK Department for Transport (2002), Transportation Research Board (2000), and Smith *et al.* (1996). The HCM2000 and COBA11 curves assume an expressway with no hills, bends, or heavy vehicles. Capacities under these idealized conditions are $V_K = 2,330$ (COBA) and $V_K = 2,350$ (HCM), and the break points V_B are 1,200 (COBA) and 1,450 (HCM). The two COBA segments are given by $S = 118 - 0.006 \cdot V$ for $V \le V_B$ and $S = 110.8 - (33/1,000)\cdot(V - V_B)$ for $V_B < V \le V_K$. The two HCM segments are given by $S = 110$ for $V \le V_B$ and $S = 110 - [(730/28)\cdot((V - 1450)/900)^{2.6}]$ for $V_B < V \le V_K$. The two additional (dotted) segments proposed by Hall, Hurdle and Banks (1992) are hand-drawn.

15 Transportation Research Board (2016).

16 This is Keeler and Small's equation (12, p. 11), for the Eastshore Freeway, rewritten to make transparent the maximum V/V_K ratio and the maximum speed.

17 See US Bureau of Public Roads (1964).

18 BPR-U, derived by Skabardonis and Dowling (1996), has values $a = 0.2$ (freeways) or 0.05 (arterials), and $b = 10$.

19 Dewees (1978) reports nine simulations from Toronto arterials; we fit the nine resulting data points, using non-linear least squares, obtaining $T_f = 2.48$ minutes, $a = 0.102$, and $b = 4.08$ for equation (3.6), and $T_f = 3.07$ minutes, $P = 14.44$ minutes, and $V_K = 1357$ veh/hr for equation (3.7). Similarly, Small (1983, pp. 32–33) finds that (3.7) approximates the pattern of travel times during the afternoon peak period on an 11-mile stretch of freeway in the San Francisco Bay area.

20 Akçelik proposes the following parameters $\{V_K, S_f, J_a\}$ for different types of roads, where $S_f = L/T_f$ (mi/hr) and L is the length of the road: freeway $\{2000, 75, 0.1\}$; uninterrupted arterial $\{1800, 62, 0.2\}$; interrupted arterial $\{1200, 50, 0.4\}$; interrupted secondary $\{900, 37, 0.8\}$; high-friction secondary $\{600, 25, 1.6\}$.

21 See for example Arnott (2013), Fosgerau (2015), and Jin (2020).

22 Equation (3.14) can be understood as follows. Let ΔN denote the change in the number of cars between two locations x and $x + \Delta x$ over the time interval from t to $t + \Delta t$. If Δt is small enough, the flow rates at the two locations can be treated as constant over time; letting ΔV denote the difference in V between the two locations, we see that the number of vehicles between x and $x + \Delta x$ builds up if incoming flow exceeds outgoing flow, *i.e.*, it builds at rate $-\Delta V$. Thus $\Delta N = -\Delta t \cdot \Delta V$. If Δx is small enough, density at the two locations can be treated as equal; letting ΔD denote the change in density over time, we see that the number of vehicles in this space of length Δx changes in proportion to the change in density: $\Delta N = \Delta x \cdot \Delta D$. Because vehicles are conserved, these two expressions for ΔN should be equal, in turn implying $\Delta V/\Delta x + \Delta D/\Delta t = 0$. When the discrete increments become infinitesimal, (3.14) is obtained.

23 After rotating the $V(D)$ curve of Figure 3.1c by 90°, shock-wave speed S_w between two states can be found geometrically as the slope of the straight line connecting these states. The traffic speed in a state

is given by the slope of the ray from the origin through that state. Under the stated assumptions, S_w is then always smaller than S_u and S_d.

24 Other phenomena found, empirically or on test tracks, include path-dependency of observed speed–density combinations (Zhang 1999) and spontaneous transitions to hypercongested equilibria in the absence of a bottleneck (Kerner and Rehborn 1997; Sugiyama *et al.* 2008). The relevance of the spontaneous transitions to observed traffic is disputed by Daganzo *et al.* (1999).

25 In the example in Section 2.3.3, we reserved symbol *p* for an explicit price, and used symbol *c* for the "money price" to the user (Table 2.3 and equation 2.36). We did this in order to indicate that it also includes any other monetary expenditures, such as fuel and car maintenance, that vary with usage. Here such expenditures are also part of cost *c*, but so are the user-perceived costs, such as travel time, valued at the amounts derived from travel demand models.

26 See Verhoef (1999). When applying conventional stability analysis, an equilibrium is stable for flow perturbations if a small increase in flow leads to average cost $c(V)$ above inverse demand $d(V)$, inducing users to reduce their inflow. An equilibrium is stable for price perturbations if a small increase in "price" (here average cost, so one could think of a speed perturbation) leads to excess supply: *i.e.*, it leads to a "price" where the supply curve is to the right of the demand curve. In conventional markets this would cause suppliers to reduce the price level; but here the "supplier" is a congestion technology rather than a profit-motivated firm, making this stability criterion of questionable relevance.

27 The same result occurs with the LWR model when discontinuous changes in traffic conditions (*V*, *D*, and *S*) are ruled out. The intuition is that, from equation (3.15), the shock wave between two hypercongested stationary states must always travel at a negative speed. This is because, with $V(D)$ downward-sloping between both states, $V_u - V_d$ and $D_u - D_d$ must have opposite signs. Therefore a change in inflow can never cause a transition between two hypercongested stationary states, or, indeed, from the maximum-flow state to any hypercongested state: the boundary to the new state can travel only backward so can never enter the road.

28 A naïve but understandable choice of *P*, defined by the instants that queuing begins and ends, would imply a time-averaged inflow *V* equal to capacity V_K. This choice would produce travel delay equal to zero according to the piecewise-linear function and $(1/2)^{1/2} \cdot (PJ_d/V_K)^{1/2}$ according to Akçelik's function.

29 It is analyzed by Hendrickson and Kocur (1981) and Newell (1987).

30 However, as will be noted later in this section, their analysis treats only the special case in which the desired schedule t_d is identical for all commuters. This implies that, in our notation, $q = 0$ and $V_d = \infty$, both achieved as limiting processes keeping $Q \equiv q \cdot V_d$ fixed. This version of the model, which we call the *basic bottleneck model*, is widely used. Here, we achieve more realism at a modest cost in complexity by retaining Vickrey's original assumption of a uniform distribution of t_d with non-zero *q* and finite V_d. In doing so we also render the assumption of zero travel time before and after the bottleneck less troublesome because the varying preference for queue-exit time could be interpreted as arising from individuals having different free-flow times T_f that are outside the model. The extra complexity seems amply justified in light of the evidence compiled by Jonathan D. Hall (2021), as discussed later in this section, that non-identical schedules are essential for explaining observed empirical congestion patterns.

31 These theoretical rates of change are compared to actual rates on congested roads in Paris by Fargier (1983, pp. 247–52) in order to estimate the behavioral parameters β/α and γ/α. He gets values much smaller than the direct behavioral estimates of Small (1982). As discussed at the end of this section, the discrepancy is consistent with the findings of Hall (2021), noted in Section 2.8.6, that most commuters are infra-marginal in the sense that they arrive exactly at their preferred time rather than balancing travel time and schedule delay costs at the margin.

32 Due to linearity in the cost function, each commuter is in fact indifferent among departure times in the "early" interval $[t_q, \tilde{t}]$, or else among departure times in the "late" interval $[\tilde{t}, t_q]$. We can remove this indeterminacy by making the quite natural assumption that commuters exit the queue in the same order as their desired queue-exit times.

33 This differs from the Arnott, de Palma and Lindsey model, for which the desired arrival times are the same for all travelers, and also equilibrium costs are the same.

34 Somewhat confusingly, the UE has sometimes been called a "user optimum," in contrast to a "system optimum" which is the socially optimal flow pattern (to be discussed in Chapter 4).

35 The following example is from Arnott and Small (1994). Suppose two bridges, *A* and *B*, cross a river. When bridge *i* carries traffic volume V_i, congestion causes its travel time (in minutes) to be $V_i/100$. Two cities a few miles apart and on opposite sides of the river are connected by two routes. Route *A* uses bridge *A* and an uncongested road that takes 15 minutes to travel; route *B* uses bridge *B* and a different

but identical road. (The roads follow the river bank on opposite sides.) Total traffic of 1,000 reaches a user equilibrium when traffic divides equally across the two routes, resulting in flows $V_A = V_B = 500$ and travel times $t_A = t_B = 15 + (500/100) = 20$. An engineer notices that the roads along the river banks are circuitous, and proposes a straight causeway connecting the far ends of the two bridges; it takes only 7.5 minutes to traverse, but to do so requires crossing both bridges. It looks like a time saver because currently each bridge has only 5 minutes of congestion, so the new route C covering both bridges and the causeway takes only 17.5 minutes. However, after the causeway is built, congestion on the bridges rises: travel time on route i is now $t_i = 15 + (V_i + V_C)/100$, for $i = A, B$, while that on route C is $t_C = 7.5 + (V_A + V_C)/100 + (V_B + V_C)/100$. Equilibrium requires that all three travel times be equal; this occurs when $V_A = V_B = 250$, $V_C = 500$, and $t_A = t_B = t_C = 22.5$. Because the causeway has enticed half the travelers onto a route with a higher marginal congestion cost than the other routes (due to its including both bridges), its availability raises travel costs for everyone compared to the situation where it had never been built.

36 See, for example, Kobayashi (1994), Arnott *et al.* (1991a), and Emmerink (1998).

37 See, for example, Lindsey *et al.* (2014).

38 For example, Jiang *et al.* (2020). This finding is similar to the way induced demand can create the Downs-Thompson paradox discussed earlier.

39 See Hall (1996) and Dong *et al.* (2006).

40 See Ramos *et al.* (2014) and Ben-Elia and Avineri (2015) for reviews of applications of behavioral economics to transportation research.

41 Mrozek and Taylor (2002) advocate including industry-specific dummy variables to reduce the influence of such factors. Doing so also reduces variation in the risk variable across any sample, so makes estimation more difficult. Viscusi and Aldy (2003), arguing against such inclusion, find the predicted VSL for US studies to be roughly three times higher than found by Mrozek and Taylor.

42 For this, we use the chain-type price index for personal consumption expenditures (PCE) in the USA, from US CEA (2021), Table B-39, which rose 42.3% between 2000 and 2020. Their reported average in 2000 prices is $6.52 million, from their Table 5 Specification 0.

43 Bellavance *et al.* (2009, p. 454) measure the income elasticity at 0.84–1.08, in their sample of mostly high-income countries.

44 Viscusi and Aldy (2003) review 39 such studies from around the world.

45 Specifically, we have updated costs other than fatalities by the average of (i) growth in nominal hourly earnings (production and non-supervisory employees) and (ii) growth in the price index for personal consumption expenditures (PCE). These two quantities grew 82.8% and 45.4%, respectively, between the 3-year period 1998–2000 and the year 2020: from US CEA (2023), Tables B-30, B-39. The average of these two growth rates is 64.1%.

46 Based on Parry's Table 2. For our tally of non-fatal injuries, we include accidents with "possible injury" but exclude those with "injury status unknown." Parry's estimates are disaggregated by severity of injury. Updated to 2020$, his figures imply that the cost of a non-fatal injury ranges from $43,000 to $251,000, with weighted average $76,000. This compares to $11.3 million for a fatal injury, which consists of our assumed VSL ($11 million) plus Parry's estimates of associated costs such as legal, insurance, and property damage.

47 See Fridstrøm *et al.* (1995), Wang *et al.* (2009), and Fridstrøm (2011). Fast traffic also discourages pedestrians and bicyclists, a direct cost to them and possibly an efficiency cost to the entire urban transportation system.

48 Such offsetting behavior was postulated by Peltzman (1975) and has been tested empirically in many contexts, mostly confirming it. For a review and an application to anti-lock brakes, see Winston, Maheshri and Mannering (2006).

49 More recent papers include Anderson (2008), Brozović and Ando (2009), Li (2012), Van Ommeren *et al.* (2013), Jacobsen (2013), and Anderson and Aufhammer (2014). This inter-vehicle externality may be diminishing as manufacturers redesign SUVs and pickup trucks to reduce their impact on cars.

50 This dominance of mortality appears to contrast with the situation in analyzing COVID-19 as an externality, for which morbidity may be a much more significant component of health costs: see Ashworth *et al.* (2022, p. 157).

51 Many researchers have documented correlations between mortality and ozone concentrations over very short time periods such as days. But some or all of such correlation is likely due to "harvesting" (more formally, "short-term mortality displacement"), whereby short-term changes in air quality determine the timing of a death that was going to occur soon for other reasons. See National Research Council (2008), especially pp. 69, 75 (note 3).

52 The authors of National Research Council (2008) conclude that ozone probably does produce deaths over a longer time period, but "[b]ecause the evidence is based on results from only one study, it warrants confirmation by other studies" (pp. 84–85).

53 "Increases of 10 μg per cubic meter in $PM_{2.5}$ and of 10 ppb [parts per billion] in ozone were associated with increases in…mortality of 7.3%…and 1.1%…, respectively" (Qian *et al.* 2017, p. 2513).

54 See their text, p. 2983. They also relate these ozone levels to NO_x control measures on power plants, controlling for endogeneity (using state-level decisions on entering an emissions trading program) and for defensive health investments, in order to estimate specifically the benefits of NO_x control.

55 This is the conclusion of National Research Council (2008, pp. 26–28). That report cites Alberini *et al.* (2004), who "find weak support for the notion that [VSL] declines with age, and then, only for [people] aged 70 or above" (Alberini *et al.*, p. 769). By contrast, Viscusi and Aldy (2003, pp. 50–53) conclude that VSL does decline with age. However they find that this decline is *not* proportional to remaining life span, and thus their results, even if valid, would not support the more radical practice in which risk of fatalities at different ages are all valued through a single constant known as the value of a statistical life year (VSLY); see National Research Council (2008, pp. 8–9). (A closely related concept, which also incorporates morbidity, is the value of a "quality-adjusted life year" or QALY; see Krupnick 2004.)

56 Population exposure depends critically on wind and the vertical mixing of the atmosphere, which these models attempt to take into account. The effect of wind is exemplified by the long-time practice of higher-income residents locating upwind of urban pollution sources, documented by Heblich *et al.* (2021).

57 From their Table 7.7, p. 144, averaging over the four instances of gasoline cars and excluding the column for CO_2. Of the total, particulates account for two-thirds, NOx for one-fourth, and sulfur dioxide and volatile organic compounds for most of the rest.

58 Cui and Levinson (2020, p. 506). We have combined their internal and external cost estimates, the former (0.09 cents/km) arising from air breathed by a car's own occupants while traveling, the latter (1.92 cents/km) from the car's effect on air breathed by everyone else.

59 The 2017 National Household Travel Survey (NHTS) tabulates average commute trip distance and time for all US commutes by automobile as 12.21 miles and 25.47 minutes, as given by Davis and Boundy (2021, Table 9.17). This includes some rural trips, which tend to be about 10% shorter in time (Burd *et al.* 2021, Table 3), so we have rounded the time upward to 26.0 minutes. The fraction of travel time due to congestion (*i.e.*, any travel time above that for free-flow conditions) is equivalent to a Travel Time Index of 1.30, defined as "The ratio of travel time in the peak period to the travel time at free-flow conditions" in Schrank *et al.* (2019), Table 1, notes; that table shows average travel time index in the largest 47 US metropolitan areas as 1.35 for the top 15 and 1.24 for others.

60 External costs raise a host of estimation issues besides those treated here. Many of them are discussed by Quinet (2004) for Western Europe, and Delucchi and McCubbin (2011) for the United States.

61 As reported in Davis and Boundy (2021, Table 11.15) for year 2019, updated to 2020 by the PCE price index.

62 Average US federal and state gasoline tax rates in 2019 were $0.184 and $0.279 per gallon, respectively: US FHWA (2021), Tables FE-101a, MF-205; we update prices by 1.0105. Average fuel consumption for automobiles was one gallon per 28.3 miles: Davis and Boundy (2021, Table 4.1).

63 The capital recovery factor is the annual expenditure in each year from 1 to T that has a *present value* of 1.0 (computed at interest rate r). The present value of an expenditure C undertaken at some time t years in the future is the amount, invested today, that would provide sufficient funds for that expenditure; if the interest rate is a constant r and compounded annually, the present value is $C/(1+r)^t$. Adding such terms from $t=1$ through $t=T$, and inverting, we obtain (3.39). If interest is compounded n times per year the CRF becomes $r/(1-\delta_n^{nT})$, where $\delta_n=(1+r/n)^{-1}$. Continuous compounding is represented by taking the limit as $n \to \infty$, which yields $CRF = r/(1-e^{-rT})$. The discrete version is more commonly used; in this chapter, we use it whenever T is an integer.

64 Data are from Davis and Boundy (2021), for 2019, updated to 2020 prices. We choose 2019 in order to avoid anomalies in car markets during the COVID-19 pandemic in 2020. New-car price: Table 11.13. Annual miles per vehicle: Table 4.1. Median lifetime: Table 3.15 (time at which survival rate of cars is 50%).

65 The real rate for US car loans in 2016–2020 was 3.28%, calculated from the 2016–2020 average annual US rates for car loans (4.76%, from US FRB 2021), minus the average annual inflation rate over the same years (1.48%, from US CEA 2021, Table B-39). We use a higher rate than this due to credit-market frictions that raise the effective cost to buyers.

66 Mean hourly earnings in 2019 were $23.51, from US CEA (2021), Table B-30; we update to 2020$.

67 The ratio of 1.7 quoted here is the value of "congestion costs generated" (per vehicle-km) for cars, averaged between urban trunk roads and other urban roads (from their Table 48), divided by "congestion costs borne" for all urban passenger cars (their Table 41). As will be discussed in Chapter 4 around equation (4.9), the said ratio of 1.7 could be generated by the BPR function of equation (3.6) when its power is 1.7. This is below the conventional power of 4 often used for single link models, but is reasonable for congested traffic averaged over space and time on networks; see our discussions of space-averaged and time-averaged congestion relationships in Section 3.3.2.

68 From US FHWA 2021, Table HF-10; we include only 1/3 of "administration and research" disbursements because we allocate the other two-thirds to road capital (included in line 8 of Table 3.3), based on the ratio of "Maintenance and traffic services" to "Capital outlay" in this same table. These are divided by vehicle-miles traveled by all vehicles, from same source, Table VM-1.

69 For the USA in 2019, this was $0.184/gal federal tax plus a weighted average over state taxes of $0.279/gal (US FHWA 2021, Table MF-121T).

70 Their point estimates for congestion cost are 18.2 €ct/pass.-km for dense traffic on rural motorways, and 41.2 €ct/pass.-km for dense metropolitan traffic. (€ct stands for Euro cent, *i.e.*, 0.01 Euro.) External costs due to climate change, not corrected for fuel duties, are between 0.8 and 1.81 €ct/pass.-km for fossil fuel cars, depending on the type of car. Air pollution varies from 0.08 to 1.9 €ct/pass.-km; noise accounts for 0.5 €ct/pass.-km in dense metropolitan traffic and 0.04 €ct/pass.-km for dense rural traffic, and external costs of accidents amount to 1.41 €ct/pass.-km in dense metropolitan conditions and 0.25 €ct/pass.-km for dense rural traffic. To convert these numbers to $ct per veh.-mile, we should multiply them by around 3.1 (1.7 for assumed vehicle occupancy in the EU numbers, times 1.14 for the exchange rate, times 1.6 km per mile). The remaining difference in the external cost of accidents is mostly due to differences in the VSL, which is around one third in the EU numbers compared to what we have used for the US numbers.

71 The role of free-flow speed in capital investment is formalized by Small and Ng (2014).

72 In the limiting special case where $q \rightarrow 0$ while keeping $Vq \equiv Q$ finite, only the second regime applies and its cost becomes $C_g(Q) = c_{bot}Q$, showing neutral scale economies in Q.

73 Parcel delivery is also moving to the air, as drone technology advances rapidly, with regulation slowly evolving. At time of writing, automated drone aircraft are performing deliveries for large customers such as Walmart, Amazon, Walgreens, and FedEx in the United States, and for supermarkets in Australia. Drones are also suited to transporting medical supplies and specimens, and providing services for mining, oil & gas, and other businesses in rural communities and remote areas. Due to safety, noise, and privacy concerns, drones are not yet permitted to fly in densely-populated areas. Nevertheless, it seems likely that experience will gradually lead to expansion of such services, which may replace many road delivery trips.

74 In Europe there are only two charger types. Category 1 uses AC delivered at the standard residential 230 V. Category 2 uses DC delivered at 400 V (https://alternative-fuels-observatory.ec.europa.eu/general-information/recharging-systems)

75 See Dimitropoulos *et al.* (2013) for a historical review of studies, and the discussion in Section 2.4.6 on general automobile ownership and usage decisions.

76 This last point substantially lowers the social benefits of EV incentives, as explored by Muehlegger and Rapson (2023).

77 See De Rubens *et al.* (2020). Yet another possibility is to provide "batteries as a service", whereby customers pay a monthly fee to use a battery; or "battery swapping", whereby discharged batteries are simply replaced at a depot with fresh batteries. Battery swapping, however, has attracted skepticism as a business model (Ulrich 2021).

78 See Anfinsen *et al.* (2019) and Daramy-Williams *et al.* (2019).

79 The degree of scale economies, as defined here, is the inverse of the cost elasticity, estimated by Kraus at 0.84 (1981, p. 20 and n. 4).

80 The corresponding capital recovery factor, from equation (3.39), is 0.0736. We update the capital value from 2019 to 2020 using the same price index as for operating costs in Section 3.4. We assume that "passenger vehicles" consists of automobiles, pickup trucks, and vans for the cost allocation in US FHWA (2000).

81 Here we assume that passenger vehicles consists of all light-duty vehicles as listed in US FHWA (2021), Table VM-1, whose VMT was 2,924 billion in 2019. We update from 2019 prices to 2020 prices using the same factor 1.0105 used earlier for operating costs.

82 Here, we allocate a small portion of "other taxes and fees" as a privately paid fixed cost: specifi-cally, 2/3 of "administration and research" disbursements, assumed to be paid for privately through various vehicle-related fees. (The other 1/3 is assumed variable: see endnote for part 6, "Govern-ment Services," of the short-run costs tabulated in section 3.4.9.) These are very arbitrary alloca-tions, acceptable for our purposes because the amounts involved are such tiny portions of costs of driving.

83 This assumes tight planning by the employer. The average vacancy rate for all US parking spaces in the late 1990s was much higher: about 50% (Cambridge Systematics *et al.*, 1998, pp. 9–17, n. 15). But as described in Section 3.6, newer planning regulations are requiring less employer parking.

84 We take the per-space cost of an urban parking structure to be the average of those for under- or above-ground structures. We assume that suburban structures and surface lots cost 60% and 30% as much, respectively, per space. For our representative urban commuter, we then average these three per-space costs (for an urban structure, a suburban structure, and a suburban surface lot). We add 20% for land costs. We update to 2020 prices using the PCE price index, as for roads.

85 See *e.g.*, Arnott (2011) and Inci (2015).

86 In the USA, the effects of minimum parking requirements are aggravated by tax laws governing employer-provided benefits, which favor parking costs relative to other transportation subsidies. See Shoup (2018, Part I).

87 See Hess (2018) and Shoup (2018d).

References

Abbas, Khaled A. and Mona H. Abd-Allah (1999) "Estimation and assessment of cost allocation models for main transit systems operating in Cairo," *Transport Reviews* 19: 353–375.

Abe, Ryosuke (2019) "Introducing autonomous buses and taxis: quantifying the potential benefits in Japa-nese transportation systems," *Transportation Research Part A: Policy and Practice* 126: 94–113.

Adler, Martin, Stefanie Peer and Tanja Sinozic (2019) "Autonomous, connected, electric shared vehicles (ACES) and public finance: an explorative analysis," *Transportation Research Interdisciplinary Per-spectives* 2: 100038.

Agnew, Carson E. (1976) "Dynamic modeling and control of congestion-prone systems," *Operations Re-search* 24(3): 400–419.

Agnew, Carson E. (1977) "The theory of congestion tolls," *Journal of Regional Science* 17: 381–393.

Akçelik, Rahmi (1991) "Travel time functions for transport planning purposes: Davidson's function, its time-dependent form and an alternative travel time function," *Australian Road Research* 21: 49–59.

Akerlof, George A. (1970) "The market for 'lemons': quality uncertainty and the market mechanism," *Quarterly Journal of Economics* 84(3): 488–500.

Alberini, Anna *et al.* (2004) "Does the value of a statistical life vary with age and health status? Evidence from the US and Canada," *Journal of Environmental Economics and Management* 48: 769–792.

Alberini, Anna (2019) "Revealed versus stated preferences: what have we learned about valuation and behavior?," *Review of Environmental Economics and Policy* 13(2): 283–298.

Anderson, Michael L. (2008), "Safety for whom? The effects of light trucks on traffic fatalities," *Journal of Health Economics* 27: 973–989.

Anderson, Michael L. (2020) "As the wind blows: the effects of long-term exposure to air pollution on mortality," *Journal of the European Economic Association* 18(4): 1886–1927.

Anderson, Michael L. and Maximilian Auffhammer (2014) "Pounds that kill: the external costs of vehicle weight," *Review of Economic Studies* 81: 535–571.

Andersson, Henrik and Nicolas Treich (2011) "The value of a statistical life," in André de Palma *et al.* (eds.) *A Handbook of Transport Economics*, Cheltenham: Edward Elgar.

Anfinsen, Martin, Vivian Anette Lagesen and Marianne Ryghaug (2019) "Green and gendered? Cultural perspectives on the road towards electric vehicles in Norway," *Transportation Research Part D: Trans-port and Environment* 71: 37–46.

Arnott, Richard (1998) "Congestion tolling and the urban spatial structure," *Journal of Regional Sci-ence* 38(3): 495–504.

Arnott, Richard (2011) "Parking economics," in André de Palma *et al.* (eds.) *A Handbook of Transport Economics*, Cheltenham: Edward Elgar, pp. 726–743.

Arnott, Richard (2013) "A bathtub model of downtown traffic congestion," *Journal of Urban Economics* 76: 110–121.

Arnott, Richard and Joshua Buli (2018) "Solving for equilibrium in the basic bathtub model," *Transportation Research Part B: Methodological* 109: 150–175.

Arnott, Richard, André de Palma and Robin Lindsey (1990) "Economics of a bottleneck," *Journal of Urban Economics* 27: 111–130.

Arnott, Richard, André de Palma and Robin Lindsey (1991) "Does providing information to drivers reduce traffic congestion?" *Transportation Research Part A: Policy and Practice* 25(5): 309–318.

Arnott, Richard, André de Palma and Robin Lindsey (1992) "Route choice with heterogeneous drivers and group-specific congestion costs," *Regional Science and Urban Economics* 22: 71–102.

Arnott, Richard, André de Palma and Robin Lindsey (1993) "A structural model of peak-period congestion: a traffic bottleneck with elastic demand," *American Economic Review* 83(1): 161–179.

Arnott, Richard, André de Palma and Robin Lindsey (1994) "The welfare effects of congestion tolls with heterogeneous commuters," *Journal of Transport Economics and Policy* 28(2): 139–161.

Arnott, Richard, André de Palma and Robin Lindsey (1996) "Information and usage of free-access congestible facilities," *International Economic Review* 37(1): 181–203.

Arnott, Richard, André de Palma and Robin Lindsey (1999) "Information and time-of-usage decisions in the bottleneck model with stochastic capacity and demand," *European Economic Review* 43: 525–548.

Arnott, Richard and Eren Inci (2010) "The stability of downtown parking and traffic congestion," *Journal of Urban Economics* 68: 260–276.

Arnott, Richard, Anatolii Kokoza and Mehdi Naji (2016) "Equilibrium traffic dynamics in a bathtub model: a special case," *Economics of Transportation* 7–8: 38–52.

Arnott, Richard and Kenneth A. Small (1994) "The economics of traffic congestion," *American Scientist* 82: 446–455.

Ashworth, Madison, Todd L. Cherry, David Finnoff, Stephen C. Newbold, Jason F. Shogren and Linda Thunström (2022) "COVID-19 research and policy analysis: contributions from environmental economists," *Review of Environmental Economics and Policy* 16(1): 153–167.

Axsen, Jonn and Benjamin K. Sovacool (2019) (eds.) "The roles of users in low-carbon transport innovations: electrified, automated, and shared mobility," *Transportation Research Part D: Transport and Environment* 71: 1–21.

Bailey, Elizabeth E. and Ann F. Friedlaender (1982) "Market structure and multiproduct industries," *Journal of Economic Literature* 20(3): 1024–1048.

Banks, James H. (1989) "Freeway speed-flow-concentration relationships: more evidence and interpretations," *Transportation Research Record: Journal of the Transportation Research Board* 225: 53–60.

Barnes, Gary and Peter Langworthy (2003) "Per mile costs of operating automobiles and trucks," *Transportation Research Record: Journal of the Transportation Research Board* 1864(1): 71–77.

Barter, Paul (2018) "Parking policies in Asian cities: conventional but instructive," in Donald C. Shoup (ed.) *The High Cost of Free Parking*, Chicago, IL: American Planning Association, Planners Press, pp. 161–170.

Basso, Leonardo J., Sergio R. Jara-Díaz and William G. Waters II (2011) "Cost functions for transport firms," in André de Palma *et al.* (eds.) *A Handbook of Transport Economics*, Cheltenham: Edward Elgar, pp. 273–297.

Bastian, Anne and Maria Börjesson (2018) "The city as a driver of new mobility patterns, cycling and gender equality: travel behaviour trends in Stockholm 1985–2015," *Travel Behaviour and Society* 13: 71–87.

Bates, John (2014) "Parking demand," in Stephen Ison and Corinne Mulley (eds.) *Parking Issues and Policies,* Volume 5, Bingley: Emerald Group Publishing Limited, pp. 57–86.

Becker, Gary S. (1965) "A theory of the allocation of time," *Economic Journal* 75(299): 493–517.

Beckmann, Martin J., C. Bartlett McGuire and Christopher B. Winsten (1956) *Studies in the Economics of Transportation*, New Haven, CT: Yale University Press.

Bellavance, François, George Dionne and Martin Lebeau (2009) "The value of a statistical life: a meta-analysis with a mixed effects regression model," *Journal of Health Economics* 28(2): 444–464.

Ben-Elia, Eran and Erel Avineri (2015) "Response to travel information: a behavioural review," *Transport Reviews* 35(3): 352–377.

Ben-Elia, Eran and Yoram Shiftan (2010) "Which road do I take? A learning-based model of route-choice behavior with real-time information," *Transportation Research Part A: Policy and Practice* 44(4): 249–264.

Bereitschaft, Bradley and Daniel Scheller (2020) "How might the COVID-19 pandemic affect 21st century urban design, planning, and development?," *Urban Science* 4(4): 56.

Bifulco, Gennaro Nicola, Roberta Di Pace and Francesco Viti (2014) "Evaluating the effects of information reliability on travellers' route choice," *European Transport Research Review* 6(1): 61–70.

Bifulco, Gennaro N., Giulio E. Cantarella, Fulvio Simonelli and Pietro Velonà (2016) "Advanced traveller information systems under recurrent traffic conditions: network equilibrium and stability," *Transportation Research Part B: Methodological* 92: 73–87.

Bigazzi, Alexander and Kevin Wong (2020) "Electric bicycle mode substitution for driving, public transit, conventional cycling, and walking," *Transportation Research Part D: Transport and Environment* 85: 102412.

Bishop, Kelly C., Nocolai V. Kuminoff, H. Spencer Banzhaf, Kevin J. Boyle, Kathrine von Gravenitz, Jaren C. Pope, V. Kerry Smith and Christopher D. Timmins (2020) "Best practices for using hedonic property value models to measure willingness to pay for environmental quality," *Review of Environmental Economics and Policy* 14(2): 260–281.

Blundell, Richard, Ran Gu, Søren Leth-Petersen, Hamish Low and Costas Meghir (2023) "Durables and lemons: private information and the market for cars," Working paper 26281, National Bureau of Economic Research (December).

Boardman, Anthony E. and Lester B. Lave (1977) "Highway congestion and congestion tolls," *Journal of Urban Economics* 4(3): 340–359.

Boarnet, Marlon G., Xize Wang and Douglas Houston (2017) "Can new light rail reduce personal vehicle carbon emissions? A before-after, experimental-control evaluation in Los Angeles," *Journal of Regional Science* 57(3): 523–539.

Börjesson, Maria and Jonas Eliasson (2012a) "The benefits of cycling: viewing cyclists as travellers rather than non-motorists," *Cycling and Sustainability* 1: 247–268.

Börjesson, Maria and Jonas Eliasson (2012b) "The value of time and external benefits in bicycle appraisal," *Transportation Research Part A: Policy and Practice* 46(4): 673–683.

Borlaug, Brennan, Shawn Salisbury, Mindy Gerdes and Matteo Muratori (2020) "Levelized cost of charging electric vehicles in the United States," *Joule* 4: 1470–1485.

Braess, Dietrich (1968) "Über ein paradoxon aus der verkehrsplanung," *Unternehmenforschung* 12: 258–268.

Braeutigam, Ronald R. (1999) "Learning about transport costs," in José Gómez-Ibáñez, William B. Tye and Clifford Winston (eds.), *Essays in Transportation Economics and Policy*, Washington, DC: Brookings Institution, pp. 57–97.

Broach, Joseph, Jennifer Dill and John Gliebe (2012) "Where do cyclists ride? A route choice model developed with revealed preference GPS data," *Transportation Research Part A: Policy and Practice* 46(10): 1730–1740.

Brozović, Nicholas and Amy W. Ando (2009) "Defensive purchasing, the safety (dis)advantage of light trucks, and motor-vehicle policy effectiveness," *Transportation Research Part B: Methodological* 43(5): 477–493.

Buehler, Ralph and Jennifer Dill (2016) "Bikeway networks: a review of effects on cycling," *Transport Reviews* 36(1): 9–27.

Burd, Charlynn, Michael Burrows and Brian McKenzie (2021) "Travel time to work in the United States: 2019," American Community Survey Reports ACS-47, US Census Bureau.

Cambridge Systematics, Inc. *et al.* (1998) *Economic Impact Analysis of Transit Investments: Guidebook for Practitioners*, Transit Cooperative Research Program Report 35, Washington, DC: National Academies Press.

Carvajal, Germán A., Olga L. Sarmiento, Andrés L. Medaglia, Sergio Cabrales, Daniel A. Rodríguez, D. Alex Quistberg and Segundo López (2020) "Bicycle safety in Bogotá: a seven-year analysis of bicyclists' collisions and fatalities," *Accident Analysis and Prevention* 144: 105596.

Chorus, Caspar G. and Harry J.P. Timmermans (2011) "Personal intelligent travel assistants," in André de Palma *et al.* (eds.) *A Handbook of Transport Economics*, Cheltenham: Edward Elgar, pp. 604–623.

Chorus, Caspar G., Eric J.E. Molin and Bert Van Wee (2006) "Travel information as an instrument to change car drivers' travel choices: a literature review," *European Journal of Transport and Infrastructure Research* 6(4): 335–364.

Christensen, Laurits R., Dale W. Jorgenson and Lawrence J. Lau (1973) "Transcendental logarithmic production frontiers," *Review of Economics and Statistics* 55(1): 28–45.

Chu, Xuehao (1995) "Endogenous trip scheduling: the Henderson approach reformulated and compared with the Vickrey approach," *Journal of Urban Economics* 37(3): 324–343.

Clifton, Geoffrey T., Corinne Mulley and David A. Hensher (2014) "Bus rapid transit versus heavy rail in suburban Sydney – comparing successive iterations of a proposed heavy rail line project to the pre-existing BRT network," *Research in Transportation Economics* 48: 126–141.

Coulombel, Nicolas and Guillaume Monchambert (2023) "Diseconomies of scale and subsidies in urban public transportation," *Journal of Public Economics*. doi:10.1016/j.jpubeco.2023.104903

Cui, Mengying and David Levinson (2020) "Internal and external costs of motor vehicle pollution," *Transportation Research Record: Journal of the Transportation Research Board*: 2674(11): 498–511.

Dafermos, Stella C. (1980) "Traffic equilibrium and variational inequalities," *Transportation Science* 14(1): 42–54.

Daganzo, Carlos F. (1997) *Fundamentals of Transportation and Traffic Operations*, New York: Pergamon.

Daganzo, Carlos F., Michael J. Cassidy and Robert L. Bertini (1999) "Possible explanations of phase transitions in highway traffic," *Transportation Research Part A: Policy and Practice* 33(5): 365–379.

Daganzo, Carlos F. and Yosef Sheffi (1977) "On stochastic models of traffic assignment," *Transportation Science* 11(3): 253–274.

Daina, Nicolò, Aruna Sivakumar and John W. Polak (2017) "Modelling electric vehicles use: a survey on the methods," *Renewable and Sustainable Energy Reviews* 68: 447–460.

Daramy-Williams, Edmond, Jillian Anable and Susan Grant-Muller (2019) "A systematic review of the evidence on plug-in electric vehicle user experience," *Transportation Research Part D: Transport and Environment* 71: 22–36.

Davis, Lucas (2019) "How much are electric vehicles driven?," *Applied Economics Letters* 26(18): 1497–1502.

Davis, Stacy C. and Robert G. Boundy (2021) *Transportation Energy Data Book,* 39th edition, Oak Ridge, TN: Oak Ridge National Laboratory (ORNL), http://tedb.ornl.gov (updated April; accessed 21 May 2021).

De Borger, Bruno and Kristiaan Kerstens (2008) "The performance of bus-transit operators," in David A. Hensher and Kenneth J. Button (eds.) *Handbook of Transport Modelling*, 2nd edition, Bingley: Emerald Group Publishing, pp. 693–714.

de Palma, André and Richard Arnott (1986) "Usage-dependent peak-load pricing," *Economics Letters* 20(2): 101–105.

de Palma, André and Robin Lindsey (2002) "Comparison of morning and evening commutes in the Vickrey bottleneck model," *Transportation Research Record: Journal of the Transportation Research Board* 1807: 26–33.

de Palma, André, Robin Lindsey and Guillaume Monchambert (2017) "The economics of crowding in rail transit," *Journal of Urban Economics* 101: 106–122.

de Palma, André, Robin Lindsey and Nathalie Picard (2012) "Risk aversion, the value of information and traffic equilibrium," *Transportation Science* 46(1): 1–26.

de Palma, André and Fabrice Marchal (2002) "Real cases applications of the fully dynamic METROPOLIS tool-box: an advocacy for large-scale mesoscopic transportation systems," *Networks and Spatial Economics* 2: 347–369.

de Palma, André and Nathalie Picard (2006) "Equilibria and information provision in risky networks with risk averse drivers," *Transportation Science* 40(4): 393–408.

De Rubens, Gerardo Zarazua, Lance Noel, Johannes Kester and Benjamin K. Sovacool (2020) "The market case for electric mobility: investigating electric vehicle business models for mass adoption," *Energy* 194(1): 116841

De Souza, Felipe, Omer Verbas and Joshua Auld (2019) "Mesoscopic traffic flow model for agent-based simulation," *Procedia Computer Science* 151: 858–863.

Delucchi, Mark and Don McCubbin (2011) "External costs of transport in the United States," in André de Palma *et al.* (eds.) *A Handbook of Transport Economics*, Cheltenham: Edward Elgar, pp. 341–368.

Denant-Boèmont, Laurent and Romain Petiot (2003) "Information value and sequential decision-making in a transport setting: an experimental study," *Transportation Research Part B: Methodological* 37: 365–386.

Deschênes, Olivier, Michael Greenstone and Joseph S. Shapiro (2017) "Defensive investments and the demand for air quality: evidence from the NOx budget program," *American Economic Review* 107(10): 2958–2989.

Dewees, Donald N. (1978) "Simulations of traffic congestion in Toronto," *Transportation Research* 12(3): 153–161.

Dimitropoulos, Alexandros, Piet Rietveld and Jos N. van Ommeren (2013) "Consumer valuation of changes in driving range: a meta-analysis," *Transportation Research Part A: Policy and Practice* 55: 27–45.

Dixit, Vinayak V., Andreas Ortmann, Elisabet Rutstrom and Satish Ukkusuri (2015) "Understanding transportation systems through the lenses of experimental economics: a review," January 8, available at SSRN: https://papers.ssrn.com/sol3/papers.cfm?abstract_id=2546881. DOI: 10.2139/ssrn.2546881

Dong, Jing, Hani S. Mahmassani and Chung-Cheng Lu (2006) "How reliable is this route? Predictive travel time and reliability for anticipatory traveler information systems," *Transportation Research Record: Journal of the Transportation Research Board* 1980(1): 117–125.

Dowling, Richard G., Rupinder Singh and Willis Wei-Kuo Cheng (1998) "The accuracy and performance of improved speed-flow functions," *Transportation Research Record: Journal of the Transportation Research Board* 1646: 9–17.

Downs, Anthony (1962) "The law of peak-hour expressway congestion," *Traffic Quarterly* 16(3): 393–409.

Else, Peter K. (1981) "A reformulation of the theory of optimal congestion taxes," *Journal of Transport Economics and Policy* 15(3): 217–232.

Emmerink, Richard H.M. (1998) *Information and Pricing in Road Transportation*, Berlin: Springer.

Emmerink, Richard H.M., Erik T. Verhoef, Peter Nijkamp and Piet Rietveld (1996a) "Information provision in road transport with elastic demand: a welfare economic approach," *Journal of Transport Economics and Policy* 30: 117–136.

Emmerink, Richard H.M., Erik T. Verhoef, Peter Nijkamp and Piet Rietveld (1996b) "Endogenizing demand for information in road transport," *Annals of Regional Science* 30(2): 201–222.

Emmerink, Richard H.M, Erik T. Verhoef, Peter Nijkamp and Piet Rietveld (1998) "Information policy in road transport with elastic demand: some welfare economic considerations," *European Economic Review* 42: 71–95

Engelson, Leonid and Mogens Fosgerau (2020) "Scheduling preferences and the value of travel time information," *Transportation Research Part B: Methodological* 134: 256–265.

Eren, Ezgi and Volkan Emre Uz (2020) "A review on bike-sharing: the factors affecting bike-sharing demand," *Sustainable Cities and Society* 54: 101882.

European Commission, Directorate-General for Mobility and Transport, Huib van Essen, Lisanne van Wijngaarden, Arnot Schroten *et al.* (2020) *Handbook on the External Costs of Transport: Version 2019-1.1*, doi:10.2832/51388

Evans, Mary F. and Laura O. Taylor (2020) "Using revealed preference methods to estimate the value of reduced mortality risk: best practice recommendations for the hedonic wage model," *Review of Environmental Economics and Policy* 14(2): 282–301.

Fargier, Paul-Henri (1983) "Effects of the choice of departure time on road traffic congestion," in VanOlin F. Hurdle, Ezra Hauer and Gerald N. Steuart (eds.) *Proceedings of the Eighth International Symposium on Transportation and Traffic Theory*, Toronto: University of Toronto Press, pp. 223–262.

Ferro, Pablo Salazar and Roger Behrens (2015) "From direct to trunk-and-feeder public transport services in the Urban South: territorial implications," *Journal of Transport and Land Use* 8(1): 123–136.

Fielbaum, Andrés, Sergio R. Jara-Díaz and Antonio Gschwender (2016) "Optimal public transport networks for a general urban structure," *Transportation Research Part B: Methodological* 94: 298–313.

Fishman, Elliot and Christopher Cherry (2016) "E-bikes in the mainstream: reviewing a decade of research," *Transport Reviews* 36: 72–91.

Fitzsimmons, Emma G. (2018) "At long last, a plan to fix New York City's Buses," *New York Times*, April 23.

Fosgerau, Mogens (2009) "The marginal social cost of headway for a scheduled service," *Transportation Research Part B: Methodological* 43(8–9): 813–820.

Fosgerau, Mogens (2015) "Congestion in the bathtub," *Economics of Transportation* 4(4): 241–255.

Fosgerau, Mogens and André de Palma (2012) "Congestion in a city with a central bottleneck," *Journal of Urban Economics* 71: 269–277.

Fosgerau, Mogens and Robin Lindsey (2013) "Trip-timing decisions with traffic incidents," *Regional Science and Urban Economics* 43(5): 764–782.

Fosgerau, Mogens and Kenneth A. Small (2013) "Hypercongestion in downtown metropolis," *Journal of Urban Economics* 76: 122–134.

Fosgerau, Mogens, Emma Frejinger and Anders Karlstrom (2013) "A link based network route choice model with unrestricted choice set," *Transportation Research Part B: Methodological* 56: 70–80.

Frank, Marguerite and Philip Wolfe (1956) "An algorithm for quadratic programming," *Naval Research Logistics Quarterly* 3(1–2): 95–110.

Fridstrøm, Lasse (2011) "A framework for assessing the marginal external accident cost of road use and its implications for insurance ratemaking," Discussion Paper No. 2011-22, International Transport Forum. Paris: OECD (July). doi:10.1787/5kg29s6x0vd8-en

Fridstrøm, Lasse, Jan Ifvar, Siv Ingebrigtsen, Risto Kulmala and Lars Krogsgård Thomsen (1995) "Measuring the contribution of randomness, exposure, weather, and daylight to the variation in road accident counts," *Accident Analysis and Prevention* 27(1): 1–20.

Friedrich, Rainer and Emile Quinet (2011) "External cost of transport in Europe," in André de Palma *et al.* (eds.) *A Handbook of Transport Economics*, Cheltenham: Edward Elgar, pp. 369–395.

Geroliminis, Nikolas and Carlos F. Daganzo (2007) "Macroscopic modeling of traffic in cities," Transportation Research Board 86th Annual Meeting No. 07-0413.

Geroliminis, Nikolas and Carlos F. Daganzo (2008) "Existence of urban-scale macroscopic fundamental diagrams: some experimental findings," *Transportation Research Part B: Methodological* 42(9): 759–770.

Gonzales, Eric J., Celeste Chavis, Yuwei Li and Carlos F. Daganzo (2011) "Multimodal transport in Nairobi, Kenya: insights and recommendations with a macroscopic evidence-based model," Transportation Research Board 90th Annual Meeting Paper 11-3045.

Graff Zivin, Joshua S. and Matthew Neidell (2012) "The impact of pollution on worker productivity," *American Economic Review* 102(7): 3652–3673.

Graff Zivin, Joshua S., Matthew J. Kotchen and Erin T. Mansur (2014) "Spatial and temporal heterogeneity of marginal emissions: implications for electric cars and other electricity-shifting policies," *Journal of Economic Behavior and Organization* 107: 248–268.

Graham, Daniel J. and Stephen Gibbons (2019) "Quantifying Wider Economic Impacts of agglomeration for transport appraisal: existing evidence and future directions," *Economics of Transportation* 19: 100121.

Greenberg, Harold (1959) "An analysis of traffic flow," *Operations Research* 7(1): 78–85.

Greenshields, Bruce D. (1935) "A study of traffic capacity," *Highway Research Board Proceedings* 14: 448–477.

Griswold, Julia B., Mengqiao Yu, Victoria Filingeri, Offer Grembek and Joan L. Walker (2018) "A behavioral modeling approach to bicycle level of service," *Transportation Research Part A: Policy and Practice* 116: 166–177.

Gschwender, Antonio, Sergio R. Jara-Díaz and Claudia Bravo (2016) "Feeder-trunk or direct lines? Economies of density, transfer costs and transit structure in an urban context," *Transportation Research Part A: Policy and Practice* 88: 209–222.

Gubins, Sergejs and Erik T. Verhoef (2014) "Dynamic bottleneck congestion and residential land use in the monocentric city," *Journal of Urban Economics* 80: 51–61.

Guo, Ren-Yong, Hai Yang and Hai-Jun Huang (2018) "Are we really solving the dynamic traffic equilibrium problem with a departure time choice?" *Transportation Science* 52(3): 603–620.

Haight, Frank (1963) *Mathematical Theories of Traffic Flow*, New York: Academic Press.

Hall, Fred L. (2002) "Chapter 2: Traffic stream characteristics," in Nathan A. Gartner, Carrol J. Messer and Ajay Rathi (eds.) *Traffic Flow Theory: A State-of-the-Art Report*, Washington, DC: US Department of Transportation, Turner-Fairbank Highway Research Center, http://www.tfhrc.gov/its/tft/tft.htm.

Hall, Fred L., Brian L. Allen and Margot A. Gunter (1986) "Empirical analysis of freeway flow-density relationships," *Transportation Research Part A: Policy and Practice* 20(3): 197–210.

Hall, Fred L. and Lisa M. Hall (1990) "Capacity and speed flow analysis of the QEW in Ontario," *Transportation Research Record: Journal of the Transportation Research Board* 1287: 108–118.

Hall, Fred L., Van F. Hurdle and James H. Banks (1992) "Synthesis of recent work on the nature of speed–flow and flow–occupancy (or density) relationships for freeways," *Transportation Research Record: Journal of the Transportation Research Board* 1365: 12–18.

Hall, Jonathan D. (2018) "Pareto Improvements from Lexus Lanes: the effects of pricing a portion of the lanes on congested highways," *Journal of Public Economics* 158: 113–125.

Hall, Jonathan D. (forthcoming) "Inframarginal travelers and transportation policy," *International Economic* Review. Prepublication version: https://papers.ssrn.com/sol3/papers.cfm?abstract_id=3424097

Hall, Randolph W. (1996) "Route choice and advanced traveller information systems on a capacitated and dynamic network," *Transportation Research Part C: Emerging Technologies* 4(5): 289–306.

Hammitt, James K. and Lisa A. Robinson (2011) "The income elasticity of the value per statistical life: transferring estimates between high and low income populations," *Journal of Benefit-Cost Analysis* 2(1): Article 1.

Hampshire, Robert and Donald Shoup (2018) "What share of traffic is cruising for parking?" *Journal of Transport Economics and Policy* 52(3): 184–201.

Hazledine, Tim, Stuart Donovan and Christine Mak (2017) "Urban agglomeration benefits from public transit improvements: extending and implementing the Venables model," *Research in Transportation Economics* 66: 36–45.

Heblich, Stephan, Alex Trew and Yanos Zylberberg (2021) "East-side story: historical pollution and persistent neighborhood sorting," *Journal of Political Economy* 129(5), doi:10.1086/713101.

Henderson, J. Vernon (1974) "Road congestion: a reconsideration of pricing theory," *Journal of Urban Economics* 1(3): 346–365.

Hendrickson, Chris and George Kocur (1981) "Schedule delay and departure time decisions in a deterministic model," *Transportation Science* 15(1): 62–77.

Hensher, David A. and Thomas F. Golob (2008) "Bus rapid transit systems: a comparative assessment," *Transportation* 35: 501–518.

Hess, Daniel Baldwin (2018) "Buffalo abandons parking requirements," in Donald C. Shoup (ed.) *The High Cost of Free Parking*, Chicago, IL: American Planning Association, Planners Press, pp. 244–254.

Hills, Peter (1993) "Road congestion pricing: when is it a good policy? A comment," *Journal of Transport Economics and Policy* 27(1): 91–99.

Holland, Stephen, Erin Mansur, Nicholas Muller and Andrew Yates (2016) "Are there environmental benefits from driving electric vehicles? The importance of local factors," *American Economic Review* 106(12): 3700–3729.

Holland, Stephen, Erin Mansur, Nicholas Muller and Andrew Yates (2020) "Decompositions and policy consequences of an extraordinary decline in air pollution from electricity generation," *American Economic Journal: Economic Policy* 12(4): 244–274.

Hörcher, Daniel, Bruno De Borger, Woubit Seifu and Daniel J. Graham (2020) "Public transport provision under agglomeration economies," *Regional Science and Urban Economics* 81: 103503.

Horni, Andreas, Kai Nagel, Kay W. Axhausen (2016) *The Multi-Agent Transport Simulation MATSim*, London: Ubiquity Press.

Hossain, Sanjana, Patrick Loa, Felita Ong, Yicong Liu and Khandker Nurul Habib (2023), "Have the determinants of bike-share demand changed in response to the covid-19 pandemic? A machine learning-based approach," Proceedings of the 58th Annual Conference of the Canadian Transportation Research Forum, pp. 276–285.

Inci, Eren (2015) "A review of the economics of parking," *Economics of Transportation* 4: 50–63.

Inman, Robert P. (1978) "A generalized congestion function for highway travel," *Journal of Urban Economics* 5(1): 21–34.

International Energy Agency (2019) "Global EV outlook 2019: scaling up the transition to electric mobility," https://www.iea.org/reports/global-ev-outlook-2019 (accessed 1 August 2021).

International Energy Agency (2021) "Policies to promote electric vehicle deployment. Global EV outlook 2021," https://www.iea.org/reports/global-ev-outlook-2021/policies-to-promote-electric-vehicle-deployment (accessed 29 June 2021).

Ison, Stephen and Corinne Mulley (eds.) (2014) *Parking Issues and Policies*, Volume 5, Bingley: Emerald Group Publishing Limited.

ITF (2015) "Urban mobility system upgrade: how shared self-driving cars could change city traffic," International Transport Forum Corporate Partnership Board Report, OECD, Paris.

ITF (2019) *Smart Use of Roads*, Research Report, International Transport Forum, https://www.itf-oecd.org/sites/default/files/docs/smart-use-roads_0.pdf

Jacobsen, Mark R. (2013) "Fuel economy and safety: the influences of vehicle class and driver behavior," *American Economic Journal: Applied Economics* 5(3): 1–26.

Jacobsen, Peter L. (2003) "Safety in numbers: more walkers and bicyclists, safer walking and bicycling," *Injury Prevention* 21(4): 205–209.

Jakob, Astrid, John L. Craig and Gavin Fisher (2006) "Transport cost analysis: a case study of the total costs of private and public transport in Auckland," *Environmental Science and Policy* 9(1): 55–66.

Jansson, Jan Owen (1980) "A simple bus line model for optimisation of service frequency and bus size," *Journal of Transport Economics and Policy* 14(1): 53–80.

Jara-Díaz, Sergio R., André Latournerie, Alejandro Tirachini and Félix Quitral (2022) "Optimal pricing and design of station-based bike-sharing systems: a microeconomic model," *Economics of Transportation* 31: 100273.

Jara-Díaz, Sergio R. and Alejandro Tirachini (2013) "Urban bus transport: open all doors for boarding," *Journal of Transport Economics and Policy* 47(1): 91–106.

Jenn, Alan (2021) "Charging forward: deploying electric vehicle infrastructure for Uber and Lyft in California," White papers, UC Davis, https://escholarship.org/uc/item/6vk0h1mj

Jiang, Gege, Mogens Fosgerau and Hong Lo (2020) "Route choice, travel time variability, and rational inattention," *Transportation Research Part B: Methodological* 132: 188–207.

Jin, Wen-Long (2020) "Generalized bathtub model of network trip flows," *Transportation Research Part B: Methodological* 136: 138–157.

Johari, Mansour, Mehdi Keyvan-Ekbatani, Ludovic Leclercq, Dong Ngoduy and Hani S. Mahmassani (2021) "Macroscopic network-level traffic models: bridging fifty years of development toward the next era," *Transportation Research Part C: Emerging Technologies* 131: 103334.

Kain, John F. (1997) "Cost-effective alternatives to Atlanta's rail rapid transit system," *Journal of Transport Economics and Policy* 31(1): 25–49.

Kazemzadeh, Khashayar, Milad Haghani and Frances Sprei (2023) "Electric scooter safety: an integrative review of evidence from transport and medical research domains," *Sustainable Cities and Society* 89, February: 104313.

Kazemzadeh, Khashayar and Frances Sprei (2022) "Towards an electric scooter level of service: a review and framework," *Travel Behaviour and Society* 29: 149–164.

Keeler, Theodore E. and Kenneth A. Small (1977) "Optimal peak-load pricing, investment, and service levels on urban expressways," *Journal of Political Economy* 85(1): 1–25.

Kerner, Boris S. and Hubert Rehborn (1997) "Experimental properties of phase transitions in traffic flow," *Physical Review Letters* 79(20): 4030–4033.

Khan, Zaid and Saurabh Amin (2018) "Bottleneck model with heterogeneous information," *Transportation Research Part B: Methodological* 112: 157–190.

Knorr, Florian, Thorsten Chmura and Michael Schreckenberg (2014) "Route choice in the presence of a toll road: the role of pre-trip information and learning," *Transportation Research Part F: Traffic Psychology and Behaviour* 27: 44–55.

Kobayashi, Kiyoshi (1994) "Information, rational expectations and network equilibria - an analytical perspective for route guidance systems," *The Annals of Regional Science* 28(4): 369–393.

Kraus, Marvin (1981) "Scale economies analysis for urban highway networks," *Journal of Urban Economics* 9(1): 1–22.

Kraus, Marvin (1991) "Discomfort externalities and marginal cost transit fares," *Journal of Urban Economics* 29(2): 249–259.

Krupnick, Alan J. (2004) *Valuing Health Outcomes: Policy Choices and Technical Issues*, Washington, DC: Resources for the Future, http://www.rff.org/rff/Publications/Reports.cfm

Kumar, Neeraj, Sudip Misra, Joel J.P.C. Rodrigues and Mohammad S. Obaidat (2015) "Coalition games for spatio-temporal big data in internet of vehicles environment: a comparative analysis," *IEEE Internet of Thing: Journal* 2(4): 310–320.

Lamotte, Raphaël and Nikolas Geroliminis (2021) "Monotonicity in the trip scheduling problem," *Transportation Research Part B: Methodological* 146: 14–25.

Leclerq, Ludovic (2007) "Hybrid approaches to the solution of the "Lighthill-Witham-Richardson" model," *Transportation Research Part B: Methodological* 41(7): 701–709.

Lee, Seungjae and Sungwhee Shin (2011) "Variable message sign operating strategies: simple examples," *Transportmetrica* 7(6): 443–454.

Levitt, Steven D. and Jack Porter (2001) "How dangerous are drinking drivers?" *Journal of Political Economy* 109(6): 1198–1237.

Li, Shanjun (2012) "Traffic safety and vehicle choice: quantifying the effects of the 'arms race' on American roads," *Journal of Applied Econometrics* 27(1): 34–62.

Li, Shanjun, Lang Tong, Jianwei Xing and Yiyi Zhou (2017) "The market for electric vehicles: indirect network effects and policy design," *Journal of the Association of Environmental and Resource Economists* 4(1): 89–133.

Li, Zhi-Chun, Hai-Jun Huang and Hai Yang (2020) "Fifty years of the bottleneck model: a bibliometric review and future research directions," *Transportation Research Part B: Methodological* 139: 311–342.

Lighthill, Michael James and Gerald Beresford Whitham (1955) *On Kinematic Waves, II: A Theory of Traffic Flow on Long Crowded Roads*, London: Royal Society.

Lindberg, Gunnar (2001) "Traffic insurance and accident externality charges," *Journal of Transport Economics and Policy* 35(3): 399–416.

Lindsey, Robin (2004) "Existence, uniqueness and congestion cost properties of equilibrium in the bottleneck model with heterogeneous users," *Transportation Science* 38(3): 293–314.

Lindsey, Robin, Terry Daniel, Eyran Gisches and Amnon Rapoport (2014) "Pre-trip information and route-choice decisions with stochastic travel conditions: theory," *Transportation Research Part B: Methodological* 67: 187–207.

Lindsey, Robin and Erik T. Verhoef (2000) "Congestion modelling," in David A. Hensher and Kenneth J. Button (eds.) *Handbook of Transport Modelling*, New York: Pergamon, pp. 353–373.

Litman, Todd (2016) *Transportation Cost and Benefit Analysis: Techniques, Estimates and Implications*, 2nd edition, Victoria Transport Policy Institute, https://www.vtpi.org/tca/

Liu, Shixu, Li-Dan Guo, Said Easa and Hao Yan (2020) "Experimental study of day-to-day route-choice behavior: evaluating effect of ATIS market penetration," *Journal of Advanced Transportation*, 8393724, doi:10.1155/2020/8393724

Lu, Xuan, Song Gao, Eran Ben-Elia and Ryan Pothering (2014) "Travelers' day-to-day route choice behavior with real-time information in a congested risky network," *Mathematical Population Studies* 21(4): 205–219, doi:10.1080/08898480.2013.836418

Mahmassani, Hani S. and Robert Herman (1984) "Dynamic user equilibrium departure time and route choice on idealized traffic arterials," *Transportation Science* 18(4): 362–384.

Mangrum, Daniel and Alejandro Molnar (2020) "The marginal congestion of a taxi in New York City," December 9, https://www.danielmangrum.com/docs/Boro_current.pdf

Manville, Michael (2014) "Parking pricing," in Stephen Ison and Corinne Mulley (eds.) *Parking Issues and Policies,* Volume 5, Bingley: Emerald Group Publishing Limited, pp. 137–155.

Marcotte, Patrice and Sang Nguyen (eds.) (1998) *Equilibrium and Advanced Transportation Modelling,* Boston, MA: Kluwer Academic Publishers.

Mariotte, Guilhem, Ludovic Leclercq and Jorge A. Laval (2017) "Macroscopic urban dynamics: analytical and numerical comparisons of existing models," *Transportation Research Part B: Methodological* 101: 245–267.

May, Adolf D. (1990) *Traffic Flow Fundamentals,* Upper Saddle River, NJ: Prentice-Hall.

May, Anthony D., Simon P. Shepherd and John Bates (2000) "Supply curves for urban road networks," *Journal of Transport Economics and Policy* 34(3): 261–290.

Mayeres, Inge and Kurt Van Dender (2002) "Chapter 7: The external costs of transport" in Bruno De Borger and Stef Proost (eds.) *Reforming Transport Pricing in the European Union,* Cheltenham: Edward Elgar, pp. 135–169.

McDonald, John F., Edmond L. d'Ouville and Louie Nan Liu (1999) *Economics of Urban Highway Congestion and Pricing,* Boston, MA: Kluwer Academic Publishers.

Meyer, John R., John F. Kain and Martin Wohl (1965) *The Urban Transportation Problem,* Cambridge, MA: Harvard University Press.

Mohring, Herbert (1972) "Optimization and scale economies in urban bus transportation," *American Economic Review* 62(4): 591–604.

Mohring, Herbert (1976) *Transportation Economics,* Cambridge, MA: Ballinger.

Mrozek, Janusz R. and Laura O. Taylor (2002) "What determines the value of life? A meta-analysis," *Journal of Policy Analysis and Management* 21(2): 253–270.

Muehlegger, Erich J. and David S. Rapson (2021) "Subsidizing low- and middle-income adoption of electric vehicles: quasi-experimental evidence from California," Working Paper 25359, National Bureau of Economic Research, December 2018, revised January 2021.

Muehlegger, Erich J. and Davis S. Rapson (2023) "Correcting estimates of electric vehicle emissions abatement: implications for climate policy," *Journal of the Association of Environmental and Resource Economists* 10(1): 263–282.

Muehlenbachs, Lucija, Stefan Staubli and Ziyan Chu (2021) "The accident externality from trucking: evidence from shale gas development," *Regional Science and Urban Economics* 88: 103630.

Mun, Se-il (2002) "Bottleneck congestion with traffic jam: a reformulation and correction of earlier result," Working paper, Graduate School of Economics, Kyoto University, Kyoto, Japan.

Muñoz, Juan Carlos, Marco Batarce and Dario Hidalgo (2014) "Transantiago, five years after its launch," *Research in Transportation Economics* 48: 184–193.

Nash, Christopher A. (1974) "The treatment of capital costs of vehicles in evaluating road schemes," *Transportation* 3: 225–242.

Nash, Christopher A. (1988) "Integration of public transport: an economic assessment," in John S. Dodgson and Neville Topham (eds.) *Bus Deregulation and Privatisation,* Aldershot: Avebury, pp. 97–118.

National Research Council (2008) *Estimating Mortality Risk Reduction and Economic Benefits from Controlling Ozone Air Pollution,* Washington, DC: National Academies Press.

Netherlands Institute for Road Safety Research (SWOV) (2022) "Road deaths in The Netherlands" (13 April), https://swov.nl/en/fact-sheet/road-deaths-netherlands (accessed 9 June 2023).

Newell, Gordon F. (1987) "The morning commute for nonidentical travelers," *Transportation Science* 21(2): 74–88.

Newell, Gordon F. (1988) "Traffic flow for the morning commute," *Transportation Science* 22(1): 47–58.

Nielsen, Thomas Alexander Sick and Sonja Haustein (2018) "On sceptics and enthusiasts: what are the expectations towards self-driving cars?" *Transport Policy* 66: 49–55.

Noland, Robert B., Kenneth A. Small, Pia M. Koskenoja and Xuehao Chu (1998) "Simulating travel reliability," *Regional Science and Urban Economics* 28(5): 535–564.

Ohta, Hiroshi (2001) "Probing a traffic congestion controversy: density and flow scrutinized," *Journal of Regional Science* 41(40: 659–680.

Parry, Ian W.H. (2004) "Comparing alternative policies to reduce traffic accidents," *Journal of Urban Economics* 56(2): 346–358.

Patriksson, Michael (2004) "Algorithms for computing traffic equilibria," *Networks and Spatial Economics* 4: 23–38.

Payne, Harold J. (1984) "Discontinuity in equilibrium freeway traffic flow," *Transportation Research Record: Journal of the Transportation Research Board* 971: 140–146.

PBSC Urban Solutions (2021) "The Meddin bike-sharing world map" (27 October), https://www.pbsc.com/blog/2021/10/the-meddin-bike-sharing-world-map (accessed 14 June 2023).

Peer, Stefanie, Erik T. Verhoef, Jasper Knockaert, Paul Koster and Yin-Yen Tseng (2015) "Long-run vs. short-run perspectives on consumer scheduling: evidence from a revealed-preference experiment among peak-hour road commuters," *International Economic Review* 56(1): 303–323.

Pels, Eric (2020) "Optimality of the hub-spoke system: a review of the literature, and directions for future research," *Transport Policy* 104: A1–A10. doi:10.1016/j.tranpol.2020.08.002.

Peltzman, Sam (1975) "The effects of automobile safety regulation," *Journal of Political Economy* 83(4): 677–725.

Pigou, Arthur C. (1920) *The Economics of Welfare*, London: Macmillan.

Pucher, John, Jennifer Dill and Susan Handy (2010) "Infrastructure, programs, and policies to increase bicycling: an international review," *Preventive Medicine* 50: S106–S125.

Qian, Di, Yan Wang, Antonella Zanobetti, Yun Wang, Petros Koutrakis, Christine Choirat, Francesca Dominici and Joel D. Schwartz (2017) "Air pollution and mortality in the Medicare population," *New England Journal of Medicine* 376(26): 2513–2522.

Quinet, Emile (2004) "A meta-analysis of Western European external costs estimates," *Transportation Research Part D: Transport and Environment* 9(6): 465–476.

Ramos, Giselle Moraes, Winnie Daamen and Serge Hoogendoorn (2014) "A state-of-the-art review: developments in utility theory, prospect theory and regret theory to investigate travellers' behaviour in situations involving travel time uncertainty," *Transport Reviews* 34(1): 46–67.

Raney, Bryan, Nurhan Cetin, Andreas Völlmy, Milenko Vrtic, Kay W. Axhausen and Kai Nagel (2003) "An agent-based microsimulation model of Swiss travel: first results," *Networks and Spatial Economics* 3: 23–41.

Rapoport, Amnon, Eyran J. Gisches, Terry Daniel and Robin Lindsey (2014) "Pre-trip information and route choice decisions with stochastic travel conditions: experiment," *Transportation Research Part B: Methodological* 68: 154–172.

Reynolds, Gretchen (2020) "E-bikes are all the rage. Should they be?" *The New York Times*, August 19, https://www.nytimes.com/2020/08/19/well/move/e-bike-safety-exercise.html

Richards, Paul I. (1956) "Shock waves on the highway," *Operations Research* 4(1): 42–51.

Rietveld, Piet (2011) "The economics of information in transport," in André de Palma *et al.* (eds.) *A Handbook of Transport Economics*, Cheltenham: Edward Elgar, pp. 586–603.

Rizzi, Luis I. and Juan de Dios Ortúzar (2006) "Estimating the willingness-to-pay for road safety improvements," *Transport Reviews* 16(4): 471–485.

Robinson, Lisa A., Michael R. Eber and James K. Hammitt (2021) *Valuing COVID-19 Mortality and Morbidity Risk Reductions in U.S. Department of Health and Human Services regulatory impact analyses*, report prepared for the U.S. Dept. of HHS (July), https://aspe.hhs.gov/reports/valuing-covid-19-risk-reductions-hhs-rias

Robinson, Lisa A. and James K. Hammitt (2016) "Valuing reductions in fatal illness risks: implications of recent research," *Health Economics* 25: 1039–1052, doi:10.1002/hec.3214

Rotemberg, Julio J. (1985) "The efficiency of equilibrium traffic flows," *Journal of Public Economics* 26(2): 191–205.

Schepers, Paul, Karin Klein Wolt and Elliot Fishman (2018) "The safety of e-bikes in The Netherlands", Discussion paper 168, International Transport Forum, Paris, https://www.itf-oecd.org/sites/default/files/docs/safety-e-bikes-the-netherlands_0.pdf

Schrank, David, Bill Eisele and Tim Lomax (2019) *2019 Urban Mobility Report*, College Station, TX: Texas A&M Transportation Institute, https://mobility.tamu.edu/umr/

Selten, Reinhard, Thorsten G.H. Chamura, Thomas Pitz, Sebastian Kube and Michael Schreckenberg (2007) "Commuters route choice behavior," *Games and Economic Behavior* 58: 394–406.

Shaheen, Susan and Adam Cohen, (2019) "Shared ride services in North America: definitions, impacts, and the future of pooling," *Transport Reviews* 39(4): 427–442, doi:10.1080/01441647.2018.1497728

Sheffi, Yosef (1985) *Urban Transportation Networks: Equilibrium Analysis with Mathematical Methods*, Englewood Cliffs, NJ: Prentice-Hall.

Shoup, Donald C. (2005) *The High Cost of Free Parking*, Chicago, IL: American Planning Association, Planners Press.

Shoup, Donald C. (2018a) "Truth in transportation planning," in Donald C. Shoup (ed.) *The High Cost of Free Parking*, Chicago, IL: American Planning Association, Planners Press, pp. 59–73.

Shoup, Donald C. (2018b) "Epilogue," in Donald C. Shoup (ed.) *The High Cost of Free Parking*, Chicago, IL: American Planning Association, Planners Press, pp. 495–500.

Skabardonis, Alexander and Richard Dowling (1996) "Improved speed–flow relationships for planning application," *Transportation Research Record: Journal of the Transportation Research Board* 1572: 18–23.

Small, Kenneth A. (1982) "The scheduling of consumer activities: work trips," *American Economic Review* 72(3): 467–479.

Small, Kenneth A. (1983) "Bus priority and congestion pricing on urban expressways," in Theodore E. Keeler (ed.) *Research in Transportation Economics* 1, Greenwich, CT: JAI Press, pp. 27–74.

Small, Kenneth A. (1999) "Economies of scale and self-financing rules with noncompetitive factor markets," *Journal of Public Economics* 74(3): 431–450.

Small, Kenneth A. (2015) "The bottleneck model: an assessment and interpretation," *Economics of Transportation* 4: 110–117.

Small, Kenneth A. and Xuehao Chu (2003) "Hypercongestion," *Journal of Transport Economics and Policy* 37(3): 319–352.

Small, Kenneth A. and Camilla Kazimi (1995) "On the costs of air pollution from motor vehicles," *Journal of Transport Economics and Policy* 29(1): 7–32.

Small, Kenneth A. and Chen Ng (2014) "Optimizing road capacity and type," *Economics of Transportation* 3: 145–157.

Small, Kenneth A. and Erik T. Verhoef (2007) *The Economics of Urban Transportation*, London: Routledge.

Smeed, Reuben J. (1968) "Traffic studies and urban congestion," *Journal of Transportation Economics and Policy* 2(1): 33–70.

Smith, Michael J. (1984) "The stability of a dynamic model of traffic assignment – an application of a method of Lyapunov," *Transportation Science* 18(3): 245–252.

Smith, W. Spencer, Fred L. Hall and Frank O. Montgomery (1996) "Comparing speed-flow relationships for motorways with new data from the M6," *Transportation Research Part A: Policy and Practice* 30(2): 89–101.

Spady, Richard H. and Ann F. Friedlaender (1978) "Hedonic cost functions for the regulated trucking industry," *Bell Journal of Economics* 9(1): 154–179.

Srinivasan, Karhik K. and Hani S. Mahmassani (2000) "Modeling inertia and compliance mechanisms in route choice behavior under real-time information," *Transportation Research Record: Journal of the Transportation Research Board* 1725: 45–53.

Steimetz, Seiji S.C. (2008) "Defensive driving and the external costs of accidents and travel delays," *Transportation Research Part B: Methodological* 42(9): 703–724.

Stenner, Hedwig T., Johanna Boyen, Markus Hein, Gudrun Protte, Momme Kück, Armin Finkel, Alexander A. Hanke and Uwe Tegtbur (2020) "Everyday pedelec use and its effect on meeting physical activity guidelines," *International Journal of Environmental Research and Public Health* 17(13): 4807.

Stern, Raphael E., Shumo Cui, Maria Laura Delle Monache, Rahul Bhadani, Matt Bunting, Miles Churchill, Nathaniel Hamilton, R'mani Haulcy, Hannah Pohlmann, Fangyu Wu, Benedetto Piccoli, Benjamin Seibold, Jonathan Sprinkle and Daniel B. Work (2018) "Dissipation of stop-and-go waves via control of autonomous vehicles: field experiments," *Transportation Research Part C: Emerging Technologies* 89: 205–221.

Storchmann, Karl (2004) "On the depreciation of automobiles: an international comparison," *Transportation* 31: 371–408.

Sugiyama, Yuki, Minoru Fukui, Macoto Kikuchi, Katsuya Hasebe, Akihiro Nakayama, Katsuhiro Nishinari, Shin-ichi Tadaki and Satoshi Yukawa (2008) "Traffic jams without bottlenecks—experimental evidence for the physical mechanism of the formation of a jam," *New Journal of Physics* 10, 033001.

Thielmann, Axel *et al.* (2020) "Batteries for electric cars: fact check and need for action. Are batteries for electric cars the key to sustainable mobility in the future?" Perspectives: Policy Brief, No. 01/2020, Fraunhofer ISI, Karlsruhe, http://nbn-resolving.de/urn:nbn:de:0011-n-6338885

Thompson, Jason Hugh, Jasper S. Wijnands, Suzanne Mavoa, Katherine Scully and Mark R. Stevenson (2019) "Evidence for the 'safety in density' effect for cyclists: validation of agent-based modelling results," *Injury Prevention* 25(5): 379–385.

Tirachini, Alejandro and Constantinos Antoniou (2020) "The economics of automated public transport: effects on operator cost, travel time, fare and subsidy," *Economics of Transportation* 21: 100151.

Transportation Research Board (2000) *Highway Capacity Manual 2000*, Washington, DC: Transportation Research Board.

Transportation Research Board (2016) *The Highway Capacity Manual: A Guide for Multimodal Mobility Analysis*, 6th edition, Washington, DC: Transportation Research Board

Tsai, Jyh-Fa, Chih-Peng Chu and Shou-Ren Hu (2015) "Road pricing for congestion and accident externalities for mixed traffic of motorcycles and automobiles," *Transportation Research Part A: Policy and Practice* 71: 153–166.

UK Department for Transport (2002) *COBA 11 User Manual, Part 5: Speed on Links*, London: Department for Transport.

Ulrich, Lawrence (2021) "How is this a good idea?: EV battery swapping > swap this technological dead-end out for better batteries, improved superchargers and more universal EV charging standards," *IEEE Spectrum*, May 13, https://spectrum.ieee.org/ev-battery-swapping-how-is-this-a-good-idea (accessed 6 August 2021).

US Bureau of Public Roads (1964) *Traffic Assignment Manual*, Washington, DC: US Bureau of Public Roads.

US CEA (2021) "Annual report of the Council of Economic Advisers," in *Economic Report of the President*, Washington, DC: US Government Printing Office, https://www.govinfo.gov/app/collection/erp/2021

US Department of Commerce (2020) "Current-cost net stock of government fixed assets," *National Data: Fixed Asset Account Tables*, Table 7.1, Bureau of Economic Analysis, https://apps.bea.gov/itable/index_fa.cfm

US FHWA (2000) *Addendum to the 1997 Federal Highway Cost Allocation Study Final Report*, Washington, DC: US FHWA, http://www.fhwa.dot.gov/policy/hcas/addendum.htm.

US FHWA (2021) *Highway Statistics 2019*, Washington, DC: US Government Printing Office, https://www.fhwa.dot.gov/policyinformation/statistics/2019/.

US FRB (2021) *Federal Reserve Statistical Release: Consumer Credit*, Release G.19 (March), https://www.federalreserve.gov/releases/g19/

Van Den Berg, Vincent A.C. and Erik T. Verhoef (2011) "Winning or losing from dynamic bottleneck congestion pricing? The distributional effects of road pricing with heterogeneity in values of time and schedule delay," *Journal of Public Economics* 95(7–8): 983–992.

Van den Berg, Vincent A.C. and Erik T. Verhoef (2016) "Autonomous cars and dynamic bottleneck congestion: the effects on capacity, value of time and preference heterogeneity," *Transportation Research Part B: Methodological* 94: 43–60, doi:10.1016/j.trb.2016.08.018.

Van Essen, Mariska, Tom Thomas, Erik Van Berkum and Caspar G. Chorus (2016) "From user equilibrium to system optimum: a literature review on the role of travel information, bounded rationality and non-selfish behaviour at the network and individual levels," *Transport Reviews* 36(4): 527–548.

van Essen, Mariska, Tom Thomas, Eric van Berkum and Caspar G. Chorus (2020) "Travelers' compliance with social routing advice: evidence from SP and RP experiments," *Transportation* 47: 1047–1070.

van Essen, Huib, *et al.* (2019) *Handbook on the External Costs of Transport, Version 2019-1.1.* CE Delft, Luxembourg: Publications Office of the European Union, https://cedelft.eu/publications/handbook-on-the-external-costs-of-transport-version-2019/

Van Ommeren, Jos, Piet Rietveld, Jack Zagha Hop and Muhammad Sabir (2013) "Killing kilos in car accidents: are external costs of car weight internalized," *Economics of Transportation* 2: 86–93.

Van Wee, Bert and Maria Börjesson (2015) "How to make CBA more suitable for evaluating cycling policies," *Transport Policy* 44: 117–124.

Varian, Hal R. (1992) *Microeconomic Analysis*, 3rd edition, New York: Norton.

Verhoef, Erik T. (1999) "Time, speeds, flows and densities in static models of road traffic congestion and congestion pricing," *Regional Science and Urban Economics* 29(3): 341–369.

Verhoef, Erik T. (2001) "An integrated dynamic model of road traffic congestion based on simple car-ollowing theory: exploring hypercongestion," *Journal of Urban Economics* 49(3): 505–542.

Verhoef, Erik T. (2003) "Inside the queue: hypercongestion and road pricing in a continuous time–continuous place model of traffic congestion," *Journal of Urban Economics* 54(3): 531–565.

Verhoef, Erik T. (2020) "Optimal congestion pricing with diverging long-run and short-run scheduling preferences," *Transportation Research Part B: Methodological* 134: 191–209.

Verhoef, Erik T., Peter Nijkamp and Piet Rietveld (1996) "Second-best congestion pricing: the case of an untolled alternative," *Journal of Urban Economics* 40(3): 279–302.

Verhoef, Erik T. and Jan Rouwendal (2004) "A behavioural model of traffic congestion: endogenizing speed choice, traffic safety and time losses," *Journal of Urban Economics* 56(3): 408–434.

Vickrey, William S. (1963) "Pricing in urban and suburban transport," *American Economic Review, Papers and Proceedings* 53(2): 452–465.

Vickrey, William S. (1969) "Congestion theory and transport investment," *American Economic Review, Papers and Proceedings* 59(2): 251–260.

Vickrey, William S. (1973) "Pricing, metering, and efficiently using transportation facilities," *Highway Research Record* 476: 36–48.

Vickrey, William S. (2019) "Types of congestion pricing models," *Economics of Transportation* 20: 100140.

Victoria Transport Policy Institute (2019) "TDM encyclopedia: evaluating safety and health impacts," TDM Impacts on Traffic Safety, Personal Security and Public Health, updated September 6, https://www.vtpi.org/tdm/tdm58.htm#_Toc65190624

Viscusi, V. Kip and Joseph E. Aldy (2003) "The value of a statistical life: a critical review of market estimates throughout the world," *Journal of Risk and Uncertainty* 27: 5–76.

Vuchic, Vukan R. (2005) *Urban Transit: Operations, Planning, and Economics*, Wiley & Sons, Inc.

Walters, Alan A. (1961) "The theory and measurement of private and social cost of highway congestion," *Econometrica* 29(4): 676–699.

Wang, Chao, Mohammed A. Quddus and Stephen G. Ison (2009) "Impact of traffic congestion on road accidents: a spatial analysis of the M25 motorway in England," *Accident Analysis & Prevention* 41(4): 798–808.

Wardrop, John G. (1952) "Some theoretical aspects of road traffic research," *Proceedings of the Institute of Civil Engineers* 1(3): 325–378.

West, Jeremy, Mark Hoekstra, Jonathan Meer and Steven L. Puller (2017) "Vehicle miles (not) traveled: fuel economy requirements, vehicle characteristics, and household driving," *Journal of Public Economics* 145: 65–81.

White, Michelle J. (2004) "The 'arms race' on American roads: the effect of sport utility vehicles and pickup trucks on traffic safety," *Journal of Law and Economics* 47(2): 333–355.

Winston, Clifford and Quentin Karpilow (2020) *Autonomous Vehicles: The Road to Economic Growth?*, Washington, DC: Brookings Institution Press.

Winston, Clifford, Vikram Maheshri and Fred Mannering (2006) "An exploration of the offset hypothesis using disaggregate data: the case of airbags and antilock brakes," *Journal of Risk and Uncertainty* 32: 83–99.

Xing, Jianwei, Benjamin Leard and Shanjun Li (2021) "What does an electric vehicle replace?," *Journal of Environmental Economics and Management* 107: 102432

Yang, Hai (1999) "Evaluating the benefits of a combined route guidance and road pricing system in a traffic network with recurrent congestion," *Transportation* 20: 299–321.

Yang, Hai and Hai-Jun Huang (1997) "Analysis of time-varying pricing of a bottleneck with elastic demand using optimal control theory," *Transportation Research Part B: Methodological* 31(6): 425–440.

Yurtsever, Ekim, Jacob Lambert, Alexander Carballo and Kazuya Takeda (2020) "A survey of autonomous driving: common practices and emerging technologies," *IEEE Access* 8: 58443–58469, doi:10.1109/ACCESS.2020.2983149

Zamir, Kiana Roshan, Arefeh Nasri, Babak Baghaei, Subrat Mahapatra and Lei Zhang (2014) "Effects of Transit-Oriented Development on trip generation, distribution, and mode share in Washington, D.C., and Baltimore, Maryland," *Transportation Research Record: Journal of the Transportation Research Board* 2413: 45–53.

Zhang, H. Michael (1999) "A mathematical model of traffic hysteresis," *Transportation Research Part B: Methodological* 33(1): 1–24.

Zhang, Fangni, Robin Lindsey and Hai Yang (2016) "The Downs–Thomson paradox with imperfect mode substitutes and alternative transit administration regimes," *Transportation Research Part B: Methodological* 86: 104–127.

Zhao, Wenjing, Zhuanglin Ma, Kui Yang, Helai Huang, Fredrik Monsuur and Jaeyoung Lee (2020) "Impacts of variable message signs on en-route route choice behavior," *Transportation Research Part A: Policy and Practice* 139: 335–349.

Zheng, Nan and Nikolas Geroliminis (2013) "On the distribution of urban road space for multimodal congested networks," *Transportation Research Part B: Methodological* 57: 326–341.

4 Pricing and usage

Having described demand and cost structures, we can now ask what happens when the two operate simultaneously: that is, when economic actors constrained by these two structures interact in markets. Our analysis of short-run equilibria in the previous chapter provided some first insights. But to obtain a more complete picture, we must also specify how suppliers take into account demand and cost structures in formulating pricing, investment, or other policies.

There are many ways to do this, each leading to an equilibrium analysis that answers a different question. For example, if we specify that firms maximize profits, we determine equilibrium in an unregulated environment. If we specify that highway capacity is fixed and there is no charge for using it, as in Chapter 3, we determine road use in short-run unpriced equilibrium. If we specify that prices are set to maximize some social objective function, we determine a short-run optimum. These and other possibilities are considered in this chapter and Chapters 5 and 6.

Our discussion is organized around policy questions. This chapter describes first-best and second-best optimal short-run pricing, aimed at maximizing social welfare. Chapter 5 discusses investments and how their financing relates to revenues from pricing, including a discussion of cost–benefit analysis. Chapter 6 considers institutional arrangements and how they facilitate or hinder the achievement of efficient pricing and investment. These institutions include public or private ownership of highways, public or private provision of public transit, regulation, and freedom of entry by firms into established markets.

The present chapter exemplifies the ramifications of a standard argument in economics: that achieving efficiency in many situations requires marginal cost pricing. This means that each economic agent, in deciding whether to undertake an activity, faces a perceived price for doing so equal to that activity's social marginal cost. Landmark works applying this principle to transportation include Dupuit (1844, 1849), Hotelling (1938), and Walters (1968). However, it is often impossible to do so in practice, so we must also consider various constraints on what prices can be charged. We then enter the world of "second-best," as exposited for general situations by Lipsey and Lancaster (1956), Baumol and Bradford (1970), and others. The occurrence of such constraints is the rule rather than the exception in applied transportation pricing, and we therefore discuss in detail and for a variety of situations how to determine second-best prices that optimize welfare given some constraints on policies. Of course, actual pricing policy often does not follow any optimization rule but rather responds to political considerations.

Section 4.1 sets the scene by discussing first-best road pricing in the context of congested highway traffic. Section 4.2 moves on to consider second-best road pricing with such examples as the inability to price all links on a network, the inability to distinguish between classes of users, the inability to vary tolls continuously over time, imperfect information by users, and distortions outside the transportation market. Section 4.3 discusses some practical applications

DOI: 10.4324/9781315157375-4

of congestion pricing, all of which involve second-best pricing. Section 4.4 considers another common problem of applied pricing: parking. Section 4.5 discusses the pricing of public transportation. Section 4.6 introduces the political economy perspective on transport pricing.

4.1   First-best congestion pricing of highways

Economists have long recognized that the principle of marginal cost pricing applies to peak-load problems in general (Bye 1926; Boiteux 1949; Steiner 1957) and to roads in particular (Pigou 1920; Knight 1924). These authors' basic concepts have been elaborated and extended by many, including Walters (1961), Mohring and Harwitz (1962), Vickrey (1963, 1969), and Strotz (1965). The resulting models have been extended and applied empirically to cities around the world.[1]

This section presents the basic economic motivation for congestion pricing. To that end, we abstract from various complications and consider a world in which traffic congestion is the sole distortion in the economy, and where fully flexible road pricing is possible. Thus, for example, we assume for now that any other externalities associated with travel are priced (*e.g.,* by a fuel tax), and we exclude so-called external benefits that may occur if the marginal social benefit of a trip exceeds the benefit considered by the traveler.

The basic idea is easily stated within the framework of highway costs developed in Chapter 3. Recall that congestion technology and the costs of travel have been placed directly into the average cost function. All congestion functions considered in Chapter 3 have an important feature in common: short-run average variable cost $c(\cdot)$ increases with the level of road use, be it expressed in traffic flow (V) as in static models, or in the total number of travelers over the peak (Q) as in dynamic models. This implies that short-run marginal social cost exceeds short-run average variable cost. Intuitively, this is because short-run marginal social cost mc includes not only the cost incurred by the traveler themselves, but also the additional cost they impose on all other travelers by adding to the congestion they encounter.[2] This additional cost is known as the *marginal external congestion cost*, here denoted *mecc*.

An efficient level of road use is obtained when each trip that is made provides benefits as least as great as its social cost, *mc*, and when no trip meeting this condition is suppressed. To obtain this situation through pricing, each traveler should face the marginal social cost of their trip. This requires a charge equal to the difference between the marginal cost and the cost already borne by the traveler, which is short-run average variable cost, *c*. This charge, known as the optimal *congestion fee* or *congestion toll*, is therefore $\tau = mc - c = mecc$.

These arguments can be formalized by determining the allocation of road space to users that maximizes *net welfare*, in practical work often operationalized as the social surplus, or the difference between aggregate consumer benefit and total cost. (Fixed cost can be ignored because it does not affect the solution.) For first-best pricing, total cost embodies all relevant resource and technological constraints; when considering second-best pricing, we will add feasibility constraints explicitly when maximizing net welfare. A useful property of such a solution where social surplus is maximized is that it is *Pareto optimal* or *Pareto efficient*, defined as an allocation that maximizes any one person's utility while holding all others' utilities constant and meeting aggregate resource and technological constraints.

We caution that social welfare can be defined more broadly than social surplus, for example, by including distributional properties, in which case maximizing it could lead to a different solution. At the same time, many social welfare functions that have been proposed and considered in the literature are "Paretian," meaning that social welfare according to that function increases, or at least does not decrease, when at least one person is made better off and no-one else is made worse off.[3] (This is true even for the so-called Rawlsian welfare function, which defines social welfare as the utility of the least well-off individual in society and thus embodies strong egalitarianism.) For all these welfare functions, the maximum is Pareto efficient, meaning that the welfare maximum also maximizes social surplus for a particular initial distribution of wealth.[4] The optimality conditions we find when maximizing social surplus are thus necessary conditions for optimization using any Paretian welfare function. To maximize such a social welfare function, some set of lump-sum transfers will then typically be needed as well, unless the initial distribution of wealth happens to be the one for which the maximization of social surplus also means that social welfare is maximized.

In the current Section 4.1, we consider first-best pricing with static congestion (Section 4.1.1) and then with dynamic congestion (Section 4.1.2).

4.1.1   Static congestion

Static models are the easiest way to understand the underlying principles of congestion pricing. They are appropriate when traffic conditions do not change too quickly, or when it is thought sufficient to focus policy attention on average traffic levels over extended periods rather than engaging in fine-tuned attempts to influence the time pattern of trips. Chapter 3 distinguished between two types of static models of traffic congestion: those assuming that traffic is in a stationary state and those dealing with time averages. The analytical derivation of optimal road prices does not differ fundamentally between these models, provided the inflow period P is kept fixed in time-averaged models. Hence, they will be treated together.

Our exposition proceeds from the simplest to the more complex versions, all using the same basic principles, followed by a discussion of distributional implications.

4.1.1.1   Single road, single time period

Consider first the case of a single road and a single time period. As before, let $d(V)$ denote the inverse demand function, and $c(V)$, the average variable cost function. In equilibrium, individuals equate their marginal willingness-to-pay $d(V)$ to generalized price, p, which is defined as average cost $c(V)$ plus toll τ:

$$d(V) = p \equiv c(V) + \tau \tag{4.1}$$

The aggregate benefit from road use, B, is the value of travel to users, as measured by the area under the demand curve up to the equilibrium travel flow:

$$B = \int_0^V d(v)\,dv. \tag{4.2}$$

Total cost, holding capacity fixed in the short run, is

$$C = V \cdot c(V) + \rho K \tag{4.3}$$

where, as before, ρK is the fixed annualized cost of capital expenditures K.

As discussed above, an appropriate measure of aggregate welfare in this setting is social surplus W, defined as total benefit minus total cost. Maximizing $W = B - C$ with respect to V yields the necessary first-order condition:

$$d(V) - c(V) - V \cdot \frac{\partial c}{\partial V} = 0 \Rightarrow d(V) = mc(V) \tag{4.4}$$

This implies, using (4.1), that the optimal price is

$$p = mc(V) = c(V) + V \cdot \frac{\partial c}{\partial V} \qquad (4.5)$$

thus yielding the usual marginal cost pricing rule. Equivalently, the optimal toll is

$$\tau = mc(V) - c(V) = V \cdot \frac{\partial c}{\partial V} = mecc \qquad (4.6)$$

Thus, the optimal congestion toll is the difference between short-run marginal and average variable costs. It is often referred to as a *Pigouvian toll*, named after Arthur Pigou (1920).

Figure 4.1 provides a graphical illustration. The left panel shows the conventional diagram of optimal congestion pricing. The unpriced equilibrium occurs at the intersection of $d(V)$ and $c(V)$; it involves traffic flow V^0 and cost c^0. The optimal flow V^1 occurs at the intersection of $d(V)$ and $mc(V)$, according to (4.4); it can be achieved by imposing the optimal fee τ shown in the diagram. The average cost c falls from c^0 to c^1, but the generalized price rises from $p^0 = c^0$ to $p^1 = c^1 + \tau$. The quantity $(c^0 - c_0) \cdot V^0$ can be interpreted as the total cost of congestion in the unpriced equilibrium. (This should not be confused with the total cost of *inefficient* congestion, which is smaller because some congestion is optimal in this example.) The gain in social surplus is depicted by the shaded *Harberger triangle*, which gives the difference between social cost saved (the area below mc) and benefit forgone (the area below d) when reducing traffic flow from V^0 to V^1.

The increase in the generalized price due to the imposition of the toll has been identified as an important reason for the opposition that road pricing typically meets, severely limiting its social and political acceptability. We discuss this further in Section 4.6.5. In anticipation of our discussion of pricing in dynamic models, we emphasize that the increase in generalized price is a rather robust result for the above static model: it applies whenever users are homogeneous with respect to their value of time, the demand function is downward-sloping, and the marginal cost exceeds the average cost.

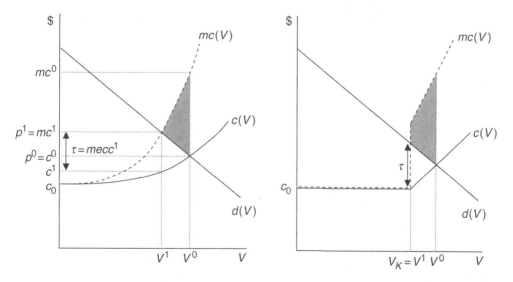

Figure 4.1 Optimal tolls in static models: smooth average cost (left panel) and piecewise linear average cost (right panel)

In many cases, the Pigouvian toll takes an intuitive form mathematically. Using the Bureau of Public Roads (BPR) congestion function of equation (3.6), average cost is given by (3.21), which we can write as

$$c = c_0 + \alpha T_f a \cdot \left(\frac{V}{V_k}\right)^b \tag{4.7}$$

where again α is the value of time, $c_0 \equiv c_{00} + \alpha T_f$ includes the value of free-flow travel time T_f, and a and b are parameters. Then,

$$mc \equiv \frac{\partial(V \cdot c)}{\partial V} = c_0 + \alpha T_f a \cdot (b+1) \cdot \left(\frac{V}{V_k}\right)^b \tag{4.8}$$

and

$$\tau = mecc \equiv mc - c = \alpha T_f ab \cdot \left(\frac{V}{V_k}\right)^b \tag{4.9}$$

In this case, the optimal congestion fee is just b times the average congestion cost c_g in the optimum, a result derived by Vickrey (1965). To determine τ numerically, (4.6) must still be solved simultaneously with the equilibrium condition (4.1), which can be written as $\tau = d(V) - c$, yielding the condition $d(V) = mc$, as also can be seen in the figure. Depending on the form of $d(V)$, this may or may not have an analytical solution.

Using instead a piecewise linear cost function based on congestion function (3.7), a corner solution is possible as illustrated in the right panel of Figure 4.1. The optimal volume is where the demand curve crosses the mc curve, namely $V_{K'}$. The optimal congestion fee is the fee that keeps demand at that level; in this case, it completely eliminates congestion. Because the cost function is kinked there, marginal cost mc is formally undefined; but conceptually, it can be interpreted as the value of the marginal trip displaced by the last traveler using the available capacity. For other demand curves, the optimum may not be a corner solution. If the demand curve were lower, so as to intersect the average cost function on its flat segment, then the optimal toll would be zero and the optimum would coincide with the unpriced equilibrium. If instead the demand curve were higher, so as to intersect $mc(V)$ on its rising segment, the optimal volume would entail some congestion, just as in the left panel. In this case, the relevant part of the cost function is

$$c = c_0 + \frac{1}{2}\alpha P \cdot \left(\frac{V}{V_k} - 1\right) \tag{4.10}$$

where P denotes the exogenous inflow period; the optimal toll is then

$$\tau = mecc \equiv mc - c = \frac{\partial(V \cdot c)}{\partial V} - c = \frac{1}{2}\alpha P \cdot \left(\frac{V}{V_k}\right) \tag{4.11}$$

Again, to determine a numerical value for the toll, this equation must be solved simultaneously with condition (4.4) for user equilibrium.

A cost function that becomes vertical, like c_{stat} in Figure 3.9, also implies a section where mc is vertical. If the marginal cost toll occurs on that section, it has an interpretation like that just described for the piecewise linear congestion function.

4.1.1.2 Single road, multiple time periods

The above model is easily extended to multiple periods of stationary-state congestion. Consider, as before, a highway of capacity V_K serving H distinct daily time periods, each of exogenous duration q_h with endogenous flow V_h under stationary traffic conditions. Then, the $q_h V_h$ users of the highway during period h incur short-run total variable cost $q_h V_h c_h$; the short-run marginal cost of adding another user is therefore

$$mc_h \equiv \frac{\partial(q_h V_h c_h)}{\partial(q_h V_h)} = \frac{\partial(V_h \cdot c_h)}{\partial V_h} = c_h + V_h \cdot \frac{\partial c_h}{\partial V_h} \tag{4.12}$$

With independent inverse demand functions $d_h(V_h)$ applying for each period, social surplus W is

$$W = \sum_h q_h \int_0^{V_h} d_h(v)dv - \sum_h q_h V_h \cdot c_h(V_h) - \rho K \tag{4.13}$$

The first-order conditions to maximize W produce optimal tolls just like (4.6):

$$\tau_h = mc_h(V_h) - c_h(V_h) = V_h \cdot \frac{\partial c_h}{\partial V_h} \tag{4.14}$$

This toll is typically higher in those periods when equilibrium demand V_h is higher, and is guaranteed to be so if $c_h''(V_h) \geq 0$ as is usual; hence, it is an example of peak-load pricing.

4.1.1.3 Network optimum, single time period

A second extension of interest concerns optimal congestion pricing on a network. Equation (3.38) presented the *user equilibrium* conditions for an unpriced network, also referred to as *Wardrop's first principle* (Wardrop 1952). Recall that subscripts l denote links, r and ρ routes, and m markets or origin–destination (OD) pairs. When link-based tolls, τ_l, are in place, these equilibrium conditions continue to hold with $c_l(V_l)$ replaced by $c_l(V_l) + \tau_l$:

$$\forall \delta_{rm} = 1 : \begin{cases} \sum_{l=1}^{L} \delta_h \cdot (c_t(V_t) + \tau_l) - d_m(V_m) \geq 0 \\ V_r \geq 0 \\ V_r \cdot \left[\sum_{l=1}^{L} \delta_h \cdot (c_t(V_t) + \tau_l) - d_m(V_m) \right] = 0 \end{cases} \tag{4.15}$$

where again $\delta_{rm} = 1$ for any route r that serves market m, $\delta_{lr} = 1$ for any link l that is part of route r, and

$$V_l = \sum_{\rho=1}^{R} \delta_{l\rho} \cdot V_\rho, \quad V_m = \sum_{\rho=1}^{R} \delta_{\rho m} \cdot V_\rho$$

The interpretation is that in a user equilibrium, all used routes for an OD pair will have equal generalized prices, all equal to marginal benefits $d_m(V_m)$ for that OD pair; and that there are no unused routes with lower generalized prices.

The optimal flow pattern, often referred to as the *system optimum* in the engineering literature, can be found by maximizing social surplus (W), now defined as the benefits in (4.2) summed over OD pairs minus the costs in (4.3) summed over links. Including non-negativity constraints for route flows, the optimization problem becomes

$$\underset{V_{r=1...R}}{\text{Max}} \ W = \sum_m \int_0^{V_m} d_m(v)dv - \sum_l V_l \cdot c_l(V_l; V_{K,l}) - \sum_l \rho \cdot K_l(V_{K,l})$$

with

$$V_l = \sum_{r=1}^R \delta_{lr} \cdot V_r \text{ and } V_m = \sum_{r=1}^R \delta_{rm} \cdot V_r \tag{4.16}$$

subject to $V_r \geq 0$ for all r.

Taking derivatives with respect to all possible route flows V_r, we obtain Kuhn–Tucker first-order conditions that are identical to (4.15), except that τ_l is replaced by $V_i \cdot (\partial c / \partial V_i)$. These conditions express *Wardrop's second principle*: in a system optimum, all used routes for an OD pair have identical marginal costs equal to the marginal benefits for that OD pair, and there are no unused routes with marginal costs lower than this. Comparing the first-order conditions of (4.16) to the equilibrium conditions (4.15), it is easy to see that the following pricing rule guarantees satisfaction of those first-order conditions:

$$\tau_l = V_l \cdot \frac{\partial c_l}{\partial V_l} \quad \text{for all } l \tag{4.17}$$

The single-road toll in (4.6) is therefore just a special case of the optimal link tolls for a full network, shown in (4.17). Link-based marginal-cost pricing throughout the network ensures that on all "active" routes (*i.e.*, with $V_r > 0$), users will enter up to the point where marginal benefits are equal to marginal cost; while a route remains "passive" (*i.e.*, $V_r = 0$) when marginal benefits on the OD pair it serves are below the marginal cost of using the route.

The tolls in (4.17) need not be the unique set of tolls achieving the optimum. The comparison between the equilibrium conditions (4.15) and the optimality conditions only tells us that the sum of link tolls over each route should be equal to the sum of marginal external costs on all the route's links. This may give some freedom in setting link-based tolls. The simplest example is when two serial links are always used together if used at all: what affects the flow pattern is not the individual link tolls but their sum, so all combinations of tolls with a given sum are equivalent. A further degree of freedom arises when demand is perfectly inelastic for all OD pairs: adding a constant to all the route-based tolls implied by (4.17) would then leave route choices unaltered, allowing a planner to choose such an added constant to meet some secondary objective.

The practical challenge of setting optimal link-based tolls is daunting given that neither the demand functions nor the link-specific speed–flow curves can be known precisely. This has raised interest in trial-and-error approaches, in which tolls are set and then adapted based on observed results. Li (2002) and Yang *et al.* (2004) develop strategies for doing this.

4.1.1.4   Heterogeneity of users

When users are heterogeneous, should tolls be differentiated across users? If so, the practical problems of toll collection are exacerbated; if not, we say the tolls can be *anonymous*.

The principle that the toll should equal marginal external congestion cost (*mecc*) does not change. However, the value of *mecc* for different users may differ for two possible reasons. First, their vehicles (*e.g.*, truck versus car) may contribute differently to congestion; in that case, optimal tolls are not anonymous. Second, they may self-sort into different parts of the network with different values of *mecc* in equilibrium. In that case, the toll can still be anonymous, but must be differentiated across links as in (4.17). For example, Verhoef and Small (2004) consider differentiated first-best tolls for a simple parallel-route network with dispersion in values of time (VOT). The route with the higher toll is faster and therefore attracts drivers with higher VOTs. The higher optimal toll on this route reflects a higher *mecc*, despite the fact that congestion is lower than on the other route; but the *mecc* imposed by a given user is not high because of that user's own value of time, but rather because of the value of time of their co-travelers, on whom they impose a congestion externality.

4.1.2   Dynamic congestion

We now discuss congestion pricing from a dynamic perspective. This enables us to develop some important principles by which pricing can cause people to make substantial changes in the time pattern of their trips. These changes, as we shall see, can produce significant benefits going beyond those produced by prices that are constant over a lengthy time period.

To this end, we focus on dynamic–equilibrium models that endogenize departure time decisions. We begin with the basic bottleneck model of Section 3.4.3, which allows for a particularly transparent analytical treatment and is recently, certainly among economists, the most widely used conceptual model of dynamic congestion pricing. We then turn to two extensions of it that we considered before – heterogeneous users and networks – and show how the insights of the basic model are modified in these more realistic situations. Finally, we describe pricing results from other types of dynamic congestion models, which open the path to still greater realism in designing pricing strategies.

4.1.2.1   First-best pricing in the basic bottleneck model

Recall that the basic bottleneck model considers a single "pure bottleneck," *i.e.*, one for which there are no delays if inflow is below capacity V_K and for which the rate of queue exits is equal to capacity when a queue exists. The basic bottleneck model further simplifies by setting free-flow travel time equal to zero and by assuming that cost parameters are identical for all users, namely the value of travel time α, the shadow prices of early and late arrivals β and γ, and the desired arrival time t^*. Total demand for passages Q is inelastic.

For ease of reference, we summarize the equilibrium conditions for this model, as derived in Section 3.4.3 in the limit where duration q of the desired queue-exit-time interval approaches zero while the total number of travelers, qV_d, remains finite at value Q. The peak starts and ends at times:

$$t_q = t^* - \frac{\gamma}{\beta+\gamma} \cdot \frac{Q}{V_K} \tag{4.18}$$

$$t_{q'} = t^* + \frac{\beta}{\beta+\gamma} \cdot \frac{Q}{V_K} \tag{4.19}$$

The queue-entry rates for early and late arrivals are given by (3.23), which ensures that the average congestion cost $\bar{c}_g$ remains constant over all queue-entry times. Adding superscripts $\bar{c}_g^0$ to denote the unpriced equilibrium, its equilibrium value $\bar{c}_g^0$ and its two components, average travel delay cost, $\bar{c}_T^0$, and average schedule-delay cost, $\bar{c}_S^0$, are

$$\bar{c}_g^0 \equiv p^0 = \delta \cdot \frac{Q}{V_K}; \; \bar{c}_T^0 = \bar{c}_S^0 = \tfrac{1}{2} \cdot \bar{c}_g^0 \qquad (4.20)$$

where $\delta = \beta\gamma / (\beta + \gamma)$. Total equilibrium costs are consequently

$$\bar{C}_g^0 = \delta \cdot \frac{Q^2}{V_K} \qquad (4.21)$$

implying marginal cost equal to

$$\overline{mc}_g^0 = 2\delta \cdot \frac{Q}{V_K} = 2\bar{c}_g^0 \qquad (4.22)$$

Figure 4.2 depicts this unpriced equilibrium graphically, by showing schedule delay cost $c_S(t')$ and travel delay cost $c_T^0(t')$ as functions of arrival time t'. Because the queue-exit rate V_b is constant over time, the time-averaged value of per-user schedule delay cost is given by the two triangular areas under $c_S(t')$ (between t_q and $t_{q'}$), divided by $(t_{q'} - t_q)$, while for travel delay cost it is the inverted triangle between $c_S(t')$ and the horizontal line at p^0, again divided by $(t_{q'} - t_q)$. The equality between these two averages, stated in (4.20), is therefore visible geometrically from the diagram.

Now consider what an optimal travel pattern must look like. The optimum can be identified by intuitive reasoning. First, as long as exits occur, the exit rate should not be below V_K, as otherwise the period of exits could be shortened, and hence, total schedule delay cost could be reduced, without increasing travel delay. Second, no queue should exist in the optimum, as otherwise total travel delay cost could be reduced without increasing schedule delay. These two observations together mean that the entry and exit rates should both be equal to V_K throughout

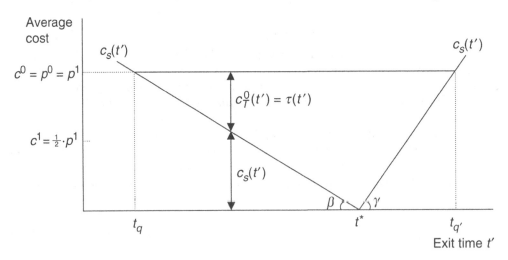

Figure 4.2 Average cost components and optimal tolls by queue-exit time in the basic bottleneck model for the unpriced equilibrium and under first-best tolling.

the peak. Third, the timing of the period of exits should be such that the schedule delay costs of the first and last drivers are equal, as otherwise total schedule delay cost could be reduced by shifting the entire pattern of exits over time. This means that exits should occur between the same instants t_q and $t_{q'}$ as in the unpriced equilibrium.

The optimum just described thus involves the same pattern of *exits* from the bottleneck as the unpriced equilibrium, but it has a different pattern of *entries*. It can be decentralized by a triangular toll schedule $\tau(t')$, with two linear segments, that replicates the pattern of travel delay costs in the unpriced equilibrium, $c_T^0(t')$:[5]

$$\tau(t') = \begin{cases} 0 & \text{if } t' < t_q \\ \beta \cdot (t' - t_q) = \delta \cdot \dfrac{Q}{V_K} - \beta \cdot (t^* - t') & \text{if } t_q \leq t' < t^* \\ \gamma \cdot (t_{q'} - t') = \delta \cdot \dfrac{Q}{V_K} - \gamma \cdot (t' - t^*) & \text{if } t^* \leq t' \leq t_{q'} \\ 0 & \text{if } t' > t_{q'}. \end{cases} \tag{4.23}$$

This toll schedule is shown in the diagram as $\tau(t')$. It results in the same constant generalized price $p^1 = p^0$ (where superscript 1 denotes the first-best tolled equilibrium) and the same pattern of schedule delay cost as in the user equilibrium, but it produces zero travel delay cost. The resulting tolled-equilibrium queue-entry pattern therefore satisfies

$$V_a^1 = V_K \tag{4.24}$$

From the figure, we find the following price and average cost levels:

$$p^1 = \delta \cdot \frac{Q}{V_K}$$

$$\bar{c}_g^1 = \tfrac{1}{2} \cdot \delta \cdot \frac{Q}{V_K}; \ \bar{c}_T^1 = 0; \ \bar{c}_S^1 = \bar{c}_g^1 \tag{4.25}$$

Total cost is therefore half as large as in the unpriced equilibrium:

$$\bar{C}_g^1 = \tfrac{1}{2} \cdot \bar{C}_g^0 = \tfrac{1}{2} \cdot \delta \cdot \frac{Q^2}{V_K} \tag{4.26}$$

The net welfare gain from optimal pricing is equal to the value of travel-time savings and therefore also to the total toll revenues generated. Neither equality is generally true in the static model of Figure 4.1.

Several points deserve emphasis. First, in contrast to most static models, no travel delays exist in the optimum. Second, the generalized price remains unchanged after imposition of the optimal toll schedule, because tolls exactly replace travel-time delays; this suggests that social acceptability should be less of a problem than is predicted by the static model in Section 4.1.1. Third, exit times and hence arrival times at the destination need not change between the un-priced equilibrium and the optimum, and no alternative to (solo) car use is required for the elim-ination of queues. In the context of the morning commute, only departure times from home have to be adjusted for queues to disappear. Moreover, if commuters retain their order of departure and their arrival times, everybody (except the very first and last driver) should depart later than in the unpriced equilibrium. This gives room for optimism about the possibility of achieving a significant reduction in queues in reality under optimal pricing. Note that these results are due to the kinked performance function for a pure bottleneck and will at best only approximately apply for models with different performance functions.

Thus far, we have assumed that total demand Q over the peak is fixed, which leaves an ambiguity in the optimal toll: any constant could be added to the toll schedule of (4.23) and still support the optimal pattern. What if, instead, total demand has nonzero elasticity with respect to generalized price? We have seen that toll schedule (4.23) produces the same constant generalized price as the user equilibrium, $p^1 = p^0$. Therefore, the two policies also produce identical total quantities demanded (Q), even if demand has some elasticity. Surprisingly, this implies that total demand Q^0 in the user equilibrium is just right when an optimal toll is in place.[6] One way to think about this puzzling result is that dynamic tolling so substantially reduces the adverse consequences of adding to total traffic that there is no longer a reason to curtail traffic, as there is in the unpriced equilibrium. Note that Q^0 in the original user equilibrium is, in fact, inefficiently high in the presence of queuing. Section 4.2.2 will show that with a time-independent or "flat" toll for this same bottleneck, which reduces the number of travelers but keeps the time patterns of queuing unaffected, it is second-best optimal to reduce the number of users when demand is price-sensitive, just like what we have seen for static congestion above.

The first-best optimality of the original volume Q^0 can be shown more formally. First, observe from (4.26) that in the optimal pattern, the marginal cost of increasing Q is

$$\overline{mc}\,_g^1 = \delta \cdot \frac{Q}{V_K} \tag{4.27}$$

which is the same as the generalized price p^1. Thus, marginal cost equals marginal benefit with the toll schedule (4.23) in place, and no additional constant needs to be added to it even though it has failed to reduce Q from its no-toll value. The toll schedule (4.23) can also be interpreted as the marginal external cost of a traveler arriving at t', defined as the difference between the (time-independent) marginal social cost (4.27) and the (time-dependent) private cost $c_g(t')$. This reflects that the marginal external cost that a driver imposes in arriving at t^* is the foregone opportunity for another driver to arrive at that same time. In the optimum, this other driver would find a slot close to the desired arrival time t^* more valuable, and the toll pattern reflects this difference exactly.

Yet another way to look at the above results is that imposing optimal time-varying tolls, through the elimination of queuing, causes the average and marginal-cost curves to rotate downward by a factor of $\frac{1}{2}$, as seen by comparing (4.20) to (4.25) and (4.22) to (4.27). The cost curves in the static models of Section 4.1.1, in contrast, do not change when pricing is imposed.

4.1.2.2   Heterogeneous users

The logic of optimal pricing in the basic bottleneck model carries over to the case where users are not identical, which of course is a more realistic assumption. Newell (1987) provides a general analysis of equilibrium at a pure bottleneck with heterogeneous commuters, each of whom minimizes a deterministic cost function belonging to a specified parametric family. He provides diagrammatic and algorithmic solutions for determining the equilibrium queuing delay function $T_D(t)$ (and, from that, the queue-entry times and resulting schedule delays for all commuters), given two cumulative distribution functions: that of desired queue-exit times, $F(t)$, and that of the cost function parameters. (The desired queue-exit rate $V_d(t)$ in the previous chapter is just $F'(t)$ in this notation.)

A few very general features can be derived from minimal assumptions on these functions. Figure 4.3 shows cumulative counts $A(t)$ of queue-entry times, $B(t)$ of queue-exit times, and $F(t)$ of desired queue-exit times. At any given queue-entry time t and desired queue-exit time t_{d}, queuing delay $T_{D}(t)$ and schedule delay $S_{D}(t) \equiv t' - t_{d} \equiv t + T_{D}(t) - t_{d}$ are the horizontal distances shown in the figure. (S_{D} is negative at the time t shown, indicating a queue-exit earlier than desired.) Denote the cost of queuing delay by $c_{T}(T_{D})$, the cost of schedule delay by $c_{S}(S_{D})$, and the derivatives of these functions with primes.[7] Each commuter chooses t to minimize $c_{T}(t) + c_{S}(t)$, leading to the following first-order condition, which must makes the sum constant over the time interval when users with the corresponding particular set of cost parameters depart:

$$c_T' \cdot T_D'(t) + c_S' \cdot \left(1 + T_D'(t)\right) = 0 \tag{4.28}$$

or

$$\frac{c_S'}{c_T'} = -\frac{T_D'(t)}{1 + T_D'(t)} \tag{4.29}$$

assuming the derivatives exist.[8] Note that the assumed first-in, first-out queue discipline implies that $T_D'(t) > -1$.

Several qualitative results follow. First, the queue grows while early travelers (those who will exit before their desired arrival times) are arriving, and it shrinks while late travelers are arriving.[9] Second, a person exiting the queue exactly at the desired time must incur the maximum travel time incurred by users with the same characteristics.[10] Third, under certain circumstances,

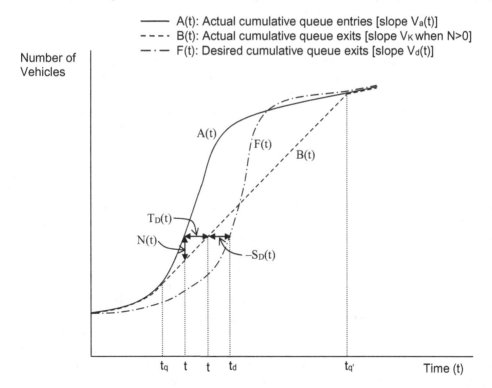

Figure 4.3 Queue entries, desired and actual queue exits.

Newell obtains a key pricing result of the basic bottleneck model for this more general model: if users have identical VOTs, a time-varying toll can be defined which has no allocative effects on the number of travelers or their time of passage through the bottleneck. Such a toll collects revenues equal to the entire cost of queuing delay in the unpriced equilibrium, and it leaves each commuter exactly as well off (before redistribution of toll revenues) as in the no-toll equilibrium. This last-mentioned result illustrates a point that emerges from simulation exercises by Arnott *et al.* (1993): the reallocation of departure times may be a greater source of benefit from time-of-day pricing than the reduction in total trips.

Now suppose heterogeneity is more limited: the desired queue-exit time t_d varies across travelers, but the per-unit costs of travel and schedule delay do not. (One example is our treatment of the bottleneck model in Chapter 3.) Hendrickson and Kocur (1981) provide an elegant and general analysis. Within limits, the heterogeneity in desired queue-exit times affects only schedule delay costs, not travel delay costs or the time pattern of queuing in the unpriced equilibrium. This is true so long as the cumulative desired exits $F(t)$, in Figure 4.3, intersect the cumulative exits $B(t)$ only once. The optimal time-varying toll is then the same as for the basic bottleneck model and will again eliminate all travel delay costs and leave schedule delay costs unaffected. Optimal tolling now reduces generalized cost by more than half (instead of exactly half as in the basic bottleneck model), because in this case, total schedule delay cost is smaller than total travel delay cost in the unpriced equilibrium – as can be seen, for example, in Figure 3.12 and equations (3.34)–(3.35).

If there are multiple intersections of $F(t)$ and $B(t)$ in Figure 4.3, the queue will wax and wane more than once over the peak in the unpriced equilibrium (but not necessarily disappear completely in between). Then, both schedule delay costs and travel delay costs are lower than in the basic bottleneck model. Arnott *et al.* (1988) show that in such equilibria, the queue-entry rates of (3.23) remain valid. Likewise, the optimal toll schedule has slopes β and $-\gamma$ just like that for the basic bottleneck model, and it again eliminates all travel delay costs and leaves schedule delay costs unaffected.

Arnott, de Palma, and Lindsey also consider the contrasting case in which distinct groups of travelers have identical desired schedules $t_d = t^*$ but different relative costs of schedule delay versus travel delay, as measured by the ratios β/α and γ/α. This model is interesting, because it shows how marginal external costs may differ between seemingly identical vehicles and because it illustrates that in the unpriced equilibrium, the ordering of travelers as well as their departure rates may be non-optimal.

Figure 4.4 illustrates this case for a simple symmetric example with two groups of users, denoted A and B. For graphical convenience, we assume that the groups are equal in size. The parameters α, β, and γ are all lower for group A; the ratios β/γ are the same for both groups; but the ratios β/α and γ/α are higher for group A. Group A could be blue-collar workers for whom all shadow prices are lower due to a lower income, but for whom scheduling is relatively more important than delays because they work in shifts.

The solid line in the upper panel shows travel delay $T_D(t')$ in the unpriced equilibrium, which is a piecewise linear function with slopes equal to β_G/α_G and $-\gamma_G/\alpha_G$ during the intervals when people from group G arrive early or late (G = A, B). Equilibrium entails temporal separation, with group A arriving closest to t^*. Both types of drivers would lose individually if either were to reschedule to an arrival time occupied by the other group. The dashed lines each extrapolate a group's experienced travel delay function as iso-price lines into the other group's arrival intervals, thus showing the required travel delays to make an arrival with these other group's drivers equally attractive as in their own interval(s). These extrapolations are always below equilibrium travel delays, confirming that there is no incentive to mix with drivers from the other group.

Drivers in group A benefit from heterogeneity, in the sense that they would be worse off if a type B driver changed and became type A.[11] This is because type B drivers spread out their

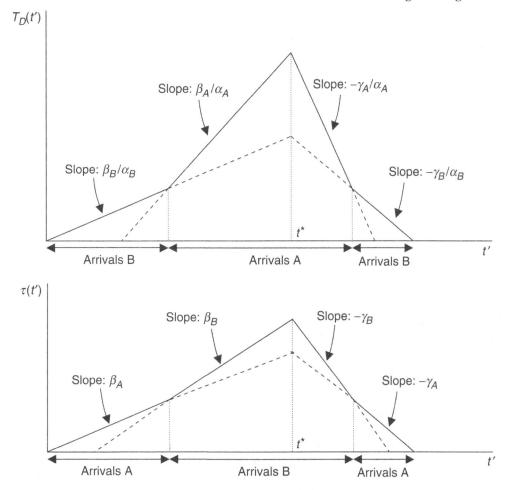

Figure 4.4 Optimal tolling in the bottleneck model with heterogeneous users.

departure times more widely and therefore cause less travel delay. The marginal external cost is therefore higher for type A drivers than for type B drivers: the identity of an extra driver is immaterial to group B, but group A prefers an additional driver to be of type B (see Arnott and Kraus 1998). As will be shown later, the second-best "flat" (time-independent) tolls would therefore differ between the two groups, making these tolls non-anonymous.

The optimal time-varying toll schedule, shown in the lower panel of Figure 4.4, eliminates all travel delays and therefore requires the slope of the toll schedule $\tau(t')$ to be equal to β_G or $-\gamma_G$ during group G's arrivals. It induces a voluntary reversal in arrival times: group B now arrives closest to t^*. Again, the dashed lines function as iso-price lines and show for each group the hypothetical toll schedule that would make its members willing to switch to the other group's arrival interval; it is below the actual toll schedule so they do not switch. The toll eliminates all travel delays, as in the basic bottleneck model, and also produces another efficiency gain: it reduces aggregate schedule delay cost because drivers in group B, with the higher β and γ, now exit the queue closer to the desired time t^*. Therefore, this example shows that additional gains may arise when users are heterogeneous due to arrival time adjustments, which do not occur with homogeneous users.

Another interesting reversal occurs: it is now group B that benefits from heterogeneity, while group A does not. This is consistent with another property: it can be shown (by comparing generalized trip prices as implied by the intersections with the horizontal axes in Figure 4.4) that before redistribution of toll revenues, group A suffers from the imposition of tolling, while group B benefits. The finding that high-value-of-time users can benefit from imposition of optimal pricing, while low-value-of-time users lose, also occurs with the static model.

The result that some users may actually benefit directly (*i.e.*, before revenues are redistributed) from the imposition of tolling is counterintuitive, but makes sense when recalling that in the bottleneck model with the homogeneous users, the generalized price remains the same when optimal tolling is implemented. Because re-ordering of travel times under optimal pricing further reduces travel cost, some groups may indeed benefit directly. Van den Berg and Verhoef (2011) confirm this using a more elaborate model with continuous distributions of preference parameters. In particular, they find that first-best pricing can leave a majority of travelers better off before revenues are redistributed.

4.1.2.3   *Networks of bottlenecks*

In reality, most pricing applications involve more than a single road. It is not necessarily straightforward to generalize from a single bottleneck to a network of bottlenecks. Arnott *et al.* (1998) provide an insightful discussion. They show that interactions between different bottlenecks may be either simpler or more complicated than between links in a conventional static network.

For example, a particularly simple result appears in the case of two bottlenecks in series, with different capacities and with no active origin or destination in between. The unpriced equilibrium, the optimum, and the optimal time-varying toll are all the same as in the absence of the higher-capacity bottleneck – regardless of which of the two bottlenecks is upstream of the other. The higher-capacity bottleneck can therefore be entirely ignored in the analysis.[12]

A more complex case is two bottlenecks in parallel. Arnott *et al.* (1990a) consider this situation with homogeneous users. The free-flow travel times T_f can then no longer be set arbitrarily to zero, unless they are equal between the two roads. Again, all travel delay costs are eliminated in the optimum. The time-varying tolls are analogous to those for a single bottleneck, and the timing of exits and the route split are identical between the unpriced equilibrium and the optimum.

One might be tempted to conclude from these examples that queuing can never be socially optimal on a network of pure bottlenecks. This is usually true, although there are counterexamples in which some queuing is optimal when drivers are heterogeneous (de Palma and Jehiel 1995). It seems hard to precisely identify the characteristics of a network that would make this happen. Nevertheless, a naïve rule that sets tolls so as to eliminate all queues, even if not optimal, will typically produce substantial efficiency gains, at least in the case of pure bottleneck congestion (de Palma *et al.* 2005). The same is not necessarily true for other types of congested networks, where substantial delays may occur at the short-run optimum even in simple models.

For all but very simple networks, numerical methods must be used to find equilibria with tolls. Rather than try and model equilibrium directly, one could consider day-to-day behavior by travelers (and possibly by toll-setting algorithms) that responds to conditions on previous days. Approach to a stable pattern would then be simulated, as discussed in Section 3.4.6. The traveler adjustments can be interpreted as travelers learning over days and adjusting behavior and expectations accordingly. Such adjustment models can be used not only to obtain equilibrium, but also to understand how traffic conditions evolve over successive days. For example, the METROPOLIS model mentioned in Section 3.4.4 uses this technique.

To determine the optimal time-varying fee in such models, we must know all the parameters and be able to solve the entire model. In practice, a way is needed to use observed data to adjust the fee in response to changed conditions. We might hope that simply setting a fee that varies instantaneously with queue length would come close to an optimum. There is at least one case where this happens, a very stylized one with perfect information known in advance (de Palma and Arnott 1986). Without advance information, the behavioral response to instantaneous toll adjustments is limited to route choice, while pre-trip decisions, such as departure time and mode choice, are based on *expected* rather than on *actual* toll and queue patterns and are therefore unaffected by instantaneous toll adjustments. Such toll adjustments may then frustrate drivers when an unexpectedly long queue is matched with an unexpectedly high toll, presumably limiting social acceptability without strongly benefiting efficiency. Using instead a day-to-day adjustment policy, with tolls known in advance on any given day, leaves drivers more time to anticipate and more ways to respond and hence may be more acceptable. The same might then be true for adjustments at yet lower frequency, as in Singapore, where toll schedules are adjusted quarterly (see Section 4.3.1).

4.1.2.4 *Alternative dynamic congestion technologies*

As indicated in Chapter 3, the bottleneck model uses a description of traffic flow that omits many details arising on real roads. More sophisticated traffic-flow models are available, as also described in Chapter 3; but they are difficult to combine with endogenous scheduling. Nevertheless, we can describe two studies that have done so, focusing on how well the insights from the basic bottleneck model hold up when extended to these more realistic settings.

Xuehao Chu (1995) investigates optimal pricing for a road that is characterized by no-propagation flow congestion as presented in Section 3.3.4, where the travel time depends solely on the flow at the road's exit at the instant that the trip is completed, $V_o(t')$. The demand side of his model is the same as for the basic bottleneck model discussed above. The optimal time-varying toll turns out to be a straightforward dynamic generalization of the standard toll for static congestion in (4.6):

$$\tau(t') = \alpha \cdot V_o(t') \cdot \frac{\mathrm{d}T(V_o(t'))}{\mathrm{d}V_o(t')} \tag{4.30}$$

This expression follows from the optimality condition that the marginal social cost of an arrival at t' should be constant throughout the period during which arrivals occur.[13]

Chu provides an interesting comparison between his model and the basic bottleneck model. Several qualitative differences are worth emphasizing. First, total schedule delay cost is smaller than total travel delay cost in the unpriced equilibrium. This is because in order to keep the generalized price p^0 constant over time, the exit rate must be higher the closer to t^* one completes the trip. Therefore, many drivers have relatively high travel delay costs and relatively low schedule delay costs. The simple geometry of Figure 4.2, which was due to the constancy of the queue-exit rate, breaks down. Second, the optimal toll does not eliminate all travel delays in Chu's model and raises total schedule delay cost. Third, applying the optimal toll lengthens the duration of the peak because it reduces the rate at which trips near the desired arrival time are completed. Fourth, applying the optimal toll raises the generalized price of traveling, because of the increased peak duration.[14] Finally, the total variable cost in Chu's model depends on the value of travel time, α, in contrast to the pure bottleneck model.

Verhoef (2003) uses a car-following model (mentioned in Section 3.3.4) to investigate optimal time-varying tolls on a road with a sudden reduction in the number of lanes by half.

This model does produce hypercongestion in the unpriced equilibrium, in the form of a slowly moving queue immediately upstream of the bottleneck. Optimal tolling eliminates such queuing, but increases the duration of the peak and therefore also raises the generalized price. Qualitatively, the differences with the basic bottleneck model are therefore similar to those found in Chu's model.

Thus, it appears that the basic bottleneck model may overestimate the benefits from optimal tolling and underestimate the resulting increase in generalized price, by exaggerating the extent to which travel delays can be eliminated without increasing scheduling costs. But opposite biases may exist in flow-based dynamic models, especially when they ignore the waste of hypercongested queuing. The simulation results of Mun (2002) and Verhoef (2003) support similar conclusions.

Verhoef's study also provides a potentially useful computational device for approximating the optimal toll schedule. Although no analytical solution for it is found, more than 99% of the possible welfare gains from tolling appear to be captured by adopting a time- and location-specific version of (4.30). Specifically, the toll for traversing a link is calculated as the integral over distance of the following time- and place-specific toll per unit distance:

$$\tau(t,x) = \alpha \cdot V(t,x) \cdot \frac{d\left[1 / S(V)\right]}{dV}\Bigg|_{V(t,x)} \tag{4.31}$$

where $S(V)$ is the stationary-state speed–flow function from which the first-order car-following equation is derived, and the combinations of times t and locations x to be considered should, of course, be mutually consistent. In other words, the logic of the basic Pigouvian toll in (4.6) not only extends to a dynamic setting with flow congestion, as shown by (4.30), but apparently also to more realistic and complex cases where congestion varies both temporally and spatially in a continuous manner. The shape of this link toll as a function of time is approximately triangular, similar to that in the basic bottleneck model. But although it eliminates hypercongestion, it does not fully eliminate travel delays. In fact, eliminating all travel delays by naïvely copying the triangular toll schedule from the basic bottleneck model is a disastrous policy in Verhoef's numerical simulations, as it produces a welfare loss (compared with the unpriced equilibrium).

A practical advantage of a toll based on (4.31) would be that it can, in principle, be set adaptively, based on local and instantaneous traffic conditions. This allows a regulator to iterate toward the desired toll by trying a toll structure, observing $V(t, x)$, and calculating (4.31) from a previously measured speed–flow relationship. The idea is similar to the trial-and-error approach to setting tolls in static models, mentioned in Section 4.1.1.

Finally, there are also reasons why the basic bottleneck model can sometimes *under*estimate the welfare gains from tolling. We already discussed how with user heterogeneity, there may be additional gains from tolling that the basic bottleneck model would miss. Another possible additional benefit from tolling is in preventing capacity reductions due to queuing, which can happen when flow is close to capacity, as described in Section 3.3.2, or when queues propagate far enough upstream to block other intersections. Hall (2018) shows that when this occurs, tolling a portion of lanes can even be Pareto-improving before redistribution of revenues. Hall (2021) confirms the idea empirically while allowing for heterogeneity of preferences. Specifically, he finds that under some plausible conditions, all users benefit from tolling when only a portion of capacity is priced and that a vast majority of users benefit even when the entire network is tolled. Van den Berg and Verhoef (2011) obtain similar results for heterogeneous users in the absence of a capacity drop; their results would clearly be reinforced when tolling increases effective capacity.

The blocking of intersections on urban networks is likely to be an important reason why empirical Macroscopic Fundamental Diagrams (MFDs), as discussed in Chapter 3, may display a hypercongested segment of the flow–density curve. If that occurs in the no-toll equilibrium, pricing may then also bring benefits of increasing throughput, allowing a shorter peak duration. Fosgerau (2015) confirms that if initial congestion in a bathtub model is so high that hypercongestion occurs, optimal pricing can reduce the duration of the peak (as it does in Jonathan Hall's analyses of expressways), with resulting large gains. Similarly, Arnott (2013) and Arnott *et al.* (2016) provide examples where tolling in a bathtub model shortens the peak by eliminating hypercongestion; in these cases, so much so that the toll reduces costs by more than toll revenues, so that travelers benefit even before revenues are redistributed.[15]

When hypercongestion translates into a reduction in capacity, it becomes even more likely that optimal tolling can reduce congestion so much that the generalized price of travel, which includes the toll, is less than with no toll. Nevertheless, the occurrence of hypercongested speeds in equilibrium does not necessarily mean that the output flow is pushed below optimal levels.[16] This is illustrated by the car-following models of Verhoef (2003), where hypercongested speeds do not diminish exit-flow capacity. In that case, optimal tolling lengthens rather than shortens the peak duration, and so raises the generalized price although it still produces welfare gains once revenues are accounted for.

4.1.2.5 Discussion

Dynamic models suggest that a main source of efficiency gains from optimal pricing is the re-scheduling of departure times from the trip origin. With heterogeneous users, additional gains may also result from changing the order of arrivals at the trip destination. Despite severe practical limitations, the basic bottleneck model and its generalizations have proven useful in generating understanding of these features. These large gains from rescheduling are even bigger if tolling prevents capacity drops that arise from hypercongestion or flow instability. It is then possible for travelers to benefit from optimal pricing even before toll revenues are recycled. However, not all models predict this, and furthermore, the occurrence and severity of capacity drops are likely to depend on the details of the network. Thus, it remains an open question whether, in practical settings, optimal tolling can produce gains for everyone in the absence of revenue recycling.

4.2 Second-best pricing

The rules for marginal cost pricing discussed in the previous section are often referred to as "first-best," because there are no constraints on the pricing instrument and there are no market distortions other than the congestion externality. Although extremely useful as a theoretical benchmark, first-best pricing is increasingly recognized to be of limited practical relevance. We therefore need to consider explicitly how such constraints and distortions alter the properties of tolls.

Because lump-sum taxes do not exist in reality and governments need budgets to pursue redistributional policy objectives or to supply public goods, any modern economy operates under second-best conditions because distortive taxes are in place – especially those on labor, but also those on a variety of goods and services. As a consequence, marginal social benefits and marginal social costs are not equalized in most markets. Any transportation policy that directly or indirectly affects equilibrium quantities in these markets will therefore create nonzero net social costs or benefits in them, which should be accounted for in the economic evaluation and design of the policy. A policy that does so in the most efficient way possible is called the second-best policy.

A policy can also be second-best when the tools for implementing it are not as flexible as assumed in the theory generating first-best rules. For example, perfect price or toll differentiation may not be possible. It is instructive to consider a simple graphical example of second-best pricing of this type, which allows us to make some basic but important points about second-best pricing before moving to more elaborate cases.

In our example, we ignore congestion but consider a pollution externality. Suppose that there are two types of cars: "clean" cars (type A) and "dirty" cars (type B), so that the marginal external costs are ranked as $mec_B > mec_A$. If we assume that the cars are otherwise identical and have equal user costs c, then total marginal costs (including the external costs) also differ: $mc_B > mc_A$. If we also assume that the two inverse demand functions d are the same, then with no government pricing the vehicle flows of the two types, V_A^0 and V_B^0, would be identical. These flows are shown in the two panels of Figure 4.5.

First-best pricing in this case would involve group-specific tolls (not shown in the diagrams), each equal to that group's *mec*. The result would be flows V_A^1 and V_B^1, producing social surplus gains as given by the areas of the shaded triangles. When tolls cannot be differentiated, however, a second-best identical toll can be determined that optimally compromises between the two first-best tolls (Verhoef *et al.* 1995). In the case sketched, with identical linear demand functions, it is exactly equal to the average of the *mec*s, shown as τ in the diagram. The potential welfare gains foregone by overpricing group A and underpricing group B, compared with first-best pricing, are given by the two bold triangles. This example is discussed further, in a more general setting, in Section 4.2.3.

This simple example already illustrates some important aspects of second-best pricing. First, tautologically, the welfare gains cannot exceed those from first-best pricing and are usually smaller (unless the constraint does not bind). Second, although tolls are not equal to marginal external costs, they are of course still related to them; in this simple example, the toll is the average of the *mec*s. And third, the key to determining the second-best toll is the trade-off between welfare gains foregone due to non-optimal pricing in the various (sub)markets involved. In this example, because equal demand sensitivities are assumed, it is optimal to have the vertical sides of the bold triangles equally long (*i.e.*, the toll is the average of the *mec*s), so that a marginal change in the toll would create a surplus loss in the one market that is exactly compensated for by a surplus gain in the other market. In diagrammatic terms, when characterizing the welfare-loss triangles from non-optimal pricing, one could say that "two small Harberger triangles are better than one large one" (Arnott and Yan 2000, p. 171).

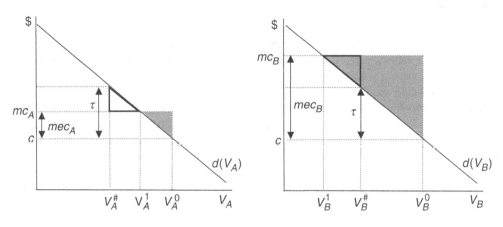

Figure 4.5 Second-best pricing for an environmental externality when tolls cannot be differentiated.

Because second-best problems come in so many variants, it is not instructive to combine all possible sources of second-best constraints into one grand exposition, even if it were possible. Rather, more insight is gained from considering different sources of second-best distortions in isolation, *i.e.*, in an otherwise first-best world. The insights will remain relevant in explaining what is going on in more realistic but complex cases, where various distortions occur simultaneously. This section considers six cases: when not every link in a network can feasibly be priced; when tolls cannot be varied smoothly over time; when tolls cannot be differentiated among different classes of users; when tolls must be set before knowing what the actual demand and/or capacity will be; when financial incentives take the form of subsidies or budget-neutral instruments such as tradable permits (perhaps to enhance political support); and when pricing affects labor supply which is already discouraged due to income or other taxes. Our discussion benefits from an earlier exposition in Lindsey and Verhoef (2001).

4.2.1 *Network aspects*

Probably, the earliest example of second-best road pricing considered in the literature concerns the case where not every congested link in a network is tolled. Reasons for this might include excessive cost for charging each link, political constraints requiring that road charging be implemented gradually, or an acceptability constraint that a toll-free alternative should always be available. Lévy-Lambert (1968) and Marchand (1968) addressed this type of problem using a simple network featuring a toll road and a parallel, untolled road between a common origin and destination.[17] This setting is still relevant today, as it describes the main constraint faced when setting a congestion toll on an express lane with parallel untolled lanes.

But the general problem of untolled links encompasses a much wider set of practical congestion-charging mechanisms. A toll cordon, as used in various cities, corresponds to a situation in which tolls are in place only on the links that define the cordon. An area charge, as applied in Central London, can be viewed as a priced "virtual" link that is added, for modeling purposes, to all routes that pass through the charging area, with all other routes unpriced. Even parking charges can be modeled in this way, by adding a tolled virtual link to all routes that end within the area subject to a parking charge.

We start our discussion with the static two-route problem just mentioned and choose this case to provide a full derivation of the second-best optimal toll. This model provides fundamental insights, which, as will be shown later, also help to understand how to price public transit when it competes with automobiles for passengers. We then go on to other second-best problems, which can be solved using similar Lagrangian approaches but for which full derivations will be suppressed for reasons of space.

4.2.1.1 *Static congestion: two routes in parallel*

The classic two-route problem considers static congestion on two parallel roads connecting a single OD pair: precisely the situation for the widely adopted policy of "managed lanes" discussed in Section 4.3.2. A congestion toll can be applied on one of the two roads (route *T*), while the other (route *U*) must remain untolled. Total traffic V is equal to the sum of traffic on the two roads, V_T and V_U, and average user cost on road R is $c_R(V_R)$.[18] Users consider the roads as pure substitutes, so Wardrop's first principle of an equilibrium across routes applies. Users are homogeneous in all respects except that willingness to pay for trips differs across users, so that overall inverse demand $d(V)$ is downward-sloping (*i.e., $d'<0$*), where inverse demand function $d(\cdot)$ pertains to the generalized price including user cost and toll.

The optimal toll on route T, τ_T, can be found by maximizing the following Lagrangian function:

$$\Lambda = \int_0^{V_T+V_U} d(v)\,dv - V_T \cdot c_T(V_T) - V_U \cdot c_U(V_U)$$

$$+ \lambda_T \cdot \left[c_T(V_T) + \tau_T - d(V_T + V_U) \right] + \lambda_U \cdot \left[c_U(V_U) - d(V_T + V_U) \right] \tag{4.32}$$

where the first three terms form the social objective of social surplus, the variables λ_R give the shadow price of the equilibrium constraint for route R, $R = T, U$, and capacities are suppressed as arguments in cost functions because we consider only the short run. The expressions in square brackets express the constraints that people choose how much to travel according to their demand curves.

The equilibrium value of a Lagrange multiplier in general reflects the marginal impact of a relaxation of the associated constraint upon the optimized value of the objective. For the Lagrangian (4.32), this means that the equilibrium value of λ_R should give the impact on social surplus of a marginal increase in the toll on route R. We therefore expect to find $\lambda_T = 0$ in the second-best optimum (τ_T should be set optimally), and $\lambda_U > 0$ when route U is congested (since surplus would be increased if a positive toll could be included in the second constraint). The first-order conditions to (4.32) confirm this:

$$\frac{\partial \Lambda}{\partial V_T} = d - c_T - V_T \cdot c_T' + \lambda_T \cdot \left(c_T' - d' \right) - \lambda_U \cdot d' = 0$$

$$\frac{\partial \Lambda}{\partial V_U} = d - c_U - V_U \cdot c_U' - \lambda_T \cdot d' + \lambda_U \cdot \left(c_U' - d' \right) = 0$$

$$\frac{\partial \Lambda}{\partial \tau_T} = \lambda_T = 0 \tag{4.33}$$

$$\frac{\partial \Lambda}{\partial \lambda_T} = c_T + \tau_T - d = 0$$

$$\frac{\partial \Lambda}{\partial \lambda_U} = c_U - d = 0$$

where primes denote derivatives. These first-order conditions can be solved to yield

$$\lambda_U = \frac{V_U \cdot c_U'}{c_U' - d'} \tag{4.34}$$

which is non-negative as expected (recall that d', the slope of the inverse demand function, is non-positive). Furthermore, λ_U increases in the congestion externality on route U (the numerator) and in the sensitivity of equilibrium demand to price changes on route U (which decreases the denominator). Both factors would indeed boost the welfare gains from introducing a marginally positive toll on route U.

Starting with the first-order condition for V_T in (4.33), we first substitute the solutions for the two Lagrange multipliers, namely (4.34) and $\lambda_T = 0$. Next, using Wardrop's condition for route T (i.e., the first-order condition for λ_T), we replace $d - c_T$ by τ_T and obtain the following second-best toll:

$$\tau_T = V_T c_T' - V_U c_U' \cdot \frac{-d'}{c_U' - d'} \tag{4.35}$$

The toll is equal to the marginal external congestion cost on route T, minus a certain fraction of the marginal external congestion cost on route U. The first term reflects the direct beneficial impacts of the toll upon congestion on route T. The second term, which including its minus sign is negative, captures the toll's indirect spillovers on route U through induced route diversion. The fraction in that term gives the number of trips added to route U per trip removed from route T. It is less than one (provided demand is not perfectly inelastic) because some of the trips removed from T are no longer made on either route.[19] Under perfectly inelastic demand ($d' \to -\infty$), the fraction becomes unity and the two effects are equally important: only route choice matters for overall efficiency with inelastic demand, and it is optimized by setting the toll on route T equal to the difference between marginal external costs on the two routes. In contrast, as demand becomes perfectly elastic ($d' = 0$), the second term vanishes: V_U cannot be affected by τ_T because it is fully determined by Wardrop's condition $d = c_U(V_U)$, with d constant. The best thing the regulator can then do is to ignore route U altogether and optimize the use of route T by perfectly internalizing the congestion externality.

This example illustrates two lessons that turn out to be more general. The first is that the difference between welfare gains from first-best and second-best pricing can typically be determined only when detailed information is available. The upper curve in Figure 4.6 illustrates this point by plotting, for the simulation model of Verhoef and Small (2004), the relative efficiency of second-best pricing – *i.e.*, its welfare gain (compared with no pricing) as a fraction of the welfare gain from first-best pricing. This relative efficiency (the top line in the figure) rises from 0 to 1 as the relative size of priced capacity increases from 0 to 1. The sigmoid shape of the curve underlines that unless a significant portion of capacity is priced, the welfare losses from spillovers on unpriced capacity, reflected in the second term of (4.35), are substantial. For example, the relative efficiency at one-third of capacity is approximately 0.3, as seen in the figure.

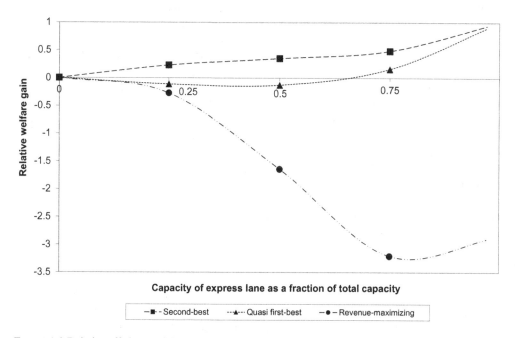

Capacity of express lane as a fraction of total capacity

—■– Second-best   ···▲··· Quasi first-best   —●– Revenue-maximizing

Figure 4.6 Relative efficiency of three express-lane pricing regimes. Source: Computed using the base-case numerical model of Verhoef and Small (2004). The "quasi-first-best" case presents previously unpublished calculations.

In general, the gains from express-lane pricing are disappointingly small in static models; as we will see, dynamic models produce more optimistic conclusions.

The second lesson from the example just discussed is that second-best pricing rules are usually more complex than first-best; compare equations (4.35) and (4.6). The reason is that second-best rules account for the indirect effects of the price.[20] Because the rules are more complex, the chance of making mistakes in setting second-best optimal tolls is also greater; accounting for this would further diminish the expected welfare gains from pricing. Moreover, more information is required: not only marginal external costs but also demand and cost elasticities must be known.

It may be thought that a safer course is to use first-best reasoning, ignoring the constraints that apply, and hope it is close enough to a true second-best solution. We call such a prescription *quasi-first-best* tolls, defined in the current example as toll $V_T \cdot c'_T$ on route T and no toll on route U. However, this is not an attractive option either because it is often far inferior to the second-best toll. It may even lead to a welfare loss compared with no pricing, as shown by the middle line in Figure 4.6: in this example, unless at least 65% of capacity is priced, the quasi-first-best toll is worse than no toll.

The third curve in Figure 4.6 shows the relative efficiency from a private (revenue-maximizing) express lane, which will be discussed in Section 6.1.

4.2.1.2   Dynamic congestion: two bottlenecks in parallel

We now consider two bottlenecks of equal capacity V_K in parallel, in a setting that is otherwise identical to the basic bottleneck model. Suppose a time-varying toll can be implemented on one of the two bottlenecks, but no toll is permitted on the other. In this case, the quasi-first-best toll (*i.e.*, (4.23) with Q taken to be only those people using the tolled road) will eliminate all travel delays for this bottleneck. Recall that the dynamic bottleneck toll does not affect the equilibrium generalized price (including scheduling costs) on that route. Thus, the toll induces no route shift and therefore produces no spillover of congestion onto the unpriced road. As a result, the relative welfare gain of this policy is exactly 50%: 100% of possible gains are obtained on one route and none on the other.

Even higher welfare gains occur using a truly optimized second-best toll on the priced link (Braid 1996). This toll takes into account the fact that with equal traffic, the marginal social cost on the tolled route (where only schedule delay cost is incurred) is lower than on the untolled route (where both schedule delay cost and travel delay cost are incurred) – in this example, it is only half as large, as can be seen by comparing equations (4.22) and (4.27) with equal values of Q. To equalize the marginal social costs, the tolled alternative should carry two-thirds of all traffic and the untolled alternative one-third. This requires a time-independent subsidy to users of the tolled route, added to the time-dependent toll, such that exactly half the users of the tolled bottleneck receive a net subsidy while the other half pay a net tax. This policy achieves two-thirds of the welfare gain from first-best pricing.[21]

4.2.1.3   Other networks

The case of two parallel routes, discussed above, is just one of many where second-best congestion pricing is relevant. A similar case arises when travelers face a mode choice between driving and using public transportation (Tabuchi 1993), where public transportation is obliged to be self-financing for political or other reasons. Due to scale economies, average cost pricing of transit causes the generalized price of a transit trip to exceed its marginal social cost, as argued in Section 3.2.1. The second-best toll on the road then exceeds marginal external cost in order to boost demand for public transportation. This can also be viewed as an example of a distortion in the economy outside the road sector, in this case making it desirable to charge road prices higher than the Pigouvian values. Such distortions are discussed more generally in Section 4.2.6.

Verhoef (2002a, 2002b) derives second-best optimal tolls for any subset of tolled links on a network of arbitrary size and shape.[22] The toll formulas are complex; (4.35) is a special case. Verhoef shows how, in larger networks, the Lagrange multipliers reflecting zero-pricing constraints may be useful in computational algorithms for finding second-best optima. A complication in such algorithms is that the interior second-best optimum need not be unique nor even exist – especially if there are untolled links with relatively high marginal external costs. If an interior solution does not exist, then the global optimum is a corner solution in which tolls are set so that for at least one OD pair, one or more links (and hence routes) are exactly balanced in their attractiveness between being used or not being used.

The formal optimization of second-best toll levels and locations is a complex problem. Ekström *et al.* (2012) propose a mixed integer linear approximation to address it; Li *et al.* (2014) specifically study the optimal locations of toll cordons. Second-best questions can also be explored by trial and error rather than by formal optimization. A typical starting point is one of several well-developed applied network models, in which route choices are determined as a user equilibrium, using either Wardrop's first principle or some stochastic route-choice mechanism. The model is then applied to pricing schemes that incorporate the researcher's view of technical, political, acceptability, equity-based, or other practical considerations. In some cases, a search is carried out over various parameters such as toll levels and number and locations of toll charging points.

The trial-and-error approach has been applied quite successfully to at least two questions. The first is how to introduce pricing incrementally by applying it to just a subset of the network, perhaps in conjunction with other policies such as free passage to high-occupancy vehicles (HOVs). Safirova *et al.* (2007) provide a good example, analyzing policies for the Washington (D.C.) metropolitan area using a model known as START that was developed in the UK. As a general rule, the best candidates for road pricing are usually found to be expressways and major urban arterial roads, because of their high traffic volumes, high speeds, and lack of close substitutes (Lindsey and Verhoef 2001).

The other question is toll-cordon design: where to place the cordon, how high to set the toll, and how to improve incrementally over a "pure" toll cordon, which we can define as a single charge applied to anyone crossing a well-defined boundary enclosing an area. For example, various researchers have applied the SATURN network model to road networks depicting Cambridge (UK), Edinburgh, and other cities.[23] Their results suggest that pure cordon tolls produce large reductions in cordon crossings with only small impacts on overall quantity of vehicle travel. They also find that the cordons can produce substantial welfare gains, but that those gains are easily lost if the toll is too high. Furthermore, in designing a cordon, simple analytical rules for choosing the tolled links produce great improvements over expert judgment. Further welfare gains can be achieved by allowing toll levels to differ at different charging points, or by using two cordons, one inside the other, with different charge levels. It is also insightful to incorporate land-use effects via models of urban structure.[24]

4.2.2   *Time-of-day aspects*

A second type of constraint on congestion tolls is when they cannot be varied freely over time. The simplest but most instructive examples again involve the basic bottleneck model.

4.2.2.1   Flat pricing of a bottleneck

Assume first that only a single fixed ("flat") toll can be charged throughout the peak period. This toll can affect the overall use Q, provided demand is not completely inelastic, but in this basic model it does not affect queue-entry rates. Therefore, the reduced-form cost functions for an un-priced equilibrium, (4.20)–(4.22), remain valid. The second-best optimal flat toll τ_F is therefore

$$\tau_F = \overline{mc}_g^0 - \overline{c}_g^0 = \delta \cdot \frac{Q}{V_K} \tag{4.36}$$

The optimal time-invariant charge (4.36) is exactly twice the time average of the optimal time-varying toll (4.23) if Q were equal; intuitively, this is because adding a new traveler to the system imposes both schedule delay and travel-time costs, instead of just the former. The relative efficiency of this second-best charge depends strongly on the elasticity of demand.

The results are a little more complex if we allow for dispersion in desired queue-exit times, as in the model of Section 3.4.3. Let V_d and q again denote the height and width of the density function describing desired queue exits (*i.e.*, people would like to exit at rate V_d over time interval q). Hence, $Q = q \cdot V_d$. The relevant average cost function is that in (3.36):

$$\overline{c}_g^0 = \delta \cdot \frac{qV_d}{V_K} \cdot \left(1 - \frac{1}{2} \cdot \frac{V_K}{V_d}\right) \tag{4.37}$$

The marginal cost now depends on whether a marginal increase in use would *intensify* the period of desired queue exits by increasing V_d, or *extend* it by increasing q.

To fix ideas, suppose one wishes to influence the decisions of developers whose buildings generate traffic according to some known process, by charging them the marginal external cost of new traffic generated assuming that tolls cannot be differentiated by time of day. The new development might then *intensify* desired queue exits if work start times are the same everywhere and buildings are all about the same distance from the bottleneck's exit. In this case, the marginal cost of one unit of traffic (an increase in Q holding q constant) is $(1/q)\partial\left(qV_d\overline{c}_g^0\right)/\partial V_d$; subtracting average cost (4.37) yields the following optimal flat toll (where superscript I denotes *intensify*):

$$\tau_F^I = \delta \cdot q \cdot \frac{V_d}{V_K} \tag{4.38}$$

which is identical to (4.36).

Alternatively, the new development might *extend* desired queue exits (raise q but not V_d) if firms practice staggered work hours, or if the development is at the edge of an already developed area. The marginal cost of one unit of traffic (an increase in Q holding V_d constant) is now $(1/V_d)\partial\left(qV_d\overline{c}_g^0\right)/\partial q$; subtracting average cost (4.37) yields the following optimal flat toll (with superscript E designating *extend*):

$$\tau_F^E = \delta \cdot q \cdot \left(\frac{V_d}{V_K} - \frac{1}{2}\right) \tag{4.39}$$

which is smaller than (4.36). Therefore, a developer (or the drivers using the new development) would be charged less for extending demand than for intensifying it, because extending demand has less impact on other users. This notion seems intuitive, so it is reassuring to see it confirmed analytically.

4.2.2.2 Coarse tolls

A more sophisticated variant of the flat toll is a coarse or "step" toll: *i.e.*, a toll that allows one or more nonzero toll values, each applying during a specific time interval chosen as part of the policy (Arnott *et al.* 1990b, 1993). The simplest such toll has a single step: it is zero except for a time interval (presumably a subset of the peak period) when it is a positive constant. Analytical derivations for this case may be cumbersome, with the degree of complexity depending on assumptions made on interactions that may arise between groups that pass the bottleneck during different periods. We consider three distinct analytical approaches to designing a coarse toll, all with the basic bottleneck model.

The simplest of the three approaches is one proposed by Laih (1994). Here, users within different intervals have separate queues, resulting in a neat analytical solution with a useful property: the relative efficiency of a step toll with m intervals is simply $m/(1 + m)$. So, for example, a single-step toll achieves one-half of possible welfare gains from tolling, a two-step toll achieves two-thirds, and so forth, approaching relative efficiency equal to one when the number of intervals goes to infinity – in which case the toll schedule converges to the optimal time-varying toll of Section 4.1.2.

Laih assumed that the road has a shoulder, so that separate physical queues are possible: one on the road and one on the shoulder. More often, users paying tolls in different time intervals are in the same queue, so Laih's results do not apply. Modeling then requires an assumption about what happens when the toll takes a step down in order for equilibrium to prevail. In the basic bottleneck model, a mass departure occurs with individuals' positions in the mass determined randomly. The size of the mass is such that the discrete increase in expected travel cost due to a greater travel time and late schedule delay exactly offsets the reduction in toll. Arnott *et al.* (1990, 1993) analyze such equilibria, finding that the second-best single-step toll produces relative efficiency gains of slightly over one-half – better, not surprisingly, than a flat toll for which only the toll level, not the starting and ending moments, can be optimized.[25]

A third approach to analyzing coarse tolls is the "braking" model of Lindsey *et al.* (2012), in which drivers are allowed to hit the brake and wait for the toll to drop before passing the toll gantry – which they would choose to do for downward toll steps occurring after their preferred queue-departure time t^*. Numerical results indicate that the relative efficiencies of step tolls in the Laih and Arnott *et al.* (1990, 1993) models are relatively close. However, because braking behavior causes the bottleneck to remain unused during some part(s) of the peak, additional costs arise that eat away some 15% of the welfare gains from step tolling. We should note that in practice braking behavior can create operational and safety problems and is usually discouraged in toll design.

In all three models, step tolling is beneficial (relative to a flat toll) because the queue drops to zero whenever the toll is about to increase. Fosgerau (2011) and Knockaert *et al.* (2016) exploit this same mechanism when proposing other, non-price dynamic traffic measures that separate groups' departure windows so that queue length can drop to zero between groups.

The analysis of step tolls is further complicated when accounting for heterogeneity.[26] The overall relative efficiency and the distributional impacts of step tolling then vary with the type of heterogeneity, as well as among analytical models. This again highlights the importance of preference heterogeneity for the assessment of transport pricing policies.

The analysis of step tolls also becomes complicated on networks. A study by de Palma *et al.* (2005) uses the dynamic queue-based METROPOLIS model, mentioned earlier, to simulate a number of second-best policies on a stylized circular network with eight radial roads connecting four concentric ring roads to a central point. OD demands are distributed around the network. They find that welfare gains are substantially higher with step tolls (in half-hour steps) than with flat tolls and also higher with area pricing (*i.e.*, pricing all trips within a cordon) than with cordon pricing. Step tolls also have a more favorable acceptability impact than flat tolls, in that they have a higher proportion of travelers whose consumer surplus change is positive (without considering use of revenues). However, area tolls have a lower acceptability impact than cordon tolls. Thus, area pricing with step tolls achieves the highest welfare gain (61% of the first-best gain), while cordon pricing with step tolls achieves the highest proportion of positive consumer surplus changes (41%), along with a substantial relative welfare gain (44%). Zheng *et al.* (2012) consider step cordon tolling for heterogeneous preferences in a numerical agent-based MFD model for Zurich and find it effective in eliminating hypercongestion.

All these results further support the cordon studies described earlier, in suggesting that pure cordons can be greatly improved upon by allowing even modest flexibility in the locations and toll levels of charge points.

4.2.3 User heterogeneity

Another second-best problem arises when the price cannot differ by user group. At least within a static model, the second-best toll is quite intuitive: it is a weighted average of the marginal external costs imposed by the different groups' users (Verhoef *et al.* 1995). A group's weight depends positively on its price sensitivity of demand. The welfare losses from undifferentiated prices generally increase in the price sensitivity of demand of those user groups whose marginal external costs differ the most from the weighted average.

Undifferentiated tolls give up two advantages of optimally differentiated tolls: they fail to secure optimal use levels within each group of travelers, and they fail to provide optimal incentives for travelers to choose among groups where this is possible. For example, tolls differentiated by pollution emissions would encourage owners of dirty cars to curtail their use (securing optimal use levels across groups) and would also encourage them to buy clean cars instead (choice among groups); other policies might achieve one objective but not the other. Without the ability to differentiate charges, supplementary policies may become desirable: for example, technological standards for emissions control in the pollution example. As another example, the inability to differentiate congestion tolls by distance traveled might justify land-use controls or spatial planning. Doing this in a second-best optimal manner requires the regulator to possess much more information than just the marginal external costs that are required for short-run optimal pricing. The risk of mistakes in second-best policies is therefore larger than for first-best policies.

In Section 4.1.2, we saw that even if users drive the same type of car, their marginal external costs in a dynamic setting can differ if their VOTs and schedule delays differ. Optimal flat tolls would then also differ and be non-anonymous (Arnott and Kraus 1998) – although that might be ruled out on the grounds of acceptability, as it would seem unfair to many people. In the context of the bottleneck model, even if individuals' preferences cannot be observed, full efficiency could be restored by varying tolls suitably over time as users with different preferences self-select into different departure intervals. Yet that may not be possible, for example, because the toll is constrained to be constant over the entire peak. Second-best optimization then calls for the same sort of weighted average toll rule as described above.

While trip-timing preferences are typically treated as exogenous, they may arise endogenously in more realistic settings. There are several examples of researchers modeling such cases analytically. Gubins and Verhoef (2014) and Fosgerau *et al.* (2018) provide examples in which individuals make residential location decisions based on transport costs; their location decisions in turn feed back into transport cost functions through their impact on trip-timing preferences. As noted earlier, traveling in an autonomous vehicle (AV) probably reduces an individual's value of travel time (VOT); thus, VOT is endogenous when automation is a consumer choice.[27] Fosgerau and Small (2017) consider endogenous trip-timing preferences arising from agglomeration externalities. They find that ignoring this mechanism biases the calculated benefits of capacity expansion and also leads to under-predicting the benefits of congestion pricing. Verhoef (2020) and Hall (2021) consider the dispersion of desired arrival times, which could result from long-run optimization of daily schedules, so that desired arrival times in the short run are chosen partly in response to the expected dynamic travel times offered by the network; in Verhoef's framework, a dynamic road toll alone then becomes second-best, as the choice of desired arrival times in the commuters' long-run problem entails a separate congestion-related externality.

4.2.4 Stochastic congestion and information

Uncertainty about actual traffic conditions is another factor that may affect the optimality of pricing rules. It is useful to distinguish between two types of uncertainty: idiosyncratic and objective.

Idiosyncratic uncertainty exists when traffic conditions are predictable, but individual travelers do not know them precisely and instead form idiosyncratic perceptions of their own travel times. The standard approach to describing behavior in this case is the Stochastic User Equilibrium (SUE), discussed in Section 3.4.4. Under reasonable conditions, a system optimum (which minimizes total travel time) can be supported as a SUE with marginal external cost tolls (Yang 1999a).

Objective uncertainty exists when traffic conditions vary unpredictably due to accidents, bad weather, demand shocks, or other factors. Section 3.4.5 already discussed many aspects of this; for example, that providing real-time travel information is guaranteed to increase welfare only in the first-best case where optimal pricing is in place. Recent research has elaborated on such potential synergies between information and road pricing.

In many situations, the benefits from pricing and information provision seem to be approximately additive – *i.e.*, equal to the sum of benefits of each instrument in isolation. Furthermore, they tend to be complementary; that is, under conditions when one instrument does not yield much benefit, the other does particularly well.[28] But such results do not apply universally. For example, benefits from information and pricing may be super-additive beyond a certain level of market penetration (Yang 1999b). Also, benefits from providing information can be negative if pricing is *non-responsive*: that is, if the toll varies according to a preset schedule instead of according to real-time conditions (de Palma and Lindsey 1998). (Note that non-responsive pricing is different from flat pricing: in non-responsive pricing, the toll can vary dramatically over time, but in a predictable fashion.)

Nevertheless, at least three studies find that if second-best non-responsive pricing is in place and *perfect* information is provided, benefits are often almost as great as those from first-best responsive pricing.[29] This suggests an attractive combination in practice. Information provision makes travelers feel that they have some control over their trip, if only in planning for unexpected delays. And non-responsive pricing avoids a psychologically treacherous feature of first-best pricing, namely that the toll is unexpectedly high just when the conditions encountered are unexpectedly bad.

4.2.5 *Monetary rewards and tradeable permits*

Despite the strong economic case for the use of pricing as an instrument to manage congestion, applications have remained scarce – as we discuss more extensively in Sections 4.3 and 4.6.5. Thus, there is strong interest in finding a policy that could offer similar incentives, but avoid the large monetary transfers from travelers to government that are associated with marginal external cost pricing. Such policies typically either modify a toll structure, replace tolls partially or entirely with a subsidy, or replace tolls with permits that can be traded in markets. The *Spitsmijden* (peak avoidance) project in the Netherlands was an early example of the subsidy approach, paying motorists to shift their departure times out of the morning peak (Knockaert *et al.* 2012). In this subsection, we review research on such policies.[30]

We begin with a comparison among several such policies within a single model. Rouwendal *et al.* (2012) use the bottleneck model to compare four incentive schemes that vary from net rewarding, via budget neutrality, to net taxation. The schemes each employ three steps (with the timing of steps optimized along with incentive levels): an "early shoulder," a "central peak" period, and a "late shoulder." The three periods jointly cover the entire morning peak. The four incentive schemes differ in average charge level. The "step toll" has three positive toll levels. The "coarse toll" has a toll in the central peak and is zero in the shoulders. The so-called fee-bate involves a subsidy in the shoulders and a toll in the central peak and is constrained to be revenue-neutral in aggregate. Finally, a pure "reward" is zero in the central peak and has a subsidy for traveling in the shoulders, like in the *Spitsmijden* experiments just mentioned.

Figure 4.7 shows how the efficiencies (relative to first-best continuously time-varying pricing) of these policies vary as functions of the overall demand elasticity. If demand is perfectly

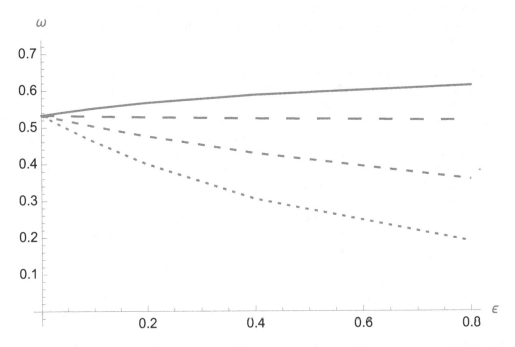

Figure 4.7 Relative efficiency (ω) of step tolls (solid), coarse tolls (large dashing), coarse feebates (medium dashing), and coarse rewards (small dashing) by absolute value of elasticity of demand in the no-toll equilibrium (ϵ). Source: Adapted (in monochrome) from Rouwendal *et al.* (2012) with permission from Elsevier.

inelastic, the four coarse schemes are equally efficient, since then only departure time matters for efficiency and it is influenced equally well by all four instruments. If demand has any elasticity, the relative efficiencies diverge. Their ranking reflects that suppressing demand becomes more important for efficiency, but harder to achieve, as the aggregate money transfer from travelers to the government is increasingly constrained. Unsurprisingly, the pure subsidy ("coarse rewards") is particularly bad when demand elasticity is high, as it induces too much travel even while attempting to channel that travel into less congested time periods.

It is hard to imagine how a policy involving pure rewards could be applied over a full network, due to the large budgetary resources it would require. Applications have accordingly been limited to small-scale experimental trials. Such experiments have generally shown that participants can be very sensitive to financial incentives, with as many as half rescheduling trips from peak to shoulder periods. It is likely that there is selection bias here: participation in such experiments is voluntary, and it is the relatively flexible travelers who are most likely to participate.

For more large-scale and long-lasting applications, revenue-neutral schemes such as feebates seem more attractive as alternatives to tolls that raise extensive revenue.[31] To the best of our knowledge, no feebate or other network-wide revenue-neutral scheme yet exists in practice although studies have considered how one might be designed. If travel demand is perfectly inelastic for all OD pairs, constants can be added to static link-based tolls to achieve revenue neutrality (Section 4.1.2). Adler and Cetin (2001) analyze the simple case of a two-route network in which the toll revenue collected from the shorter route is transferred to users on the longer route. However, designing a scheme in which only some links are tolled and that is both revenue-neutral and Pareto-improving is difficult even with homogeneous users (Bagloee and Sarvi 2017).

Another policy similar to tolls and toll–subsidy schemes that can be designed to be budget-neutral is tradable permits, in which individuals are allocated a limited number of permits to travel toll-free.[32] Making the permits tradeable at a free-market price means the marginal financial incentive is always present for anyone wanting to travel during a priced time period. Part of a policy often called "cap-and-trade," they are frequently proposed to deal with environmental externalities or common pool depletion, including air and water pollution, fishing, motor-vehicle fuel efficiency, and carbon dioxide emissions (see Chapter 7). While most operational applications involve trading among firms, tradable permits can also be used to allocate property rights to scarce or overused resources to individuals. Here, we examine applications to road traffic externalities, analyzed, for example, by Goddard (1997) and Verhoef *et al.* (1997).

In the deterministic partial-equilibrium setting of Figure 4.1, a tradable permit scheme can replicate the effects of an optimal tolling scheme, provided transaction costs for traders are negligible. When V^1 permits are distributed, their equilibrium price is then τ. Since only drivers to the left of V^1 are willing to pay the permit price, the equilibrium number and composition of users who use permits and make trips are the same as with a toll. However, users pay nothing to the regulator if permits are distributed for free (*i.e.*, "grandfathered"); instead, a user either pays some other permit holders (if purchased in a market) or foregoes the opportunity to sell the permit at that same price. Thus, the marginal incentives are identical: the only analytical difference would be income effects, which are ignored in Figure 4.1.

However, the equivalence between tradable permits and tolls disappears in more elaborate settings. Suppose, for example, that demand or supply conditions are stochastic and the regulator cannot adjust either the toll or number of permits issued once the uncertainty is resolved. This situation is analogous to Weitzman's (1974) analysis of quantity versus price instruments for pollution control, discussed in Chapter 7. Thus, for example, De Palma *et al.* (2018) study such a case on a road network with a single OD pair connected by two parallel links. They find that a permit typically performs better than a toll when marginal external congestion cost is steeper than inverse demand, both as functions of traffic. In contrast, Lindsey *et al.* (2023) study capacity shocks in a model with serial links and find that a toll is generally superior. More generally, De Palma and Lindsey (2020) show that results depend in predictable ways on the relative slopes and curvature of cost functions. Intuitively, a tradable permit performs well if first-best usage levels are similar across the uncertain states that define the stochastic situation, while a toll performs well if first-best congestion charges are similar across states. Furthermore, tradable permits often have more favorable outcomes from the perspective of equity and political acceptability.[33] Even dynamic pricing has at least a theoretical counterpart in the form of tradeable permits; in some cases, however, multiple equilibria may exist, which would require the government to regulate the permit price in order to realize the first-best optimum (Bao *et al.* 2019).

Implementing an actual tradable permit scheme is practical only if a market for trading can be designed at reasonable cost and travelers understand how to use it. These issues have been tentatively explored in experimental studies (*e.g.,* Brands *et al.* 2020). It seems too early to make any definitive statements on the prospects for tradable permits in the regulation of transport externalities on a large scale. Nevertheless, further research is justified by theoretical results, especially on budget-neutral schemes, along with promising early experiments and the possibility to combine environmental objectives with congestion relief.

4.2.6   Interactions with other distorted markets

The imposition of prices in transportation, as well as the use of the revenues, may have non-marginal welfare effects in other markets when these markets do not function efficiently. Such distortions can be considered constraints, from the point of view of transportation pricing, in the sense that they could be eliminated with appropriate instruments but such instruments are assumed unavailable.

An important example is that of labor markets. Income taxes lower the nominal wage paid to labor, while indirect taxes (*e.g.*, sales or value-added taxes) tend to increase the price level and thereby to reduce the real wage. In both cases, the taxes create an incentive against work that will reduce labor supply below its efficient level unless the incentive is offset in other ways; the resulting cost to the economy is called the *deadweight loss* of the existing tax system.

A congestion toll, or indeed any Pigouvian tax, will tend to discourage labor supply even if there is no direct connection with commuting, because it raises the average cost of living faced by workers and therefore lowers the real wage rate earned by those workers. Thus, it will aggravate the deadweight loss of labor taxation, just as do other indirect taxes. That aggravation may be partially mitigated if toll revenues are used to reduce the original distorting labor tax. If revenues are spent in some other way, for example, as lump-sum compensations to groups thought to be hurt by the tolls, the aggravation may instead be enhanced (because a higher non-wage income discourages labor supply) and can become quite severe (Parry and Bento 2001). Thus, revenue uses have implications for efficiency as well as for equity and political feasibility.

Tax interactions with other distorted markets are a very general issue in public finance, arising whenever two different taxes affect the same consumption or production decision. This issue is treated within environmental economics under the term *double dividend*, as it refines a simpler argument that environmental externality taxes create two types of benefit: one by correcting the externality and the other by creating public revenues that can reduce the deadweight loss of other taxes. This latter dividend is called the *revenue-recycling effect* of the externality tax. However, Bovenberg and de Mooij (1994) and several other authors show that there is a third effect, called the *tax-interaction effect*, which is that described in the previous paragraph and which tends to offset the revenue-recycling effect.[34]

In fact, in several quantitative analyses, the adverse tax-interaction effect more than fully offsets the beneficial revenue-recycling effect – even when revenue is in fact "recycled" by reducing other tax rates. This reduces the welfare benefits of the externality tax below those calculated in a partial-equilibrium framework, as used so far in this chapter. In that case, the optimal externality tax is somewhat smaller than the Pigouvian value. However, this conclusion depends on the assumption that the taxed good and leisure are substitutes in overall consumer demand, in which case people respond to the tax by increasing consumption of leisure, thereby reducing labor supply. If instead the taxed good is *complementary* to leisure, or even a sufficiently mild substitute (relative to other goods), taxing it will *increase* labor supply. In that case, the tax-interaction effect has the opposite sign, and thus, the optimal tax is *higher* than the Pigouvian value. West and Williams (2007) find this to be the case for gasoline. Perhaps motor fuel and leisure are complements because people like to drive in their leisure time. Fuel taxes are discussed further in Section 7.2.

For a congestion tax, the impact on labor supply is probably quite strong, as much of it is borne by commuters. This makes it all the more important to take labor-market distortions into account. Parry and Bento (2001) find that because of this, the general-equilibrium effects of road pricing are large and very sensitive to the allocation of revenues. Specifically, the interaction with a tax-distorted labor market is so large as to possibly more than offset its beneficial effects as an externality tax if revenues are not used to offset labor taxes. On the other hand, when revenues are used to reduce distorting taxes on labor, the usual efficiency advantage of the congestion tax is magnified (partly because of its beneficial effects on commuting times, which further reduce the labor-tax distortion). With revenues used this way, welfare gains are twice as large as would be predicted by the standard partial-equilibrium analysis. Van Dender (2003) generalizes the Parry–Bento model, obtaining similar – though less extreme – results using more realistic assumptions. Tikoudis *et al.* (2015) explore, in a monocentric general-equilibrium setting, how the spatial variation of tax interaction and tax recycling effects feed back into the optimal spatial pattern of road pricing. Complications that arise when space is considered stem from the spatial variation of the elasticity of labor supply and of the marginal utility of income. Both impact the optimal spatial toll and revenue-recycling schedules, on top of the impact of spatial variation of congestion.

The interaction between transportation taxes and labor markets depends also on the extent to which labor supply adjusts through changes in number of days worked away from home – hence is sensitive to commuting costs – versus number of hours worked per day. Hirte and Tscharak-tschiew (2020) analyze this distinction formally, showing that an optimal tax on transportation is bracketed by values computed from assuming that all labor adjustment occurs alternately through days commuting or through hours worked per day.

The underlying assumption that labor taxes are distorting is not universally accepted. Kaplow (1996) argues that the distortion may be offset by other aspects of public spending, notably because people with higher earnings also receive more benefits from public services and therefore view these services as offsetting some of their tax burden. The extent to which this effectively reduces the deadweight loss of the labor tax, and thus its impacts on second-best Pigouvian tax rules, depends on the specific fiscal regime, which varies from nation to nation. It also depends on the extent to which the benefits from public services are public in nature. If an individual's reduction in hours worked reduces the total labor tax paid but not the amount of benefits derived from public services, a distortion remains in place.

4.2.7 Second-best pricing: a conclusion

First-best analysis of congestion pricing provides important insights; but because constraints and distorted markets abound in reality, second-best analysis is the only way to translate those insights into practical advice in policy design. The resulting pricing rules are more complex, as they reflect indirect effects. They also require more information. Both traits increase the chance of making mistakes in setting prices, possibly with serious adverse consequences. Yet ignoring indirect effects can result in very poorly performing policies.

Fortunately, second-best models do provide some general guidance as to which factors are most important to consider. For example, toll cordons can be designed that achieve a high proportion of theoretically possible benefits; but they do not necessarily look like what an expert would intuitively draw on a map. Relaxing typical constraints, such as that all cordon crossings must be tolled at the same amount or that the toll must be flat over the entire peak period, can significantly improve results. Providing information on traffic conditions seems like a good idea, yet may sometimes be harmful if tolls are absent or if they are set *ex ante* based on expected traffic conditions. Second-best policies that prevent large net financial flows away from travelers, such as budget-neutral toll–subsidy schemes or tradable permits, may still be rather effective.

Finally, taxes affecting labor supply can greatly influence the welfare effects of congestion tolls, and accounting for them introduces an important efficiency factor in choosing how to use toll revenues – generally favoring using them to offset those taxes creating the distortion.

Most of the constraints we have considered are in reality "soft" constraints, reflecting judgment about how to account for the regulatory costs (*i.e.*, costs due to technical, bureaucratic, or political factors) of toll collection. If those costs could be incorporated into the objective function, then maximizing it would achieve what we might call *broadly first-best* pricing. By contrast, the conventional definition of first-best ignores those costs, so in fact is only *narrowly first-best* (Milne *et al.* 2000). The broadly first-best pricing problem cannot be formulated unless the relevant costs can be quantified. But in many cases, a second-best analysis (one assuming hard constraints) may be a good approximation. Thus, it might be said that to apply second-best pricing can be a broadly first-best policy. This, of course, leaves open the possibility that future developments could change regulatory costs and thus make certain constraints obsolete. Advances in tolling technology and the development of smartcards to pay for public transit are cases in point.

4.3   Congestion pricing in practice

Even ignoring tolling in the ancient world, road pricing has a long history, with turnpikes dating back at least to the seventeenth century in Great Britain and the eighteenth century in the USA (Levinson 1998). Road pricing for congestion management is more recent. The earliest modern application is Singapore's Area License Scheme (ALS), established in 1975. Since then, other applications have appeared, varying from single facilities such as bridges or toll roads to tolled express lanes as in the USA and larger schemes in several European cities. We describe here selected applications where managing congestion is explicitly or potentially a significant goal in the design of the pricing scheme.[35]

4.3.1   *Full congestion pricing in large cities*

We begin with cordon and area-based pricing schemes that have been implemented in five cities. Table 4.1 lists some of their main features. These examples differ in many details. Some charge per crossing (with time-of-day variation), while others use a flat daily charge between specific hours. All except Singapore dedicate revenues, mainly to public transit. All that have been subject to cost–benefit analysis have been found to yield positive net benefits, except Singapore.[36]

4.3.1.1   Singapore

In 1975, Singapore implemented the first operational congestion pricing scheme in the world, the ALS. A license had to be purchased and displayed on the windscreen before entering the central "Restricted Zone" (RZ) during designated peak hours; compliance was monitored manually at control points. Peak hours and tolls were adjusted a number of times. When first implemented, the ALS caused a large reduction in traffic within the RZ, but diversion of some traffic to outside it.

In 1995, Singapore extended the ALS with a Road Pricing Scheme, which added some pricing of expressways. Traffic volumes on tolled expressways dropped, but some drivers rerouted to major bypass roads (Goh 2002). The instances of traffic diversion with the ALS and road pricing scheme illustrate the second-best character of these tolling systems and the empirical relevance of the two-route problem of Section 4.2.1.

In 1998, Singapore switched to the current Electronic Road Pricing (ERP) system, which features tolls on arterials, expressways, three RZs in the central business district (CBD), and the Orchard cordon. Charges are deducted using microwave technology from an in-vehicle unit when passing under an ERP gantry. Charges vary by time of day, often in 30-minute steps and sometimes in incremental 5-minute steps (to discourage motorists from changing speed in order to pay a lower toll). Tolls on expressways and arterials are adjusted quarterly to maintain target speeds.

Singapore is now upgrading ERP with satellite-based technology that will provide real-time road traffic updates and other information, as well as enabling distance-based charges (Tan 2021). In-vehicle units will be replaced by more elaborate "on-board units" (OBUs) comprising an antenna, a touchscreen display, and a processing unit (Tan 2020). The initially planned 2020 start was delayed, and the system is unlikely to be fully operational before 2025 (Tan 2021).

4.3.1.2   London

In 2003, London introduced the London Congestion Charge (LCC) in its central area covering 22 square kilometers. The charge is paid once per day and applies to vehicles driving or parking on public roads in the area as well as for entering and exiting. Vehicles are identified by number plates using Automated Number Plate Recognition (ANPR) technology. The charge now operates from 7:00 a.m. to 6:00 p.m. weekdays, with shorter hours on weekends.

The LCC was initially successful in reducing traffic entering the zone and circulating within it. Congestion, measured as the difference between actual and free-flow speed, decreased by 30% within the zone, leading also to an improvement in travel-time reliability. Travelers adjusted in various ways: switching to public transportation, carpooling, changing destination or departure time, and altering routes to bypass the cordoned area. Large reductions in driving were facilitated by the fact that, even before the LCC was introduced, only 10% of people entered the city center by car during the morning peak.

Net revenues from the charge were lower than forecast, for several reasons (Santos 2008): fewer than expected chargeable vehicles, but more exempt and discounted vehicles, entering the zone;[37] greater toll evasion; and high collection cost, partly because of the large number of video cameras required.

The LCC has undergone many changes over the years, including a series of toll increases, elimination of some exemptions, reallocation of road space to other modes, and a Western Extension that nearly doubled the size of the charged area operated between 2007 and 2011. Average travel speeds within the tolled zone have tended to fall back to their pre-LCC levels. In 2019, an Ultra Low Emission Zone was introduced with an additional charge of £12.50 on passenger vehicles that do not meet certain emission standards.[38]

Table 4.1 Characteristics of urban road pricing schemes

	Singapore electronic road pricing (ERP)	London congestion charge	Stockholm congestion tax	Gothenburg congestion tax	Milan Ecopass	Milan area C
Inception	September 1998	February 2003	August 2007 (after seven-month trial in 2006)	January 2013	January 2008 (replaced by Area C scheme 2012)	January 2012
Goals	Primary: congestion relief Secondary: promote transit	Primary: congestion relief Secondary: promote transit	Primary: congestion relief Secondary: promote transit and reduce pollution	Primary: revenue generation Secondary: congestion relief and reduce pollution	Primary: pollution reduction Secondary: congestion relief	Reduce traffic and pollution, and promote public transport
Tolled area or infrastructure	Expressways, arterial roads and cordon charges for three restricted zones around CBD	22-km^2 area around city center (extension to west in effect 2007–2010)	Cordon around 30-km^2 inner-city area plus Essingeleden motorway	Cordon around central Gothenburg	Restricted zone of 8 km^2 in city center	Same as Ecopass
Toll application	Per passage; inbound crossings of restricted zones	Paid daily; includes parking on public roads	In- and outbound crossings; 18 control points	In- and outbound crossings and E6 main road passing the city; 36 control points	Paid daily; 43 control points	Same as Ecopass

(Continued)

Table 4.1 (Continued)

	Singapore electronic road pricing (ERP)	London congestion charge	Stockholm congestion tax	Gothenburg congestion tax	Milan Ecopass	Milan area C
Time variation	Varies separately by time of day for arterials, expressways, and CBD; often zero; charges change in 5- or 30-minute steps; charge levels reviewed quarterly	Charge of £15 from 7:00 a.m. to 10:00 p.m. every day	Weekdays 6:30 a.m.– 6:30 p.m.: SEK 11–35. Daily max SEK 105 (SEK 135 during peak seasons)	Weekdays 6:00 a.m.– 6:30 p.m.: SEK 9–22 (except July). Daily max SEK 60	Flat charge 7.30 a.m.– 7.30 p.m. weekdays. €2–€10 depending on emission standard. Bans most-polluting vehicles October 15–April 15	Flat charge 7.30 a.m.–7.30 p.m. weekdays. €2 for residents, €3 for "service vehicle," €5 standard rate. Bans certain diesel vehicles
Toll differentiation by vehicle and user characteristics	Differentiated by four vehicle types	Exemptions: battery electric and hydrogen fuel cell vehicles (ends Dec. 2025). Discounts: 90% for residents. Surcharge: £12.50 for most vehicles not meeting Ultra Low Emission Zone stndrd.	Exempt: traffic between Lidingö Island and the rest of the county that spends less than 30 minutes within the charging zone Discounts: none	Discounts: only one crossing per hour charged	Discounts: 50% rebate for first 50 entries annually, 40% rebate for second 50 entries. Residents of restricted zone can buy annual pass for 25× cost of daily charge	Discounts: 40 free days per year for Area C residents

4.3.1.3   Stockholm

The Stockholm Congestion Tax was implemented in 2007, following a seven-month trial the previous year and subsequent approval in a referendum. It is treated as a tax for legal reasons. It is mostly a cordon scheme, but with one additional expressway charged. As in London, a majority of commuters used public transport before the tax was introduced. Also as in London, there were some surprises: a greater-than-expected reduction in the number of vehicles crossing the cordon, reductions in traffic flows further out from the toll zone, smaller percentage shifts from driving to public transport, and no evidence of more carpooling or telecommuting (Eliasson *et al.* 2009).

The Stockholm application differs from that in London in two significant ways. First, the fee is paid each time a vehicle crosses into or out of the cordon; but the fee is not paid for driving or parking within the charging zone; also, there is a daily maximum charge. Second, within the charging period (6:30 am–6:30 pm), the tax varies by hour, with higher charges during the morning and evening peaks. Toll revenues are used to fund bus, metro, and rail service, as well as park-and-ride facilities.

4.3.1.4   Gothenburg

The Gothenburg scheme was implemented in 2013. Although it was modeled on Stockholm, its primary goal was to generate revenue rather than relieve congestion. Congestion was less severe than in Stockholm, and the share of commuting trips by public transport was much lower. The tax is applied on vehicles not only entering and exiting the city, but also on some main roads passing by. This forestalls problems with traffic diversion which, as noted above, initially occurred in Singapore.

Although charge rates are much lower than in Stockholm, a much larger fraction of the population regularly pays the charge due to the extensive charged area. As a result, total revenue generated is similar (West and Börjesson 2020).

4.3.1.5   Milan

In 2008, a pollution charge called Ecopass was introduced in an 8 km² central sector of Milan. Ecopass succeeded in reducing pollution as motorists replaced older polluting vehicles with newer vehicles that were exempt from paying the charge (Rotaris *et al.* 2010).[39] However, this response undermined another goal of Ecopass: limiting congestion. In 2012, it was replaced by a new scheme, called Area C, which is levied within the same area but has a primary goal of targeting congestion. (This followed a referendum in which the revised scheme received 79% support.) As Beria (2015) describes, during the first year of operation the new scheme proved effective in alleviating both congestion and pollution: vehicle entrances into the center fell by 31%, and emissions fell by 18% and 35% for particulate matter and CO_2, respectively.

4.3.2   *Value pricing in North America*

Congestion pricing has gained momentum in the USA since federal legislation began funding congestion pricing pilot projects under the so-called Value Pricing Program and started to allow states to introduce limited pricing on Interstate highways. Virtually all the examples in place are *managed lanes*, where pricing is applied to specific lanes on a multi-lane expressway – an example of the problem of two roads in parallel discussed in Section 4.2.1. Usually, the policy is combined with free, or at least lower-cost, travel for high-occupancy vehicles (HOVs), in which case the managed lane is called a High Occupancy/Toll (HOT) lane. Poole (2020) provides a thorough history highlighting changing strategies over time.

Some of these projects introduced congestion pricing on previously existing untolled infrastructure, almost always by converting one or more dedicated HOV lanes into HOT lanes. Since prices are designed to maintain high speed despite the free entry by HOVs, such conversions can be viewed as filling unused capacity on the previous HOV lane with paying low-occupancy vehicles. Early examples are California's *FasTrak* scheme, implemented in 1999 on Interstate 15 (I-15) near San Diego; and the *QuickRide* scheme on the Katy Freeway and on US290, starting in 1998 and 2000, respectively, near Houston, Texas.

Somewhat more popular in the USA is using tolls to finance new infrastructure. One early and well-studied example was initiated in 1995 as a time-varying toll on a new set of express lanes added to the Riverside Freeway (State Route 91, known as SR-91). This is a heavily peaked commuter route in Orange County, California, leading to employment centers in Orange and Los Angeles Counties. Initially a private undertaking, the so-called 91 Express Lanes, it changed to public ownership and control in 2003 for reasons discussed in Section 6.1.4. A similar example, though not strictly a HOT lane, is Highway 407 near Toronto, Canada. It opened in 1997 as a privately financed highway; because it roughly parallels a major free expressway, it is sometimes considered an example of managed lanes.

Sometimes the two approaches are combined, converting an HOV lane while adding new capacity to it. Examples include the Metro Express Lanes on I-10 in Los Angeles County (opened in 2013) and the I-66 Express Lanes inside the Capital Beltway near Washington, D.C. (opened in 2017). A typical installation includes many complexities. For example, on I-10 a portion of the route was expanded, while another was not; the occupancy criterion defining HOVs changes depending on time of day.

In the San Diego and Los Angeles schemes and several others, the toll is responsive; *i.e.,* it is varied in real time, depending on congestion, in order to maintain a target speed. (This procedure is also called *dynamic pricing*, although it is only indirectly related to pricing principles for the dynamic models discussed in this chapter.) Researchers have identified various algorithms for adjusting prices to maintain efficient flow (Lombardi *et al.* 2021).

Yet another type of value pricing adds time-of-day toll variation to existing toll facilities. Such policies have typically introduced only small rate variations, yet appear sometimes to have encouraged rescheduling of trips. For example, one year after off-peak toll discounts of 20% began for crossing the Hudson River into New York City, morning peak traffic had fallen by 7% and evening peak traffic by 4%, with overall traffic stable (DeCorla-Souza 2004).

Managed lanes appear, on the surface, to offer a Pareto improvement in comparison with the same capacity being either unpriced or subject to HOV restrictions. However, this statement depends on several conditions including low transaction costs, maintaining flow on the flat portion of a speed–flow curve, and no change in the occupancy definition of HOVs or in which vehicles are exempt. These conditions may interfere with other goals and require sophisticated management. Hall (2020) analyzes conditions under which managed lanes improve the welfare of all identified groups of travelers, before accounting for use of revenues.

4.3.3   Other road pricing schemes

A number of other tolling schemes have been implemented or proposed around the world.[40] Among them are cordon toll rings in three Norwegian cities.[41] Consistent with long-standing Norwegian tolling policy, the toll rings were created primarily to raise revenue. However, the possibility of using tolls to manage demand was proposed in the early 2000s, and the toll rings in

Bergen and Oslo were converted to congestion charges in 2016 and 2017, respectively (Meloche 2019). Tolls in various cities are now differentiated by time of day, vehicle fuel type, and emissions characteristics. Another change is that toll revenues are less often allocated primarily to finance road construction.[42]

Many large-scale urban and national road pricing schemes have been proposed but not implemented for reasons reviewed in Section 4.7.

Congestion pricing schemes continue to be proposed in the USA. These include San Francisco (Jenn 2019), Portland (Portland Bureau of Transportation 2021), and Seattle (Seattle Department of Transportation 2019). A plan to introduce a cordon toll in New York City failed in 2008, despite widespread political support. Another plan for New York was agreed on in 2019, to address congestion, air pollution, and funding for public transit (Krohnengold 2020); as of this writing it is scheduled to begin in mid-2024.

Congestion pricing has occasionally been implemented on individual bridges, roads, and traffic lanes. Broadly speaking, this has induced changes in travel behavior similar to the changes observed from the larger schemes. For example, peak-period tolls on the San Francisco-Oakland Bay Bridge in 2010 reduced the total number of car trips on the bridge, shifted some from peak to off-peak hours, and reduced peak-period travel times and travel-time variability (Foreman 2016).

4.3.4   *Distance-based tolling*

The road pricing systems described above mostly employ electronic toll collection (ETC) technologies and video cameras to collect tolls on portions of a road network. The infrastructure is costly and, because part of the network is untolled, traffic diversion occurs. These drawbacks have motivated interest in distance-based or *vehicle-km traveled* (VKT) pricing schemes that cover all roads and require less infrastructure. VKT schemes are also viewed as a potential long-run replacement for fuel taxes, which are becoming less viable for revenue generation as conventional vehicles become more fuel-efficient and electric vehicles gain market share.

VKT tolling schemes have been implemented for heavy goods vehicles in a number of European countries. Some schemes initially used tachographs and smartcards, or dedicated short-range communication technology. Satellite-based systems are becoming increasingly common, and some differentiate toll rates by engine emissions.[43] Until recently, separate on-board units (OBUs) were required by each country. However, a recent European Union regulation now stipulates that road users need only choose a single subscription contract, a single service provider, and a single OBU to travel throughout Europe.[44] Smartphone tolling apps are now emerging as a cheaper alternative to OBUs for universal tolling (BEMobile 2021).

Distance-based pricing for passenger vehicles has not advanced as quickly as for trucks. Plans for the UK and the Netherlands were dropped in 2007 and 2010, respectively. Nevertheless, distance-based tolls for light private vehicles are prevalent on conventional toll roads, where they mainly serve the purpose of revenue generation.[45]

Interest in satellite-based tolling systems has led to several pilot projects in Europe, Australia, and the USA. The state of Oregon has been the leader in the USA, with two pilot projects testing various collection technologies and measuring consumer responses. Technologies included on-board diagnostics devices (which record aggregate mileage but not vehicle movements), collection during refueling, use of the Global Positioning System, and a smartphone app.[46] Oregon now has an optional program called "OReGO," open to all Oregon residents, that charges 1.9 cents per mile driven on Oregon roads in lieu of fuel taxes.

Washington State has also researched network-wide tolling since the early 2000s. In 2018, it conducted a pilot project with over 2,000 participants who could choose among various options for mileage reporting. Preferred options were an electronic odometer plug-in device (56%), manual odometer reading (28%), and a smartphone app (14%).[47]

Distance-based tolls have some clear advantages over conventional tolls and fuel taxes because they can differentiate charges according to time, place, duration, and possibly real-time driving conditions as well. They also have some drawbacks. Collection costs are higher than for fuel taxes (since the latter are paid by a relatively small number of fuel distributors); they provide no incentive for fuel savings; and some collection technologies raise concerns about privacy and equity. Each of these drawbacks is also shared by some other types of tolls. Jenn (2019) and Moore (2021) provide further discussion.

4.3.5   *Implications of autonomous vehicles*

As discussed in earlier chapters, autonomous vehicles (AVs) have the potential to revolutionize road transportation by reducing the value of travel time, improving safety, curbing emissions, and reducing the space required for parking, among other effects. Ostrovsky and Schwarz (2018) argue that autonomy may also make road pricing more beneficial and convenient, for several reasons. First, as already noted, reductions in the time and other costs of travel will very likely encourage driving and increase congestion, despite potentially increasing road capacity – thereby boosting the benefits from congestion pricing. Second, since autonomous vehicles will have information on the road network and the route being taken, efficient tolls can be computed in real time and communicated to the passenger or to a pre-programmed algorithm within the vehicle's operating system. Third, tolls can be conveniently computed and presented at the same time a passenger enters information about the planned trip. If, furthermore, AVs become part of Mobility as a Service (MaaS), rather than privately owned, passengers will already be accustomed to paying an explicit monetary price for each trip, so adding a toll to the cost may elicit less opposition.[48]

Tscharaktschiew and Evangelinos (2019) focus on a different aspect of vehicle autonomy, which could cause it to decrease the benefits from congestion pricing. They assume that travelers can choose the level of automation at which they will operate their vehicle. More automation potentially saves time and reduces the value of time; but it also may cause anxiety or inconvenience due to concerns about privacy, software hacking, legal liability, ability to recover manual control in the event of an emergency, and so on. At higher levels of congestion, the relative importance of VOT increases, so travelers opt for more automation. A congestion toll, by reducing congestion, reduces the privately optimal level of automation, which undoes part of the benefit of the toll. Using a numerical example, Tscharaktschiew and Evangelinos find that the (second-best) optimal toll may sometimes be close to zero due to this effect.

Van den Berg and Verhoef (2016) consider autonomous driving in the basic bottleneck model, where autonomous cars can have two types of impact already noted in our discussion: they can increase capacity (as vehicles can safely travel closer together), and they can reduce the cost of travel time. Due to endogenous scheduling, both have external effects on other drivers: the first effect shortens the peak, whereas the second leads to longer queues. The net external effect on other drivers if an individual switches to an autonomous vehicle is therefore uncertain *a priori*.

4.3.6   *Conclusions*

Several general lessons can be drawn from experience with congestion pricing to date. One is that none of the schemes that have been implemented or planned follows first-best pricing principles. For example, cordon tolls and area charges do not price usage outside their boundaries, and usually, they either lack time differentiation or vary in discrete steps. For this reason, the efficiency of early schemes in Singapore and London has been strongly challenged.[49] Similarly, HOT-lane pricing focuses on maintaining smooth travel conditions on the priced lanes while ignoring traffic conditions elsewhere.

A particular example of not following first-best pricing is that most schemes have incorporated toll discounts and exemptions when they were launched. Studies leading to congestion charging in London argued against discounts and exemptions, but they were implemented nevertheless for political reasons. Proposed exemptions are a controversial aspect of the proposed congestion charge for New York City. According to Komanoff (2019), exempting just 10% of trips would reduce the travel-time savings notably and reduce estimated net benefits from $3.71 billion to $3.43 billion. Moreover, since the New York scheme is supposed to meet a net revenue target to fund capital projects, granting more exemptions may force tolls to be higher than otherwise (Krohnengold 2020).

A second lesson is that road pricing schemes cannot be designed simply by copying working schemes elsewhere; rather, they need to be tailored to individual city characteristics such as road network topology, scope of public transit service, and the structure of local government. Furthermore, those cities with successful programs tend to have high density, good public transit systems, low vehicle ownership, and strong national-level social safety nets, making their experience hard to duplicate elsewhere.

4.4   Pricing of parking

As shown in Chapter 3, parking accounts for a large part of the social costs of automobile trips in major cities; its external costs can be large. Here, we will find that these inefficiencies are quite sensitive to parking prices, making them a good target for policy.

Many demand studies have shown that parking prices affect behavior such as the type and location of parking, parking duration, time of travel, trip destination, trip frequency, and mode of travel. For example, eliminating free parking reduced the number of solo drivers by 19%–81% in four sites in Los Angeles, and by 20% in Ottawa. In eight California case studies, the number of solo commuters fell by 17% for employers affected by a 1992 law requiring them to "cash out" employer-paid parking by offering a cash allowance as an alternative.[50]

The principles of efficient pricing of parking are similar to those of road congestion pricing (Arnott 2011). In the balance of this section, we review parking pricing studies, beginning with those that focus on search congestion, drawing on some of the models described in Section 3.6.5 on parking.

4.4.1   Parking pricing with search congestion

In Arnott and Inci's (2006) model, drivers have a common destination downtown and park in undifferentiated spaces on the street. If a vacancy is available, they park immediately, whereas if parking is saturated, they cruise until a spot opens up. Since cruising is wasteful, it is optimal to raise the parking fee until cruising is eliminated. (This is analogous to a congestion fee that completely eliminates bottleneck queues.) The time cost of cruising is converted into parking fee revenue, with no excess burden. Furthermore, parking fees may at least partially counteract the welfare loss resulting from the interaction of parking policies with other distorting taxes, just as in the case of congestion (Section 4.2.6).

In the study by Anderson and de Palma (2004), drivers are bound for the CBD, for which some parking spaces are closer than others. They prefer to park nearby, so congestion due to parking search is worse near the center. The socially optimal parking distribution can be achieved using a spatially differentiated parking charge that falls with distance from the center. The authors show that this fee structure arises in equilibrium if parking spaces are privately operated and the market is monopolistically competitive.[51]

The two studies just described do not consider off-street (garage) parking, whose existence raises several complications (Arnott 2006). First, garages exhibit scale economies due to the fixed space needed for parking ramps. Partly for this reason, garages are distributed discretely in space, giving them a degree of market power. Second, price competition between garages may be limited by capacity constraints that prevent a garage from accommodating customers from rivals. Further complications exist in the long run if garage capacities, and perhaps locations, are endogenous. Arnott (2006) shows that to support a social optimum, two policy instruments may be needed: a subsidy per parker to offset the inefficiency from garages pricing above marginal cost, and a lump-sum tax per garage to offset excessive entry in a zero-profit equilibrium that results in inefficiently small garage market areas. Due to the considerable analytical complexities that arise, most studies either ignore these complications or finesse them away.

Calthrop and Proost (2006) analyze a market with competition between publicly provided on-street parking and privately provided off-street parking whose locations are exogenous. The two kinds of parking are assumed to be perfect substitutes, and drivers choosing on-street parking have to search for a space. Thus, in equilibrium, the generalized prices of the two types of parking are equalized. If off-street parking is supplied competitively, the optimal on-street parking charge would be equal to the off-street charge in order to eliminate search. But if garage operators exercise market power, the second-best optimal on-street charge is somewhat higher than the first-best level, in order to encourage adequate use of off-street parking despite its noncompetitive price.

Using quite a different model with an explicit representation of space, Qian and Rajagopal (2014) consider a general network with multiple origins and destinations, as in Section 3.4.4, but without road congestion. Parking is available at public lots, but not on the street. Drivers have to search for an empty space within a lot and then walk to their final destination. No car leaves a parking lot during the time horizon considered, so search cost at each lot increases as it fills up. The model is "quasi-dynamic" in that the departure flows from each origin continuously vary over clock time, but are exogenous. Drivers choose where to park with a goal of minimizing the sum of their driving, searching, and walking time costs. The authors show that the socially optimal allocation of drivers to lots is generally not unique. Any optimal flow pattern can be achieved by charging parking fees that differ by lot, but in a manner depending on clock time (or occupancy, which varies by clock time). Importantly, optimal fees do not depend on a user's origin or destination and are thus anonymous in the same sense as in Section 4.1. This last property would not hold with road congestion since the marginal external cost of a trip would then depend on a driver's origin and destination and the route they choose.

4.4.2 *Parking pricing and road traffic congestion*

So far, the discussion has ignored road traffic congestion, which complicates analysis of parking pricing because parking fees influence not only parking activity but also traffic flows. To a degree, parking fees can serve as a sort of cordon toll by increasing the generalized cost of automobile trips – and, in fact, are often viewed as alternatives to cordon tolls. Indeed, such fees could be structured as a two-part tariff, with the variable component proportional to parking duration and a fixed component that includes the average external congestion cost caused by a marginal parker (Jansson 2010; Arnott 2011).[52] By reducing both cruising and congestion, as well as generating scarce public revenue, parking fees could thus possibly yield a triple dividend.[53]

In practice, parking fees are likely to be a highly imperfect way to control traffic congestion. They do not depend on how far or on what links a driver travels. The time variation of parking fees, even if permitted, is hard to synchronize with the intensity of traffic congestion. Furthermore, parking fees do not apply to through traffic, which causes congestion and may actually increase if parking fees succeed in reducing those trips bound for parking spaces (a form of induced demand). Privately owned parking spaces also may remain unpriced unless their use is discouraged by policies such as cashing out free parking.

Despite these caveats, reducing traffic congestion can be a useful side benefit of charging for parking. This is demonstrated in Arnott and Rowse (2009), who extend the base model in Arnott and Inci (2006) to include both garage parking and traffic congestion. Road space is allocated either to on-street parking or to lanes for moving traffic. An increase in on-street parking space results in less road capacity and slower travel. Equilibrium in the model is derived in a way similar to Calthrop and Proost (2006). If the on-street fee is low, only a small fraction of road space should be allocated to parking and the cruising that results is very costly. If the on-street fee is higher, the (second-best) optimal amount of curbside space can be much higher. The fee thus creates benefits from both less cruising and less cruising-caused congestion.

The externality caused by parking depends on how long a vehicle is parked. Parking duration by commuters is relatively fixed, but for shopping and certain other types of trips, drivers may shorten their visits if hourly parking rates increase. For example, when on-street parking fees were raised in Dublin by 50%, average parking duration dropped from 90 to 76 minutes with an implied price elasticity of about −0.3 (Kelly and Clinch 2009).

Some cities encourage parking turnover by imposing time limits or by increasing the hourly rate for each successive hour parked. These policies can reduce cruising by deterring long-term parkers. But higher parking turnover exacerbates congestion if it leads to more trips, which happens if the price elasticity of parking dwell time exceeds one in magnitude (Nourinejad and Roorda 2017). In fact, the second-best policy, when parking fees are used to address underpriced traffic congestion, is a fixed rather than an hourly fee (Glazer and Niskanen 1992).

4.4.3   Parking pricing with endogenous trip timing

In the literature reviewed so far, trip timing has not been modeled explicitly. We now address this limitation, beginning with models with a single spatial dimension, *i.e.,* parking occurs along a single travel route.

Arnott *et al.* (1991) combine the bottleneck model described in Section 3.4.3 with an analysis of parking. All drivers travel along a single route from a common origin to a common destination such as the CBD. In addition to choosing when to depart, they decide where to park along the commuting route. Drivers are perfectly informed about parking availability, so there is no search. If parking is free, drivers park "outward" in order of increasing distance from the destination. Later travelers thus have to walk further, which spreads out the arrival period relative to the standard bottleneck model and increases total schedule delay costs. A judiciously chosen location-dependent parking fee can induce parking "inward" instead and thereby can improve efficiency. If the fee is combined with a time-varying congestion toll, queuing can be eliminated and the social optimum achieved.

Fosgerau and de Palma (2013) add an evening commute to the above model, while allowing the parking fee to be duration-dependent and paid continuously at a rate that varies by time of day. When the morning and evening departure time decisions are separate, the fee can reduce – but generally not eliminate – queuing in either period. Surprisingly, under certain conditions the parking fee schedule can be chosen to fully eliminate queuing in both periods and support the social optimum even though no road tolls are imposed. Zhang *et al.* (2008) find similar results.

Qian and Rajagopal (2015) again analyze the morning commute in isolation, but now including congestion due to search for parking at lots along the route. Users prefer lots that are closer to the destination. Expected search time at a lot is a strictly increasing function of occupancy and the number of other vehicles searching in the lot at the same time. They then examine a parking fee schedule for each lot that is chosen to achieve a constant arrival rate of commuters at the lot entrance. Compared to the equilibrium with no parking fees, this policy shortens the travel period and reduces total schedule delay costs – as in Arnott *et al.* (1991). It also attracts more commuters to the farther and less convenient lots by setting lower fee schedules there and offering early-bird parking discounts – similar to Anderson and de Palma (2004). Parking fees thus succeed in efficiently redistributing parking demand over both time and space. Using a case study of parking at Stanford University, the authors obtain a total cost savings of 28% from parking pricing, with further gains possible if search time can be reduced by giving drivers information on where to find vacant spaces.

It is also possible to create analytical parking models in two-dimensional space, although additional assumptions are required. An example is Arnott (2006).

4.4.4 *Optimal occupancy*

Municipalities often impose time limits or set parking fees to encourage turnover. However, as noted above, rapid turnover can exacerbate traffic congestion. Such policies are also inconvenient for drivers whose business requires long stays. Vickrey (1954) addresses these considerations, proposing that parking fees be varied responsively to maintain a target occupancy rate rather than rate of turnover. Vickrey recognizes that, due to search costs and randomness in demand, the optimal average occupancy rate is well under one. Shoup (2006) advocates an 85% target, which, as described below, has been influential in guiding practice.

Determining the optimal occupancy rate is not simple, because it depends on supply and demand conditions that are very local. Arnott (2014) explores this dependency, showing that the optimal target occupancy rate increases with demand intensity. The reason is that when demand is strong, the marginal social benefit from travel is high and more trips should be accommodated; to do so, higher throughput is required and this necessitates an increase in parking occupancy. A further consideration is that the optimal target also depends on the number of parking places over which occupancy is measured. Due to the law of large numbers, occupancy on a long block with many spaces is more predictable than on a short block with few spaces (Shoup 2018b). The optimal occupancy rate therefore increases with block size.

Modern technology has enabled some cities to implement fees that vary by time and location in a way similar to that proposed by Vickrey and Shoup. A case in point is the SF*park* Experiment, conducted by the San Francisco Municipal Transportation Agency (SFMTA) from 2011 to 2013 and continued afterward in modified form.[54] In its pilot form, which targeted selected areas, pre-announced time-varying meter rates on each block were adjusted every 6–8 weeks, with a goal of maintaining occupancy rates between 60% and 80%. Each day was split into three time bands, and separate rates were set for weekdays and weekends. Hourly rates were raised by $0.25 if occupancy exceeded 80%, and reduced by $0.25 if occupancy fell below 60%, unless doing so would violate an overall permitted range of prices.[55]

The San Francisco experiment produced favorable results (Primus 2018): average search times, double parking, and citations per meter fell; use of SF*park* garages by short-term parkers rose while use by commuters dropped; vehicle-miles traveled fell; and transit speeds increased. Unexpectedly, large price differences developed between adjacent blocks. On average, the hourly meter rates fell, yet net parking revenue rose slightly.

The results of SF*park* illustrate that suitable parking rates may be difficult to predict, but can be set by trial and error. Moreover, in most locations drivers now need information only on prices, not on occupancies, in order to decide where they want to park. In January 2018, San Francisco expanded SF*park* to all the city's metered parking spaces and city-owned garages and lots (De Scant 2018). Other cities have followed its example, including Los Angeles, New York, Washington, D.C., and Seattle in the USA and Calgary in Canada.[56] Technological developments, including cell phone payment and license-plate recognition, have facilitated such policies.

The simple pricing algorithm used by SF*park* has some imperfections. One is that with small price changes ($0.25) and long periods between adjustments (6–8 weeks), occupancy rates were slow to adjust toward the target range. A more fundamental problem is that *average* occupancy rates may not be the best overall metric of parking availability. Chatman and Manville (2014) propose instead using the *minimum* vacancy rate; Millard-Ball *et al.* (2014) propose using a demand-weighted probability that a block is full. Furthermore, Fabusuyi and Hampshire (2018) argue that the parking fee on a given block should be based not only on the observed occupancy on that block, but also on occupancies in nearby blocks and on whether the rate was changed in the previous period.[57] Some of these suggestions have been adopted by SF*park*.

Another limitation is that SF*park* and other existing systems used predetermined fee schedules rather than varying fees responsively to real-time changes in demand conditions. Real-time or online pricing might be justified if parking demand is highly unpredictable, but drivers may have difficulty adapting to prices if they fluctuate rapidly or by large amounts.

4.4.5   Summary

It seems clear that eliminating subsidized parking for employees in high-density business districts is a high priority for improved efficiency in urban transportation. Doing so would reduce expenditures on parking facilities, free up land for other uses, and favorably alter the modal mix on congested roads. Charging more for on-street parking would have similar advantages and would in addition reduce congestion from cruising. Fears that such charges would undermine the economic vitality of business districts do not seem to be supported by the limited and disparate empirical evidence (Rye and Koglin 2014).

There are several aspects of parking for which further research would yield considerable benefits. For example, Marsden (2014) argues that research on parking pricing has focused too narrowly on trip-making, with inadequate consideration of how parking policy affects the local economy, the environment, and social equity. Pricing could also be better coordinated with land-use planning. Finally, as noted in Section 2.1.5, new practices and technologies such as car sharing, ride-sourcing, parking-sharing programs, and AVs are likely to impact the nature of parking demand, and hence, the way parking policies work.

4.5   Pricing of public transit

We now turn to pricing for public transit. While the technologies and institutions are different from those dealt with so far in this chapter, the basic principle of marginal cost pricing is the same. As a result, the pricing rules and their derivations bear surprising similarities and indeed can sometimes be viewed as extensions of the models already discussed. This topic is thoroughly reviewed by Hörcher and Tirachini (2021).

Setting prices for transit service involves at least three issues: the average fare level, the fare structure, and the incentive effects of transit subsidy programs.

4.5.1   *Fare level*

Under a simple but unrealistic condition, pricing of public transit looks just like congestion pricing for highways: namely, if the only market failure is crowding. Hörcher and Graham (2018)
show that this remains true even if bus frequency and/or capacity is adjusted optimally – in
which case the crowding externality is partially or fully absorbed by the operator through additional operating costs, incurred to reduce the deleterious effect of marginal ridership on crowding. This is analogous to a highway authority adjusting capacity to manage congestion: the
externality may be partially but not entirely ameliorated.

But passenger crowding is not the only market failure for public transit. Equally important is
the Mohring effect discussed in Section 3.2.1: additional ridership makes it economically feasible to reduce waiting time or other types of inconvenience caused by infrequent schedules. In
that section, we noted this situation creates increasing returns to scale when the user inputs (*e.g.*,
waiting time) are accounted for in the cost function; as a result, the optimal transit fare would
not fully cover average costs. In fact, in the simple model presented there, the optimal fare is
zero whenever there are empty seats. The Mohring effect applies even if there is also crowding,
but then the two effects interact and the optimal fare is no longer zero. In fact, it is equal to the
short-run external cost of crowding given bus frequency and capacity.

The problem is more complex if a competing mode is not priced optimally. The case most often
considered is underpricing of peak-hour automobile travel, which corresponds to the rather common situation where the policymaker seeks to address car congestion by making public transport
more attractive. Second-best solutions for such cases confirm our intuition that underpricing of
congested car traffic creates a case for luring travelers from car to transit via lower fares. In other
words, underpriced car congestion justifies a higher subsidy of transit service, especially if the
cross-elasticity of demand between transit and auto is high relative to transit's own-price elasticity.[58]

These two arguments for transit subsidies – scale economies and underpriced automobile
travel – can be understood through a concrete model that generalizes the two-route problem for
car congestion, presented in Section 4.2.1. The generalization is in two directions. First, the two
competing alternatives are no longer required to be perfect substitutes. Second, one of them (representing public transit) has scale economies based on user-supplied inputs, as just discussed. As
with the two-route problem, we take a second-best approach, where one of the competing alternatives, now representing automobile travel, cannot be priced optimally. The result is a second-best
optimal transit fare that is similar to the second-best road toll (4.35) in the two-route problem,
but modified in two ways corresponding to the two directions of generalization just described.

For simplicity, we consider rail transit only, assuming it does not directly interact with automobiles on the roads; we assume automobile occupancy to be 1.0. Let q_A and q_R be the numbers
of automobile and rail trips per unit of time, with vehicle flow rate $V_A = q_A$. Under the reasonable
assumption that income effects in demand are negligible (see Section 2.2.5), the joint demand
for these two types of travel can be derived from a benefit function $B(q_A, q_R)$, which expresses
the consumer benefits from these amounts of travel as their total willingness to pay for the
particular combination $\{q_A, q_R\}$.[59] $B(\cdot)$ is therefore a generalization of the area under an inverse
demand curve to the case of more than one good. An important property is that the inverse demand for either type of travel, given the amount consumed of the other type, is given by the corresponding partial derivative of the benefit function, just as it is in our earlier models of multiple
time periods and multiple roads:[60]

$$d_k(q_A, q_R) = \frac{\partial B(q_A, q_R)}{\partial q_k}, \ k = A, R \tag{4.40}$$

Furthermore, the cross-partial second derivatives of $B(\cdot)$ are negative when auto and rail are substitutes in demand, positive when complements, and zero when independent.

Let $C_A(\cdot)$ and $C_R(\cdot)$ be the total cost functions for auto and rail, including both user costs and (if applicable) agency operating costs:

$$C_A = C_{A\text{-}users} \equiv q_A \cdot c_A(q_A)$$

$$C_R = C_{R\text{-}agency} + C_{R\text{-}users} \equiv q_R \cdot c_{R\text{-}agency}(q_R) + q_R \cdot c_{R\text{-}users}(q_R) \tag{4.41}$$

Note that the average agency and user costs of rail, $c_{R\text{-}agency}$ and $c_{R\text{-}users}$, play important roles in transit finance and in user satisfaction, respectively. Both may be decreasing functions of q_R due to scale economies. Note furthermore that in this formulation, the costs on the two modes are independent of each other. Recall that the generalized price of mode k ($k = A, R$) is defined as the average user cost $c_{k\text{-}users}$ plus toll or fare payment τ_k, and the user equilibrium conditions are such that marginal benefits are equalized to this price for each transportation good:

$$\partial B / \partial q_A = c_A(q_A) + \tau_A$$
$$\partial B / \partial q_R = c_{R\text{-}users}(q_R) + \tau_R \tag{4.42}$$

Social surplus can be defined as benefits minus cost:

$$W = B(q_A, q_R) - C_A(q_A) - C_R(q_R) \tag{4.43}$$

First, we can check that the first-best solution gives the expected marginal cost prices for each mode. The first-order conditions for maximizing (4.43), after substituting (4.42), produce the following first-best prices:

$$\tau_A = q_A c'_A$$
$$\tau_R = q_R c'_{R\text{-}users} + c_{R\text{-}agency} + q_R c'_{R\text{-}agency} \equiv \chi_R \tag{4.44}$$

which indeed confirm our expectations. The optimal road tax is the familiar Pigouvian toll. The optimal transit fare is the average agency cost, with downward adjustments for any scale economies in user costs (first term) and in agency costs (last term). For later reference, we define the short-hand notation that we introduced for the right-hand side of (4.44),

$$\chi_R \equiv q_R c'_{R\text{-}users} + c_{R\text{-}agency} + q_R c'_{R\text{-}agency}$$

to be applicable even when we depart from first-best conditions. Thus, χ_R can be thought of as the quasi-first-best toll, *i.e.*, the toll calculated from the first-best formula also when evaluated at other values of the quantity variables.

Now consider the second-best solution, where the auto toll is fixed at zero. We set up a Lagrangian that closely resembles (4.32):

$$\begin{aligned}\Lambda = {}& B(q_A, q_R) - C_A(q_A) - C_R(q_R) \\ & + \lambda_A \cdot \left[c_A(q_A) - \partial B / \partial q_A \right] + \lambda_R \cdot \left[c_{R\text{-}users}(q_R) + \tau_R - \partial B / \partial q_R \right] \end{aligned} \tag{4.45}$$

The solution to maximizing this Lagrangian also closely resembles that of (4.32). We find that $\lambda_R = 0$, and substituting this and the constraints (4.42) into the first-order conditions with respect to q_A and q_R, we obtain the following optimality conditions:

$$\tau_R - \chi_R - \lambda_A B_{AR} = 0$$
$$-q_A c'_A + \lambda_A (c'_A - B_{AA}) = 0 \tag{4.46}$$

where B_{AR} and B_{AA} are second derivatives of $B(q_A, q_R)$. The second-best transit fare is therefore

$$\tau_R = \chi_R - q_A c'_A \cdot \frac{-B_{AR}}{c'_A - B_{AA}} \tag{4.47}$$

This fare, also derived by Ahn (2009), equals the non-internalized marginal cost of transit, χ_R, minus a term that reflects the demand interaction between the rail and car markets. This latter term multiplies the marginal congestion externality on the road, $(q_A c'_A)$, by a weight depending on demand sensitivities and marginal congestion cost. So far, this sounds just like our description of the optimal second-best road toll in the two-route problem (4.35). However, the weight here is somewhat different, depending not only on the slope B_{AA} of the auto-inverse demand curve (note that B_{AA} itself is negative) but also on the cross-effect $-B_{AR}$. This weight is equal to the number of new road travelers per rider deterred from rail, known as the *diversion coefficient*.[61]

Equation (4.47) can be understood better by considering some special cases. When the two types of travel are perfect substitutes, $B_{AR} = B_{AA} < 0$ and both are equal to d', the slope of the combined inverse demand curve for auto and rail trips together. In that case, (4.47) becomes the same as (4.35), except that it replaces the quasi-first-best road toll on the priced alternative with the quasi-first-best rail fare. When the two types of travel are imperfect substitutes, the second term in (4.47) remains negative but is smaller in absolute value than for the case of perfect substitutes. This is because the cross-derivative in the numerator is smaller in absolute value than the second derivative in the denominator – reflecting the fact that auto and rail trips substitute imperfectly for each other, which also makes it less attractive from an efficiency perspective to lower the rail fare in order to reduce auto congestion. When the cross-elasticity of demand is zero, the second term in (4.47) becomes zero: quasi-first-best pricing of rail transit ($\tau_R = \chi_R$) is then optimal, because automobile use cannot be affected anyway. Finally, when the two goods are complements, so that B_{AR} is positive, the second term in (4.47) becomes positive. We then raise the rail fare beyond marginal cost in the transit market alone because doing so reduces automobile traffic. (An example of complementarity would be if congestible auto traffic included many people traveling to a subway station.)

It is easy to show that if some nonzero price τ_A is being charged for autos, equation (4.47) still holds with $q_A c'_A$ replaced by $q_A c'_A - \tau_A$. In other words, the effect of car congestion on optimal transit fare depends on the *uninternalized* congestion externality. We can also rewrite χ_R in terms of average and marginal rail costs, based on cost function (4.41), and state the result in terms of the per-user transit subsidy σ_R required to cover deficits from second-best pricing. Doing so yields

$$\sigma_R \equiv c_{R\text{-agency}} - \tau_R = (ac_R - mc_R) + (q_A c'_A - \tau_A) \cdot \frac{-B''_{AR}}{c'_A - B''_{AA}} \tag{4.48}$$

As a policy prescription, (4.48) applies to a welfare-maximizing agency; offering this per-unit subsidy to a profit-maximizing rail operator would not be second-best as that operator would not adjust frequency optimally as assumed in deriving (4.48).

Equation (4.48) clearly shows the two sources of second-best transit subsidies in our model. The first is scale economies: if average cost exceeds marginal cost (for agency and user costs combined), it is desirable to subsidize the difference. The second is automobile congestion: insofar as lowering transit price is effective in diverting automobile users, it is desirable to use subsidies to encourage that result. The second effect is likely to be large in magnitude in many situations, which leads to an important observation. The size of this component of the optimal transit subsidy depends directly on the degree of underpricing of automobile traffic. If optimal congestion pricing were in place, so that $\tau_A = mec_A$, that term would disappear and the efficient subsidy would be much smaller, thereby greatly ameliorating the incentive problems associated with subsidies. Thus, congestion pricing of automobiles can be viewed as a solution not only to problems of traffic congestion and road finance but also to problems of transit finance.

This argument raises the objection that we have ignored the deadweight loss of the taxes required to finance transit subsidies – that is, their adverse effects on economic output over and above the actual revenue raised. This is true, but we have also ignored a less obvious factor that tends to offset such deadweight loss. It is the same phenomenon involving other distorting taxes, discussed in Section 4.2.6, only working in reverse. There, we noted that a Pigouvian *tax*, even though implemented for efficiency reasons, raises the cost of living and thereby lowers the real wage, thus aggravating any deadweight loss caused by using labor taxes to finance public expenditures. By the same reasoning, a *subsidy* that is implemented for efficiency reasons, as described here, reduces the cost of living and thereby tends to ameliorate the deadweight loss from labor taxes. This advantage of subsidies may in large part offset the deadweight loss of financing them – all the more so if transit use is complementary with labor supply so that transit subsidies directly lower the ancillary costs of being employed.

This and other models of second-best transit pricing have been used to investigate optimal transit subsidies for specific cities. They typically encompass some, but not all, pertinent factors such as variation in conditions over times and locations, substitutability of demand across times and locations, transit-agency operating policies, externalities from transit vehicles, and crowding on transit vehicles. Consequently, results vary greatly. For example, Parry and Small (2009) estimate optimal subsidies to be very large for both rail and bus in three cities: London, Washington (D.C.), and Los Angeles – over 90% of operating costs in London (before its congestion charge was implemented) under their preferred parameters.

Basso and Silva (2014) simulate bus-only transit systems in London (also, without the congestion charge) and in Santiago, Chile. Their optimal subsidies are similar to those of Parry and Small: 55% of operating costs for Santiago and over 100% for London. Optimal frequencies are notably higher in Santiago, and much higher in London, with the subsidy than without.

Basso and Silva also compare transit subsidies with two other policies: road congestion pricing and dedicated bus lanes, all within the same model. In London, congestion pricing creates more than double the social benefits of a transit subsidy. In both London and Santiago, dedicated bus lanes create far greater welfare gains than subsidies. In both cases, the presence of either of these alternative policies greatly weakens the case for a transit subsidy. Thus, it seems that direct measures to control car congestion, or at least to keep it from spilling over to public transit, are more cost-effective than the indirect policy of using low transit fares to entice drivers away from cars.

Strommer et al. (2023) note that more recent evidence on crowding – as reviewed in Section 2.7.3 of this book – tends to suggest larger values for crowding costs than those used by Parry and Small. Strommer et al. find that recalibrating the Parry–Small model with these larger values produces somewhat smaller optimal transit subsidies. (This is because the crowding externality tends to offset the forces producing optimal subsidies.) They find furthermore that even during off-peak periods, crowding costs for the three cities studied by Parry and Small are comparable in magnitude (but of course opposite in sign) to scale economies.

Proost (2018) notes that optimal peak-period subsidies are sensitive to the diversion coefficient, which directly influences the amount of congestion reduction achieved by subsidizing transit. Proost cites empirical European evidence for a diversion coefficient in the range 0.15–0.35 – considerably smaller than the value of 0.5 for peak periods used by Parry and Small, hence implying smaller subsidies. However, there is a countervailing factor: in a realistic world where congestion varies by location, what matters for optimal subsidies is not how many auto drivers are diverted in total, but how many are diverted from the most congested parts of the road network. As noted in Chapter 2, Michael Anderson (2014) produces strong evidence that ridership on Los Angeles rail transit is drawn disproportionately from more congested roads. As a result, he finds that the existence of a rail transit route reduces auto congestion by nearly six times as much as would be predicted from a homogeneous road network, at least over a period of a few weeks. Anderson's result applies to the complete cessation of the rail transit system; we hope that this kind of fine-tuned measurement of diversion will be made for other situations as well.

4.5.2 Fare structure

The problem is more complex if demand differs by time period and the operator cannot alter vehicle size between time periods. How does this affect the pressures of Mohring effects and competition from underpriced automobile? Parry and Small (2009) and Basso and Silva (2014) address these two forces and others. They both distinguish between peak and off-peak periods, as well as account for imperfect substitutability in demand, user crowding on transit, the impact of traffic congestion on bus speed, and endogenous transit vehicle size. Parry and Small model simultaneous rail and bus transit, with limited substitutability in demand between them, while Basso and Silva model bus only, but allow the transit supplier to optimize the distance between bus stops. The results of these two studies mostly show that diversion from congested auto is the most important factor when transit frequency is high, while scale economies are more important when frequency is low. The former condition holds in peak periods, and the latter condition tends to dominate in off-peak periods though this feature varies across cities.

Proost (2018) examines two sets of numerical simulations of these types of models, one for Stockholm and one for Paris. The results suggest that major welfare gains are available from differentiating peak and off-peak services; specifically, making peak service more expensive and more frequent than current practice, with the opposite for off-peak service. For example, one of these simulations is by Börjesson *et al.* (2017), who estimate optimal bus fares and frequencies for a commuting corridor in Stockholm, in the presence of its road pricing system. Compared to existing conditions, second-best pricing of transit would more than double the fare in the peak and would lower it to zero off-peak, while optimal frequency would rise about 25% above existing in the peak, but fall by more than half in the off-peak. Surprisingly, 60% of the welfare gains from optimizing both fare and frequency can be obtained from adjusting frequency alone; doing so also has a small favorable impact on the operating deficit.[62] We caution that in many cities or corridors, the low optimal off-peak frequency calculated in an economic model might be overruled by policies to provide basic access to all residents even where demand is low.

Hörcher and Graham (2018) analyze transit with two time periods theoretically, paying special attention to crowding costs and constraining peak and off-peak service to use the same vehicles. Several interesting results emerge when demands are inelastic. First, the equilibrium level of crowding does not depend strongly on passenger volumes; this is because the operator adds frequency to offset most of the greater demand during peak periods. Second, the optimal transit fare equals the external crowding cost, in analogy with road pricing. Third, most surprisingly, the marginal subsidy is identical in the two time periods: the discount in optimal fare below marginal operating cost is the same for peak and off-peak travel. This result relies upon the assumptions that (i) crowding cost depends on vehicle occupancy and vehicle capacity only through their ratio (the load factor), and (ii) vehicle operating cost is proportional to vehicle size. The model developed by the authors allows one to relax these assumptions, using numerical simulation to obtain results.

The fare structure may also be designed to pursue distributional goals. Some of the simulations mentioned earlier distinguish various income groups, permitting a distributional analysis. In addition, transit agencies often offer discounts to narrowly defined subgroups such as elderly people. This may be a more cost-effective distributional strategy than subsidizing transit fares across the board, since many transit users are well-off financially – especially users of high-quality radial commuting services. Such motivations are studied more formally, especially for developing countries, by Tirachini and Proost (2021).

4.5.3   *Incentive effects of subsidies*

In practice, most transit systems in the world's richer countries are highly subsidized, whether for reasons discussed here or for other reasons. However, subsidy programs inevitably have rules that distort the decisions of the transit operators.

One such distortion occurs in programs that subsidize capital but not operating costs. Not surprisingly, this tends to cause recipients to use a higher ratio of capital to other inputs than otherwise. Such effects can be very large, as measured, for example, by Frankena (1987) for Ontario, Canada. A particular form of capital bias can occur in the choice among types of transit, by encouraging local authorities to build capital-intensive rail systems in locations where corridor volumes do not justify them. In fact, many newer rail systems have extremely high costs compared with buses, and many rail transit initiatives have severely over-predicted demand and underpredicted cost (Flyvbjerg *et al.* 2003, 2005).

Subsidizing operating costs has its own incentive problems. Several studies have found that subsidies cause operating costs to increase, even after controlling for the possible reverse causation (*i.e.*, that high costs require more subsidies); and that this tendency is worse when the source of the funds is a level of government remote from the operator.[63] Another effect is to cause output to increase (Obeng 2011); sometimes, notably in the USA, this has taken the form of inefficient expansion of service to low-density suburbs.

These results are discouraging for the prospects of achieving optimal pricing of public transit. We can offer three responses.

First, subsidy programs can be designed to minimize adverse incentives – for example, by basing subsidies on ridership. A great deal of research has gone into studying specific design mechanisms basing subsidies on riders (*e.g.*, Sun and Zhang 2018), on service levels offered (Ling *et al.* 2019), or on other factors.

Second, a subsidy can be combined with a concession scheme in which the right to operate transit is determined by competitive bidding. We consider this approach in Section 6.3.1.

Third, the welfare loss from overpricing transit may be small in cases where traffic congestion is not a factor, since many estimates suggest a relatively low own-price elasticity of transit use, at least in the short run – although estimates naturally differ over time and place.[64] Indeed, evidence on privately provided transit service suggests that unsubsidized transit is already viable in many markets.[65] Simulation studies suggest it would become much more so if congestion and parking were priced anywhere near their marginal cost, and in that case, the other main argument for subsidies (to relieve traffic congestion) would also be diminished or eliminated. Thus, one solution to institutional difficulties with transit subsidies is to raise prices both for transit and for competing forms of urban transportation, as argued strongly by Proost (2018).

4.5.4 *Political considerations of transit subsidies*

We have tried to present the main economic advantages and disadvantages of transit subsidies. However, two questions remain. What actually determines the shape of subsidy programs within a democratic political system? And why do these programs persist despite what many observers see as extreme inefficiencies?

Borck (2008) offers several possible answers. The first is a traditional answer, known as the capture theory: participants in the industry succeed in lobbying legislative, administrative, and regulatory bodies for subsidies. Support for this theory includes the high percentage of subsidies that, as we have noted, is captured by workers in the form of higher wage rates (Winston 2000). A second possible answer assumes that demand for public transit is less income-elastic than are tax payments, so transit subsidies are desired by low-income but not high-income citizens. Then, because the income distribution is skewed to the right (*i.e.*, more people are far above the median than far below it), the median citizen wants more transit than the average citizen, resulting in a pressure toward subsidizing transit if the median voter is decisive politically. The role of median voters will be considered further in the next section.

4.6 Political economy of pricing

User charges for transportation generally do not adhere to marginal cost pricing principles and often are not imposed at all. In the case of roads and parking, as we have shown, congestion charges have only been implemented in a few cities, charges are not differentiated efficiently, discounts and exemptions are prevalent, and parking prices deviate drastically from what economic theory prescribes.

Research on the political economy of urban transportation seeks to explain these facts. Two central explanations are public dislike of prices and conflicting goals of multiple governments that control prices. More broadly, studies of political economy in urban transportation draw on literature in public economics and public choice, accounting for several characteristics of transportation such as the prevalence of externalities, network structure, and interaction between private and public providers. In this section, we examine several of these factors.

4.6.1 *Tax competition*

Governments presumably consider the well-being of various groups of residents and other stakeholders. But they often have incentives to ignore the needs of those outside their dominion and to generate revenue from such people where possible. When two or more governments operate in such an environment, they are said to engage in *tax competition*. De Borger and Proost (2012b) review much of this literature as it pertains to transportation.

Interactions between governments can be horizontal or vertical. *Horizontal interactions* exist when the tax base is mobile between jurisdictions. For example, travelers may have a choice between two routes that traverse different cities or regions. By reducing its prices, one jurisdiction can gain market share and perhaps increase revenue, at the expense of the other jurisdiction, leading to inefficiently low taxes. Levinson (2001) shows empirically that states in the USA are more likely to levy tolls on their major through roads when non-residents account for a larger share of the traffic.

Vertical interactions exist when two or more governments impose taxes on the same tax base, and are common when they have overlapping responsibilities and powers. For example, in the USA, federal and state governments both levy fuel taxes. If one government increases its tax rate, the revenue collected by the other government goes down due to less traffic. If governments ignore this fiscal externality, each seeking to increase its own revenues, resulting tax rates are inefficiently high due to the well-known *double marginalization* effect.

A variant of horizontal interaction occurs when a government can impose taxes on people who lack standing in its jurisdiction – we may call them *non-residents*. The resulting equilibrium depends on whether or not the government can discriminate between residents and non-residents. If it can, it may levy higher taxes on non-residents. If not, it may instead raise taxes on certain goods and services, such as through highways, that are heavily used by non-residents. Either response is called *tax exporting*. The toll on German roads that was to be introduced in 2016 provides a good example. Under this policy, both German and foreign road users were to pay a road toll by acquiring a 10-day, 2-month, or annual pass. However, German drivers would be fully compensated for this, through a simultaneous cut in annual vehicle taxes. The net revenues from the scheme would therefore be entirely due to foreigners. The implied discrimination was sufficient that European Court of Justice invalidated the plan in 2019.

Tax competition may instead also lead to lower taxes, notably when the tax base is mobile – a normal feature in transport applications. Luxemburg successfully applies relatively low fuel taxes in order to attract international traffic to purchase fuel, suggesting it believes that fuel demand by foreigners is price-elastic.

We describe here a number of studies of tax competition.

4.6.1.1 Horizontal competition

De Borger *et al.* (2005) study the simple case of two governments controlling congestion-prone links in parallel through tolls. Some traffic is regional in nature, meaning it can choose between the links, whereas local traffic is forced to use the home link. The authors consider cases both where the governments can and where they cannot discriminate between regional and local traffic. When they can discriminate, governments engage in tax exporting and set excessive tolls on transit traffic; less obviously, they impose high tolls on local traffic as well in order to reduce congestion, which attracts regional traffic and therefore revenue. When they cannot discriminate, they choose a toll above marginal external cost, due to their revenue-maximizing incentive with respect to regional traffic. This results in a lower welfare for both residents and non-residents compared with an efficient level of tax. The authors also consider a case where only local traffic can be tolled, which produces still lower welfare, because the effects of congestion on non-residents are ignored. The overall lesson here is that despite the fiscal distortion due to being able to tax non-residents, the ability to do so improves welfare when congestion is important.

4.6.1.2 Vertical competition

Proost and Sen (2006) study vertical competition using a simulation model that features a region containing a city and its periphery, with all residents commuting by car to the city center.[66] Car travel creates congestion and pollution. The city sets a parking fee that all travelers pay, while the regional government controls a cordon toll paid by only those living outside the city. In choosing prices, the city government seeks to maximize the welfare of city residents, while the regional government seeks to maximize welfare for all residents. All these features have important counterparts in real metropolitan areas.

The result depends on the institutional regime, two of which are considered. In the first, the two governments set prices simultaneously without sharing revenues. This yields a Nash equilibrium in which the city government sets the parking fee above marginal external cost (*mec*); the regional government partly compensates for this by setting its toll below what it otherwise would, since the parking fee and toll are partly substitutes for internalizing congestion and pollution externalities. These two effects tend to counter each other, so welfare is only modestly compromised by the existence of tax competition.

In the second regime, the regional government acts as a Stackelberg leader (an assumption justified by noting that in reality, a regional government may contain more than one such city). The regional government sets the cordon toll above the Nash equilibrium level in order to induce the city government to reduce its parking fee. This response again keeps inefficiencies in check; note, however, that the relative sizes of the parking fee and toll (each defined here as a constant per trip) differ substantially in these two regimes.

In either the Nash or Stackelberg regime, welfare is raised further if the regional government shares some of the cordon toll revenues with the city government. Doing so induces the city government to lower the parking fee in order to boost regional traffic and hence its share of regional toll revenue. Such revenue sharing may therefore be mandated by a higher level of government in order to reduce the ill effects of tax competition.

In a different setting, however, vertical competition can be very damaging to welfare. Ubbels and Verhoef (2008) consider two road links in series, one a regional road traveled by suburban residents and the other a city road traveled by city residents and by some but not all suburban residents. The authors derive equilibria for a number of variants of the game, involving Nash or Stackelberg behavior. In all cases, equilibrium welfare is far below the first-best optimum.

Watling *et al.* (2015) consider a more general situation, with both horizontal and vertical competition involving road tolls. Two regions are served by a network with multiple links and OD pairs, with the price on each link controlled by one of the two regions. The authors show numerically that the Nash equilibrium can result in tax exporting and double marginalization, causing tolls to be so excessive that welfare is lower than with no tolls at all.[67] Some of the welfare loss is mitigated if governments are required to share their revenue with each other; although tolls can then end up too low because each region disregards the congestion costs borne by the other region's citizens, just as in Proost and Sen (2006).

4.6.2 *Political economy of government decision-making*

In the studies presented so far, governments are assumed to maximize the total utility of agents within their jurisdiction. In democracies, however, governments have to gain or retain power through elections. In order to take this into account, the motivations and/or institutional features that affect government decisions must be considered.

Following the path-breaking analysis of Downs (1957), it is common to assume that elections are determined by majority voting and that, as a result, governments seek to maximize the utility of the median voter. Some studies go further and take into account intensity of preferences, which may govern whether citizens bother to vote and whether stakeholders lobby for or against policies. Furthermore, some studies recognize that agents with strong preferences can form interest groups that can have an outsize effect on outcomes – as indeed has been observed when small interest groups block large-scale transportation infrastructure projects and road pricing initiatives.[68] Other public choice mechanisms have been considered as well, such as one that explicitly models decisions that determine who enters electoral competition (Osborne and Slivinsky 1996).

Citizen support for fiscal measures depends not only on objective impacts but also on perceptions and values that are not easily accommodated in a standard economics framework. Road pricing especially has provided a wonderful laboratory to study these, and transportation researchers have provided extensive analysis of the several case studies available. We cover this material in Section 4.6.5.

We begin here with models based on majority voting as determined by the median voter. A good example is De Borger and Proost (2012a), who explore the support for road pricing. In their basic model, individuals choose between driving and not traveling. They then vote whether or not to adopt a road toll which, if adopted, will be set at an optimal Pigouvian level with revenues distributed uniformly to all citizens. If a toll is implemented, all non-drivers gain; those who continue to drive lose in aggregate; and those who stop driving may either gain or lose. Thus, a toll is approved if the fraction of the population who drive initially is small. These results are consistent with the fact, noted in Section 6.3, that cities adopting road pricing tend to have comparatively low proportions of trips by automobile.

When voter uncertainty is introduced, however, results change markedly. De Borger and Proost consider two types of such uncertainty, both still assuming voters correctly forecast the effects of the toll on congestion and aggregate revenue. *Idiosyncratic uncertainty* concerns whether a voter who drives will continue doing so after a toll is introduced, while *political uncertainty* concerns how efficiently toll revenues are used. To model idiosyncratic uncertainty, the authors suppose that a voter's anticipated benefit follows a uniform probability distribution, with a range specified by the authors; with their parameter choices, the result is that *all* those who initially drive vote against the toll. This is true even though a majority of them will in fact benefit once uncertainty is resolved. Political uncertainty is found to have similar effects. Parallel findings persist in a two-mode model, in which individuals also have a public transport option.

Russo (2013) and De Borger and Russo (2018) introduce another factor: explicit distributions of voter preferences, among both city and suburban residents. In Russo's model, all trips are made to the city center, either by car or by bus. A regional government controls a toll paid by both suburban and city residents who choose car. Revenues are rebated lump sum to all residents. Russo shows that if the median suburban voter has sufficiently stronger preferences than the median city voter for driving (relative to bus), the regional government does not implement a toll because it would be paid disproportionately by suburban residents. This result is consistent with observed strong opposition to tolls by suburban residents, even in high-transit-use cities such as Stockholm and New York. De Borger and Russo then introduce an elaborate geographical setup, in which conflicts of interest exist between many subgroups. A common result is that support for a toll is strengthened if public transport is easily accessible and if toll revenues are dedicated to public transport. Again, this seems consistent with several cases where congestion tolls are combined with well-publicized improvements to public transit.

4.6.3   Political economy of parking fees

The rarity of efficient parking pricing calls out for political explanations.[69] One that has been explicitly invoked is lobbying by downtown retailers, who often face competition from retailers in suburbs with low-cost parking. De Borger and Russo (2017) analyze this factor by modeling a linear city with downtown retailers at one end and large outlying retailers at the other. All shoppers travel in cars that create a negative externality. The city government maximizes a weighted sum of social welfare and lobbying contributions. Downtown retailers lobby for a lower parking fee in the city, and outlying retailers lobby for a higher one. The incentive to lobby increases with the profit margin from a sale. If the downtown margin is high enough compared with the suburban margin, the government responds to its retailers' lobbying by setting the fee below the optimal level. If retailers sell differentiated goods and consumers can shop at both locations, then the parking fee does not affect demand at the outlying stores, so only downtown retailers lobby and the government sets an even lower parking fee.

We note, however, that the approach just described assumes that downtown retailers' business is adversely affected by high parking fees, or at least that they think it will be. In fact, many before-and-after studies have found little or no such adverse effect, especially where public transit is prevalent (ITF 2021).

Lobbying over downtown parking policy occurs not only by retailers but also by certain groups of residents. Specifically, people living in neighborhoods near business districts, such as downtown, dislike competition for space from shoppers. They often lobby for residential permits giving them exclusive access to on-street parking in their neighborhoods, as part of any program of parking fees. However, these same downtown residents also care about the vitality of downtown shopping, which depends on business from all residents – partly due to agglomeration economies, which foster desirable product variety. Molenda and Sieg (2013) employ a model that captures these two opposing forces. Reserving space for downtown residents reduces those residents' total parking costs, but also hurts downtown business and thus the product variety on offer. The city government thus makes a trade-off, whose result depends on how much weight is given to lobbying.

4.6.4   Distributional effects of pricing

Road tolls, parking fees, and other price-based travel-demand management policies affect consumers and firms, residents and non-residents, government budgets, and other stakeholders. As the studies reviewed above show, the welfare-distributional effects can influence attitudes toward and decisions on tolls and parking fees. Parking fees and tolls have different patterns of incidence, which may help explain their rather distinct histories of adoption.

4.6.4.1   Defining equity

It is one thing to describe distributional effects of policy; but what can we say about them from a normative perspective? The usual starting point for this question is *equity*, which immediately demands a definition.[70]

Many dimensions of distributional patterns may be considered in such a definition. Here, we focus on three. *Horizontal equity* concerns the extent to which individuals with similar characteristics and circumstances are treated similarly. Often, it is invoked in favor of a user-pays or benefits-received principle: the costs of providing a good or service should be paid by those who use it or benefit from it. Horizontal equity is also consistent with a different principle, namely that those who create negative externalities should pay for the costs.

Vertical equity concerns the relative treatment of individuals who differ with respect to income, physical ability, social class, and other characteristics. Vertical equity is most often analyzed with respect to income. A tax or fee is deemed to be *progressive* if the pecuniary cost it imposes increases more than proportionally with income and *regressive* if less than proportionally.

Spatial equity is about relative treatment of people living, working, or shopping in different geographical locations. An example of its use would be designing a toll cordon to avoid especially high costs to people whose locations require frequently crossing toll stations for ordinary travel. Spatial equity is closely related to environmental equity, which considers who suffers exposure to noise, pollution, and other externalities.

Dimensions of equity can conflict. For instance, a toll consistent with the user-pays principle, aimed at achieving horizontal equity, may not promote vertical or spatial equity. Furthermore, the presumed distributional effects that underlie equity pronouncements may be ephemeral: fiscal and other burdens are shifted through markets for land, labor, and commercial space in ways many people do not recognize. In the case of pricing or tax policies, the burdens may also be shifted by how revenues are used.

4.6.4.2   Equity of congestion pricing

We now consider specifically the distributional effects of road pricing. Let us preview some rather intuitive conclusions. First, road pricing tends to be regressive in its direct impacts, if only mildly so in some cases. Second, it is less regressive if public transport provides a good alternative to driving. Third, individuals living within a cordon or tolled area fare better than those living outside it. Fourth, individuals and firms that lack flexibility to reschedule trips are at a disadvantage relative to those who are flexible.

Some initial observations can be drawn from the Pigouvian toll diagram in Figure 4.1. In that diagram, if individuals are identical except for their willingness to pay (*i.e.*, their position on the demand curve), everyone who drove before the toll was implemented is made worse off, whether or not they continue to drive. The only gain is to the public sector, in the form of toll revenues. Thus, a key policy consideration is whether these revenues can be used in ways that compensate drivers for their direct losses.

On the other hand, if individuals are heterogeneous, there is variation among them in a road toll's incidence. Those with sufficiently high VOT may gain even without compensation, because the monetary value of travel-time savings to them exceeds the toll. Moreover, some high-VOT individuals who were deterred by congestion from driving may start to drive. Since high-VOT travelers benefit more, or lose less, from tolling, the direct impact (not counting the use of toll revenues) is likely to be regressive. This is mitigated somewhat by the tendency of overall travel to increase with income.

The distributional effects of the congestion pricing schemes reviewed in Section 4.3 have been assessed in a number of studies. Some representative findings are summarized here.

London: Santos (2008) reviews the distributional effects of the initial £5-per-day London Congestion Charge, introduced in 2003. She concludes that the 90% of entrants who did not use a car gained from the charge, since they benefited from quicker trips, less pollution, and less noise without having to pay or change their behavior. Some commuters with high VOT who continued to drive also gained, as did some drivers who circulate extensively within the tolled zone during the day. In contrast, commercial vehicles did not do as well because rigid delivery requirements and schedules prevented them from canceling or retiming trips.

Stockholm: Two studies consider the direct impact of the Stockholm congestion charge on welfare, prior to accounting for use of toll revenues. Karlström and Franklin (2009) find that all income groups incurred losses on average, and in an irregular pattern: from lowest to highest quintile, the average annual losses were €321, €199, €35, €348, and €219. The irregularity results partly from differences by quintile in who drove across the cordon. More recently, Eliasson (2019) concludes that the Stockholm tax is slightly regressive across income deciles; it is more regressive for those residents living close to the charging boundary – an example of spatial inequity. After comparing different charging schemes for Stockholm, Kristoffersson *et al.* (2017) somewhat discouragingly conclude that the most efficient pricing scheme is also the least equitable.

Gothenburg: West and Börjesson (2020) determine that the congestion tax in Gothenburg is more regressive than the one in Stockholm, again before considering revenue uses. One reason is a higher level of car dependence at all income levels. Another is that high-income workers have greater access than in Stockholm to company cars, for which employers typically pay congestion charges incurred, even for non-working trips.

Milan: Beria (2015) examines the effects of Milan's Area C charge during its first year of operation. Overall, most people appear to have benefited. Residents inside the cordon rarely exceeded their allotment of 40 free entrances per year, and only 4% paid more than €1 per day. Furthermore, only a small fraction of people entered the central city by car before the charge was imposed. Meanwhile, reductions in traffic and pollution benefited drivers, users of other modes, and inner-city residents. Beria also takes into account that revenues were dedicated to public transport and other sustainable transport policies, which in his analysis benefited nearly everyone.

Managed lanes: As discussed in Section 4.3, managed lanes may come close to offering a Pareto improvement under the right circumstances. One limitation, however, is that they generate relatively little revenue compared with other congestion pricing schemes. Hence, if distributional concerns do arise, revenues may be insufficient to fully address them.

Distance-based tolls: Since no full-scale adoption of distance-based tolls has occurred, their welfare-distributional effects are still largely conjectural. Nevertheless, there is reason to believe that using them to replace fuel taxes would benefit low-income households because, on average, those households own older and less fuel-efficient vehicles and pay higher fuel taxes. Rural residents might also benefit since they typically own less fuel-efficient vehicles (Moore 2021). Heyndrickx *et al.* (2021) study the distributional impacts of road pricing in the Flanders region of Belgium, highlighting that even though road pricing is mildly regressive when looking at aggregated income classes, differences within classes may diverge widely so that support or opposition for road pricing may depend mainly on individual characteristics other than just income.

Pollution reduction: Reducing pollution is often a motivating factor for road pricing. How does that influence equity? The first question is whether congestion pricing in fact does reduce pollution. Several studies, reviewed by Hosford *et al.* (2021), suggest it does. As expected, the largest resulting benefits are realized inside the toll scheme's boundaries. Currie and Walker (2011) show that, in fact, reducing traffic congestion reduces premature and low-weight births. Various other studies find that pollution imposes particularly high costs on lower-income individuals.[71] Together, these findings suggest that lower-income individuals gain disproportionately from the favorable health impacts of any policy that reduces road traffic.

4.6.5 Public acceptability

Public opposition to road pricing is very widespread.[72] Mostly, the extent of opposition cannot be explained by the observable distributional patterns just discussed. Yet many citizens maintain that tolling is inequitable, raising objections along all three of the horizontal, vertical, and spatial dimensions. As it is impossible in practice to design a pricing scheme that leaves no one worse off, there is always someone who will feel it inequitable – although many analysts have suggested that the status quo itself is inequitable.[73]

4.6.5.1 Other reasons for opposition

Further investigation has identified several likely reasons for opposition besides the patterns of incidence.

Mobility is considered a basic right, so the use of roads should not be charged. This objection applies primarily to existing toll-free roads. On the surface, it seems at odds with the fact that drivers routinely pay for driving licenses, vehicle registration, fuel taxes, parking, and all vehicle operating expenses. The objection also ignores that a basic right does not imply it should be free; compare, for example, the right to own property or the right to residence.

Road pricing constitutes double taxation. People object to paying tolls for roads that have already been financed by taxes and other revenue sources. For the same reason, motorists often view on-street parking as common property, not a service to be purchased. This objection ignores that travel creates external costs that are additional to the (historical) costs of building roads, parking spaces, and other infrastructure.

There is no practical substitute: People object to tolls if they cannot avoid them. Sometimes this objection can be bypassed by requiring that a reasonable alternative to a toll road exist. For example, such a requirement is imposed on toll roads in Spain and in British Columbia, Canada.[74]

Doubts about the goals of tolling: Tolls may be used to alleviate congestion, reduce pollution, raise revenues, and for other purposes. Some public opposition may occur if the goals of a given proposed scheme are unclear, or deemed unimportant.

Scheme complexity: People often dislike complex price structures. The cordon schemes proposed for Edinburgh and Manchester, in the UK, were opposed partly for this reason. The original Milan Ecopass charge was a complicated function of vehicle fuel type, emission class, and vehicle type; the much simpler Area C plan was far more popular.[75]

Loss of privacy: Motorists fear having their vehicle movements recorded. Privacy concerns were partly responsible for the failure of Hong Kong to follow up on its technologically successful road pricing experiment in 1983–1985. Privacy concerns can be mitigated to some extent by technological design, but there will always remain trade-offs between privacy and other goals of the policy.

4.6.5.2 Attitudes before and after implementation

Public support for tolling increased after implementation in London, Stockholm, Trondheim, Oslo, Bergen, Milan, and Gothenburg.[76] Many explanations for the change have been suggested. Börjesson *et al.* (2016) test several hypotheses in the case of the Gothenburg charge, including the following:

1 *Benefits were larger than expected.* People may not have anticipated certain responses to tolling, such as shifts from car to public transport, that reduce its adverse impacts.[77]
2 *Benefits of accompanying measures.* The scheme included better public transport and more bicycle lanes, which may not have been fully appreciated before implementation.
3 *Reframing.* Congestion pricing may be reframed post-implementation, for example, by describing it initially as a fiscal policy but later as an environmental policy.
4 *Loss aversion.* Before implementation, individuals may place greater weight on the prospective monetary costs (a loss) than on travel-time savings (a gain). After implementation, they value the two more objectively, or might even reverse the weights as they come to view the post-implementation situation as the new status quo.[78]
5 *Smaller downsides than expected.* Some adverse effects, such as crowding on public transit, may turn out to be milder than feared.
6 *Status quo bias.* People may simply resist change, due perhaps to the so-called endowment effect or to transaction costs. Once a toll is in effect, it becomes the status quo.

However, Börjesson *et al.* find little or no empirical support for the first four hypotheses and limited support for the other two. Thus, attitudinal changes to congestion pricing remain something of a mystery.

4.6.6 Policy lessons

The analysis and evidence summarized above suggest some lessons on implementation of road and parking pricing. The following four factors appear well attested to contribute to success:

Prior assessments and debate: Such public scrutiny prior to implementation occurred extensively in London and Stockholm, as described by Small and Gomez-Ibañez (1998).

Consolidated decision-making: Many successful pricing programs have had a single level of government and/or a single agency in charge. Examples are road pricing in London, Stockholm, and Milan, as well as parking pricing in San Francisco and in Nottingham, UK (Ison and Mulley 2014).

Simplicity and clarity: Pricing can be used to pursue multiple objectives, but this complicates planning and makes the program difficult to explain. An advantage of the SFpark initiative, for example, was its exclusive focus on managing parking demand to make parking more easily available.

Public engagement: Involving the public and other stakeholders from the early planning stages can help to overcome opposition. National Academies (2020) suggests several measures such as stakeholder interviews, advisory groups, data provision, and publicizing revenue uses.

Four other factors have more ambiguous effects:

Trials and Referenda: The track record is mixed. Two successes of this strategy can be cited: The Stockholm Congestion Tax and Milan's Plan C. By contrast, referenda prior to trials failed in Edinburgh and Manchester, and the authorities in Gothenburg ignored the negative results of a referendum.

Policy packages and revenue dedication: One approach is to combine unpopular pricing instruments in a package with more popular measures that enhance travel choices, such as improved public transit or infrastructure. Such supplementary measures can magnify the intended effects of tolls as well as appeal to the public. Sometimes, revenues are dedicated by law to these purposes, which may reassure a wary public. For example, this policy was integral to the opening of a HOT lane leading from Jerusalem to Tel Aviv in Israel, since it is well integrated with new a subsidized park-and-ride lot intermediate between the two cities (Cohen-Blankshtain *et al.* 2020). But dedicating revenues can limit control over budgets and otherwise restrict later choices.

Discounts and exemptions: Most of the major urban congestion pricing schemes feature various discounts and exemptions, which no doubt contributed to public support; but since they weaken incentives to alter travel behavior, they can undermine the project's goals, and they also complicate enforcement.

Monetary Rewards and Tradeable Permits: These schemes, described in Section 4.2.5, are similar to discounts in that they seem to enhance acceptability but could partly undermine congestion relief by encouraging excessive travel.

Summary on policy: Much has been learned about factors leading to successful implementation of pricing policies, but much is still uncertain. What is clear is that the political economy of road and parking pricing involves considerations well beyond those appearing in most economic models.

4.7 Conclusions

How important is it to "get the prices right," meaning set them at marginal social cost? Transportation researchers have offered conflicting views. For example, the European Commission's transportation research program (EXTRA 2001) suggests that the concept of marginal social cost pricing can be translated into practical pricing or taxation measures using even then existing technology; and furthermore, that simple second-best approaches such as cordon tolls can achieve most of the benefits of a theoretically optimal solution. Delucchi (2000), by contrast, argues that the effects of such pricing, especially as constrained by practical considerations, would be too modest to solve pressing problems of traffic congestion and transit deficits and that other social concerns, such as distributional equity and the environment, further erode the case for pricing.

We think both of these views are extreme. The constraints that operate in real-world applications will indeed lower the benefits to be reaped from pricing. But both theoretical and practical advances have found many ways to apply pricing even with such constraints and to alleviate social concerns over its impacts. For example, it is by now well accepted that social costs formerly thought to be unquantifiable, such as pollution and safety externalities, can be incorporated into formal policy analysis. Furthermore, we have shown that many feasibility constraints can also be explicitly modeled and taken into account. An important benefit of such explicit modeling has been to demonstrate how certain practical limitations posed for simplicity, such as equal tolls at all entry points through a cordon, can be relaxed slightly with major resulting welfare gains. Furthermore, tractable models can be built that account for traveler behavior, such as trip scheduling, that has too often been taken as fixed. We have seen that doing so considerably changes the nature of optimal pricing in a way that alleviates some of the most feared effects. Such behavioral changes are perhaps the primary reason why toll policies cause less financial harm, and reap greater travel-time savings, than more naïve analyses would predict.

We do agree that under currently foreseeable constraints, marginal cost pricing will not eliminate congestion or transit deficits. And we agree that it will not end reliance on automobile travel. Regulations such as pollution standards will continue to play an important role. Nevertheless, we believe pricing can substantially tame the many problems now associated with both transit and automobile transportation. Because the problems are significant, the potential role of pricing is important even though it cannot solve all problems by itself.

Our views are well within the range of the professional opinion of economists, but there remains a wide range of opinion about specific features: how complex to make it, how politically feasible it is, how well it would guide investment, whether it should be accompanied by privatization, its distributional effect, and how revenues should be spent (Lindsey 2006). In our view, such diversity is a healthy sign that economics does not neglect practical considerations, but rather is struggling with the best way to rigorously account for them.

Notes

1 Examples include Smeed (1968), Keeler and Small (1977), Santos (2004), de Palma *et al.* (2006), Anas and Hiramatsu (2013), and De Lara *et al.* (2013).

2 Formally, total cost is $Vc\,(V)$, so marginal cost is $mc(V) = c(V) + Vc'(V)$ (by the product rule of differentiation). With rising average cost, *i.e.*, $c'(V) > 0$, we see that $mc(V)$ exceeds $c(V)$ for any positive V.

3 See, for example, Atkinson and Stiglitz (2015) for proposed welfare functions.

4 Because social surplus depends on Marshallian demand functions and therefore on the distribution of income and initial wealth, there is no unique maximum of social surplus as it changes with redistribution of wealth. As a consequence of non-uniqueness, social surplus can be maximized at distinct maxima of different social welfare functions, for which the distribution of utility levels may be quite different. Thus, for Paretian welfare functions, maximizing social surplus is a necessary though not sufficient condition for welfare maximization. For these reasons, we follow conventional economic theory in seeking to maximize social surplus as one step in the broader objective of maximizing welfare, and we sometimes refer to the two concepts interchangeably for simplicity.

5 For exit times outside the period $[t_q, t_{q'}]$, the zero tolls shown in (4.23) are more than sufficiently high to support the optimal pattern. Negative tolls would even be allowed so long as $\tau(t') > p^0 - c_S(t')$.

6 It also implies that (4.26) still holds, even when demand is elastic.

7 This is a slight change of notation from Chapter 3, where c_T and c_S are functions of t. Here, c'_T refers to (dc_T / dT_D) so that, by the chain rule, the time derivative of $c_T(T_D(t))$ is $c'_T T'_D$. Similarly for c_S.

8 Because $T_D = (V - V_K)/V_K$ when there is a queue, equation (4.29) is consistent with the departure rates of (3.23) in the basic bottleneck model, where $c'_T = \alpha$, $c'_S = -\beta$ for early arrivals, and $c'_S = \gamma$ for late arrivals.

9 Proof: We know that c'_T is positive and that c'_S has the same sign as S_D (the latter because c_S is by definition minimized at $S_D = 0$). For early exits, c'_S is therefore negative; so equilibrium condition (4.29)

requires that $T'_D(t) > 0$ (growing queue). It also requires that $c'_T > |c'_S|$: a consistency condition identical to the previously noted requirement $\beta < \alpha$ in the basic bottleneck model, where $c'_T = \alpha$ and $c'_S = -\beta$. For late exits, (4.29) requires that $T'_D(t) < 0$ (shrinking queue).

10 If c_T, c_S, and F are everywhere differentiable, then $c'_S = 0$ implies $T'_D = 0$; *i.e.*, $T_D(t)$ must be a maximum where c_S is a minimum. If these functions are not differentiable, it remains true that in equilibrium any alternative travel moment offering a less desired arrival time and a longer travel delay can never be more attractive.

11 This is an example of a general result. Using the bottleneck model with multiple discrete groups of travelers, Lindsey (2004) shows that when users travel with users unlike themselves, they incur a trip cost that is never higher (and often lower) than when traveling with an equal number of users like themselves. The intuition is that a greater similarity of preferences worsens congestion.

12 To eliminate travel delays, the optimal entry rate must be equal to the lower capacity, and the optimal time-varying toll is set accordingly. The higher-capacity bottleneck therefore remains inactive in the first-best optimum and is irrelevant. In the unpriced equilibrium, the higher-capacity bottleneck may become active when it is located upstream of the other bottleneck; but even so total queuing time is independent of whether or not the higher-capacity bottleneck exists.

13 Mun (1999) combines Xuehao Chu's (1995) approach with a downstream pure bottleneck, finding that the optimal toll is described by (4.30) during the shoulders of the peak (where the exit rate is below the bottleneck's capacity) and takes on the basic bottleneck form with slopes β and $-\gamma$ at other times.

14 The toll and travel delay are both zero for the first and last driver arriving, in the unpriced equilibrium as well as in the optimum. The generalized trip price in both regimes, which is equalized for all drivers, must be equal to the sum of the values of free-flow travel time and schedule delay for the first or the last driver. The fourth result therefore follows from the lengthening of the peak under optimal tolling.

15 It is of course possible to design an example where the no-toll equilibrium timing of trips is actually socially optimal, so that tolling has no useful role. Fosgerau (2015) does so in the simplest version of his model, in which homogeneous users have inelastic demand; a similar result has been noted for ski-lift pricing by Barro and Romer (1987).

16 See Frascaria *et al.* (2020) for a fuller discussion.

17 Pigou (1920) considered the same network, but because he assumed the untolled road to be uncongested, the optimal toll on the other road was first-best rather than second-best. The model is further developed by Verhoef *et al.* (1996).

18 Thus, c_T here refers to user cost on the tolled road (route T), not to travel delay cost in the sense of Section 4.1.2.

19 More precisely, consider a toll increase that results, after a new equilibrium is established with new amounts of congestion, in a change in generalized price $\Delta p \equiv \Delta p_T = \Delta p_U$. Write the ratio of trips added on U to trips removed from T as $-(\Delta V_U/\Delta V_T)$. Because the roads are perfect substitutes, the change in total trips must equal $\Delta p/d'$ in order to be consistent with the overall inverse demand curve $d(p)$. Therefore, $\Delta V_T + \Delta V_U = \Delta p/d'$. Also, to be consistent with congestion, the change in generalized price on road U is given by $c_U'\Delta V_U$. (The same is not true on the road T because the toll is also changing.) Therefore, $\Delta V_T + \Delta V_U = c'_U \Delta V_U/d'$, which can be solved for $-(\Delta V_U/\Delta V_T) = -d'/(c'_U - d')$.

20 This is a particular application of the so-called envelope theorem, which applies to a differentiable objective function. That theorem states that indirect effects of a marginal change in a choice variable upon the objective are zero when evaluated in the full optimum. For first-best pricing on general networks, the changes in other link flows that would follow from a marginal increase in one of the link tolls have a zero net welfare effect, because all other links in the network are optimally priced and only carry traffic from OD pairs for which marginal benefits and marginal costs are equated. The reader may verify that if the first-best general network problem of equation (4.16) were solved using the Lagrangian technique of (4.32) and using route-based tolls as policy instruments, all route-specific multipliers would indeed be equal to zero in the optimum. Indirect effects therefore vanish in first-best optima.

21 Total cost under this policy, with overall demand of Q, two equal capacities V_K, and two-thirds of the traffic taking the tolled road, can be determined by substituting $\frac{1}{3}Q$ in (4.21) and $\frac{2}{3}Q$ in (4.26) and adding the costs thus obtained, which yields $\frac{1}{3}\delta Q^2 / V_K$. Total cost in the unpriced equilibrium and in the first-best optimum can be found from (4.21) and (4.26), respectively, with V_K replaced by $2 \cdot V_K$. The results are $\frac{1}{2}\delta Q^2 / V_K$ and $\frac{1}{4}\delta Q^2 / V_K$. Thus, the relative welfare gain of the policy (its welfare gain compared with an unpriced equilibrium divided by the welfare gain of first-best pricing) is therefore $(\frac{1}{2} - \frac{1}{3})/(\frac{1}{2} - \frac{1}{4}) = \frac{2}{3}$.

22 Chen and Bernstein (2004) address the same problem with multiple user groups.

23 See Santos *et al.* (2001), May *et al.* (2002), and Sumalee *et al.* (2005). The latter two studies, as well as Zhang and Yang (2004) and Fan (2017), use a genetic algorithm to facilitate search through many possible configurations of charge points and toll levels.

24 For example, Mun *et al.* (2003, 2005), Anas and Hiramatsu (2013), and De Lara *et al.* (2013).

25 Xuehao Chu (1999) obtains similar relative efficiencies of coarse and flat tolls, using a static model that applies for each of many discrete time intervals, with users choosing among them according to a nested logit model.

26 For example, Xiao (2011), Van den Berg (2014), Chen *et al.* (2015), and Li *et al.* (2017).

27 Van den Berg and Verhoef (2016) consider this case.

28 These results are derived by Verhoef *et al.* (1996) in a static model and by El Sanhouri and Bernstein (1994) in a dynamic one.

29 Verhoef *et al.* (1996), de Palma and Lindsey (1998), and Yu *et al.* (2023).

30 Reviews include Krabbenborg *et al.* (2021) and Balzer *et al.* (2021).

31 Chapter 7 discusses feebates in relation to fuel efficiency.

32 Tradable permits may be viewed as a response to Coase's (1960) insight that externalities exist because of missing property rights.

33 See, for example, Wang *et al.* (2012) and Akamatsu and Wada (2017).

34 See especially Goulder *et al.* (1997) and Parry and Oates (2000). For an elegant and very general synthesis, see Kreiner and Verdelin (2012).

35 Lehe (2019) reviews the major urban schemes, while Croci (2016) compares three European examples. Button (2020) summarizes the history of thought on road pricing and how it contributed to applications of congestion pricing. Congestion pricing technologies are reviewed by de Palma and Lindsey (2011) and Clements *et al.* (2021).

36 See Santos (2008) for London, Eliasson (2009) for the Stockholm congestion-charging trial, West and Borjesson (2020) for Gothenburg, and Rotaris *et al.* (2010) and Danielis *et al.* (2012) for Milan's Ecopass. No full cost–benefit analysis appears to have been done for either Singapore's successive road pricing schemes or for the Area C plan in Milan, although Gibson and Carnovale (2015) conclude that the air pollution reductions of the latter yield large welfare gains.

37 According to D'Artagnan Consulting and Ian Wallis Associates (2018), 50% of traffic received discounts or exemptions.

38 A number of studies have investigated the effects of the LCC on traffic-related externalities. Li *et al.* (2012) determined that from 2003 to 2005, the charge reduced car accidents but increased bicycle and motorcycle accidents. Green *et al.* (2020) found that CO, NO, and PM10 emissions dropped; but NO_2 emissions increased due to a shift toward diesel-powered buses and taxis which are exempt from the charge. Tang (2020) concludes that the LCC increased housing values within the charging zone by reducing congestion, pollution, accidents, and noise. See also https://tfl.gov.uk/modes/driving/congestion-charge/.

39 Similarly, the Stockholm Congestion Tax boosted sales of ethanol cars, while they were exempt from the tax (2006–2009) although the increase was not very large (Mannberg *et al.* 2014).

40 In Europe, small-scale congestion-charging schemes were implemented in Durham, UK, in 2002 (The Chartered Institution of Highways & Transportation), in Valletta, Malta, in 2007 (Attard and Enoch 2011) and in Palermo, Italy, in 2016. https://www.worldtravelguide.net/guides/europe/italy/palermo/gettingaround/

41 Small and Gómez-Ibáñez (1998) describe the first three toll rings established in Bergen (1986), Oslo (1990), and Trondheim (1991). The toll ring in Trondheim was discontinued in 2005 but resumed operation in 2010.

42 For further details, see Meloche (2019) and Baranzini *et al.* (2021).

43 See GNSS Consulting (2022).

44 See the European Commissions's "Interoperable Europe" website https://joinup.ec.europa.eu/interoperable-europe

45 See, for example, Schubert *et al.* (2022) for European policy.

46 See Jenn (2019) for more details.

47 For an update, see Washington State Transportation Commission (2024).

48 Traveling in AVs could also affect how tolls alter travel behavior. Finkelstein (2009) finds that people are less responsive to conventional tolls that are paid electronically than those paid manually. One explanation for this is that electronic payment is less salient, particularly if it is delayed (as is the case with credit card payments). Thus, observing a toll up front (at the beginning of an AV trip), rather than *en route*, could increase its salience – making it a more effective policy tool but perhaps inducing

opposition. On the other hand, tolls may have a lesser effect if they comprise only a small portion of an easily observed total monetary cost of a trip.

49 See, for example, Santos (2005) and Richards (2006).

50 Inci (2015) summarizes the effects on parking demand of residential parking fees, shopping mall parking fees, working place parking charges, and employer "cash out" policies. Shoup (2018a, Part II) provides an in-depth analysis of setting appropriate prices for on-street parking.

51 Specifically, parking operators have to be sufficiently small to take the utility of drivers as given, but large enough to internalize the parking-congestion externalities that drivers who use their facilities experience.

52 If privately operated garages charge fees above marginal cost, they help to alleviate congestion – although their price markups are unlikely to match the external costs of trips.

53 This is shown by Arnott *et al.* (2005, Chap. 2).

54 The trial is described and evaluated in San Francisco Municipal Transportation Authority (2014). San Francisco Municipal Transportation Authority (2018) describes updated rules and fees. See also Pierce and Shoup (2018) and Inci (2015, Section 6) for discussions. The SFMTA also implemented a number of changes at its parking garages, including adjusting rates to smooth entries and exits, modifying the early-bird rate period to reduce congestion, and providing better information to drivers on off-street parking locations and occupancy rates.

55 The city chose a target occupancy range, rather than a single-occupancy rate, since it wanted parking fees to change infrequently (Primus 2018). Occupancy rates were initially monitored using sensors below the pavement, which proved to be costly and unreliable; occupancies are now estimated using meter payment data rather than being measured directly.

56 The Los Angeles system, LA Express (http://www.laexpresspark.org/), is summarized in Ghent (2018). For Calgary, see https://www.calgaryparking.com/findparking/onstreetrates. Berkeley also has a parking management project (http://www.goberkeley.info/) that is a cheaper and lower-tech version of SF*park*; see Deakin (2018).

57 In fact, SFMTA now takes previous changes into account by using time-series data to predict how occupancy varies with parking rates.

58 Classic models, largely followed here, were developed by Glaister (1974) and Henderson (1977, Chap. 7). Dodgson and Topham (1987) add distributional preferences, distorting taxes, and cost-sharing by higher levels of government. Proost (2018) provides a non-technical summary.

59 See, for example, Arnott and Yan (2000, Note 3) for the conditions required. Our model is in fact similar to that of Arnott and Yan except that our rail mode is characterized by scale economies instead of congestion.

60 See equations (4.13)–(4.14) and (4.32)–(4.33). Here, q_A plays the role that V_A plays in those equations; but here we do not assume independence across demand functions. From (4.40), we see that the usual symmetry of second derivatives of $B(\cdot)$ implies symmetry of the Slutsky matrix of derivatives of the demand functions, $(\partial d_i / \partial q_j)$, $i, j = A, R$. This shows that because we treat the marginal utility of income as constant, our ordinary (Marshallian) demand functions are also compensated (Hicksian) demand functions: See Varian (1992) and our discussion of income effects in Section 2.2.5.

61 The logic is similar to that explained for two-route road pricing in the note following equation (4.35).

62 These simulations also show that raising the road toll from its existing value would create a welfare gain, but not by nearly as much as the transit reforms. By contrast, Kilani *et al.* (2014) find that in Paris, introducing road pricing (where there is none to start with) would create very large welfare gains, whereas raising or lowering transit prices (undifferentiated by time) would make a comparatively small difference: See Proost (2018, Table 2) or Kilani *et al.* (2014, Table 16).

63 See, for example, Savage (2004) and De Borger and Kerstens (2000).

64 See Section 2.1.3 for a review of transit price elasticities. Holmgren (2007) in his meta-analysis reports fare elasticities ranging from −0.009 to −1.32, with a mean value of −0.38. Even when the fare elasticity is low, drastic fare changes, such as the complete elimination of fares by making public transport free, may still induce relatively sizable increases in demand: See, for example, Cats *et al.* (2017).

65 See Tang and Lo (2010) for Hong Kong, Buehler, and Pucher (2011) for Germany. In the case of Hong Kong, the rail service achieves financial viability only through cross-subsidies from property development over rail stations.

66 The model they use is called TRENEN-II URBAN MODEL.

67 This result also occurs in a model by De Borger *et al.* (2007) of two links in series. They refer to this as a Prisoner's Dilemma, because everyone is better off by refraining from tolling, but each government has an incentive to institute a toll if the other does not.

68 See, for example, Feitelson and Salomon (2004) and Schaller (2010).
69 See Button (2006), Arnott (2011), and Inci (2015) for more extended discussions of these political factors.
70 For comprehensive reviews in the transportation arena, see Levinson (2010), van Wee (2011), and National Research Council (2011).
71 Manville and Goldman (2018) investigate this claim by simulating freeway tolling in the ten most congested urbanized areas in the USA. They find that residents who live close to freeways are both poorer on average and more exposed to pollution.
72 See, for example, Schaller (2010), Hensher and Li (2013), Noordegraaf *et al.* (2014), Eliasson (2019), and Selmoune *et al.* (2020).
73 National Research Council (2011).
74 Relevant policies are described in Bueno *et al.* (2017) and British Columbia Ministry of Transportation (2003), Rule 2.3.
75 As a perhaps extreme example of complexity, users of the I-10 Express Lanes in Los Angeles have to carry a transponder; those using them as carpools have to carry a separate "switchable" transponder to identify when they are traveling as a carpool. The operator advises users not to carry both kinds of transponders at the same time unless one is placed in a Mylar bag and to consult the manufacturer about where to mount a transponder if they have a metal oxide windshield. Perhaps it is not a coincidence that this plan faced considerable opposition despite that no one loses from it according to conventional analysis.
76 See Börjesson *et al.* (2016) for study references.
77 A study by Dal Bó *et al.* (2018), using laboratory experiments with games, supports the idea that individuals often overlook changes in the behavior of other people. Subjects played a simple prisoners' dilemma game and then voted on whether to switch to another game that had a better Nash equilibrium for all, but that offered lower payoffs if no one changed behavior. Most subjects preferred the original game.
78 De Borger and Fosgerau (2008) find strong evidence using survey data in support of loss aversion in the money and travel-time dimensions.

References

Ahn, Kijung (2009) "Road pricing and bus service policies," *Journal of Transport Economics and Policy* 43(1): 25–53.

Akamatsu, Takashi and Kentaro Wada (2017) "Tradable network permits: a new scheme for the most efficient use of network capacity," *Transportation Research Part C: Emerging Technologies* 79: 178–195.

Anas, Alex and Tomoru Hiramatsu (2013) "The economics of cordon tolling: general equilibrium and welfare analysis," *Economics of Transportation* 2(1): 18–37.

Anderson, Michael L. (2014) "Subways, strikes and slowdowns: the impacts of public transit on traffic congestion," *The American Economic Review* 104(9): 2763–2796.

Anderson, Simon P. and André de Palma (2004) "The economics of pricing parking," *Journal of Urban Economics* 55: 1–20.

Arnott, Richard (2006) "Spatial competition between parking garages and downtown parking policy," *Transport Policy* 13(6): 458–469.

Arnott, Richard (2011) "Parking economic," in André de Palma *et al.* (eds.) *A Handbook of Transport Economics*, Cheltenham: Edward Elgar, Chap. 31, pp. 726–743.

Arnott, Richard (2013) "A bathtub model of downtown traffic congestion," *Journal of Urban Economics* 76: 110–121.

Arnott, Richard (2014) "On the optimal target curbside parking occupancy rate," *Economics of Transportation* 3: 133–144.

Arnott, Richard, André de Palma and Robin Lindsey (1988) "Schedule delay and departure time decisions with heterogeneous commuters," *Transportation Research Record: Journal of the Transportation Research Board* 1197: 56–67.

Arnott, Richard André de Palma and Robin Lindsey (1990a) "Departure time and route choice for the morning commute," *Transportation Research Part B: Methodological* 24(3): 209–228.

Arnott, Richard, André de Palma and Robin Lindsey (1990b) "Economics of a bottleneck," *Journal of Urban Economics* 27: 111–130.

Arnott, Richard, André de Palma and Robin Lindsey (1991) "A temporal and spatial equilibrium analysis of commuter parking," *Journal of Public Economics* 45(3): 301–335.

Arnott, Richard, André de Palma and Robin Lindsey (1993) "A structural model of peak-period congestion: a traffic bottleneck with elastic demand," *American Economic Review* 83(1): 161–179.

Arnott, Richard, André de Palma and Robin Lindsey (1998) "Recent developments in the bottleneck model," in Kenneth J. Button and Erik T. Verhoef (eds.) *Road Pricing, Traffic Congestion and the Environment: Issues of Efficiency and Social Feasibility*, Cheltenham: Edward Elgar, pp. 79–110.

Arnott, Richard and Eren Inci (2006) "An integrated model of downtown parking and traffic congestion," *Journal of Urban Economics* 60: 418–442.

Arnott, Richard, Anatolii Kokoza and Mehdi Naji (2016) "Equilibrium traffic dynamics in a bathtub model: a special case," *Economics of Transportation* 7–8: 38–52.

Arnott, Richard and Marvin Kraus (1998) "When are anonymous congestion charges consistent with marginal cost pricing?" *Journal of Public Economics* 67(1): 45–64.

Arnott, Richard, Tilman Rave and Ronnie Schöb (2005) *Alleviating Urban Traffic Congestion,* Cambridge, MA: MIT Press.

Arnott, Richard and John Rowse (1999) "Modeling parking," *Journal of Urban Economics* 45(1): 97–124.

Arnott, Richard and An Yan (2000) "The two-mode problem: second-best pricing and capacity," *Review of Urban and Regional Development Studies* 12: 170–199.

Atkinson, Anthony B. and Joseph E. Stiglitz (2015) *Lectures in Public Economics,* Updated Edition, Princeton, NJ: Princeton University Press.

Attard, Maria and Marcus Enoch (2011) "Policy transfer and the introduction of road pricing in Valletta, Malta," *Transport Policy* 18(3): 544–553.

Balzer, Louis, Jesper Provoost, Oded Cats and Ludovic Leclercq (2021) "Tradable mobility credits and permits: state of the art and concepts," DIT4Tram Deliverable 4.1, Universite Gustave Eiffel, https://dit4tram.eu/pdf/2021-12-dit4tram-deliverable-D4-1.pdf (accessed 27 June 2023).

Bao, Yue, Erik T. Verhoef and Paul Koster (2019) "Regulating dynamic congestion externalities with tradable credit schemes: does a unique equilibrium exist?," *Transportation Research Part B: Methodological* 127: 225–236.

Baranzini, Andrea, Stefano Carattini and Linda Tesauro (2021) "Designing effective and acceptable road pricing schemes: evidence from the Geneva Congestion Charge," *Environmental and Resource Economics* 79: 417–482.

Barro, Robert J. and Paul M. Romer (1987) "Ski-lift pricing, with applications to labor and other markets," *American Economic Review* 77(5): 875–890.

Basso, Leonardo J. and Hugo E. Silva (2014) "Efficiency and substitutability of transit subsidies and other urban transport policies," *American Economic Journal: Economic Policy* 6(4): 1–33.

Baumol, William J. and David F. Bradford (1970) "Optimal departures from marginal cost pricing," *American Economic Review* 60(3): 265–283.

BEMobile (2021) "The evolution and future developments of GNSS tolling," *BEMobile*, October 18, https://be-mobile.com/de/news/the-evolution-and-future-developments-of-gnss-tolling (accessed June 28 2023).

Beria, Paolo (2015) "Effectiveness and monetary impact of Milan's road charge, one year after implementation," *International Journal of Sustainable Transportation* 10(7): 657–669.

Boiteux, Marcel (1949) "La tarification des demandes en pointe: application de la theorie de la vente au cout marginal," *Revue Générale de l'Électricité*. Reprinted in English translation as "Peak-load pricing," *Journal of Business* 33(2) (1960): 157–179.

Borck, Rainald (2008) "The political economy of urban transit," in International Transport Forum, *Privatisation and Regulation of Urban Transit Systems*, OECD Publishing, Paris, pp. 23–46. doi:10.1787/9789282102008-3-en.

Börjesson, Maria, Jonas Eliasson and Carl Hamilton (2016) "Why experience changes attitudes to congestion pricing: the case of Gothenburg," *Transportation Research Part A: Policy and Practice* 85: 1–16.

Börjesson, Maria, Chau Man Fung and Stef Proost (2017) "Optimal prices and frequencies for buses in Stockholm," *Economics of Transportation* 9: 20–36.

Bovenberg, A. Lans and Ruud A. de Mooij (1994) "Environmental levies and distortionary taxation," *American Economic Review* 84(4): 1085–1089.

Braid, Ralph M. (1996) "Peak-load pricing of a transportation route with an unpriced substitute," *Journal of Urban Economics* 40(2): 179–197.

Brands, Devi K., Erik T. Verhoef, Jasper Knockaert and Paul R. Koster (2020) "Tradable permits to manage urban mobility: market design and experimental implementation," *Transportation Research Part A: Policy and Practice* 137: 34–46.

British Columbia Ministry of Transportation (2003) "Guidelines for tolling," http://www.th.gov.bc.ca/tolling/index.htm

Buehler, Ralph and John Pucher (2011) "Making public transport financially sustainable," *Transport Policy* 18(1): 126–138.

Bueno, Paola Carolina, Juan Gomez and Jose Manuel Vassallo (2017) "Seeking factors to increase the public's acceptability of road-pricing schemes: case study of Spain," *Transportation Research Record: Journal of the Transportation Research Board* 2606: 9–17.

Button, Kenneth J. (2006) "The political economy of parking charges in 'first' and 'second-best' worlds," *Transport Policy* 13(6): 470–478.

Button, Kenneth J. (2020) "The transition from Pigou's ideas on road pricing to their application," *Journal of the History of Economic Thought* 42(3): 417–438. doi:10.1017/S105383721900035X

Button, Kenneth J. and Erik T. Verhoef (eds.) (1998) *Road Pricing, Traffic Congestion and the Environment: Issues of Efficiency and Social Feasibility*, Cheltenham: Edward Elgar.

Bye, Raymond Taylor (1926) "The nature and fundamental elements of costs," *Quarterly Journal of Economics* 41(1): 30–62.

Calthrop, Edward and Stef Proost (2006) "Regulating on-street parking," *Regional Science and Urban Economics* 36(1): 29–48.

Cats, Oded, Yusak O. Susilo and Triin Reimal (2017) "The prospects of fare-free public transport: evidence from Tallinn," *Transportation* 44: 1083–1104.

Chatman, Daniel. G. and Michael Manville (2014) "Theory versus implementation in congestion-priced parking: an evaluation of SF*park*, 2011–2012," *Research in Transportation Economics* 44: 52–60.

Chen, Mei and David H. Bernstein (2004) "Solving the toll design problem with multiple user groups," *Transportation Research Part B: Methodological* 38(1): 61–79.

Chen, Honhyu, Yu Nie and Yafeng Yin (2015) "Optimal multi-step toll design under general user heterogeneity," *Transportation Research Part B: Methodological* 81: 775–793.

Chu, Xuehao (1995) "Endogenous trip scheduling: the Henderson approach reformulated and compared with the Vickrey approach," *Journal of Urban Economics* 37(3): 324–343.

Chu, Xuehao (1999) "Alternative congestion pricing schedules," *Regional Science and Urban Economics* 29(6): 697–722.

Clements, Lewis M., Kara M. Kockelman and William Alexander (2021) "Technologies for congestion pricing," *Research in Transportation Economics* 90: 100863.

Coase, Ronald (1960) "The problem of social cost," *Journal of Law and Economics* 3: 1–44.

Cohen-Blankshtain, Galit, Hillel Bar-Gera and Yoram Shiftan (2020) "Congestion pricing with minimal public opposition: the use of High-occupancy Toll lanes and positive incentives in Israel," Discussion papers No. 2020/09, International Transport Forum, OECD Publishing, Paris. doi:10.1787/ead92f06-en

Croci, Edoardo (2016) "Urban road pricing: a comparative study on the experiences of London, Stockholm and Milan," *Transportation Research Procedia* 14: 253–262.

Currie, Janet and Reed Walker (2011) "Traffic congestion and infant health: evidence from E-ZPass," *American Economic Journal: Applied Economics* 3(1): 65–90.

d'Artagnan Consulting and Ian Wallis Associates (2018) "Review of international road pricing initiatives, previous reports and technologies for demand management purposes," Final report, MinistryofTransport,https://www.transport.govt.nz/assets/Uploads/Land/Documents/3e828706f5/ASTPP-Scheme-review1.8.pdf

Dal Bó, Ernesto, Pedro Dal Bó and Erik Eyster (2018) "The demand for bad policy when voters underappreciate equilibrium effects," *The Review of Economic Studies* 85(2): 964–998.

Danielis, Romeo, Lucia Rotaris, Edoardo Marcucci and Jérôme Massiani (2012) "A medium term evaluation of the Ecopass road pricing scheme in Milan: economic, environmental and transport impacts," *Economics and Policy of Energy and the Environment*. doi:10.3280/EFE2012-002004.

De Borger, Bruno, Fay Dunkerley and Stef Proost (2007) "Strategic investment and pricing decisions in a congested transport corridor," *Journal of Urban Economics* 62(2): 294–316.

De Borger, Bruno and Mogens Fosgerau (2008) "The trade-off between money and travel time: a test of the theory of reference-dependent preferences," *Journal of Urban Economics* 64(1): 101–115.

De Borger, Bruno and Kristiaan Kerstens (2008) "The performance of bus-transit operators," in David A. Hensher and Kenneth J. Button (eds.) *Handbook of Transport Modelling*, 2nd edition, Bingley: Emerald Group Publishing, pp. 693–714.

De Borger, Bruno and Stef Proost (2012a) "A political economy model of road pricing," *Journal of Urban Economics* 71: 79–92.

De Borger, Bruno and Stef Proost (2012b) "Transport policy competition between governments: a selective survey of the literature," *Economics of Transportation* 1: 35–48.

De Borger, Bruno, Stef Proost and Kurt Van Dender (2005) "Congestion and tax competition in a parallel network," *European Economic Review* 49(8): 2013–2040.

De Borger, Bruno and Antonio Russo (2017) "The political economy of pricing car access to downtown commercial districts," *Transportation Research Part B: Methodological* 98: 76–93.

De Borger, Bruno and Antonio Russo (2018) "The political economy of cordon tolls," *Journal of Urban Economics* 105: 133–148.

De Lara, Michel, André de Palma, Moez Kilani and Serge Piperno (2013) "Congestion pricing and long-term urban form: application to Paris region," *Regional Science and Urban Economics* 43: 282–295.

de Palma, André and Richard Arnott (1986) "Usage-dependent peak-load pricing," *Economics Letters* 20(2): 101–105.

de Palma, André and Philippe Jehiel (1995) "Queuing may be first-best efficient," Discussion paper 95-20, THEMA (Théorie Economique, Modélisation et Applications), Université de Cergy-Pontoise, Cergy-Pontoise, France.

de Palma, André, Moez Kilani and Robin Lindsey (2005) "Comparison of second-best and third-best tolling schemes on a road network," *Transportation Research Record: Journal of the Transportation Research Board* 1932: 89–96.

de Palma, André and Robin Lindsey (1998) "Information and usage of congestible facilities under different pricing regimes," *Canadian Journal of Economics* 31: 666–692.

de Palma, André and Robin Lindsey (2011) "Traffic congestion pricing methodologies and technologies," *Transportation Research Part C: Emerging Technologies* 19(6): 1377–1399.

de Palma, André and Robin Lindsey (2020) "Tradable permit schemes for congestible facilities with uncertain supply and demand," *Economics of Transportation* 21: 100149.

de Palma, André, Robin Lindsey and Stef Proost (eds.) (2006) *Modelling of Urban Road Pricing and its Implementation*, Special issue of *Transport Policy* 13. Amstersam: Elseiver.

de Palma, André, Stef Proost, Ravi Seshadri and Moshe Ben-Akiva (2018) "Congestion tolling - dollars versus tokens: a comparative analysis," *Transportation Research Part B: Methodological* 108: 261–280.

De Scant, Skip (2018) "San Francisco rolls out dynamic parking rate model," *Automation*, January 3, http://www.govtech.com/fs/San-Francisco-Rolls-Out-Dynamic-Parking-Rate-Model.html

Deakin, Elizabeth (2018) "Parking limits: lean demand management in Berkeley," in Donald C Shoup. (ed.) *Parking and the City*, London: Routledge, pp. 316–321.

DeCorla-Souza, Patrick (2004) "Recent U.S. experience: pilot projects," in Georgina Santos (ed.) *Road Pricing: Theory and Evidence*, Amsterdam: Elsevier JAI, pp. 283–308.

Delucchi, Mark (2000) "Should we try to get the prices right?" *Access* 16: 14–21.

Dodgson, John S. and Neville Topham (1987) "Benefit–cost rules for urban transit subsidies," *Journal of Transport Economics and Policy* 21(1): 57–71.

Downs, Anthony (1957) *An Economic Theory of Democracy*, New York: Harper & Row.

Dupuit, Jules (1844) "De l'influence des peages sur l'utilité des voies de communication," *Annales des Ponts et Chaussees*. Translated by Elizabeth Henderson as "On tolls and transport charges," *International Economic Papers* 11 (1962): 7–31.

Dupuit, Jules (1849) "De la mesure de l'utilité des travaux publics," *Annales des Ponts et Chaussees* 8. Translated by R. H. Barback as "On the measurement of the utility of public works," *International Economic Papers* 2 (1952): 83–110.

Ekström, Joakim, Agachai Sumalee and Hong K. Lo (2012) "Optimizing toll locations and levels using a mixed integer linear approximation approach," *Transportation Research Part B: Methodological* 46: 834–854.

El Sanhouri, Ibrahim and David Bernstein (1994) "Integrating driver information and congestion pricing systems," *Transportation Research Record: Journal of the Transportation Research Board* 1450: 44–50.

Eliasson, Jonas (2009) "Cost-benefit analysis of the Stockholm congestion charging system," *Transportation Research Part A: Policy and Practice* 43(4): 468–480.

Eliasson, Jonas, Lars Hultkrantz, Lena Nerhagen and Lena Smidfelt Rosqvist (2009) "The Stockholm congestion-charging trial 2006: overview of effects," *Transportation Research Part A: Policy and Practice* 43(3): 240–250.

EXTRA (2001) "Getting prices right: results from the transport research programme," European Commission, DG Energy and Transport, Consortium for EXploitation of TRAnsport Research, Brussels, Belgium. Luxembourg: Office for Official Publications of the European Communities, 2001, ISBN 92-894-1549-5.

Fabusuyi, Tayo and Robert Cornelius Hampshire (2018) "Rethinking performance based parking pricing: a case study of SFpark," *Transportation Research Part A: Policy and Practice* 115: 90–101.

Fan, Wei (2017) "Social welfare maximization by optimal toll design for congestion management: models and comprehensive numerical results," *Transportation Letters* 9(2): 81–89.

Feitelson, Eran and Ilan Salomon (2004) "The political economy of transport innovations," in Michel Beuthe, Veli Himanen, Aura Reggiani and Luca Zamparini (eds.) *Transport Developments and Innovations in an Evolving World*. Berlin Heidelberg GmbH: Springer-Verlag, pp. 11–26.

Finkelstein, Ami (2009) "E-ZTAX: tax salience and tax rates," *The Quarterly Journal of Economics* 124(3): 969–1010.

Flyvbjerg, Bent, Matte K. Skamris Holm and Søren L. Buhl (2003) "How common and how large are cost overruns in transport infrastructure projects?," *Transport Reviews* 23: 71–88.

Flyvbjerg, Bent, Matte K. Skamris Holm and Søren L. Buhl (2005) "How (in)accurate are demand forecasts in public works projects? The case of transportation," *Journal of the American Planning Association* 71(2): 131–146.

Foreman, Kate (2016) "Crossing the bridge: the effects of time-varying tolls on curbing congestion," *Transportation Research Part A: Policy and Practice* 92: 76–94.

Fosgerau, Mogens (2011) "How a fast lane may replace a congestion toll," *Transportation Research Part B: Methodological* 45: 845–851.

Fosgerau, Mogens (2015) "Congestion in the bathtub," *Economics of Transportation* 4(4): 241–255.

Fosgerau, Mogens and André de Palma (2013) "The dynamics of urban traffic congestion and the price of parking," *Journal of Public Economics* 105: 106–115.

Fosgerau, Mogens, Jinwon Kim and Abhishek Ranjan (2018) "Vickrey meets Alonso: commute scheduling and congestion in a monocentric city," *Journal of Urban Economics* 105: 40–53. doi:10.1016/j.jue.2018.02.003

Fosgerau, Mogens and Kenneth A. Small (2017) "Endogenous scheduling preferences and congestion," *International Economic Review* 58(2): 585–615.

Frankena, Mark W. (1987) "Capital-biased subsidies, bureaucratic monitoring and bus scrapping," *Journal of Urban Economics* 21(2): 180–193.

Frascaria, Dario, Neil Olver and Erik T. Verhoef (2020) "Emergent hypercongestion in Vickrey bottleneck networks," *Transportation Research Part B: Methodological* 139: 523–538.

Ghent, Peer (2018) "LA express park," in Donald Shoup (ed.) *Parking and the City*, London: Routledge, pp. 378–388.

Gibson, Matthew and Maria Carnovale (2015) "The effects of road pricing on driver behavior and air pollution," *Journal of Urban Economics* 89: 62–73.

Glaister, Stephen (1974) "Generalised consumer surplus and public transport pricing," *Economic Journal* 84(336): 849–867.

Glazer, Amihai and Esko Niskanen (1992) "Parking fees and congestion," *Regional Science and Urban Economics* 22(1): 123–132.

GNSS-consulting (2022) "Using satellite positioning for all-electronic tolling," January 31, https://www.gnss-consulting.com/using-satellite-positioning-in-all-electronic-tolling

Goddard, Haynes C. (1997) "Using tradeable permits to achieve sustainability in the world's large cities: policy design issues and efficiency conditions for controlling vehicle emissions, congestion and urban decentralization with an application to Mexico City," *Environmental and Resource Economics* 10: 63–99.

Goh, Mark (2002) "Congestion management and electronic road pricing in Singapore," *Journal of Transport Geography* 10(1): 29–38.

Goulder, Lawrence H., Ian W. H. Parry and Dallas Burtraw (1997) "Revenue-raising versus other approaches to environmental protection: the critical significance of preexisting tax distortions," *RAND Journal of Economics* 28(4): 708–731. doi:10.2307/2555783

Green, Colin P., John S. Heywood and Maria Navarro Paniagua (2020) "Did the London congestion charge reduce pollution?," *Regional Science and Urban Economics* 84: 103573.

Gubins, Sergejs and Erik T. Verhoef (2014) "Dynamic bottleneck congestion and residential land use in the monocentric city," *Journal of Urban Economics* 80: 51–61.

Hall, Jonathan D. (2018) "Pareto improvements from Lexus Lanes: the effects of pricing a portion of the lanes on congested highways," *Journal of Public Economics* 158: 113–125.

Hall, Jonathan D. (2020) "Can tolling help everyone? Estimating the aggregate and distributional consequences of congestion pricing," *Journal of the European Economic Association*. doi:10.1093/jeea/jvz082

Hall, Jonathan D. (forthcoming) "Inframarginal travelers and transportation policy," *International Economic* Review. Prepublication version: https://papers.ssrn.com/sol3/papers.cfm?abstract_id=3424097

Henderson, J. Vernon (1977) *Economic Theory and the Cities*, New York: Academic Press.

Hendrickson, Chris and George Kocur (1981) "Schedule delay and departure time decisions in a deterministic model," *Transportation Science* 15(1): 62–77.

Hensher, David A. and Zheng Li (2013) "Referendum voting in road pricing reform: a review of the evidence," *Transport Policy* 25: 186–197.

Heyndrickx, Christophe, Toon Verheukelom and Stef Proost (2021) "Distributional impact of a regional road pricing scheme in Flanders," *Transportation Research Part A: Policy and Practice* 148: 116–139.

Hirte, Georg and Stefan Tscharaktschiew (2020) "The role of labor-supply margins in shaping optimal transport taxes," *Economics of Transportation* 22: 100156.

Holmgren, Johan (2007) "Meta-analysis of public transport demand," *Transportation Research Part A: Policy and Practice* 41(10): 1021–1035.

Hörcher, Daniel and Daniel J. Graham (2018) "Demand imbalances and multi-period public transport supply," *Transportation Research Part B: Methodological* 108: 106–126.

Hörcher, Daniel and Alejandro Tirachini (2021) "A review of public transport economics," *Economics of Transportation* 25: 100196.

Hosford, Kate, Caislin Firth, Michael Brauer and Meghan Winters (2021) "The effects of road pricing on transportation and health equity: a scoping review," *Transport Reviews* 41(6): 766–787.

Hotelling, Harold (1938) "The general welfare in relation to problems of taxation and of railway and utility rates," *Econometrica* 6(3): 242–269.

Inci, Eren (2015) "A review of the economics of parking," *Economics of Transportation* 4: 50–63.

Ison, Stephen and Corinne Mulley (eds.) (2014) *Parking Issues and Policies*, Volume 5, Bingley: Emerald Group Publishing Limited.

ITF (2021) "Reversing car dependency: summary and conclusions," ITF Roundtable Reports No. 181, OECD Publishing, Paris.

Jansson, Jan Owen (2010) "Road pricing and parking policy," *Research in Transportation Economics* 29: 346–353.

Jenn, Alan (2019) "Lessons learned for designing programs to charge for road use, congestion and emissions," A white paper from the National Center for Sustainable Transportation, National Center for Sustainable Transportation, ITS UC Davis Institute of Transportation Studies (December) https://escholarship.org/uc/item/9n8571hf

Kaplow, Louis (1996) "The optimal supply of public goods and the distortionary cost of taxation," *National Tax Journal* 49(4): 513–533.

Karlström, Anders and Joel P. Franklin (2009) "Behavioral adjustments and equity effects of congestion pricing: analysis of morning commutes during the Stockholm Trial," *Transportation Research Part A: Policy and Practice* 43(3): 283–296.

Keeler, Theodore E. and Kenneth A. Small (1977) "Optimal peak-load pricing, investment and service levels on urban expressways," *Journal of Political Economy* 85(1): 1–25.

Kelly, J. Andrew and J. Peter Clinch (2009) "Temporal variance of revealed preference on-street parking price elasticity," *Transport Policy* 16(4): 193–199.

Kilani, Moez, Stef Proost and Saskia van der Loo (2014) "Road pricing and public transport pricing reform in Paris: complements or substitutes?," *Economics of Transportation* 3: 175–187.

Knight, Frank (1924) "Some fallacies in the interpretation of social costs," *Quarterly Journal of Economics* 38(4): 582–606.

Knockaert, Jasper, Yin-Yen Tseng, Erik T. Verhoef and Jan Rouwendal (2012) "The Spitsmijden experiment: a reward to battle congestion," *Transport Policy* 24: 260–272.

Knockaert, Jasper, Erik T. Verhoef and Jan Rouwendal (2016) "Bottleneck congestion: differentiating the coarse charge," *Transportation Research Part B: Methodological* 83: 59–73.

Komanoff, Charles (2019). "KOMANOFF: congestion pricing carveouts will steal millions of hours and billions of bucks," March 28, 2019. *Streetsblog New York*, https://nyc.streetsblog.org/2019/03/28/komanoff-congestion-pricing-carveouts-will-steal-millions-of-hours-and-billions-of-bucks

Krabbenborg, Lizet, Chris Bergen and Eric Molin (2021) "Public support for tradable peak credit schemes," *Transportation Research Part A: Policy and Practice* 145: 243–259.

Kreiner, Claus Thustrup and Nicolaj Verdelin (2012) "Optimal provision of public goods: a synthesis," *Scandinavian Journal of Economics* 114(2): 384–408. doi:10.1111/j.1467-9442.2011.01686

Kristofferson, Ida, Leonid Engelson and Maria Börjesson (2017) "Efficiency vs equity: conflicting objectives of congestion charges," *Transport Policy* 60: 99–107.

Krohnengold, Benjamin (2020) "Keeping the streets clear: advancing transportation equity by limiting exemptions under New York City's Central Business District Tolling Program," *Fordham Urban Law Journal*, https://ir.lawnet.fordham.edu/ulj/vol47/iss4/8.

Laih, Chen-Hsiu (2004) "Effects of the optimal step toll scheme on equilibrium commuter behaviour," *Applied Economics* 36(1): 59–81.

Lehe, Lewis (2019) "Downtown congestion pricing in practice," *Transportation Research Part C: Emerging Technologies* 100: 200–223.

Levinson, David M. (1998) "Road pricing in practice," Button, Kenneth J. and Erik T. Verhoef (eds.) (1998) *Road Pricing, Traffic Congestion and the Environment: Issues of Efficiency and Social Feasibility*, Cheltenham: Edward Elgar, pp. 14–38.

Levinson, David M. (2001) "Why states toll: an empirical model of finance choice," *Journal of Transport Economics and Policy* 35(2): 223–238.

Levinson, David M. (2010) "Equity effects of road pricing: a review," *Transport Reviews* 30(1): 33–57.

Lévy-Lambert, Hubert (1968) "Tarification des services à qualité variable – application aux péages de circulation [Pricing of variable-quality services – application to road tolls]," *Econometrica* 36(3–4): 564–574.

Li, Michael Z. F. (2002) "The role of speed–flow relationship in congestion pricing implementation with an application to Singapore," *Transportation Research Part B: Methodological* 36(8): 731–754.

Li, Haojie, Daniel J. Graham and Arnab Majumdar (2012) "The effects of congestion charging on road traffic casualties: a causal analysis using difference-in-difference estimation," *Accident Analysis and Prevention* 49: 366–377.

Li, Zhi-Chun, William H. K. Lam and S. C. Wong (2017) "Step tolling in an activity-based bottleneck model," *Transportation Research Part B: Methodological* 101: 306–334.

Li, Zhi-Chun, Ya-Dong Wang, William H. K. Lam, Agachai Sumalee and Keechoo Choi (2014) "Design of sustainable cordon toll pricing schemes in a monocentric city," *Networks and Spatial Economics* 14: 133–158.

Lindsey, Robin (2004) "Existence, uniqueness and congestion cost properties of equilibrium in the bottleneck model with heterogeneous users," *Transportation Science* 38(3): 293–314.

Lindsey, Robin (2006) "Do economists reach a conclusion on road pricing? The intellectual history of an idea," *Econ Journal Watch* 3: 292–279, www.econjournalwatch.org.

Lindsey, Robin and Erik T. Verhoef (2001) "Traffic congestion and congestion pricing," in Kenneth J. Button and David A. Hensher (eds.) *Handbook of Transport Systems and Traffic Control*, New York, NY: Emerald, pp. 77–105.

Lindsey, Robin, Vincent A. C. van Den Berg and Erik T. Verhoef (2012) "Step tolling with bottleneck queuing congestion," *Journal of Urban Economics* 72(1): 46–59.

Lindsey, Robin, André de Palma and Pouya Rezaeinia (2023) "Tolls vs tradable permits for managing travel on a bimodal congested network with variable capacities and demands," *Transportation Research Part C: Emerging Technologies* 148: 104028.

Ling, Shuai, Ning Jia, Shoufeng Ma, Yanfei Lan and Wandi Hu (2019) "An incentive mechanism design for bus subsidy based on the route service level," *Transportation Research Part A*: Policy and Practice 119: 271–283.

Lipsey, Richard G. and Kelvin J. Lancaster (1956) "The general theory of second best," *Review of Economic Studies* 24(1): 11–32.

Lombardi, Claudio, Luís Picado-Santos and Anuradha M. Annaswamy (2021) "Model-based dynamic toll pricing: an overview," *Applied Sciences* 11(11): 4778.

Mannberg, Andrea, Johan Jansson, Thomas Pettersson, Runar Bränlund and Urban Lindgren (2014) "Do tax incentives affect households' adoption of 'green' cars? A panel study of the Stockholm congestion tax," *Energy Policy* 74: 286–299.

Manville, Michael and Emily Goldman (2018) "Would congestion pricing harm the poor? Do free roads help the poor?," *Journal of Planning Education and Research* 38(3): 329–344.

Marchand, Maurice (1968) "A note on optimal tolls in an imperfect environment," *Econometrica* 36(3–4): 575–581.

Marsden, Greg (2014) "Parking policy," in Ison, Stephen and Corinne Mulley (eds.) *Parking Issues and Policies*, Volume 5, Bingley: Emerald Group Publishing Limited, pp. 11–32.

May, Anthony D. *et al.* (2002) "The impact of cordon design on the performance of road pricing schemes," *Transport Policy* 9(3): 209–220.

Meloche, Jean-Philippe (2019) "Towards a new era in road pricing? Lessons from the experience of first movers," Cirano Cahier Scientifique 2019S-35 (December), https://econpapers.repec.org/paper/circirwor/2019s-35.htm

Millard-Ball, Adam, Rachel Weinberger and Robert Hampshire (2014) "Is the curb 80% full or 20% empty? Assessing the impacts of San Francisco's parking experiment," *Transportation Research Part A: Policy and Practice* 63: 76–92.

Milne, David S., Esko Niskanen and Erik T. Verhoef (2000) "Operationalisation of marginal cost pricing within urban transport," research report 63, Government Institute for Economic Research (VATT), Helsinki, Finland, http://ideas.repec.org/p/fer/resrep/63.html.

Mohring, Herbert and Mitchell Harwitz (1962) *Highway Benefits: An Analytical Framework*, Evanston, IL: Northwestern University Press.

Molenda, Inga and Gernot Sieg (2013) "Residential parking in vibrant city districts," *Economics of Transportation* 2: 131–139.

Moore, Adrian (2021) "How Florida can use mileage-based user fees to fund roads," *Reason Foundation*, June 22, https://reason.org/commentary/how-florida-can-use-mileage-based-user-fees-to-fund-roads/

Mun, Se-il (1999) "Peak-load pricing of a bottleneck with traffic jam," *Journal of Urban Economics* 46(3): 323–349.

Mun, Se-il (2002) "Bottleneck congestion with traffic jam: a reformulation and correction of earlier result," Working paper, Graduate School of Economics, Kyoto University, Kyoto, Japan.

Mun, Se-il, Ko-ji Konishi and Kazuhiro Yoshikawa (2003) "Optimal cordon pricing," *Journal of Urban Economics* 54(1): 21–28.

Mun, Se-il, Ko-ji Konishi and Kazuhiro Yoshikawa (2005) "Optimal cordon pricing in a non-monocentric city," *Transportation Research Part A: Policy and Practice* 39(7–9): 723–736.

National Academies of Sciences, Engineering and Medicine (2020) *Emerging Challenges to Priced Managed Lanes*, Washington, DC: The National Academies Press. doi:10.17226/25924

National Research Council (2011) "Equity of evolving transportation finance mechanisms," Transportation Research Board Special Report 303, National Academy Press, Washington, DC, http://onlinepubs.trb.org/onlinepubs/sr/sr303.pdf

Newell, Gordon F. (1987) "The morning commute for nonidentical travelers," *Transportation Science* 21(2): 74–88.

Noordegraaf, Diana Vonk, Jan Anne Annema and Bert van Wee (2014) "Policy implementation lessons from six road pricing cases," *Transportation Research Part A: Policy and Practice* 59: 172–191.

Nourinejad, Mehdi and Matt J. Roorda (2017) "Impact of hourly parking pricing on travel demand," *Transportation Research Part A: Policy and Practice* 98: 28–45.

Obeng, Kofi (2011) "Indirect production function and the output effect of public transit subsidies," *Transportation* 38: 191–214.

Osborne, Martin J. and Al Slivinsky (1996) "A model of political competition with citizen-candidates," *Quarterly Journal of Economics* 111(1): 65–96.

Ostrovsky, Michael and Michael Schwarz (2018) "Carpooling and the economics of self-driving cars," Working paper 24349, National Bureau of Economic Research.

Parry, Ian W. H. and Antonio M. Bento (2001) "Revenue recycling and the welfare effects of congestion pricing," *Scandinavian Journal of Economics* 103(4): 645–671.

Parry, Ian W. H. and Wallace E. Oates (2000) "Policy analysis in the presence of distorting taxes," *Journal of Policy Analysis and Management* 19(4): 603–613.

Parry, Ian W. H. and Kenneth A. Small (2009) "Should urban transit subsidies be reduced?" *American Economic Review* 99(3): 700–724.

Pierce, Gregory and Donald Shoup (2018) "SFpark: pricing parking by demand," in Donald Shoup (ed.) *Parking and the City*, London: Routledge, pp. 344–353.

Pigou, Arthur C. (1920) *The Economics of Welfare*, London: Macmillan.

Poole, Robert W., Jr. (2020) "The impact of HOV and HOT lanes on congestion in the United States," Discussion papers No. 2020/08, International Transport Forum, OECD Publishing, Paris. doi:10.1787/0b353b17-en

Portland Bureau of Transportation (2021) "Task force recommendations and next steps," https://www.portland.gov/sites/default/files/2021/2020_0714_poem_recommendations_adopted.pdf

Primus, Jay (2018) "*SFpark*," in Donald Shoup (ed.) *Parking and the City*, London: Routledge, pp. 322–343.

Proost, Stef (2018) "Reforming private and public urban transport pricing," Discussion paper 2018/15, International Transport Forum, OECD Publishing, Paris. doi:10.1787/3567dda4-en.

Proost, Stef and Ahksaya Sen (2006) "Urban transport pricing reform with two levels of government: a case study of Brussels," *Transport Policy* 13(2): 127–139.

Qian, Zhen (Sean) and Ram Rajagopal (2014) "Optimal dynamic parking pricing for morning commute considering expected cruising time," *Transportation Research Part C: Emerging Technologies* 48: 468–490.

Qian, Zhen (Sean) and Ram Rajagopal (2015) "Optimal dynamic pricing for morning commute parking," *Transportmetrica A: Transport Science* 11(4): 291–316.

Richards, Martin G. (2006) *Congestion Charging in London: The Policy and the Politics*, Basingstoke, Hampshire: Palgrave Macmillan.

Rotaris, Lucia, Romeo Danielis, Edoardo Marcucci and Jérôme Massiani (2010) "The urban road pricing scheme to curb pollution in Milan, Italy," *Transportation Research Part A: Policy and Practice* 44(5): 359–375.

Rouwendal, Jan, Erik T. Verhoef and Jasper Knockaert (2012) "Give or take? Rewards versus charges for a congested bottleneck," *Regional Science and Urban Economics* 42(1–2): 166–176.

Russo, Antonio (2013) "Voting on road congestion policy," *Regional Science and Urban Economics* 43(5): 707–724.

Rye, Tom and Till Koglin (2014) "Parking management," in Ison, Stephen and Corinne Mulley (eds.) *Parking Issues and Policies*, Volume 5, Bingley: Emerald Group Publishing Limited, pp. 157–184.

Safirova, Elena, Sébastien Houde and Winston Harrington (2007) "Marginal social cost pricing on a transportation network: a comparison of second-best policies," Discussion paper DP 07-52, Resources for the Future.

San Francisco Municipal Transportation Authority (2014) "SFpark: Pilot project evaluation: the SFMTA's evaluation of the benefits of the SFpark Pilot Project," http://direct.sfpark.org/wp-content/uploads/eval/SFpark_Pilot_Project_Evaluation.pdf (accessed 29 June 2023).

San Francisco Municipal Transportation Authority (2018) "Drive & park in San Francisco: resources for getting around by car," https://www.sfmta.com/drive-park

Santos, Georgina (ed.) (2004) *Road Pricing: Theory and Evidence*, Research in Transportation Economics, Volume 9, Amsterdam: Elsevier.

Santos, Georgina (2005) "Urban congestion charging: a comparison between London and Singapore," *Transport Reviews* 25(5): 511–534.

Santos, Georgina (2008) "London congestion charging," in Gary Burtless and Janet Rothenberg Pack (eds.) *Brookings Wharton Papers on Urban Affairs,* Washington, DC: The Brookings Institution, pp. 177–207.

Santos, Georgina, David Newbery and Laurent Rojey (2001) "Static versus demand-sensitive models and estimation of second-best cordon tolls: an exercise for eight English towns," *Transportation Research Record: Journal of the Transportation Research Board* 1747: 44–50.

Savage, Ian (2004) "Management objectives and the causes of mass transit deficits," *Transportation Research Part A: Policy and Practice* 38(3): 181–199.

Schaller, Bruce (2010) "New York City's congestion pricing experience and implications for road pricing acceptance in the United States," *Transport Policy* 17: 266–273.

Schubert, Daniel, Christa Sys, Thierry Vanelslander and Athena Roumboutsos (2022) "No-queue road pricing: a comprehensive policy instrument for Europe?," *Utilities Policy* 78(5): 101413.

Seattle Department of Transportation (2019) Seattle congestion pricing study: phase 1 summary report (May), https://www.seattle.gov/a/99095#page=28

Selmoune, Aya, Qixiu Cheng, Lumeng Wang and Zhiyuan Liu (2020) "Influencing factors in congestion pricing acceptability: a literature review," *Journal of Advanced Transportation* 2020: 4242964.

Shoup, Donald C. (2006) "Cruising for parking," *Transport Policy* 13(6): 479–486.

Shoup, Donald C. (2018a) *Parking and the City*, London: Routledge. doi:10.4324/9781351019668

Shoup, Donald C. (2018b) "Popular parking meters," in D. Shoup (ed.) *Parking and the City*, London: Routledge, pp. 311–315.

Small, Kenneth A. and José A. Gómez-Ibáñez (1998) "Road pricing for congestion management: the transition from theory to policy," in Kenneth J. Button and Erik T. Verhoef (eds.) (1998) *Road Pricing,*

Traffic Congestion and the Environment: Issues of Efficiency and Social Feasibility, Cheltenham: Edward Elgar, pp. 213–246.

Smeed, Reuben J. (1968) "Traffic studies and urban congestion," *Journal of Transportation Economics and Policy* 2(1): 33–70.

Steiner, Peter O. (1957) "Peak loads and efficient pricing," *Quarterly Journal of Economics* 71(4): 585–610.

Strommer, Tamás, Daniel Hörcher and András Munkácsy (2023) "Crowding externalities and optimal subsidies in public transport: revisiting the Parry-Small model," *Research in Transportation Economics* 100: 101324. doi:10.1016/j.retrec.2023.101324.

Strotz, Robert H. (1965) "Urban transportation parables," in Julius Margolis (ed.) *The Public Economy of Urban Communities*, Washington, DC: Resources for the Future, pp. 127–169.

Sumalee, Agachai, Tony May and Simon Shepherd (2005) "Comparison of judgmental and optimal road pricing cordons," *Transport Policy* 12: 384–390.

Sun, Yanshuo and Lei Zhang (2018) "Microeconomic model for designing public transit incentive programs," *Transportation Research Record: Journal of the Transportation Research Board* 2672(4): 77–89.

Tabuchi, Takatoshi (1993) "Bottleneck congestion and modal split," *Journal of Urban Economics* 34(3): 414–431.

Tan, Christopher (2020) "Parliament: distance charging several years away, 'premature' to decide on lowering road tax when ERP 2.0 rolls out," *Strait Times*, October 15 https://www.straitstimes.com/singapore/transport/parliament-no-decision-yet-to-lower-road-tax-when-erp-20-rolls-out

Tan, Christopher (2021). "Roll-out of satellite-based ERP system delayed by global chip shortage," *Strait Times*, November 17, https://www.straitstimes.com/singapore/transport/transition-to-next-erp-system-delayed-by-global-chip-shortage

Tang, Cheng Keat (2020) "The cost of traffic: evidence from the London congestion charge," *Journal of Urban Economics* 121(1): 103302.

Tang, Siman B. and Hong K. Lo (2010) "On the financial viability of mass transit development: the case of Hong Kong," *Transportation* 37: 299–316.

The Chartered Institution of Highways & Transportation (n.d.) "Durham City centre road charging scheme," https://www.ciht.org.uk/media/8057/durham_city_centre_road_charging_scheme.pdf.

Tikoudis, Ioannis, Erik T. Verhoef and Jos van Ommeren (2015) "On revenue recycling and the welfare effects of second-best congestion pricing in a monocentric city," *Journal of Urban Economics* 89: 32–47.

Tirachini, Alejandro and Stef Proost (2021) "Transport taxes and subsidies in developing countries: the effect of income inequality aversion," *Economics of Transportation* 25(3): 100206.

Tscharaktschiew, Stefan and Christos Evangelinos (2019) "Pigouvian road congestion pricing under autonomous driving mode choice," *Transportation Research Part C: Emerging Technologies* 101: 79–95.

Ubbels, Barry and Erik T. Verhoef (2008) "Governmental competition in road charging and capacity choice," *Regional Science and Urban Economics* 38: 174–190.

Van den Berg, Vincent A. C. (2014) "Coarse tolling with heterogeneous preferences," *Transportation Research Part B: Methodological* 64: 1–23.

Van den Berg, Vincent A. C. and Erik T. Verhoef (2011) "Winning or losing from dynamic bottleneck congestion pricing? The distributional effects of road pricing with heterogeneity in values of time and schedule delay," *Journal of Public Economics* 95(7–8): 983–992.

Van den Berg, Vincent A. C. and Erik T. Verhoef (2016) "Autonomous cars and dynamic bottleneck congestion: the effects on capacity, value of time and preference heterogeneity," *Transportation Research Part B: Methodological* 94: 43–60.

Van Dender, Kurt (2003) "Transport taxes with multiple trip purposes," *Scandinavian Journal of Economics* 105(2): 295 310.

van Wee, Bert (2011) *Transport and Ethics: Ethics and the Evaluation of Transport Policies and Projects*, Cheltenham UK and Northampton, MA, USA: Edward Elgar.

Verhoef, Erik T. (2002a) "Second-best congestion pricing in general static transportation networks with elastic demands," *Regional Science and Urban Economics* 32(3): 281–310.

Verhoef, Erik T. (2002b) "Second-best congestion pricing in general networks: heuristic algorithms for finding second-best optimal toll levels and toll points," *Transportation Research Part B: Methodological* 36(8): 707–729.

Verhoef, Erik T. (2003) "Inside the queue: hypercongestion and road pricing in a continuous time–continuous place model of traffic congestion," *Journal of Urban Economics* 54(3): 531–565.

Verhoef, Erik T. (2020) "Optimal congestion pricing with diverging long-run and short-run scheduling preferences," *Transportation Research Part B: Methodological* 134: 191–209.

Verhoef, Erik T., Peter Nijkamp and Piet Rietveld (1995) "Second-best regulation of road transport externalities," *Journal of Transport Economics and Policy* 29(2): 147–167.

Verhoef, Erik T., Peter Nijkamp and Piet Rietveld (1996) "Second-best congestion pricing: the case of an untolled alternative," *Journal of Urban Economics* 40(3): 279–302.

Verhoef, Erik T., Peter Nijkamp and Piet Rietveld (1997) "Tradeable permits: their potential in the regulation of road transport externalities" *Environment and Planning B: Planning and Design* 24(4): 527–548.

Verhoef, Erik T. and Kenneth A. Small (2004) "Product differentiation on roads: constrained congestion pricing with heterogeneous users," *Journal of Transport Economics and Policy* 38(1): 127–156.

Vickrey, William S. (1954) "The economizing of curb parking space," *Traffic Engineering* 29 (November): 62–67.

Vickrey, William S. (1963) "Pricing in urban and suburban transport," *American Economic Review, Papers and Proceedings* 53(2): 452–465.

Vickrey, William S. (1965) "Pricing as a tool in coordination of local transportation," in John R. Meyer (ed.) *Transportation Economics: A Conference of the Universities – National Bureau Committee for Economic Research*, New York: Columbia University Press, pp. 275–296.

Vickrey, William S. (1969) "Congestion theory and transport investment," *American Economic Review, Papers and Proceedings* 59(2): 251–260.

Walters, Alan A. (1961) "The theory and measurement of private and social cost of highway congestion," *Econometrica* 29(4): 676–699.

Walters, Alan A. (1968) *The Economics of Road User Charges*, World Bank staff occasional papers no. 5, Baltimore, MD: Johns Hopkins University Press.

Wang, Xiaolei, Hai Yang, Daoli Zhu and Changmin Li (2012) "Tradable travel credits for congestion management with heterogeneous users," *Transportation Research Part E: Logistics and Transportation Review* 48(2): 426–437.

Wardrop, John G. (1952) "Some theoretical aspects of road traffic research," *Proceedings of the Institute of Civil Engineers* 1(3): 325–378.

Washington State Transportation Commission (2024) *Forward Drive: Sustaining Washington State's Transportation System Into the Future* (January). https://waroadusagecharge.org/library.html#final-report-anchor

Watling, David, Simon Shepherd and Andrew Koh (2015) "Cordon toll competition in a network of two cities: formulation and sensitivity to traveller route and demand responses," *Transportation Research Part B: Methodological* 76: 93–116.

Weitzman, Martin L. (1974) "Prices versus quantities," *Review of Economic Studies* 41(4): 477–491.

West, Jens and Maria Börjesson (2020) "The Gothenburg Congestion charges: cost–benefit analysis and distribution effects," *Transportation* 47: 145–174.

West, Sarah and Roberton C. Williams III (2007) "Optimal taxation and cross-price effects on labor supply: estimates of the optimal gas tax," *Journal of Public Economics* 91: 593–617.

Winston, Clifford (2000) "Government failure in urban transportation," *Fiscal Studies* 21(4): 403–425.

Xiao, Feng, Qian Zhen and H. Michael Zhang (2011) "The morning commute problem with coarse toll and nonidentical commuters," *Networks and Spatial Economics* 11: 343–369.

Yang, Hai (1999a) "System optimum, stochastic user equilibrium and optimal link tolls," *Transportation Science* 33(4): 354–360.

Yang, Hai (1999b) "Evaluating the benefits of a combined route guidance and road pricing system in a traffic network with recurrent congestion," *Transportation* 20: 299–321.

Yang, Hai, Qiang Meng and Der-Horng Lee (2004) "Trial-and-error implementation of marginal-cost pricing on networks in the absence of demand functions," *Transportation Research Part B: Methodological* 38(6): 477–493.

Yu, Xiaojuan, Vincent A. C. van den Berg and Zhi-Chun Li (2023) "Congestion pricing and information provision under uncertainty: responsive versus habitual pricing," *Transportation Research Part E: Logistics and Transportation Review* 175: 103119.

Zhang, Xiaoning, Hai-Jun Huang and H. M. Zhang (2008) "Integrated daily commuting patterns and optimal road tolls and parking fees in a linear city," *Transportation Research Part B: Methodological* 42(1): 38–56.

Zhang, Xiaoning and Hai Yang (2004) "The optimal cordon-based network congestion pricing problem," *Transportation Research Part B: Methodological* 38(6): 517–537.

Zheng, Nan, Rashid A. Waraich, Kay W. Axhausen and Nikolas Geroliminis (2012) "A dynamic cordon pricing scheme combining the Macroscopic Fundamental Diagram and an agent-based traffic model," *Transportation Research Part A: Policy and Practice* 46(8): 1291–1303.

5 Investment

While pricing, as discussed in the previous chapter, may be the economist's knee-jerk reflex to transportation problems, most policy makers consider capital investment to be a more natural response. From the economic perspective, pricing and investment are both important and complementary instruments in managing transportation. It is thus wise to consider them jointly; moreover, the best choice for the one depends on the choices made for the other. The question can thus be asked: What are the consequences of optimizing investment, with or without optimal (or suboptimal) pricing in place?

In practice, investment is motivated by many political and economic factors. One is the frequent perception that current levels of capital stock are grossly inadequate. Such perceptions are not always grounded in actual data. An example is the US stock of highway capital: despite widespread belief that its condition is poor and getting worse,[1] statistics do not support this view. The US Federal Highway Administration classifies highway condition based on the International Roughness Index (IRI); the majority of highways typically fall in the "good" range, and conditions have modestly improved since the early 1990s.[2]

The other primary motivation for investment is inadequate capacity to handle travel volumes. For highways, this means increased traffic congestion. This may or may not call for further investment. Thus, it is very useful to have analytical tools to help with such decisions.

To this end, in this chapter we add choice of capital stock to our analytical framework. In the terminology introduced in Chapter 3, this means moving from a short-run to a long-run analysis. Section 5.1 discusses capacity choice for highways. We focus on the interactions and interrelations between pricing and capacity choice, and between toll revenues and capacity cost, under first-best and second-best conditions. We also address the perennial question: Is it possible to build our way out of congestion? Section 5.2 extends the framework to lumpy investments or other discrete policy changes, introducing a very general technique known as cost-benefit analysis.

5.1 Capacity choice for highways

We return to the framework of Section 4.1, in which we sought to maximize the difference between benefits and costs, and now apply it to the choice of highway capacity. In this way, we can generalize the capacity results of Section 3.5, obtained as part of finding long-run cost functions, to more complex situations. Treating optimal pricing and capacity within the same framework also makes transparent the close relationship between revenues and capacity costs, a relationship of great importance for financing capacity.

We first re-derive the rule for determining first-best optimal highway capacity under optimal road pricing. This enables us to consider the relationship between capacity cost and the revenues from optimal pricing – first within a basic model and then considering more complex settings.

DOI: 10.4324/9781315157375-5

Next, we turn to one type of second-best capacity choice, namely, capacity choice when pricing is constrained to be suboptimal. We will see, for example, that with underpricing, the threat of "induced traffic" causes a downward adjustment of second-best capacity. We also consider the impacts of unpriced congestion elsewhere upon second-best capacity choice for a priced link that is part of a larger network. We conclude this section by discussing the potential effects of using "naïve" investment rules that ignore behavioral responses to capacity expansion.

5.1.1   Basic results: capacity choice with first-best pricing and static congestion

A basic difference between pricing and capacity choice is that road capacity cannot be varied over the day, while traffic demand does vary. This complicates the choice of capacity to one of finding a compromise between what would be the best choices for specific times of day. We therefore consider the multi-period static model of Section 4.1.1 as our starting point.

5.1.1.1   Optimizing capacity

We earlier defined social welfare $W = B - C$ for this model as equation (4.13), which we now rewrite making explicit its dependence on road capacity V_K:

$$W = \sum_h q_h \int_0^{V_h} d_h(v)dv - \sum_h q_h V_h \cdot c_h(V_h; V_K) - \rho \cdot K(V_K). \tag{5.1}$$

Earlier, we maximized W with respect to the vehicle flows V_h and obtained the marginal cost pricing rule (4.14) for each time period:

$$\tau_h = V_h \cdot \frac{\partial c_h}{\partial V_h}. \tag{5.2}$$

The first-order conditions for flow and optimal pricing results in (5.2) naturally remain valid when now we also maximize W with respect to capacity V_K, to obtain an investment rule. Doing so is identical to minimizing C given vehicle flows V_h, since B (the first term in W above) does not depend directly on V_K. This problem is therefore the same case already considered when deriving the long-run cost function of Section 3.5, except that here we do not limit $K(V_K)$ to be linear. The first-order condition for maximizing W therefore yields the same optimal investment rule derived before as equation (3.44):

$$\rho \cdot K'(V_K) = -\sum_h q_h V_h \cdot \frac{\partial c_h(\cdot)}{\partial V_K}. \tag{5.3}$$

The marginal cost of adding capacity (on the left-hand side) is equated to the resulting marginal user cost savings from lower congestion (on the right). These cost savings are calculated holding flows V_h constant: The envelope theorem assures this is correct, because we are dealing with a marginal change from a first-best optimal starting point since pricing follows (5.2). That is, because marginal benefits and marginal social costs of flows are equalized through optimal pricing according to (5.2), any indirect marginal benefits or costs of capacity changes via traffic flows have zero net welfare effects. Section 5.1.3 will show that such indirect effects must be taken into account when first-best pricing is not in place.

5.1.1.2 *Self-financing of capital cost*

The congestion fees derived in Section 4.1 may be viewed as charges for the use of capacity, which is scarce because it is expensive. It is natural, then, to ask whether the fees will bring in enough revenue to cover the cost of capacity.

By combining investment rule (5.3) with pricing rule (5.2), total revenue can be related to total cost. To do so, we need first to relate $\partial c_h / \partial V_h$ to $\partial c_h / \partial V_K$. This is easy for any model in which c_h depends only on the volume–capacity ratio V_h / V_K, a condition interpretable as *constant returns to scale in congestion technology*. Under this assumption, we can use the quotient rule and chain rule of differentiation to show that:

$$V_K \cdot \frac{\partial c_h(\cdot)}{\partial V_K} = -V_h \cdot \frac{\partial c_h(\cdot)}{\partial V_h}$$

which is an example of Euler's theorem.[3] Under optimal pricing and capacity choice as defined by equations (5.2) and (5.3), we get the following equation for total revenue R:

$$R \equiv \sum_h q_h V_h \tau_h = -\sum_h q_h V_h V_K \cdot \frac{\partial c_h}{\partial V_K} = V_K \rho \cdot K'(V_K). \tag{5.4}$$

This can be simplified by using the economies-of-scale indicator s_K introduced in Section 3.5.4, which was defined as the ratio of average to marginal capacity cost:

$$s_K = \frac{K(V_K)}{V_K \cdot K'(V_K)}. \tag{5.5}$$

Using (5.5), we find that (5.4) implies the following *degree of self-financing*:

$$\frac{R}{\rho \cdot K(V_K)} = \frac{1}{s_K}. \tag{5.6}$$

The ratio of total revenue to total capacity cost is equal to $1/s_K$, which is also the elasticity of capacity cost with respect to capacity. We refer to this as the *self-financing result*.

Optimal fees therefore exactly cover the cost of providing capacity if there are *neutral scale economies in capacity provision* ($s_K = 1$); we call this equality *exact self-financing*. A deficit arises under economies of scale ($s_K > 1$), and a surplus under diseconomies of scale ($s_K < 1$). This was demonstrated for transportation by Mohring and Harwitz (1962), and is simply an extension of the result in equation (3.4) to this more complex formulation of capacity costs and (congestion) pricing. Note that the self-financing result applies no matter how $K(V_K)$ is constructed, so long as s_K is defined as above. For example, $K(V_K)$ may or may not entail constant input prices. Of course, for the result to represent actual financial balance for a highway provider, $K(V_K)$ must reflect the provider's actual costs.

The benchmark result of exact self-financing when $s_K = 1$ thus requires three technical assumptions to be fulfilled:

  I constant returns to scale in the congestion technology;
 II neutral scale economies in capacity provision; and
III perfect divisibility of capacity.

How likely are these assumptions to be satisfied? As far as assumptions I and II are concerned, the units of capacity to satisfy II can be freely chosen, which means that what eventually matters is only the combined effect of the two assumptions. Our earlier discussion in Section 3.5.4 suggests that, overall, there are probably mild economies of scale in major cities, which may disappear altogether in very large cities. Thus, the degree of self-financing in (5.6) may be close to one.

Condition III seems unrealistic on the face of it, given that the number of lanes of a road must be an integer. But, as noted in Section 3.5, capacity can be fine-tuned in various ways besides adding lanes – such as widening lanes, adding shoulders, or straightening the road – so it is less discrete than might first appear. Nevertheless, indivisibility of capacity is likely to be important for suburban streets and rural roads. As shall be seen shortly, the exact results of this section break down when capacity is imperfectly divisible, although the amount of deviation from exact self-financing is not necessarily very large as long as conditions I and II remain fulfilled.

For public transport, it is (even) more of an open question whether or not the degrees of scale economies, and therewith self-financing, are close to one in practice. Hörcher and Tirachini (2021) review some of the relevant studies. To fully appreciate the matter, it is important to recall that the waiting time cost function capturing the Mohring effect, as discussed in Section 3.2.1, exhibits strong economies of scale. For example, the simple square root rule that we derived for a basic model implies that the optimal fare is zero, so that self-financing appears to be out of reach under optimal policies. Crowding externalities in public transport, on the other hand, introduce an analog to road congestion as treated in our analysis of highways. Thus, the capital costs of vehicles may be needed either to alleviate waiting time costs or to alleviate crowding; the former has strong scale economies, the latter not necessarily. Hörcher and Graham (2018) find in a stylized model that, as a consequence, the degree of self-financing in public transport may vary between zero and one depending on whether waiting time or crowding cost dominates in the user cost function. Börjesson *et al.* (2019) more specifically find that for bigger cities (Stockholm in their study), high crowding costs seem to dominate so that full cost recovery is approximated, while in smaller cities (Karlstad) waiting time dominates, implying a lower degree of self-financing and hence larger subsidies under optimal policies.

5.1.1.3   *Implications of the self-financing result*

It is useful to note some policy implications of the self-financing result, before we describe how it holds up under various generalizations of the model. Our discussion focuses on situations where assumptions I–III are reasonable approximations, so that exact self-financing nearly applies.

First, when applicable, the exact self-financing results provide a necessary condition for optimal capacities and prices – namely, financial balance including capital costs – that is more readily observable than variables entering the first-order conditions for optimal capacities and prices. Thus, the self-financing result provides a practical check on whether the road system is efficient. It has certain other advantages, as well. First, self-financing promotes public acceptability of road pricing because road finance can be perceived as fair (since roads are paid for by users) and transparent (since it depends on observable money flows). Second, under certain conditions, the exact self-financing result provides an iterative way for a road authority (or private providers) to achieve first-best optimal capacity: namely, by expanding road capacity whenever short-run optimal congestion pricing yields revenues that exceed the incremental capital cost of capacity.[4] The market would thus indicate whether expansion is socially warranted, just as in competitive private markets. Third, the self-financing result implies that other taxes are less needed to sustain the road sector, which is good for economy-wide efficiency when these other taxes cause distortions.

On the other hand, the self-financing result has some practical qualifications. First, there will be many possible combinations of capacity and toll that produce the same (zero) profit for the operator, only one of which is efficient. Second, the annualized cost of capital coincides with financial outlays only if the financing mechanisms for capital recovery exactly reproduce social costs. This is typically not the case for many reasons: taxes on capital, explicit or hidden capital subsidies, financial mechanisms for risk-sharing, inadequate accounting standards, separation of ownership and control of private corporations, and financial fraud.

The most important qualification is the proviso of optimal pricing. To institutionalize self-financing the way it occurs in private markets when roads are not in public hands, a degree of competition among road operators would be needed that is difficult to achieve in practice – otherwise, they have incentives to price according to other objectives (see Section 6.1), which destroys the equality between optimal revenues and capacity cost. And, as we will see in Section 5.1.3, even for public management the self-financing rule of equation (5.6) breaks down once pricing becomes second-best.

We warn against the possible erroneous conclusion that, when assumptions I–III are fulfilled, all revenues from optimal congestion tolling should be used to finance further capacity expansions. This interpretation of the self-financing result confuses current investment expenditures with the annualized cost of capital. It is one of the possible erroneous interpretations of the self-financing theorem discussed by Verhoef and Mohring (2009), who demonstrate that acting on such interpretations can create substantial welfare losses which increase over time (see also Section 5.1.3).

Highway improvements designed to increase free-flow speeds or to improve safety, independent of capacity, do not engender congestion fees under optimal pricing and therefore are not included in the self-financing result. (Equivalently, it could be said that they are a source of fixed cost in the function relating capital cost to capacity, therefore creating economies of scale in capacity.) But many such improvements simultaneously increase capacity. It is possible that a substantial portion of highway investments in rural or even suburban areas falls into this category (Larsen 1993).[5] To better understand this issue, we need empirically estimated models in which free-flow speed and/or safety are also affected by capital investment. Small and Ng (2014) provide such a model, and suggest that uniform design standards, such as characterize the US Interstate Highway System, result in excessive free-flow speeds in urban areas where high free-flow speed is especially expensive. Similarly, modeling safety as a dimension of capital investment would be a valuable undertaking.

5.1.2 Self-financing in more complex settings

This section considers a number of complications in which the self-financing result carries over in some form, either exactly or as an approximation under certain conditions. Our discussion follows and sometimes draws from earlier reviews such as Lindsey and Verhoef (2000) and Lindsey (2012).

5.1.2.1 Discrete capacity

Especially for smaller roads, assumption III in the previous subsection, involving continuous capacity, is often unrealistic. Discreteness of capacity generally causes the self-financing result to break down. This is most easily seen for a road for which demand is so small that it will never be congested once constructed at minimum feasible capacity. The revenues from optimal road pricing are then zero, and the road cannot be self-financing.

Figure 5.1 illustrates the problem more generally. The heavy solid line marked *lratc* shows the long-run average total cost, where the total means that it includes both average user cost c

$

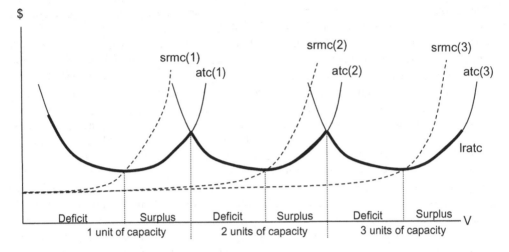

Figure 5.1 Surpluses and deficits with discrete capacity.

and per-user capacity cost $\rho \cdot K/V$ (with K optimized, in a discrete fashion, with respect to V). This *lratc* curve is the lower envelope of many U-shaped short-run average total cost $atc(l)$ curves, each valid for a different discrete number of lanes (denoted l). A different short-run marginal cost function $srmc(l)$ applies for every segment of the *lratc* curve, and each $srmc(l)$ curve cuts the *lratc* curve through its relevant local minimum. In any short-run optimum, the optimal toll is the difference between $srmc$ and c (with c not drawn in the figure), and the per-user capacity cost is the difference between atc and c. Thus, if V is such that $srmc < atc$ at the optimum, a deficit occurs; if $srmc > atc$, there is a surplus. Only by coincidence would the inverse demand function (also not drawn in the figure) cut the relevant $srmc$ curve at its intersection with the associated atc, so that exact self-financing would apply.

Nevertheless, if the general trend of *lratc* is neither up nor down, we have a discrete analog of neutral scale economies and it is more or less equally probable to have a deficit or surplus with optimal pricing and capacity. In that case, the self-financing result will approximately hold under certain conditions likely to prevail in practice. First, if the number of possible capacity values is large and the difference between them small, then *lratc* will approach a horizontal line and self-financing will approximately apply. Second, if demand grows steadily over time, periods of deficit and surplus will tend to alternate, causing the discounted net deficit or surplus to be small. Third, on a network of many roads, deficits and surpluses on individual roads can be pooled, causing most of them to cancel. These considerations make the discreteness issue less important in practice than would appear from Figure 5.1.

5.1.2.2 *Short-run dynamics*

We next consider dynamic congestion. Does the self-financing result of equation (5.6) remain intact? Arnott and Kraus (1998a) have shown that this is indeed the case under rather general conditions.

The basic bottleneck model for a single period, extended to incorporate elastic demand, can illustrate this. Recall from equation (4.25) that the average user cost under optimal pricing for this model amounts to $\bar{c}_g^1 = \bar{c}_S^1 = \frac{1}{2}\delta \cdot Q/V_K$. This equation is proportional to the total number of trips Q and to the inverse of capacity V_K, implying that the congestion technology exhibits constant returns to scale. The appropriate social objective can next be written as a single-period variant of (5.1), with q_h normalized to 1 and Q replacing V_h. Because the average optimal time-varying toll $\bar{\tau}$ is equal to $\bar{c}_g^1$, it is also equal to $Q \cdot \partial \bar{c}_g^1 / \partial Q$. Equation (5.2) therefore remains valid (with adapted notation). Because (5.3) also still applies (again with adapted notation), the self-financing result of equation (5.6) again applies.

Surprisingly, the result goes through even if the time pattern of tolls is not optimal, so long as the toll *level* is optimized subject to that pattern. To understand this, recall from equation (4.36) how to determine a second-best optimal flat price for the basic bottleneck model with elastic demand: namely, by solving its reduced-form time-independent representation, as if it were a static model with an average user cost function $\bar{c}_g^0 = \delta \cdot Q / V_K$. This user cost function exhibits constant returns to scale in the congestion technology, so leads to the same self-financing result as before. The same is true for coarse tolls. We see, then, that the essential aspect of a pricing scheme that makes the self-financing result applicable is not that prices be first-best, but rather that prices equal marginal costs – provided the latter are determined subject to some constraint. As explained in Chapter 4, that is the case in this example: Second-best flat pricing of a bottleneck sets a toll equal to the marginal external cost given that departure times are not affected by the toll. It thus qualifies as marginal cost pricing, although it is second-best in nature, and it leads to self-financing under conditions I–III.

5.1.2.3 Long-run dynamics

Arnott and Kraus (1998b) consider a variety of situations when capacity need not be fixed over the period of analysis, accounting for depreciation, maintenance, adjustment costs, and irreversibility of investments. They find that the self-financing theorem remains valid in present value terms, provided that the size of capacity additions is optimized conditional on the timing of investments. This holds irrespective of whether capacity is added continuously or in discrete units, and whether or not the timing of investments is optimal.

5.1.2.4 Networks

Yang and Meng (2002) demonstrate that if the self-financing result holds for every individual link in an optimally priced network, it holds also for the network as a whole, despite the demand interdependencies across links. This is another example of the envelope theorem at work: We can ignore the indirect effects of policy variables (link tolls, link capacities) upon other markets (other links) in welfare analysis provided optimality conditions on these other markets are fulfilled. In other words, one can then analyze each link individually, and derive (5.6) for it, without worrying about network spillovers.[6] Section 5.1.3 will show that this is no longer true when some links are not optimally priced.

5.1.2.5 Heterogeneity

Arnott and Kraus (1998a) address heterogeneity across users, finding that it does not undermine the self-financing theorem as long as marginal cost pricing applies to all users. But if practical considerations prevent tolls from being differentiated optimally among users, for example with identical pricing applied to two user groups in the model of Figure 4.4, the self-financing result generally breaks down.

User heterogeneity in relation to capacity choice also raises the question of whether segregation of traffic onto different roads or lanes is desirable. Such segregation generally becomes more attractive as cross-congestion effects (congestion that one group inflicts on another) become stronger relative to own-congestion effects (congestion inflicted on members of one's own group). If cross-effects are high in both directions for all pairs of groups, appropriate segregation can arise spontaneously; but if they predominate in only certain directions, regulation or pricing may be required to bring about an optimal degree of segregation.

Consider, for example, the case where cars travel faster than trucks, due, for example, to safety regulations or vehicle capabilities. Separation may then be desirable, depending on discreteness of capacity and any resulting cost premium. But these cross-effects are asymmetric, since passenger cars prefer to avoid sharing lanes with trucks less than vice versa. Thus, car-only lanes, truck-only lanes, or lane-specific truck tolls may be desirable in order to enforce separation. De Palma *et al.* (2008) further study the merits of segregating cars and trucks by accounting for congestion delay, safety, values of travel time, and capacity indivisibilities.

Another possibility is to segregate users by value of time, enabling the planner to optimize toll and capacity separately for two substitute facilities. Simulations by Verhoef and Small (2004) and Small *et al.* (2006) suggest that the benefits of such segregation are likely negligible if first-best pricing can be practiced; but they can be substantial if one is restricted to no pricing or to second-best pricing of just one roadway (*i.e.*, priced express lanes). Small *et al.* (2006) also find that segregation permits a compromise pricing scheme, involving differentiated tolls on both roadways, that achieves higher welfare than second-best pricing of an express lane, with much lower direct impacts on users (measured as consumer surplus loss before accounting for revenue uses). All these results depend critically on the existence of substantial differences among users in value of time, differences which exist empirically in the above-mentioned papers and other studies discussed in Section 2.7.3.

Yet another possibility is to segregate vehicles with different numbers of passengers by reserving certain lanes for high-occupancy vehicles (HOVs), either on the highway itself or on metered entry ramps. Mohring (1979) and Small (1983) estimate the welfare gains from such restricted lanes on city streets and on expressways, respectively, finding substantial welfare gains under somewhat ideal conditions. Dahlgren (1998), however, finds that only in rather exceptional circumstances does an HOV lane outperform a general-purpose lane: specifically, when there is high initial congestion and when the initial proportion of HOVs falls within a rather narrow range. Small *et al.* (2006) get more favorable results for HOV lanes, but they also depend strongly on the factors identified by Dahlgren and on relatively highly elastic demand. These results assume no pricing is possible; if instead marginal cost pricing is in effect, then the welfare gain from segregating HOVs is essentially negligible (Small 1983; Yang and Huang 1999). Konishi and Mun (2010) confirm that local circumstances determine whether or not converting regular lanes into HOV or HOT lanes produces a societal gain.

5.1.2.6   Road maintenance

So far, we have ignored road damage, road maintenance cost, and the choice of durability (*e.g.*, thickness of the pavement) in construction. These aspects are treated in some detail by a few studies, of which we consider two. Here, we focus on implications for self-financing.

Newbery (1989) considers whether the combination of optimized congestion charges and road-damage charges would cover the cost of constructing and maintaining roads, taking into account maintenance costs due to pavement damage and the extra construction costs undertaken to limit such damage. Newbery shows that self-financing holds in this broader sense, provided that heavy vehicles uniformly affect user and maintenance costs on the entire width of the road – a condition that may be thought of as an extension of neutral scale economies of road use. This result requires certain rather strong technical assumptions, such as that capital costs incurred to make the road stronger are proportional to capacity (for example, the same road thickness must be applied to all lanes even if not all are traveled by heavy vehicles).

Small *et al.* (1989) reach a similar conclusion empirically, without adopting Newbery's assumptions. They treat congestion and road damage in a multi-product framework, where the products are number of trips and the total weight of their loads (more precisely, the number of standardized units of road damage done by the heavy loads). Even though they find substantial economies of scale in providing for each product separately, this is balanced by diseconomies of scope in that the presence of heavy trucks makes it more expensive to handle large volumes of passenger cars. (Diseconomies of scope imply that if there were no indivisibilities, it would be cheaper to segregate trucks and cars.) Overall, neutral scale economies approximately hold.

5.1.2.7 *Variable input prices*

Contrary to the conventional assumptions, in urban areas the supply function of land for roads (*i.e.*, its price as a function of amount purchased) is likely to be upward-sloping, since taking more land for roads drives up its scarcity value for other uses. The distinction between returns to scale (a property of production functions) and economies of scale (a property of cost functions) then becomes important. A general-equilibrium analysis by Berechman and Pines (1991) demonstrates that constant returns to scale in the production function for roads implies that optimal revenues equal imputed costs, which include the amount of land multiplied by its equilibrium price (once road capacity is optimized). For a road authority that has to take prices as given, imputed land costs would coincide with actual land costs. But a road authority with market power in the land market will account for the rising supply function in its cost function, which will then show a degree of scale economies, s_K, that is less than the degree of returns to scale in production. Small (1999) shows that optimal revenues are then determined by degree of scale economies, s_K, of the actual cost function, just as in equation (5.6). Thus, self-financing still applies: if $s_K = 1$, revenues equal costs when prices and capacity are optimal.

This point has practical relevance. As mentioned in Section 3.5.4, many studies ignoring the rising supply price of land find economies of scale in road building. To the extent that these economies are offset by the rising supply price of land, the end result is closer to one where self-financing applies.

5.1.2.8 *Other externalities*

The self-financing result equates revenues from congestion charges to capacity costs. That equality remains even if other road charges are levied to cover externalities affecting nonusers, such as pedestrian injuries, noise, and air pollution. These charges do not change the user cost or capacity cost functions, so the relationships already established for congestion remain valid although they will now describe equilibrium at a different (lower) traffic volume. Thus, if conditions I–III hold, optimal congestion charges exactly cover capacity costs; hence, the revenues from charges for any other externalities create a financial surplus. If externalities other than congestion also affect average user cost (*e.g.*, accidents), and if those externalities are included in marginal cost prices, then self-financing still holds provided technical conditions analogous to I–III hold for these other externalities as well.

5.1.2.9 *Demand uncertainty*

How are capacity rules affected if the demand for travel that will apply after capacity is chosen is not known with certainty? Suppose, for example, the inverse demand function in period h can take on different positions on different days, with known probabilities. The self-financing result then continues to hold in expected value terms and also asymptotically over a sufficiently long planning period, given responsive pricing and perfect information. The proof in the previous subsection applies in this case, with h reinterpreted as an index also indicating states of nature in a certain time period, so that q_h indicates the duration of the period multiplied by the probability of the state.

As another example, suppose future demand conditions depend on exogenous developments that are still uncertain at the time of investment. Again, the road operator may have expectations that take the form of a set of future demand functions with associated probabilities. First-best pricing now depends on which demand function(s) materialize; it will lead to a deficit if demands are below expectations (since both the tolls and the use levels are lower than expected), and to a surplus in the opposite case. The *expected* surplus, however, is still zero, because the interpretation of q_h remains as just given. An operator who faces this type of uncertainty, who holds unbiased expectations, and who can pool uncorrelated risks of many roads may thus expect a zero budget over the entire network provided $s_K = 1$.[7]

5.1.3 Second-best highway capacity

Capacity choice under first-best pricing provides an important benchmark, but in practice, investment decisions are made under more constrained conditions. We now ask how this affects capacity choice. We first consider suboptimal pricing on the road whose capacity is being chosen, and then on other roads within a network. Finally, we address the case where public funds can be raised only at some efficiency cost to the economy.

5.1.3.1 Capacity choice with suboptimal pricing

Researchers have long considered capacity choice in a second-best world where the optimal congestion fee cannot be charged. The problem can be analyzed within the multi-period static model by fixing arbitrarily determined tolls τ_h^A for each period h. The objective function (5.1) is then augmented by adding a Lagrangian term for this constraint, becoming:

$$\Lambda = \sum_h q_h \cdot \int_0^{V_h} d_h(v)dv - \sum_h q_h V_h \cdot c_h(V_h;V_K) - \rho \cdot K(V_K)$$
$$+ \sum_h \lambda_h \cdot \left[c_h(V_h;V_K) + \tau_h^A - d_h(V_h) \right] \tag{5.7}$$

The first-order conditions for maximizing (5.7) with respect to V_h, V_K, and λ_h can be solved to yield the following second-best investment rule:

$$\rho \cdot K'(V_K) = -\sum_h (q_h V_h - \lambda_h) \cdot \frac{\partial c_h}{\partial V_K}, \quad h = 1,...,H \tag{5.8}$$

with

$$\lambda_h = q_h \cdot \frac{V_h \cdot (\partial c_h / \partial V_h) - \tau_h^A}{(\partial c_h / \partial V_h) - d'(V_h)}$$

The second-best policy rule deviates from the first-best rule, unless the Lagrange multipliers are all zero – which would require, in each period h, that toll $t^A{}_h$ be set optimally or that demand be perfectly inelastic ($d'_h = -\infty$). We assume finite d'_h for purposes of discussion. Then, if τ_h^A is below its optimal value, λ_h must be positive and the marginal benefits of capacity expansion are calculated as if fewer than $q_h V_h$ travelers benefit from the expansion. (With overcharging, the opposite occurs.) This reflects that with undercharging, the social benefit of an additional user is smaller than the private benefit because of the congestion externality. Limiting capacity is one way to discourage this additional user from entering the road.

While the Lagrangian multipliers in equations (5.8) reduce second-best capacity below its first-best value at any given value of flows V, those flows are of course different from their first-best values. Typically, in the period of undercharging the flow will be greater than the first-best value, which has an effect on (5.8) opposite to that just described. Therefore, whether in the end second-best capacity is smaller or larger than first-best capacity depends on demand and cost elasticities and their impact on equilibrium use levels (d'Ouville and McDonald 1990). Still, Wheaton (1978) shows that if the toll starts at its first-best level and is reduced marginally, optimal capacity increases – at least in a single-period model. Wilson (1983) derives more general conditions under which second-best road capacity with underpricing exceeds the first-best level. Thus, it seems likely that lack of pricing should be compensated for by building more and bigger roads. Or, to put it another way: optimal pricing would probably allow us to get by with less pavement.

The self-financing result of equation (5.6) generally breaks down under arbitrary pricing and second-best capacity choice. This is of course obvious for the case where tolls are zero.

5.1.3.2   *Induced traffic*

Whether or not second-best capacity is greater than first-best, equation (5.8) shows clearly that a naïve application of cost–benefit analysis to an incremental capacity increase will mislead if there is underpricing (so that $\lambda_h > 0$). Capacity should then not be expanded just because travel-time savings to existing users would be valued at more than the cost of expansion. Rather, the marginal social benefit of such expansion is lowered by the fact that expansion reduces the equilibrium generalized price and therefore attracts new traffic, known as *induced traffic* or *induced demand*.[8]

The problem is especially acute if demand is highly elastic. To see why, consider again the left panel of Figure 4.1, illustrating equilibrium congestion in a simple static model. If demand were highly elastic, meaning the inverse demand curve were nearly flat, then the equilibrium average cost is little affected if inverse demand is shifted to the left (demand-limiting policies) or if the cost curve is shifted to the right (capacity-augmenting policies). The second-best investment rule in (5.8) reflects this ineffectiveness as follows: With perfectly elastic demand and zero tolls, $\lambda_h = q_h V_h$ so the right-hand side of (5.8) – which expresses the marginal benefit of capacity expansion – is zero. The reason is that any expansion will be filled up with new traffic whose marginal benefit (height of the inverse demand curve) equals its average cost, so that the new traffic yields no net gain in social surplus. Furthermore, infra-marginal traffic does not benefit because, with perfectly elastic demand, equilibrium average cost does not change. Note that in this case, traffic expands exactly proportionally to capacity, *i.e.*, the elasticity of traffic with respect to capacity is one.

Even in less extreme situations, induced traffic represents the release of potential traffic that is deterred by congestion itself. Such traffic consists of people who, because of congestion, have been choosing an alternative route, mode, time of day, or home or workplace location, or who did not travel at all. It is sometimes called *latent demand* because in the initial situation it is unobserved, yet in a sense lies just beneath the surface. Unfortunately, latent demand is prevalent in just those areas where capacity expansion seems most needed – namely, in high-density urban areas during times when congestion is severe. Under such conditions, the release of latent demand is likely to undo much of the congestion relief that capacity expansion or demand reduction might otherwise bring about.

The undesirable filling up of new unpriced capacity by induced traffic is sometimes called the "fundamental law of highway congestion" (Downs 1962). It has long formed the basis for debates over highway investment policy, from Smeed (1968) to today. While rarely if ever true in its extreme form (in which new capacity is completely filled by induced traffic), it can come uncomfortably close to the truth in practical situations (SACTRA 1994; Downs 2004). The elasticity of traffic with respect to road capacity might be expected to be high (i) when initial congestion is high (so there is more discouraged traffic); (ii) when the facility is a small part of a larger network (so there are more alternative routes as sources of diverted traffic); and (iii) when it is measured over a longer time period (so more adjustments can take place). While Downs considered mainly diversion from other roads, traffic is also frequently diverted from other time periods, as indeed has been reported in assessments of major highway improvements.[9]

How large is induced traffic in practice? We report here on measurements of an elasticity of traffic volume with respect to capacity, which we call an "induced-traffic elasticity." As we show formally below, a value of one (meaning that traffic volume grows in proportion with road capacity) corresponds to an infinite demand elasticity if this proportional growth leaves travel cost unchanged.

A first requirement for empirical measurement is to distinguish the exact road network and time period(s) under consideration – which determines whether traffic diversions are measured as such or simply averaged out over a broader travel environment. The induced-traffic elasticity is expected to be greater the more constricted are the routes and time periods for which it is defined. The studies described below use broad time periods, such as all-day traffic volumes or volumes during a broadly defined peak period.

Furthermore, it is important to account for reverse causality: Namely, that road capacity is chosen endogenously as road authorities respond to actual or anticipated traffic. A standard econometric technique to deal with such endogeneity is to use one or more instrumental variables, in this case ones that help predict road construction but that do not directly predict usage.

Earlier studies of major urban highways often reported elasticities in the range 0.4–0.8.[10] For urban expressways, some more recent studies have found long-run elasticities close to or even above 1.0. Two of these studies – Duranton and Turner (2011) for the USA and Hsu and Zhang (2014) for Japan – use as instrumental variables the inclusion of a given road segment on a decades-old transportation plan. It is plausible that such a plan is exogenous to traffic at the time of the study, conditional on current capacity. A third study – Hymel (2019) for the USA – uses as instruments political variables related to Congressional funding for new highway capacity. Hymel also uses a partial adjustment model on a long panel dataset (see our Section 2.1.2) and so is able to measure both one-year and long-run elasticities – the latter being three to five times the former in most specifications. In these studies, failure to use instrumental variables is found to cause the induced-traffic elasticity to be underestimated by roughly 10%–30%.

It is important to remember that these studies are for a particular component of a road network, so finding an elasticity of one does not imply a linear relationship between measures of aggregate capacity and aggregate travel. At least two of the three results just cited are for expressways.[11] Thus, some of the induced traffic almost certainly came from other road types, as indeed was Downs's initial hypothesis. Duranton and Turner do look for diversion to expressways with auxiliary estimates (see their Table 11), not finding much; however, their data do not include smaller urban streets, which often are part of routes that are alternatives to expressways.

When Duranton and Turner apply the same technique to major roads other than expressways, they find smaller elasticities – again consistent with Downs's original hypothesis.

It is helpful to recognize that the induced-traffic elasticity is not itself a behavioral one: Rather, it is the end result of an equilibrium mechanism. However, it can easily be related to behavioral elasticities, which have been well studied. Doing so reveals that such behavioral elasticities are compatible only with an induced-traffic elasticity that is far less than one when measured for total daily traffic aggregated over a large network.

We first relate the induced-traffic elasticity to the elasticity of traffic with respect to travel-time cost. Suppose aggregate traffic V is a function of travel-time cost, $\bar{c}_T$, as in Section 3.4. Suppose further that $\bar{c}_T$ is a function of $v \equiv V/C$, with C a measure of aggregate capacity. That is:

$$V = f(\bar{c}_T)$$

$$\bar{c}_T = g(v)$$

Then equilibrium traffic volume is the solution of:

$$V = f(g(V / C)).$$

An exogenous change in capacity causes traffic to respond as follows, where V_C denotes a total derivative:

$$V_C = f' \cdot g' \cdot \left(V_C / C - V / C^2 \right).$$

Converting to elasticity form, using E_{xy} to denote elasticity of x with respect to y, and writing $\Gamma \equiv \bar{c}_T$ for easier-to-read notation, we have:

$$E_{VC} \equiv V_C \frac{C}{V} = \frac{C}{V} f' g' \cdot \left(\frac{V_C}{C} - \frac{V}{C^2} \right)$$

$$= \frac{f'g'}{C} \left(E_{VC} - 1 \right)$$

$$= E_{V\Gamma} E_{\Gamma v} \cdot \left(E_{VC} - 1 \right).$$

Solving for E_{VC},

$$E_{VC} = \frac{-E_{V\Gamma} E_{\Gamma v}}{1 - E_{V\Gamma} E_{\Gamma v}}. \tag{5.9}$$

This can be one only if the numerator tends to infinity, *i.e.*, either traffic is infinitely elastic with respect to congestion cost, or congestion cost is infinitely elastic with respect to volume–capacity ratio. The latter would occur on the vertical portion of the stationary-state average cost function shown in Figure 3.8, but is implausible for an aggregate relationship. Thus, an induced-traffic elasticity of one would imply an infinitely elastic response of traffic to travel-time cost. Of all the evidence considered in Chapter 2, none remotely suggests that as a possibility.

In fact, other evidence suggests that response to travel-time cost, summarized as E_{VT}, is modest, certainly nothing approaching negative infinity. One can see this by examining a closely related elasticity, namely that with respect to fuel cost. To understand their relationship, suppose traffic is a function not only of travel-time cost, but of a generalized price that includes travel-time and other costs, as postulated in Section 2.3. We may write this as:

$$V = f(c),$$

where c consists of travel-time costs, fuel costs, and other components:

$$c = \Gamma + c_F + c_{other}.$$

Then, the elasticities of traffic volume with respect to each of these components are very simply related to each other. Specifically:

$$E_{Vc} = E_{V\Gamma} \frac{c}{\Gamma} = E_{V,c_F} \frac{c}{c_F}$$

where E_{V,c_F} is the elasticity of traffic volume with respect to fuel cost. It follows that the induced-traffic elasticity is related to the fuel-cost elasticity by the ratio of the average values of these cost components:

$$E_{V\Gamma} = E_{V,c_F} \frac{\Gamma}{c_F}.$$

A great deal of research has gone into measuring E_{V,c_F} due to its importance for certain energy policies. We review this evidence extensively in Section 7.1.4. A reasonable summary is that its long-run value is around -0.3. The ratio of average private travel-time cost to average private fuel cost is considered in Section 3.4.9, for an urban commuting trip in a large US city: the ratio computed there is $\$0.42/\$0.09 = 4.67$. Thus, these estimates would place the elasticity $E_{V\Gamma}$ at around -1.4. As for $E_{\Gamma v}$, the other quantity appearing in (5.9), our review in Section 3.3.2 suggests that it is modest once travel time and volume-capacity ratios are averaged appropriately over time and space. If that elasticity is one, as implied by the basic bottleneck model, then our calculations imply that induced-traffic elasticity (5.9) is 0.58. While these calculations are very approximate, and no doubt the number differs greatly across cities of the world, there is no plausible story that would make the induced-traffic elasticity close to one for traffic aggregated over space and time.

Anas (2024) points to another reason why the Duranton-Turner study should not be taken to imply widespread existence of perfectly elastic demand. This is because capacity in their study is measured, as is typical, as aggregate lane-miles within a geographical area. But this means the overall capacity of a a traffic network can be expanded either by extending the network or by widening the roads within it. Suppose the former occurs for an expressway network, so that new expressway capacity serves markets previously unserved by expressways. If the new capacity then attracts the same amount of traffic per unit of highway capacity as previously existing capacity does, aggregate measures of vehicle miles traveled and of highway capacity would increase in the same proportion; but traffic on individual links would not. Given the long-run nature of the Duranton-Turner methodology, and the extensive development of outlying urban land in the USA via expansion of road networks, this process may well help explain their results. Thus, a better characterization of their main result might be: high-capacity highway extensions into newly developing parts of urban areas tend to attract or enable development that rapidly fills up their capacity to the same extent as existing capacity is filled.

Indeed, other researchers have observed that if some new capacity takes the form of extending the road network into new origins and destinations, induced travel can occur with an elasticity even greater than one. Hsu and Zhang (2014) derive this result analytically, and measure it empirically for the national expressway system in Japan, finding an elasticity of around 1.3. Garcia-López *et al.* (2022) find evidence for it in Europe. These authors suggest that such results could even occur on portions of the network not part of the expansion, if extending the road system geographically generates new trips that also use the roads whose impact is being measured. This can be expected when exurban land is newly opened to development by extending high-capacity roads to it. A similar result is reported for Chinese cities by Chen and Klaiber (2020).

We caution that even where a Downs-law mechanism might result in large induced traffic, it cannot result in overall worse congestion. This is because it is congestion itself that drives the mechanism causing induced demand. Anas (2024) demonstrates this rigorously using a variety of urban models.

As already noted in connection with Figure 4.1, the problem of releasing latent demand occurs not only with policies that shift the cost curve to the right, but also with those that shift the demand curve to the left. Thus, demand management policies and improved transit, when implemented as measures to relieve congestion, are also vulnerable to producing induced traffic.

What about the benefits of capacity expansion? In the simplest case, capacity expansion has no benefits if demand is perfectly elastic (*i.e.*, the induced-traffic elasticity is one), as already noted. In more realistic cases, there may still be benefits even if the induced-traffic elasticity is one, for at least two reasons. First, newly generated traffic permits new activities to be undertaken that may yield benefits not fully reflected in the demand for transport. Second, some of the induced traffic most likely reflects traffic that previously used other roads or time periods that were underpriced; relieving conditions at those alternate locations or times may in turn confer substantial benefits to residents or other travelers.

Pricing measures, in contrast to many other polies, do not induce new demand; at least not when the value of time is equal for all users. This is because pricing operates on the demand and supply curves differently than other policies. Specifically: pricing does not shift the demand or cost curves in the left panel of Figure 4.1 either to the right or left, but rather inserts a wedge between the cost curve and the generalized price perceived by users. Thus, it does not attract latent demand and it is able to reduce congestion and produce welfare gains, even when demand is quite elastic. Furthermore, if pricing is in place, capacity expansion is no longer frustrated by latent demand, as can be seen from the investment rule in (5.8): the closer τ_h^A approaches its optimal value, the smaller is λ_h and therefore the higher are the marginal benefits from capacity expansion (the right-hand side of (5.8)) for given flows. Thus, pricing is especially well suited to overcome the policy limitations imposed by induced traffic.

Does the existence of induced demand mean it is impossible to "build our way out of congestion"? Not really – with realistic demand elasticities, there is always some theoretical amount of capacity that will eventually eliminate severe congestion. The relevant questions are whether that amount is affordable in practice, desirable from the perspective of the implications for the living environment, and whether capacity expansion is an efficient response to the problem. Capacity expansion may provide congestion relief in many smaller cities, but in large ones it is less likely to do so and whatever benefits it conveys can usually be obtained much more efficiently through pricing.

5.1.3.3   *Network spillovers*

Another type of second-best situation occurs when it is not the toll on the road itself that is imperfect, but the tolls on other roads in the network. We consider the case where tolls on other roads are completely absent, and discuss how this affects a given road's second-best optimal capacity. It turns out that the answer depends on whether the unpriced capacity is parallel to or in series with the road whose capacity is under consideration. (More generally, the question is whether travel on the unpriced links is a substitute or complement to that on the link in question.) We therefore consider two extreme cases, defining for each a simple two-link network in which both toll and capacity can be optimized for one link (T), while an unpriced link (U) of fixed capacity exists either parallel to or in series with link T. We simplify by considering a single period only, whose duration q_h is normalized to one.

Consider first the case where the links are parallel. We already treated pricing for this case using the Lagrangian function (4.32); we need only modify it to include capacities and their costs:

$$\Lambda = \int_0^{V_T+V_U} d(v)dv - V_T \cdot c_T(V_T;V_{KT}) - V_U \cdot c_U(V_U;V_{KU}) - \rho \cdot K_T(V_{KT}) - \rho \cdot K_U(V_{KU})$$
$$+\lambda_T \cdot \left[c_T(V_T;V_{KT}) + \tau_T - d(V_T+V_U) \right] + \lambda_U \cdot \left[c_U(V_U;V_{KU}) - d(V_T+V_U) \right] \quad (5.10)$$

where V_{KT} and V_{KU} are the capacities of the two links (with V_{KU} fixed) and where $d(\cdot)$ is the inverse demand function for the entire corridor. The first-order conditions (with respect to V_T, V_U, V_{KT}, λ_U, and λ_T) can be solved to yield:

$$\tau_T = V_T \cdot \frac{\partial c_T}{\partial V_T} - V_U \cdot \frac{\partial c_U}{\partial V_U} \cdot \frac{-d'}{(\partial c_U / \partial V_U) - d'} \quad (5.11)$$

$$\rho \cdot K_T'(V_{KT}) = -V_T \cdot \frac{\partial c_T}{\partial V_{KT}}. \quad (5.12)$$

The second-best toll (5.11) is the same as second-best toll (4.35), while the second-best capacity rule (5.12) is identical to the first-best rule (5.3). Thus, the toll on link T is set to account for the underpriced parallel link, while the capacity of link T is set to minimize the cost incurred by its users.

Because the investment rule for V_{KT} is the same as the first-best rule, we already know that revenues under a first-best toll would balance capacity cost under the conditions for the self-financing result. But, revenues under the second-best toll (5.11) are smaller than this because the toll is smaller. Therefore, the self-financing result breaks down.

How does the second-best highway capacity compare to first-best capacity in this example? We are not aware of any systematic analyses of this question. We can say something about the case where capacities on both links can be optimized. Suppose users are homogeneous and the links are equally long; then the optimal capacity of the untolled link is zero so that, effectively, the link is eliminated while the tolled link is expanded to first-best capacity. This result would change with sufficient dispersion in values of time, since it may then be desirable to leave an untolled link available for the lowest-value-of-time drivers. However, the relatively small numerical difference that Verhoef and Small (2004) find between optimal tolls on parallel links for heterogeneous drivers suggests that the second-best capacity for an untolled link would still be very small.

Now suppose the unpriced link U is in series with link T, with a single origin at one end and single destination at the other so that all traffic must use both links. The Lagrangian function is now:

$$\Lambda = \int_0^V d(v)dv - V \cdot \left[c_T(V,V_{KT}) + c_U(V,V_{KU}) \right] - \rho \cdot K_T(V_{KT}) - \rho \cdot K_U(V_{KU}) \quad (5.13)$$
$$+\lambda \cdot \left[c_T(V,V_{KT}) + c_U(V,V_{KU}) + \tau_T - d(V) \right].$$

The first-order conditions with respect to V, V_{KT}, and λ imply:

$$\tau_T = V \cdot \left(\frac{\partial c_T}{\partial V} + \frac{\partial c_U}{\partial V} \right) \tag{5.14}$$

$$\rho \cdot K_T'(V_{KT}) = -V \cdot \frac{\partial c_T}{\partial V_{KT}}. \tag{5.15}$$

Not surprisingly, the toll rule (5.14) perfectly internalizes the congestion externalities on both links jointly, and therefore exceeds the first-best toll for link T whenever link U is congested. The investment rule again has the familiar first-best form. With a first-best investment rule and a toll higher than the first-best value, we can see that now a surplus occurs at link T, compared to the degree of self-financing as given in (5.6). As a matter of fact, in this simple example the toll will raise sufficient revenues to finance the entire network if both capacities are optimized with neutral scale economics.

Therefore, unpriced congestion elsewhere in the network does not seem to affect the optimal investment rule for a tolled road. Of course, because flows will differ between first-best and second-best optima, the equilibrium *size* of the second-best capacity for link T is generally different from first-best. The self-financing result also breaks down. The two examples above suggest that, for links in larger networks, surpluses will result if the network contains mostly unpriced complements, and deficits will result if the network contains mostly unpriced substitutes.

5.1.3.4 *Marginal cost of public funds*

As a third source of second-best pricing and capacity choice, we consider the case, also discussed in Section 4.2.6, when it is costly to raise government funds because taxes are distortionary. This situation can be quantified in terms of the *marginal cost of public funds* (MCF), defined as the cost to society of raising one dollar of tax revenue. A value greater than one indicates an imperfect, distortionary tax system. In practice, the value need not be a constant, but may depend on the specific taxes or expenditure categories affected by a proposed transportation investment (Kleven and Kreiner 2006).

Intuition tells us that when the relevant MCFs exceed one, an optimal policy would try to increase revenues from congestion tolls as this could replace other distortionary taxes as a revenue-generating mechanism. But, as noted in Section 4.2.6, this intuition is counteracted by the fact that congestion tolls themselves aggravate the distortion (insofar as it is caused by taxes on labor income) by raising the cost of living, thus making a dollar of earned income less valuable. Intuition also tells us that a high MCF would reduce the desirability of expanding road capacity at public expense; although again, this effect is at least partially offset by the fact that road capacity reduces congestion, which effectively reduces the cost of living. More in-depth analyses are provided by Van Dender (2003) and Proost et al. (2007).

We can extend our model to show how investment rules are affected. We allow the MCF to take one value $(1 + \lambda_\tau)$ for the uses of toll revenues, and another value $(1 + \lambda_K)$ for funds required for new capacity. In order to keep the analysis simple, we let λ_τ incorporate some of the general-equilibrium effects of prices just discussed. (Thus, a high λ_τ indicates that the toll revenues replace highly distorting taxes, that they are spent on particularly high-value public services, or that the toll's congestion relief reduces the distorting effects of other taxes or policies.) Hence, λ_τ is smaller than would be measured by a partial-equilibrium analysis of the tax system, and can even be negative. In one particular case, where travel and work are perfectly complementary (commuting being the only travel motive) and revenues are spent reducing a distorting tax on labor, then the damage done by a higher generalized price of travel is exactly offset by the advantageous use of revenues (Parry and Bento 2001): that is, $\lambda_\tau = 0$.

With a single road, still denoted as link T with toll t_T, the objective then becomes:

$$\Lambda = \int_0^V d(v)\,dv - V \cdot c(V, V_k) + \lambda_\tau V \cdot \left[d(V) - c(V, V_K) \right] - \left(1 + \lambda_K\right)\rho \cdot K(V_K) \tag{5.16}$$

where we have inserted the equilibrium condition $\tau_T = d - c$ in calculating toll revenues in the third term on the right-hand side. (Note that toll revenues are a transfer so would not appear except for the fact that they have the extra welfare value λ_τ per dollar of revenue.) The first-order conditions with respect to V and V_K are:

$$d - c \equiv \tau_T = V \cdot \frac{\partial c}{\partial V} - \frac{\lambda_\tau}{1 + \lambda_\tau} \cdot V \cdot d' \tag{5.17}$$

$$\left(1 + \lambda_K\right)\rho \cdot K'(V_K) = -\left(1 + \lambda_\tau\right)V \cdot \frac{\partial c}{\partial V_K}. \tag{5.18}$$

Note that each term in these equations is positive. When $\lambda_\tau > 0$, indicating that the value of revenue used exceeds any harm from raising the cost of travel, the optimal toll in (5.17) is above the conventional Pigouvian toll (*mecc*), confirming the intuition mentioned above. When $\lambda_\tau = 0$, (5.17) reproduces the conventional Pigouvian toll (*mecc*), confirming the Parry-Bento result. When $\lambda_\tau < 0$, we obtain a result common in the literature on environmental externalities (*e.g.*, Bovenberg and de Mooij 1994): tax distortions cause the optimal toll to be smaller than the Pigouvian toll.[12]

The investment rule (5.18) is somewhat more surprising. The prescription that marginal user benefits equal marginal investment cost is modified in a direction that depends on the relative sizes of λ_τ and λ_K. If they are equal, the conventional investment rule of (5.3) re-emerges, even if each MCF exceeds 1. The intuition is as follows. In the conventional first-best optimum of (5.3), we optimize traffic volume given capacity, and capacity given the traffic volume. We then find that the marginal cost of capacity expansion should be equated to the negative of the product of the traffic volume and the slope of the average cost function. But the latter is also equal to the additional revenue from pricing when, following a marginal increase in capacity, the toll is adjusted to keep traffic volume constant at the optimized value; *i.e.*, the toll is raised by an amount equal to the decrease in average cost. The marginal cost of capacity is then exactly equal to the marginal increase in toll revenue. If we now multiply the marginal cost of capacity and the additional toll revenues in (5.15) by identical MCF's, we find the same optimality condition: the distortions from financing capacity and raising tolls exactly balance each other in the (second-best optimal) investment rule.[13] Another special case occurs if $\lambda_\tau = 0$. Then, (5.18) states that marginal user benefits are equated to marginal investment cost, but with the latter inflated by its relevant MCF.

It is difficult to recommend empirical values for MCF because its value varies greatly, not only by situation but also by the assumptions used in calculating it – including whether or not the public expenditures being financed will tend to reduce labor supply through income effects.[14] Some typical values for the USA and UK, based on literature reviews, lie between 1.12 and

1.25.[15] A case can be made for using a smaller value if one believes that the tax distortions are offset by other factors, such as a tendency for public services to be spent in a way that favors those with higher incomes (Kaplow 1996); or that labor taxes partly or fully offset distortions in the opposite direction due to people's concern for relative status, which would cause them to overwork in a sort of arms race to outdo their neighbors in consumption ability.[16] On the other hand, several authors have argued that tax distortions are larger, for a variety of reasons including tax avoidance (Feldstein 1999) and non-marginal tax disincentives for labor-force participation (Kleven and Kreiner 2006). Kleven and Kreiner also find that several European nations other than the UK have considerably higher MCFs than this, as much as 3.5 for Denmark, due to higher marginal tax rates and higher transfers to people not working.[17]

5.1.4   Naïve investment rules

Finally, we address a question important for the interpretation of conventional investment analysis, but rarely analyzed. This is the question of whether and how a planner's misperceptions of the true preference structure of travelers, or the true congestion technology, or a misinterpretation of the Mohring-Harwitz rule, might lead to systematic biases in capacity choice and associated welfare losses. We discuss a few examples. The first involves the neglect of induced traffic, the second of rescheduling; the others involve misunderstandings of the self-financing theorem.

5.1.4.1   Ignoring induced traffic

Applied investment analysis often overlooks the problem of induced traffic. How this affects investment decisions depends on whether the neglect stems from a misperception of the actual demand elasticity or from the erroneous use of the conventional first-best investment rule (5.3) where the second-best rule (5.8) is appropriate.

Let us first consider, as a benchmark, the case with optimal pricing in place – admittedly irrelevant to current practice. In this case, an erroneous mixing up of the conventional investment rule (5.3) and the second-best rule (5.8) would be harmless because, with all $\lambda_h = 0$ in (5.8), the rules are identical. But, if demand is erroneously assumed to be highly inelastic, optimal flow and capacity will be underpredicted, leading to an unpleasant surprise once the new capacity is opened. Even so, the mistake could be corrected iteratively by further adjusting capacity to the newly revealed level of traffic demanded, presuming such iterations would be convergent even if the planner does not learn about demand responses; or, the mistake could be avoided in the next iteration.

Now consider the more realistic case where no toll can be charged and the regulator is aware of the second-best rule (5.8), but erroneously assumes that demand is completely inelastic. Again, there will be an unexpected increase in demand after an expansion. There are now two possibilities. The first is that the regulator learns from the previous experience, adjusts the estimate of demand elasticity to the correct value, and ends up in the second-best optimum. The second is that the regulator is unable or unwilling to learn, instead treating the newly observed flow V as an exogenous shock to an inelastic demand function. This regulator ends up in an equilibrium where (5.8) is satisfied under the incorrect assumption that $\partial d_h/\partial V_h = -\infty$, hence $\lambda_h = 0$. That is, the regulator inadvertently applies the first-best rule because, in the mistaken belief that demand is inelastic, the first-best and second-best rules coincide. This equilibrium is the same as that attained in yet another case, where the regulator knows about induced traffic but mistakenly applies the conventional first-best rule (5.3) to analyze investment. This is perhaps the most common case, since the second-best investment rule is not widely known in practice.

To determine the impacts of mistakenly applying the first-best investment rule, let us define two alternate expressions for the marginal benefit of capacity expansion: the true value MB_K, equal to the right-hand side of (5.8), and the naïve value MB_K^n, equal to the right-hand side of (5.3). The regulator expands capacity until MB_K^n equals the marginal cost of capacity. But since $MB_K < MB_K^n$ at any given set of traffic volumes, this means the road will be overbuilt for the situation: the last increment of capacity was not actually worth its cost.

5.1.4.2 *Ignoring rescheduling of trips*

Another type of naïve cost-benefit analysis would ignore endogenous scheduling and the implied departure-time adjustments that a capacity expansion may induce. Intuitively, one may expect two errors in opposite directions from this mistake. On the one hand, capacity expansion leads to a stronger concentration of trip completion times (peak narrowing), causing aggregate scheduling cost to fall – a benefit that is ignored in the naïve analysis. On the other hand, peak narrowing limits the ability of the capacity expansion to reduce congestion, so savings in travel-delay cost are likely to be less than predicted in the naïve analysis.

To illustrate: suppose the world operates according to the bottleneck model of Section 3.4.3, with uniformly dispersed desired queue-exit times. What happens when the regulator is ignorant of scheduling costs and tries to optimize capacity subject to a static congestion model such as one based on the US Bureau of Public Roads (BPR) congestion function of equation (3.7)?

To keep it simple, we assume that total demand Q is fixed and this is correctly perceived by the regulator. We observe the system in equilibrium when capacity is V_K^0 (assumed less than the desired queue-exit rate V_d), and we wish to assess the benefits of expanding it slightly to V_K. The true marginal benefit is then found by differentiating the average cost $\bar{c}_g$ of equation (3.36) and multiplying by Q:

$$MB_K = -Q \cdot \frac{\partial \bar{c}_g}{\partial V_K}\bigg|_{V_K = V_K^0} = \delta \cdot \left(\frac{Q}{V_K^0}\right)^2. \tag{5.19}$$

But, under our assumptions, the regulator instead uses a naïve measure of marginal benefit, MB_K^n, computed under the following assumptions: first, average congestion cost (call it c_g^n) consists only of travel-time cost; second, for a given demand, c_g^n is inversely proportional to $(V_K)^b$ as in the BPR function; and third, the initial value of c_g^n is the observed average travel-delay cost, which we know from the true model is $\bar{c}_T = \frac{1}{2}\delta \cdot Q/V_k^0$ (equation 3.34). Thus, the regulator uses the following naïve average cost as a function of V_K:

$$c_g^n = \left(\frac{1}{2}\delta \cdot \frac{Q}{V_K^0}\right) \cdot \left(\frac{V_K^0}{V_K}\right)^b. \tag{5.20}$$

Differentiating, evaluating the result at $V_K = V_K^0$, and multiplying by Q yields the naïve marginal benefit:

$$MB_K^n = -Q \cdot \frac{\partial c_g^n}{\partial V_K}\bigg|_{V_K = V_K^0} = \frac{1}{2}b\delta \cdot \left(\frac{Q}{V_K^0}\right)^2 = \frac{1}{2}b \cdot MB_K. \tag{5.21}$$

We see that the naïve calculation underestimates true marginal benefits when $b < 2$ and overestimates them when $b > 2$. Which of the two mistakes dominates – ignoring scheduling benefits or overestimating travel time benefits – therefore depends on the curvature of the naïve cost function. This is because the convexity determines how seriously travel-delay savings are overestimated: with small b that error is small and overshadowed by the naïve neglect of scheduling-cost savings, but with large b the mistaken forecast of reduced congestion is the more serious mistake.

It seems quite likely that the error in computing marginal benefits could be large, in either direction. If the conventional BPR value of $b = 4$ is used, marginal benefits would be overestimated by 100%. But if the BPR function were fit using observed data generated by the bottleneck model (here assumed to be the true one), we know from equation (3.36) that it would appear linear, *i.e.*, $b = 1$; then marginal benefits would be underestimated by 50%.

Other examples can be considered. What if the observed pattern of queue-exit times is thought to be fixed, when it really is determined by the bottleneck model? Small (1992) finds in that case that $MB_K^n = \frac{1}{2}(\alpha / \delta) \cdot MB_K$. Using the empirical values $(\alpha/\beta) = 1.631$ and $(\alpha/\gamma) = 0.417$ from equation (2.30), $\frac{1}{2}(\alpha/\delta) = 1.02$, so the marginal benefit is overestimated by just 2%. But Henderson (1992) considers the same question in the context of the no-propagation model already mentioned in Section 3.3.4. He finds that under a mild parameter restriction, the marginal benefit is always overestimated, causing the road to be overbuilt.

It appears, then, that ignoring trip scheduling in investment analysis can cause serious mistakes. However, there seems to be no general rule as to which direction those mistakes will take, or how big they will be. This makes solid structural dynamic modelling even more important for the evaluation of road investments when primarily motivated by the occurrence of dynamic peak congestion.

5.1.4.3 *Misinterpreting the Mohring-Harwitz result*

Verhoef and Mohring (2009) investigate the quantitative importance of three naïve interpretations of the self-financing theorem. They apply a numerical static model of traffic congestion, using a classic BPR function with a power of 4, a linear inverse demand curve with a reference (*i.e.*, initial equilibrium) elasticity of −0.35, a reference speed of half the maximum speed, and a capacity cost function that was calibrated to match the average capital cost of road capacity in the Netherlands for a 60 km highway.

The first misinterpretation was already briefly mentioned in Section 5.1.1. It concerns the case where the interest cost of capital is ignored and all revenues are allocated to new investment, rather than repaying the capital cost of existing capacity. This leads to a recurrent pattern of (over-)investments. Starting from the assumed base equilibrium, after 20 years the social surplus of the highway has fallen back to its initial value, and keeps falling further as overinvestment continues. The exact speed of this process obviously depends upon the choice of parameters, functional forms, and base equilibrium; the result, however, appears robust and gives a strong warning against making this mistake in formulating road pricing policies.

The second error Verhoef and Mohring consider is when the self-financing rule is followed even though there are economies or diseconomies in capital investment costs. Under the auxiliary assumption that toll and capacity are set to maximize social welfare under a self-financing constraint, the loss of social surplus is modest; increasing only gradually with the deviation of the capital cost elasticity from 1. These results suggest that the political advantages of self-financing may be achieved at only a modest sacrifice of social surplus, even when scale economies make it less than fully efficient.

The third error is to apply the self-financing constraint to a single road link while ignoring unpriced congestion elsewhere on the network. This was shown in Section 5.1.3 to be inefficient.

Verhoef and Mohring assume parallel unpriced congestion, and find the welfare losses to be substantial, naturally increasing with the size of unpriced capacity.

All in all, our analysis of naïve investment rules suggests that the devil is in the details: incomplete evaluation of optimal investments in road capacity may cause substantial societal cost. It pays to apply solid economic analysis before "starting the dig"; all the more so as political forces often militate in favor of rapid action in the form of large road capacity investments. This brings us to the second main topic of the chapter: cost-benefit analysis.

5.2   Cost-benefit analysis

The investment analysis we have described thus far depends on the possibility of incremental investments whose purpose is to enlarge a well-defined measure of capital such as "capacity." It also assumes that the relevant benefits and costs can be described as continuous functions. Sometimes, these conditions are not met. More generally, it is often necessary to analyze policy initiatives that are arbitrarily defined and may have little to do with any describable optimality conditions. It then becomes useful to have a more general method for comparing benefits and costs of proposed projects.

Cost-benefit analysis (CBA) is a set of tools for making such comparisons. As its name implies, it focuses on assessing negative and positive societal effects in economics terms; thus, it is not by itself a complete political decision-making mechanism. Nevertheless, it can incorporate many factors that are sometimes considered non-economic – just as we showed in Chapter 3 that cost functions can incorporate air pollution, noise, and risk of injury and death. Indeed, the way that was done illustrates a central principle of cost-benefit analysis: namely, that benefits can be measured as the willingness of individuals to pay for them.

One appeal of cost-benefit analysis is that it can identify the economic actors affected by a project or policy and measure the value to each of them, thereby permitting some description of the distribution of a project's or policy's benefits. However, price changes in ancillary markets may drastically alter this distribution by shifting benefits or costs from one group to another. A classic example is that land rents and land prices in areas made more accessible will increase through the normal working of land markets, as these locations become more desirable compared to others. Other markets that may shift transportation benefits are those for labor and for retail goods and services. Thus, the distribution of the immediate (*i.e.*, direct) costs and benefits may be quite misleading as a guide to the true, eventual distributional effects of a policy or an investment.

The net benefits to various groups created by these shifts are sometimes called *indirect* or *secondary* effects. The shifts in secondary markets may create genuine additional net social benefits when these other markets are distorted; two examples are considered in Section 5.2.5. But they also create the danger of double-counting, where, for example, the beneficiary of a transfer is explicitly identified but the loss from that same transfer is ignored. This becomes even more problematic if the costs and benefits considered are restricted to those affecting firms or people in a specific jurisdiction. Such a restriction is sometimes even mandated by government policy, in which case it refers to who has *standing* in analogy to a legal process (Boardman *et al.* 2018, pp. 7–8). As we will see in Chapter 7, standing has special importance in computing benefits related to control of climate change, due to their international nature.

We begin by explaining some basic principles embodied in cost-benefit analysis and why they provide a useful reference point for summarizing project impacts. We then consider just a few of the many measurement issues that afflict cost-benefit analysis. We go on to illustrate by describing studies of investments in high-speed rail. The topic is vast, but our goal is modest: to help the reader understand the implications of particular analytical choices that have been used in, or are suggested for, particular applications.[18]

5.2.1 *Willingness to pay*

The starting point for measuring costs or benefits is *willingness to pay*: that amount of money that an individual or firm could pay after a proposed change and still be equally well off (by its own evaluation). This concept incorporates consumer sovereignty: *i.e.*, the belief that individuals are the best judge of the value to them of their consumption decisions – better, for example, than policy makers or civil servants. This does not mean that externalities are to be ignored – on the contrary, the willingness-to-pay principle allows one to assess how much people care about relieving the externality. The principle does, however, exclude analysts' or governments' beliefs about the inherent worth of activities unless those beliefs can be articulated in terms of benefits that people, as individuals, will appreciate. For example, fostering a healthy ecology is often thought to have its own moral value; cost-benefit analysis can account for this but only insofar as that value can be translated into valued improvements.

Given enough data and analytical capability, willingness to pay measures can encompass the so-called "use values" of ecological systems, such as better health, more pleasant living conditions, or more reliable resource availability for current and future residents of the Earth. They also encompass non-use values, *i.e.*, the intrinsic value people assign to the existence of certain species or other ecological goods, even if they do not directly contribute otherwise to an individual's well-being – for example, species living in the deep sea that the individual is unlikely to ever encounter in real life. The point is, the cost-benefit analyst's job is to measure what ordinary citizens are willing to pay for such things, not what a government body thinks is important; there is, of course, room for the latter in decision-making, but the idea of CBA is to make such judgments explicit when they override individual preferences.

The willingness-to-pay principle has actually been present throughout the analysis of this book. For example, in Chapter 2 we measured the values of travel time and reliability from the way individuals trade them against price in travel-demand models; they are simply travelers' willingness to pay for time savings or reliability improvements. The costs defined in Chapter 3 measure the collective willingness to pay by individuals and transportation providers for any savings in their required inputs of time, fuel, labor, and other things. The area under a demand curve, introduced in equation (4.2) as a benefit measure, is an approximate indicator of travelers' collective willingness to pay for the quantity of travel consumed.

Figure 5.2 illustrates the relationship between willingness to pay and the demand curve. The downward sloping line depicts the demand for bus trips as a function of generalized price (see Section 2.3.3) by users with identical values of time.[19] These users differ in other ways, causing some but not all to choose the bus at a given generalized price. Suppose a service improvement speeds up the buses and thereby lowers the generalized price from p^0 to p^1. There are Q^0 existing users, each willing to pay $(p^0 - p^1)$ for the improvement; their aggregate willingness to pay is therefore the rectangular area $p^0 AF p^1$. The improvement also attracts Q^1-Q^0 new users; some (those most easily attracted) are willing to pay almost (p^0-p^1) for the improvement, while others (those just barely attracted) are willing to pay very little. Adding them together, aggregate willingness to pay for new users is the triangular area ABF. The total willingness to pay for the change, from both existing and new users, is therefore the trapezoid $p^0 ABp^1$. This area is the change in consumer surplus (*i.e.*, gross consumer benefits minus total amount paid), which changes from triangle GAp^0 to triangle GBp^1.

Recall that generalized price consists of a monetary charge τ (a road toll, or a public transport fare) plus user cost, the latter consisting (in this example) of travel time valued according to the user's preferences, $v_T \cdot T$. Suppose now T is reduced to $T+\Delta T$, where $\Delta T < 0$, by measures with aggregate resources cost ΔC.

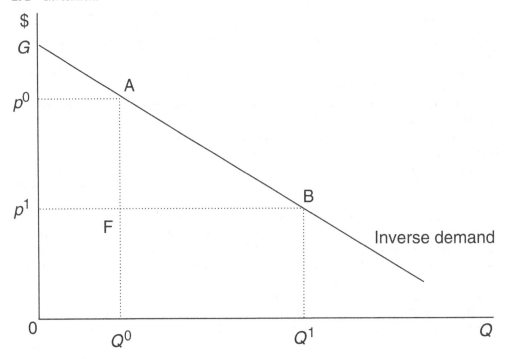

Figure 5.2 Benefits to existing and new users

Allowing both money price and user cost to change, we can then write the change in consumer surplus as:

$$\Delta CS = -Q^0 \Delta p + \int_{Q^0}^{Q^1} \left[p(Q) - p_1 \right] dQ$$

$$\approx -Q^0 \Delta p - \frac{1}{2} \Delta p \Delta Q$$

$$= -\left(Q_0 + \frac{1}{2} \Delta Q \right) \Delta \tau - \left(Q_0 + \frac{1}{2} \Delta Q \right) v_T \Delta T \tag{5.22}$$

where the linear approximation in the second line becomes exact when demand is exactly linear, as drawn here. Equation (5.22) represents gains to consumers; the third line shows that it is positive if T is lowered enough: specifically, if $v_T \Delta T \geq \Delta \tau$ Producers (possibly including government) incur some cost ΔC, and also gain or lose revenues, for a total change in producer profit[20]

$$\Delta \Pi = -\Delta C + \left(Q_0 + \frac{1}{2} \Delta Q \right) \Delta \tau. \tag{5.23}$$

Net social benefits are the sum of (5.22) and (5.23):

$$\Delta W \equiv \Delta CS + \Delta \Pi$$

$$= \left\{ -\left(Q_0 + \frac{1}{2} \Delta Q \right) \Delta \tau - \left(Q_0 + \frac{1}{2} \Delta Q \right) v_T \Delta T \right\} + \left\{ \left(Q_0 + \frac{1}{2} \Delta Q \right) \Delta \tau - \Delta C \right\}.$$

$$= \left\{ -\left(Q_0 + \frac{1}{2} \Delta Q \right) v_T \Delta T \right\} - \left\{ \Delta C \right\} \tag{5.24}$$

The third line of (5.24) follows from the second because the change in fare revenues cancel out: it offsets the benefits to consumers, but adds to profits of producers, and we weigh these effects equally in this example (ignoring a possible reweighting due to the marginal cost of public funds).

The second and third lines in (5.24) in fact represent two different ways of grouping the component costs and benefits (here indicated by curly brackets). The second line, sometimes called *surplus* accounting, shows net benefits to users and those to producers. It is needed for calculating the distribution of net benefits. The third line, sometimes called *resource-cost* accounting, shows benefits and costs of the physical changes that occur (here, a saving ΔT in travel time).[21] This is the version needed if a benefit–cost ratio is to be reported, as then the ratio is unaffected by purely financial flows. We caution that studies are not always explicit about which accounting version is being described.

It is worth noting that the change in consumers' aggregate generalized payments $p^1Q^1 - p^0Q^0$ (*i.e.*, the difference between areas of rectangles p^0AQ^00 and p^1BQ^10) creates an opportunity for them to spend more money or time on other things. Since these "payments" are already incorporated in the costs and benefits, it would be double-counting to include them as benefits in other markets. This result changes if prices in those other markets do not reflect social marginal costs; we discuss one example of such a case in Section 5.2.5.

Figure 5.2 and the approximation in the second line of equation (5.22) reflect a very useful rule of thumb for calculating the net benefits to new users of a decrease in generalized price. With a linear demand curve as drawn, area ABF is half the number of newly attracted users multiplied by the reduction in generalized price. If demand is not exactly linear but the change in quantity is fairly small, this statement is still a reasonable approximation, known as the "rule of half." The rule of half remains valid for sets of interdependent markets such as travel networks serving multiple origin–destination pairs, and remains exact when also the cross-demand effects are linear. Suppose, for example, we expand capacity of part of a road network, as described earlier in this chapter. We can denote the equilibrium quantities (travel flows) in market m before and after an investment in a road network as V_m^0 and V_m^1, respectively; and the corresponding generalized prices as p_m^0 and p_m^1. The rule of half then states that the change in aggregate consumer surplus over the full network is given by:

$$\Delta CS = -\sum_{m=1}^{M} V_m^0 \Delta p_m - \sum_{m=1}^{M} \tfrac{1}{2} \cdot \left(V_m^1 - V_m^0 \right) \cdot \Delta p_m$$
$$= -\sum_{m=1}^{M} \tfrac{1}{2} \cdot \left(V_m^0 + V_m^1 \right) \cdot \Delta p_m.$$

In the last line, we see that this measure of benefits is the sum (over markets) of the average use, before and after the investment, multiplied by the reduction in generalized price – a very intuitive result. This approximation greatly simplifies the estimation of benefits, because it is not necessary to measure all the interdependent demand curves, but only the initial and final quantities in each market and the changes in generalized prices. This is very helpful for back-of-the-envelope computations. For a more detailed analysis of a project's or policy's benefits, it is desirable to base benefit estimates directly upon the utility or demand functions used in the models through which the final quantities are computed, not only for improved accuracy but also to avoid inconsistencies between assumed behavior and benefits attached to that behavior.

Some inputs that are part of the generalized price p are not freely traded in markets. We have already seen how to deal with these in the case of users' time, for which we imputed a value. But observable monetary prices also need not fully or correctly reflect social values. For example, price controls on gasoline sometimes result in informal fuel rationing. As a result, many consumers who purchase rationed fuel would be willing to pay more than its resource cost; others might be willing to pay less due to time and effort required by the rationing scheme. In such cases, the analyst may be able to calculate a *shadow price*, different from the market price, that reflects true resource cost. This is the same issue, but now applied to users, as that requiring producer costs to be adjusted to reflect the true resource costs when input markets are distorted.

Most projects have diverse effects that will benefit some people and harm others. Granted that we can measure each person's willingness to pay (negative if they are harmed), why should we be interested in the result of adding them all together? The answer is that by doing so, cost-benefit analysis can identify projects that are *potential Pareto improvements*: *i.e.*, projects for which winners could compensate losers, leaving all better off. For example, a new highway interchange may save enough people time that they could compensate those harmed by extra noise and traffic. Mechanisms exist for such compensation, but they are far from perfect; as a result, few if any projects can be strict Pareto improvements and thereby achieve unanimous support. Indeed, one can argue that it is precisely the absence of such unanimity that creates the need for cost-benefit analysis to aid public decision-making.

Nevertheless, if projects were consistently analyzed and undertaken only when they are potential Pareto improvements, it could be expected that the losers from some projects would be winners from others. Given enough randomness in the effects of different projects, "most persons ... would be better off by reason of the program as a whole" (Hotelling 1938, pp. 258–259). If so, the joint result of many potential Pareto improvements would be a strict Pareto improvement after all. This argument is formalized by Polinsky (1972) and supported through simulation by Zerbe (2020), who explores an important qualification: the result is destroyed by too high a correlation in the individualized impacts of various projects.

5.2.2   Demand and cost forecasts

The most critical component of a cost-benefit analysis is simply predicting what will happen. The desirability of a new or improved facility depends especially on how much it will cost and how many people will use it. Yet, as already noted in Section 4.5.3, there are wide disparities between forecast and realized results of transportation infrastructure projects, for both costs and demands. Furthermore, the discrepancies are generally not random or neutral in sign, but instead are biased toward making projects look more favorable than they turn out to be.

Flyvbjerg *et al.* (2004, 2005) analyze the factors determining the size and direction of forecasting errors based on worldwide samples of over 200 projects. For cost projections, they find that errors grow rapidly with the time it takes to build the project. Public and private projects show similar patterns, except that state-owned enterprises lacking financial transparency are less accurate. For demand projections, forecast errors for rail projects are especially large and show optimism bias; those for roads are also large in magnitude but show little bias. Some authors have found smaller inaccuracies and biases for toll roads (Bain 2009).

The authors of National Academies (2020) compile a comprehensive database of traffic forecasts for road projects, mostly from the USA but some also from Denmark, Norway, Sweden, and the UK. They find plenty of inaccuracy but only a modest bias, about 6%; more accuracy for larger projects; and less accuracy for longer time horizons. They also find that forecasts have improved over time, and that they are better when developed using formal traffic models. Highlighting the importance of economic conditions, they find an important predictor of forecast inaccuracy is the unemployment rate in the year a new road opens.[22]

By contrast, Flyvbjerg and Bester (2021) find overwhelming bias in cost estimates from over 1,200 transportation projects from around the world and covering nearly a century. They measure average cost overruns on specific investment types, with results ranging from 24% for roads to 40% for rail and bus rapid transit projects.[23] They report little systematic difference in bias by time, geography, or level of economic development. Benefit estimates also show bias, but much less so, ranging from 4% for roads and bridges to roughly 34% for rail and bus rapid transit.[24]

Various proposals have been made to reduce such discrepancies and, especially, to eliminate biases that systematically cause poor investments to be undertaken. Recommended actions include sensitivity analysis, limiting the time horizon, and subjecting forecasting procedures to independent audits. Most important, perhaps, is to systematically collect before-and-after data and to regularly perform and report comparisons. Flyvbjerg and Bester (2021) go on to propose that financial or legal incentives be applied to forecasters and planners. They also advocate systematic "de-biasing" of forecasts, by applying an observed distribution of forecast errors, such as those they estimate, to adjust any particular result before using it for public decisions. This sounds sensible, but creates a challenge in making such a procedure consistent over time, as forecasters will learn about and react to such post-analysis adjustments.

Two explanations for the systematic bias in forecasts have been put forward: That errors are due to strategic attempts to favor investments or that observed discrepancies are due to selection bias that occurs during the process determining which investments get implemented.

Clear evidence of bias goes back at least to Wachs (1989, 1990), who uncovered, through interviews, strong politically motivated processes leading to misrepresentation in demand forecasts for urban transportation investments. As a result, he was a strong advocate for addressing this with professional ethics guidelines for planners (Wachs 2013). Cadot *et al.* (2006) find statistically that infrastructure investments in France's regions from 1985 to 1992 were strongly influenced by measures of political factors. Bent Flyvbjerg and associates have long found evidence of bias in demand forecasts (as described in Chapter 2) as well as in cost forecasts. Flyvbjerg and Bester (2021) summarize and extend this analysis. They firmly believe that the main reason for bias is strategic, while acknowledging that some selection bias is possible.

Eliasson and Fosgerau (2013), by contrast, argue the observed cost overruns and demand overestimations for realized projects can be explained by selection bias: if only those projects that looked good on paper when originally analyzed went on to pass the decision-making stage, the observed set of implemented investments will contain a disproportionate number of forecast errors that favor implementation (*i.e.*, low cost or high demand). The authors demonstrate both theoretically and using simulations that under plausible conditions, selecting projects for implementation based on *ex ante* predicted payoffs causes the average selected project to have a higher payoff than the average potential project, even if random forecasting errors are quite large; and, importantly, that the magnitude of this selection bias is comparable to what has been observed in practice.

Thus, it appears that both factors are important. We agree with many other professionals that at a minimum, measures to reduce systematic bias are warranted. Flyvbjerg and Bester (2021) argue further that such measures must be part of an overall plan to improve the political process of investment choice – consistent with our view that cost-benefit analysis is ultimately part of such a political process and so must be designed to support good outcomes within it.

5.2.3   *Discounting future costs and benefits*

We already mentioned how costs or benefits incurred over time can be converted to an equivalent present value or an equivalent constant annualized flow (Section 3.4.9). The basic principle is that any expenditure C undertaken in year t could be funded by investing some smaller amount PV today (year 0) and regularly reinvesting its financial yield. Assuming a constant interest rate r, compounded annually, they are related by $PV \cdot (1 + r)^t = C$; *i.e.*, $PV = C/(1 + r)^t$.

The quantity PV is called the *present value* of the future expenditure. More generally, a series of expenditures C_t in years $t = 1, ..., T$ has present value

$$PV = \sum_{t=1}^{T} \frac{C_t}{(1+r)^t}.$$ (5.25)

The same principle works for benefits if one assumes that people have access to capital markets at interest rate r. This is because, if they were required to pay an amount PV in conjunction with receiving a stream of benefits $\{B_t\}$ over time, they could borrow or lend in the capital markets in order to be just as well off in each year as before, provided PV is given by (5.25) with C_t replaced by B_t.

However, capital markets are far from perfect and many transactions are carried out at interest rates different from the one observed in formal capital markets. On the one hand, consumers can usually receive only low rates on their savings, if they even have any; so they may be willing to trade money against time only at a low rate, called the *marginal rate of time preference*. On the other hand, businesses pay taxes on their investment returns, causing them to undertake socially productive investment only when its rate considerably exceeds the rate at which they can raise capital (through borrowing or by issuing equity shares). If a proposed project displaces private investment subject to such taxes, the appropriate rate for cost-benefit analysis would be the before-tax rate of return to private capital, sometimes called the *value of marginal product of capital*. These arguments have led analysts to widely different opinions about the appropriate interest rate for discounting benefits in CBA, known as the *discount rate*. Since the choice of discount rate strongly affects present values in the distant future, such debates are particularly fierce for the evaluation of climate change effects, as discussed in Chapter 7.

When inflation is expected, the value of future consumption or cost savings brought about by investing capital today will be less than the nominal returns indicated by financial accounts; this is accounted for by defining a *real rate of interest* approximately equal to $r = n - \pi$, where n is any particular nominal rate of interest and π is the rate of inflation.[25]

How would these discount rates be measured? Let's start with the consumption-oriented measure, the marginal rate of time preference. This is conventionally measured using the Ramsey (1928) model of an economy steadily growing (in real terms) at rate g while optimizing the rate of investment to maximize an inter-temporal social welfare function. Suppose that the welfare function embodies a "pure" rate of time preference ρ over utilities achieved at different times, and also incorporates an elasticity η of marginal social utility with respect to average consumption at a given time. The former is based on consumers' preferences, the latter on social preferences over distributions across different consumers. Thus, a positive value of η can be viewed as representing aversion to inter-temporal inequality of achieved utilities (*i.e.*, inequality across generations). The Ramsey model shows that capital markets adjust so that capital earns a rate of return:

$$r_{SW} = \rho + g\eta.$$

Here, we follow Goulder and Williams (2012) in subscripting this discount rate by SW to indicate it is relevant to maximizing a social welfare function. Goulder and Williams list three computations in the literature, using plausible values for these underlying parameters. These computations result in values of r_{SW} between 1.4% and 4.3% for very long-term investments. Moore *et al.* (2013) measure r_{SW} at 3.5% for ordinary capital investments.

Turning to the investment-oriented measure, the marginal product of capital, we again follow Goulder and Williams by denoting it as r_F. It is measured as the pre-tax financial rate of return on capital, which incorporates both a risk-free interest rate (*e.g.*, that on safe government long-term bonds) and a risk premium reflecting uncertainty in the returns that will actually be realized.[26] It also incorporates any tax wedge reflecting capital taxes. Taylor (2018) reviews more than a century of asset returns on equities (*i.e.*, stocks), housing, and bonds, for sixteen highly developed nations in Western Europe plus Japan, Australia, and the USA. He finds typical real interest rates of 1%–3% on risk-free bonds, and 6%–8% on equities and housing. Taylor therefore concludes that risk premia have averaged 4%–5%. In fact, the risk premia have been more stable than either the risk-free returns or total returns, as the latter vary with macroeconomic conditions. Burgess and Zerbe (2013) estimate r_F to be 7%, in the middle of the range found by Taylor.

The results of cost-benefit analyses, especially of long-lived investments, can vary enormously depending on whether r_{SW} or r_F is used as a discount rate. Moore *et al.* (2013) and Burgess and Zerbe (2013) make strong cases for r_{SW} and r_F, respectively. They appear to agree that the issue hinges on whether one assumes that the project's costs are financed by current taxes or by government borrowing. The former implies a reduction in current consumption, whereas the latter causes the government to compete in capital markets, crowding out private investments via interest rate changes. The estimates of these two rates quoted above, namely $r_{SW} = 3.5\%$ and $r_F = 7\%$, are close to the low and high rates recommended by US OMB (2003) for evaluation of US public projects.[27]

Each of these estimates contains uncertainty, as both depend on several auxiliary quantities that are not easily measured. Indeed, the assumptions behind the two rates involve projecting both a "business as usual" scenario describing what will happen without the project, and a macroeconomic scenario describing how the project affects current and future interest rates, taxes, and investment – including the institutional factors governing tax rates and central bank policy. In reality, economies and government decision-making processes are too complex for either of the two suggested approaches to hold in pure form. It is common, therefore, to advocate a real interest rate somewhere in the middle of the range defined by the two alternate proposals. This would be about 5% for the United States on average, while recognizing that the appropriate rate may vary greatly across situations, nations, and over time.

We suggest a lower rate of 4% for the US transportation investments, however, for two reasons. First, most such investments are not funded by private debt and so do not carry the default risk of private firms (with its implication for including a risk premium in the discount rate). Second, uncertainty in the appropriate discount rate requires that one compute the *expected* present value of benefits, in a probabilistic sense; this has been shown to be equivalent to computing a present value under *certainty* but using a lower discount rate (Weitzman 2001; Moore *et al.* 2013).

When turning to the extremely long-term investments in climate-change mitigation, we will choose a still lower rate, as explained in Section 7.3.2. The main reason is that the second effect just mentioned, caused by uncertainty in the discount rate itself, is stronger, the longer the time horizon.

The sensitivity of the present value of benefits to the discount rate is even more pronounced if benefits are small at the beginning and grow rapidly over time, as is typical of new transportation facilities in areas undergoing population growth. Partly because of this, cost-benefit practitioners have often found it easy to manipulate the results to favor an outcome that they desire by altering their assumed interest rate. As a damper to such practices, government agencies often promulgate rules, or at least guidelines, for how other agencies and private parties should choose interest rates and other key analytical elements when presenting cost-benefit analyses of government projects.[28] In addition, it is near universal to recommend or require that sensitivity analysis be undertaken by recomputing results at different interest rates.

5.2.4 Distortions

Often, observable or market prices do not reflect the true social cost of a resource whose valuation is needed for a cost-benefit analysis. Examples include labor markets, in which search costs and macroeconomic phenomena may prevent the market from clearing as would a perfectly competitive market;[29] resources such as petroleum and food whose production is subsidized or otherwise regulated; and information. These non-market effects are sometimes treated by adjusting the observed price; for example, the social cost of fuel might be computed at a price reflecting externalities. Alternatively, non-market effects can be estimated and incorporated explicitly, *e.g.* by estimating the ancillary benefits or costs of a policy through its effects on climate or local pollution, and including them as additional costs or benefits.

A very common distortion is the effects of taxes that fund government expenditures. In Section 4.2.6, we analyzed how this affects pricing, and in Section 5.1.3 how it affects second-best optimal highway capacity. The same issues affect measurement of the costs of any investment or policy that changes governments' fiscal balances.

Calthrop *et al.* (2010) provide a general treatment of how distortions affect CBA. Their results imply that a marginal road investment dI creates an additional social cost due to fiscal distortions equal to:

$$dC = MCF \cdot \left(1 - \frac{\partial R}{\partial T}\frac{\partial T}{\partial I}\right)dI, \tag{5.26}$$

where MCF is the marginal cost of public funds as defined earlier; R is total government revenue (including from distorting taxes); and T is users' travel times.[30] The term MCF captures the exacerbation of tax or other distortions, just as in Section 5.1. The term multiplying it captures how alleviation of congestion may alter revenues, *e.g.* through fuel taxes or labor-supply shifts due to changed commuting cost. Needless to say, (5.26) is more of a framework than a concrete result: the real challenge of transport appraisal in a world of distortions is to quantify and measure its components.

5.2.5 Wider economic benefits and network effects

Promoters of projects like to highlight various benefits such as jobs created, real-estate development induced, economic activity attracted, or industrial activities facilitated by a transportation improvement. Indeed, such "wider economic benefits" are often promoted as the project's primary rationale. As we have discussed, many such impacts are not net benefits additional to what can be measured from the demand for the use of the facility, but rather transfers from other locations, or conversions of direct benefits, already measured in conventional cost-benefit analysis, to another form.

For example, consider the benefits of "industrial reorganization," by which transportation improvements enable firms to create more efficient systems of distribution or of production.[31] Mohring and Williamson (1969) show that these benefits, while quite possibly real, are already captured in the demand curve for transportation that is the basis for conventional benefit measurement. To illustrate: consider again Figure 5.2 and suppose it represents demand for urban freight travel by industrial firms. The ability to reorganize distribution or production through cheaper transportation is represented by the amount the firms are willing to pay for the Q^1–Q^0 new trips that make this reorganization possible. Thus, area ABF already captures their value to firms.

Nevertheless, some societal benefits do not fully accrue to people using the infrastructure to be evaluated, and may then not be fully reflected in the demand for its use. Such benefits are often referred to as the *wider economic benefits* of transport infrastructure improvement: basically, encompassing all benefits that are not reflected through surplus measures that can be derived from market demand functions. Such effects may in fact be either positive or negative, and arise when the markets from which the demand for transport is derived do not function perfectly (*e.g.*, SACTRA 1999). The measurement of this type of wider economic benefit is entirely legitimate and, when done correctly, should not lead to double counting. Such effects are likely to be important in at least three situations, each indeed involving the pre-existence of failures in the markets served by the new or improved infrastructure.

First, transportation improvements may reduce the market power of firms by promoting trade among previously isolated locations. Jara-Díaz (1986) illustrates this process with a model of two firms, each initially a monopolist within its own region; a transportation improvement creates social benefits, not reflected by the transport demand curve, by reducing their monopoly power. Similarly, improved transportation can create social benefits by reducing firms' monopsony power over their labor, as demonstrated empirically by Brooks *et al.* (2021) for an expressway in India. These types of wider benefits of transportation projects are especially important in developing economies and isolated rural areas, where inter-regional trade is significantly impeded by high transportation costs, enhancing local market power.[32]

A second reason why transport demand functions need not perfectly reflect social benefits concerns the existence of distortionary taxes, as discussed in Section 5.2.4 above. The argument fully parallels the discussion in Section 4.2.6 on how labor taxes might affect second-best congestion tolls for commuters. Also, for the assessment of the benefits of discrete improvements through infrastructure investments, the labor tax would create a wedge between the marginal private benefits (willingness to pay), which are depressed because of the tax, and the marginal social benefits, for which the tax revenues count as a gain for the government that compensates for the loss to travelers. The same is true for fuel taxes – irrespective of whether these may reflect marginal environmental external costs, which are measured separately and considered as a social cost in a complete CBA. The wedge can be interpreted as creating wider economic benefits from transport projects, as it is not reflected by the inverse demand for transport.

A third source of wider economic effects is *economies of agglomeration*, that is, cost reductions made possible when a large number of firms exist in proximity. These economies are at the heart of why cities exist, and so are widespread and significant. When an additional firm locates in an urban area, it reaps some of these advantages but creates benefits that are external to itself, by adding to density benefits experienced by other firms. This phenomenon involves a reciprocal externality, very much like congestion except it conveys positive rather than negative benefits. Good transportation enlarges the effective size of an urban agglomeration by enabling more firms and households to interact, thereby enhancing labor matching, knowledge sharing, and other sources of urban agglomeration (*e.g.*, Duranton and Puga 2004). Agglomeration economies may thus drive a wedge between the societal benefits of transport infrastructure improvement and the users' willingness to pay for them, justifying the consideration of wider economic benefits in infrastructure appraisal (Venables 2007). Graham and Gibbons (2019) discuss a number of methodological challenges that have to be overcome to put this seemingly simple advice into sound practice. And Eliasson and Fosgerau (2019) point to a potential pitfall in doing so: not all agglomeration forces constitute market failures. For example, the benefits from labor market matching may be partly reflected already in the demand for transport, so counting them as a wider would be partly double-counting.

Economies of agglomeration are commonly called "external economies" in the literature on urban economics, because they arise from beneficial effects of economic activity that are not captured by the firm or other decision-maker undertaking that activity. The connection to transportation is indirect: improved transportation better facilitates such activities, so creating transportation infrastructure may lead to some such "wider" benefits, since it is helping to partially correct a market failure in urban development. However, the transportation itself is not necessarily what creates this wider benefit: for example, encouraging shoppers to travel to more distance retail outlets would do so only if it encourages greater product differentiation. And, making a detour on the way to such outlets without stopping, so an expansion of transport activities alone, certainly will not generate agglomeration benefits. For this reason, we do not call them "external economies" within a transportation context.

The magnitude of agglomeration economies is the subject of extensive research, with results usually summarized as the elasticity of productivity as a function of economic size or density. Combes and Gobillon (2015) survey empirical estimations, finding the most reliable estimates of the agglomeration elasticity with respect to economic density tending to be in the range 0.04–0.07 (Combes and Gobillon, p. 299).

How much are these agglomeration economies enhanced by transportation improvements? Glaeser and Ponzetto (2010) model theoretically how improved transportation and communications raise productivity by facilitating the spread of ideas within cities. For example, Bailey *et al.* (2020) document a concrete example: they find that inter-zonal social contacts within the New York metropolitan area are strongly influenced by transportation costs, even when the communications themselves are via social media. Duranton and Puga (2001) show how transportation improvements also lead to innovative product development in diversified cities. The key role of transportation is further highlighted by findings that agglomeration effects attenuate rapidly with distance (Rosenthal and Strange 2020).

Empirical evidence supports the hypothesis that transportation infrastructure can enhance urban productivity. For example, transportation-induced productivity elasticities have been measured for the UK, with typical estimates also in the range 0.04–0.07 (Graham and Gibbons 2019).[33] Such results have been applied widely to cost-benefit studies of transportation investments, sometimes suggesting that including agglomeration effects substantially increase net benefits.[34] Researchers have begun to formally incorporate general-equilibrium location models in order to consistently measure secondary effects on transportation variables such as travel times, and on the spatial reallocation of population and economic activity. In one example, Tsivanidis (forthcoming) finds that the spatial reorganization induced by the TransMilenio system in Bogotá (Colombia), a large investment in bus rapid transit, probably added 20%–40% to its benefits and substantially changed its impacts on income distribution.[35] As another example, Anas and Chang (2023) determine that agglomeration economies will contribute substantially to benefits from the Grand Paris Express project, a very large and long-term plan for new rail and bus service connecting outlying areas of Paris circumferentially.

In very well-developed urban areas, incremental transportation improvements may have smaller effects because most locations are already well connected. By way of analogy, Fernald (1999) finds evidence that the US Interstate Highway System created substantial productivity gains in its early years, but that later additions had much smaller effects – presumably due to diminishing returns.

Incorporating wider economic effects into cost-benefit analysis is now recognized as appropriate, but doing so needs sophistication. A transportation improvement may attract nearby economic activity from other locations, in which case any local agglomeration benefits must be weighed against possible agglomeration losses elsewhere. Furthermore, agglomeration benefits are substantially affected by the overall tax system (Kanemoto 2013). For all these reasons, government guidelines for project evaluation sometimes spell out how to measure the effects and avoid double-counting. Graham and Gibbons (2019) provide a good example of this process in the UK.

Some of the interactions that are important to agglomeration take place in offices or between nearby locations. The COVID-19 pandemic suddenly and dramatically changed the nature of in-person communications, at least for a time, as workers learned to interact virtually. This will create the opportunity for much fruitful research into how such communications affect agglomeration. Based on older research, they are probably mainly complementary with transportation (Salomon 1985; Mokhtarian 1990, 2009). It seems that people prefer to interact electronically with others whom they sometimes see in person – so that long-distance digital contacts, whether private or professional, may eventually result in additional travel for purposes of physical meetings. As we write, researchers and others who are interested in the role of urban downtowns – real estate developers, building owners, corporate managers, and public transportation officials – are attempting to determine the extent to which the COVID-induced shift will persist and how it will change commuting. Early indications are that following relaxation of COVID restrictions, commuting patterns partially bounced back to pre-COVID levels, while working from home became popular as a longer-term option. Whatever the final outcome, these changes will have significant implications for both the direct and the indirect benefits of transportation investments.

5.2.6 Example: High-speed rail

One type of investment that is very expensive, and ripe for more cost-benefit analysis, is high-speed rail. This set of technologies, introduced first in Japan and France, has become an important part of many national and international transportation policies, especially in Europe and China. While not strictly a form of urban transportation, high-speed rail has profound effects on urban development and on the way urban transit systems are configured to work with it. For example, Zheng and Kahn (2013) suggest that China's high-speed trains will relieve transportation problems in China's very large cities by moving some economic activity to smaller (but still large) cities connected to them.

High-speed rail is an example of an investment with very large initial capital cost and a long payoff period. For this reason, uncertainty in the elements of a cost-benefit analysis becomes magnified in the final result. With so much money at stake, not to mention personal interests in the various local impacts, it is no surprise that many high-speed rail projects are controversial. Good economic analysis cannot remove these features, but it can help by narrowing the range of argument.

One complication is that high-speed rail is not a single well-defined type of transportation, but rather covers a range of possibilities. Campos and de Rus (2009) distinguish four methods, which they call "exploitation models," for how high-speed technology can be applied, depending on the nature of the rail infrastructure and vehicle stock. The highest level of service is provided by *exclusive* infrastructure and vehicles, such as Japan's Shinkansen. Other models involve various forms of sharing with conventional rail: *mixed high-speed*, in which some trackage consists of upgraded conventional tracks; *mixed conventional*, in which the high-speed lines are also open to some conventional trains; and *fully mixed*, in which high-speed and conventional trains can both use either type of track. The mixed high-speed model is exemplified by the French Train à Grande Vitesse (TGV); mixed conventional by the Spanish Alta Velocidad Española (AVE); and fully mixed by the German intercity (ICE) service.[36] These options offer trade-offs between high service quality (at high cost) at one extreme and operational flexibility at the other. For example, when freight and passenger traffic are mixed, several diseconomies of scope come into play, such as maintenance activities slowing down passenger trains and difficulty in designing track to handle both high speeds and heavy loads.

With these different operational models, it is easy to see that cost-benefit analysis will require measuring very specific cost components, including (in the mixed models) infrastructure and operational costs of various vehicle types on various track types. Thus, there is likely no single answer to whether or not a given high-speed rail link passes a cost-benefit test. Nevertheless, it is possible to give tentative answers for specific cases. This is the goal of the retrospective evaluation by de Rus (2012) of the first AVE line, 471 km long, opened in 1992 between Madrid and Seville. During its first year, its traffic consisted of new trips (15%) and diverted trips: from air (45%), from conventional train (26%), from car (12%), and from bus (2%).

We provide in Table 5.1 some summary results of de Rus's complete calculation of costs and benefits for this line, all discounted to the time when construction began (1987). (They are expressed here at 2020 price levels.) We also show the percentage that each component comprises of total benefits or of total costs. The base case uses a real discount rate of 5%, reflecting the high interest rates that prevailed when the line was built. An alternative calculation is shown using a discount rate of 3%. These calculations do not include environmental benefits, such as those related to carbon dioxide emissions.

These results are unfavorable for this line, with a cost-benefit ratio of 67% in the base case and 86% at the lower discount rate. (As noted earlier, a lower discount rate substantially enlarges the benefits because they occur later than most of the costs.) De Rus suggests that the main reason for this poor performance is relatively low demand for all trips in this corridor.

The relative magnitudes are instructive. The largest *cost* is the initial investment in infrastructure. Next comes operation and maintenance costs, which (like benefits) are sensitive to the interest rate because they are shown as present discounted values at the time of initial construction. If we instead presented annualized costs, it would be capital (*i.e.*, investment) that is sensitive to the discount rate, its costs being smaller at lower interest rates as explained earlier.

The largest *benefit* is time savings for trips formerly taken using land transportation. Next is cost savings for those same trips, and also for trips by air (for which time savings are minimal).

Table 5.1 Costs and Benefits of Madrid-Seville High-Speed Rail (1987 present values, expressed in millions of 2020 Euros)

	Discount rate 5%		Discount rate 3%	
	Amount	% of total	Amount	% of total
Costs				
Infrastructure investment	4,635	60.6%	5,026	50.8%
Infrastructure maintenance	633	8.3%	994	10.0%
Rolling stock investment	359	4.7%	490	4.9%
Rolling stock operation & maintenance	2,023	26.4%	3,386	34.2%
Total costs	7,651	100.0%	9,896	100.0%
Benefits				
Time savings (conventional train & car)	1,548	30.4%	2,656	31.3%
Time savings (air)	176	3.5%	302	3.6%
Cost savings (conventional train & car)	1,325	26.0%	2,172	25.6%
Cost savings (air)	839	16.5%	1,371	16.2%
Accidents	254	5.0%	391	4.6%
Generated demand	879	17.2%	1,467	17.3%
Other (congestion, savings on bus)	77	1.5%	132	1.6%
Total benefits	5,100	100.0%	8,490	100.0%
Total benefits/total costs	0.667		0.858	

Source: de Rus (2012), Table 2 and RI (2024).

These are measured using resource-cost accounting, as defined in Section 5.2.1. Another significant benefit is "generated demand," *i.e.*, the value to new travelers on this corridor of the improved options. It is measured by the area under their demand curve less fares paid (which again are netted out by operator revenue, so not incorporated explicitly in resource-costs accounting).

Many of these quantities are far from simple to measure. Time savings, for example, include faster line-haul speed relative to car, partially offset by increased access time. For air travel, the opposite holds: high-speed rail is slower in the line haul but faster for access. Thus, the relative values of access and line-haul time are critical to the calculation of the time-savings component of benefits. These relative values depend on specific conditions: for example, the extent of security required for rail boarding and the convenience (or possibly inconvenience) of having a car at the destination, as one would if traveling by car. Furthermore, air travel is a highly complex market typically involving route-specific oligopoly or monopoly power, strategic interactions between firms, and much government intervention; thus, the full resource costs of a new mode that is highly competitive with air are far from transparent.[37] These are just some of many limitations in our ability to provide generalizable results from this specific case study.

De Rus goes on to a retrospective analysis of another Spanish AVE line, that connecting Madrid to Barcelona, which opened in 2008. Its results are even less favorable, showing a benefit–cost ratio of 0.56 and 0.77 at the higher and lower discount rates, respectively. De Rus calculates that demand would have to more than double for benefits to exceed costs. These results are far from definitive, yet they suggest extreme caution in building such expensive infrastructure in a region whose population density is not especially great and which is relatively isolated from other large population centers. The pessimistic results of de Rus's analyses of these two high-speed rail lines are in line with a later overall evaluation by an independent Spanish fiscal monitoring organization (AIReF 2020).

As already mentioned, a broader picture of high-speed rail is made difficult by the importance of local conditions. Nevertheless, it is helpful to have at hand a description of the range of values of key parameters experienced in cities around the world. Campos and de Rus (2009) provide just this kind of analysis, carefully estimating costs of infrastructure, maintenance, investment, and maintenance of rolling stock, and environmental costs (which are found to be small) for high-speed rail in a variety of European countries under various conditions. Results such as these, expanded and updated regularly, could be a valuable starting point for first-pass evaluations of possible new routes. Two summary comments by Campos and de Rus are worth highlighting: first, that demand for this transport technology is promising when the population density is high; and second, that "this is a very expensive and risky alternative method of transport" (Campos and de Rus 2009, p. 27). We would add that even if including environmental benefits would substantially change their numbers, this second conclusion would still apply to a modified question: how promising is high-speed rail as a policy to achieve goals for greenhouse gas emissions, relative to other policies?

5.2.7 Conclusion: the use and misuse of cost-benefit analysis

In the end, cost-benefit analysis is undertaken to inform decision-makers, including members of the public who may influence those decisions. One can hope that by making the impacts of a project transparent and by quantifying them in consistent ways, the decision-making process – inherently political – can be guided toward better decisions. As a technical process, cost-benefit analysis is of course prone to mistakes in implementation and interpretation – see, for example, Nardinelli (2018). As a political process, it will inevitably be subjected to pressures to misuse it for the benefit of particular interest groups. Professionals and public officials can reduce both kinds of misuse by developing clear procedural guidelines and articulating them both to practitioners and to the public.[38] Furthermore, the cost-benefit analyses themselves need to be transparent, as well as technically sound, so that such misuse can be identified.

One way to ensure that users can understand the implications of particular assumptions is through sensitivity analysis. One type of such analysis is *risk analysis*. It postulates specific probability density functions for uncertain parameters, then uses Monte Carlo simulation to compute the corresponding frequency distribution of any particular result of interest. This has the advantage of making uncertainty explicit. Yet, there is a danger: formalizing uncertainty may lead to a false sense of precision about how uncertainty can be characterized. For example, even if uncertainty about each parameter is accurately known, it may be hard to guess how such uncertainties are correlated across parameters. Furthermore, in many cases – especially in developing nations – the outcome may be affected more by administrative competence, sabotage, or breakdown of related markets than by the elements formalized in risk analysis (Jenkins 1997). And, sensitivity analysis alone cannot uncover the kinds of systematic bias discussed earlier.

Another point of concern in CBA applications is distributional effects. Users of CBA outcomes understandably focus on the more easily conveyed summary indicators about a project, such as the cost-benefit ratios for different project variants. Yet distributional considerations are often at least as important as such efficiency-driven considerations. Underlying the overall values for aggregate cost and benefit components is often detailed information on effects for different groups in society, be they distinguished by location or by socioeconomic characteristics. A careful presentation of such results can help in weighing distributional considerations in the final decision-making, including decisions on possible auxiliary redistributional policies. If done well, such information can foster a decision process that is consistent with improving overall societal welfare while incorporating informed public input and enhancing understanding.

A final consideration is that the increased weight that societies are putting on achieving environmental sustainability targets, coupled with the difficulties that sometimes exist in valuing these in monetary terms, creates new challenges for CBA practices. OECD (2018), for example, considers a wide range of challenges including valuing the distant future, weighing the benefits of ecosystems and biodiversity, coping with subjective well-being, and valuing health. By no means, therefore, should CBA be thought of as a complete set of tools and methods.

5.3 Conclusions

Long-lived transport investments can be analyzed either as a problem of optimizing over a continuously varying quantity of capital stock, or as a problem of choice among well-defined discrete packages. Either way, the analysis completes the characterization of long-run cost functions. If done the second way, it also becomes part of a more general technique, cost-benefit analysis, which can be used to analyze other proposals such as pricing or regulatory changes. Indeed, it has become common for governments to mandate such analyses of a wide range of government initiatives, in order to increase the burden of proof on proposed actions that might have adverse economic effects. Whether this actually affects decisions is another matter, but there is some evidence that it does at least in some nations (Eliasson *et al.* 2013).

Like pricing, investment analysis can be considered under first- or second-best conditions. The latter are of course far more prevalent; in several cases, we can identify the way investment rules should be modified to account for constraints, especially constraints on pricing the facility in question or other facilities that interact with it. Furthermore, we can sometimes describe the potential misallocations due to applying first-best rules (which might be thought of as common-sense cost-benefit analysis) to what are really second-best situations.

The COVID-19 pandemic has created some new challenges for investment analysis. Especially, it has created enormous changes in personal behavior and business conditions that greatly affect travel. Because transportation investments tend to be long-lived and expensive, such changes add a risk to undertaking such investments before the implications of these changed conditions are fully understood. As noted by Pisarski (2020), this factor especially lends strength to a case for delaying new investments that depend on extensive commuting travel. A more formal way to approach this is to model the option value of waiting before making a decision, which involves probabilistic calculations analogous to those used to define the value of options in financial markets. Boardman *et al.* (2018, Chap. 12) provide an extended explanation.

Of course, many factors besides those considered in formal economic models, including cost-benefit analyses, enter into public investment decisions. To take just one example, rail transit systems are frequently advocated as solutions to problems of local or global air pollution. In principle, these factors can be incorporated into cost-benefit analysis, as described extensively in this book. Yet, many people may consider such calculations inadequate or even irrelevant, given the widespread understanding that pollution is a serious public health danger and climate change a worldwide threat. Thus, for example, there is increasing evidence that local air pollution adversely affects child development, which is mostly not accounted for in studies of the costs of pollution. This is just one of many reasons why cost-benefit analysis is best regarded as a supplement to, not a replacement of, political decision-making.

Indeed, all public investment decisions are part of a political process. The goal of investment analysis is not to create rigid criteria that must be followed to the exclusion of all others, but rather to use economic principles to cast light on the real implications of a given project. Thus, to be useful, it needs to be not only technically sound, but transparent to all who have a stake in the decisions.

Notes

1 For example, the widely publicized "grades" for US highways compiled by the American Society of Civil Engineers (ASCE 2021) have hovered between D– and D+ for many years. ASCE is a professional organization representing a group heavily involved in designing infrastructure.

2 In 2019, the percentage of US highways classified as in "poor" condition ranged from only 1.9% for rural interstates to 12.1% for urban principal arterials (other than interstates). These statements and that in the text are documented in Poole (2018, p. 2), Duranton *et al.* (2020), and Feigenbaum *et al.* (2020). Bridges present a more complex and less optimistic picture. It is still true that significant portions of US highways and bridges are in need of repair, and that the system of finance is struggling to keep up as the system ages: See for example National Academies (2019).

3 Euler's theorem states that if a differentiable function $c(x)$ of variables $x \equiv (x_i)$ is homogeneous of degree k, *i.e.*, if $c(tx) = t^k c(x)$ for all positive scalars t, then $\Sigma_i x_i \cdot (\partial c / \partial x_i) = k \cdot c(x)$. In our case, c_h is homogeneous of degree $k = 0$ in its two arguments.

4 To see why, observe that for a given demand function, the short-run optimal congestion toll and the associated road use per unit of capacity are both decreasing in capacity. This can be verified graphically in the left panel of Figure 4.1, by imagining how a larger capacity would imply equality of $d(V)$ and $mc(V)$ at some price p lower than p^1; this in turn would imply an equilibrium user cost c lower than c^1, hence an equilibrium ratio V/V_K lower than V^1/V_K and a lower optimal toll τ. With exact self-financing, short-run optimal toll revenues per unit of capacity therefore exceed the unit cost of capacity when total capacity is below optimal, and fall short of it when total capacity is above optimal. Lindsey (2012, note 20) proves algebraically that the cost recovery ratio is a strictly decreasing function of capacity under optimal road pricing, so that only for the optimal capacity does exact self-financing occur if the relevant technical conditions I-III apply.

5 Jansson (1984, Chap. 10) models it as a type of scale economy, whereas Larsen treats it as a quality variable that is produced jointly along with capacity.

6 Of course, a full network analysis is still necessary in order to predict the traffic volumes that appear in the link-specific equation (5.6).

7 Lindsey (2009) extends this result to include capacity uncertainty, and imperfect information of users about the state. Lindsey and de Palma (2014) extend it, as well as the result of Arnott and Kraus (1998b), to long-run uncertainty about investment costs, user costs, and demand. Cost recovery is sensitive to variability in the growth rate of demand.

8 These terms, plus "induced travel" and "latent demand," tend to be used synonymously. Lee *et al.* (2002) suggest the following useful distinction: induced traffic is a change in traffic resulting in movement along a short-run demand curve, whereas induced demand is a shift in the short-run demand curve (perhaps also a movement along a long-run demand curve). Here, "short-run" should be defined as a time period over which demand factors, such as vehicle fleet or land uses, are kept constant. Other authors, notably Cervero (2003), distinguish between the effects of a capacity expansion on traffic on the facility itself ("induced travel") and the effects on all traffic in the region ("induced demand"). We do not attempt here to maintain this distinction rigorously, partly because we use "latent demand" for a particular kind of potential induced traffic.

9 For example, opening a new section of the M25 London Orbital Motorway apparently caused peak narrowing on a competing bridge (Mackie and Bonsall 1989, p. 415).

10 For example, Noland (2001), Cervero (2003), and studies reviewed by Goodwin (1996). Cervero attributes one-fourth of the elasticity he measures to land-use changes.

11 Hymel measures capacity as expressways only. The logic of his paper suggests that the usage variable is also expressways only, but its description is ambiguous on this point.

12 If the revenue objective were entirely dominant ($\lambda_t \to \infty$), the toll in (5.17) would be identical to the revenue-maximizing congestion toll that we will encounter in Chapter 6, equation (6.5).

13 Even for a profit-maximizing road operator, to be considered in Chapter 6, we will see that investment rule (5.3) still applies, for essentially the same reason.

14 If they do, then the labor-supply elasticity appearing in the formula for MCF is typically a compensated elasticity; if not, it is an uncompensated elasticity, which is larger in magnitude.

15 Small et al. (1999) suggests 1.25 as a central result from literature reviewed. Parry and Small (2005, Note 15) choose central assumptions for the uncompensated labor-supply elasticity (0.2) and for the average tax rate (0.35 for the USA, 0.45 for the UK), from which we calculate the MCF as $1 + MEB_L$ using their equation (9d); the resulting MCF is 1.12 for the USA and 1.20 for the UK.

16 See, for example, Ng (1987). Wendner and Goulder (2008) offer some empirical evidence that relative-status concerns are large enough to greatly reduce the size of the conventionally measured MCF.

17 Kleven and Kreiner (2006, Table 3, Scenarios S5–S9). The five nations considered, in ascending order of the estimated MCF under most scenarios, are the UK, Italy, France, Germany, and Denmark.

18 A fuller treatment is provided by many authors including Boardman *et al.* (2018) and de Rus (2021). We forego the fascinating implications for cost-benefit analysis of non-standard utility functions or behavior in the absence of any utility function: Bernheim (2016) considers such matters in depth.

19 The line is drawn as an "inverse demand curve," meaning it shows price on the vertical axis and quantity on the horizontal axis.

20 This "profit" includes any "factor surplus," indicating net excess (if any) of returns to factors of production, like labor or capital, over and above their resource cost: See Boardman *et al.* (2018, Section 3.3.1).

21 See de Rus (2012, pp. 30–33), or Boardman *et al.* (2018, Sect. 3.3) on equivalence of these approaches; the names we give them are from de Rus. Note that resource-cost accounting does not include toll payments or revenues, because they cancel each other.

22 Because it is difficult to measure demand over extended time periods, especially as conditions and perhaps the facility itself evolve, comparisons of actual to forecast demand often use first-year usage as the measure of actual demand – as explained, for example, by Flyvbjerg and Bester (2021).

23 We quote here results for BRT, Rail, Tunnels, Bridges, and Roads in their Table 1. We group BRT and rail together since there are so few BRT projects. The authors also analyze other public investments, such as dams and power plants. Their larger sample includes over 2,000 projects from 104 countries.

24 The authors note that these numbers may overstate the true bias somewhat due to selection bias in their statistical sample. Nevertheless, this issue seems unlikely to account for the very large biases observed. The distributions of errors, for both costs and benefits, also show very large kurtosis, *i.e.* "fat tails," indicating the existence of many estimates far from the averages just described.

25 More precisely, the real interest rate r is implicitly defined by the equation $(1 + r) \cdot (1 + \rho) = 1 + n$. If π is small, the solution to this equation is approximately $r = n - \pi$.

26 The risk premium disappears in a portfolio of many investments that are fully diversified relative to each other and uncorrelated with overall consumption. However, most private investments cannot meet these conditions, especially because returns depend on overall economic growth. Neither can

public investments, due to overall budgetary limitations and practical constraints on the menu of possible investments.

27 US OMB gives the 7% as the "default" rate, based on the presumption that most projects compete with private capital investment; the lower rate is recommended if the project can be shown to mainly reduce consumption.

28 Manuals or directives for practitioners include US OMB (2003); Asian Development Bank (2013) (which contains a thorough exposition of theory and measurement as well as a review of guidelines from other nations); and European Commission DG Regional and Urban Policy (2013). The latter mandates rates (for projects under its purview) of 4% for financial analysis and either 3% or 5% (depending on the country) for economic analysis: See pp. 42, 55, and Annexes I and II. The Netherlands Ministry of Finance (2020) mandates a discount rate of 2.25%, citing arguments similar to those by Moore *et al.* discussed here and the slightly negative risk-free real rates prevailing at its time of writing.

29 Boardman *et al.* (2018, Sect. 6.2) and Haveman and Farrow (2011) discuss the complexities of how to measure and account for labor-market distortions in cost-benefit analysis.

30 This equation is a simplification of equation (18) of Calthrop *et al.* (2010), omitting the first term on the right-hand side of that equation, which depicts direct measurement of benefits and costs. They calculate each term at a constant level of government fiscal surplus or deficit, thus implicitly assuming in the term omitted here that taxes are raised or other expenditures lowered so as to maintain this balance.

31 For a rigorous study defining and measuring such benefits, see Shirley and Winston (2004).

32 Rouwendal (2012) provides a more extended theoretical treatment.

33 These numbers are the economy-wide weighted average in their Table 3 and the agglomeration elasticity for car travel in their Table 4.

34 Examples include Shefer and Aviram (2005) for a light-rail line in Tel Aviv, Israel, and Hazledine *et al.* (2017) for two public transit projects in Auckland, New Zealand.

35 Allen and Arkolakis (2022) engage in a similar exercise for the entire USA, as they analyze the impacts of segment-specific US highway investments on economic activity, taking into account the endogenous adjustment of the entire system of urban geography.

36 China's high-speed network mostly uses the "exclusive" model; but this followed a long development period using other models, including conventional track upgrades, improved vehicles, and, in some cases, laying exclusive high-speed rails alongside conventional rails. Wikipedia provides a detailed history. In the USA, a high-speed line between Los Angeles and San Francisco (and points beyond) is currently under construction with plans to fully open during the 2030s (though the plans' realism is debatable). Its planning began with the "exclusive" model, but moved to one that is fully mixed within each of its end-point regions (ostensibly as an interim measure), thereby providing auxiliary benefits in the form of upgrading conventional commuter rail.

37 Adler *et al.* (2010) provide an excellent example of modeling such a market in competition with high-speed rail, applying it to a variety of proposals for expansion of high-speed rail throughout Europe. They also compute cost-benefit ratios, obtaining largely favorable results.

38 Abelson (2020) analyzes guidelines from selected agencies in five nations, all from the perspective of conforming with principles laid out by Boardman *et al.* (2018).

References

Abelson, Peter (2020) "A partial review of seven official guidelines for cost-benefit analysis," *Journal of Benefit Cost Analysis* 11(2): 272–293.

Adler, Nicole, Eric Pels and Christopher A. Nash (2010) "High-speed rail and air transport competition: game engineering as tool for cost-benefit analysis," *Transportation Research Part B: Methodological* 44: 812–833.

AIReF (2020) *Transport Infrastructure Study: Spending Review, Phase II.* Madrid: Independent Authority for Fiscal Responsibility (July), https://www.airef.es/en/spending-review-phase-ii (accessed 5 March 2024).

Allen, Treb and Costas Arkolakis (2022) "The welfare effects of transportation infrastructure improvements," *Review of Economic Studies* 89(6): 2911–2957.

Anas, Alex (2024), " 'Downs's Law' under the lens of theory: Roads lower congestion and increase distance traveled," *Journal of Urban Economics* 139: 103607.

Anas, Alex and Huibin Chang (2023) "Productivity benefits of urban transportation megaprojects: a general equilibrium analysis of 'Grand Paris Express'," *Transportation Research Part B: Methodological* 174: 102746. doi:10.1016/j.trb.2023.03.006

Arnott, Richard and Marvin Kraus (1998a) "When are anonymous congestion charges consistent with marginal cost pricing?" *Journal of Public Economics* 67(1): 45–64.

Arnott, Richard and Marvin Kraus (1998b) "Self-financing of congestible facilities in a growing economy," in David Pines, Efraim Sadka and Itzhak Zilcha (eds.) *Topics in Public Economics: Theoretical and Applied Analysis*, Cambridge: Cambridge University Press, pp. 161–184.

American Society of Civil Engineers (2021) *2021 Report Card for America's Infrastructure*, ASCE, https://infrastructurereportcard.org/making-the-grade/

Asian Development Bank (2013) *Cost-Benefit Analysis for Development: A Practical Guide*. Mandaluyong City, Philippines: Asian Development Bank.

Bailey, Michael, Patrick Farrell, Theresa Kuchler and Johannes Stroebel (2020) "Social connectedness in urban areas," *Journal of Urban Economics* 118: 103264.

Bain, Robert (2009) "Error and optimism bias in toll road traffic forecasts," *Transportation* 36(5): 469–482.

Berechman, Joseph and David Pines (1991) "Financing road capacity and returns to scale under marginal cost pricing," *Journal of Transport Economics and Policy* 25(2): 177–181.

Bernheim, B. Douglas (2016) "The good, the bad, and the ugly: a unified approach to behavioral welfare economics," *Journal of Benefit Cost Analysis* 7(1): 12–68.

Boardman, Anthony E., David H. Greenberg, Aidan R. Vining and David L. Weimer (2018) *Cost–Benefit Analysis: Concepts and Practice*, 5th edition, Cambridge University Press.

Börjesson, Maria, Chau Man Fung, Stef Proost and Zifei Yan (2019) "Do small cities need more public transport subsidies than big cities?," *Journal of Transport Economics and Policy* 53(4): 275–298.

Bovenberg, A. Lans and Ruud A. de Mooij (1994) "Environmental levies and distortionary taxation," *American Economic Review* 84(4): 1085–1089.

Brooks, Wyatt, Joseph P. Kaboski, Illenin O. Kondo, Yao Amber Li and Wei Qian (2021) "Infrastructure investment and labor monopsony power," *IMF Economic Review* 69: 470–504. doi:10.1057/s41308-021-00144-6

Burgess, David F. and Richard O. Zerbe (2013) "The most appropriate discount rate," *Journal of Benefit-Cost Analysis* 4(3): 391–400.

Cadot, Olivier, Lars-Hendrik Röller and Andreas Stephan (2006) "Contribution to productivity or pork barrel? The two faces of infrastructure investment," *Journal of Public Economics* 90: 1133–1153.

Calthrop, Edward, Bruno De Borger and Stef Proost (2010) "Cost-benefit analysis of transport investments in distorted economies," *Transportation Research Part B: Methodological* 44(7): 850–869.

Campos, Javier and Ginés de Rus (2009) "Some stylized facts about high-speed rail: a review of HSR experiences around the world," *Transport Policy* 16(1): 19–28.

Cervero, Robert (2003) "Road expansion, urban growth, and induced travel: a path analysis," *Journal of the American Planning Association* 69(2): 145–163.

Chen, Wei and H. Allen Klaiber (2020) "Does road expansion induce traffic? An evaluation of vehicle-kilometers traveled in China," *Journal of Environmental Economics and Management* 104: 102387.

Combes, P.-P. and L. Gobillon (2015) "The empirics of agglomeration economies," in: Gilles Duranton, J. Vernon Henderson and William C. Strange (eds.) *Handbook of Regional and Urban Economics*, Volume 5, Amsterdam: Elsevier, pp. 247–348.

Dahlgren, Joy (1998) "High occupancy vehicle lanes: not always more effective than general purpose lanes," *Transportation Research Part A: Policy and Practice* 32(2): 99–114.

d'Ouville, Edmond L. and John F. McDonald (1990) "Optimal road capacity with a suboptimal congestion toll," *Journal of Urban Economics* 28(1): 34–49.

de Palma, André, Moez Kilani and Robin Lindsey (2008) "The merits of separating cars and trucks," *Journal of Urban Economics* 64(2): 340–361.

de Rus, Ginés (2012) "Economic evaluation of the high speed rail," Report for the Expert Group on Environmental Studies, Ministry of Finance, Sweden (May), https://www.researchgate.net/publication/259558449_Economic_Evaluation_of_the_High_Speed_Rail (accessed 24 November 2021).

de Rus, Ginés (2021) *Introduction to Cost-Benefit Analysis*, 2nd edition. Cheltenham: Edward Elgar.

Downs, Anthony (1962) "The law of peak-hour expressway congestion," *Traffic Quarterly* 16(3): 393–409.

Downs, Anthony (2004) *Still Stuck in Traffic: Coping with Peak-Hour Traffic Congestion*, Washington, DC: Brookings Institution Press.

Duranton, Gilles, Geetika Nagpal and Matthew A. Turner (2020) "Transportation infrastructure in the US," Working paper 27254, National Bureau of Economic Research.

Duranton, Gilles and Diego Puga (2001) "Nursery cities: urban diversity, process innovation, and the life cycle of products," *American Economic Review* 91(5): 1454–1477.

Duranton, Gilles and Diego Puga (2004) "Chapter 48: Micro-foundations of urban agglomeration economies," In: J. Vernon Henderson and Jacques-François Thisse (eds.) *Handbook of Regional and Urban Economics*, Volume 4, Amsterdam: Elsevier, pp. 2063–2117. doi:10.1016/S1574-0080(04)80005-1

Duranton, Gilles and Matthew A. Turner (2011) "The fundamental law of road congestion: evidence from US cities," *American Economic Review* 101: 2616–2652.

Eliasson, Jonas, Maria Börjesson, James Odeck and Morten Welde (2013) "Does benefit–cost efficiency influence transport investment decisions?" *Journal of Transport Economics and Policy* 49(3): 377–396.

Eliasson, Jonas and Mogens Fosgerau (2013) "Cost overruns and demand shortfalls – deception or selection?" *Transportation Research Part B: Methodological* 57: 105–113.

Eliasson, Jonas and Mogens Fosgerau (2019) "Cost-benefit analysis of transport improvements in the presence of spillovers, matching and an income tax," *Economics of Transportation* 18: 1–9.

European Commission DG Regional and Urban Policy (2013) *Guide to Cost–Benefit Analysis of Investment Projects: Economic appraisal tool for Cohesion Policy 2014-2020*, Brussels: European Commission Directorate-General for Regional and Urban policy.

Feigenbaum, Baruch, Spence Purnell, and Joseph Hillman (2020) 25th Annual Highway Report, Reason Foundation (November). https://reason.org/policy-study/25th-annual-highway-report/

Fernald, John G. (1999) "Roads to prosperity? Assessing the link between public capital and productivity," *American Economic Review* 89(3): 619–638.

Flyvbjerg, Bent and Dirk W. Bester (2021) "The cost-benefit fallacy: why cost-benefit analysis is broken and how to fix it," *Journal of Benefit Cost Analysis* 12(3): 395–419.

Flyvbjerg, Bent, Matte K. Skamris Holm and Søren L. Buhl (2004) "What causes cost overrun in transport infrastructure projects?" *Transport Reviews* 24: 3–18.

Flyvbjerg, Bent, Matte K. Skamris Holm and Søren L. Buhl (2005) "How (in)accurate are demand forecasts in public works projects? The case of transportation," *Journal of the American Planning Association* 71(2): 131–146.

Garcia-López, Miquel-Angel, Ilias Pasidis and Elisabet Viladecans-Marsal (2022) "Congestion in highways when tolls and railroads matter: evidence from European cities," *Journal of Economic Geography* 22(5): 931–960.

Glaeser, Edward L. and Giacomo A.M. Ponzetto (2010) "Did the death of distance hurt detroit and help New York?," in: Edward P. Glaeser (ed.) *Agglomeration Economics*, Chicago and London: University of Chicago Press, Chpt. 10, pp. 303–337.

Goodwin, Phil B. (1996) "Empirical evidence on induced traffic," *Transportation* 23: 35–54.

Goulder, Lawrence H., and Roberton C. Williams III (2012) "The choice of discount rate for climate change policy evaluation," *Climate Change Economics* 3(4): 1250024. doi:10.1142/S2010007812500248

Graham, Daniel J. and Stephen Gibbons (2019) "Quantifying wider economic impacts of agglomeration for transport appraisal: existing evidence and future directions" *Economics of Transportation* 19: 100121. doi:10.1016/j.ecotra.2019.100121

Haveman, Robert H., and Scott Farrow (2011) "Labor expenditures and benefit-cost accounting in times of unemployment," *Journal of Benefit Cost Analysis* 2(2): 7.

Hazledine, Tim, Stuart Donovan and Christine Mak (2017) "Urban agglomeration benefits from public transit improvements: extending and implementing the Venables model," *Research in Transportation Economics* 66: 36–45.

Hörcher, Daniel and Daniel J. Graham (2018) "Demand imbalances and multi-period public transport supply," *Transportation Research Part B: Methodological* 108: 106–126.

Hörcher, Daniel and Alejandro Tirachini (2021) "A review of public transport economics," *Economics of Transportation* 25: 100196.

Hotelling, Harold (1938) "The general welfare in relation to problems of taxation and of railway and utility rates," *Econometrica* 6(3): 242–269.

Hsu, Wen-Tai and Hongliang Zhang (2014) "The fundamental law of highway congestion revisited: evidence from national expressways in Japan," *Journal of Urban Economics* 81: 65–76.

Hymel, Kent (2019) "If you build it, they will drive: measuring induced demand for vehicle travel in urban areas," *Transport Policy* 76: 57–66.

Jansson, Jan Owen (1984) *Transport System Optimization and Pricing*, Chichester: John Wiley & Sons.

Jara-Díaz, Sergio R. (1986) "On the relation between users' benefits and the economic effects of transportation activities," *Journal of Regional Science* 26(2): 379–391.

Jenkins, Glenn P. (1997) "Project analysis and the World Bank," *American Economic Review Papers and Proceedings* 87(2): 38–42.

Kanemoto, Yoshitsugu (2013) "Evaluating benefits of transportation in models of new economic geography," *Economics of Transportation* 2: 53–62.

Kaplow, Louis (1996) "The optimal supply of public goods and the distortionary cost of taxation," *National Tax Journal* 49(4): 513–533.

Kleven, Henrik Jacobsen and Claus Thustrup Kreiner (2006) "The marginal cost of public funds: hours of work versus labor force participation," *Journal of Public Economics* 90(10–11): 1955–1973.

Konishi, Hideo and Se-il Mun (2010) "Carpooling and congestion pricing: HOV and HOT lanes," *Regional Science and Urban Economics* 40(4): 173–186.

Larsen, Odd I. (1993) "Road investment with road pricing – investment criteria and the revenue/cost issue," in Antti Talvitie, David Hensher and Michael E. Beesley (eds.) *Privatization and Deregulation in Passenger Transportation*, Second International Conference on Privatization and Deregulation in Passenger Transportation, Espoo, Finland: Viatek Ltd., pp. 273–281.

Lee, Douglass, Jr., Lisa A. Klein and Gregorio Camus (2002) "Induced traffic and induced demand," in US Federal Highway Administration, *Highway Economic Requirements System – State Version: Technical Report, Appendix B*, Washington, DC: US Federal Highway Administration, http://rosap.ntl.bts.gov/view/dot/58541.

Lindsey, Robin (2009) "Cost recovery from congestion tolls with random capacity and demand," *Journal of Urban Economics* 66(1): 16–24.

Lindsey, Robin (2012) "Road pricing and investment," *Economics of Transportation* 1(1–2): 49–63.

Lindsey, Robin and André de Palma (2014) "Cost recovery from congestion tolls with long-run uncertainty," *Economics of Transportation* 3: 119–132.

Lindsey, Robin and Erik T. Verhoef (2000) "Congestion modelling," in David A. Hensher and Kenneth J. Button (eds.) *Handbook of Transport Modelling*, New York: Pergamon, pp. 353–373.

Mackie, Peter J. and Peter W. Bonsall (1989) "Traveller response to road improvements: implications for user benefits," *Traffic Engineering and Control* 30: 411–416.

Mohring, Herbert (1979) "The benefits of reserved bus lanes, mass transit subsidies, and marginal cost pricing in alleviating traffic congestion," in Peter Mieszkowski and Mahlon Straszheim (eds.) *Current Issues in Urban Economics*, Baltimore, MD: Johns Hopkins University Press.

Mohring, Herbert and Mitchell Harwitz (1962) *Highway Benefits: An Analytical Framework*, Evanston, IL: Northwestern University Press.

Mohring, Herbert and Harold F. Williamson, Jr. (1969) "Scale and 'industrial reorganisation' economies of transport improvements," *Journal of Transport Economics and Policy* 3(3): 251–271.

Mokhtarian, Patricia L. (1990) "A typology of relationships between telecommunications and transportation," *Transportation Research Part A: General* 24: 231–242.

Mokhtarian, Patricia L. (2009) "If telecommunication is such a good substitute for travel, why does congestion continue to get worse?" *Transportation Letters* 1: 1–17.

Moore, Mark A., Anthony E. Boardman and Aidan R. Vining (2013) "More appropriate discounting: the rate of social time preference and the value of the social discount rate," *Journal of Benefit-Cost Analysis* 4(1): 1–16.

Nardinelli, Clark (2018) "Some pitfalls of practical Benefit-Cost Analysis, "*Journal of Benefit Cost Analysis* 9(3): 519–530.

National Academies of Sciences, Engineering, and Medicine (2019) *Renewing the national commitment to the Interstate Highway System: A foundation for the future*. Washington, DC: The National Academies Press. doi:10.17226/25334

National Academies of Sciences, Engineering, and Medicine (2020) *Traffic Forecasting Accuracy Assessment Research*, Washington, DC: The National Academies Press. doi:10.17226/25637

Newbery, David M. (1989) "Cost recovery from optimally designed roads," *Economica* 56(222): 165–185.

Ng, Yew-Kwang (1987) "Relative-income effects and the appropriate level of public expenditure," *Oxford Economic Papers* 39(2): 293–300.

Noland, Robert B. (2001) "Relationships between highway capacity and induced vehicle travel," *Transportation Research Part A: Policy and Practice* 35(1): 47–72.

Organisation for Economic Co-operation and Development (OECD) (2018) *Cost-Benefit Analysis and the Environment*, Organisation for Economic Cooperation and Development, Paris.

Parry, Ian W.H. and Antonio M. Bento (2001) "Revenue recycling and the welfare effects of congestion pricing," *Scandinavian Journal of Economics* 103(4): 645–671.

Parry, Ian W.H. and Kenneth A. Small (2005) "Does Britain or the United States have the right gasoline tax?" *American Economic Review* 95(4): 1276–89.

Pisarski, Alan (2020) "Five steps to guide transportation spending and planning during Coronavirus pandemic," *Commentary*, August 19, Reason Foundation, https://reason.org/commentary/five-steps-to-guide-transportation-spending-and-planning/

Polinsky, A. Mitchell (1972) "Probabilistic compensation criteria," *Quarterly Journal of Economics* 86(3): 407–425.

Poole, Robert W., Jr. (2018) *Rethinking America's Highways: A 21st-Centry Vision for Better Infrastructure*. Univ. of Chicago Press.

Proost, Stef, Bruno De Borger and Pia M. Koskenoja (2007) "Public finance aspects of transport financing and investment," in André de Palma, Robin Lindsey and Stef Proost (eds.) *Investment and the Use of Tax and Toll Revenues in the Transport Sector*, Research in Transport Economics, Volume 19, Amsterdam: Elsevier JAI, pp. 59–80.

Ramsey, Frank P. (1928) "A mathematical theory of saving," *Economic Journal* 38: 543–559.

RI (2024) "Euro area Consumer Price Index: 1996 to 2024," https://www.rateinflation.com/consumer-price-index/euro-area-historical-cpi/

Rosenthal, Stuart S., and William C. Strange (2020) "How close is close? The spatial reach of agglomeration economies," *Journal of Economic Perspectives* 34(3): 27–49.

Rouwendal, Jan (2012) "Indirect effects in cost-benefit analysis," *Journal of Benefit-Cost Analysis* 3(1): 1–27.

SACTRA (Standing Advisory Committee on Trunk Road Assessment) (1994) *Trunk Roads and the Generation of Traffic*, London: Her Majesty's Stationery Office.

SACTRA (Standing Advisory Committee on Trunk Road Assessment) (1999) *Transport and the Economy*, London: Her Majesty's Stationary Office.

Salomon, Ilan (1985) "Telecommunications and travel: substitution or modified mobility?," *Journal of Transport Economics and Policy* 19: 219–235.

Shefer, Daniel and Haim Aviram (2005) "Incorporating agglomeration economies in transport cost–benefit analysis: the case of the proposed light-rail transit in the Tel-Aviv metropolitan area," *Papers in Regional Science* 84(3): 487–507.

Shirley, Chad and Clifford Winston (2004) "Firm inventory behavior and the returns from highway infrastructure investments," *Journal of Urban Economics* 55(2): 398–415.

Small, Kenneth A. (1983) "Bus priority and congestion pricing on urban expressways," in Theodore E. Keeler (ed.) *Research in Transportation Economics*, Volume 1, Greenwich, CT: JAI Press, pp. 27–74.

Small, Kenneth A. (1992) *Urban Transportation Economics*, Fundamentals of Pure and Applied Economics, Vol. 51, Chur, Switzerland: Harwood Academic Publishers.

Small, Kenneth A. (1999) "Economies of scale and self-financing rules with noncompetitive factor markets," *Journal of Public Economics* 74(3): 431–450.

Small, Kenneth A. *et al.* (1999) *Valuation of Travel-Time Savings and Predictability in Congested Conditions for Highway User-Cost Estimation*, National Cooperative Highway Research Program report 431, Washington, DC: National Academies Press.

Small, Kenneth A. and Chen Ng (2014) "Optimizing road capacity and type," *Economics of Transportation* 3: 145–157.

Small, Kenneth A., Clifford Winston and Carol A. Evans (1989) *Road Work: A New Highway Pricing and Investment Policy*, Washington, DC: Brookings Institution Press.

Small, Kenneth A., Clifford Winston and Jia Yan (2006) "Differentiated road pricing, express lanes, and carpools: exploiting heterogeneous preferences in policy design," *Brookings-Wharton Papers on Urban Affairs* 7: 53–96.

Smeed, Reuben J. (1968) "Traffic studies and urban congestion," *Journal of Transportation Economics and Policy* 2(1): 33–70.

Taylor, Alan M. (2018) "The rate of return on everything," *NBER Reporter*, No. 4. Cambridge, MA: National Bureau of Economic Research, https://www.nber.org/reporter

The Netherlands Ministry of Finance (2020) Rapport Werkgroep discontovoet 2020, *Rijksoverheid*, 9 October, https://www.rijksoverheid.nl/documenten/kamerstukken/2020/11/10/rapport-werkgroep-discontovoet-2020

Tsivanidis, Nick (forthcoming) "Evaluating the impact of urban transit infrastructure: evidence from Bogotá's TransMilenio," *American Economic Review*. Pre-publication version at https://www.nicktsivanidis.com/research

US OMB (2003) *Regulatory Analysis*, circular no. A-4, revised, Washington, DC: US Office of Management and Budget, https://obamawhitehouse.archives.gov/omb/circulars_a004_a-4/

Van Dender, Kurt (2003) "Transport taxes with multiple trip purposes," *Scandinavian Journal of Economics* 105(2): 295–310.

Venables, Anthony J. (2007) "Evaluating urban transport improvements: cost-benefit analysis in the presence of agglomeration and income taxation," *Journal of Transport Economics and Policy* 41(2): 173–188.

Verhoef, Erik T. and Herbert Mohring (2009) "Self-financing roads," *International Journal of Sustainable Transportation* 3(5–6): 293–311.

Verhoef, Erik T. and Kenneth A. Small (2004) "Product differentiation on roads: constrained congestion pricing with heterogeneous users," *Journal of Transport Economics and Policy* 38(1): 127–156.

Wachs, Martin (1989) "When planners lie with numbers," *Journal of the American Planning Association* 55(4): 476–479.

Wachs, Martin (1990) "Ethics and advocacy in forecasting for public policy," *Business and Professional Ethics Journal* 9(1 & 2): 141–157.

Wachs, Martin (2013) "The past, present, and future of professional ethics in planning," in Naomi Carmon and Susan S. Fainstein (eds.) *Policy, Planning, and People: Promoting Justice in Urban Development*, Philadelphia, PA: University of Pennsylvania Press, pp. 101–119.

Weitzman, Martin L. (2001) "Gamma discounting," *American Economic Review* 91(1): 260–271.

Wendner, Ronald and Lawrence H. Goulder (2008) "Status effects, public goods provision, and the excess burden," *Journal of Public Economics* 92: 1968–1985. DOI: https://doi.org/10.1016/j.jpubeco.2008.04.011

Wheaton, William C. (1978) "Price-induced distortions in urban highway investment," *Bell Journal of Economics* 9(2): 622–632.

Wilson, John D. (1983) "Optimal road capacity in the presence of unpriced congestion," *Journal of Urban Economics* 13(3): 337–357.

Yang, Hai and Hai-Jun Huang (1999) "Carpooling and congestion pricing in a multilane highway with high-occupancy-vehicle lanes," *Transportation Research Part A: Policy and Practice* 33(2): 139–155.

Yang, Hai and Qiang Meng (2002) "A note on 'Highway pricing and capacity choice in a road network under a build-operate-transfer scheme'," *Transportation Research Part A: Policy and Practice* 36(7): 659–663.

Zerbe, Richard O. (2020) "The consent justification for Benefit–Cost Analysis," *Journal of Benefit Cost Analysis* 11(2): 319–340.

Zheng, Siqi, and Matthew E. Kahn (2013) "China's bullet trains facilitate market integration and mitigate the cost of megacity growth," *Proceedings of the National Academy of Sciences*. doi:10.1073/pnas.1209247110.

6 Industrial organization of transportation providers

So far, we have discussed desirable investment and pricing policies. We now turn to a discussion of the forms of institutional structure that can best bring them about. The dominant organizational form for providing urban transportation services to individual users, especially in developed nations, is public ownership. This is supplemented by regulation of those firms allowed to operate privately. Observers increasingly question the efficacy of these arrangements.

A fundamental characteristic of private transportation markets is their tendency toward scale economies. This tendency has long been recognized in inter-city transportation industries such as ocean shipping and railroads, whose fixed costs take tangible forms like terminals and rail track. But scale economies also affect industries, such as airlines and trucking, where users place a premium on fast and reliable transfers across various links in a large network. Scale economies on individual links – which can exist due to indivisibilities and to efficiencies of operating large vehicles – then become important, as firms seek to intensively use those links to provide convenient service for many origin–destination pairs. Scale economies are one of the classic rationales for regulating transportation services.

Both urban roads and urban public transit services also operate on networks that collect users with diverse origins and destinations onto high-capacity links in order to take advantage of link-specific scale economies. In Chapter 3, we noted that for urban roads, this is at least partially counteracted by diseconomies of intersections and scarcity of urban land. For public transit, however, we saw in Section 3.2.1 that the nature of scheduled services creates a type of scale economy that also affects low-volume links such as feeder links. Where scale economies occur, marginal cost prices do not cover average costs, so in order for private firms to operate in such markets, they must either receive subsidies or forgo marginal cost pricing. In either case, market power may arise, creating questions about whether and how to regulate private firms.

Of course, transportation is only one of many industries for which the question of private versus public operation arises. This seemingly simple question encompasses a wide range of aspects to be traded off, including social, economic, organizational, cultural, technical, practical, and historical matters; and the details often vary between industries. Analyses of transportation industries have been important in developing more general conclusions in the economics literature, as well as in applying more general results to specific cases. For example, as discussed later, transportation has been important for developing, analyzing, and testing public–private partnerships (PPPs), which may be regarded as intermediate between regulation and full privatization (Engel *et al.* 2014, 2021). Thus, the study of industrial organization in transportation continues to provide insights of widespread interest.

This chapter, then, reviews issues related to private operators in urban transportation. Section 6.1 discusses profit-maximizing price and capacity choice for private highway operators and

DOI: 10.4324/9781315157375-6

compares these to the welfare-maximizing choices described in earlier chapters. Section 6.2 discusses regulation and franchising of private highways, while Section 6.3 does the same for transit services and new transportation modes.

6.1   Private roads: theory

Some observers suggest that many of the recent difficulties with financing and pricing publicly owned highways could be overcome through a return to private ownership, which was common in the nineteenth century. For the textbook benchmark of perfect competition among road suppliers, first-best congestion pricing would be the equilibrium outcome (Knight 1924; DeVany and Saving 1980). Even under the more realistic conditions of monopoly or oligopoly, private ownership would provide some form of congestion pricing, as we shall see – although not at first-best price levels. Naturally, the outcomes and hence the desirability of private ownership depend critically on market structure, which includes the nature of the highway network and the relationship among suppliers. This section examines how such outcomes can be analytically characterized.

6.1.1   Single road with static congestion

We start with an unregulated private monopolist on a single road, using the same multi-period benefit–cost framework developed in Chapter 5. But instead of choosing capacity and tolls so as to maximize welfare $W \equiv B - C$, as in equation (5.1), we now assume the monopolist maximizes profit Π, equal to its revenues minus its own costs:

$$\Pi = \sum_h q_h \cdot V_h \cdot \tau_h - \rho \cdot K(V_K), \tag{6.1}$$

where again h denotes a time period of duration q_h. We ignore any variable cost for the supplier, such as volume-dependent maintenance or depreciation; these would be simply passed on to the consumer as part of the price, so would not lead to new insights. The user equilibrium condition from equation (4.1), equating marginal benefit $d(V)$ to the generalized price $p \equiv c(V) + \tau$, of course remains valid for each period h. It is convenient to directly substitute this condition into the objective function:

$$\Pi = \sum_h q_h V_h \cdot \left[d_h(V) - c_h(V_h; V_K) \right] - \rho \cdot K(V_K). \tag{6.2}$$

We can then maximize (6.2) with respect to capacity V_K and flows V_h.

Maximizing with respect to capacity produces, perhaps surprisingly, the first-best condition already encountered in (5.3):

$$\rho \cdot K'(V_K) = -\sum_h q_h \cdot V_h \cdot \frac{\partial c_h(\cdot)}{\partial V_K}. \tag{6.3}$$

For given flows V_h, the monopolist chooses capacity to minimize total social cost, including user cost. This is important, as it shows that the monopolist is cost-conscious, even with those resources supplied by its customers. The intuition is that for any given flows V_h resulting from some generalized prices $p_h = c_h + \tau_h$, the monopolist would like to minimize user cost c_h and thus maximize toll τ_h, while maintaining that generalized price. Every dollar reduction in total user cost can in that way be turned into an extra dollar of toll revenues for given flow levels. The monopolist therefore faces the optimal incentive to minimize the sum of user cost and capital cost, just as in welfare-maximization.

Maximizing (6.2) with respect to traffic volume, however, does not yield the first-best rule derived previously. Instead, we obtain the following condition:

$$\tau_h = V_h \cdot \frac{\partial c_h}{\partial V_h} - V_h \cdot \frac{\partial d_h}{\partial V_h} - \sum_{i \neq h} \frac{q_i}{q_h} \cdot V_i \cdot \frac{\partial d_i}{\partial V_h}. \tag{6.4}$$

The first term on the right-hand side is equal to the first-best toll in (4.14) and (5.2). Thus, the profit-maximizing toll does at least partly internalize the congestion externality. However, two extra terms are added, which take into account demand elasticities. With downward-sloping demand functions and substitutability across time periods, both terms are positive, so the toll is higher than optimal – just what we would expect from a monopolist.

When demands in different time periods are independent of each other, the last term disappears and (6.4) simplifies to

$$\tau_h = V_h \cdot \frac{\partial c_h}{\partial V_h} - V_h \cdot \frac{\partial d_h}{\partial V_h} \Leftrightarrow p_h \cdot \left(1 - \frac{1}{|\varepsilon_h|}\right) = mc_h \Leftrightarrow \frac{p_h - mc_h}{p_h} = \frac{1}{|\varepsilon_h|}, \tag{6.5}$$

where ε_h is the own-period price elasticity of demand with respect to generalized price (p_h), and where mc_h is defined, as before, as $\partial(V_h c_h)/\partial V_h = c_h + \partial c_h/\partial V_h$: that is, as marginal social cost.[1] Equation (6.5) resembles the familiar monopoly rule equating marginal revenue to marginal cost, but here the price and marginal cost both include user costs c_h. As usual with monopoly solutions, it is valid only when demand is elastic ($|\varepsilon_h| > 1$); otherwise only a negative mc_h could satisfy (6.5). Phrased differently, with a positive mc_h, the profit-maximizer would not choose a price at a level for which demand is inelastic: raising the price would then increase profits.

The monopolist internalizes the congestion externality because it has an interest in making its service attractive, so that users will pay more for it. When choosing the toll, just as when choosing capacity, the monopolist would like to reduce user cost in order to charge a higher toll. In doing so it is constrained by users' demand elasticities, as in conventional monopoly problems, but now also by the congestion technology. In fact, as we can see from the first of equations (6.5), the upward slope of the average user cost function (representing congestion) affects the toll in exactly the same way as the downward slope of the inverse demand function; indeed, the inverse demand function $\tau_h(V_h)$ as viewed by the monopolist, that is, the function relating the toll and the volume, is given by $\tau_h(V_h) = d_h(V_h) - c_h(V_h; V_K)$.

Because the monopolist takes marginal social cost into account in setting price, it practices a form of congestion pricing – but it then adds a markup represented by the bracketed term in the second equation in (6.5). This term multiplies the entire user-perceived price p_h, not just the toll τ_h. As a result, a substantial fee may be charged even during times when the optimal congestion fee is zero. An example of this in practice is the fact that the private operator of the express lanes on State Route 91 (SR-91) in southern California between 1995 and 2002 (see Section 4.3.2), in setting its time-varying fee, chose a non-zero fee even during night-time hours.

In the special case of perfectly elastic demand ($|\varepsilon_h| = \infty$), the demand-related monopolistic markup vanishes and the monopolist undertakes socially optimal pricing and investment. This is the case in the classic analyses by Pigou (1920) and Knight (1924). Although important as a benchmark, it is of limited use in practice.[2]

Note also from (6.5) that the monopolist's fractional markup on marginal social cost, as given by the "Lerner index" $(p_h - mc_h)/p_h$, is set to equal the inverse of the absolute value of the demand elasticity $|1/\varepsilon_h|$. Again, this is consistent with conventional microeconomics.

A similar relationship holds with "Ramsey pricing", when social welfare is maximized subject to a minimum profit constraint (Ramsey 1927; Baumol and Bradford 1970). We can derive the Ramsey result in this case by maximizing surplus B–C subject to a minimum constraint $\Pi^{\#}$ on profit Π, the latter defined in (6.2). Thus, we maximize the Lagrangian function:

$$\Lambda = \sum_h q_h \cdot \int_0^{V_h} d_h(v)\,dv - \sum_h q_h V_h \cdot c_h(V_h;V_K) - \rho \cdot K(V_K)$$

$$+ \lambda \cdot \left\{ \sum_h q_h V_h \cdot \left[d_h(V_h) - c_h(V_h;V_K) \right] - \rho \cdot K(V_K) - \Pi^{\#} \right\},$$

where λ is the Lagrange multiplier associated with the profit constraint. The first-order condition for capacity V_K is unchanged: once again, V_K is chosen to minimize total social cost. The first-order condition for volume V_h, however, changes. It may be solved to yield

$$\tau_h = V_h \cdot \frac{\partial c_h}{\partial V_h} - \frac{\lambda}{1+\lambda} \cdot V_h \cdot \frac{\partial d_h}{\partial V_h} \Leftrightarrow p_h \cdot \left(1 - \frac{\lambda}{1+\lambda} \cdot \frac{1}{\varepsilon_h} \right) = mc_h$$

$$\Leftrightarrow \frac{p_h - mc_h}{p_h} = \frac{\lambda}{1+\lambda} \cdot \frac{1}{|\varepsilon_h|} \quad,$$

where again *mc* denotes marginal social congestion cost. This equation resembles a well-known result for Ramsey pricing, but adapted here to incorporate a mutual externality and user-supplied costs.[3] When the constraint is not binding, implying $\lambda = 0$, the equation confirms that we are back at first-best pricing. When the constraint becomes increasingly hard to satisfy, so that $\lambda \to \infty$, the toll approaches the profit-maximizing toll of (6.5). Likewise, note that the conditions for the profit-maximizing toll (6.5) and capacity (6.3) are indeed also the same as those for a public operator practicing second-best pricing and investment, as in the setting of Section 5.1.3, if the marginal cost of public funds for the latter is infinite.[4]

6.1.2   Single road with dynamic congestion

In models with endogenous scheduling, demands at different times within the peak period are determined by individual travelers' tradeoffs between travel delay and schedule delay. Does this affect a monopolist differently from a welfare-maximizer?

Arnott et al. (1993) show that if the monopolist charges only a time-invariant fee, the problem is exactly like that just analyzed. This happens because we can then simply use the equilibrium average and marginal cost functions from (4.20) and (4.22), using them in (6.2) to solve the monopolist's maximization problem. However, if a time-varying fee is possible, one might wonder whether the travelers' tradeoffs across time periods set up varying time-specific elasticities to be exploited by a monopolistic road owner. If so, the monopolist would choose a *pattern* of time variation that differs from the optimal pattern.

This question can be answered within the basic bottleneck model, as used in Section 4.1.2. We consider a downward-sloping inverse demand function $d(Q)$. For convenience, we follow de Palma and Lindsey (2002) and decompose the time-varying toll $\tau(t')$ (for an exit at time t') into a time-independent "base toll" τ_0 and a purely time-varying component $\tau_v(t')$ that is zero for the first and last users to travel. This enables us to distinguish between the monopolist's choice of toll level t_0 and toll pattern $\tau_v(t')$. What we find is that the toll *pattern* is unaffected by monopoly – that is, it is the same as the optimal toll pattern, whereas the toll *level* is higher for a monopolist by exactly the same amount (and for the same reasons) as in the static result (6.5).

The reasoning is as follows. First, consider the toll *pattern*. A revenue-maximizer would set the toll pattern so as to eliminate any queuing because queuing time can be replaced by toll revenues without affecting the generalized price p – exactly as we argued in the previous subsection when considering profit-maximizing investment. The toll schedule must therefore be at least as steep as the optimal one. But given the absence of queuing, the revenue-maximizer would also not make the toll schedule steeper than the optimal one. If it did, this would create periods within the peak where the bottleneck remains idle, but then it would be possible to extract some revenue from the earliest or the latest driver by shifting that driver to an empty time slot within the peak, for which this driver is willing to pay more because of lower scheduling cost. The purely time-varying toll component will consequently follow the same pattern as the first-best time-varying toll of (4.23).

Now consider the toll *level*. To see how the base toll τ_0 is chosen, recall from (4.25) that with this time-varying toll pattern, users adjust so that their average congestion-related user cost is made up solely of schedule delay costs. This amounts to $\bar{c}_g^1 = \frac{1}{2}\delta \cdot Q/V_K$, where Q is the total number of trips over the rush-hour and δ is a composite measure of how costly it is to deviate from the desired schedule. Users furthermore pay tolls, which also have an average of $\bar{c}_g^1$. Thus, we can write

$$\bar{c}_g^1(Q;V_K) = \bar{\tau}_v(Q;V_K) = \tfrac{1}{2}\delta \cdot \frac{Q}{V_K}. \tag{6.6}$$

With the additional base toll added, generalized price, which must be equalized across users for them to be in equilibrium, is

$$\begin{aligned} d(Q) \equiv p &= \tau_0 + \bar{\tau}_v(Q;V_K) + \bar{c}_g^1(Q;V_K) \\ &= \tau_0 + \delta \cdot Q/V_K \end{aligned} \tag{6.7}$$

Profit is toll revenue from the base toll and from the variable toll, less capital cost, or

$$\Pi(Q,V_K) = Q \cdot \left[d(Q) - \bar{c}_g^1(Q;V_K) \right] - \rho \cdot K(V_K). \tag{6.8}$$

This equation is just like (6.2) with one time period h, with $q_h V_h$ replaced by Q, and with c_h replaced by $\bar{c}_g^1$. So it leads to first-order conditions with the same properties as (6.3) and (6.4): namely, capacity is chosen efficiently (given Q), and the toll level is set to account for marginal congestion cost (through $\bar{\tau}_v$) but with a monopoly markup (through τ_0). Writing out explicitly the first-order condition with respect to Q (and suppressing V_K as an argument in the functions), we have

$$d(Q) - \bar{c}_g^1(Q) + Q \cdot d'(Q) - Q \frac{\partial \bar{c}_g^1}{\partial Q} = 0,$$

where d' is the slope of the inverse demand curve. Equation (6.6) implies that the fourth term is equal to $-\bar{\tau}_v$. Because $d - \bar{c}_g^1 - \bar{\tau}_v = \tau_0$, we find

$$\tau_0 = -Q \cdot d'(Q). \tag{6.9}$$

There are two ways that we can interpret the base toll in (6.9) as a markup over marginal cost. First, as argued in Section 4.1.2, the time-varying toll component $\tau_v(t')$ is equal to the time-varying marginal external congestion cost *mecc* for a user exiting at t'. With the base toll τ_0 set according to (6.9), the total toll $\tau(t')$ is therefore equal to $mecc(t')$ plus a time-independent demand-related markup.

Alternatively, we can rewrite (6.9) in a form like (6.5) by defining the marginal cost of adding a new user, given the optimal toll pattern:

$$mc = \partial(Q \cdot \bar{c}_g^1) / \partial Q = \bar{c}_g^1 + Q \cdot \partial \bar{c}_g^1 / \partial Q = 2\bar{c}_g^1.$$

Then, the generalized price is

$$p = \tau_0 + \bar{\tau}_v + \bar{c}_g^1 = \tau_0 + 2\bar{c}_g^1 = \tau_0 + mc$$

so that (6.9) becomes (6.5) with the h subscripts removed and $1/|\varepsilon|$ defined as $-(Q/p) \cdot d'(Q)$.

The main insights from the static model on profit-maximizing tolling and capacity choice therefore survive in the basic bottleneck model.

6.1.3   Heterogeneous users

When individuals' values of time differ, another rather fundamental deviation between conditions for optimality and those for profit maximization is created. This is because the monopolist, in absence of price discrimination, naturally considers the preferences only of marginal travelers (those nearly indifferent to using the highway in question) when assessing the impact of the price on the quantity, whereas conditions for optimality reflect the preferences of all travelers, including the infra-marginal ones.

We can elaborate using the analysis of David Mills (1981). Mills considers the situation when there is correlation between willingness to pay (WTP) to make a trip and value of time (VOT) – that is, when people accounting for one portion of the demand curve have different values of time than those accounting for other portions. Then the monopolist may allow too much or too little congestion compared to the optimum because changes in revenues resulting from a marginal change in price depend on just the marginal user. The monopolist thus ignores the benefits or costs for others. For example, suppose users with a relatively high WTP also have relatively high values of time. The existence of these users tends to increase the level of the first-best toll because they would benefit a lot from reduced congestion. But such users do not affect the marginal revenue of the operator – the left-hand side of the second of equations (6.5) – because they will take trips regardless of marginal changes in congestion. (Hence, they are called infra-marginal users.)

More generally, a first-degree perfectly discriminating monopolist would have to discriminate both by individuals' WTP for making a trip *and* by their VOT, in order to achieve the conventional results of (1) extracting the entire consumer surplus (turning it into monopoly profits) and (2) reproducing first-best optimal use levels. This is because both margins for discrimination are needed to determine the toll at which a traveler would be deterred from the trip under congested conditions. It is highly unlikely that a supplier would have this amount of information, if only because these values typically differ between days for any given individual.[5] Still, the conceptual point – that first-degree price discrimination could theoretically eliminate inefficient allocative consequences of monopoly pricing – is relevant for contemplating possible regulatory policies toward monopoly. Specifically, allowing some price discrimination, with excess profits taxed in a lump-sum fashion or extracted by the public through competitive bidding, might provide a way to reap the advantages of private road provision while minimizing the disadvantages.

Needless to say, these extra complications reduce the attraction of a policy creating a private monopoly road operator. Nevertheless, the policy might be favored if it is the most practical means of financing needed highway capacity, for example, if the marginal cost of public funds is very high or public budgets are politically constrained. We return to this motivation in the next subsection.

6.1.4 *Private toll lanes: the two-route problem revisited*

One way to allow a private road operator to implement pricing, while limiting its market power, is to maintain a close substitute that is free of tolling. In fact, this arrangement – known as *managed lanes* – is of increasing practical interest. Usually, it is combined with discounted or free travel for carpools.

We analyzed a similar situation under the rubric of second-best pricing and investment (in Sections 4.2.1 and 5.1.3), by positing two parallel links that are perfect substitutes for each other: one tolled (route T) and the other untolled (route U). There, we maximized welfare (benefits minus costs) subject to a user equilibrium constraint on each link, as summarized in the Lagrangian problem of equations (4.32) and (5.9). Here, we instead assume that a private operator would maximize profit, subject to the same constraints. This means maximizing the Lagrangian function:

$$\Lambda = V_T \cdot \tau_T - \rho \cdot K_T(V_{KT})$$
$$+ \lambda_T \cdot \left[c_T(V_T; V_{KT}) + \tau_T - d(V_T; V_U) \right] + \lambda_U \cdot \left[c_U(V_U; V_{KU}) - d(V_T; V_U) \right], \tag{6.10}$$

where $d(\cdot)$ is again the inverse demand curve for the entire corridor. The first-order conditions can be solved to yield

$$\tau_T = V_T \cdot \frac{\partial c_T}{\partial V_T} - V_T \cdot d'(V) \cdot \left(\frac{\partial c_U / \partial V_U}{(\partial c_U / \partial V_U) - d'(V)} \right) \tag{6.11}$$

$$\rho \cdot K_T'(V_{KT}) = -V_T \cdot \frac{\partial c_T}{\partial V_{KT}}, \tag{6.12}$$

where d' and K' denote derivatives.[6] The investment rule (6.12) has the familiar first-best structure indicating that conditional on travel volumes, capacity is chosen to minimize total social cost.

The toll formula in (6.11), however, is not second-best or even quasi first-best, as can be seen by comparing it with (4.35) and (4.6). Its first term shows that the profit maximizer internalizes the congestion externality on the road under its control, just like the public operator as depicted in (4.35). The second term of the toll formula gives the demand-related markup, positive because d' is negative, which depends on how demand for the tolled link is affected both by congestion (on the untolled link) and by the overall corridor demand elasticity. This second term is a fraction, defined by the term in large brackets, of the markup that would apply if there were no free alternative – that is, the markup that occurs in the profit-maximizing toll (6.5) for a single road. This fraction is zero when the competing route U is uncongested since then demand for the toll road itself is perfectly elastic even if overall demand d is not perfectly elastic. The fraction rises to one as congestion on route U becomes highly sensitive to traffic ($\partial c_U/\partial V_U \rightarrow \infty$) since then traffic on the free route is effectively fixed, and so inverse demand for the toll road has the same slope d' as total inverse demand.

It is illuminating to compare (6.11) term by term with the corresponding second-best toll of equation (4.35). In both cases, the congestion externality on the toll road itself is accounted for through the usual term reflecting marginal external congestion cost on the toll road, which we may denote $mecc_T$. Where they differ is in how they account for congestion on the competing road. In computing the second-best toll of (4.35), a positive term is *subtracted* from $mecc_T$ to account for congestion spillover to route U. But in computing the profit-maximizing toll of (6.11), a positive term is *added* to $mecc_T$ to account for the additional revenue that can be extracted when congestion on the free road is heavy so that it becomes a less competitive alternative. Thus, the profit-maximizing toll is higher than the second-best toll. It is no surprise, then, that the welfare gains from applying a profit-maximizing toll are below the already small gains from second-best tolling. Indeed, they may well be negative when compared to the unpriced situation for the same capacity; this situation is in fact illustrated by the lowest curve in Figure 4.6. This is why Liu and McDonald (1998), in their study of partial pricing on southern California's SR-91, find a substantial efficiency *loss* in moving from no pricing to revenue-maximizing pricing on the express lanes, whereas they find a small but positive welfare *gain* from second-best pricing.

Why, then, is private ownership of express lanes receiving such favorable attention as a policy option? There are several reasons why it might be desirable in practice, despite these theoretical results. First, although we have compared alternative regimes for a given amount of capacity, private ownership may in fact be the key to providing *new* capacity – as was true for SR-91 in California. In that case, the relevant comparison is between a single free road and the same road augmented by a privately operated express road. Computing the welfare gain then involves knowing the capital cost of the new capacity. Nevertheless, if the private road is a financial success and there are no adverse spillovers elsewhere on the network, then the net benefits of adding and pricing the express road cannot be negative: the free road offers travel at least as fast as before, the toll road is used only voluntarily (hence, its users must be at least as well off as they were on the free road), and the operator makes non-negative profits.

A second reason is user heterogeneity. Small and Yan (2001) and Verhoef and Small (2004) find that even holding total capacity fixed, the welfare losses from profit maximization (as compared to no pricing) become smaller and may, in some cases, turn into gains, when users have heterogeneous values of time. The reason is the same as for public express lane pricing, discussed in Section 4.2.1, and involves socially beneficial self-selection of users according to VOT.

A third reason for private express lane ownership is favorable impacts of revenue-maximizing pricing on departure times. As shown using the basic bottleneck model, revenue-maximizing pricing leads to a toll pattern over time that reduces or even eliminates queuing. This remains true when an unpriced alternative exists and represents a potentially huge welfare gain (de Palma and Lindsey 2000).

Finally, the two roads may be imperfect substitutes. An example is the 407 Express Toll Route in suburban Toronto, Canada, a privately operated road that parallels, several miles distant, the main east–west freeway through the city center. Imperfect substitutability reduces congestion spillovers and thus might decrease the distortions from revenue-maximizing pricing, although it could also increase them by strengthening the operator's market power.[7] Viton (1995) analyzes a model incorporating these factors.

Designing concession agreements when two roads closely compete is not easy – a particular case of the more general issues discussed in Section 6.2. This difficulty is illustrated by the privately built, financed, and operated Express Lanes on SR-91 in southern California described earlier. These lanes were ultimately converted to public ownership due to a non-compete clause in the original contract that precluded expansion of competing capacity on parallel untolled routes, including the untolled lanes of SR-91 itself. This clause became problematic after congestion had grown worse on the untolled lanes, apparently much sooner than the government had envisaged when signing the original contract. Similarly, citizens of Sydney, Australia, became incensed when competing roads were closed as part of a franchise agreement with the builder of the Cross City Tunnel. These experiences emphasize the differences in interest between public and private road operators: whereas heavy congestion on parallel connections is good news for a private operator, it is generally bad news from the public perspective.[8] In Section 6.2, the ways in which franchise agreements attempt to reconcile such differences are considered in more detail.

6.1.5 Competition in networks

Private ownership has also been analyzed in various network configurations other than the classic two-route problem with a single, unpriced substitute. If more than one private operator is active in the market, the results depend on the sequence in which they make decisions. The most common assumption is that they decide simultaneously and that a Nash equilibrium is reached. Alternatively, one operator may act as a Stackelberg leader and move first. Three or more operators may act sequentially, one after the other. The timing of decisions matters for both toll settings and capacity choice. We look first at the short-run case in which capacities are fixed.

De Palma and Lindsey (2000) consider various ownership regimes for a network of two parallel links characterized as interacting bottlenecks. One result is that a duopoly of two private operators engaged in Bertrand-Nash price competition, each operating one of the links, achieves most of the potential efficiency gains from first-best pricing (over 90% in their base case with time-varying tolling). A mixed duopoly, with one public and one private operator, can be even more efficient – consistent with more general results from oligopoly theory.[9]

For more general networks, we can appeal to the more general results of Economides and Salop (1992) involving substitutes and complements. These results suggest that price competition among producers of goods that are substitutes (*e.g.*, operators of competing parallel roads) leads to lower prices than a combined monopolistic producer. By contrast, competition among producers of complements (*e.g.*, operators of serial links) leads to higher prices (but lower total profits) than a single monopoly: each firm applies a conventional demand-related markup, each of which must be paid by a consumer who desires the firms' complementary goods.[10] Thus, in a general network of privately owned or operated roads, the results of various degrees of toll competition depend on whether the private operators control parts of the network that are predominantly substitutable (parallel) or complementary (serial).

This idea can be formally illustrated by considering two extreme cases of dividing control of a single corridor with only regional traffic. We allow a number F of identical revenue-maximizing firms to control different parts of the corridor, with F varying between one (monopoly) and infinity (perfect competition). Each firm's capacity and costs are fixed. In one case, the corridor is divided into F equal-capacity parallel roads, each operated by a different (and otherwise unregulated) firm. Total corridor traffic V divides across the roads according to the Wardrop conditions, constrained by $\Sigma_f V_f = V$. In the other case, the corridor is divided serially into F segments, each controlled by a different firm. The total corridor traffic level V then applies to each firm. In both cases, because the firms are otherwise identical, we consider only symmetric equilibria – that is, outcomes for which all firms have identical tolls, traffic, and hence revenues.

First, we consider the case of parallel roads that are perfect substitutes, a case analyzed by Engel *et al.* (2004). The equilibrium toll for firm f can be derived by maximizing the following Lagrangian:

$$
\Lambda_f = V_f \cdot \tau_f + \lambda_f \cdot \left[c_f(V_f) + \tau_f - d\left(V_f + \sum_{g \neq f} V_g \right) \right]
$$
$$
+ \sum_{g \neq f} \lambda_f^g \cdot \left[c_g(V_g) + \tau_g - d\left(V_f + \sum_{h \neq f} V_h \right) \right]
$$

(6.13)

where $d(\cdot)$ is the inverse demand function for the entire corridor, and each term in square brackets represents a user equilibrium constraint. The first-order conditions can be solved to yield the following toll formula:

$$
\tau = \tau_f = V_f \cdot \left(c'_f - d' \right) + \frac{-(F-1)d'}{c'_{-f} - (F-1)d'} \cdot V_f d'
$$

(6.14)

where τ is the toll that each user will pay for a trip; τ_f is the toll for a specific firm (these are identical across firms and equal to τ because of symmetry); c_f is the user cost function for the road controlled by firm f; and c_{-f} is the user cost function for any other road (symmetry of course implies that in equilibrium, $c_f = c_{-f}$). The primes thus each indicate a derivative with respect to the relevant traffic volume. Equation (6.14) shows that the toll is equal to the monopolistic toll of (6.5) when $F = 1$, while it approaches the first-best toll of (4.6) when $F \to \infty$.[11] These results are intuitive and suggest that the equilibrium toll level is closer to the first-best level when the number of firms is larger so that each firm has little market power.

Now consider when individual firms occupy serial segments, each carrying the same traffic V as determined by the inverse demand curve.[12] The Lagrangian for firm f is now

$$
\Lambda_f = V\tau_f + \lambda \cdot \left\{ c_f(V) + \tau_f + \sum_{g \neq f} \left[c_g(V) + \tau_g \right] - d(V) \right\},
$$

(6.15)

where $c_g(V)$ is now the average user cost incurred just on the segment operated by firm g, so that the user cost for the entire trip is $c = \Sigma_g c_g$. The first-order conditions yield the following firm-specific toll:

$$
\tau_f = V \cdot \left(c'_f + \sum_{g \neq f} c'_g - d' \right).
$$

(6.16)

This firm thus internalizes not only the congestion on its own road segment $(V \cdot c'_f)$, but also that on each other firm's segment $(V \cdot c'_g)$. The reason is that congestion on the other firms' segments affects the firm's marginal revenues in exactly the same way as congestion on its own segment. Since every firm internalizes the congestion on the entire road, the combined toll facing the traveler over-internalizes congestion if $F > 1$. Furthermore, each firm applies a demand-related markup $(-V \cdot d')$ that is identical to what a single monopolist would charge; thus, this markup gets charged F times when considering the entire trip. Writing this formally, the total trip toll τ is

$$\tau = \sum_f \tau_f = F \cdot V \cdot (c' - d'), \tag{6.17}$$

which (for a given V) is exactly F times the monopoly toll of (6.5) – which already exceeds the first-best toll. We therefore now find the opposite result to the parallel competition case: here, the lower the number of firms, the closer the overall toll approaches the efficient level – although even with one firm it will never reach that level unless demand is perfectly elastic. An ever-larger number of firms produces an ever-larger total trip toll and hence drives demand toward zero.[13]

These opposing results for the extreme cases are exactly in the direction predicted by the general analysis of Economides and Salop (1992), as just discussed. Thus, the desirability of private road ownership and the ideal number of competitors depend critically on the network configuration and the distribution of firms over that network. Generally, an increase in competition among substitute roads would bring equilibrium tolls closer to first-best levels, while the opposite applies for complementary roads. This suggests that private operators, if allowed on a network, should insofar as possible each serve a full-length corridor, but should face competition when doing so.

These results are derived for identical roads and homogeneous users. It is more difficult to determine the characteristics of equilibrium if either roads or users are heterogeneous. We first consider roads that can differ in length (measured in km) and/or capacity (measured in maximum flow of vehicles per hour). De Palma and Lindsey (2000) show numerically, for the case of bottleneck queuing congestion, that private duopolists perform most efficiently when their roads have the same lengths and capacities. For given aggregate lengths and capacities, efficiency drops as one road gets shorter or acquires more capacity, giving the firm that operates it more market power.

Next, we consider heterogeneity of users. An obvious situation of interest would be heterogeneous values of travel time (VOTs). In that case, the distinction between marginal and infra-marginal users is again relevant, typically causing each operator to provide an inefficient level of congestion for users of its road. Efficiency can be improved if, as in Verhoef and Small (2004), the operators provide differentiated levels of service on the two roads, with one operator setting a high toll and accommodating users with high VOTs, while the other operator sets a lower toll and serves the low VOT users. But there is no guarantee this will happen – indeed, Calcott and Yao (2005) show that if a Bertrand-Nash price equilibrium exists in such a situation, it is inefficient in both the extent of toll differentiation and the resulting aggregate traffic volume.

Consider now a longer-run situation, where firms compete by choosing both capacity and toll.[14] The timing of decisions matters. Three cases have been studied for a setting in which firms operate parallel links between the same origin and destination. The simplest case is a one-stage game in which firms choose their capacities and tolls simultaneously. The profit function of each firm is then the same as a monopolist's, except that instead of facing the full market demand for travel, each firm faces a residual demand curve equal to market demand less the traffic captured by its rivals. The results therefore parallel those derived in Section 6.1.1. Each firm sets a toll equal to the marginal external cost of congestion on its link plus a markup that varies inversely with the price elasticity of its residual demand curve. Each firm also chooses a capacity that minimizes the sum of capacity costs and the congestion delay costs borne by users of its facility. If the assumptions of the self-financing result hold,[15] the combined capacity and toll choices therefore result in the same volume-to-capacity ratio as for a public welfare-maximizing firm operating the same link. Thus, each firm chooses the socially optimal service quality on its link, but with a higher toll and a lower traffic volume than the corresponding first-best optimum.

The second case is a two-stage game. In stage 1, firms simultaneously choose their capacities, anticipating the tolls that will be set in stage 2, and in stage 2, they simultaneously choose their tolls.[16] In this game, firms behave strategically and hold back on capacity in order to soften toll competition in stage 2. Relative to the simultaneous-moves game, volume-to-capacity ratios are higher, service quality is lower, and welfare is further below the first-best optimum.

The third case, studied by Van den Berg and Verhoef (2011), is a multi-stage Stackelberg game in which firms choose their capacities in sequence and then choose tolls simultaneously once all links are built. Firms in this game have conflicting incentives. As in the two-stage game, they gain from restricting capacity to limit toll competition. But the firms that choose capacities early also gain from investing heavily in capacity, in order to induce later firms to invest less. Van den Berg and Verhoef show that the first firm "overinvests" in capacity, whereas the last "underinvests." They find numerically that welfare can be higher or lower than in the two-stage game.

In summary, the studies reviewed above come to mixed conclusions about the allocative efficiency of markets in which private operators compete freely. Although a private operator will build and operate a link only if it is profitable, profitability is neither a necessary nor sufficient condition for an added link to be welfare-improving. Furthermore, if a monopolist or a firm in an oligopoly operates multiple links that are either substitutes or complements for each other, there is no guarantee that each link will be profitable (Yang *et al.* 2009). Moreover, a private firm may set capacity and/or toll of a link far from the first-best amount; thus, unfettered competition may be rather inefficient. An alternative is to regulate private road operators, a topic to which we now turn.

6.2 Regulation and franchising of private roads

If roads are controlled by a private operator, its local monopoly power provides a potentially strong economic rationale for some form of government regulation. Moreover, it is impractical to allow unrestricted free entry of private road operators given the physical nature of road investment, including its network aspects, lumpiness, irreversibility, right-of-way requirements, and land-use implications. Under what institutional setup, then, can private roads contribute most to social welfare? The question gains relevance with the growing interest in and importance of private involvement in road operations throughout the world. This section explores various dimensions of such institutional arrangements, particularly explicit agreements known as PPPs.[17] Comprehensive reviews, from which we draw heavily, include Small (2010), Estache *et al.* (2011), and Engel *et al.* (2021).

Engel *et al.* quantify the extent of PPP activity in Europe and in developing nations. In Europe, PPP investment grew steadily from the early 1990s through 2006, when it peaked at over €226 billion; it then diminished modestly through 2018, the latest year for which data are shown. In developing countries, it has peaked three times: in 1997, 2006, and 2015, showing substantial fluctuation in number of projects and a gradual increase in average size of project. These figures include all PPP projects, of which roughly one-third are in transportation.

Private involvement is motivated by many factors, both political and economic. Politically, one factor is that private capital is sought to expand investment when public budgets are tight. Small (2010) suggests this can be an economic rationale as well since restrictions on public budgets are not necessarily efficient and so an alternative may improve efficiency. A second factor is that using a PPP can circumvent restrictions on government debt: typically, the PPP is not treated as debt even though it may be effectively the same thing by forcing the government to forego revenues that it otherwise would receive. Engel *et al.* (2021) note that some accounting standards used by governments have been modified to better cope with this (probably inefficient) motive, but with mixed success. A third political factor is ideological: private infrastructure is a way to reduce the relative size of the public sector in the economy.

Economic factors include the hope that private management will be more efficient than public management. Engel *et al.* (2021) describe several potential sources of such efficiency gains: for example, more specialized management teams, better integration of design and operations, better control of the duration of construction (which has major implications for capital cost), and stronger incentives to restrict investment to projects with good traffic potential. We would add innovative design, as exemplified by Saenz de Ormijana and Rubio (2015), and innovative financing. A second economic factor, discussed further below, is the desire to reallocate risk from taxpayers to private investors – or more generally, to ensure that the parties who can bear each type of risk most cheaply are the ones that do so. A third possible factor is that the public may more readily accept road pricing if it arises from a private entity.

There are few if any truly standardized formats for PPPs, but several categories are generally recognized. The most basic is build–operate–transfer (BOT). Under such a scheme, the concessionaire finances, builds, operates, and maintains the road – usually to predefined specifications – while collecting tolls for a specified period such as 30 years, after which control is transferred to the government. The design-BOT format is similar, but the private party also designs the road. Another format is leasing, where the government sells to a private operator the right to operate and charge users for an existing road for a specified time period; prominent examples are the Chicago Skyway and the Indiana Toll Road, two adjacent portions of US Interstate Route 90 in the USA for which long-term leases were sold in 2005 and 2006, respectively.[18]

As an alternative to tolls, systems of "shadow tolls" have also been used in certain countries including the UK, Finland, and the Netherlands. In this case, users do not pay tolls, but the authority remunerates the concessionaire depending on the degree of utilization. A shadow toll may be better or worse, from the point of view of social welfare, than a privately set toll – depending on all the considerations discussed in Section 6.1.

Experience with highway franchising has not always been positive. Engel *et al.* (2021) highlight two pitfalls: the frequent use of government guarantees, and renegotiations in the face of financial trouble. Guarantees reduce the incentives to control construction costs, while the prospect of renegotiations encourage bidders to submit overoptimistic bids on the assumption that discrepancies will be made up later. Engel *et al.* attribute these problems mainly to the fact that most franchises are awarded for a fixed period. They therefore propose and analyze a variable-term contract, in which the franchise is awarded to the bidder that requires the *least present value of revenue* (LPVR) from tolling. In the LPVR auction, each possible revenue stream is converted to a present value through procedures defined in advance as part of the request for bids. The bidder then specifies an amount for this present value that, once reached through the accumulation of toll revenues, ends the term of the franchise. Assuming there are multiple bidders, the smallest such bid wins the franchise. Such an approach is likely to limit the need for guarantees and for contract renegotiations, thereby saving very substantial costs of renegotiations and removing the distorting impacts that such practices exert on both the original franchise and the subsequent operations.

Alternative criteria for auctions that have been used in practice include total cost, duration of the construction period, the toll rate at opening, and the length of the concession (World Bank 2006). Verhoef (2007) finds that the toll rates and capacities chosen may in fact depend strongly upon which of these criteria is used. His analysis considers static congestion, homogeneous travelers, neutral scale economies, and competitive auctions, while allowing for unpriced congestion elsewhere on the road network. Surprisingly, a criterion based on maximizing traffic flow can often reproduce the zero-profit second-best outcome. An exception is when the road would produce something akin to a Braess paradox, but such a situation would represent a planning failure at the very start of the process.

A key element of franchising is how various risks, especially of uncertain future demand, are shared between the government and the private operator. The parties to the agreement (including financial institutions providing capital to the franchisee) vary in several ways relevant to efficient risk sharing: diversification in their stakeholders' portfolios, access to capital markets, information about contingencies, and ability to influence these contingencies. It is important to take account of these variations in order to minimize the overall cost of risk-bearing – as well as to provide incentives against any use of private information to gain market power.

Because of the difficulty of foreseeing every contingency, a franchise agreement may include some form of price and/or capacity regulation. Otherwise, competition to win the franchise would push bidders toward a profit-maximizing combination of capacity and toll, which, as we have seen, may be far from socially optimal. But setting rigid toll rates in advance makes future changes highly political and may discourage pricing policies that are in the public interest. One solution to this is regulations that limit the rate of return on the project, as specified, for example, in the franchise for the 91 Express Lanes described in Section 6.1.4. In addition, a price control may incentivize a private operator to cut back on quality (*e.g.*, through poor maintenance). This leads to a prescription to include quality standards in the franchise, although it may be difficult to define and measure all the relevant quality dimensions over the duration of the franchise. All these possibilities highlight a basic dilemma: having more conditions in the franchise may make it better serve the public interest, but also creates opportunities for incompetence, political manipulation, and corruption on the part of the public authority. Thus, the ideal balance may differ depending on the capabilities and integrity of public management.

A skeptic might well argue that given such complexities, public road provision should remain the preferred option. A more pragmatic viewpoint is that private road operation should be an option when conditions warrant. Such conditions could include competition from substitute road links, an inefficient public road supplier, political limitations on the public sector's ability to implement pricing, inefficient constraints on public budgeting, relatively small external effects other than congestion, and the ability of the government to create and manage an effective auction mechanism. These conditions vary across locations and across time: thus, for example, the long experience with motorway networks in France and Spain illustrates how changing conditions and goals have led to a changing extent to which the networks were privatized (Small 2010).

We conclude, then, that it is impossible to state in general that either private or public road provision is more desirable. The extent to which the conditions just described apply can be expected to vary strongly across nations, regions, and over time. Fortunately, many degrees and forms of privatization are possible and understanding these conditions is the key to choosing among them.

6.3   Privately provided transit services

Over the last several decades, many cities and nations have privatized or deregulated public transit services. A few have also tightened or modified regulations in an attempt to address problems with service. This has created opportunities to compare results of alternatives ranging from public ownership and operation, through various public coordinating or regulatory roles, to fully deregulated private provision. Hörcher and Tirachini (2021) provide a succinct review.

Dissatisfaction with public control has been fueled by huge budgetary commitments to urban public transit. Some research has attributed transit's tenuous finances to wage increases, overly capital-intensive operations, and various perverse incentives built into subsidy programs. Public ownership also invites political interference, which may deter timely investments. Solving these distinct problems may lead to differing policy recommendations: for example, cost control may require competition, whereas raising funds for investment may require some monopoly power. Indeed, as we have already seen in the case of road franchises, there is a tension between the desire to limit the pricing power of private operators and the desire to maximize the value of the government's asset.

In this section, we review the main forms that private-sector involvement takes, followed by an analysis of likely outcomes. We identify the various design elements of contracts between transit authorities and operators, and note their strengths and limitations. We then briefly review empirical evidence on the extent to which private operators display lower costs and/or higher labor productivity. We go on to examine the actual experience with several cases of privatization and deregulation. Finally, we examine the economics of several forms of transportation that somewhat resemble public transit and that often involve private providers: ride-sourcing, ride-sharing, and Mobility as a Service (MaaS).

6.3.1   Forms of privatization

While discussing private highways, we have already seen that there are many intermediate positions between the extremes of full public operation and unregulated private ownership. With transit, there are even more dimensions along which such intermediate positions can be defined since not only infrastructure provision but also ongoing operation must be considered.

The least drastic form of privatization is *tendering*, also called *contracting* or *contracting out*. In this arrangement, the public authority retains full control over network design and services offered, but it contracts with private firms to carry out specific parts of this overall design such as operating prespecified bus runs or maintaining rolling stock (*i.e.*, vehicles). An example of tendering is the private bus operators with which London Transport contracted in the early phases of UK deregulation during the 1980s.

Going somewhat further, the public authority can *franchise* some of these services by licensing private firms to operate them under less specific guidelines.[19] The franchise is for a specified period of time, ranging from two or three years in Sweden to several decades in parts of South America (Nash 2005).

Going further still, the market to provide certain services may be simply turned over to one or more private firms, as is common, for example, with telecommunications and electricity in many nations. This could be a *regulated monopoly*, in which a single firm is allowed to provide services under tightly controlled terms of price and service quality. This form of privatization entails the so-called "competition *for* the market," in contrast to "competition *in* the market." If freedom of entry is allowed, the regulations over price and service may be relaxed on the assumption that competition will produce a desirable result just as for other goods in a largely market economy. Depending on how completely such regulations are relaxed, the result is some degree of *privatization with deregulation*. In virtually all cases, government oversight is maintained over such things as safety, financial disclosure, and matters covered by general business policies.

Naturally, the relative advantages of different forms of privatization depend on the nature of the industry. A primary consideration is whether or not the market is a natural monopoly, meaning that costs display scale or scope economies that are strong enough to make it (unacceptably) inefficient to have more than one producer. Natural monopoly is often thought to characterize infrastructure (*e.g.*, rail track and large bus terminals) but not operations. However, as shown before, transit operations are also subject to scale economies when they require substantial access costs on the part of users. Thus, transit operations may also be a natural monopoly and it is no coincidence that free entry into privatized transit markets has often led to consolidation of the market by one or at most a very few firms.

6.3.2 *Market structure and competitive practices*

If markets are left partially or fully unregulated, what will happen? This question has been addressed specifically for public transport through theoretical, empirical, and simulation analysis.

A first question is whether private firms could operate profitably without subsidies. Case studies have identified some favorable conditions: for example, two potentially profitable markets for conventional urban transit in the USA are high-quality express service from affluent suburbs to large employment centers, and local bus service serving low-income people in high-density areas.[20] More generally, as seen in Section 5.1.1, the ability of a public transit provider to self-finance from fare revenues when pricing optimally depends on its degree of scale economies: prospects are poor at low ridership volumes but are much better in large dense cities.

Despite this potential, nearly all existing transit systems are heavily subsidized. Hong Kong is an exceptional case in which all mass transit services are both commercially operated and profitable. As Tang and Lo (2010) explain, Hong Kong has favorable conditions for rail and bus transit including a high population density, compact development, and low car ownership. This has encouraged the government to forego direct subsidies to either rail or bus service. Nevertheless, both modes are subsidized indirectly. The rail operator receives revenues from non-core commercial activities and has exclusive rights to property development above rail stations.[21] The bus operator is exempt from fuel taxes, some registration taxes, and license fees, and like other road vehicles, it does not pay for road infrastructure other than tolls on a few roads. Thus, even in Hong Kong, transit is not fully self-financing.

A second question is whether private operation produces desirable results. To analyze this question, we have to consider the complexities of competition under various market conditions.

One line of inquiry is the nature of unregulated and imperfectly competitive equilibria in which two or more firms compete. Often, these are modeled as some variation of a Bertrand equilibrium, in which each firm assumes that the price and quality of service offered by other firms are fixed. Several of these studies were part of a vigorous policy debate over deregulation of bus services in the UK in the 1980s. For example, Evans (1987) considers an unregulated non-cooperative oligopoly with free entry: he finds a symmetric equilibrium which exhibits higher fares and higher service frequency than would result from welfare-maximization, even subject to a breakeven constraint. However, in Evans' simulations, welfare in the oligopolistic case falls only slightly short of that from welfare maximization, whereas it far exceeds (at most demand levels) that from monopoly. Hence, Evan's results are supportive of deregulation as a viable policy when the market is likely to accommodate two or more firms.

But will oligopolistic structure emerge in an unregulated market? Dodgson and Katsoulacos (1988b) examine entry conditions for local bus service, finding a wide range of market conditions under which just two firms share the market. Assuming consumers do not take advantage of posted timetables, the firms differentiate their products in order to increase their market power, with one using minibuses to provide high frequency at a high fare, and the other using double-decker buses to supply lower frequency at a lower fare. Similarly, Viton (1981) finds that two transit firms would significantly differentiate their products if they engaged in Cournot-like competition, in which each assumes the other will respond to its actions so as to maintain its customer base.

The results of these latter studies raise the question whether differentiated service is socially desirable. Gronau (2000) addresses this using a model with two potential modes that differ in travel speed, and two groups of travelers that differ in values of time (VOT); high VOT passengers choose the faster and more expensive mode. Gronau shows that the social benefit of having two modes, rather than one, increases with the number of travelers and with dispersion in VOT, while it decreases with costs due to waiting time and boarding and alighting times. This illustrates a basic tradeoff: differentiating service helps cater to diverse preferences, but it also inhibits consolidation of traffic to exploit economies of density.

Despite the theoretical possibility of oligopoly, experience in the UK suggests that in most deregulated local bus markets, one firm becomes dominant through superior efficiency, predatory practices, mergers, or luck. Thus, the question arises whether it is necessary to regulate such a firm in order to prevent the high price and low ridership expected from a monopoly. A key question here is whether *potential* entry by competitors would serve to discipline a monopolist's decisions about price and service. An extreme case is a perfectly *contestable* market, in which the prospect of hit-and-run entry is sufficiently threatening to force a monopolist to choose competitive fare and service policies. Contestability requires that the entrant have low barriers to entry and exit (the latter requiring an absence of sunk costs, which are discussed in Section 3.1), and also that the incumbent be unable to change fares and service levels quickly (Baumol *et al.* 1982).

Some features of urban transit, such as low scale economies in providing vehicle-hours of service, favor low barriers to entry and exit. However, other factors do create entry barriers (Gagnepain *et al.* 2011). Entrants may incur substantial costs in training staff, securing access to terminal facilities, establishing a system of travel cards, gaining efficiency through learning-by-doing, and establishing a reputation for good service. Used bus equipment may be costly or hard to obtain, and incumbent operators may withhold surplus buses from the second-hand market. Thus, many forms of investment by a new entrant cannot be fully retrieved if the incumbent monopolist responds quickly by lowering fares or increasing service quality. If the incumbent can credibly threaten to do so even temporarily, in order to drive out the entrant, it is said to be capable of *predation*, which discourages entry. Dodgson and Katsoulacos (1988a) analyze when a rational incumbent would respond in this way, showing that informational asymmetries can lead to successful predation.

Indeed, the limited empirical evidence suggests that transit markets are partially but not perfectly contestable. Evans (1988) describes the experience in Hereford, UK, where transit service was deregulated beginning in 1981. Following a brief period of intense competition, the dominant firm drove out all its rivals except in one small segment of its market. Fares ultimately returned nearly to the levels that prevailed prior to the experiment, but service levels remained substantially higher. Evans thus suggests that potential entry constrains a monopolist's service levels, which cannot be quickly increased in response to entry, but does not constrain its fares. As we will see in Section 6.3.4, this conclusion is consistent with results of more widespread deregulation of local bus service in Great Britain starting in 1986.

Such experience is consistent with a broader theory of competition with differentiated products (Schmalensee 1978). In such a market, the threat of potential entry will typically cause a monopolist to offer an excessive number of products in order not to leave an open niche for a competitor. In the context of public transit, this might simply be offering service at many times of day. The reason is that the monopolist can protect its high profits on each product through price predation, giving it a strong incentive to maintain dominance in each product, but it cannot so easily protect against new products because doing so would require immediately matching an entrant's product characteristics.

Van der Veer (2002) further explores these issues using numerical simulations on a prototype bus line. He finds that, as expected, a profit-maximizing monopolist would like to offer service that is *less* frequent than would be optimal, but if needed to deter entry, it will instead offer service that is *more* frequent than optimal. Van der Veer finds similar inefficiencies regarding other dimensions of service quality. Ironically, these can be partly ameliorated if the government offers a per-rider subsidy, preferably combined with a lump-sum payment required of the firm (as would occur with a competitive franchising). The ridership-related subsidy encourages a lower price and better quality of service, while requiring the lump-sum payment (assumed to apply equally to a potential entrant) reduces the incentive to oversupply service because it makes entry more difficult.

The models described above mostly assume constant returns to scale in producing intermediate outputs such as annual bus-kilometers of service. Importantly, they also (implicitly) assume that any economies of scale due to user-supplied time are at a system level, rather than a firm level: for example, the traveler cares only about total bus frequency on his or her route, not about the frequency provided by a given firm. This, however, raises troubling questions about the viability of a non-integrated system of urban transit. What if it is not feasible for each firm to use the same stops, for example, because they use vehicles of different sizes or because major terminals are owned by one firm? What if consumers care about the reputations of firms in whose vehicles they entrust their well-being? What if the unregulated equilibrium entails differentiated products, for example, high-fare express and low-fare local service (as in some of the models just discussed), so that travelers with a strong preference for one cannot benefit from the extra service frequency offered by the other? In all these situations, scale economies are lost by allowing multiple providers because the waiting times of a given firm's riders are not diminished by an increase in service supplied by other firms. Nash (1988) emphasizes the importance of system integration in realizing these user cost savings and also reminds us that several other sources of economies of scale and scope, such as through ticketing of passengers and scheduling of drivers, occur in an integrated system. The implication is that efficiency may be lost unless a central authority takes a proactive role in coordinating service.

Transit services in developing nations often operate quite differently from those in the developed world. Broadly speaking, they entail informal, freewheeling, and rather chaotic competition. There are several reasons for this (Cervero and Golub 2007). First, gaps in government agencies' managerial capacity typically make it less likely that regulations will be consistently enforced or that other policies will be consistently implemented. Second, the widespread availability of low-wage labor and the difficulty with which small businesses can raise capital create the possibility of very small companies – thus, many developing cities are characterized by hundreds of separate bus companies, many operating informally. Third, the potentially chaotic competitive situation is exacerbated by another trait: a high modal share for bus transit, arising because many residents cannot afford cars. All three of these factors tend to produce a great deal of bus congestion.

Informal transit services do have some virtues. They are flexible and can deviate from standard routes to accommodate passenger requests or be redeployed if market conditions change. Small transit vehicles can maneuver on narrow and crowded streets more easily than full-size buses. Operators sometimes collaborate by organizing route associations that provide more frequent and reliable service, thus partially addressing the desire to exploit scale economies.

However, informal services have a number of drawbacks. They can be sporadic. Operators may ignore unserved low-density routes and interlope on high-density routes with scheduled services. Drivers may not be adequately trained, and vehicles may not be insured or meet safety standards. Often, the vehicles create noise and air pollution. Evasion of taxes and fees is common. On-the-road competition can encourage aggressive and dangerous driving, as bus drivers attempt to poach passengers from competitors.[22] Due to these traits, bus transit contributes substantially to high levels of congestion, air pollution, and traffic accidents in large developing cities.

To reduce the problems associated with on-the-road competition, Klein *et al.* (1997) have proposed a system of "curb rights" whereby individual firms are granted exclusive rights to pick up passengers at specified locations and times of day. The system would enable firms to establish reputations for serving their designated markets and thus to attract passengers without the threat of rivals stealing their business. Operators could license their rights to others so that vehicle breakdowns, illness, or other shocks would not disrupt regular service. To be sure, designing a workable system of curb rights is a challenging task and to our knowledge none has yet been implemented, except in a few instances of inter-city bus service.

6.3.3 Contract design

Tendering, franchising, and other forms of privatization require contracts between a governmental authority or regulator and firms that provide transit service. The comprehensive theory of regulation developed by Laffont and Tirole (1993) is applicable. It is based on two key considerations: information asymmetries between regulators and firms, and efficient sharing of risks.

Information asymmetries are near universal in any setting with private firms interacting with public agencies. Urban transit is no exception. Firms typically know more about factors that determine costs – such as the number of buses required to serve a network, fuel consumption, how traffic congestion affects costs, and so on (Gagnepain and Ivaldi 2017). Firms may also know more about local demand and how it depends on frequency and other aspects of service quality. We note that these same factors are also important to the franchising of private roads (Section 6.2).

Furthermore, risks to transit providers arise with respect to both costs and demand. Costs are impacted by many unpredictable factors including fuel price fluctuations, wage disputes, and problems with reliability and maintenance of equipment – especially of equipment involving new types of infrastructure or vehicles. Demand is affected by such things as the general state of the economy, the supply of competing modes and newly emerging modes, and lifestyle changes. In general, it is efficient to allocate risks to the party that has more control over them, and/or is more able to bear the risks.

A central conclusion of Laffont and Tirole's theory is that by offering an appropriate menu of contractual options, firms subject to such risks can be induced to implicitly reveal their information and to voluntarily make desirable choices. Such contracts avoid moral hazard problems with the operator, such as failing to maintain reliable service; they also address adverse selection problems by offering terms that are unattractive to inefficient firms.

In practice, local authorities have limited resources and often lack enough information to design contracts as prescribed by economic theory.[23] Most contracts take one of three forms (Sheng and Meng 2020). The simplest form is a *management contract*, in which the regulator retains fare revenue and bears operational costs, while the operator receives a fixed profit – this is a form of cost plus contract that is often used for construction. A second form is a *gross-cost contract* (the "Scandinavian model" in Preston's (2005) terminology) in which the regulator again keeps fare revenues, but the operator incurs costs; these contracts have been used in Sweden, Norway, Copenhagen, London, Helsinki, Rome, Auckland, and Las Vegas, among other places. In this case, firms bid on the payment at which they will offer specified services. Since the payment does not depend on the costs actually incurred, the contract is a type of fixed-price contract, which transfers cost risks to the operator.

Management and gross-cost contracts avoid on-the-road competition and related problems with safety and noise. But they do not give incentives to boost demand, deter fare evasion, or provide good-quality service. These drawbacks are potentially overcome by the third type: the *net-cost contract*, in which the operator keeps fare revenue and bears both cost and demand risks. Competitive bids specify the amount of subsidy required or, perhaps, the amount of profits the firm is willing to return to the government. In addition to instilling incentives to attract riders and minimize fare evasion, net-cost contracts give operators an incentive to modify aspects of service such as routes. They also ease the regulator's task of planning and monitoring. However, one drawback is that firms may be less able to bear risk than government, as noted in Section 6.2, resulting in higher bids and less competition for the contract.[24] Another drawback is that a net-cost contract would require fare restrictions to prevent a profit-maximizing monopolistic outcome.

Given the tradeoffs between instilling incentives, allocating risks, and monitoring performance, some transit systems employ hybrid payment schemes. A generic scheme combines a fixed payment, a component based on vehicle kilometers to encourage supply, a component based on passenger kilometers to encourage ridership, and a component depending on other performance indicators, such as punctuality.[25] A limitation of performance standards is that they may be difficult to define and monitor. Another is that they could interfere with operators' needed discretion to improve service and boost demand by designing routes, adjusting timetables, marketing, and other actions.

Contract duration is another design consideration, just as we saw for road franchising. Long contracts encourage operators to maintain infrastructure and vehicles and to take other actions with long-term payoffs. However, long contracts invite complacency and monopoly behavior, and they give incumbents an extended period of experience that puts other potential operators at a disadvantage. Long contracts are also more likely to lead to renegotiations due to changes in economic conditions, technological developments, or other factors that affect either party to the contract. That prospect may, in turn, also encourage candidate operators to submit unrealistic bids in the belief that they can later negotiate better terms, just as we saw for private roads.

A general and fundamental limitation is that contracts are always incomplete since it is not possible to specify contractual obligations for, or even to envisage, all eventualities. This is one reason for negotiations. Preferably, contracts may specify specific mechanisms for negotiation between the regulator and operator during the contract period. Such negotiation may even be warranted if an operator is cost-efficient and has performed well.

Some local authorities in the UK and Sweden have gone further and formed voluntary quality partnerships with transit firms to improve bus services in urban areas (Hrelja *et al.* 2018). Such partnerships allow lessons from experience to be implemented during the contract period and facilitate transparency and monitoring. Similar to the case with long contracts, however, this practice creates learning advantages for the incumbent and so may increase the difficulty for other firms to compete for contracts.

6.3.4   *Efficiency of public and private providers*

Two types of studies have attempted to compare the costs or productivities of public and private transit operators. The first type compares firms across cities, often estimating cost functions to control for factors other than the type of ownership. The second examines the results in a given city when tendering or franchising of transit services is introduced. Frick *et al.* (2008) and Karlaftis (2008) review these studies carefully.

6.3.4.1   *Comparisons across areas*

Cross-sectional studies have reached varying conclusions about whether or not private operators are more efficient than public operators. These studies are complicated by potential biases that may make private operators falsely appear more efficient. Public operators often experience sharper daily peaks, and a public authority may take over previously failing private firms or spin off its more successful operations, thereby leaving it with less inefficient operations at any point in time. After accounting for these factors, Iseki (2010), in one of the most careful analyses, finds modest cost savings (per vehicle hour) from contracting out in the USA – around 5% to 8%. Likewise, using data for transit systems in Europe, Karlaftis and Tsamboulas (2012) find that contracting out results in greater efficiency as measured by the costs of supplying vehicle kilometers, with net-cost contracts performing better than gross-cost contracts. However, they obtain the opposite ranking for costs per passenger kilometer: public systems rank the best, and systems with net-cost contracts rank the worst.[26]

More recently, using panel data for US bus transit agencies from 1997–2014, Sarriera *et al.* (2018) estimate that private operators have on average 16.4% lower costs per vehicle-revenue-mile than directly operated services. Contracting out reduces costs by more when the public sector provides some of the service: Sarriera *et al.* conjecture that this is because simultaneous public-sector operations encourage private firms to operate efficiently so that privatization will not be reversed.

6.3.4.2   *Before-and-after comparisons*

Preston (2005) and Karlaftis (2008) review a number of cases where publicly operated bus and rail services switched to a tendering system. Again, the evidence is mixed, but generally positive for privatization. Cost savings and/or productivity improvements have been reported for several cases in Sweden, Spain, Australia, New Zealand, and the USA. For bus services, most cases reported have shown some immediate reductions in unit costs, averaging around 20% if services remained unchanged and more if services were restructured.

By contrast, subsidy incentives to increase bus ridership have been found to be ineffective. For example, Vigren and Pyddoke (2020) assess a case in Sweden where a subsidy per passenger was added to existing gross-cost contracts, finding that ridership did not increase significantly. They attribute this to three factors: the per-passenger payments were too low, the operator lacked the freedom to modify service, and service was already of high quality – thereby leaving little scope to attract more riders.

For rail service, the experience with tendering is less favorable than for bus. Rail service has higher fixed costs and involves a more complex relationship between infrastructure and operations. These traits create more scope for strategic bidding and predatory pricing as means for firms to attempt to control the market. Attempts to privatize the infrastructure itself have been the most problematic, as we will discuss in Section 6.3.5. As with many economic policies, success depends in part on the particular mechanism used and how well it matches conditions of the local market. Transit systems vary widely in terms of network size, exposure to traffic congestion, competition from other modes, susceptibility to shocks, and so on. In light of this, and given the many dimensions of contracts, it is not surprising to find a lot of variation in outcomes.

6.3.4.3   Conclusions

While results of private transit provision are promising, the evidence is not straightforward. Rather, it supports the conclusion that the most important factors are not so much ownership itself, but factors that affect management incentives. This observation provides a useful background for the next subsection, in which we examine the practical experience with institutional changes in public transit.

6.3.5   Experience with privatization and deregulation

The statistical studies just reviewed can be supplemented with an analysis of the practical experience in privatization and deregulation of public transit services. Nash (2005) is particularly helpful. Here, we focus on two special cases that have proven illuminating: Great Britain starting in 1985, and developing nations.

6.3.5.1   Great Britain since 1985

A set of far-reaching and varied privatization experiments began with the British Transport Act of 1985.[27] Three quite different experiments can be distinguished. *Outside London*, urban bus services were mostly privatized and free entry permitted, with municipal operators required either to privatize or to operate on a commercial basis. (Subsidies were allowed but had to be made available on equal terms to all firms.) *Within London*, the public bus operator (London Transport) was retained but was required to tender services through competitive contracts, while maintaining central control over schedules, routes, and fares. The *London Underground*, by contrast, was unaffected by the 1985 Act, but later – between 2003 and 2010 – its infrastructure maintenance and investment activities were spun off through PPPs.

We look first at the experience in urban areas outside London. The main results were large service increases (as measured by vehicle-kilometers), higher fares, lower patronage, and substantial cost savings. Real wages for drivers stabilized (after a prior increase) but did not substantially decline, implying that the observed cost savings represent improved productivity. Much of the service increase was due to a switch to smaller buses, called minibuses. The higher fares resulted not from the new market structure but from a drastic reduction in government subsidies that was made simultaneously with deregulation.

The patronage decline was the biggest surprise. Several studies from the mid-1990s compare patronage with counterfactual scenarios to see how much of the decline was due to deregulation (Small and Gómez-Ibáñez 1999). Some results suggest that fare increases alone cannot explain the decline, with authors suggesting that lack of integration of service among competing operators may have diminished the quality of service. Neither is the decline explained by transitional difficulties, as it continued throughout the 1990s and beyond.

The nature of competition varied among metropolitan areas. In most cases, any serious competition was soon eliminated by aggressive increases in route frequency, predatory pricing, or mergers. Mackie *et al.* (1995) explain this consolidation, at least in part, as reflecting inherent advantages of incumbents such as local knowledge. Scale economies of the kind described in Chapter 3 may also help explain it.

Next, we consider London's bus service. The experience there is in some ways similar: more service, higher fares, and dramatic cost reductions. However, patronage did not fall, but instead increased.[28] This last observation offers some support to the hypothesis that users benefit from the integrated planning of service offerings that continues in London. It also reflects a much more moderate subsidy-cutting program in London than elsewhere.

Finally, we consider the London Underground. The central government set up PPPs consisting of three separate contracts with private consortia of firms, each with a mandate to maintain and improve the infrastructure of a specific group of Underground lines. (No private firm was given authority to operate trains.) These contracts were competitively bid, with one consortium winning two of the three contracts. London Underground Limited (LTL), a public agency, retained responsibility for train operations and fare collection and was given somewhat circumscribed responsibility to monitor the contracts. The 30-year contracts called for frontloading of expenditures by the private firms, covered by private financing arranged by the consortia as part of their bids, in order to speed up needed upgrades.

The contracts were forced through by the national government over the strenuous objections of the Mayor of London, leading academics, and others due to financial, operational and safety concerns.[29] And indeed, serious problems arose over time due to project revisions, contractual ambiguities, poor corporate governance and leadership, cost escalation, and insufficient information about costs on the part of LTL. By 2010, both consortia had been either forced into "administration" (akin to bankruptcy) or bought out at a loss to shareholders.

The London Underground's adverse experience with PPPs is consistent with more general concerns about separating responsibility for transportation infrastructure and operations. The pros and cons of separation have long been debated with respect to long-distance rail service, the main concerns being high transactions costs and potential loss of economies of scope.[30]

6.3.5.2   Developing nations

Section 6.3.2 reviewed the prevalence in developing nations of on-the-road competition and its attendant problems. Policy makers have attempted to address these problems, with differing degrees of success. Experience in two South American cities, with strikingly different results, is illustrative. In Bogotá, Colombia, the TransMilenio project, begun in 2000, establishes a single public company to design the bus network, to oversee tendering of routes to private operators, and to organize a centralized (and separately tendered) fare collection system (Estache and Gómez-Lobo 2005, pp. 153–55). At the same time, several elements of bus rapid transit were added, including exclusive bus lanes and enclosed bus stops. Operators work on gross-cost contracts, so they have no incentive to compete for passengers. In its first year, very favorable results were reported on trip times, bus-related accidents, and air pollution concentrations. Subsequently ridership has risen substantially, despite periodic complaints about crowding and safety at stations.[31]

A broadly similar project, Transantiago, began operating in Santiago, Chile, in 2006, with many of the same goals.[32] It followed an earlier system of competitive tendering based on net-cost contracts, introduced in 1991, which had reduced the number of buses in central Santiago and lowered fares, but had failed to improve service quality or to eliminate dangerous on-street competition and high accident rates. Transantiago involved a major redesign of services: the network was restructured in a hub-and-spoke configuration, resulting in 27% fewer buses; fares were integrated (including transfers to and from the state-owned and operated subway system) using a single contactless smart card; and net-cost contracts replaced gross-cost contracts.[33] Partly this was an attempt to replace costly and low-quality bus service by better trunk service, and to make fuller use of the modern Metro system.

Like many big changes in transport policy, this innovation was not carried out in isolation, but rather in conjunction with other major policy changes intended to improve service quality and safety. In particular, the new system reduced the number of licensed private providers, giving each exclusive rights over its designated service area. Considerable investment in new vehicles and in exclusive bus lanes was also planned. However, these investments had not been fully completed when the new service was initiated. In addition, the "trunk and feeder" character of the service was enforced by certain trip restrictions that were unpopular. These facts created public resentment.

The resulting system did eliminate on-street competition, but it created some new problems: gaps in network coverage, increased waiting and travel times, more transfers, and more crowding. In addition, congestion occurred at bus stops, fare evasion increased, and the public deficit increased as well. It also appears that that car travel increased (Gallego *et al.* 2013). The result was widespread complaints and very adverse publicity. Over time, the situation improved, and within five years, the system was meeting at least some of its goals: metro ridership doubled, most trips involved a single fare, bus speeds rose, and some express bus service was introduced. Ironically, one of the ultimate successes – segregated bus lanes offering expedited travel – was itself a source of controversy because local business and residents viewed some of them as substitutes for a desired new Metro line.

In part, the difficulties experienced by Transantiago resulted from an ill-designed restructuring of routes and too large a reduction in the number of buses. The design of contracts was also not ideal. Fares were adjusted to maintain roughly constant revenues, which reduced the incentive to provide service. Rigidity of the contracts provided little scope to deal with problems as they arose, and the threat to cancel contracts due to poor performance was not considered credible; indeed, contracts were instead renegotiated several times.

In 2019, Transantiago was renamed Red Metropolitana de Movilidad (Metropolitan Mobility Network) or "Red" for short. Other changes were made, such as introducing electric buses and buses with low floors. Nevertheless, as of 2022, Transantiago had not yet met all its goals. One lesson from its rocky history is the danger of overhauling an entire transit system at once. Bogotá and other Latin American cities phased in changes gradually, with better results.

6.3.6   *Ride-sourcing, ride-sharing, and Mobility as a Service*

Private entrepreneurs and firms, in addition to providing conventional transit service, sometimes fill market niches with other services that, like public transit, involve strangers sharing a vehicle. Examples include subscription commuter buses, semi-scheduled jitney services by vans or minibuses, airport shuttle vans, demand-responsive services, shared-ride taxi, shared ride-sourcing services, and commuter vanpools. These services, sometimes called "paratransit," are often discouraged or prohibited outright when transit service is publicly provided or heavily regulated, in order to avoid competition with formal public transit. Thus, one outcome of deregulation or privatization of formal transit services may be the spontaneous emergence of paratransit services.

More drastic innovations are now occurring due to the use of digital and web-based technologies to improve the interface between users and service providers. Here, we focus on three such innovations: ride-sourcing, ride-sharing, and Mobility as a Service (MaaS).

6.3.6.1 Ride-sourcing

Ride-sourcing was briefly discussed in Section 2.1.5. Ride-sourcing companies, formally known as transportation network companies (TNCs), serve as two-sided digital platforms that match passengers with vehicle drivers. Unlike taxicabs, drivers cannot legally be hailed from the street; instead, customers request rides using smartphones or other mobile devices. Some drivers work for TNCs full time, but many drivers work only part time on days they choose. TNCs offer various types of service differentiated by vehicle capacity, comfort, reservations priority, and ability to book rides in advance.[34] Ride-sharing, meaning a single vehicle serving two or more passengers with different itineraries, may also be provided, as discussed below. TNCs often vary fares according to market conditions; during periods of high demand, this enhances efficiency by simultaneously discouraging demand and encouraging supply.

As a relatively new transportation mode, ride-sourcing has been beneficial to visitors to a city, as well as to residents who do not own a vehicle, cannot drive, or want to drink. Response times can be quicker than for taxis, and fares often lower. Its relationship to other travel modes is the subject of active research. For example, it may either substitute for or complement public transit, as noted in Section 2.1.5: where public transport service is good, ride-sourcing can boost ridership by providing a feeder role, but it seems that more often it replaces public transit trips.[35]

Thus, it is no surprise that Mangrum and Molnar (2020), Diao *et al.* (2021), and other studies have found that ride-sourcing increases total vehicle travel and slows traffic. The former study takes advantage of a natural experiment in the form of a change in taxi regulations that permitted a form of ride-sourcing. The substitution for public transit is exacerbated, in terms of effects on congestion, by ride-sourcing's low load factors and by extra distances traveled while empty, called "deadheading," as drivers move to pick up their next customer.

Official attitudes toward ride-sourcing have varied widely. Some cities initially banned it while others encouraged it. Regulations differ with respect to driver licensing requirements, insurance, fares, and the number of drivers permitted to operate in a given area. Moreover, most TNCs have treated drivers as independent contractors, rather than employees, but some jurisdictions have challenged this in court or legislated otherwise, seeking to impose minimum wages and/or other employee protections. A few have also imposed restrictions on charges relating to congestion.[36]

6.3.6.2 Ride-sharing

Ride-sharing allows two or more parties with different origins and/or destinations to take parts of their trips in the same vehicle at the same time. Ride-sharing services are often supplied by TNCs, and by public agencies or other private companies using vans, buses, or jitneys – the latter, also called dollar vans, are privately owned buses operated, sometimes illegally, in areas that are under-served by public transit.[37]

Some analysts believe that autonomous vehicles (AVs) will be implemented predominantly as a form of shared mobility, rather than being privately owned. Consequently, much of the recent literature on ride-sharing has focused on AVs – hence called shared autonomous vehicles (SAVs). Here we discuss ride-sharing both in conventional vehicles and in SAVs.

Several business models have been proposed for SAVs (Stocker and Shaheen 2017). They differ according to what type of entities own and operate vehicles, and how many of them are permitted in a given area. Ride-sourcing can be requested either on-demand or via reservation, the latter being especially convenient for regular trips. Reservation-based systems enable better planning of routes and schedules and thus improve vehicle availability, reduce deadheading, and reduce the needed fleet size (Narayanan *et al.* 2020). Fares can be based on distance, duration, and/or trip origin and destination, and they may be varied dynamically according to current or anticipated demand.

Ride-sharing provided as part of an organized system has several advantages over traditional carpooling. It can reduce the costs of parking and vehicle capital, relax scheduling constraints, and perhaps reduce emissions through special-purpose regulations and through better access to electric charging stations.[38] With SAVs, further cost savings are possible because there is no human driver, and because coordination among vehicles and route adjustments will be easier. Travel will probably be safer. The VOT for passengers may be lower than in conventional vehicles, assuming passengers have more space and/or can access amenities such as communication portals and video screens. The economics of ride-sharing are best in areas of high population density where demand is high, and hence, deadheading distances can be short.

In a series of projects, Kara Kockelman and collaborators have studied the design and operation of SAV services using an agent-based simulation model known as POLARIS. It combines an activity model (ADAPTS, mentioned in Section 2.6), a dynamic "mesoscopic" traffic-flow model (noted in Section 3.4.4), and a dispatching model. Gurumurthy *et al.* (2020) describe results for two US locations: Bloomington (Indiana) and the greater Chicago area. The authors find that a centralized dispatching strategy is important if cost and congestion are to be kept low while still providing good service quality (as measured by response time and percentage of requests that are accommodated). Their results especially favor a strategy of proactively repositioning unused vehicles from areas with a surplus to those with a shortage of vehicles relative to nearby demand. A typical feasible scenario involves about 40% of vehicle travel to be empty because it either is being repositioned or is *en route* to a customer. This fraction is comparable to that actually observed in private ride-sourcing operations serving individual (unshared) trips with simpler algorithms. Other studies have shown that, as expected, the fraction of empty trips decreases with larger AV fleets (Adler *et al.* 2019).

Ride-sharing has two disadvantages. One is that picking up and dropping off two or more sets of passengers increases average travel time and uncertainty about arrival time. The other is a loss of privacy and possible concerns for personal safety when traveling with strangers – especially in an AV. The importance of these and other factors for SAVs has been investigated in several studies. Barbour *et al.* (2019) determine from a survey of American Automobile Association (AAA) members that the biggest concerns, in order of decreasing frequency, are SAV safety, travel time uncertainty, privacy, longer travel times, and cost. Individuals who can easily find parking are less inclined to use SAVs, as are those with longer commutes (possibly because of greater uncertainty about arrival time). Using data from a web-based survey, Lavieri and Bhat (2019) find that users are less averse to the presence of strangers when commuting than on leisure-activity trips: an encouraging result for alleviating congestion during peak periods.

6.3.6.3 *Mobility as a Service*

MaaS is an ambitious attempt to arrange seamless personal door-to-door travel service using a single digital platform, typically combining public transit with other motorized and non-motorized modes. Instead of obtaining services from individual transport service providers, travelers convey trip requests to a MaaS platform operator   also called a broker or aggregator (Ho *et al.* 2018). The operator determines the best combination of modes and service types for the customer and purchases the component services from the providers – possibly providing the traveler with a menu of choices. The traveler then makes a single combined payment to the operator. The concept is described and analyzed by ITF (2021), from which we draw.

The services offered on MaaS platforms can span public and private motorized and non-motorized modes of transport. Existing platforms typically charge a fixed monthly subscription which provides for unlimited use of public transport and discounted rates for other modes.[39] Services may provide ride-sharing, or alternatively sequential sharing of the same vehicle – as with car-sharing and bicycle hire. Services may or may not include an option for reservations; routes and timetables might be either fixed or flexible. In order to encourage a more uniform approach to this type of service, an organization known as MaaS Alliance was founded in 2016 as a PPP.[40]

Experience with MaaS is still limited and its financial viability is unclear. MaaS has some promising features: easier trip planning for travelers, potential reductions in travel time, and greater capacity utilization of vehicles (similar to ride-sharing). Price and quality competition among service providers may be enhanced by the fact that the MaaS operator searches for each customer's best options. Yet, there are also obstacles. One is that service providers need to share data and use a common accounting system for their payments. Another is that by breaking service into short trip segments – for example, the so-called first- and last-mile trip segments added to a trip by public transit – there may be inadequate scope for profitable commercial service. A third is that by facilitating use of motorized modes, MaaS may draw passengers away from public transport, undermining its financial viability and contributing to congestion. Finally, demand for MaaS may also be tepid (Ho *et al.* 2018).[41]

Implementing MaaS on a regional scale is complicated by the fragmented nature of regional transport governance. Given the rapid evolution of transport markets and the introduction of new modes, it seems wise to introduce regulations cautiously and make them easy to revise. The MaaS platform itself could be operated as a utility that provides access on equal terms to service providers, following the example of vertical separation of infrastructure and operations for long-distance rail service followed in Europe.

6.4 Conclusions

Dissatisfaction with publicly provided transportation infrastructure and services has sparked continued interest in applying free-market principles to urban transportation. Current research suggests that although the transportation sector is far from meeting the conditions under which unregulated markets are fully efficient, selective use of private enterprise can improve incentives and bring about significant cost savings. Much is being learned about the effects of specific regulatory measures on market structure and performance, both from more fine-tuned theoretical models and from careful examination of the many experiments being carried out around the world.

New transportation technologies are disrupting the status quo. This creates many opportunities for private enterprise, as well as challenging questions about what regulatory stance will best protect the public interest while promoting efficiency in constantly evolving urban transportation markets.

Notes

1 This result is equivalent to that of Mohring (1985) for a monopolist owner of a congested port (his equation (4), for one time period only). The equivalence involves converting his demand curve (stated as a function of fee τ) to one that is a function of generalized price p.

2 Recall from Section 5.1.3 that an induced-traffic elasticity of one would imply this case. As we argued there, that could occur only for very congested express roads that are close substitutes for other congested roads. In that case, monopoly pricing of the express roads would not be optimal because it would ignore external effects of congestion on other roads; see also the discussion in Section 6.1.4 below.

3 It is derived in a more conventional context, for example, by Oum and Tretheway (1988), who go on to generalize it to handle externalities imposed by the price-setting firm on society in general.

4 This can be seen, for the case of a single time period of duration normalized to one, by letting $\lambda_\tau = \lambda_K \to \infty$ in (5.17) and (5.18).

5 To state these points differently: a monopolist is limited by what might be called a consumer's net willingness to pay (the toll that can be charged without losing the consumer's business). That net WTP depends not only on an individual's gross WTP (*i.e.,* the gross benefit from making a trip), but also costs incurred including vehicle operating cost, travel time, and VOT of the car's occupants. A monopolist may be able to observe some correlates with these factors – for example vehicle occupancy (which affects both gross WTP and aggregate VOT applying to the vehicle), total trip distance (which affects gross WTP and demand elasticity), and vehicle type. But, the monopolist's information will be incomplete, and practical and legal constraints may limit how the information is exploited.

6 The toll formula (6.11) is derived in this way, for the case of fixed capacities, by Verhoef, Nijkamp and Rietveld (1996). It could be derived alternatively by using the user-equilibrium conditions to translate total demand for the corridor into demand just for the toll road, then applying (6.5).

7 Since 1999, the 407 Express Toll Route (ETR) (https://www.407etr.com/en/index.html) has been operated by 407 International Inc. It now runs in series with another toll road, Highway 407 East (https://on407.ca/en/highway/highway/background.html), which opened in 2019 and is owned and operated by the Province of Ontario. The Province sets tolls, but 407 ETR provides tolling and customer services on the Province's behalf. It is not public knowledge whether 407 International Inc. and the Province coordinate their tolls.

8 Another instance is the Northern Boulevard Peripherique in Lyon, which opened as a privately tolled link in 1997. The contract stipulated a reduction in capacity of a free parallel alternative in order to assure adequate demand for the tolled link. In response to legal challenges, the original capacity of the alternative was restored, the toll was reduced, and a public corporation took over operations (Raux and Souche 2004).

9 Mixed duopoly can be less efficient if the public link has a small capacity. The private operator then has considerable market power and sets a high toll, resulting in too little traffic on its link. The public operator attempts to redress the imbalance by raising its toll, which leaves tolls on both routes higher than with a private duopoly. This potential disadvantage of mixed duopoly does not arise in a Stackelberg game in which the public operator can set its toll first.

10 This latter result is closely related to "double marginalization," which occurs with vertically organized monopolistic producers of intermediate and final goods. With double marginalization, however, the upstream firm faces the downstream firm's marginal revenue function as its inverse demand function. With pure complements as discussed in the main text, the firm faces the market inverse demand function, shifted downward by the prices charged by the other firms. Double marginalization in urban transport would occur when a privately owned transit firm needs to travel on a private highway without substitutes, or when a private transit operator depends on the private operator of a transit station.

11 This is because the fraction on the right-hand-side approaches one as F approaches infinity, hence the toll approaches $V_f c_f'$.

12 Two examples somewhat like this case are the privatization of two separate US toll roads: the Chicago Skyway and the Indiana Toll Road. These roads, in adjacent states, cover parts of the same interstate highway route (I-90) and so carry a lot of through traffic. Perhaps the problem of excessive tolling, illustrated in this paragraph, is part of the reason why two large firms (Cintra Concesiones de Infraestructuras de Transporte and Macquarie Infrastructure Group) were included in *both* of the consortia that won the separate franchise auctions for the two roads. These firms have an interest in internalizing the combined revenue potential from the two roads and therefore could have influenced their respective consortia to bid more, on the expectation that such internalization would be realized, thus yielding higher total revenues.

13 De Borger *et al.* (2007) find that similar mechanisms are relevant when different governments control different parts of a corridor.

14 This summary draws on Lindsey (2012).

15 That is, travel cost functions are homogeneous of degree zero in demand and capacity, capacity costs are homogeneous of degree one, and capacity is perfectly divisible (see Section 5.1)..

16 This timing is plausible given the high cost, construction time, and irreversibility of investment in road capacity. By comparison, adjusting tolls is typically much easier.

17 See Nash (2005) for a more general analysis of privatization in transportation.

18 See footnote to Section 6.1.5 on serial links.

19 Precise definitions vary. Preston (2005) defines tendering as "firms bidding for the right to operate services" (p. 65) and defines franchising as a particular type of tendering, involving "contracting out some of the tactical…as well as operational functions" with an emphasis on arrangements that "expose bidders to revenue risk" (p. 66).

20 See Gómez-Ibáñez and Meyer (1993) and studies cited therein.

21 Similarly, some urban rail services in Japan achieve profitability from revenues at shops, hotels, and other Japan Rail-owned services (ITF 2021c, p.82).

22 Herrera and Lopez (2022) explain some of these practices using a stylized model in which bus drivers alter their speeds based on the distance separating them from rival buses. They find that due to perturbations such as traffic lights and accidents, no equilibrium is likely to persist for long, and drivers alternate between such tactics as racing, leapfrogging, and hanging back.

23 This gap is documented for France by Gagnepain and Ivaldi (2002), who find significant departures from contracting arrangements that would be optimal given the Laffont-Tirole theory. Concession contracts used in practice are analyzed by Gómez-Lobo and Briones (2014) and Sepúlveda and Galilea (2020), with particular attention to Latin America.

24 See Estache and Gómez-Lobo (2005). Hensher *et al.* (2016) find through surveys that private transit operators tend to be risk averse.

25 See Gómez-Lobo and Briones (2014). Sepúlveda and Galilea (2020), using a simulation model calibrated for Santiago, Chile, illustrate how a combination of payments for frequency and payments per passenger can improve system performance as measured by social surplus. Some systems also employ bonuses and penalties whereby a portion of the contract fee is added or deducted according to performance (Sheng and Meng 2020).

26 Karlaftis and Tsamboulas (2012) do not attempt to explain this reversal. One potential explanation is that systems with contracts charged higher fares, which suppressed ridership so that the cost of a vehicle hour was spread over fewer passengers.

27 Useful reviews include Small and Gómez-Ibáñez (1999, Section 5.5), Darbéra (2004), and Nash (2005, Section 4).

28 Darbéra (2004, Fig. 10). According to Transport for London (2014), total bus passenger-km increased by 70% from 2000 to 2012. Trip rates generally increased for all age groups and both genders.

29 Information in this paragraph is taken from Gannon (2011), Centre for Public Impact (2018) and Porcher (2022).

30 See Nash (2011) for an extensive and authoritative assessment.

31 Ridership and financial data for 2021–2022 are provided in TransMilenio (2022). A Wikipedia article provides details and citations. It reports that daily ridership "quickly reached 800,000 after the system opened," and rose (following expansions) to over 2 million in September 2018. https://en.wikipedia.org/wiki/TransMilenio (accessed 30 Dec 2022).

32 This summary draws on Gómez-Lobo and Briones (2014) and Hurtubia and Leondhardt (2021). See also Muñoz *et al.* (2014).

33 Briones (2009) provides details (in Spanish).

34 Uber, one of the largest TNCs, also allows customers to make multiple stops on one trip, and some types of service can be hired by the hour rather than per trip (https://www.uber.com/us/en/ride/uberx/).

35 For example, evidence suggests that ride-sourcing tends to draw ridership from other modes rather than generate new trips (ITF 2021c, Table 5, p.60). The impact on taxi demand has been particularly strong – as reflected by a steep decline in the values of taxi medallions.

36 New York in 2019 levied a "congestion surcharge" on all for-hire vehicle trips, including taxis and ride-source vehicles, within a "congestion zone" in Manhattan; however it was not differentiated by time of day (New York Department of Taxation and Finance 2022). Chicago in 2020 introduced a congestion tax on TNCs, differentiated by car occupancy (City of Chicago 2022).

37 Our definition of ride-sharing excludes forms of shared mobility that entail using vehicles in sequence: examples include as peer-to-peer rentals between individual owners (*e.g.*, via Turo), and short-term rentals managed by firms such as Car2Go (Santos 2018).

38 For example, the California Clean Miles Standard will require SAV fleets and TNCs to eliminate CO_2 greenhouse gas emissions by 2030 (California Public Utilities Commission 2022).

39 For example, Whim Helsinki allows travelers to use five modes of public transport as well as shared bicycles and several brands of e-scooters, taxis, and rental cars. Users can purchase tickets for single trips or subscription passes offering specified rates or discounts. Whim has been established in several other European cities and in Greater Tokyo.

40 See http://maas-alliance.eu/
41 Ho *et al.* also suggest that individuals are less sensitive to the long-run costs of vehicle ownership and usage than to the recurrent cost of an MaaS subscription – consistent with a common finding that individuals underestimate the full cost of driving (Andor *et al.* 2020). This can make it difficult to price MaaS services profitably.

References

Adler, Martin, Stefanie Peer and Tanja Sinozic (2019) "Autonomous, connected, electric shared vehicles (ACES) and public finance: an explorative analysis," *Transportation Research Interdisciplinary Perspectives* 2: 100038.

Andor, Mark A., Andreas Gerster, Kenneth T. Gillingham and Marco Horvath (2020) "Running a car costs much more than people think: stalling the uptake of green travel," *Nature* 580: 453–455.

Arnott, Richard, André de Palma and Robin Lindsey (1993) "A structural model of peak-period congestion: a traffic bottleneck with elastic demand," *American Economic Review* 83(1): 161–179.

Barbour, Natalia, Nikhil Menon, Yu Zhang and Fred Mannering (2019) "Shared automated vehicles: a statistical analysis of consumer use likelihoods and concerns," *Transport Policy* 80: 86–93.

Baumol, William J. and David F. Bradford (1970) "Optimal departures from marginal cost pricing," *American Economic Review* 60(3): 265–283.

Baumol, William J., John C. Panzar and Robert D. Willig (1982) *Contestable Markets and the Theory of Industry Structure*, New York: Harcourt Brace Jovanovich.

Briones, Ignacio (2009) "Transantiago: Un problema de información," *Estudio Públicos* 116: 37–91. doi:10.38178/cep.vi116.422, https://www.estudiospublicos.cl/index.php/cep/article/view/422/653

Calcott, Paul and Shuntian Yao (2005) "Competition between highway operators: can we expect toll differentiation?," *Papers in Regional Science* 84(3): 615–626.

California Public Utilities Commission (2022) "Clean miles standard," https://www.cpuc.ca.gov/regulatory-services/licensing/transportation-licensing-and-analysis-branch/clean-miles-standard (accessed 2 January 2023).

Centre for Public Impact (2018) "The London underground's failed PPP," January 31, https://www.centreforpublicimpact.org/case-study/london-undergrounds-failed-ppp

Cervero, Robert and Aaron Golub (2007) "Informal transport: a global perspective," *Transport Policy* 14(6): 445–457.

City of Chicago (2022) "City of Chicago Congestion Pricing," Department of Business Affairs and Consumer Pricing, https://www.chicago.gov/city/en/depts/bacp/supp_info/city_of_chicago_congestion_pricing.html (accessed 2 January 2023).

Darbéra, Richard (2004) "L'expérience anglaise de dérégulation des transports par autobus [Bus services deregulation in the UK]," *Cahiers Scientifiques du Transport* 46: 25–44. Lyon: Association Française des Instituts de Transport et de Logistique (In French with English summary), http://www.afitl.com/CST/precedents-numeros/article.php?id=18.

De Borger, Bruno, Fay Dunkerley and Stef Proost (2007) "Strategic investment and pricing decisions in a congested transport corridor," *Journal of Urban Economics* 62(2): 294–316.

de Palma, André and Robin Lindsey (2000) "Private roads: competition under various ownership regimes," *Annals of Regional Science* 34: 13–35.

de Palma, André and Robin Lindsey (2002) "Private roads, competition, and incentives to adopt time-based congestion tolling," *Journal of Urban Economics* 52(2): 217–241.

DeVany, Arthur S. and Thomas R. Saving (1980) "Competition and highway pricing for stochastic traffic," *Journal of Business* 53(1): 45–60.

Diao, Mi, Hui Kong and Jinhua Zhao (2021) "Impacts of transportation network companies on urban mobility," *Nature Sustainability* 4: 494–500.

Dodgson, John S. and Yannis Katsoulacos (1988a) "Models of competition and the effect of bus service deregulation," in John S. Dodgson and Neville Topham (eds.) *Bus Deregulation and Privatisation: An International Perspective*, Aldershot: Avebury, pp. 45–68.

Dodgson, John S. and Yannis Katsoulacos (1988b) "Quality competition in bus services," *Journal of Transport Economics and Policy* 22(3): 263–281.

Economides, Nicholas and Steven C. Salop (1992) "Competition and integration among complements, and network market structure," *Journal of Industrial Economics* 40(1): 105–123.

Engel, Eduardo, Ronald Fisher and Alexander Galetovic (2004) "Toll competition among congested roads," in *Topics in Economic Analysis and Policy 4: Article 4*. Berkeley, CA: BE Press. Earlier version: Technical working paper T239, National Bureau of Economic Research, 1999, https://www.nber.org/papers/t0239.

Engel, Eduardo, Ronald Fisher and Alexander Galetovic (2014) *The Economics of Public-Private Partnerships: A Basic Guide*, Cambridge University Press.

Engel, Eduardo, Ronald Fisher and Alexander Galetovic (2021) "When and how to use public-private partnerships in infrastructure: lessons from the international experience," in Glaeser, Edward L. and James M. Poterba (eds.) *Economic Analysis and Infrastructure Investment*, Cambridge, MA: National Bureau of Economic Research, Published from NBER working paper 26766, https://www.nber.org/papers/w26766.

Estache, Antonio and Andrés Gómez-Lobo (2005) "Limits to competition in urban bus services in developing countries," *Transport Reviews* 25: 139–158.

Estache, Antonio, Ellis Juab and Lourdes Trujillo (2011) "Public-private partnerships in transport," in André de Palma *et al.* (eds.) *A Handbook of Transport Economics*, Cheltenham: Edward Elgar, pp, 708-725.

Evans, Andrew (1987) "A theoretical comparison of competition with other economic regimes for bus services," *Journal of Transport Economics and Policy* 21(1): 7–36.

Evans, Andrew (1988) "Hereford: a case study of bus deregulation," *Journal of Transport Economics and Policy* 22(3): 283–306.

Frick, Karen Trappenberg, Brian Taylor and Martin Wachs (2008) "Contracting for public transit services in the US: evaluating the tradeoffs," International Transport Forum, Privatisation and Regulation of Urban Transit Systems, ITF Round Table No. 141, OECD Publishing, Paris, 2008, pp. 47–65, doi:10.1787/9789282102008-en

Gagnepain, Philippe and Marc Ivaldi (2002) "Incentive regulatory policies: the case of public transit systems in France," *RAND Journal of Economics* 33(4): 605–629.

Gagnepain, Philippe and Marc Ivaldi (2017) "Economic efficiency and political capture in public service contracts," *Journal of Industrial Economics* 65(1): 1–38.

Gagnepain, Philippe, Marc Ivaldi and Catherine Vibes (2011) "Competition in local bus services," in André de Palma *et al.* (eds.) *A Handbook of Transport Economics*, Cheltenham: Edward Elgar, pp. 744–762.

Gallego, Francisco, Juan-Pablo Montero and Christian Salas (2013) "The effect of transport policies on car use: evidence from Latin American cities," *Journal of Public Economics* 107: 47–62.

Gannon, Mark (2011) "A re-examination of the public-private-partnership discourse: was PPP the way to upgrade London underground's infrastructure?" Paper delivered at the European Transport Conference, Glasgow. https://www.worldtransitresearch.info/research/4381/

Gómez-Ibáñez, José A. and John R. Meyer (1993) *Going Private: The International Experience with Transport Privatization*, Washington, DC: Brookings Institution.

Gómez-Lobo, Andrés and Julio Briones (2014) "Incentives in bus concession contracts: a review of several experiences in Latin America. *Transport Reviews* 34(2): 246–265.

Gronau, Reuben (2000) "Optimum diversity in the public transport market," *Journal of Transport Economics and Policy* 34(1): 21–42.

Gurumurthy, Krishna Murthy, Felipe de Souza, Annesha Enam, and Joshua Auld (2020) "Integrating supply and demand perspectives for a large-scale simulation of shared autonomous vehicles," *Transportation Research Record* 2674(7): 181–192.

Hensher, David A., Chinh Ho and Louise Knowles (2016) "Efficient contracting and incentive agreements between regulators and bus operators: the influence of risk preferences of contracting agents on contract choice," *Transportation Research Part A: Policy and Practice* 87: 22–40.

Herrera, Fernanda and Sergio I. Lopez (2022) "Bus operators in competition: a directed location approach," *Research in Transportation Economics* 95: 101220.

Ho, Chinh Q., David A. Hensher, Corinne Mulley and Yale Z. Wong (2018) "Potential uptake and willingness-to-pay for mobility as a service (MaaS): a stated choice study," *Transportation Research Part A: Policy and Practice* 117: 302–318.

Hörcher, Daniel and Alejandro Tirachini (2021) "A review of public transport economics," *Economics of Transportation* 25: 100196.

Hrelja, Robert, Tom Rye and Caroline Mullen (2018) "Partnerships between operators and public transport authorities. Working practices in relational contracting and collaborative partnerships," *Transportation Research Part A: Policy and Practice* 116: 327–338.

Hurtubia, Ricardo and Janus Leondhardt (2021) "The experience of reforming bus concessions in Santiago de Chile", International Transport Forum Discussion Papers, No. 2021/09, OECD Publishing, Paris.

Iseki, Hiroyuki (2010) "Effects of contracting on cost efficiency in US fixed-route bus transit service," *Transportation Research Part A: Policy and Practice* 44(7): 457–472.

ITF (2021) *The Innovative Mobility Landscape: The Case of Mobility as a Service. International Transport Forum Policy Papers,* No. 92, Paris: OECD Publishing.

Karlaftis, Matthew G. (2008) "Privatisation, regulation and competition: a thirty-year retrospective on transit efficiency," International Transport Forum, Privatisation and Regulation of Urban Transit Systems, ITF Round Table No. 141, OECD Publishing, Paris, pp. 47–65, 67–108. doi:10.1787/9789282102008-en

Karlaftis, Matthew G. and Dimitrios Tsamboulas (2012) "Efficiency measurement in public transport: are findings specification sensitive?" *Transportation Research Part A: Policy and Practice* 46(2): 392–402.

Klein, Daniel B., Adrian T. Moore and Binyam Reja (1997) *Curb Rights: A Foundation for Free Enterprise in Urban Transit*, Washington, DC: Brookings Institution Press.

Knight, Frank (1924) "Some fallacies in the interpretation of social costs," *Quarterly Journal of Economics* 38(4): 582–606.

Laffont, Jean–Jacques and Jean Tirole (1993) *A Theory of Incentives in Procurement and Regulation*, Cambridge, MA: MIT Press.

Lavieri, Patrick S. and Chandra R. Bhat (2019) "Modeling individuals' willingness to share trips with strangers in an autonomous vehicle future," *Transportation Research Part A: Policy and Practice* 124: 242–261.

Lindsey, Robin (2012) "Road pricing and investment," *Economics of Transportation* 1(1–2), 49–63.

Liu, Louie Nan and John F. McDonald (1998) "Efficient congestion tolls in the presence of unpriced congestion: a peak and off-peak simulation model," *Journal of Urban Economics* 44(3): 352–366.

Mackie, Peter J., John Preston and Chris Nash (1995) "Bus deregulation ten years on," *Transport Reviews* 15: 229–251.

Mangrum, Daniel and Alejandro Molnar (2020) "The marginal congestion of a taxi in New York City," December 9, https://www.danielmangrum.com/docs/Boro_current.pdf

Mills, David E. (1981) "Ownership arrangements and congestion-prone facilities," *American Economic Review* 71(3): 493–502.

Mohring, Herbert (1985) "Profit maximization, cost minimization and pricing for congestion-prone facilities," *Logistics and Transportation Review* 21: 27–36.

Muñoz, Juan Carlos, Marco Batarce and Dario Hidalgo (2014) "Transantiago, five years after its launch," *Research in Transportation Economics* 48: 184–193.

Narayanan, Santhanakrishnan, Emmanouil Chaniotakis and Constantinos Antoniou (2020) "Shared autonomous vehicle services: a comprehensive review," *Transportation Research Part C: Emerging Technologies* 111: 255–293.

Nash, Christopher A. (1988) "Integration of public transport: an economic assessment," in John S. Dodgson and Neville Topham (eds.) *Bus Deregulation and Privatisation*, Aldershot: Avebury, pp. 97–118.

Nash, Christopher A. (2005) "Privatization in transport," in Kenneth J. Button and David A. Hensher (eds.) *Handbook of Transport Strategy, Policy and Institutions*, Bingley: Emerald, pp. 65–81, pp. 97–113.

Nash, Christopher A. (2011) "Competition and regulation in rail transport," in André de Palma *et al.* (eds.) *A Handbook of Transport Economics*, Cheltenham: Edward Elgar, pp. 763–778.

New York Department of Taxation and Finance (2022) "Congestion surcharge," https://www.tax.ny.gov/bus/cs/csidx.htm (accessed 2 January 2023)

Oum, Tae Hoon and Michael W. Tretheway (1988) "Ramsey pricing in the presence of externality costs," *Journal of Transport Economics and Policy* 22(3): 307–317.

Pigou, Arthur C. (1920) *The Economics of Welfare*, London: Macmillan.

Porcher, Simon (2022) "A case study of the London underground's PPP failure." doi:10.2139/ssrn.3597476

Preston, John (2005) "Tendering of services," in Kenneth J. Button and David A. Hensher (eds.) *Handbook of Transport Strategy, Policy and Institutions*, Bingley: Emerald, pp. 65–81.

Ramsey, Frank P. (1927) "A contribution to the theory of taxation," *Economic Journal* 37(145): 47–61.

Ramsey, Frank P. (1928) "A mathematical theory of saving," *Economic Journal,* 38: 543–559.

Raux, Charles and Stéphanie Souche (2004) "The acceptability of urban road pricing: a theoretical analysis applied to experience in Lyon," *Journal of Transport Economics and Policy* 38(2): 191–216.

Saenz de Ormijana, Fidel, and Nicolas Rubio (2015) "Innovation capture through the alternative technical concept process in PPPs in Texas: a tool for financial viability," in Zhanmin Zhang, Cesar Queiroz and C. Michael Walton (eds.) *Advances in Public-Private Partnerships: Proceedings of the Second International Conference on Public-Private Partnerships.* doi:10.1061/9780784480267

Santos, Georgina (2018) "Sustainability and shared mobility models," *Sustainability* 10/9: 3194. doi:10.3390/su10093194

Sarriera, Javier Morales, Frederick P. Salvucci and Jinhua Zhao (2018) "Worse than Baumol's disease: the implications of labor productivity, contracting out, and unionization on transit operation costs," *Transport Policy* 61: 10–16.

Schmalensee, Richard (1978) "Entry deterrence in the ready-to-eat breakfast cereal industry," *Bell Journal of Economics* 9(2): 305–327.

Sepúlveda, Juan Pablo, and Patricia Galilea (2020) "How do different payment schemes to operators affect public transport concessions? A microeconomic model," *Transport Policy* 93: 27–35.

Sheng, Dian and Qiang Meng (2020) "Public bus service contracting: a critical review and future research opportunities," *Research in Transportation Economics* 83: 100938.

Small, Kenneth A. (2010) "Private provision of highways: economic issues," *Transport Reviews* 30(1): 11–31.

Small, Kenneth A. and José A. Gómez-Ibáñez (1999) "Urban transportation," in Paul Cheshire and Edwin S. Mills (eds.) *Handbook of Regional and Urban Economics, Vol. 3. Applied Urban Economics*, Amsterdam: North-Holland, pp. 1937–1999.

Small, Kenneth A. and Jia Yan (2001) "The value of 'value pricing' of roads: second-best pricing and product differentiation," *Journal of Urban Economics* 49(2): 310–336.

Stocker, Adam, and Susan Shaheen (2017) "Shared automated vehicles: review of business models," Prepared for the Roundtable on Cooperative Mobility Systems and Automated Driving, Discussion Paper No. 2017-09, International Transport Forum, OECD, Paris (July), https://www.itf-oecd.org/shared-automated-vehicles-review-business-models

Tang, Siman B., and Hong K. Lo (2010) "On the financial viability of mass transit development: the case of Hong Kong," *Transportation* 37: 299–316.

TransMilenio (2022) *Transmilenio en cifras abril 2022*. Informe No. 79, TransMilenio S.A. (May), https://www.transmilenio.gov.co/loader.php?lServicio=Tools2&lTipo=descargas&lFuncion=descargar&idFile=48593

Transport for London (2014) "Long-term trends in travel behaviour: cross-sectional cohort analysis of London residents' trip rates, car ownership and work-related travel," Strategic Analysis, TfL Planning, September, https://content.tfl.gov.uk/long-term-trends-in-travel-behaviour-cross-sectional-cohort-analysis.pdf

Van den Berg, Vincent A.C. and Erik T. Verhoef (2012) "Is the service quality of private roads too low, too high, or just right when firms compete Stackelberg in capacity?," *Transportation Research Part B: Methodological* 46(8): 971983.

Van der Veer, Jan Peter (2002) "Entry deterrence and quality provision in the local bus market," *Transport Reviews* 22(3): 247–265.

Verhoef, Erik T. (2007) "Second-best road pricing through highway franchising," *Journal of Urban Economics* 62(2): 337–361.

Verhoef, Erik T., Peter Nijkamp and Piet Rietveld (1996) "Second-best congestion pricing: the case of an untolled alternative," *Journal of Urban Economics* 40(3): 279–302.

Verhoef, Erik T. and Kenneth A. Small (2004) "Product differentiation on roads: constrained congestion pricing with heterogeneous users," *Journal of Transport Economics and Policy* 38(1): 127–156.

Vigren, Andreas and Roger Pyddoke (2020) "The impact on bus ridership of passenger incentive contracts in public transport," *Transportation Research Part A: Policy and Practice* 135: 144–159.

Viton, Philip A. (1981) "On competition and product differentiation in urban transportation: the San Francisco Bay Area," *Bell Journal of Economics* 12(2): 362–379.

Viton, Philip A. (1995) "Private roads," *Journal of Urban Economics* 37(3): 260–289.

World Bank (2006) *Toll Roads and Concessions*, Washington, DC: World Bank, http://www.worldbank. org/transport/roads/toll_rds.htm.

Yang, Hai, Feng Xiao and Haijun Huang (2009) "Private road competition and equilibrium with traffic equilibrium constraints," *Journal of Advanced Transportation* 43(1): 21–45.

7   Transportation, energy, and climate

As preceding chapters have made clear, special attention to the economic characteristics of transportation is amply motivated by its crucial economic role and special features. As though that were not enough, another aspect propels it to center stage: its key role in energy consumption, along with concerns about petroleum markets and climate change. Worldwide, transportation accounts for 65% of oil consumption and 15% of greenhouse gas (GHG) emissions.[1] These facts have led to strong policies intended to reshape transportation: for example, promoting public transit and high-speed rail, regulating vehicle energy efficiency, mandating electric vehicles or lower-carbon fuels, and taxing vehicles based on GHG emissions.

The academic community has responded with an outpouring of research on exactly how transportation activities use energy and how energy-related policies affect transportation decisions. This chapter reviews such research, with primary emphasis on motor vehicles. A recurrent theme is potential market failures. They fall mostly into three groups, related to climate change, technology adoption, and oil markets.

The first group is relatively straightforward: Burning fossil fuels produces carbon dioxide (CO_2), a GHG that accounts for the majority of human-induced climate change in the form of global warming.[2] The amount of CO_2 released is directly proportional to the amount of fuel burned, more specifically to its carbon content; its long-term warming effects are closely related to worldwide *cumulative* CO_2 emissions. Release of CO_2 does not affect a user directly, so any climate-related damage is an external cost to the current and future world population at large. We consider how to measure this externality in Section 7.3.

The second group involves consumer perceptions of the monetary value of vehicle technologies that affect fuel efficiency. The question is whether consumers undervalue the savings they would receive from efficiency improvements, relative to objective estimates – possibly due in part to characteristics of markets for these vehicles and for their finance. If so, the market may produce an inefficiently fuel-intensive vehicle stock, causing consumers to spend too much on fuel even when they do not account for environmental externalities, thus also exacerbating the climate-related market failure.

The third group of market failures involves petroleum markets. Leiby (2007) and others have identified three broad problems resulting from petroleum consumption that especially depend on oil imports: imperfect competition in oil markets, macroeconomic instability, and international conflicts. Sometimes their effects are quantified into an "oil premium," but this is problematic: they are not easily described as externalities, nor is their relationship to aggregate oil consumption or oil imports necessarily close.[3] For these reasons, and because interest in the oil premium has waned, we do not treat it here.

DOI: 10.4324/9781315157375-7

There are of course other potential market failures indirectly related to energy use, such as vehicle safety and pollutants whose emissions are correlated with energy use. These are covered in other parts of the book, especially Sections 3.4 and 3.5.

We proceed by first examining the demand for motor vehicle fuel and its disaggregation into demands for fuel efficiency and for vehicle usage (Section 7.1). We then consider policies to reduce fuel use (Section 7.2). Next, we consider explicitly the role that climate change should play in designing such policies, including a discussion of the social cost of emissions of CO_2 (Section 7.3). The last section of the chapter presents a brief summary conclusion.

7.1   Fuel price, fuel efficiency, and motor vehicle usage

The most common transportation policies aimed at energy use concern "light-duty vehicles," *i.e.*, cars, vans, sport utility vehicles (SUVs), and pickup trucks. We focus here on this class of vehicles, which for brevity we sometimes call "motor vehicles" or just "cars." Several policies influence such vehicles' fuel efficiency: fuel taxes, fuel efficiency standards, mandates for use of alternatives to conventional fuels, and tax policies that levy fees or provide rebates to vehicle purchase depending on the vehicle's fuel efficiency.

To analyze such policies, it is crucial to understand several things: the workings of private vehicle markets (especially manufacturers' decisions about vehicle characteristics); the pricing and market shares of different classes of vehicles; and vehicle usage. This involves a set of inter-related decisions. Manufacturers commit years in advance to the main outlines of product lines they will introduce; they then make medium- and short-term adjustments in response to shifts in fuel prices, consumer preferences, policy mandates, and other factors. Consumers choose among the resulting set of offerings in a given year, knowing these vehicles will last many years. Consumers also decide how much to drive and, in households with more than one vehicle, how to allocate their usage across the different vehicles. In addition, consumers decide whether and when to sell a vehicle, which may then turn up as a used vehicle for sale in the same or some other location.

Most research has condensed this process into two components: how vehicle efficiency responds to fuel price and how usage responds to fuel cost per kilometer. Sometimes, the results are summarized by two elasticities: the elasticity $\varepsilon_{E,PF}$ of vehicle efficiency (E) with respect to fuel price (P_F) and the elasticity $\varepsilon_{M,PM}$ of vehicle use (M) with respect to fuel cost per kilometer ($P_M \equiv P_F/E$). (Note that here P_M excludes other cost components of driving that are discussed in Chapter 3.) Together, these elasticities determine the overall price elasticity $\varepsilon_{F,PF}$ of fuel use (F). Using definitions $F = M/E$ and $P_M = P_F/E$ to differentiate F and M totally with respect to fuel price (keeping in mind that M is implicitly a function of both P_F and E), we obtain

$$\varepsilon_{F,PF} = -\varepsilon_{E,PF} + \varepsilon_{M,PM} \cdot \left(1 - \varepsilon_{E,PF}\right) \tag{7.1}$$

The equation presumes that usage depends on fuel price solely via the fuel cost per kilometer, not independently on fuel price and fuel efficiency. This assumption may be questioned, which we consider in our empirical survey.

Separate measurement of the two components that determine fuel use is important, because specific policies affect these components quite differently. For example, fuel taxes raise the cost of driving per kilometer, whereas fuel efficiency mandates lower it; whether this matters depends on the magnitude of $\varepsilon_{M,PM}$. We describe research on fuel demand and its components in Section 7.1.2. In Section 7.1.3, we focus on a particularly important market failure possibly embedded in $\varepsilon_{E,PF}$ – namely the alleged failure of consumers and/or manufacturers to optimize investment in fuel efficiency. Finally, in Section 7.1.4, we consider the empirical magnitude of $\varepsilon_{M,PM}$ known as the "rebound effect." But first, we consider an essential distinction that is often ignored in empirical studies, namely the time period over which fuel efficiency and vehicle use respond to changing conditions.

7.1.1 Dynamics of demand responses

If fuel price or fuel efficiency is changed exogenously, a variety of responses will occur over different time frames. For example, a sudden change in fuel price may cause consumers to delay filling a gas tank for a few days, to reallocate household vehicles among family members over a few weeks, to change trip patterns over a few months, to alter vehicle purchase decisions over a few years, or to alter residential or work locations and thereby affect urban structure for decades. Most such changes accumulate, so that the longer the time period, the greater the elasticity in magnitude; but this is not always the case, as illustrated by a commuter who switches to public transit initially in response to a gasoline price increase, but later buys a second and more fuel-efficient car and switches back to driving.

Unfortunately, most of this detail is lost in the majority of studies. If a study considers time at all, it may simply distinguish between "short run" and "long run," which usually means roughly less than or greater than two years. Even that distinction is frequently ignored, leaving the reader to interpret from the nature of the empirical model what time periods of response are captured by the stated results. For example, a monthly time series would capture short-run responses, whereas cross-sectional analyses would capture longer-run responses provided markets were reasonably stable when data were recorded. Some authors helpfully discuss what types of variation in their data are primarily responsible for the estimated coefficients and what that implies for the time period over which the measured responses most likely occur. These subtleties are often missing from the summary conclusion, which can lead to careless comparisons of results.

Ideally, an empirical study would incorporate explicit dynamics into the empirical specification, for example, by including the values of one or more variables at other (usually earlier) times. Such a "lag structure" has a cost in terms of precision of estimates, so it is not always feasible, especially if the researcher wishes the specification to be flexible. One useful compromise, which adds only one additional variable, is the partial adjustment model introduced in Section 2.1.2.

In the present context, the partial adjustment model usually works as follows. Average fuel efficiency E_t in year t (or more typically, its logarithm) is assumed to change from its value one year ago toward a new "desired" value (e.g., $\log E_t^* \equiv \gamma' \cdot z_t$, with the right-hand side denoting the regression equation of interest), with adjustment speed $(1 - \alpha)$:

$$\log E_t = \log E_{t-1} + (1-\alpha)\left(\log E_t^* - \log E_{t-1}\right) + u_t$$

where u_t is a stochastic term. Equivalently, we have a simple linear specification:

$$\log E_t = \alpha \log E_{t-1} + \beta' z_t + u_t \; ; \beta = (1-\alpha)\gamma$$

Given this specification, the expected value of $\log E_t$ would converge asymptotically to $\log E_t^*$ if all variables z_t remained constant for infinitely many past periods. If the k-th variable z^k is logarithm of fuel price, then β^k and $\beta^k / (1-\alpha)$ are, respectively, the short-run and long-run values of the elasticity $\varepsilon_{E,PF}$ defined earlier.

Studies that employ the partial adjustment model have produced a wide variety of estimates for α and hence for the ratio $1/(1-\alpha)$ of long-run to short-run responses. Small and Van Dender (2007) estimate $\alpha = 0.79$ for vehicle distance traveled and 0.85 for fleet vehicle efficiency, whereas Li *et al.* (2009) estimate $\alpha = 0.07$ for new-car purchases; both studies use panel data across locations and years. The difference is probably due in large part to the very disaggregate definition of the dependent variable in Li *et al.* and also to Small and Van Dender's accounting for serial correlation across years.[4] This illustrates how difficult it is to disentangle the many dynamic aspects of economic decisions, especially those involving capital goods. This makes it especially difficult to forecast changes over various time periods. Indeed, some attempts to add even a single lagged dependent variable have led to insufficient precision to give useful results on the dynamics. An example is Klier and Linn (2010, p. 142), who use monthly data, for which the dynamics are probably more complex and subject to greater random error than for annual data.

7.1.2   Empirical results: demand for motor vehicle fuel

Many studies, especially older ones, focus solely on the combined effects of the two components in equation (7.1). This has the advantage of avoiding some difficult data issues in measuring usage, in favor of measuring fuel consumption, which is often available from tax records. It also avoids difficulties in defining and measuring the fuel efficiency of vehicles, which depends, for example, on driving behavior, temperature, and use of amenities such as air conditioning.

Graham and Glaister (2002) and Goodwin *et al.* (2004) review a number of studies, both concluding that the overall price elasticity for fuel consumption is typically around −0.3 in the short run and −0.6 in the long run. Brons *et al.* (2008) obtain similar results from a meta-analysis,[5] while an international review by Dahl (2012) finds typical values to be about half as large. Indeed, several researchers have found lower elasticities using more recent data (*i.e.*, from the 1990s or early 2000s). For example, Hughes *et al.* (2008) find a short-run elasticity in the USA (based on aggregate monthly time series) of −0.21 to −0.34 during 1975–1980 (consistent with the reviews just noted), but only about one-fifth as large during 2001–2006. Hughes *et al.* speculate that the decrease might be due to increased dependence on automobile travel, for example, due to suburbanization and more working household members, or to higher fuel efficiency (due largely to regulations), which reduces the financial impact of high fuel prices on driving.

Litman (2013) argues that some factors contributing to lower fuel-use elasticities around the turn of the millennium were temporary and that the fall in elasticity magnitudes is being reversed by more recent trends such as stagnant incomes, lower workforce participation, higher fuel prices, increased traffic congestion, and increased use of public transit. One of these factors – fuel prices – has proven quite volatile with no clear trend, and another – traffic congestion – seems to make little difference, based on empirical work described later in this chapter. Thus, Litman's argument remains speculative.

Dahl (2012) observes that studies distinguishing long-run responses from short-run responses tend to find long-run elasticities about twice as large as cross-sectional studies. She suggests that more formal dynamic tests using cointegration could determine which are more reliable (p. 12). Dahl's review also reveals a point that we return to in Section 7.1.4: there is some tantalizing evidence of asymmetry in responses to rising versus falling fuel prices.

Some recent studies have introduced more careful controls for endogeneity of fuel prices, which in aggregate markets are simultaneously determined with quantity of fuel demanded. A good example is Li *et al.* (2014), who use crude oil prices as instruments for gasoline prices (at the level of annual averages for individual states in the USA), on the assumption that state-level shocks in the demand for gasoline will have negligible impacts on world oil prices.[6] These authors add another important feature, which is to decompose retail fuel price into the pretax price and the fuel-tax component. They find that gasoline demand is three times as responsive to taxes as to overall fuel price. They speculate that this results from greater visibility and greater perceived permanence of changes in tax rates.[7] Similarly, Cropper *et al.* (2018) note that the few before-and-after studies of a carbon-tax implementation – specifically in British Columbia, Canada, in 2008 – find somewhat higher elasticities than most of the literature. They suggest this may be because people regarded the changes as more stable and predictable than other sources of price variation typically observed in empirical studies.

Recent research has raised a concern that fuel-price elasticities may be underestimated in magnitude due to aggregation over space and time. Levin *et al.* (2017) analyze data on U.S. urban retail fuel-purchase transactions by individual consumers, using daily price information. They include fuel prices lagged by one to 20 days in order to capture reallocations of fuel purchases over very short periods, interpreting the sum of coefficients (of contemporaneous and all lagged prices) as a short-run response occurring over a few months. This results in somewhat higher elasticities than other estimates applicable to a similar time (2006–2009). They show that if their data are artificially aggregated over space to the level of a state in the USA, and/or over time to the level of a month, the estimates decrease in magnitude by roughly one-third. Aggregating to the national level depresses the magnitudes far more.[8] Levin *et al.* interpret this finding as indicating downward bias in virtually all other empirical studies. We expect that others will further investigate the nature and extent of aggregation bias, now that large disaggregated datasets are becoming more widely available.

Regarding aggregation over space, microdata permit a more detailed look at variations across consumers. For example, Wadud *et al.* (2010) analyze distributional effects of energy policies. One challenge is to find sources of price variation across individuals that are independent of other potential influences such as urbanization.

Regarding aggregation over time, the use of daily data as in Levin *et al.* (2017) could provide insights into the short-term dynamics of consumer response to fuel prices. However, knowledge of much longer-term dynamics is needed to better inform policy, since most policies of interest would create changes that last for years. New data may facilitate such knowledge, yet there are serious barriers: complex dynamic models are likely to suffer from lack of robustness to the many uncertain facets of manufacturer and consumer behavior.

Finally, we should mention a problem that affects this topic in common with virtually all empirical studies in economics and other fields: publication bias. Specifically, there is strong evidence that statistically significant results (in the theoretically expected direction) have a much greater probability of being published (and perhaps of even being issued as working papers) than other results. Havranek *et al.* (2012) document this clearly for estimates of the price elasticity of gasoline. They do so primarily by showing that the standard error of reported studies is related to the estimated elasticity in a highly asymmetrical manner, with large elasticities often reported even with quite large standard errors, but small elasticities reported only with very tight standard errors (typically so the ratio, which is the t-statistic, is 2.0 or higher). Havranek *et al.* apply a correction for this in a meta-study of 202 estimates from 41 studies published between 1978 and 2010; they find the correction reduces the magnitude of the average elasticity by more than half. (Their preferred short- and long-run estimates are −0.09 and −0.31.)

7.1.3   *Empirical results: fuel efficiency and the energy efficiency gap*

More interesting than the overall demand for fuel are the determinants of its two components: fuel efficiency of vehicles and how much those vehicles are used. We consider the first in this subsection.

First, a comment about terminology. Many datasets and empirical studies are from the USA, so the US system of units based on gallons and miles has become very common. Indeed, the abbreviation MPG for miles per gallon is often used as a synonym for the very concept of fuel efficiency.[9] Thus, in many cases it is impractical to discuss US-based research in terms of metric units.

As already noted, changes in fuel markets – whether via price, regulation, or quantity controls – affect both sides of the transaction between motor vehicle manufacturers and their customers; on each side, the participants have a variety of possible responses. It is unsurprising, then, that researchers have taken a variety of approaches. Some use a purely demand-side approach, estimating discrete-choice models of consumer purchase behavior. Others are supply-oriented, looking at manufacturer decisions in detail. Still others look at changes in market equilibria and either ignore the separate roles of demand and supply or distinguish them using auxiliary information. We consider all three approaches.

7.1.3.1   Demand-side studies

Many studies have estimated consumers' response to fuel price, fuel efficiency, vehicle prices, and other factors in their vehicle purchase decisions. This literature is part of the broader literature on automobile demand that we review in Section 2.4.6. Most studies focus on consumers, but occasionally the decisions of fleet managers (*e.g.*, for rental companies or government fleets) are also considered; some evidence suggests that the two sectors exhibit similar behavior with respect to fuel efficiency (Leard *et al.* 2019). This literature includes studies of both revealed and stated preferences.

Ever since Hausman (1979) found strong "myopia" in purchases of air conditioners, studies of other consumer durables have highlighted consumers' intertemporal trade-off between energy efficiency and purchase price. Typically, this is done by comparing the estimated marginal rate of substitution between operating and capital costs to an objective calculation based on various discount rates. For example, Mannering and Winston (1985) find that for automobile purchase, consumers use implicit discount rates of roughly 16%–20%, much higher than market rates and thus potentially implying myopic behavior.[10] Many similar results have appeared since – for example, an estimate by Cambridge Econometrics (2008) of 6%–19% using survey data from the UK. Nevertheless, a review by Greene (2010) finds the issue of myopia still unsettled. We return to it in far more detail following our review of studies of supply-side and market-equilibrium responses.

7.1.3.2   Supply-side studies

Manufacturers can respond to changing markets in many ways. One of the simplest is to make short-term pricing adjustments in order to achieve the aspired sales volumes for vehicles that are already produced, are in production, or are necessary for long-term production plans to which the manufacturer is committed.

Langer and Miller (2013) derive theoretical pricing rules for a market characterized by Bertrand competition and use data on four large US manufacturers' weekly pricing adjustments in order to estimate parameters reflecting responsiveness. Their results show significant responses to fuel-price changes, indicating that a $1.00/gallon price increase would result in price incentives that add a $340/vehicle wedge between the lowest and highest quartiles of the efficiency distribution. Busse *et al.* (2013) obtain a very similar result.

Langer and Miller point out several implications of this process. First, the price adjustments are large enough to suggest that over a long time horizon, in which manufacturers can shift production plans, substantial changes in market shares and hence in the resulting average vehicle efficiency would result. Second, studies whose vehicle-price data exclude short-term adjustments around the list price will obtain estimates of price sensitivity that are biased downward in magnitude. (This is mainly an issue for studies based on short-term data.) The authors estimate this downward bias at 14% of the true magnitude.

Langer and Miller also find a bigger response for changes within a vehicle type than between types, suggesting that fuel prices will not cause large changes in the mix of vehicle types. This is consistent with several other studies, which fail to find much response in the mix of sizes or vehicle classifications.[11]

It is unclear whether vehicles relying partly or wholly on electrical propulsion should be regarded as separate "types" in the sense just mentioned. Indeed, the answer may vary over time as consumers become more accustomed to such vehicles in the marketplace. There is sufficient market experience with gasoline-electric hybrid vehicles ("hybrids") to draw some tentative conclusions about their role. Beresteanu and Li (2011) analyze hybrid market shares, finding a substantial responsiveness to fuel prices with an elasticity of around 0.8.[12]

Most empirical studies of the supply side of vehicle manufacturing have relied on econometric techniques using market data. But forecasting often requires the consideration of available technologies that are not currently being used. This requires that market information be supplemented with engineering information about such technologies. Whitefoot *et al.* (2017) accomplish this by incorporating a design model used by motor vehicle manufacturers for their planning, combined with cost information used by the US government in its regulatory impact analyses. They run the design model for numerous combinations of assumed conditions (*e.g.*, fuel prices) and desired performance characteristics (*e.g.*, energy efficiency and acceleration), generating a dataset that can then be analyzed statistically in the same way as market data. This approach produces a cost function measured over a wide range of characteristics, which in turn helps overcome one of the challenges of market-based econometric analyses: the correlation among observed and unobserved vehicle characteristics. Just like purely econometric analyses, the cost function can be combined with a separately estimated demand model to analyze various scenarios; we describe how the authors do this in Section 7.2.

7.1.3.3   *Market-equilibrium responses*

Rather than explicitly model demand and supply, some studies take a reduced-form approach, examining how one or more market outcomes are related to factors of interest, such as fuel efficiency. Li *et al.* (2009) consider quantity outcomes. The authors construct two panel datasets, one for new vehicles and one for used vehicles, each containing numbers of vehicles sold or retired and their characteristics. They do this for nine years, 20 metropolitan statistical areas (MSAs), and up to 68 cells each consisting of a vehicle segment (*i.e.*, a group of similar models of vehicle) and up to 20 quantile intervals for fuel efficiency (*e.g.*, one such interval contains all vehicle models within a given vehicle segment whose fuel efficiencies lie between the 60th and 65th percentiles). We refer here to each cell as an "MPG cell." The result is over 6,000 observations on new-car sales and a similar number on used-car retirements.[13]

The authors' preferred new-vehicle specification has the following form, for MPG cell c, metropolitan area m, and year t:

$$q_{c,m,t} = \alpha q_{c,m,t-1} + \left(\beta_1 + \frac{\beta_2}{E_{c,t}} \right) P_{m,t}^F + \gamma Z_{c,m,t} + u_{c,m,t}$$

where $q_{c,m,t}$ is the logarithm of vehicle sales, E is fuel efficiency, P^F is fuel price, Z is a set of control variables (including E), and u is a random term. The key is the term in parentheses:

it implies that price will differentially affect sales of vehicles of different efficiencies. The resulting estimates[14] of β_1 and β_2 imply that higher gasoline price increases the sales of vehicles with $E > 23.3$ mi/gal while decreasing sales of less efficient vehicles. The estimated value of α, namely 0.068, implies that the ratio of long-run (asymptotic limit) to short-run (one-year) responses is $1/(1 - 0.068) = 1.07$. Note this equation contains no vehicle price, so it is a reduced-form quantity regression.

The used-vehicle retirement model employed by Li *et al.* has a similar form, except the dependent variable is the logarithm of the conditional survival probability[15] and the lagged dependent variable is omitted. To compensate for this more constrained dynamic structure, serial correlation is allowed in the error term *u*. Resulting estimates imply that high fuel price encourages retirement of most used vehicles, but it encourages retention of those more efficient than the 80th percentile of MPG.

Using this equation, the authors can simulate the composition of the combined vehicle fleets of the 20 MSAs under hypothetical changes in fuel prices, in order to determine the magnitudes of market responses. These simulations reveal that nearly all the response comes through changes in the new-vehicle fleet, not through used-vehicle retirement. The short-run (one-year) fuel-price elasticity of new-vehicle sales is −0.19, which implies a long-run elasticity of −0.19 × 1.07 = −0.20.

Let us now turn to substitution among vehicle characteristics. This is of special interest because fuel efficiency and certain dimensions of performance, especially acceleration, can use the same technology; by simply tuning it differently, the manufacturer can increase one at the expense of the other. For example, manufacturers can quickly increase fuel efficiency by sacrificing some acceleration. If markets are smooth and efficient, the marginal costs of doing so this way (including loss of consumer value) or through adding technology are equalized in equilibrium. Hence, either adjustment could serve as a basis for measurement of the cost of higher fuel efficiency.

But automobiles markets are neither smooth nor efficient, or necessarily in equilibrium. They are not smooth or always in equilibrium because technology is constantly developing through exogenous discoveries, as well as through carefully planned and funded research and development. They are not efficient because of oligopolistic rivalry, consumer misinformation, inherent uncertainty, and well-documented behavioral biases of consumers that preclude full rationality. Just to take one example of the latter, consumers are subject to "MPG illusion": the mistaken belief that a given numerical change in fuel efficiency (*e.g.,* from 10 to 12 MPG or from 40 to 42 MPG) always yields the same change in annual fuel consumption – whereas in reality, fuel consumption is proportional to the *inverse* of efficiency.[16]

Two studies, one by Knittel (2012) and one by Leard *et al.* (2023), find that most or all of the fuel efficiency gains achieved under US fuel efficiency regulations were achieved by diverting technological gains that otherwise would have been used for enhanced performance. In both cases, the authors measure the production frontier, whose slope is the marginal trade-off between performance and efficiency. The rate of expansion of this production frontier is a measure of technological development and/or the adoption of existing but unused technology. What is missing from both studies is an account of the cost of expanding that frontier and an assessment of whether manufacturers are efficiently equating the two margins mentioned above.

The main insight of these studies is the strong substitutability within the production function between fuel efficiency and performance. This is important for two reasons. First, it is very likely that consumers exhibit very different degrees of rationality in evaluating these two dimensions of vehicles. One dimension (fuel efficiency) is subject to uncertainty about its value due to unknown future fuel prices and usage rates; it is also subject to limits on numerical literacy, including the MPG illusion just mentioned; and, let's face it, it is boring to most people – by all accounts far down on the list of criteria consumers report that they consider when purchasing vehicles. The other dimension (performance) is for many consumers the part of owning a car that feeds their self-image and their perceived social rank, as well as generating its own non-internalized externalities; it is also the focus of intensive advertising aimed at emotional responses that consumers may rationally prefer to avoid given their long-term preferences. Thus, it seems unlikely that the market will produce an efficient trade-off between them.

The second reason why substitutability matters is that in its presence, empirical work needs to account not only for the observed cost of vehicles but also for consumers' (possibly irrational) valuation of performance. As we discuss below, Leard *et al.* (2023) find that consumers' valuation of lost performance, when they consider vehicle usage, fully offsets their fuel-cost savings from tightening US efficiency standards beyond their 2012 level.

These observations highlight the importance of the two questions just raised: are financial gains from fuel efficiency improvements underestimated or otherwise undervalued, and is vehicle performance overvalued at the moment of purchase, relative to consumers' true long-term preferences? If either answer is yes, rational manufacturers will not offer attribute bundles that are socially efficient, even aside from externalities. We focus especially on the first question, for which there is a great deal of empirical study.

7.1.3.4   *Is fuel efficiency underprovided?*

Some of the studies just reviewed suggest that there may be a significant market failure in the processes that determine the fuel efficiencies of motor vehicles. Such a market failure could arise on the demand side, the supply side, or in market transactions. The possibility that such a phenomenon exists is called the *energy efficiency gap*, as it implies a gap between actual and socially optimal outcomes.

On the demand side, do consumers fully account for the cost savings they will receive from purchasing a more efficient vehicle? The possibility that they do not is sometimes called the *energy efficiency paradox*, because consumers seem not to do what is in their own best interests over time.[17] How could this occur? Possibilities are reviewed by Helfand and Wolverton (2011) and Gerarden *et al.* (2017). Consumers may suffer from inattention to fuel efficiency (lack of "salience") as they navigate the complexities of choosing among vehicles offered on the market. They may subjectively associate fuel efficiency with poor performance, even if the two are actually unrelated, perhaps due to the trade-off discussed earlier; or they may otherwise be poorly informed about fuel efficiency. They have difficulty objectively calculating the implications of fuel efficiency for their future costs, as already noted and as amply documented by Turrentine and Kurani (2007). They may exhibit excessive caution about spending more on fuel efficiency whose future value is uncertain.[18] Vehicles may be "positional goods," which place consumers in a social ranking based on the most readily observable characteristics so that there is an externality in consumption, rather than being purely consumption items.

Finally, consumers may exhibit inconsistent preferences, acting on impulse but later regretting it – a phenomenon we call *myopia* because it implies decisions based on shorter time horizons than the consumer would use in a more considered choice. There is in fact plenty of evidence, as well as theory, for consumers widely displaying preferences that are inconsistent over time (see, *e.g.,* Thaler 2017, pp. 1800–1801).

On the other hand, an apparent energy paradox might not be real. It is possible that consumers perceive quality differences correlated with energy efficiency that are invisible to the analyst: In that case, we can say that the measurable energy savings are offset by a loss of *hidden amenities*.

Also, there is evidence that consumer preferences vary widely, which implies that a feature that would benefit an average consumer will be only partially adopted. Hence, an analyst who incorrectly assumes that everyone is average may observe an energy paradox when there is none. If regulation is nonetheless adopted to meet other objectives, heterogeneity favors incorporating regulatory flexibility to accommodate differences among consumers. As it happens, most energy policies under consideration are flexible in this sense – unlike the case of conventional air pollution, where governments typically prohibit sales of cars that exceed a certain emissions level.[19]

Even if a demand-side paradox exists, its normative implications depend on its source. If the source is inattention, poor information, cognitive limits, or principal-agent problems, then each consumer's individual welfare can be improved by forcing buyers to purchase more fuel-efficient cars than they would purchase voluntarily. In that case, consumers would arguably recognize that they are better off with the choice forced on them by regulation, even if they opposed the regulation beforehand. The same is true if caution about uncertain fuel prices reflects a lack of information that is known to policymakers. Also, if vehicles are positional goods, market intervention would theoretically make all of them better off (unless it induces them to find some other socially unproductive way to show off), but individually they might now perceive the result negatively. Finally, if the problem is inconsistent preferences, the welfare implications are ambiguous – being an example of a large class of cases revealed by "behavioral economics" to have welfare implications that do not fit conventional methods of analysis (see, *e.g.*, Bernheim 2016).

On the supply side, an energy efficiency gap may occur if manufacturers provide less fuel efficiency than consumers desire, especially if their desires are congruent with socially optimal outcomes (for example, if appropriate Pigouvian taxes are in place). Why might this happen? Manufacturers also face uncertainty, affecting the returns on investments in technology development, and so may forego investments with positive expected returns. They face long time lags in their ability to fully adjust to changes in consumer preferences. And they compete with each other through product differentiation, branding, bundling of attributes, and marketing, which may result in their emphasizing some quality dimensions and de-emphasizing others relative to customer preferences. If manufacturers de-emphasize energy efficiency, this will result in an energy efficiency gap.

Now consider when demand and supply interact in markets. Institutional features of those markets may produce an energy efficiency gap. For example, consumers may face inefficient markets for loans, resulting in interest rates higher than those appropriate for social cost–benefit analysis. (This could occur, for example, if consumers choose cheaper but energy-inefficient vehicles in order to stay within lenders' credit limits.) As another example, interests among market participants may conflict, such as when the vehicle driven by a consumer is chosen by a rental company – an example of an "agency problem." Yet another possibility is the well-known problem of adverse selection in used-vehicle markets, which can drive down the unobservable quality of vehicles on offer (Akerlof 1970).

We now turn to the empirical evidence for an energy efficiency gap. Empirical tests are difficult not only because of the complexity of markets for light-duty vehicles, but because the question is inherently about a long-term dynamic decision problem: What should a consumer pay to save on future fuel costs over a period of perhaps 15 years? The answer depends on several factors: vehicle lifetimes (more precisely, the distribution of vehicle retirements, including those due to vehicle crashes); vehicle usage patterns over their lifetimes; expectations of future fuel prices; and, especially, the discount rates that measure consumers' true preferences over current and future consumption. Some of these factors are hard to observe.

The difficulty is illustrated by an influential study by Busse *et al.* (2013), notable for its careful econometric methodology controlling for various sources of endogeneity and omitted variables. Their data are individual new- and used-vehicle purchase transactions. This study is often described as finding no myopia. The authors are slightly more circumspect, summarizing their results as "showing little evidence of consumer myopia" (abstract, p. 220). Yet, even this conclusion is overstated: it is based on the overlap between the range of computed implicit real discount rates, under alternate parametric assumptions, and the range of real market interest rates faced by the middle four-fifths of people in their sample. These ranges are huge: [−6.8%, +20.9%] and [−0.9%, +9.0%], respectively.[20,21] It seems the authors consider the null hypothesis of a perfectly functioning market compelling enough to highlight their inability to firmly reject it, even though it is rejected by a large fraction of the particular comparisons they display.

Three other recent studies with extensive econometric controls, two from the USA and one from Europe, are explicit about which estimates their authors believe are most credible. Allcott and Wozny (2014) use monthly average prices by model and year of used vehicles sold at auction; like Busse *et al.*, their data are from the USA for years 1999–2008. They present results using a measure that is equivalent to the implicit discount rate: namely, they compare (i) the revealed marginal rate of substitution (MRS) between fuel efficiency and vehicle price to (ii) the MRS that would apply to a fully rational consumer. The latter is the ratio between the present value of future fuel-cost savings and the measured fuel efficiency of the vehicle at purchase, with the calculation based on rational expectations for future prices and other factors.[22] The ratio between quantities (i) and (ii) is the *valuation ratio*. If the consumer is fully rational and informed, with an implicit discount rate equal to the market rate (*i.e.*, no myopia), and all other sources of market failure are absent, then the valuation ratio will be 100%. All-cott and Wozny present this calculation for a wide variety of assumptions; at their preferred assumptions, the estimated valuation ratio is 76%, indicating a substantial undervaluation of fuel savings. They note that under these same preferred assumptions, Busse *et al.* find an implicit discount rate of 13%, which is above most of the range of interest rates that Busse *et al.* consider to be market rates.

A second study, by Grigolon *et al.* (2018), makes use of a feature of European vehicle markets: the existence of many models offering diesel and gasoline cars that are otherwise nearly identical. Diesel cars are more expensive, but incur significantly lower fuel costs; furthermore, the trade-off varies across different European fuel-tax structures. The authors analyze a 14-year panel data set consisting of thousands of distinct vehicle models, each varying by engine type and facing the vehicle- and fuel-tax regimes of seven different countries. By using vehicle-model fixed effects, the authors isolate the diesel vs. gasoline decision, which is readily apparent and comprehensible to consumers. Their central estimate of the valuation ratio is 91%. The ratio that would apply to decisions between less easily observed and quantified differences in fuel efficiency is most likely smaller.

A third study is by Leard *et al.* (2023), who use more recent US data and thus avoid the troublesome 2007–2009 recession. Their data come from surveys designed specifically for this purpose and conducted by a market research firm. Their approach, like that of Busse *et al.*, relies on two reduced-form estimations involving the market for vehicles: one explains market price and the other market quantity. Each is a function of two vehicle characteristics (fuel cost per mile and performance as measured by either acceleration or torque) and of a set of demand- or cost-shifting variables. Instrumental variables for fuel cost and performance, along with fixed effects, serve to separately identify the two equations.[23] The results can then be used to "back out" the underlying demand and marginal cost curves for vehicles, as illustrated by Figure 7.1. This figure depicts a shift in both demand and marginal cost curves resulting from an increase in fuel efficiency – due, respectively, to added value of the vehicle to the consumer and to extra manufacturing cost. The observed shifts in market price and quantity are l_1 and (Q_2-Q_1), respectively,[24] whereas the shift in value to the consumer, which we desire to measure, is (l_1+l_2). Like

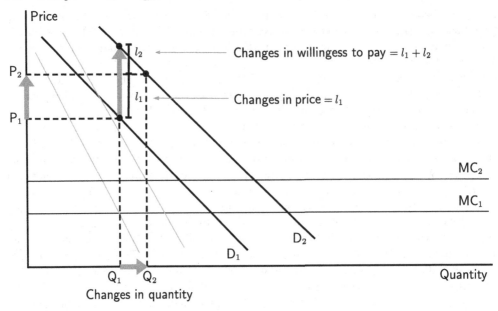

Figure 7.1 Changes in market price, market quantity, and willingness to pay for a fuel efficiency improvement.

Source: Figure 3 from Leard *et al.* (2023). With permission from © 2023 by the President and Fellows of Harvard College and the Massachusetts Institute of Technology.

Busse *et al.*, Leard *et al.* (2023) use an assumed price elasticity of demand (namely −3.0, based on other studies) to calculate this quantity from the observed market shifts; they then check their calculation for robustness to this assumed elasticity.

The magnitude of the upward shift of demand curve D can be used to compute the implicit real discount rate that consumers are using to value the improved fuel efficiency. Their results imply this discount rate is 12.2%, which again is well above the range of market rates faced by most consumers and thus represents a significant energy efficiency paradox. Equivalently, the authors describe their result as a valuation ratio of 54%, based on a real market interest rate of 1.3% (the average financing rate reported by their survey respondents, less inflation). In other words, the demand curve shifts upward by only 54% of the amount one would calculate using this market interest rate.[25]

Leard *et al.* (2023) also measure the marginal trade-off in consumers' utility between fuel efficiency and performance. They measure a very high valuation of performance, which they describe as follows: based on other literature, manufacturers could increase performance by 3%–6% at the same cost as increasing fuel efficiency by 1%, an MRS of 3–6; whereas consumers' marginal rate of substitution was about 0.33. In other words, the MRS in production was 9–18 times higher than that in consumption! This suggests to us that manufacturers were strongly constrained by the fuel efficiency standards in effect during the time period of the study; otherwise, they would have continued the historically strong trend of regular performance enhancements as documented by Knittel (2012). Indeed, as noted by Gerarden *et al.* (2017, p. 1509), most modern empirical studies of the energy efficiency gap for motor vehicles observe choices made under some version of fuel efficiency standards, which restrict vehicle offerings and thus may prevent consumers with high implicit discount rates from exhibiting them in the market. This biases such studies against finding myopia.

Taken as a whole, the newer studies support the older literature in finding consumer under-valuation of future fuel savings. While there is plenty of uncertainty in the results, it seems to us that one could be unpersuaded by the evidence for market failure only by starting with a very strong prior belief of full rationality and perfect markets. Since modern behavioral theory and direct observation of behavior already cast doubt on this belief, there is little reason to adopt it; more likely, observed behavior reflects a substantial energy efficiency gap. Whether or not its size is sufficient to justify fuel efficiency policies currently in place or under discussion is another question, which we take up in Section 7.2.

7.1.4 Empirical results: motor vehicle usage and the rebound effect

Motor fuel usage (*e.g.*, in gallons) by a given vehicle equals vehicle usage (miles) divided by vehicle fuel efficiency (miles/gallon).[26] Both respond to fuel price and, of course, to various control variables. Viewed as separate quantities for which demand can be expressed, fuel efficiency and usage are inherently interdependent. As already discussed, the demand for fuel efficiency – expressed through demand for specific vehicle models – depends on current and expected future fuel price as well as expected usage. As for vehicle usage, it is natural to posit that fuel price enters demand as a component of the total price of driving, which includes the "fuel cost of driving," defined as fuel price divided by fuel efficiency. Thus, the demand for each component of motor fuel usage depends directly on the other.

One consequence of this interdependence is that policies aimed at improving fuel efficiency have dual effects: one directly through reduced fuel for each vehicle-mile and the other indirectly through increased vehicle usage due to a lower fuel cost of driving. The two effects are in opposite directions. The indirect effect has occasionally been viewed as secondary, something of an analytical nuisance, and so acquired the name "rebound effect." But in fact, the rebound effect can have large impacts on the overall welfare evaluation of policies toward fuel efficiency. It not only directly offsets the desired reduction in fuel usage, which has its own role in social welfare trade-offs through implications for emissions and resource depletion, but in addition, vehicle usage often produces other strong externalities. Thus, the magnitude of the rebound effect is important to policy evaluation and has attracted much empirical attention.[27]

The fact that fuel efficiency and usage are chosen simultaneously creates a definitional problem for the rebound effect: what does it mean to say it is the response of usage to efficiency? Following and simplifying Small and Van Dender (2007), we can define the rebound effect within a two-equation system:

$$\begin{aligned} M &= M(P_M, X_M) \\ E &= E(M, P_F, R_E, X_E) \end{aligned} \qquad (7.2)$$

where, as before, M is vehicle usage (vehicle-miles or vehicle-kilometers), E is fuel efficiency, P_F is the price of fuel, and $P_M \equiv P_F/E$ is the fuel price of driving. Variable R_E represents some regulatory policy that directly influences fuel efficiency, while X_M and X_E are other control variables. The rebound effect can then be defined as the price elasticity $\varepsilon_{M,PM} \equiv (\partial M/\partial P_M) P_M/M$ from the first of these equations.

Equations (7.2) can be estimated by two-stage least squares or other methods that recognize the endogeneity of P_M in the first equation (via its definition in terms of E) and that of M in the second equation. For statistical estimation, the set of variables X_M must contain at least one that is omitted from the set (R_E, X_E), and (R_E, X_E) must contain at least one variable that is omitted from X_M. These so-called exclusion restrictions are the critical assumptions that identify the model (*i.e.*, that allow us to estimate the two equations as a structural system rather than simply to trace the path of observed market equilibria as prices vary). The exclusion restrictions implicitly define instrumental variables, which are variables that directly influence only one of the dependent variables.

What does empirical evidence tell us about the rebound effect? Researchers continue to reach varied conclusions, for many reasons. First is the inherently dynamic nature of the response, especially that of E as described in the previous subsection. The second is a consequence of the first: results differ depending on whether a study relies primarily on variation over time or over cross sections, the latter usually leading to estimates that are smaller in magnitude. Third, most datasets lack much exogenous variation in fuel efficiency, the explanatory variable of primary interest. Most studies therefore rely on combining fuel efficiency and fuel price into a single variable P_M, as in (7.2). But this introduces a fourth problem: there is no solid evidence that this simplification is empirically valid, and considerable evidence against it as detailed below. Since it is fuel *price* that provides most of the exogenous variation used by most studies, this leaves the rebound effect itself (the response to fuel *efficiency*) only tenuously estimated.

One way to alleviate the first two problems is to use combined cross-sectional time-series data, sometimes known as panel data (see Section 2.4.4). Another approach is to use high-frequency data, such as monthly or even daily, to enlarge the number of time-series observations; but that measures short-run effects, whereas policy analysis typically requires knowledge of longer-run adjustments. Yet another approach is to take advantage of specific policy changes or other events that are credibly exogenous and thus create a natural experiment; this approach is enhanced in some newer studies by collecting individual transaction data, leading to much larger datasets and hence more precision in estimation.

Gillingham *et al.* (2016) provide an excellent review of empirical findings, focusing on studies they deem most credible in controlling for endogeneity. They tabulate results for six US studies: four studying the rebound effect itself and two studying gasoline demand, of which the rebound effect is a component per (7.1). The findings for short- to medium-run elasticities vary between −0.045 and −0.458; *i.e.*, rebound effects when stated in percentage terms vary from 4.5% to 45.8% – a distressingly large range. The authors also review studies from fifteen low- and middle-income countries, finding a similar range of magnitudes.

The lowest-magnitude estimate just quoted, 4.5%, comes from Small and Van Dender (2007), who use cross-sectional time-series data to estimate an elaborated version of (7.2).[28] This study differs from most others by estimating not a single constant elasticity across their 35 years of data (1966–2001), but an elasticity that varies linearly according to income and the fuel cost of driving – which means the second equation in (7.2) is a quadratic function of fuel cost P_M. They find the elasticity to be strongly influenced by income and moderately influenced by P_M. As a result, the magnitude of the rebound effect declines dramatically over their sample: the long-run elasticity is −0.22 averaged over the entire sample (comparable to many other studies) but only −0.11 over the last five years of the sample. The short-run elasticities are one-fifth of these values.[29] A few other studies support a decline in the rebound effect, either directly across time (Hughes *et al.* 2008, for the USA), as a function of income (De Borger *et al.* 2016, for Denmark), or both (Greene 2012).

Hymel and Small (2015) use the same data source as Small and Van Dender, but extend it through 2009, finding that the reduction in magnitude up to 2001 was partially reversed starting in 2004. They are able to account for some of this reversal by adding two control variables intended to indicate fuel-price salience, namely news coverage and fuel-price volatility.

Perhaps the most serious weakness of the empirical literature on the rebound effect is the need in most studies to assume the fuel economy E enters the demand for driving only through the composite variable $P_M \equiv P_F/E$, as in (7.2). Several studies have attempted to test this assumption; virtually none can accept it with any reasonable confidence, yet very few can definitively reject it due to inadequate variation in fuel efficiency. An exception is De Borger *et al.* (2016), who use Danish microdata to show that the response to fuel efficiency (*i.e.*, the rebound effect) is considerably smaller than that to fuel price. There is in fact growing evidence from other studies that this is the case.[30]

Jeremy West *et al.* (2017) make use of a natural experiment, namely the arbitrary eligibility criterion for a US "cash for clunkers" subsidy program in 2009, to provide a rare direct estimate of the response of usage to fuel efficiency, independently of fuel price. They analyze individual-level data on people who were close to the eligibility threshold (18 mi/gal for their existing car), some just below and some just above, to see how the fuel efficiency of new cars purchased affected their driving. At the same time, they examine how the program's subsidies for more efficient cars affected choices of other vehicle traits, such as weight and horsepower. They find that fuel efficiency and performance were negatively related in new-car purchases, leading to measurable reductions in performance as a result of higher fuel efficiency. They note that lower performance would affect amount of driving in an opposite direction to higher fuel efficiency and find empirically that the offset is complete – *i.e.*, they measure the combined response of driving to be zero or possibly even negative. This study is a good reminder that when using a rebound effect for policy, one needs to give close attention to what other quantities besides fuel efficiency will be changed by the policy.[31]

There is one tantalizing finding that is not well confirmed or understood. Hymel and Small (2015) find that consumer response to changes in fuel cost of driving is much greater if that cost is increasing than if it is decreasing. Such asymmetry, also known as demand hysteresis, may reflect sunk capital investments, the undesirability of reversing technological advances or government policies (Gately and Huntington 2002), or just the salience of a change to travelers. This finding is clouded by the inability to separate effects of efficiency and price, so that it is unclear which variable produces the behavioral asymmetry. Leard *et al.* (2017) find a similar asymmetry in a study of how monthly changes in fuel costs affect new-car purchases.[32]

Dimitropoulos *et al.* (2018) provide a useful meta-analysis of rebound studies. In a summary regression, they analyze estimates from 74 studies, relating the estimates to gross domestic product (GDP) per capita, gasoline price per liter, and population density. The regression predicts long-run rebound effects ranging from 15% at conditions similar to the USA to 65% for low-income countries with very high fuel prices and population densities. These results, while higher than much of the evidence we have reviewed, are consistent with the dependence on income found by Small and Van Dender (2007): In their regression, the rebound effect declines by 0.4 percentage points for each $1,000 in increased GDP and in addition by 0.7 percentage points for each year, together implying much smaller rebound effects in the future than those observed from past data.[33]

Considering all this evidence, it appears that the rebound effect for motor vehicle travel is relatively small, especially in rich countries; but there is still a lot of uncertainty and it no doubt varies across situations. The most important research innovations needed are (i) to more rigorously model dynamics; (ii) to further study consumers' response to efficiency separately from fuel price; (iii) to study asymmetric responses to exogenous changes in fuel efficiency; and (iv) to see whether the dependence on income is robust.

7.2   Policies to reduce motor vehicle fuel consumption

In this section, we consider a few of the most common approaches aimed at reducing fuel use by motor vehicles. Broadly, they are divided between those aimed at the fuel efficiency of new vehicles (Section 7.2.1) and fuel-tax policies, which target all factors affecting fuel consumption (Section 7.2.2).

7.2.1   *Promoting vehicle fuel efficiency*

A popular approach to reducing fuel consumption is to regulate or otherwise influence the efficiency of vehicles on the road. This is sometimes done by providing tax incentives for efficiency or by encouraging the retirement of older inefficient vehicles. Often, it is done by direct regulation of new vehicles. We refer to direct regulation by its US name, Corporate Average Fuel Economy (CAFE).

Due to the many interacting actions spurred by such policies, a simulation model is usually needed for policy design, although some conclusions can be drawn from a single well-specified statistical study. We highlight three such simulation studies here, each illustrating a different approach. We then consider some specific features of policy programs and some empirical estimates of their impacts.

7.2.1.1   *Economic simulation model*

Jacobsen (2013) offers a very detailed model based on full rationality, a strong theoretical derivation of optimization conditions by both consumers and producers, econometric estimation consistent with that theory, and ample allowance for heterogeneity among consumers and producers. The model assumes there is no energy paradox. Jacobsen includes several features that are lacking from most other studies, finding them quite important quantitatively. First, the model includes used-car markets, interacting consistently with new-car markets and scrappage decisions. Second, it considers that domestic manufacturers may perceive a shadow cost to any violation of CAFE standards, perhaps for political or public relations reasons, in addition to any monetary penalties. Third, the model has demand and supply functions for each vehicle type, which depend on prices for other vehicle types: A type here means a vehicle in one of ten size classes, one of five age ranges, and one of seven manufacturers (two of which are aggregates of several manufacturers).

The importance of these features is seen in some of the conclusions from using the model to analyze a tightening of CAFE standards. We describe here results of the simpler version of the model, in which the standards are of a pure form (not varied by car attributes) and technology is fixed. Conclusions include, first, that used-car prices rise and the stock of used cars shifts toward larger, more fuel-inefficient cars, due to the relative scarcity of such cars in the new-car market. These shifts reduce the effectiveness of the policy and make it substantially more regressive, because lower-income people are over-represented among used-car buyers.[34] Second, domestic US manufacturers treat the standard as binding, even though they could increase profits by paying fines instead. As a result, their sales and profits are adversely impacted, in some cases severely so. Third, in contrast, foreign producers choose to pay fines and fill the gap left by domestic firms in the market for larger and less efficient vehicles. This ability to buy exemption from the standards reduces the policy's effectiveness. Fourth, the standard achieves the vast majority of its fuel savings through changes in vehicle mix (*i.e.*, through changes among the set of existing vehicle size classes, ages, and manufacturers). These savings come at a very high welfare cost.[35]

Jacobsen provides two alternatives to the main simulation model. One allows endogenous technological change to help meet increased standards, with costs based on an independent assessment (US National Research Council 2002). The other combines this with an approximation to the actual footprint-based standard, which varies by the area covered by the vehicle's wheels. (In the approximation, the standard is set in such a way as to remove all incentive to change vehicle mix.) In both versions, vehicle mix ceases to play much of a role; instead, the fuel savings now arise mainly from the application of technology, and the welfare cost per ton of CO_2 is roughly one-third of its value in the simpler model.

7.2.1.2   Composite simulation model

A different simulation approach is illustrated by Small (2012). Rather than derive a model from full rationality, Small adopts the well-known National Energy Modeling System (NEMS), a simulation model used by the US Energy Information Agency for official projections. He adapts it to better represent producer pricing behavior and goes on to calculate welfare effects separately for the various sub-markets involved, especially for vehicle-type choice and vehicle usage.

An advantage of this approach is that NEMS is based on extensive empirical observation and so captures many complexities of the markets, including details of CAFE and other regulations. The modeling system also contains an extremely detailed list of potential technologies and their costs, allowing modeled firms to apply technology in a very flexible way to meet standards. As for the energy efficiency gap, NEMS takes observed behavior as given, without dictating an interpretation of its causes. Small therefore calculates welfare using two alternate assumptions: either that the energy efficiency gap implied by NEMS is real (*i.e.*, that consumers are not optimizing), or alternatively that the gap is only apparent, meaning that observed behavior is caused by unobserved disamenities associated with fuel economy.

A disadvantage of this approach is that the welfare calculations are complex and only approximate, unable to fully account for all interactions among market segments. One could counter, however, that the true workings of these markets cannot be captured by a typical economic optimization model if in fact participants do not act according to its rather stringent behavioral assumptions.

Small (2012) simulates the gradual tightening of CAFE enacted under the Obama administration for cars produced between 2016 and 2025.[36] Energy savings are achieved in these simulations mainly by adopting new-vehicle technologies; vehicle mix plays only a small role, consistent with Jacobsen's results. Small finds that the welfare costs of reducing GHGs in this way are drastically affected by two factors: (i) whether the energy efficiency gap is real or only apparent and (ii) whether externalities of motor vehicles that are unrelated to energy or climate change are taken into account.

To better understand these results, consider the implications of changing one or both of these factors. We begin with the most favorable case for the CAFE policy: assuming the gap is real and that other externalities are negligible. In that case, the welfare cost is negative – *i.e.*, the policy is beneficial even without counting its climate benefits.[37] This is because it mitigates the inefficiency of the energy paradox – namely by correcting consumers' mistaken decisions to forego substantial fuel-cost savings.

Now suppose we change just the second of these assumptions and assume that the external costs of driving (excluding climate costs) are at the preferred values in Small's simulations. In that case, the welfare cost becomes positive, though very small – far smaller than many other climate mitigation measures being adopted. The reason this case raises the welfare cost of CAFE is the rebound effect, discussed earlier, in the presence of unpriced local externalities.[38]

Suppose next we change not only the second assumption but also the first – *i.e.*, we now assume the apparent efficiency gap is not real, and we also account for non-climate-related driving externalities. Then, the welfare cost becomes quite large – comparable to current estimates of the cost of carbon – hence bringing CAFE into the realm of policies that are possibly but debatably beneficial.[39] The difference from the previous case arises because under these assumptions, the policy no longer alleviates assumed consumer misperceptions. Allcott *et al.* (2014) and Parry *et al.* (2014) similarly find that accounting for a real energy efficiency gap in welfare calculations greatly increases the net benefits of efficiency standards.

Together, these simulations suggest a case of "the tail wagging the dog." That is, the original objective of the policy – reducing climate costs – tends to be overshadowed by the policy's favorable and unfavorable side effects. Those side effects are (1) overcoming the energy efficiency gap, via direct regulation of efficiency, and (2) encouraging more driving, via the rebound effect. The overall evaluation of the policy turns out to depend as much on the size of these side effects as on the climate change benefits themselves.

7.2.1.3   *Engineering design model*

Given that technological changes seem to account for most results of applying fuel efficiency standards, it is natural to focus greater attention on them and less on the intricacies of vehicle-type choice. As noted earlier, Whitefoot *et al.* (2017) do this by developing a tractable version of an actual design model used by automobile manufacturers and nesting it within a conventional discrete-choice model of vehicle-type choice.

The engineering design model is simulated nearly 30,000 times using different combinations of vehicle characteristics, focusing especially on those that are adjustable in the "medium run" – defined as one to six years after a new regulation is announced. The results define iso-technology relationships between performance (acceleration) and fuel efficiency, with vehicle weight and various technology indicators as parameters. (Technology indicators include such options as advanced alternators and low-resistance tires.) Unit production costs are also calculated for each simulation, permitting estimation of a function relating costs to the same variables. The model of vehicle-type choice is mixed (random coefficients) logit (as discussed in Section 2.4.2), estimated from results of a custom-designed household survey. As is standard, instrumental variables (IVs) are used to control for endogeneity of price and attributes, while being careful to exclude from the set of IVs any variables that the model treats as adjustable in the medium run.

This framework is used to simulate a substantial change in stringency of the US CAFE standards that occurred between 2006 and 2014. In order to understand the role played by vehicle performance in this process, the same simulations are carried out with two versions of the model: one allowing full freedom in the design process and the other constraining acceleration (for a given car model) to be held constant. When acceleration trade-offs are allowed, the aggregate reductions in fuel consumption are four times as large as otherwise, and the cost in terms of lost consumers' surplus is 42% smaller. This is because manufacturers use reduced performance to help achieve the standards: for example, in the unconstrained model, acceleration time (0–60 mi/hr) rises by about 8% due to the regulations. These results show dramatically that curtailing vehicle performance can be an important and beneficial part of the response to fuel efficiency regulations. Furthermore, changes in vehicle mix play a much smaller role when performance can be freely altered: in the unconstrained model, vehicle size, as measured by footprint, rises hardly at all. The share of light trucks increases in both versions of the model, but considerably less so when acceleration trade-offs are allowed. Thus, the model suggests that consumers will settle for small reductions in performance, rather than changing their vehicle-type choices, if that proves the most economical way for manufacturers to meet the more stringent standards.

Simulations by Liu *et al.* (2014) similarly find that technology, not vehicle mix, accounts for most of manufacturers' anticipated responses to US CAFE standards.

The results from engineering design models thus suggest that fuel efficiency standards are much more effective, and less costly, than estimated by models that focus solely on vehicle mix or on technology changes that hold performance constant. They also suggest that making the standards footprint-based may do less damage than would appear from models that lack fully flexible technology options. We caution that the importance of vehicle mix may change with advancing technology, especially if electric vehicles become substantially cheaper.

There is independent evidence that the US standards are, in fact, less costly to meet than would be inferred from a model based on achieving them through changes in vehicle mix. Anderson and Sallee (2011) take advantage of a regulatory quirk to provide a more direct estimate of compliance cost. The US regulation allows a significant credit, in meeting the standard, for flexible-fuel vehicles that can use either gasoline or ethanol as fuel. This is a true loophole in the sense that, at least at the margin, the regulation serves no actual environmental purpose because many such vehicles are sold in states lacking ethanol fueling stations. Anderson and Sallee derive a first-order profit-maximization condition for when a gasoline vehicle would be reconfigured as a flexible-fuel vehicle (a quite simple operation costing \$100–\$200 per car) as part of a manufacturer's strategy to meet the standard. The manufacturer will make this conversion whenever doing so is cheaper than improving fuel efficiency of gasoline-powered vehicles. Because the number of such conversions is observable, Anderson and Sallee can use this condition to infer the marginal cost of improving fuel efficiency. Doing so, they find a marginal cost of only \$9–\$27 per vehicle for an improvement of one mile per gallon, which is on the order of one-tenth Jacobsen's (2013) estimates for US domestic manufacturers.[40]

7.2.1.4 Attribute-based regulations

Like many other kinds of regulation, fuel efficiency standards or other programs promoting fuel efficiency are usually implemented not uniformly, but in relationship to one or more attributes that are thought to affect compliance cost or perhaps that reflect other social or political goals. The most common is some measure of size or weight of the vehicle, but some programs apply more arbitrary distinctions. Such programs have been implemented in China, Japan, the USA, and many other countries.

Attribute basing of standards has at least two effects. First, it can be designed to lower the compliance cost of a given reduction in fuel use, by forcing the biggest improvements on those model vehicles for which marginal compliance cost is lowest. Second, it distorts the market for the attribute itself by encouraging designs that emphasize attribute values for which standards are more lenient. This may increase compliance cost by inducing wasteful expenditures on the attribute. If the attribute itself has an external cost, this response also adds a welfare burden by exacerbating that externality.

Ito and Sallee (2018) provide an elegant theory, which applies either to regulatory standards or to an attribute-based subsidy. This theory demonstrates both the rationale and the drawback of attribute basing: it potentially can lower compliance cost by putting the most stringent regulation on those vehicles that can comply most cheaply, but it also distorts attribute choice. As described in Chapter 2, there is strong evidence that larger and heavier vehicles have negative safety costs when they collide with smaller vehicles, making this distortion a potentially severe disadvantage.

Ito and Sallee apply this theory to the weight-based subsidy scheme for purchase of high-efficiency cars as implemented in Japan beginning in 2009. The subsidy acts like a fine for exceeding an efficiency standard and is an example of a partial feebate policy (see Section 4.2.5).[41] The subsidy schedule contains kinks or "notches" in the relationship between the attribute (weight), which result in bunching of vehicle offerings just above the set of discrete weights that define different efficiency standards. That bunching is part of the distortion in the attribute market but also provides a way to identify the cost relationships econometrically. Using a panel dataset of individual model car designs before and after the regulations, the authors show that indeed many model cars were redesigned to be both heavier and more fuel-efficient, with a strong tendency to land just above one of the weight notches. Furthermore, the authors use the observations on car redesigns to infer all the relevant cost parameters.

The results strikingly demonstrate the adverse effects that attribute basing can have in practice. Simulations indicate that the scheme implemented has private compliance costs of $2,132 per car, twice as high as would a scheme that allows efficient compliance trading. In addition, it results in cars on average 3% heavier, with a resulting increased cost of fatalities of $677 per car.[42] A second-best optimal flat subsidy (*i.e.*, one not based on weight) would have even higher compliance costs ($3,605/car) but would have a safety *benefit* of $627/car due to manufacturers using lighter cars to increase fuel efficiency. Thus, the safety disadvantage of the scheme adopted nearly offsets its favorable effect on compliance cost, relative to a subsidy not based on weight. Both aspects could be improved by allowing firms to trade among vehicle models in determining the standards on which the subsidy is based.

Leard *et al.* (2017) similarly find that for US fuel efficiency standards, being based on vehicle footprint causes substantial increases in vehicle footprint.

Chen *et al.* (2021) consider attribute basing of a more arbitrary nature in the subsidy program that operated in China in 2010 and 2011. Specific model cars were offered the subsidy, a new list of models being announced every few months with little or no advance notice or explanation except that all were relatively fuel-efficient. Here, the attribute is the specific model car, and the potential distortion is substitution between similar models that were or were not eligible for subsidy. The authors find that nearly half the cars receiving the subsidy were purchased as substitutes for other cars within the top quartile of fuel efficiency, substantially reducing the cost-effectiveness of the program. By their calculations, the program's welfare costs exceeded its environmental benefits by roughly a factor of four.[43]

7.2.1.5   *Analytical issues*

The design of fuel efficiency standards may embody sources of inefficiency that are omitted from most economic analyses. For example, the fuel efficiency of a vehicle, as measured in official tests, is an imperfect proxy for actual fuel efficiency – which depends on driving behavior, tire pressure, and other factors. Furthermore, future fuel prices are unknown when efficiency standards are announced, so many of the adjustments that consumers and manufacturers could make as fuel prices evolve are not incentivized (Kellogg 2018).

Another problem is that there is large variation in amount of driving across vehicle models, causing emissions to differ even between two vehicles with the same actual fuel efficiency. Grigolon *et al.* (2018) measure heterogeneity in annual amount of driving across different vehicle models, finding it quite important to program evaluation. Jacobsen *et al.* (2020) measure total vehicle-kilometers driven over vehicles' lifetimes, which they observe from consumer surveys that include vehicle retirements; they estimate that this heterogeneity reduces the overall welfare gain of a fuel efficiency standard by three-fourths.

Greenstone *et al.* (2017) propose to reform efficiency standards so as to bypass both attribute basing and most of the problem of heterogeneity in amount of driving. Their proposal would apply a "cap-and-trade" policy to new-car purchases, with the cap based solely on estimated lifetime fuel consumption for that model vehicle. Cap-and-trade means that permits are issued for fuel consumption up to the cap, but manufacturers can trade these permits in markets, selling them if they do better than the cap and buying them if they would otherwise fail to meet it. In a well-functioning market, the permit prices act just like a feebate centered about the cap; however, in this case the cap is based on estimated lifetime fuel consumption rather than on estimated vehicle fuel efficiency.

7.2.1.6 *Other policies*

A policy closely related to efficiency standards is the feebate policy mentioned earlier. As the name implies, the policy specifies fees for less energy-efficient vehicles and rebates for more energy-efficient vehicles, compared with some baseline standard. A feebate can be revenue-neutral, as in the congestion pricing example in Section 4.2.5, but need not be. Feebates also exist in one-sided versions: the Japanese weight-based program discussed earlier, as well as programs in Sweden and Canada, contain only the rebate part, whereas the "gas-guzzler tax" in the USA contains only the fee part. A feebate system has the advantage of causing little or no increase in the average cost of driving, thus bypassing an appreciable share of the distributional and tax-interaction effects of fuel or carbon taxes (see next subsection). As discussed in Section 4.2.5, feebates are second-best: they provide a subsidy to those imposing relatively low external costs, whereas charging them a (low) tax would be first-best optimal. Feebates have been implemented in France, as the "bonus/malus" program, starting in 2008.[44]

Durrmeyer and Samano (2017) consider in greater depth the short-term properties of feebate policies, with manufacturers' reactions restricted to changing vehicle prices (*i.e.*, holding constant technology and the set of models offered for sale). They derive several interesting theoretical results comparing feebates with efficiency standards, taking into account the market power of manufacturers. As expected, the policies can be made equivalent if manufacturers offer identical sets of vehicles, have identical costs, and choose to comply with a standard rather than pay fines. But if any of these properties are absent, feebates are preferable under a wide variety of conditions because they better allocate the cost of reducing fuel use among manufacturers. For example, if one manufacturer is unconstrained by the chosen average level of fuel efficiency, it does not have an incentive to change under the CAFE standard but does under a feebate due to the ability to increase its rebates. The authors also consider efficiency credit trading under CAFE, showing that if it is allowed (as in the USA since 2011), the standard again becomes equivalent to a feebate policy provided that all firms comply rather than pay fines. Durrmeyer and Samano estimate their model econometrically for France and the USA, finding significant differences in the relative performance of the two policies: feebates are much more efficient than standards in France, but only slightly more so in the USA.

Small (2012), previously discussed, analyzes feebates, as well as emission standards, accounting for the possibility that manufacturers endogenously choose technologies. He finds that a feebate policy can be constructed to closely match the US CAFE standard in its impacts.

A popular substitute for efficiency standards is scrappage programs, which subsidize the purchase of new fuel-efficient vehicles on condition that an older inefficient vehicle is retired. The primary motivation for such programs is often economic stimulus, especially to help motor vehicle producers cope with economic fluctuations. Economic analyses reveal that these programs are not very cost-effective as fuel efficiency programs, but they may in the right circumstances

368 Transportation, energy, and climate

stabilize a new-vehicle market that has been disrupted by economic conditions such as the 2007 financial crises and the coronavirus disease 2019 (COVID-19) pandemic.[45]

Other policies aim to promote greater fuel efficiency by subsidizing development of new technology. They are possibly justified by commercial barriers to research and development such as industry-wide scale economies. Their effectiveness varies greatly with specifics, and like most industrial policies, they are easily subject to diversion of funds to politically well-connected people.

7.2.2 Fuel taxes

Standard economics suggests that the most efficient policy to reduce fuel use would be to tax it directly. The price and income elasticities for fuel, discussed earlier, are a good starting point for analyzing such a tax. But they do not answer all the interesting questions, such as distributional effects. Also, there are subtleties to the tax's welfare effects – especially the existence of pre-existing distortions, which we also noted in connection with congestion fees (Section 4.2.6). Researchers have dealt with these in a variety of ways.

First, let us consider distributional effects directly. A common view is that the fuel tax is regressive, because the income elasticity of vehicle usage is less than one: Therefore, fuel-tax payments rise less than proportionally to income. However, Sarah West (2004) shows that the fuel-price elasticity of a given group of drivers also varies by income, in such a way as to counteract that regressivity: Low-income people respond more to the tax by curtailing fuel use. As a result, she finds that the US fuel tax in the late 1990s was progressive over the lower ranges and mildly regressive in the upper ranges, with middle-income consumers paying the most and incurring the greatest lost consumers' surplus (as percentages of income).[46] Furthermore, the fuel tax is not found to be regressive in many studies that use consumption, rather than income, as the basis for comparison of tax burdens.

As noted in Chapter 2, Bento et al. (2009), like West, use a version of the Dubin–McFadden model to estimate vehicle choice and usage. They embed this demand system within a broader model of several interacting car markets. It includes a supply function for new cars (taking into account fuel efficiency requirements) and equations describing the evolution of the used-car fleet, including vehicle scrappage as a function of endogenous used-car prices. The entire model is estimated simultaneously using full information maximum likelihood, based on a large sample of US households from the 2001 National Household Transportation Survey. The results of Bento et al. confirm West's findings regarding progressivity.[47,48]

Parry and Small (2005) use a more conventional public-finance approach to examine the fuel tax, especially how it interacts with other taxes. They postulate a general-equilibrium model of an economy with consumer utility depending on leisure, consumer goods, vehicle travel, and various characteristics of the environment as well as government services. The government funds services through taxes on labor and fuel. This permits computation of an optimal fuel tax accounting for many of the factors discussed in this book. Specifically, the tax includes three components. The first is an "adjusted Pigouvian tax" component, consisting of the external cost of fuel use and vehicle usage, divided by the marginal cost of raising public funds (i.e., divided by one plus the marginal excess burden). The second is a "Ramsey tax" component, resulting from the tax-interaction and revenue-recycling effects discussed in Section 4.2.6. The third is a "congestion feedback" component reflecting the favorable effect of lower congestion on labor supply.

A key theoretical result is that in computing the adjusted Pigouvian tax, many of the external costs of driving enter in a diluted form, because they depend on vehicle usage rather than directly on fuel consumption. To see why, suppose fuel consumption F generates marginal cost mec^F, due to climate change or other aspects of fuel markets; in addition, vehicle usage M produces distance-related costs mec^c and mec^M, the first due to congestion and the second due to local air pollution and safety.[49] Then, the adjusted Pigouvian tax includes the larger factor:

$$MEC_F \equiv mec^F + r_F^M \cdot E \cdot \left(mec^c + mec^M \right) \tag{7.3}$$

where the r_F^M is the ratio of elasticities of vehicle usage and fuel consumption, each with respect to fuel price (see Section 7.1):

$$r_F^M = \frac{\varepsilon_{M,PF}}{\varepsilon_{F,PF}} \tag{7.4}$$

This "dilution factor," when multiplied by E, gives the change in mileage per unit change of fuel consumption, accounting for all substitution effects. Based on an empirical review, Parry and Small set $r_F^M = 0.4$ (the two elasticities in the ratio are taken to be 0.22 and 0.55, respectively). The full quantity in (7.3) is called the "marginal external cost of fuel use."

It is very common for analysts to describe external costs such as $(mec^c + mec^M)$ in terms of a fuel equivalent by multiplying by fuel efficiency E. But this is quite misleading as a guide to a tax on driving, because it does not incorporate the dilution factor r_F^M. It would apply if fuel prices affected only vehicle usage; but ample evidence suggests that they also affect vehicle efficiency, which reduces the ability of a fuel tax to control such distance-related externalities.

Marshalling empirical evidence for the parameters in their model, Parry and Small estimate optimal tax rates in the USA and UK for the year 2000, expressed in US dollars, to be $1.01/gal and $1.34/gal, respectively. Roughly three-fourths of this is due to the externality; the rest is mostly the combined tax-interaction and revenue-recycling effects. Furthermore, the externality portion (*i.e.*, the adjusted Pigouvian tax) consists mostly of external costs of pollution, congestion, and accidents, even with the dilution factor applied; this would be true even if they had used the higher social cost of carbon (SCC) that applies today (see Section 7.3.2). These optimal tax rates are much larger than current gasoline taxes in the USA, but actually smaller than those in the UK.[50] More recent estimates using the same methodology (Coady *et al.* 2019) show the UK fuel tax to be approximately the efficient level, in part because congestion costs have risen.

Parry and Small also find that large benefits would be reaped by lowering fuel taxes and implementing instead a tax on vehicle usage, sometimes called a tax on "vehicle-miles traveled" (VMT). In that case, the overall tax burden on vehicles in the UK would go up instead of down, compared to current policy. A similar conclusion is reached for the entire EU by Proost *et al.* (2009).

To better understand the various (tax) interactions involved in the above matters and the relationship between fuel and VMT taxes, we set out here a simplified but instructive version of Parry and Small's model, including an explicit congestion component. We remind the reader that this is a general-equilibrium model, ostensibly incorporating all the indirect economic effects of what happens in fuel markets.

Let a representative consumer maximize utility

$$U\left(x, L, M \right)$$

where L is labor supplied, M is annual vehicle usage (in km), and x is a composite "good" consisting of four parts: a numeraire good X (itself again composite, with price normalized to one); a perceived cost of time lost in travel; social costs C^S generated by other users; and government services and transfer payments G:

$$x = X - \alpha TM - C^S + G \tag{7.5}$$

Here, T is travel time per km and α is value of travel time ($/hr). Thus, x incorporates, in an additive fashion as a single index, several things valued or disvalued by the consumer. (The assumption that x is a simple additive function of its variables is not in the original Parry–Small paper, but is made here to simplify the model.) Note that neither labor supplied nor amount of travel is a component of the composite good x, but instead each is made an additional argument in the utility function. This is because labor and travel are not plausibly considered to be perfectly substitutable with other components of x; hence they are not appropriate to model additively. And, of course, x, representing composite consumption, does not itself include income, but rather will appear as an expenditure in the consumer's budget constraint.

We now turn to this budget constraint. Labor receives pretax wage rate w and labor income is taxed at rate τ_L, which we refer to for simplicity as the "labor-tax rate." The consumer is responsible for fuel costs, other running costs c^0 per km, road-toll payments τ_M per km, and vehicle ownership cost $K(E)$ per year. The latter is increasing in vehicle fuel efficiency E. Thus, the consumer's own budget constraint is

$$X + \left[c^0 + \left(p_F / E \right) + \tau_M \right] M + K(E) = wL\left(1 - \tau_L\right)$$

where $p_F \equiv p_F^0 + \tau_F$ is the retail price of fuel, p_F^0 is pretax fuel price, and τ_F is the fuel-tax rate. We can rewrite this budget constraint in terms of our composite commodity x by using (7.5) to replace X:

$$x + \alpha TM + C^S - G + \left[c^0 + \left(p_F / E \right) + \tau_M \right] M + K(E) = wL\left(1 - \tau_L\right)$$

It is convenient to group those terms proportional to M together, thereby creating a composite price of driving, denoted here p_M:

$$x = wL\left(1 - \tau_L\right) - p_M M - K(E) - C^S + G \tag{7.6}$$

where

$$p_M \equiv c^0 + \alpha T + \left(p_F / E \right) + \tau_M \tag{7.7}$$

The consumer's problem is to choose L, x, M, and E so as to maximize the following Lagrangian function:

$$\Lambda = U\left(x, L, M\right) + \lambda \cdot \left[wL\left(1 - \tau_L\right) - p_M M - K(E) - C^S + G - x \right] \tag{7.8}$$

where λ, the Lagrangian multiplier, plays the usual role of a marginal utility of income since it is the increase in the objective function (utility) that would occur if an arbitrary money income were added to the terms in square brackets. The first-order conditions for this maximization are

$$U_x = \lambda$$
$$\frac{U_L}{\lambda} = -w\left(1 - \tau_L\right)$$
$$\frac{U_M}{\lambda} = p_M \tag{7.9}$$
$$K'(E) = p_F M / E^2$$

To analyze the effects of policy, we take into account some society-wide constraints. These are a government budget constraint and technological conditions that determine travel time and social costs. We consider social costs of two types: those related directly to aggregate vehicle usage (*e.g.*, air pollution and risk of injury) and those related to fuel use (*e.g.*, climate change). We define these society-wide constraints as follows:

$$
\begin{aligned}
G &= \tau_L wL + \tau_M M + \tau_F \cdot (M/E) \\
T &= T(M) \\
C^S &= C^{SM} + C^{SF} \equiv mec^M \cdot M + mec^F \cdot M/E
\end{aligned}
\tag{7.10}
$$

where $T(M)$ is a convex increasing congestion function; mec^M is the (fixed) marginal external cost of vehicle usage excluding congestion (due, for example, to local air pollution and accidents); and mec^F is the (fixed) marginal external cost of fuel use. The quantity mec^F may be thought of as the social cost of CO_2, which is defined later in Section 7.3.2, multiplied by the rate of CO_2 production from burning fuel. An implicit assumption in (7.10) is that the society under consideration is small enough that these social costs can be approximated as linear functions of aggregate mileage and fuel consumption.

We can now compute the incremental welfare change from raising either or both of the transportation tax rates by infinitesimal amounts $d\tau_M$ and/or $d\tau_F$. Because this is a general-equilibrium model where all interactions are accounted for, we can define this welfare change as the change in utility divided by the marginal utility of income (the latter division putting utility in monetary units). We first write this welfare change as a function of the (endogenous) quantity changes – namely dL, dM, and dx – that result from the (exogenous) changes in tax rates. This gives

$$
\begin{aligned}
dW &\equiv \frac{dU}{\lambda} = \frac{U_x}{\lambda} dx + \frac{U_L}{\lambda} dL + \frac{U_M}{\lambda} dM \\
&= dx - w \cdot (1 - \tau_L) dL + p_M dM
\end{aligned}
\tag{7.11}
$$

where in the last equality we have used the first three of the first-order conditions (7.9) to substitute for U_x, U_L, and U_M, respectively. We can eliminate dx from the equation by stating it in terms of changes in other quantities.: to do this, we use the combined definition and personal budget constraint summarized as (7.6); the last of first-order conditions (7.9) (which relates vehicle ownership cost to amount of driving); and the society-wide constraints (7.10). Doing so, we find that (7.11) simplifies, as detailed in an endnote.[51] What remains is

$$
\begin{aligned}
dW &= w\tau_L dL - M_x \left[\alpha T'(M) dM \right] + \tau_M dM + \tau_F dF - mec^M dM - mec^F dF \\
&\equiv w\tau_L dL + \left(\tau_M - \tau_M^* \right) dM + \left(\tau_F - \tau_F^* \right) dF
\end{aligned}
\tag{7.12}
$$

where we have defined the Pigouvian externality tax rates

$$
\begin{aligned}
\tau_M^* &= M\alpha T' + mec^M \\
\tau_F^* &= mec^F.
\end{aligned}
\tag{7.13}
$$

Each term in the second line of (7.12) includes a change in tax revenue due to change in behavior: labor supply (first term), vehicle usage (second term), and fuel consumption (third term). This is simply the efficiency loss due to distorting free markets with taxes. In the latter two cases, however, this welfare loss applies only insofar as the current tax rate is higher than the Pigouvian value.

Note that τ^*_M and τ^*_F would be first-best optimal rates in the absence of labor taxes. But they are not optimal here because, if the road and fuel taxes were both set to these values, there would still be a welfare change $w\tau_L dL$ from the last increment in the fuel tax. Normally, we would expect this to be negative, since raising the fuel tax raises the cost of living and hence lowers the real wage rate. Thus, if τ^*_M is in fact charged as a mileage fee, the optimal fuel tax is less than τ^*_F, reflecting the trade-off between wanting to correct the fuel-related externality $(mec)^F$, but not wanting to further exacerbate the labor-related distortion.

We can derive explicitly the optimal fuel-tax rate, given any arbitrary rates for the other two taxes, by setting $dW=0$ in (7.12) and solving for τ_F. This yields

$$\tau^{opt}_F = \tau^*_F + \left(\tau^*_M - \tau_M\right)\frac{dM}{dF} - w\tau_L\frac{dL}{dF} \tag{7.14}$$

Here, we have written ratios of infinitesimal changes dM, dF, and dL, so must remember they are caused by a change in τ_F, or equivalently by a change in p_F.

Equation (7.14) is more meaningful if we divide each infinitesimal change by the increment in fuel price $(d\tau_F \equiv dp_F)$ and define compensated elasticities:

$$\varepsilon_{L,PF} \equiv \frac{dL}{dp_F}\frac{p_F}{L}$$

$$\varepsilon_{M,PF} = \frac{dM}{dp_F}\frac{p_F}{M}$$

$$\varepsilon_{F,PF} = \frac{dF}{dp_F}\frac{p_F}{F}$$

(We call them compensated elasticities, as an approximation, because the process governing the changes represented by the derivatives involves returning the revenues to the consumer in some form, via the government budget constraint.) Then, substituting these elasticity definitions into (7.14) yields[52]

$$\tau^{opt}_F = \left[\tau^*_F + r^M_F \cdot E \cdot \left(\tau^*_M - \tau_M\right)\right] - \frac{w\tau_L L}{F} \cdot \frac{\varepsilon_{L,PF}}{\varepsilon_{F,PF}} \tag{7.15}$$

where r^M_F is defined by (7.4). Equation (7.15) permits us to explain many points in the "double-dividend" literature.

First, the primary component of the optimal fuel tax – the term in square brackets – is the marginal external cost of fuel use as defined by (7.3), namely $MEC_F \equiv \tau^*_F + r^M_F \cdot E \cdot \tau^*_M$, except that here τ^*_M is replaced by $\tau^*_M - \tau_M$, the uninternalized portion of external cost of usage. (Recall from definition (7.3) that MEC_F incorporates the *dilution factor* r^M_F, applied to the simple per-liter or per-gallon equivalent of the mileage externality – the latter here written $E \cdot \tau^*_M$.)

Second, the optimal fuel tax is in fact less than MEC_F because of the interaction with the labor tax represented by the last term of (7.15). That term is the tax-interaction effect, described earlier, specifically the version that applies if incremental fuel-tax revenues are used to increase government services or transfers, G. The term is negative because of its minus sign and the fact that both elasticities in the ratio are expected to be negative. It reflects the fact that raising the fuel tax, hence the cost of living, reduces the real wage received by a potential worker and therefore discourages labor supply (assuming labor supply is an increasing function of that real wage); this in turn lowers tax revenue but without any first-order utility gain since the consumer was already optimizing. Eq (7.15) tells us that because of this disadvantage of the fuel tax, we would optimally set it lower than would be called for purely by considerations of controlling externalities.

Third, the tax-interaction effect is especially strong if labor supply and fuel use are complementary, because that increases the magnitude of the elasticity $\varepsilon_{L,PF}$. If, for example, vehicles are used mainly for commuting, then making commuting more expensive has a stronger effect on labor supply and so more strongly exacerbates the labor-tax distortion. If, instead, vehicle usage is complementary with leisure, as, for example, if vehicles are used largely for pleasure trips, the opposite is true.

Fourth, buried within the tax-interaction term shown here is an interaction with congestion, which Parry and Small isolate explicitly – though numerically they find it to be small. This interaction occurs because by reducing vehicle usage, congestion is reduced and this counteracts the tendency of the fuel tax to raise the cost of living. This effect could become quite large in the special case of taxes aimed mostly at commuters, so that labor and vehicle usage are highly complementary – as in the models by Parry and Bento (2001) and Van Dender (2003) mentioned in Chapter 4.

Now suppose that instead of using fuel-tax revenue to increase government services or transfers, the revenue is "recycled" by using it to lower the pre-existing distorting tax rate τ_L. Then, the change dL in labor is smaller in magnitude, so the first term in (7.12) and the corresponding last term in (7.15) are each smaller in magnitude. In that case, these terms each contain both the tax-interaction and revenue-recycling effects, which are disentangled in the more elaborate accounting of Parry and Small (2005). Thus, if revenue is recycled so as to reduce distortionary taxes, both the optimal tax rate and the ensuing welfare gain from applying it are greater.

It might be thought that the effect of a fuel tax on labor supply would be so small, given that fuel expenditures are a small fraction of labor income, that the tax-interaction effect would be negligible. But we see in (7.15) that the labor-supply response to fuel price is multiplied by the ratio of labor-tax revenues ($w\tau_L L$) to the fuel-tax base (F). So, although the distortion of concern here may be small relative to labor-tax revenues, it is not necessarily small relative to fuel-tax revenues. To put it differently, because labor supply is such a big part of an economy, even small impacts on labor supply can have big welfare effects.

It is worth noting that *any* incremental policy that raises the cost of living produces a similar tax-interaction effect, which reduces its benefits and makes it optimal to apply it less strongly than otherwise. Thus, direct regulatory policies such as fuel efficiency standards have the same disadvantage, though in practice they are much smaller in magnitude because such policies have smaller impacts on consumer prices.

Although we have represented the pre-existing distorting tax as a labor tax, a similar adverse interaction can occur with any pre-existing tax whose tax base is diminished by the response to the policy being analyzed.

Finally, we note that eq (7.12) allows us alternatively to analyze a tax on vehicle usage, sometimes called a "vehicle-miles traveled (VMT) tax" (see Section 4.3.4). Again, we set $dW=0$, but now solve for τ_M given a value of τ_F. The result, whose derivation is similar to that of (7.15), is

$$\tau_M^{opt} = \left[\tau_M^* + \left(1 - \varepsilon_{E,PM}\right) \cdot \left(1 / E\right) \cdot \left(\tau_F^* - \tau_F\right) \right] - w\tau_L \frac{dL}{dM} \qquad (7.16)$$

The term in square brackets is directly analogous to that in (7.15): here, we augment the Pigouvian VMT tax (consisting of congestion fee plus tax on other externalities) with a component reflecting uninternalized fuel-related externalities, converted to a mileage basis by dividing by E, but diluted to the extent that consumers respond to the tax by increasing fuel efficiency.

In this case, the dilution factor is $(1 - \varepsilon_{E,PM})$. The last term in (7.16) is again a tax-interaction effect (perhaps in combination with a revenue-recycling effect) and can be viewed as simply the loss of labor-tax income for each unit that usage is reduced.

Returning to (7.15), when leisure and fuel are complements, as appears to be the case empirically (West and Williams 2007), the optimal fuel tax is *greater* than the Pigouvian value τ^*_M. Indeed, West and Williams find it to be about 35% greater in the USA. To think about this simplistically, we could posit that taxing fuel is helpful because it reduces people's desire to take recreational trips, working harder instead – which the labor tax inefficiently discourages in this model setting.

The impact of a fuel tax is diminished if a fuel efficiency standard already exists. This is because, if the standard is binding, a marginal increase in fuel tax will not increase the fuel efficiency of new vehicles, at least as it is measured for regulatory purposes. The fuel tax, by contrast, may cause fuel efficiency to increase due to consumer choices or driver behavior; in addition, unlike the efficiency standard, the fuel tax reduces vehicle use.

Fuel taxes address another externality, not treated by Parry and Small: they influence choice of speed because, in free-flowing traffic on high-speed roads, fuel consumption per kilometer rises with speed. As noted in Section 3.4.5, traffic accidents create external costs related, usually positively, to speed. Thus, a fuel tax helps motivate drivers to slow down and thus drive more safely. Tscharaktschiew (2020) models this and many other speed-related externalities, finding that in Germany (and, he suspects, in other European countries), the fuel tax is high enough to overcome the main accident externality of speed, thus greatly reducing the case for speed limits on main highways. (This observation includes the fuel tax's indirect impact via the rebound effect.) Interestingly, a behavioral market failure resulting from imperfect information – namely a tendency of drivers to overestimate time savings from increasing their speed – is also potentially significant according to Tscharaktschiew's estimates, restoring the case for speed limits if it exists. Tscharaktschiew's model is general equilibrium in nature, containing many of the same features as that of Parry and Small (2005). Note that Tscharaktschiew's model ignores the behavioral trade-off between safety and travel-time losses, which, according to the studies reviewed in Section 3.3.4, might also call for an upward adjustment in speeds chosen.

One problem in implementing fuel taxes is that many trips may cross boundaries between areas with independent rate-setting authority. This can create inefficient incentives to local authorities and even small countries. They may set the tax too high as a way of shifting financial burdens to neighboring communities, a practice known as *tax exporting*, or they may set the tax too low because each authority competes with neighbors for the taxable transactions, a practice known as *tax competition*. De Borger and Proost (2012b) suggest that competition is likely to dominate if fuel taxes are used, due to the physical mobility of the tax base (fuel), which is carried by drivers across jurisdiction borders, whereas exporting tends to dominate if road tolls are used or if most trips are local, since then the tax base is fixed in location. Tax exporting and competition are discussed more fully in Section 4.7.1.

7.3 Motor vehicles and climate change

Transportation plays a significant, though not dominant, role in climate change. It accounts for an estimated 15% of GHG emissions worldwide, as noted earlier. Just under half of this total is due to road passenger vehicles, based on their proportion (45%) of worldwide oil consumption.[53] Their role is somewhat larger within the Organisation for Economic Co-operation and Development (OECD), perhaps amounting to a bit less than 9% of total GHG emissions.[54]

However, current shares do not tell a full story since it is not efficient to reduce GHG emissions by the same proportions in all sectors of the economy. To better understand the role of transportation, we need to compare its control costs to those of other sectors. Following standard economic principles, we would start with marginal control costs. Because the reductions required are non-marginal, in fact quite large, we would then track these control costs over a proposed mitigation path (*i.e.*, a proposed path over time for GHG emission reductions).

Such non-marginal mitigation scenarios are the subject of much current research. Fortunately, the details are not needed for most transportation analysis because the pertinent results are summarized in an extremely useful number, the *social cost of carbon* (SCC), as a function of time. This number summarizes the damage caused by a marginal increase in emissions of CO_2 from any source. It is closely related to the *shadow price of carbon*, defined here as the marginal policy-imposed cost of CO_2 emissions (now or in the future) from activities that are subject to those policies. The difference between them is that the social cost measures the cost of damages produced, whereas the shadow price measures the cost of mitigating measures taken. We discuss these concepts at length in Section 7.3.2.

But first, we begin with a rough intuitive look at the role of transportation relative to other sectors in GHG control. After discussing the SCC (Section 7.3.2), we consider two policies: a carbon tax (Section 7.3.3) and promotion of alternative fuels (Section 7.3.4).

7.3.1   *The role of motor vehicles in greenhouse gas control*

A great deal of research is being directed at mitigation policies of all kinds, in all sectors. It is not easy to assess this research comparatively. One study that does so, and thereby exemplifies the principle of comparing marginal control costs, is the McKinsey and Company cost abatement curve developed by Enkvist *et al.* (2010). The curve depicts the estimated cost per ton of CO_2 removed for individual mitigation actions, ordered from the lowest to highest cost. Only policies that can abate at a cost of €80 per ton CO_2 or less are considered. Such a curve makes it easy to see which measures would be adopted in a least-cost response to any given target price of carbon.

For a price of carbon of €80/tCO_2, only two measures for transportation fit this criterion according to the McKinsey abatement curve: hybrid cars and plug-in hybrid cars. Together, they are estimated to have a potential to abate 2.6 GtCO_2e per year in 2030, about 4% of projected worldwide emissions at that time and 7% of total abatement potential under the criterion just stated.[55] By contrast, several other sectors, especially power generation and forestry, have much greater potential. These estimates would suggest that transportation might play a slightly less than proportional role in optimal mitigation policy and that within that role, fuel efficiency improvements and partial electrification are the most promising approaches.

We do not pass judgment on whether this study is a good current guide, but we do call attention to the likelihood that optimal policy will be highly targeted, rather than applying across the board to every activity. We also note that the McKinsey study assigns a *negative* cost to a large number of policy measures, including the two transportation measures just mentioned. This assessment relies on the existence of unexploited technological possibilities that pay for themselves: in the case of highway transportation, on the existence of an energy efficiency paradox. Without the offsetting benefits from overcoming the energy efficiency paradox, the transportation measures would be quite expensive, requiring heavier investment costs than measures delineated for other sectors with considerably greater abatement potential (Enkvist *et al.* 2010, Exhibit 8).

7.3.2   *The social cost of carbon*

Transportation analysts rarely need to know the full details of the macroeconomic and geo-physical bases for projecting climate change and its impacts. For most purposes, the relevant information is summarized in a single quantity: the social cost of CO_2 ($SCCO_2$), a name which we – like most other writers – more often abbreviate as the social cost of carbon, *i.e.*, the SCC.[56] This quantity summarizes the entire chain of effects of GHG emissions, working through atmospheric and oceanic concentrations of gases, short- and long-term cumulative effects on climate, and the time path of resulting damages expressed in monetary terms (*i.e.*, in equivalent reductions in consumption, summarized as a present discounted value). The SCC thus tells us, by definition, what additional cost is attributable to GHGs arising from any source. It is typically described in US$ per metric ton of CO_2, abbreviated as being in units of ($/tCO_2$). If used in a context where other GHGs, such as methane, water vapor, nitrous oxide, and ozone, are also being assessed for their global warming potential relative, we express the units as per metric ton of CO_2 equivalent ($/tCO_2e$).

In an optimized scenario, but only then, SCC also tells us the marginal cost of making further reductions. In non-optimal, more realistic scenarios, marginal control costs may differ from the SCC and a more specific analysis is needed to determine the real cost of reducing emissions by any particular policy. Just to give one example, the cost of providing incentives for electric vehicles includes not only the monetary cost of the electricity they use but also the cost of ordinary air pollution as well as GHGs emitted in the generation of electricity. This may require an elaborate model of the electrical generation industry to account for both physical power flows around the grid and market responses that determine how generating companies respond to a local increase in demand. We return to such models in Section 7.3.4.

It is possible to consider a partially optimized scenario, where a country or region sets a target for quantity reductions in CO_2. Whether or not this target is itself optimal, it can be achieved at lowest cost by comparing policies whose costs include the shadow price of carbon, which is equated across the economy. (Equivalently, the comparison of policies could include reduced emissions as a benefit.) In other words, the shadow price of carbon, for any given time path of emissions, reflects the price that, if actually charged, would result in achieving that time path in a socially cost-minimizing fashion. Formally, it is the value achieved by the Lagrange multiplier on an economy-wide constraint that emissions must not exceed the target, within a sub-optimization problem aimed at meeting the target at lowest cost. When such targets are in place, this shadow price effectively replaces the SCC in policy analyses; some authors may even call it the SCC, but strictly speaking the concepts of shadow price and SCC are distinct. Much of what we say here applies to both.

In both actual and hypothetically optimized scenarios, the SCC is expected to rise rapidly over time, due to strong nonlinearity in damages as a function of temperature and, to the usual rising marginal control cost as controls are tightened. Together these forces give the atmospheric system a trait akin to a finite resource whose value increases as it is depleted.

Measuring the SCC has absorbed much professional attention. Nordhaus (2017) provides a good overview of methodology and a sample of results. He summarizes the results of a comprehensive economic-geophysical model system of a type called an integrated assessment model (IAM).[57] Nordhaus's model, known as DICE-2016R (for Dynamic Integrated model of Climate and the Economy, Regional version), includes an economic component projecting baseline GHGs emissions, a geophysical component deriving impacts of those emissions on future average global temperature, and another economic component describing damage in terms of a percentage reduction in world economic output. The geophysical component summarizes results of the voluminous scientific research into the greenhouse effect.

Each component of an IAM requires a great deal of information and sophistication. For example, a key parameter in the geophysical part of the model is *equilibrium climate sensitivity*, defined as the long-term change in world temperature that would result from a permanent doubling of the global-average atmospheric CO_2 concentration from its pre-industrial level. Nordhaus calibrates this parameter so that his simplified climate model reproduces results from other studies using more elaborate models with multiple data sources; the calibrated parameter is 3.1°C. In other words, in a hypothetical stable situation where CO_2 concentrations were twice their pre-industrial values, the average global temperature would be 3.1°C warmer than the pre-industrial temperature.

Another key parameter (actually a set of parameters) describes the damage function, relating reduction in world output to temperature change. This has been the subject of extensive research by the Intergovernmental Panel for Climate Change and many academic economists.[58] Based on a meta-analysis of results of such studies, Nordhaus settles on a quadratic damage function as a function of temperature, whose parameters imply that global income would be 2.1% less due to a 3°C warming above 1990 levels and 8.5% less for a 6°C warming. Note the strong nonlinearity. Nordhaus also provides confidence bands for this function, which unsurprisingly are quite wide.

A third key parameter is the real discount rate, r, needed to compare future damages or benefits to the present. Specifically, the discount factor $(1 + r)^{-t}$ determines the weights of damages or investment costs t years in the future relative to today. Given the nature of climate change, an investment today to reduce GHG emissions provides a stream of benefits realized mostly in the very far future, measured in decades and even centuries. For this reason, small variations in r can make huge differences in the economic evaluation of such an investment.[59] In many models, r is determined endogenously from more basic parameters describing normative preferences about valuing welfare of future generations in light of risk aversion.[60,61]

Nordhaus (2017) chooses parameters leading to an average value of $r = 4.25\%$ per year as his central case, based on market data. Because of the importance of discount rate to climate policy results, he also presents results using alternate values.[62] The first panel of Table 7.1 summarizes these calculations of the SCC, converted to 2020 prices.[63] As expected, the SCC rises over time, much more so under scenarios that tightly constrain temperature increases. (The baseline, a forecast under existing policies, projects temperature to rise to slightly more than 4°C above its 1990 level by year 2100.) Nordhaus's central estimate of SCC for the near future (2025) is US$51 per metric ton CO_2,[64] rising by somewhat more than 3% annually during the next quarter century. These results are broadly similar to those compiled by an official US government panel known as the Interagency Working Group (IWG), also shown in the table.[65]

Next, we show preliminary values from a 2023 version of DICE, not yet finalized at time of writing and reported in a working paper (Barrage and Nordhaus 2023). These values demonstrate that changes in scientific knowledge over the eight years between the two models substantially raise the estimates of SCC, consistent with the widespread understanding that potential climate risk is toward the higher end of the previously estimated range of uncertainty. The values also demonstrate that estimates of mitigation costs have declined, resulting in a lower shadow price of carbon in the constrained scenario (2.0°C) even than that in the earlier somewhat less constrained scenario (2.5°C).[66] We note in passing that Barrage and Nordhaus find a constraint at 1.5°C temperature rise to be infeasible, so do not show values for that scenario.

At the same time, the much larger values of SCC sometimes suggested do not arise mainly from new scientific understandings, but rather from other modeling assumptions – usually involving discounting or adjusting for risk. These larger values are exemplified by the results of a model called the Greenhouse Gas Impact Value Estimator (GIVE), developed mainly at

Resources for the Future (Rennert *et al.* 2022). This model incorporates a number of complex refinements to methodology, including Monte Carlo formulations of uncertainties that simultaneously surround several critical components of the models: socioeconomic projections, GHG emissions, climate sensitivity, and damage functions, with endogenous discounting computed for each model run in the Monte Carlo exercise – a procedure the authors call *stochastic growth discounting*. (Projections of GHG emissions, of course, require projecting worldwide policies that in reality will be influenced by these very quantities being calculated.) The final panel in Table 7.1 shows results from the GIVE model. Many of these refinements are those recommended by a study of the US National Academies, as described and recommended by Carleton and Greenstone (2022).

Clearly, an appropriate value for the SCC, like most other inputs into policy toward long-term investments, is subject to continuing debate and research, all of which enhances not only our knowledge of key parameters but also our understanding of the underlying

Table 7.1 Estimates of the social cost of carbon (US$ per metric ton CO_2 in 2020$)

	2015	*2025*	*2050*
DICE-2016R			
Baseline with current policy ($r = 4.25\%$)[a]	36	51	118
Optimal policy	36	51	121
Baseline except $r = 5\%$	23	30	57
Baseline except $r = 3\%$	92	111	182
Hold temperature change below 2.5°C	213[b]	329[b]	1,166[b]
US Interagency Working Group – July 2015 update			
Low estimate ($r = 5\%$)	13	17	32
Central estimate ($r = 3\%$)[a]	44	56	84
High estimate ($r = 2.5\%$)	68	82	115
High impact ($r = 3\%$, 95th percentile cost estimate)	127	168	257

	2020	*2025*	*2050*
DICE-2023			
Baseline with current policy ($r = 3.9\%$)	62	73	151
Optimal policy[a]	54	63	128
Baseline except $r = 5\%$	33	39	78
Baseline except $r = 3\%$	88	**104**	172
Hold temperature change below 2.0°C	86[b]	101[b]	238[b]
GIVE			
Preferred estimate, current policy ($r = 2\%$)[a]	185	238[c]	
Alternate estimate, current policy ($r = 3\%$)	80	103[c]	

[a] Indicates the scenario preferred by that set of authors. The **bold** value indicates value used for central case in calculations in this book.
[b] Value shown is the shadow price of carbon when the constraint is binding; see text endnote.
[c] Projected by us from 2020 value, using average ratios of 2025 to 2020 values for the three preferred models above (see note a).

Discount rate *r* is that assumed for discounting future consumption and investment quantities.

Sources: Calculated from Nordhaus (2017), Table 1, reprinted with permission from PNAS; US Interagency Working Group (2016), Table ES-1; Barrage and Nordhaus (2023), Table 7; Rennert *et al.* (2022). Price updates use "PCE Total" price index from US CEA (2023), Table B-39.

mechanisms producing them. For purposes of this chapter, as well as for the tabulation of automobile costs in Section 3.4.9, it is helpful to choose a single value to use in various calculations and comparisons. For that purpose, we adopt here the DICE-2023 estimate for 2025 at a discount rate of 3% – a rate which is lower than the rate we use for evaluating ordinary capital investments but consistent with our arguments in Section 5.2.3 when deriving that rate. That value for SCC is $104/tCO$_2$. We consider a plausible range to be from half to twice this amount.[67] This value incorporates a "near-term risk-free discount rate" of 2%, which means that parameters are set to produce an endogenous schedule of discount rates that begins at 2% for the earliest years. (As the authors note, the SCC would fall to less than half as much by changing to a 3% near-term discount rate.)

What does a value of $104/tCO$_2$ for the SCC mean for transportation analysis? Aside from leakage of refrigerants from air conditioners and very modest emissions of other gases, the climate damage from transportation is directly proportional to CO$_2$ emissions. These emissions are in turn proportional to the carbon content of fuel consumed, either directly in the vehicle's engine or indirectly during manufacture and disposal of batteries and vehicles. For gasoline-powered automobiles, CO$_2$ emissions are approximately 2.36 metric tons per 1,000 L,[68] so that our posited SCC amounts to $0.245 per liter of gasoline or $0.929/gal. This is a useful benchmark for various policy analyses, to which we return in the next subsection.

The true range of possible values for SCC may be even wider than suggested by Table 7.1, as there is great uncertainty in each of the components that go into the models used to calculate it. Just as one example, the damage function in DICE-2016R has a standard deviation of roughly 2.2%–2.4% of income, based on its statistical fit from estimates in the literature: this standard deviation is actually larger than the function's value at 3°C. Taking into account the main quantifiable sources of uncertainty within the DICE model – economic growth, equilibrium temperature sensitivity, and the damage function – Nordhaus reports that his SCC estimate for year 2015 has an 80% confidence band (10th–90th percentile values) that covers an eleven-fold difference in values. If one considers all the other uncertainties in IAMs, ranging from simplified model structures to the unquantifiable possibility of a catastrophic climate disruption, the uncertainty is even more daunting and will surely not be eliminated within a time frame helpful for current policy analysis. Indeed, some analysts argue that IAMs inherently undervalue some severe risks that scientists have emphasized yet that cannot be quantified in monetary terms (Heal and Millner 2014). All these uncertainties create an inherent limit on our confidence in any policy prescription based on the SCC or on the models underlying it, as emphasized by Weitzman (2009). Even so, this number is a valuable starting point for assessing the efficacy of many transportation policies, including those considered in this chapter and throughout this book.

A wildcard in SCC calculation, and indeed in all climate policy, is the potential role of geoengineering.[69] Scientists have described several ways that deliberate action could counteract the global warming from GHGs. One is placing small reflective particles in the upper atmosphere; others attempt to modify the reflectivity of the earth's surface or its cloud cover. Such policies have unknown environmental side effects and do not deal with acidification and other problems caused by high CO$_2$ concentrations. They may also exacerbate the free-rider problem inherent in obtaining international agreements to reduce GHG emissions. Nevertheless, geoengineering may have appeal as an emergency measure. It also appears financially feasible, raising the prospect that in the absence of a broad international agreement on GHG control, individual countries that are especially vulnerable might take action on their own regardless of adverse effects on other countries. It is unknown at this point what impact such scenarios would have on the SCC.

7.3.3   *Carbon taxes*

The policy toward climate change that is most widely advocated among economists is a carbon tax: *i.e.*, a tax on CO_2 emissions (and, insofar as practical, on other GHGs in proportion to their warming effects). As a first pass, the ideal rate would be the social cost of CO_2. Using the value calculated in the previous subsection, this begins at a value that is significant yet entirely manageable by markets – for example, the value $0.245 per liter of gasoline is about twice the existing average tax rate on motor vehicle fuels in the United States and well within or even below the range found in many other countries. The optimal tax rate would then rise sharply over a few decades, forcing ever more stringent shifts in technology and behavior, but with ample time to develop them.

Under some rather drastic simplifying assumptions, a carbon tax is equivalent to a *cap-and-trade* scheme (also considered in Section 4.2.5). In such a scheme, the government issues a fixed volume of emissions permits, perhaps by auction or by some allocation mechanism, then allows emitters to buy and sell them. Cap-and-trade is in fact implemented in many parts of the globe – though rarely for the transportation sector. For example, the long-standing Emissions Trading System (ETS) in Europe has operated since 2005; many smaller systems operate in individual countries or, in the USA, in individual states and in consortia of states. Stavins (2022) provides a thorough review of the relative merits of carbon taxes and cap-and-trade policies in practice.

Cap-and-trade has considerable political advantages, because adept use of the allocation mechanism can build political support and perhaps ameliorate undesired distributional impacts. But these very traits also open it to political manipulation or corruption. This can lead both to public disillusionment and to real inefficiency. One source of inefficiency would be to collect revenue from initial sale of permits but waste it on expenditures with low public benefits.

Cap-and-trade has another advantage if the public's goal is a specific target for emissions or their climate effects. Because of uncertainty about technology and consumer response, the actual emissions reductions could be quite different from the planned target. This difficulty is exacerbated by the long-term dynamics of supply: many sources of future carbon emissions are embedded in geological reserves of fossil fuels, which remain a potential emissions source depending on future economic conditions. Heal and Schlenker (2019), using data on world fossil fuel reserves and extraction costs, argue that the levels of carbon tax currently envisioned would postpone rather than eliminate the use of most oil and gas reserves, making it impossible to achieve currently accepted climate targets. If they are correct, a policy built around a carbon tax would need to incorporate very large increases over time, to well over $200 per ton CO_2, in order to maintain the desired emissions reductions. Such values are comparable to the 2050 shadow prices for a 2°C constraint estimated by Barrage and Nordhaus (2023), as discussed earlier.

Another complex issue is how uncertainty affects the choice between a tax and a cap-and-trade policy. There is a standard result here, due to Weitzman (1974), which applies when compliance costs are uncertain.[70] This result states that an environmental tax (such as a carbon tax) is preferred to a quantity policy (such as a cap-and-trade policy) when marginal compliance costs are a steep function of pollution reduction, and/or when marginal benefits are a flat function (*i.e.*, approximately constant). To understand this, suppose first that marginal benefits are relatively constant, but marginal compliance costs depend sharply on the amount of abatement: in that situation, mandating a fixed quantity reduction is risky. This is because doing so creates the danger either of very large abatement costs being incurred (if abatement turns out to be more expensive than forecast), or of too little abatement (if it turns out to be cheaper than forecast). Now suppose the opposite, *i.e.,* that marginal benefits depend strongly on the amount of abatement (for example, if the world is near a climate tipping point), whereas marginal compliance costs are nearly constant: then, setting a fixed price is risky. This is because if the price turns out to be inefficiently low *ex post*, the low price would allow very high pollution damages; if it turns out to be inefficiently high *ex post*, the high price could cause substantial economic harm with little benefit. We should add that in this context, any fixed target for CO_2 reductions should be averaged over many years, since cumulative emissions are mainly what determine the climate damage.

The Weitzman result may be overturned in a setting where policies are regularly updated (Pizer and Prest 2020). Suppose that firms engaging in carbon trading under a cap-and-trade policy can accurately foresee policy changes; suppose further that these changes are optimal and that intertemporal trading is permitted. In such a scenario, permit prices react to information more quickly than the policies themselves do, causing firms to make efficient adjustments. Unfortunately, permit prices may then fluctuate wildly during times of policy uncertainty, causing disruption in capital markets.

There is another source of inefficiency for either carbon taxes or cap-and-trade: the neglect of other distorting taxes in their design. Such distortions are typically exacerbated by both policies because they raise energy prices and hence the prices of goods that are the basis for these other taxes. This is the same argument made in Section 4.2.6 with respect to congestion taxes and in Section 7.2.2 with respect to fuel taxes. Aldy *et al.* (2010, pp. 920–921) explain it specifically for carbon policy. To recap, the price of labor is distorted by any income or payroll tax, causing the price paid by an employer to be higher than the effective price received by a worker. A carbon tax increases this disparity by reducing the effective buying power of the worker's after-tax wage, creating a welfare loss called the *tax-interaction effect*. Revenues from the carbon tax (or any other Pigouvian tax) offer the opportunity to partially counteract those distortions through tax-rate reductions, creating a *revenue-recycling effect*.

This way of using revenues may interfere with using them to build political support. Nevertheless, studies suggest that CO_2 permits are in fact extremely valuable to firms, and typical allocation schemes used to build support by giving permits to existing emitters tend to overcompensate them. As a result, the failure to use revenues to lower distortionary taxes may cause substantial inefficiency, so much so that a permit policy might actually even provide a net loss of welfare (Bovenberg *et al.* 2008).

With a carbon tax, the allocation of revenues is explicit. This may make it more politically feasible to use them to reduce existing taxes, or to fund high-priority programs that might otherwise require raising other taxes. Thus, revenue recycling is more likely to take place efficiently with a tax than with cap-and-trade. Counteracting this benefit, however, is that there may be pressure to use carbon-tax revenues exclusively for environmentally related policies, whether or not they are cost-effective. As an example, a carbon tax imposed by the State of California has revenues partly dedicated by law to building a high-speed rail line. Yet another possibility is that the revenues can be used for explicit lump-sum rebates, as in Canada; these rebates do not reduce distorting taxes and could even further discourage already distorted labor supply through income effects, as in Parry and Bento (2001).

The carbon tax has another advantage: It is a simple, easily observed carbon price that is an indicator of national or regional effort toward climate control. This has been suggested as a critically needed step in forging and monitoring international agreements (Nordhaus 2015; Cramton *et al.* 2017). This trait also facilitates adjustment as new information is learned, for example, about the link between carbon emissions and climate. Aldy (2020) and Metcalf (2020) propose and analyze automatic updating provisions for carbon-tax legislation. Pollitt and Dolphin (2022) consider the many practical issues in one particular proposal: extending the European Union's ETS to include transportation and building heating.

How would a carbon tax affect urban transportation? This question is very similar to asking about the implications of a fuel tax. Parry and Small (2015) consider some magnitudes, including the potential for using revenues to overcome deficiencies in transportation funding.

The first point is that a carbon tax at the rate discussed here would impose a cost on drivers that is smaller than recent estimates of other external costs of driving. We made this point in Section 3.4.9 for peak-period commuting, where both congestion and local air pollution impose heavier costs due to the density of people affected. Here, we show that the result holds even for overall car use, where other externalities are smaller, again using the USA as an example. The left bar of Figure 7.2 depicts the climate externality (based on the SCC) along with other external costs per liter of fuel consumed.[71] The mileage-related components shown in that bar are quite large, partly because they do not incorporate the dilution of the response to a fuel tax that occurs when it is used to address a mileage-related externality, as explained in Section 7.2.2. It is clear that with this magnitude of SCC, climate costs are significant, but they are still considerably smaller than the other components of the marginal external cost of fuel use. This would remain true even if we double the assumed value of the SCC, which, as shown above, would also approximate estimates of the current shadow price of meeting a maximum 2°C temperature increase.

The right-hand bar in the figure considers an optimal fuel tax, which is smaller than the total external cost as explained in Section 7.2.2. Here, the carbon component is a greater proportion, but still it accounts for less than one-third of the optimal tax.[72] By way of comparison, the carbon-tax portion alone of this efficient tax is about double current excise-tax rates on fuel in the United States – though it is well below those in Europe, which in early 2022 ranged from $0.40 to $0.97 per liter and averaged $0.65 (Tax Foundation 2022).

Two implications of this comparison are worth noting. First, in the USA and other countries where the fuel tax is far below an optimal level, adding a carbon tax to it would have beneficial effects on other externalities. Indeed, in some cases these side effects of climate policy may be more important than the direct effects. Second, climate change is just one argument, and not necessarily the strongest one, for high fuel taxes. These conclusions may change over time as the SCC increases. Furthermore, they depend on the absence of better-targeted policies toward congestion and accidents. As noted earlier, for example, many analysts already urge a move toward kilometer-based taxes (*i.e.*, taxes proportional to distance driven) on practical grounds; such a move would eventually make existing fuel taxes much closer to an optimal transportation policy for climate change.

Turning to revenues generated, Parry and Small (2015) consider a gap in infrastructure finance much discussed in the USA: that between tax revenues flowing into the Highway Trust Fund and current federal capital expenditures on highways and public transit. They calculate that revenues from an optimal fuel tax would largely close the gap – though they would not necessarily fund all desirable capital improvements. However, such revenues would be subject to erosion as technology for fuel efficiency improves.

More generally, the relatively modest role of carbon taxes in Figure 7.2 drives home a broader conclusion: Climate is an important consideration in transportation policy, but far from

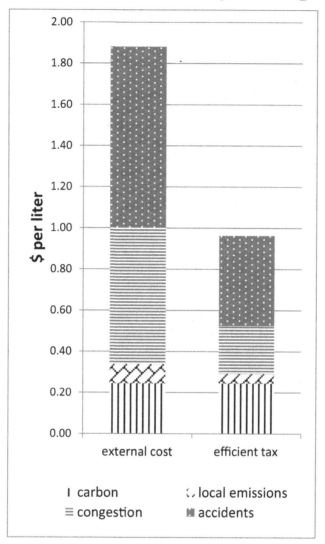

Figure 7.2 Components of external costs and optimal fuel tax. Calculations by the authors, following figure 12.3 from Parry and Small (2015). Reproduced by permission of Taylor & Francis Group.

the dominant one. Policy needs to deal more effectively with the external costs of congestion
and accidents and with financing roads and public transit. The advent of automated vehicles may
help by reducing the number of accidents, but is likely to make congestion and transit deficits
worse, ensuring that those issues will need continued attention.

7.3.4   *Alternative fuels*

A popular approach to reducing use of fossil fuels such as gasoline is to mandate stated proportions of transportation energy that must come from other sources such as ethanol, other biofuels,

and electricity. Two types of policies predominate. A biofuel mandate requires a particular proportion (or total amount) of transportation fuel supplies to be made from specified biological products. A low-carbon fuel standard (LCFS) mandates that the net emissions of CO_2 resulting from the transportation sector be limited to a specific fraction of what would be emitted by conventional fuels.

Policies mandating biofuels began in earnest with the Renewable Fuel Standard (RFS), in place since 2005 in the USA. Wise and Cole (2015) document 22 countries plus the European Union with biofuel mandates in place. The three largest are in the USA, Brazil, and the European Union with its Renewable Energy Directive. Other large biofuel producers are Argentina, China, India, and Indonesia.[73] Most such policies mandate biofuel as a stated fraction of fuel use, though in the USA the mandate is for specific annual consumption volumes.

As of 2015, Brazil and the USA were blending ethanol and biodiesel into their transportation fuel supplies so as to comprise 22% and 9%, respectively. Nearly all current mandates are fulfilled by "first-generation" biofuels, which are made from agricultural products: mainly ethanol from sugarcane and corn sugar and biodiesel fuel from the oil in palm fruits, soybeans, and rapeseed. Current regulations call for gradually shifting the burden toward "second-generation" biofuels such as perennial grasses and forestry and agricultural residues; but the technologies for extracting fuel from such cellulosic materials have not achieved commercial success.

First-generation biofuels compete directly with agriculture, and so have raised great concern about effects on world food supplies (Wise and Cole 2015; Chakravorty *et al.* 2017). If food were just a commodity and produced competitively, this concern would be fully accounted for in the production cost; but actually, food is a highly politicized product with major ethical and geopolitical implications. First-generation biofuels are also criticized as not meeting the goal of reducing GHGs, due to the high energy use in fertilizing, tilling, and processing these crops, not to mention the deforestation that may occur as their use bids up prices of agricultural land. Khanna *et al.* (2021) review empirical evidence suggesting that biofuel mandates have pushed up both food and fuel prices modestly, making both of these responses plausible; but that such effects diminish over time. Furthermore, the price responsiveness of aggregate agricultural land supply is low, thus limiting the impact of such price changes on carbon emissions.

Even if it works, is a biofuel mandate (or some other carbon-intensity standard) an efficient policy? Holland *et al.* (2009) show that under competitive conditions, such a policy is equivalent to a tax on emissions combined with a subsidy to the particular inputs that qualify to meet the mandate. That subsidy partially offsets the tax in determining the fuel price, resulting in a below-market consumer price and thus inefficiently high fuel consumption.

However, the tax-interaction effect may alter that conclusion. Goulder *et al.* (2016) analyze the situation for a policy proposed for electricity generation, known as a Renewable Portfolio Standard (RPS) or Clean Energy Standard (CES), which is essentially the same as a biofuel mandate although the favored fuels are somewhat different. Using a computable general-equilibrium model of the USA economy, the authors find that because of the implicit input subsidy, the CES has a much smaller tax-interaction effect than a carbon tax. When each policy is enacted at a level to achieve relatively small emission reductions, they find the CES is actually less costly. This result depends partly on conditions unique to electricity, such as high capital intensity and the availability of nuclear power as a low-carbon fuel. Thus, whether it might ever apply to biofuel mandates for the transportation sector remains unclear.

Finally, we consider programs promoting electric vehicles in order to "decarbonize" the transportation sector. Electric vehicles of course use electric power, which is partly generated by fossil fuels. As noted in Section 3.5.3, tracing the carbon content of electric power leaves some doubt as to the net carbon reduction, but this problem is diminishing as generation shifts to less carbon-intensive energy sources. Such a trend is incorporated formally into a model of transition dynamics by Holland *et al.* (2021). However, it is the *marginal* power source for an electric vehicle that determines its climate impact, and the complexities of electric power markets and networks make it difficult to determine that source. It depends not only on where the power used in a given location comes from, but also on how producers adjust to the particular patterns of time of day, season, and intermittency of both the new demand and the existing sources. For example, if coal-fired plants provide "base power," and other sources are used to cover variations over time, the combination of markets and network management may prolong the retention of those coal-fired plants. We also reiterate the point in Section 3.5.3 that battery manufacturing and disposal create GHG emissions and other environmental problems.

Dynamics of a transition to electric power create some unexpected policy implications. Holland *et al.* (2021) model this process with attention to three additional factors, all of which interact: falling costs of electric vehicles, electric vehicles becoming closer substitutes for conventional ones, and dynamic fleet optimization by consumers. The upshot is that a simple ban on gasoline vehicles, while usually harmful, can be beneficial if electric vehicles become good enough substitutes. But a more promising policy, they find, is a quota on the cumulative production of gasoline vehicles, with market-based options for intertemporal trading.

In the long run, for the world to meet currently adopted emissions goals, vast shifts in the electric power industry will be required. If that occurs, the carbon content of electricity will drop to near zero, and the generating cost of electricity (which will be higher than it is today) will become the appropriate input to any cost–benefit or cost-effectiveness analysis of electric vehicles.

7.4   Conclusions

Each of the topics of this chapter could fit well into a previous chapter. For example, demand for different types of automobiles is a type of travel demand (Chapter 2); environmental costs are a type of transportation cost (Chapter 3); and the pricing of energy follows a logic similar to other transportation-pricing analyses (Chapter 4). Nevertheless, these topics are united by common practical concerns related to the energy industry and by particular policy issues related to energy sources. Thus, grouping the topics together, as we have done here, helps provide guidance to analysts who confront these practical concerns. Doing so also reminds transportation researchers of the significance of these particular topics for transportation policy. The scarcity of energy sources and the magnitudes of their environmental impacts both compel us to consider carefully the way transportation uses energy and how the resulting spillovers affect analytical results and policy recommendations.

Notes

1   Oil consumption is for 2017, from International Energy Agency (2019), computed for oil products as the ratio of transport to total final consumption. A slightly lower estimate, 59%, is provided by US Energy Information Administration (2019, p. 78). The estimate for greenhouse gas emissions is for 2013, from Center for Climate and Energy Solutions (2019), figure entitled "Global manmade greenhouse gas emissions by sector, 2013."

2   See Nordhaus (2013, Chaps. 4, 5), IPCC (2013), and Hsiang and Kopp (2018) for the science behind greenhouse gases. In brief, these gases allow solar radiation to penetrate the earth's atmosphere but

prevent much of the resulting heat from escaping back into space. Because the effects of rising temperature are highly variable across the globe, the term *global warming* has mostly been replaced by *climate change* in current parlance. We use the terms interchangeably, with the reminder that climate change here means change whose underlying cause is rising global temperatures, as opposed to local climatic effects of activities such as urbanization, agriculture, wildfires, and deforestation.

3   For discussion and related research, see Borenstein (2008), Delucchi and Murphy (2008), and Kilian (2008).

4   Indeed, Li *et al.* estimate $\alpha = 0.64$ in the one specification where they use a control for serial correlation. The two values for α just quoted for Li *et al.* (2009) are the coefficients of the lagged dependent variable from specifications (1) and (2), respectively, in their Table 2.

5   Their Table 6 reports regressions on 312 distinct elasticity estimates from 43 studies, assuming that a theoretical relationship holds among the estimates and that all are influenced the same way by various factors such as country, year, and methodology. Adjusting their "baseline values" (last two rows of the table) to apply to the USA, Canada, and Australia (by adding the coefficient of variable UCA), we see their base estimates are −0.32 for short run and −0.70 for long run. These magnitudes would be diminished by 0.18 for studies including dynamics, which we argue in the text are preferable.

6   Other authors have used fuel-tax changes themselves as instruments for changes in fuel prices. When this is done using monthly data, it leads to very large and implausible estimates of price elasticity, as noted by Coglianese *et al.* (2017), because consumers can anticipate announced price changes and alter the timing of their purchases accordingly. Coglianese *et al.* bypass this problem by including leads and lags, leading to more reasonable elasticity estimates. However, if indeed consumers respond more to changes in fuel tax than to the pretax component of price, as found by Li *et al.* (2014), fuel tax is an invalid instrument because it affects consumption directly, even conditionally on overall fuel price.

7   A similar result is found by Rivers and Schaufele (2015) in Canada and by Tiezzi and Verde (2016) in the USA.

8   Based on their Table 4, first row of reported elasticities.

9   The conversion factors are 3.7854 L/gal (US) and 1.609 km/mile. Hence, 1 mi/gal = 0.4251 km/L. Writers in the UK and many British Commonwealth countries occasionally use the "imperial gallon," which is 4.546 L (1.2 US gallons).

10 Specifically, when all three of the time periods they describe are combined, the implicit discount rates are 19.6% for single-vehicle households (their Table 1) and 16.7% for two-vehicle households (their Table A2).

11 Such studies include Greene *et al.* (2005) using a nested logit model of automobile demand and Small (2012) using a large-scale simulation model.

12 The elasticity is computed approximately by us, based on their Table 9, years 2001 and 2004, for which hypothetical gasoline price reductions of 14% and 25%, respectively, result in estimated hybrid market share reductions of 11% and 19%. The authors estimate that 2006 hybrid sales "would have been 37% lower had gasoline prices stayed at their 1999 level" (abstract).

13 Data include both annual sales and changes in the number of vehicles registered for use, from which retirements can be calculated. The authors restrict attention to vehicles over ten years old to minimize the effect of vehicles that are sold or moved across cities, rather than retired.

14 Namely, $\beta = 1.145$ and $\beta_2 = -26.70$, from their Table 2, specification (1).

15 That is, the dependent variable for a given year is the logarithm of the probability that a vehicle still in operation the previous year will continue in operation in the current year.

16 For example, a consumer traveling 10,000 miles per year will save $10,000 \times [(1/10) - (1/12)] = 167$ gallons of fuel per year from the first upgrade mentioned in the text, but only $10,000 \times [(1/40) - (1/42)] = 12$ gallons from the second upgrade. This behavioral trait is documented by Larrick and Soll (2008) and Allcott (2013).

17 Many authors use interchangeably the terms *energy efficiency gap*, *energy efficiency paradox*, and *myopia*. We follow Gerarden *et al.* (2017) by distinguishing among these terms as described in the text.

18 This argument is often described as "risk aversion," a well-known property of consumers facing gambles. But actually, a fuel-efficient car is a hedge against high future fuel costs, which a risk-averse consumer should favor. The real argument is one of *loss aversion* (Greene 2011), the tendency to avoid potential changes from the status quo that make them worse off: in this case, by spending extra for a fuel-efficient car that turns out not to save them money.

19 The importance of heterogeneity is emphasized by Houde and Aldy (2017), who also consider how policies aimed directly at curbing behavioral or information biases, such as energy labeling of

products, can change the optimal level of other policies, such as fuel taxes. Houde and Aldy use the term *microfrictions* to describe both behavioral biases and transactions costs, the latter playing a role similar to what we have termed "hidden costs."

20 The implicit real discount rates (each defined as the rate for discounting future fuel-cost savings that makes the observed responses rational) are presented in their Table 9, for a wide variety of assumptions: three fuel efficiency quartile comparisons, two types of markets (used or new), four alternate demand elasticities for new vehicles, and three alternate sources of information about usage and vehicle survival rates. The market real interest rates faced by their sample are calculated from survey respondents' stated rates on auto loans, less the inflation rate, and are stated on their p. 246.

21 A less extreme example of the same tendency to summarize results as failing to reject the null hypothesis of full rationality is Dreyfus and Viscusi (1995), who use a hedonic price function rather than an explicit demand study to examine the ratio between coefficients of operating cost and vehicle price. They estimate an implicit discount rate of 11%–17%, concluding that "This range includes the prevailing rate of interest for car loans…and is consequently consistent with market rates."

22 These other factors include future vehicle usage and the evolution of a vehicle's fuel efficiency as it ages.

23 Two key improvements over other studies are that they use more disaggregated controls to eliminate the biasing effects of unobserved attributes, and they add enough vehicle fixed effects to ensure that they are measuring the response to variations in fuel efficiency, not in fuel price.

24 The sign of $(Q_2 - Q_1)$ is theoretically ambiguous; it could be negative if the marginal cost curves were further apart. It is shown here as positive, consistent with the authors' empirical results.

25 As mentioned in the previous note, the quantity of vehicles purchased (Q_2) in this example rises as fuel efficiency is increased, because the value consumers place on it is greater than the amount by which it raises marginal cost. But quantity would rise even more if consumers valued it fully.

26 Some authors use the terms *intensive margin* and *extensive margin* for vehicle usage and vehicle efficiency, in analogy with capital markets where increased use of capital can take place either by using a given capital asset more intensively or by extending the quantity of capital assets.

27 As Gillingham *et al.* (2016) point out, however, the additional driving has a direct *positive* effect on welfare, since it is a form of increased consumption. In fact, the very recognition that fuel-cost savings are a welfare benefit is an acknowledgment that income they free up for additional consumption is beneficial to consumers.

28 Small and Van Dender add a third equation to (7.2) explaining total size of the vehicle fleet. Data are a cross-sectional time series for 51 "states" of the USA (50 states plus District of Columbia). Equations are estimated in logarithms, so that the estimated coefficients are elasticities.

29 Hence, the value of −0.045 quoted by Gillingham *et al.* (2016) is the short-run elasticity for the entire sample, as correctly stated in the description in their Table 1 though incorrectly stated in footnote b of that table. The ratio of short- to long-run elasticities in Small and Van Dender's specification is that described here in Section 2.1.2 for a lagged-adjustment model.

30 See especially Greene (2012); also Gillingham (2011), Table 3.4 and Section 3.1.3; and Hymel and Small (2015, p. 97). By contrast, Linn (2016) finds a *higher* response to efficiency than to price; but as he notes, this may be because the former is long run and the latter short run. In addition, the former is not stable to alternative specifications (his Table 6), suggesting to us that despite Linn's careful controls for endogeneity, the problem of finding enough truly exogenous variation in fuel efficiency remains to be solved.

31 It is possible to define "rebound effects" that incorporate various expected ancillary shifts in behavior, from spending freed-up income on other goods (are they more or less energy-intensive?) to posited macroeconomic effects (Borenstein 2015). Such definitions of rebound are even less likely to be stable across time, geography, and policy regimes than the narrower definition used here. We therefore agree with Gillingham *et al.* (2016) that it is generally better to identify empirical information about major expected shifts than to try to incorporate them all into a single definition of "rebound."

32 For example, their Table 4, p. 681, shows that one specification estimated in first differences yields a cost-per-mile elasticity of −6.04, which increases in magnitude to −14.96 for price changes that represent the third of a consecutive series of three monthly price rises. The difference between the two (−8.92) is statistically significant. Several other specifications show suggestive asymmetry, but not quite significant at conventional levels. This study is of reduced-form market responses, not just demand-side responses.

33 These numbers are based on their Table V, plus the regression results described on p. 171.

34 Jacobsen and Van Benthem (2015) confirm the importance of scrappage to the effectiveness of fuel efficiency standards. See also Bento *et al.* (2018).

35 The estimated welfare cost is $616 (in 2001 US dollars) per metric ton of CO_2 mitigated in the tenth year of the program. See Section 7.3.2 for an interpretation of this magnitude.

36 The new standards were adopted with the proviso that the increases starting in 2022 would be subject to a "mid-term review." This led to a series of regulatory and court battles. At time of writing, a schedule of increasingly tight standards, similar to the original schedule, remains in effect.

37 This is also the conclusion of the official regulatory analysis of these same standards by US National Highway Traffic Safety Administration (2012).

38 Namely, the welfare cost is $4/t$CO_2$ as calculated from Small (2012), Table 6, by dividing the NPV of "Pavley CAFE" (row 7) by CO_2 removed (row labeled "Energy-related CO_2").

39 In this case, the policy cost becomes $85/t$CO_2$. This figure is the net present value of costs expressed in US 2007 dollars per metric ton of carbon dioxide emissions eliminated. See Section 7.4 for interpretation of such magnitudes.

40 Jacobsen's estimates (his Table 3) are $52–$438 per vehicle. Anderson and Sallee's estimate of marginal compliance cost is below the level of the fine for noncompliance (approximately $55/vehicle per mile/gallon excess). Thus, their results are explained with no need for a self-perceived penalty for being out of compliance, which as discussed earlier is how Jacobsen reconciles his high marginal cost estimates with the existence of an option to pay a fine instead of improving fuel efficiency.

41 A true feebate defines a graduated fee and rebate (subsidy) schedule for purchase of fuel-inefficient and fuel-efficient vehicles, respectively. The subsidy programs in China and Japan involve only the rebate component.

42 These figures are based on the upper panel ("logit estimates") of their Table 4, which is also the basis for their own verbal summaries.

43 Based on their Table 9, top row, which assumes a deadweight loss of raising public funds of 30%, the welfare cost per vehicle whose efficiency was raised by the program was US$3,436, while the benefit (with discount rate 3%) was $884. They also compute a break-even value for the deadweight loss of raising public funds, finding it was negative which implies that compliance costs exceeded benefits even when the deadweight loss is ignored.

44 This program is described and analyzed by D'Haultfoeuille *et al.* (2014); they find that the rebate portion was so generous as to substantially subsidize car travel overall, causing CO_2 emissions to *increase* despite the promotion of fuel efficiency. Adamou *et al.* (2014) analyze feebate policies for Germany; they find that a full feebate scheme can be welfare enhancing, but one limited to rebates is welfare reducing, even accounting for the benefits of CO_2 reduction.

45 See Jacobsen and van Benthem (2015), Grigolon *et al.* (2016), and Cantos-Sánchez *et al.* (2018) for programs in the USA, Europe, and Spain, respectively.

46 To estimate these elasticities, West estimates vehicle choice and usage jointly, using a model similar to that of Dubin and McFadden described in Chapter 2.

47 That is, when revenues are distributed proportionally to income (so as not themselves to influence progressivity), the burden as a proportion of income is highest for middle incomes. Bento *et al.* consider other ways of distributing revenues as well.

48 Bento *et al.* (2009) also find, consistent with our section 7.2.1, that changes in vehicle mix play a very small role in reducing fuel use: instead, more than 95% of the reduction caused by a fuel tax is due to less driving. This seems to us implausibly high. It arises in part because they measure a larger usage elasticity (rebound effect) than most studies. Furthermore, they use a cost function for improving fuel economy, based on US National Research Council (2002), that is relatively conservative about technological possibilities. They do not model the full range of potential manufacturer decisions as revealed by Whitefoot *et al.* (2017).

49 Regulation of local air pollutants typically sets them proportionally to vehicle usage, so they are often assumed to produce a distance-based rather than fuel-based externality.

50 Parry and Small consider only gasoline, but the same principles apply to diesel fuel for road use. The *dilution factor* is directly relevant to the debate over whether the fuel tax on diesel should be lower than on gasoline due to its greater energy efficiency, as diesel is typically worse than gasoline for local air pollution. One could argue that European policies that encourage diesel (some of which have subsequently been phased out or reversed) are justified despite high local-pollution externalities because of this dilution factor; this argument would disappear if diesel emissions were optimally controlled through other means.

51 These cancelations work as follows. From (7.6),

$$dx = w\left(1 - \tau_L\right)dL - wLd\tau_L - p_M dM - Mdp_M - K'(E)dE - dC^S + dG .$$

Inserting this into (7.11), we note that the two terms in dL cancel each other, as do the two terms in dM. This leaves the remaining terms:

$$dW = -wLd\tau_L - Mdp_M - K'(E)dE - dC^S + dG .$$

Using (7.7) to compute dp_M, using the last of (7.9) to compute K', and recalling that fuel price p_F includes the tax fuel tax τ_F, we have

$$dW = -wLd\tau_L - M\left(\alpha dT + \frac{d\tau_F}{E} - \frac{p_F}{E^2}dE + d\tau_M\right) - \frac{p_F M}{E^2}dE - dC^S + dG.$$

The two terms proportional to dE cancel each other. We can move the terms involving changes in tax rates to the beginning of the right-hand side, so that

$$dW = -wLd\tau_L - Md\tau_M - Fd\tau_F - M\alpha dT - dC^S + dG,$$

where we have simplified the notation by defining fuel consumed $F \equiv M/E$. We now make use of society-wide constraints (7.10) to rewrite these last three terms:

$$-M\alpha dT = -M\alpha T'dM$$

$$-dC^S = -mec^M dM - mec^F dF$$

$$dG = wLd\tau_L + w\tau_L dL + \tau_M dM + Md\tau_M + Fd\tau_F + \tau_F dF.$$

Substituting these quantities into the equation for dW leads to several cancelations of terms, and each of those involving dM and dF factor neatly into two pieces, one involving an actual tax rate and the other involving a first-best Pigouvian tax rate. The result is equation (7.12).

52 This result makes use of the simple ratios of infinitesimal quantities in (7.14), along with these definitions of elasticities:

$$\frac{dM}{dF} = \frac{dM / dp_F}{dF / dp_F} = \frac{\varepsilon_{M,PF} M / p_F}{\varepsilon_{F,PF} F / p_F} = r_F^M \cdot E$$

$$\frac{dL}{dF} = \frac{dL / dp_F}{dF / dp_F} = \frac{\varepsilon_{L,PF} L / p_F}{\varepsilon_{F,PF} F / p_F} = \frac{L}{F}\frac{\varepsilon_{L,PF}}{\varepsilon_{F,PF}}.$$

53 See International Transport Forum (2018, Figure 1), citing International Energy Agency statistics. The figure shows all transportation (including aviation and freight) to be 55%, and road transportation 25%, of all oil consumption in 2015. Non-transportation uses, in order of importance, are industrial, commercial, and residential – all of which include heating and cooling of buildings.

54 Within the OECD, road transportation accounted for 50.1/63.0 = 79.5% of transportation oil consumption in 2017, from Statista (2019). Within the USA, light-duty passenger vehicles accounted for 72% of oil consumption for road transportation in 2018, from Davis and Boundy (2021, Table 1.15). Combining these shares yields 0.15 × 0.795 × 0.72 = 8.6% as a rough estimate of how much light-duty vehicles contribute to all greenhouse gases.

55 One $GtCO_2e$ is one metric gigaton (*i.e.*, 10^9 metric tons or 10^{12} kilograms) of carbon dioxide or of other greenhouse gases adjusted to equivalent global warming potential. Global emissions under "business as usual" are given as 65.6 $GtCO_2e$ (Enkvist *et al.* 2010, p. 4). Abatement potential of transportation and of all measures are given in their Exhibit 7, p. 9. Enkvist *et al.* (2007) contains a more complete methodological explanation.

56 The use of the shorter terminology is due partly to the tendency of carbon atoms to move through the earth's atmospheric, oceanic, and biological systems, taking many forms but eventually producing (usually) carbon dioxide (CO_2), which is the most quantitatively important greenhouse gas. Many older studies expressed SCC instead as per ton of carbon itself; those values can be converted to values expressed per ton of CO_2 by multiplying them by 3.667, which is just the atomic weight of carbon dioxide (44) divided by that of carbon (12). Unfortunately, many writers do not state which measure

they are using. See National Academies (2017). Another problem is that US writers are not always clear whether "ton" is a metric ton or a US ton. Sometimes ton is spelled using the British spelling, tonne, to indicate it is a metric ton. In this book, SCC always refers to SC-CO$_2$.

57 See Weyant (2017) and National Academies (2017) for excellent reviews of IAMs.

58 Kolstad and Moore (2020) provide a good review of one approach to measuring such damages empirically, based on time series and cross-sectional weather observations.

59 For example, the present discounted value of $1 billion incurred 100 years in the future is $1 billion × $(1 + r)^{-100}$ = $370 million if $r = 0.01$, but only $7.6 million if $r = 0.05$.

60 For example, an "optimal policy" scenario seeks to maximize an intergenerational utility function that accounts for aversion to intergenerational income inequality: namely, consumption stream $\{c_t\}$ over time provides utility $U = \sum_t (1+\rho)^{-t} U(c_t)$, with a constant-elasticity time-specific utility function $U(c_t) = c_t^{1-\eta} / (1-\eta)$. Parameter η, the consumption-elasticity of utility, measures the degree of aversion to income inequality in consumption (similar to income inequality): in this context, it adds to the amount that future generations' utilities are discounted to the extent they are richer than the current generation. Letting g be the growth rate of future output, the standard Ramsey model of intergenerational optimization in a growing economy implies that the resulting market discount rate is $r = \rho + \eta g$, as described in Section 5.2.3, where ρ is a "pure" utility discount rate. Nordhaus chooses a value for ρ (1.5% in DICE-2016R, 1.0% in DICE-2023), uses empirical evidence on η (typically finding it somewhat greater than one), and adds projections of growth rate g, to determine the utility discount rate ρ from this Ramsey equation.

61 There is controversy over the ethical interpretation of market interest rates for discounting future costs and benefits in climate analysis. At one extreme is Stern (2007), who argues that an ethical approach to future generations' utility requires overriding the market in choosing r. He thus sets $\rho = 0.1\%$/year in the Ramsey model (see previous endnote); it is nonzero only because future generations might not be alive regardless of climate change. With assumed growth rate $g = 1.3\%$/year and inequality-aversion parameter $\eta = 1.0$, Stern computes the discount rate for consumption as $r = \rho + \eta g = 1.4\%$/year (Stern 2007, Box 6.3, pp. 183–185). Many critics see this rate as far too low: See Nordhaus (2007) and the symposium edited by Stavins et al. (2008). See Buchholz and Schymura (2011) for a good review of ethical considerations in choosing discount rates.

62 While in most scenarios the endogenous discount rate declines over time, the alternate values use a constant discount rate. There are good arguments for imposing a discount rate that declines as a function of the time span to which it is applied (Weitzman 2001). These arguments include uncertainties in consumption or in the applicable discount rate itself. Arrow et al. (2014) provide a thorough review, and show that with reasonable estimates of relevant theoretical parameters, a declining discount rate may imply a doubling or even tripling of the SCC (pp. 158-159) compared to a constant discount rate starting at the same value. A difficulty with time-varying discount rates, aside from creating inconsistency in long-range decisions, is that they can imply implausible assumptions about the nature of uncertainty in future consumption, causing some to doubt their theoretical underpinnings (Gollier 2014, 2016).

63 In all DICE models, costs incurred in various regions of the world are converted to US dollars at purchasing power parity.

64 One metric ton = 1,000 kg = 1.1023 US tons. Other greenhouse gases, such as methane, are conventionally converted to the amount of carbon dioxide that has an equivalent impact on trapping heat in the atmosphere; in that case, the measurement unit is sometimes written as tons CO$_2$-equivalent (tCO$_2$e), as we have done in Section 7.3.1.

65 See US Interagency Working Group (2016). See Greenstone et al. (2013) for a good account of the Interagency Working Group methodology. A proposed road map for updates of the official SCC used in the USA is the main topic of a National Academies (2017) study. An executive order mandating such updates was issued by the then-new US President in January 2021. The IWG stated its results in 2007 prices; we update to 2020 prices using the Personal Consumption Expenditure (PCE) price index for all items, which is 21.4% higher in 2020 than in 2007 and 16.0% higher than in 2010.

66 In these constrained scenarios, the values shown each represent the shadow price of the constraint: Barrage and Nordhaus call it the SCC because they interpret the constraint as indicating that damage costs rise to infinity at any temperature above this constraint, in which case the shadow price equals the social cost when the constraint is binding. These values are somewhat higher than the

ranges recommended by World Bank (2017) for a similar shadow price, which are $45–89 in 2025 and $78–156 in 2050, all in 2017 prices.

67 The "optimal policy" scenario of Barrage and Nordhaus, using DICE-2023, is approximately half this amount, whereas the preferred value of Rennert *et al.* (2021), using GIVE, is approximately twice this amount. Both of these values are shown in Table 7.1 (DICE-2023 and GIVE panels, rows labeled with footnote a, middle column).

68 Based on carbon content of 2.433 kg per gallon, from Davis and Boundy (2021, Table 12.12). This number is multiplied by 3.667 to convert carbon to CO_2 by weight and divided by 3.785 liters/gallon.

69 See US National Research Council (2015) for a comprehensive review.

70 If there is only uncertainty about the marginal benefits of abatement, price and quantity instruments perform equally well because they support the same amount of abatement that does not depend on the realized value of marginal benefits.

71 This figure is calculated by us following the procedure developed for Parry and Small (2015, Figure 12.3), but with monetary units in US 2020 dollars, SCC equal to $104/$tCO_2$, and US accident costs at $0.143/mile as per Chapter 2. The "carbon" portion of the external cost is computed at the fuel efficiency that occurs at the optimal tax level (part of the calculation of that tax level); hence, it is identical to the "carbon" po rtion of the optimal fuel tax.

72 This "efficient tax" is not necessarily second-best optimal if fuel efficiency regulations are in place, because they prevent the adjustments in fuel efficiency that optimality assumes. If such regulations remain binding upon raising the fuel tax, the "dilution" of a fuel tax's impacts on congestion and accidents no longer applies because the tax no longer encourages fuel efficiency improvements; on the other hand, congestion and accident externalities may reduce the benefits from the fuel efficiency regulations themselves, as discussed in Section 7.2.1.

73 See Wise and Cole (2015), Appendices A and B. The count is from the two tables entitled "OECD" and "Producers Meeting High Mandates." This paper is also the source for much of the discussion in the next two paragraphs.

References

Adamou, Adamos, Sofronis Clerides and Theodoros Zachariadis (2014) "Welfare implications of car fee-bates: a simulation analysis," *Economic Journal* 124 (August): F420–F443.

Akerlof, George A. (1970) "The market for 'lemons': quality uncertainty and the market mechanism," *Quarterly Journal of Economics* 84(3): 488–500.

Aldy, Joseph E. (2020) "Carbon tax review and updating: institutionalizing an act-learn-act approach to U.S. climate policy," *Review of Environmental Economics and Policy* 14: 76–94.

Aldy, Joseph E., Alan J. Krupnick, Richard G. Newell, Ian W.H. Parry and William A. Pizer (2010) "Designing climate mitigation policy," *Journal of Economic Literature* 48(4): 903–934.

Allcott, Hunt (2013) "The welfare effects of misperceived product costs: data and calibrations from the automobile market," *American Economic Journal: Economic Policy* 5(3): 30–66.

Allcott, Hunt, Sendhil Mullainathan, and Dmitry Taubinsky (2014) "Energy policy with externalities and internalities," *Journal of Public Economics* 112: 72–88.

Allcott, Hunt and Nathan Wozny (2014) "Gasoline prices, fuel economy, and the Energy Paradox," *Review of Economics and Statistics* 96(5): 779–795.

Anderson, Soren T. and James M. Sallee (2011) "Using loopholes to reveal the marginal cost of regulation: the case of fuel-economy standards," *American Economic Review* 101(4): 1375–1409.

Arrow, Kenneth J., Maureen L. Cropper, Christian Gollier, Ben Groom, Geoffrey M. Heal, Richard G. Newell, William D. Nordhaus, Robert S. Pindyck, William A. Pizer, Paul R. Portney, Thomas Sterner, Richard S. J. Tol, and Martin L. Weitzman (2014) "Should governments use a declining discount rate in project analysis?" *Review of Environmental Economics and Policy* 8(2): 145–163.

Barrage, Lint and William D. Nordhaus (2023) "Policies, projections, and the social cost of carbon: results from the DICE-2023 model," Working paper 31112, National Bureau of Economic Research, http://www.nber.org/papers/w31112

Bento, Antonio M., Lawrence H. Goulder, Mark R. Jacobsen and Roger H. von Haefen (2009) "Distributional and efficiency impacts of increased US gasoline taxes," *American Economic Review* 99(3): 667–699.

Bento, Antonio M., Kevin Roth and Yiou Zuo (2018) "Vehicle lifetime trends and scrappage behavior in the U.S. used car market," *Energy Journal* 39(1). doi: 10.5547/01956574.39.1.aben.

Beresteanu, Arie and Shanjun Li (2011) "Gasoline prices, government support, and the demand for hybrid vehicles in the United States," *International Economic Review* 52(1): 161–182.

Bernheim, B. Douglas (2016) "The good, the bad, and the ugly: a unified approach to behavioral welfare economics," *Journal of Benefit Cost Analysis* 7(1): 12–68.

Borenstein, Severin (2008) "Cost, conflict and climate: U.S. challenges in the world oil market," Center for the Study of Energy Markets Working paper #177, University of California Energy Institute (June).

Borenstein, Severin (2015) "a microeconomic framework for evaluating energy efficiency rebound and some implications," *Energy Journal* 36(1): 1–21.

Bovenberg, A. Lans, Lawrence H. Goulder and Mark R. Jacobsen (2008) "Costs of alternative environmental policy instruments in the presence of industry compensation requirements," *Journal of Public Economics* 92: 1236–1253.

Brons, Martijn, Peter Nijkamp, Eric Pels and Piet Rietveld (2008) "A meta-analysis of the price elasticity of gasoline demand: a SUR approach," *Energy Economics* 30: 2105–2122.

Buchholz, Wolfgang and Michael Schymura (2011) "Intertemporal evaluation criteria for climate change policy: basic ethical issues," in: Houshan Kheradmand (ed.) *Climate Change - Socioeconomic Effects*, InTech, Chap. 20, https://www.intechopen.com/chapters/19646 (accessed 26 Jul 2021).

Busse, Meghan R., Christopher R. Knittel and Florian Zettelmeyer (2013) "Are consumers myopic? Evidence from new and used car purchases," *American Economic Review* 103(1): 220–256.

Cambridge Econometrics (2008) *Demand for Cars and their Attributes*, Final report for the Department for Transport. Cambridge, UK: Cambridge Econometrics (January). https://docplayer.net/13429423-Demand-for-cars-and-their-attributes.html (accessed 10 March 2024).

Cantos-Sánchez, Pedro, Eva Gutiérrez-i-Puigarnau and Ismir Mulalic (2018) "The impact of scrappage programmes on the demand for new vehicles: evidence from Spain," *Research in Transportation Economics* 70: 83–96.

Carleton, Tamma and Michael Greenstone (2022) "A guide to updating the US government's social cost of carbon," *Review of Environmental Economics and Policy* 16(2): 196–218.

Center for Climate and Energy Solutions (2019) *Global Emissions*, https://www.c2es.org/content/international-emissions (accessed 12 September 2019).

Chakravorty, Ujjayant, Marie-Hélène Hubert, Michel Moreaux and Linda Nøstbakken (2017) "The long-run impact of biofuels on food prices," *Scandinavian Journal of Economics* 119(3): 733–767.

Chen, Chia-Wen, Wei-Min Hu and Christopher R. Knittel (2021) "Subsidizing fuel efficient cars: evidence from China's automobile industry," *American Economic Journal: Economic Policy*, 13(4): 152-184. doi: 10.1257/pol.20170098

Coady, David, Ian W.H. Parry, Nghia-Piotr Le and Baoping Shang (2019) "Global fossil fuel subsidies remain large: an update based on country-level estimates," Working Paper 19-89, International Monetary Fund (May), https://www.imf.org/en/Publications/WP/Issues/2019/05/02/Global-Fossil-Fuel-Subsidies-Remain-Large-An-Update-Based-on-Country-Level-Estimates-46509 (accessed 10 March 2024).

Coglianese, John, Lucas W. Davis, Lutz Kilian and James H. Stock (2017) "Anticipation, tax avoidance, and the price elasticity of gasoline demand", *Journal of Applied Econometrics* 32: 1–15.

Cramton, Peter, Axel Ockenfels and Jean Tirole (2017) "Translating the collective climate goal into a common climate commitment," *Review of Environmental Economics and Policy* 11(1): 165–171.

Cropper, Maureen L., Richard D. Morgenstern and Nicholas Rivers (2018) "Facilitating retrospective analysis of environmental regulations," *Review of Environmental Economics and Policy* 12(2): 359–370.

D'Haultfoeuille, Xavier, Pauline Givord and Xavier Boutin (2014) "The environmental effects of green taxation: the case of the French Bonus/Malus," *Economic Journal* 124 (August): F444-F480.

Dahl, Carol A. (2012) "Measuring global gasoline and diesel price and income elasticities," *Energy Policy* 41: 2–13.

Davis, Stacy C. and Robert G. Boundy (2020) *Transportation Energy Data Book*, Oak Ridge National Laboratory, Edition 38, Report ORNL/TM-2019/1333 (January).

De Borger, Bruno, Ismir Mulalic and Jan Rouwendal (2016) "Measuring the rebound effect with micro data: a first difference approach," *Journal of Environmental Economics and Management* 79: 1–17.

De Borger, Bruno, and Stef Proost (2012) "Transport policy competition between governments: a selective survey of the literature," *Economics of Transportation* 1: 35–48.

Delucchi, Mark and James J. Murphy (2008) "US military expenditures to protect the use of Persian Gulf oil for motor vehicles," *Energy Policy* 36: 2253– 2264.

Dimitropoulos, Alexandros, Walid Oueslati and Christina Sintek (2018) "The rebound effect in road transport: a meta-analysis of empirical studies," *Energy Economics* 75: 163–179.

Dreyfus, Mark K. and W. Kip Viscusi (1995) "Rates of time preference and consumer valuations of automobile safety and fuel efficiency," *Journal of Law and Economics* 38: 79–105.

Durrmeyer, Isis, and Mario Samano (2017) "To rebate or not to rebate: fuel economy standards *versus* feebates," *Economic Journal* 128 (December): 3076–3116.

Enkvist, Per-Anders, Jens Dinkel and Charles Lin (2010) "Impact of the financial crisis on climate economics: Version 2.1 of the global greenhouse gas abatement cost curve," McKinsey & Co., https://www.mckinsey.com/capabilities/sustainability/our-insights/impact-of-the-financial-crisis-on-carbon-economics-version-21 (accessed 10 March 2024).

Enkvist, Per-Anders, Tomas Nauclér and Jerker Rosander (2007) "A cost curve for greenhouse gas reduction," *McKinsey Quarterly* 2007(1): 35–45, https://www.mckinsey.com/capabilities/sustainability/our-insights/a-cost-curve-for-greenhouse-gas-reduction (accessed 10 March 2024).

Gately, Dermot and Hillard G. Huntington (2002) "The asymmetric effects of changes in price and income on energy and oil demand," *Energy Journal* 23(1): 19–55.

Gerarden, Todd D., Richard G. Newell and Robert N. Stavins (2017) "Assessing the energy-efficiency gap," *Journal of Economic Literature* 55(4): 1486–1525.

Gillingham, Kenneth (2011). *The Consumer Response to Gasoline Price Changes: Empirical Evidence and Policy Implications*, Ph.D. Dissertation, Dept. of Management Science and Engineering, Stanford University

Gillingham, Kenneth, David S. Rapson and Gernot Wagner (2016) "The rebound effect and energy efficiency policy," *Review of Environmental Economics and Policy* 10(1): 68–88.

Gollier, Christian (2014) "Discounting and growth," *American Economic Review: Papers & Proceedings* 104(5): 534–537.

Gollier, Christian (2016) "Gamma discounters are short-termist," *Journal of Public Economics* 142: 83–90.

Goodwin, Phil B., Joyce Dargay and Mark Hanley (2004) "Elasticities of road traffic and fuel consumption with respect to price and income: a review," *Transport Reviews* 24(3): 275–292.

Goulder, Lawrence H., Marc A.C. Hafstead and Roberton C. Williams III (2016) "General equilibrium impacts of a federal clean energy standard," *American Economic Journal: Economic Policy* 8(2): 186–218.

Graham, Daniel J. and Stephen Glaister (2002) "The demand for automobile fuel: a survey of elasticities," *Journal of Transport Economics and Policy* 36(1): 1–25.

Greene, David L. (2010) "How consumers value fuel economy: a literature review," Report No. EPA-420-R-10-008. US Environmental Protection Agency (March).

Greene, David L. (2011) "Uncertainty, loss aversion, and the markets for energy efficiency," *Energy Economics* 33, 608–616.

Greene, David L. (2012) "Rebound 2007: analysis of U.S. light-duty vehicle travel statistics," *Energy Policy* 41: 14–28.

Greene, David L., Philip D. Patterson, Margaret Singh and Jia Li (2005) "Feebates, rebates and gas-guzzler taxes: a study of incentives for increased fuel economy," *Energy Policy* 33: 757–775 with "Corrigendum" 33: 1901–1902.

Greenstone, Michael, Elizabeth Kopits and Ann Wolverton (2013) "Developing a social cost of carbon for US regulatory analysis: a methodology and interpretation," *Review of Environmental Economics and Policy* 7(1): 23–26.

Greenstone, Michael, Cass Sunstein and Sam Ori (2017) "The next generation of transportation policy," Policy Proposal 2017-02, The Hamilton Project, Brookings Institution (March), https://www.hamilton-project.org/papers/the_next_generation_of_transportation_policy (accessed 10 March 2024).

Grigolon, Laura, Nina Leheyda and Frank Verboven (2016) "Scrapping subsidies during the financial crisis – Evidence from Europe," *International Journal of Industrial Organization* 44: 41–59.

Grigolon, Laura, Mathias Reynaert and Frank Verboven (2018) "Consumer valuation of fuel costs and tax policy: evidence from the European car market," *American Economic Journal: Economic Policy* 10(3): 193–225.

Hausman, Jerry A. (1979) "Individual discount rates and the purchase and utilization of energy-using durables," *Bell Journal of Economics* 10(1): 33–54.

Havranek, Tomas, Zuzana Irsova and Karel Janda (2012) "Demand for gasoline is more price-inelastic than commonly thought," *Energy Economics* 34: 201–207.

Heal, Geoffrey and Antony Millner (2014) "Uncertainty and decision making in climate change economics," *Review of Environmental Economics and Policy* 8(1): 120–137.

Heal, Geoffrey and Wolfram Schlenker (2019) "Coase, Hotelling and Pigou: the incidence of a carbon tax and CO_2 emissions," Working paper 26086, National Bureau of Economic Research, https://www.nber.org/papers/w26086

Helfand, Gloria and Ann Wolverton (2011) "Evaluating the consumer response to fuel economy: a review of the literature," *International Review of Environmental and Resource Economics* 5: 103–146.

Holland, Stephen P., Jonathan E. Hughes and Christopher R. Knittel (2009) "Greenhouse gas reductions under low carbon fuel standards?" *American Economic Journal: Economic Policy* 1(1): 106–146.

Holland, Stephen P., Erin T. Mansur and Andrew J. Yates (2021) "The electric vehicle transition and the economics of banning gasoline vehicles," *American Economic Journal: Economic Policy* 13(3): 316–344.

Houde, Sébastien and Joseph E. Aldy (2017) "The efficiency consequences of heterogeneous behavioral responses to energy fiscal policies," NBER Working Paper 24103.

Hsiang, Solomon and Robert E. Kopp (2018) "An economist's guide to climate change science," *Journal of Economic Perspectives* 32(4): 3–32.

Hughes, Jonathan E., Christopher R. Knittel and Daniel Sperling (2008) "Evidence of a shift in the short-run price elasticity of gasoline demand," *Energy Journal* 29(1): 113–134.

Hymel, Kent and Kenneth A. Small (2015) "The rebound effect for automobile travel: asymmetric response to price changes and novel features of the 2000s," *Energy Economics* 49: 93–103.

International Energy Agency (2019) "World Energy Balances," in *IEA World Energy Statistics and Balances*. Organisation for Economic Cooperation and Development, Paris, https://www.oecd-ilibrary.org/energy/world-energy-balances_25186442 (accessed 10 March 2024).

International Transport Forum (2018) "Towards road freight decarbonisation: trends, measures and policies", ITF Policy Papers, OECD, Paris, https://www.itf-oecd.org/towards-road-freight-decarbonisation (accessed 30 April 2020).

IPCC (2013) "Technical Summary," in: *Climate Change 2013: The Physical Science Basis. Contribution of Working Group I to the Fifth Assessment Report of the Intergovernmental Panel on Climate Change* [Stocker, T.F., D. Qin, G.-K. Plattner, M. Tignor, S.K. Allen, J. Boschung, A. Nauels, Y. Xia, V. Bex and P.M. Midgley (eds.)].Cambridge, UK and New York: Cambridge University Press, https://www.ipcc.ch/report/ar5/wg1/ (accessed 10 March 2024).

Ito, Koichiro and James M. Sallee (2018) "The economics of attribute-based regulation: theory and evidence from fuel economy standards," *Review of Economics and Statistics* 100(2): 319–336.

Jacobsen, Mark R. (2013) "Evaluating US fuel economy standards in a model with producer and household heterogeneity," *American Economic Journal: Economic Policy* 5(2): 148–187.

Jacobsen, Mark R., Christopher R. Knittel, James M. Sallee and Arthur A. van Benthem (2020) "The use of regression statistics to analyze imperfect pricing policies," *Journal of Political Economy* 128(5): 1826 – 1876.

Jacobsen, Mark R. and Arthur A. van Benthem (2015) "Vehicle scrappage and gasoline policy," *American Economic Review* 105(3): 1312–1338.

Kellogg, Ryan (2018) "Gasoline price uncertainty and the design of fuel economy standards," *Journal of Public Economics* 160: 14–32.

Khanna, Madhu, Deepak Rajagopal and David Zilberman (2021) "Lessons learned from US experience with biofuels: comparing the hype with the evidence," *Review of Environmental Economics and Policy* 15(1): 67–86.

Kilian, Lutz (2008) "The economic effects of energy price shocks," *Journal of Economic Literature* 46(4): 871–909.

Klier, Thomas and Joshua Linn (2010) "The price of gasoline and new vehicle fuel economy: evidence from monthly sales data," *American Economic Journal: Economic Policy* 2: 134–153.

Knittel, Christopher R. (2012) "Automobiles on steroids: product attribute trade-offs and technological progress in the automobile sector," *American Economic Review* 101: 3368–3399.

Kolstad, Charles D. and Frances C. Moore (2020) "Estimating the economic impacts of climate change using weather observations," *Review of Environmental Economics and Policy* 14: 1–24.

Langer, Ashley and Nathan H. Miller (2013) "Automakers' short-run responses to changing gasoline prices," *Review of Economics and Statistics* 95(4): 1198–1211.

Larrick, Richard P. and Jack B. Soll (2008) "The MPG illusion," *Science* 320: 1593–1594.

Leard, Benjamin, Joshua Linn and Virginia McConnell (2017) "Fuel prices, new vehicle fuel economy, and implications for attribute-based standards," *Journal of the Association of Environmental and Resource Economists* 4(3): 659–700.

Leard, Benjamin, Joshua Linn and Yichen Christy Zhou (2023) "How much do consumers value fuel economy and performance? Evidence from technology adoption," *Review of Economics and Statistics* 105(1): 158–174. doi:10.1162/rest_a_01045

Leard, Benjamin, Virginia McConnell and Yichen Christy Zhou (2019) "The effect of fuel price changes on fleet demand for new vehicle fuel economy," *Journal of Industrial Economics* 67(1): 127–159. doi:10.1111/joie.12198

Leiby, Paul N. (2007) "Estimating the energy security benefits of reduced U.S. oil imports," Paper No. ORNL/TM-2007/028, Oak Ridge National Laboratory, July 23.

Levin, Laurence, Matthew S. Lewis and Frank A. Wolak (2017) "High frequency evidence on the demand for gasoline," *American Economic Journal: Economic Policy* 9(3): 314–347.

Li, Shanjun, Joshua Linn and Erich J. Muehlegger (2014) "Gasoline taxes and consumer behavior," *American Economic Journal: Economic Policy* 6: 302–342.

Li, Shanjun, Christopher D. Timmins and Roger H. von Haefen (2009) "How do gasoline prices affect fleet fuel economy?" *American Economic Journal: Economic Policy* 1: 113–137.

Linn, Joshua (2016) "The rebound effect for passenger vehicles," *Energy Journal* 37(2): 257–288.

Litman, Todd (2013) "Changing North American vehicle travel price sensitivities: implications for transport and energy policy," *Transport Policy* 28: 2–10.

Liu, Changzheng, David L. Greene and David S. Bunch (2014) "Vehicle manufacturer technology adoption and pricing strategies under fuel economy/emissions standards and feebates," *Energy Journal* 35(3): 71–89.

Mannering, Fred and Clifford Winston (1985) "A dynamic empirical analysis of household vehicle ownership and utilization," *RAND Journal of Economics* 16(2): 215–236.

Metcalf, Gilbert E. (2020) "An emissions assurance mechanism: adding environmental certainty to a U.S. carbon tax," *Review of Environmental Economics and Policy* 14: 114–130.

National Academies of Sciences, Engineering, and Medicine (2017), *Valuing Climate Damages: Updating Estimation of the Social Cost of Carbon Dioxide*, Washington, DC: National Academies Press. doi:10.17226/24651.

Nordhaus, William D. (2007) "A review of the Stern Review on the economics of climate change," *Journal of Economic Literature* 45(3): 686–702.

Nordhaus, William D. (2013) *The Climate Casino: Risk, Uncertainty, and Economics for a Warming World*. New Haven, CT: Yale University Press.

Nordhaus, William D. (2015) "Climate clubs: overcoming free-riding in international climate policy," *American Economic Review* 105(4): 1339–1370.

Nordhaus, William D. (2017) "Revisiting the social cost of carbon," *Proceedings of the National Academy of Sciences* 114(7): 1518–1523.

Parry, Ian W.H. and Antonio M. Bento (2001) "Revenue recycling and the welfare effects of congestion pricing," *Scandinavian Journal of Economics* 103(4): 645–671.

Parry, Ian W.H., David Evans and Wallace E. Oates (2014) "Are energy efficiency standards justified?" *Journal of Environmental Economics and Management*, 67: 104–125.

Parry, Ian W.H. and Kenneth A. Small (2005) "Does Britain or the United States have the right gasoline tax?" *American Economic Review* 95: 1276–1289.

Parry, Ian W.H. and Kenneth A. Small (2015) "Implications of carbon taxes for transportation policies," in Ian W.H. Parry, Adele Morris and Roberton C. Williams III (eds.) *Implementing a US Carbon Tax: Challenges and Debates*, Routledge, Chapter 12.

Pizer, William A. and Brian C. Prest (2020) "Prices versus quantities with policy updating," *Journal of the Association Environmental and Resource Economists* 7(3): 483–518.

Pollitt, Michael G. and Geoffroy G. Dolphin (2022) "Should the EU ETS be extended to road transport and heating fuels?," *Economics of Energy and Environmental Policy* 11(2). doi:10.5547/2160-5890.11.1.mpol

Proost, Stef, Eef Delhaye, Wouter Nijs and Denise Van Regemorter (2009) "Will a radical transport pricing reform jeopardize the ambitious EU climate change objectives?" *Energy Policy* 37: 3863–3871.

Rennert, Kevin, Brian C. Prest, William A. Pizer, Richard G. Newell, David Anthoff, Cora Kingdon, Lisa Rennels, Roger Cooke, Adrian E. Raftery, Hana Ševčíková and Frank Errickson (2021) "The social cost of carbon: advances in long-term probabilistic projections of population, GDP, emissions, and discount rates," Brookings Paper on Economic Activity (Fall 2021): 223–275.

Rennert, Kevin, Frank Errickson, Brian C. Prest, Lisa Rennels, Richard G. Newell, William Pizer, Cora Kingdon, Jordan Wingenroth, Roger Cooke, Bryan Parthum, David Smith, Kevin Cromar, Delavane Diaz, Frances C. Moore, Ulrich K. Müller, Richard J. Plevin, Adrian E. Raftery, Hana Ševčíková, Hannah Sheets, James H. Stock, Tammy Tan, Mark Watson, Tony E. Wong and David Anthoff (2022) "Comprehensive evidence implies a higher social cost of CO2," *Nature* 610 (27 October): 687–692.

Rivers, Nicholas and Brandon Schaufele (2015) "Salience of carbon taxes in the gasoline market," *Journal of Environmental Economics and Management* 74: 23–36.

Small, Kenneth A. (2012) "Energy policies for passenger motor vehicles," *Transportation Research Part A: Policy and Practice* 46(6): 874–889.

Small Kenneth A. and Kurt Van Dender (2007). "Fuel efficiency and motor vehicle travel: the declining rebound effect," *Energy Journal* 28: 25–51.

Statista (2019) "Distribution of oil demand in the OECD in 2017 by sector," https://www.statista.com/statistics/307194/top-oil-consuming-sectors-worldwide (accessed 17 September 2019).

Stavins, Robert N. (2022) "The relative merits of carbon pricing instruments: taxes versus trading," *Review of Environmental Economics and Policy* 16(1): 62–82.

Stavins, Robert N., Carlo Carraro and Charles D. Kolstad, eds. (2008) "Symposium: the economics of climate change: the *Stern Review* and its critics," *Review of Environmental Economics and Policy* 2(1): 45–113.

Stern, Nicholas (2007) *The Economics of Climate Change: The Stern Review*. Cambridge and New York: Cambridge University Press. Pre-published by the UK HM Treasury as *Stern Review on the Economics of Climate Change* (2006) https://webarchive.nationalarchives.gov.uk/ukgwa/20100407172811/https://www.hm-treasury.gov.uk/stern_review_report.htm (accessed 10 March 2024).

Tax Foundation (2022) "Gas taxes in Europe," Washington, DC: Tax Foundation (July) https://taxfoundation.org/data/all/eu/gas-taxes-in-europe/ (accessed 10 March 2024).

Thaler, Richard H. (2017) "Behavioral Economics," *Journal of Political Economy* 125(6): 1799–1805.

Tiezzi, Silvia and Stefano F. Verde (2016) "Differential demand response to gasoline taxes and gasoline prices in the U.S.," *Resource and Energy Economics* 44: 71–91.

Tscharaktschiew, Stefan (2020) "Why are highway speed limits really justified? An equilibrium speed choice analysis," *Transportation Research Part B: Methodological* 138: 317–351.

Turrentine, Thomas S. and Kenneth S. Kurani (2007) "Car buyers and fuel economy?" *Energy Policy* 35: 1213–1223.

US CEA (2023) "Annual report of the Council of Economic Advisers," in *Economic Report of the President*, Washington, DC: US Government Printing Office, https://www.govinfo.gov/app/collection/erp/2023 (accessed 2 June 2023)

US Energy Information Administration (2019) *International Energy Outlook 2019*, https://www.eia.gov/outlooks/ieo/ (accessed 29 April 2020).

US Interagency Working Group on Social Cost of Greenhouse Gases (2016) Technical Update of the Social Cost of Carbon for Regulatory Impact Analysis, August, https://www.epa.gov/sites/default/files/2016-12/documents/sc_co2_tsd_august_2016.pdf (accessed 10 March 2024).

US National Highway Traffic Safety Administration (2012) *Corporate Average Fuel Economy for MY 2017-MY 2025 Passenger Cars and Light Trucks: Final Regulatory Impact Analysis*, August, https://www.nhtsa.gov/document/cafe-final-regulatory-impact-analysis-2012 (accessed 10 March 2024).

US National Research Council (2002) *Effectiveness and Impact of Corporate Average Fuel Economy (CAFE) Standards*. Washington, DC: National Academy of Sciences Press.

US National Research Council (2015) *Climate Intervention: Reflecting Sunlight to Cool Earth*, Washington, DC: National Academies Press. doi:10.17226/18988.

Van Dender, Kurt (2003) "Transport taxes with multiple trip purposes," *Scandinavian Journal of Economics* 105(2): 295–310.

Wadud, Zia, Daniel J. Graham and Robert B. Noland (2010) "Gasoline demand with heterogeneity in household responses," *Energy Journal* 31: 47–74.

Weitzman, Martin L. (1974) "Prices versus quantities," *Review of Economic Studies* 41(4): 477–491.

Weitzman, Martin L. (2001) "Gamma discounting," *American Economic Review* 91(1): 260–271.

Weitzman, Martin L. (2009) "On modeling and interpreting the economics of catastrophic climate change," *Review of Economics and Statistics* 91(1): 1–19.

West, Jeremy, Mark Hoekstra, Jonathan Meer and Steven L. Puller (2017) "Vehicle miles (not) traveled: fuel economy requirements, vehicle characteristics, and household driving," *Journal of Public Economics* 145: 65–81.

West, Sarah E. (2004) "Distributional effects of alternative vehicle pollution control policies," *Journal of Public Economic* 88: 735–757.

West, Sarah E. and Roberton C. Williams III (2007) "Optimal taxation and cross-price effects on labor supply: estimates of the optimal gas tax," *Journal of Public Economics* 91: 593–617.

Weyant, John (2017) "Some contributions of integrated assessment models of global climate change," *Review of Environmental Economics and Policy* 11(1): 115–137.

Whitefoot, Kate S., Meredith L. Fowlie and Steven J. Skerlos (2017) "Compliance by design: influence of acceleration trade-offs on CO_2 emissions and costs of fuel economy and greenhouse gas regulations," *Environmental Science and Technology* 51(18): 10307–10315.

Wise, Timothy A. and Emily Cole (2015) "Mandating food insecurity: the global impacts of rising biofuel mandates and targets," Working paper No. 15-01, Global Development and Environmental Institute, Tufts University.

World Bank (2017) *Guidance Note on Shadow Price of Carbon in Economic Analysis* (English). Washington, DC: World Bank Group (12 November), http://documents.worldbank.org/curated/en/621721519940107694/Guidance-note-on-shadow-price-of-carbon-in-economic-analysis

8 Conclusion

Our review of transportation economics has revealed several themes that characterize contemporary urban transportation research. We now turn to an assessment of how these themes are likely to evolve and how they may influence the character of urban transportation research in the future.

8.1 Continuing themes

8.1.1 Scheduling and reliability

In chapters 2 and 3, we identified scheduling and reliability as significant, intertwined factors in travel decisions and in the cost of travel. This has long been understood, yet we expect to see several further developments. Researchers are likely to refine tools to extract measures of reliability from the plethora of new and rapidly expanding (big) data sources that are described in Chapter 2. New tools to predict reliability in advance should improve the analysis of traffic incidents. More data will also help identify the different points in time at which a traveler makes use of information – further clarifying, for example, the "value of urgency" mentioned in Section 2.7.4. We expect that continuing improvement of temporal and spatial resolution of data will spur ongoing further development in the conceptual and empirical modelling of scheduling behavior, including both individuals and households and allowing for interactions between them.

8.1.2 Safety

The cost of traffic accidents, identified in Chapter 3, is arguably larger than the cost of unreliability. As economies grow, especially developing economies, people will place ever larger values on safety. This is a concern not only for car travel, but even more so for motorcycles, e-bikes, scooters, and bicycles. With the desired greening of transport and the popularity of e-bikes and e-scooters, increasing numbers of vulnerable travelers in urban traffic may be expected, and also greater speed differences. All this will make traffic accidents a more prominent part of transportation economics.

Economics has long experience with analyzing people's willingness to pay for reduced probability of accidental injury or death. It has shorter but useful experience with analyzing the incentives affecting safety that market participants face, *e.g.* through speed choice or vehicle maintenance, and how those incentives interact with the legal system, the health care system, driver behavior, congestion, traffic regulations, vehicle characteristics, and strategies and policies of insurance companies. Thus, economists have much to add to this topic, and we can

DOI: 10.4324/9781315157375-8

expect their analyses to demonstrate that safety affects every aspect of transportation analysis, from travel demand to institutional design.

8.1.3 *Design of road pricing schemes*

As described in Chapter 4, second-best analysis has become essential to using economic models to inform policy. A barrier to its use is that each situation seems to require a distinct model to understand it, making it difficult to draw general lessons for policies such as road pricing. One possible route is to develop summary measures of success of a proposed pricing system, both empirically and through modelling, and relate those measures statistically to the characteristics of the system. We might call this a meta-second-best analysis: a formal analysis of the results of individual second-best analyses. Such an approach could target aggregate welfare effects and other important aspects such as public acceptability and distributional impacts. This approach might find inspiration in the work by Vonk Noordegraaf *et al.* (2014).

Such an analysis would need to incorporate several elements. First is reliability, including the possibilities for integrating traffic information into road pricing in a two-pronged strategy to improve reliability. Second is distribution: by consistently quantifying the distributional impacts of pricing implementations, tests of the effect of distribution acceptability would become more rigorous. Third is dynamics: especially, the use of dynamic models to create better measures of how scheduling decisions determine the results of road pricing.

To fully appreciate differences between policy scenarios, the analyses should ideally be carried out in frameworks that capture the role of spatial feedbacks, and that account for interactions with (distorted) markets behind the demand and supply conditions in transport. Labor, housing, real estate, and land markets are logical candidates. An important balance to strike in such an endeavor is to profit as much as possible from the potential of exploiting big data and machine learning, while not losing the strengths of structural modelling, microeconomic consistency, and conceptual clarity. These comments, of course, apply to much transportation analysis, not just that of road pricing.

Finally, we hope that second-best analyses will fully incorporate user heterogeneity, both in order to provide better understanding and predictions of behavioral responses, and to more fully incorporate the themes of distribution and inclusion. Among other benefits, this could help identify possible niche products in urban transportation. Deregulation in other transportation industries, such as aviation and freight transportation, has led to an explosion of new products and services, including finely graduated classes of service and long-term specialized contracts. Nothing comparable has occurred in urban transportation, but we see no lack of possibilities. Might smaller delivery vehicles be used if encouraged by targeted pricing incentivizes? Could a highway authority offer a priced express lane with guaranteed travel time to an airport at certain hours? Would autonomous vehicles attract more shared rides if priced according to prevalent congestion? Targeted road pricing, perhaps combined with road investments, might make some such niche markets financially feasible.

8.1.4 *Sustainability*

Environmental problems are prominent effects of transportation activities. We expect the importance of local air pollution to remain high, especially in developing nations; and that of carbon emissions to increase even further as climate change progresses and governments attempt to achieve carbon neutrality in many economic sectors.

We also think that both local and global air emissions can be well addressed using currently known analytical and policy tools. The most efficient tools frequently involve incentives, especially carbon pricing of some sort; but those are not the only possible tools. Our analyses suggest that the near-term responses to pricing tools, as well as to the most promising regulatory tools, are primarily technological rather than behavioral. For example, both fuel taxes and fuel-efficiency regulations achieve their results most strongly through changes in engine technology, and somewhat less strongly through changes in behavior such as driving less or purchasing smaller cars. This is why policies targeted toward particular technological improvements can be effective – just as past policies toward local air pollution have been successful, even if not fully efficient, by mandating specific equipment such as catalytic converters for automobiles.

An important question is to what extent this remains true if environmental standards become more binding over the coming decades. For example, if economies become fully climate-neutral by 2050, as many hope, the required changes are likely to go beyond a technology fix such as full electrification. Rather, with rising societal shadow prices of meeting the increasingly strict policy objectives, more behavioral margins would become relevant in meeting these targets. Furthermore, as the cost of meeting these objectives increases, so does the importance of efficiency, and hence the potential societal value of economic analysis. If, by contrast, international cooperation fails to achieve the reductions in carbon emissions that are currently targeted, it is likely that technological, more than behavioral, responses to environmental policy will continue to predominate. Under either scenario, understanding the impacts of policies requires looking at the details of how transportation is provided and used, and at the trade-offs among behavioral margins and between them and technological standards.

8.1.5   *Urban goods movement*

Moving goods continues to play important roles in urban areas. Freight transport naturally often concentrates around ports, airports, and other hubs for shipments serving intra- and interregional trade. This occupies valuable land and generates significant rail and truck travel. At the same time, intra-urban goods delivery has become even more prominent: Even as just-in-time delivery to manufacturers appears to wane, prompt delivery to individual consumers has grown in importance. Both factors add to pressure on the ability of roadways to handle traffic. New technologies now coming on line, such as drones and ground-based robotic delivery vehicles, will further complicate the picture.

Trucking, whether involved in urban deliveries or longer-range shipments, is especially sensitive to congestion because it involves paid drivers, expensive equipment, and valuable cargo. This makes congestion-control measures all the more important, and also affects their design since values of time, vehicle dimensions, and typical time patterns of movements all differ from those of passenger cars. Truckers also tend to be part of professional associations and unions that have important public input into formulation of policies toward congestion. As one example, trucking associations in the United States have been resistant to broad pricing policies, but less so to proposals for tolled truck-only roads.

Trucks remain significant contributors to environmental problems, – notably air pollution, noise, and climate change. As is the case with passenger vehicles, we expect that, especially in the shorter run, most solutions to these problems will be through changes in vehicle technology. Nevertheless, modal shifts, especially from trucks to rail for inter-urban shipments, can play a role as well.

8.2   Emerging themes

In preceding chapters, we have written about several themes that have already received attention and are likely to become yet more prominent. One is the strategic use of information and better understanding of its benefits and its unexpected side effects. Automation, especially of vehicles, will sooner or later transform some aspects of urban transportation, probably in combination with greater use of artificial intelligence to guide private and public decisions. The interaction of automation with information is rich in possibilities. Another such issue is the health implications of active modes, including related safety issues. The production and use of big data will be an ongoing project. This in turn will increase the availability of ever-growing temporal, spatial, and individual resolution of information, making it likely that methods from machine learning will be integrated into empirical transportation modelling.

Another broad theme is that of regulation of markets in the sharing economy. It is clear that often, governments have difficulty anticipating the explosive growth that firms in the sharing economy can undergo; this is in large part due to the ability to greatly reduce costs in markets characterized by external scale economies among consumers. Concerns over the impacts of Airbnb on urban neighborhoods and hospitality industries, or of Uber on taxi firms and public transit, are illustrations. Furthermore, some emerging technologies for urban transportation can thrive only when external scale economies can be exploited. This is likely the case for Mobility as a Service; for automated driving; and for the sharing of cars, bikes and rides. This raises not only the classic dilemma between technological efficiency and market power, but also questions about market access and the control of supply by one or a few firms. These questions become even more complex because they interact importantly with societal concerns over the sustainability, safety, congestion, and inclusiveness of urban transport.

Security, in many forms, is likely to continue gaining in importance for transportation. Travel can be disrupted with long-lasting consequences by shocks such as natural disasters, infrastructure failures, labor strikes, and terrorist attacks. Furthermore, climate change threatens to create further shocks due to rising sea levels, extreme weather events, and, in cold climates, the melting of permafrost that underlies roads and other infrastructure. The effects of such shocks depend strongly on the vulnerability of transport links and the degree of network redundancy, issues that can be brought into rigorous economic analysis.

A different form of security for transportation involves disruptions in electricity supply. Even as the likely demand for electricity grows, an increased frequency of extreme conditions – droughts, fires, strong winds, and even cold weather – is adversely affecting electricity supply. The impact of such shocks similarly depends on the quality of individual links and on network redundancy, in this case of the electrical grid. Given the growing interdependence between transportation and electricity, research on their nexus should have a high payoff. We expect that big data and new research methods, such as machine learning, should improve understanding of extreme events and the most practical ways to ameliorate their effects, whether through protection or relocation of critical facilities, creation of redundant networks, or other means.

Cybersecurity is yet another security issue for transportation. It is already a concern for technologies that track individuals' movements for various reasons; it is also a concern for autonomous vehicles. Research has shown how AVs could be attacked through their control and autonomous-driving systems, as well as through vehicle-to-vehicle, vehicle-to-infrastructure, and vehicle-to-network communications (Kim *et al.* 2021).

One further issue is the role of behavioral economics, which deals with individual behavior that, at least on the surface, does not seem to pursue rational self-interest. As noted in Section

2.2, there is ample evidence of frequent departures from the simplest postulates of conventional demand analysis. There is no lack of examples in transportation. For one, travelers often underestimate the variable monetary costs of car travel: for example, they may consider only fuel costs and ignore costs of vehicle maintenance, vehicle depreciation, and accident risks. This misperception may contribute to the so-called "car effect" that may bias individuals toward car travel (Garcia-Sierra *et al.* 2015). Another example is overestimating the travel time of non-chosen routes (Vreeswijk *et al.* 2014), or overestimating the travel time savings of express lanes (as noted in Section 2.7.3). A third example is that drivers appear less sensitive to payments made electronically than those paid manually – a potential consideration for acceptability of pricing (Finkelstein 2009). A fourth is non-linear response to prices as they are raised from zero to some small value (Lehe 2019).

A further example is habitual behavior that persists when better alternatives exist. For example, people who move to a new city may initially experiment with travel-related choices, such as where to shop, until they find a satisfactory – although not necessarily optimal – outcome. Such behavior could be caused by myopically discounting the expected benefits of search. It could also result from a rational process of economizing on cognitive effort, a process sometimes called "rational inattention," as illustrated by Jiang *et al.* (2020). Habitual behavior can be disrupted by shocks, such as a subway strike, leading to long-term shifts in behavior (Larcom *et al.* 2017).

Yet another example of apparently irrational behavior is the energy efficiency paradox, discussed in Section 7.1.3, in which purchasers of cars appear to undervalue the monetary savings they will receive from greater fuel efficiency. As noted there, one potential source of this bias is a simple misperception of how fuel-efficiency ratings translate into cost savings.

These examples raise several questions. How large are these departures, and how persistent are they? What types of decisions do they most affect? When might they cause economic incentive systems to fail in their purpose, or even have perverse effects? How can incentives be altered to account for this? To address such questions, several approaches to research might be helpful.

First, the insights of the "credibility revolution" in empirical economics can be brought to transportation, as is in fact already happening. This is to say that empirical estimates can be designed to answer very specific questions, such as the responses to a particular policy innovation, taking advantage of natural experiments that eliminate some sources of spurious correlation. This approach typically involves estimating "reduced-form" economic models, meaning that the environment, however complex, is taken for what it is rather than trying to hold constant specific factors analytically. This has the advantage of minimizing tenuous theoretical assumptions, though it has the disadvantage of limiting the ability to extrapolate results to other situations.

As a second approach, laboratory experiments can play a larger role in our field. These offer the potential to place experimental subjects in situations comparable to those in which behavior might conflict with simple optimizing models. Other fields of economics have already developed a rich set of tools and results for such experiments.

Third, the insights of behavioral economics, an active field in its own right, can be better integrated into transportation research. Bowles (2016) argues that the very use of economic incentives based on self-interest may "crowd out" the more civic-minded behavior on which a healthy polity depends. Bowles provides several examples of how such incentives could be modified to avoid this drawback, and we encourage research on how such approaches might improve transportation policy. Indeed, the "messaging" proposed by Bowles is akin to some of the recommendations for how to improve public acceptance of pricing measures, as we review in Section 4.6.5.

Fourth, more can be learned about dissipation over time in behavior that appears non-rational. There are already hints in the experience to road pricing that people who say they will act in a way that appears non-rational act differently when presented with an actual situation. Often, their behavior adjusts fairly quickly toward optimization as they gain experience with implementation, and furthermore their acceptance of pricing schemes tends to increase over time – provided they retain trust in the authority that is implementing the pricing program.

Finally, the literature on "nudge" suggests many possibilities to alter behavior simply by redefining the default that occurs if a consumer takes no overt action. The classic example is investment portfolios for a retirement program: many people simply accept the default option, especially if it is difficult for them to evaluate various options. One can imagine examples being developed for transportation policy, for example in vehicle purchase or route choice.

8.3   Trends in transportation research

The themes described above imply the continuation or acceleration of certain trends that also characterize the wider field of economics. First, theory is becoming more applied – a result of both the growing availability of data and the increasing desire for empirically validated policy advice. Second, economic models are incorporating more complexity; in the transportation field this often stimulates collaboration among branches of economics and between economists and – among others – engineers, psychologists, environmental scientists, and geographers. Third, the modeling of individual economic actors is becoming more sophisticated: it is now possible to simultaneously consider multiple margins of traveler behavior – such as departure time, speed, and safety precautions – as well as the strategic behaviors of public and private operators.

Complexity is a two-edged sword. It can make research more readily applicable to real policy questions, but it also can make it more esoteric and difficult to understand. We think the former is happening more often than the latter, and that the resulting applicability to policy is very important. Thus, we believe that, on balance, complexity is helping economists to give better policy advice and to interact productively with policy-making professionals.

Transportation research not only benefits from research in other fields, but also stimulates it. For example, past developments in transportation economics, such as analysis of peak-load pricing and the random-utility model for discrete choice, were generalized for wide applications throughout the field of economics. We see no reason that this should not recur, especially because transportation problems are so pervasive and inherently interesting to so many people. It is most likely to recur if transportation economics remains open to influence from broader trends in economic research and in other allied fields. Without doubt, this activity will be fueled by an unending stream of new and interesting problems arising from society's mobility needs.

References

Bowles, Samuel (2016) *The Moral Economy: Why Good Incentives Are No Substitute for Good Citizens*, New Haven, CT: Yale University Press.

Finkelstein, Ami (2009) "E-ZTAX: tax salience and tax rates," *The Quarterly Journal of Economics* 124(3): 969–1010.

Garcia-Sierra, Mata, Jeroen C. J. M. van den Bergh and Carme Miralles-Guasch (2015), "Behavioural economics, travel behaviour and environmental-transport policy," *Transportation Research Part D: Transport and Environment* 41: 288–305. doi:10.1016/j.trd.2015.09.023.

Jiang, Gege, Mogens Fosgerau and Hong K. Lo (2020) "Route choice, travel time variability, and rational inattention," *Transportation Research Part B: Methodological* 132: 188–207.

Kim, Kyounggon, Jun Seok Kim, Seonghoon Jeong, Jo-Hee Park and Huy Kang Kim (2021) "Cybersecurity for autonomous vehicles: review of attacks and defense," *Computers & Security* 103: 102150

Larcom, Shaun, Ferdinand Rauch and Tim Willems (2017) "The benefits of forced experimentation: striking evidence from the London underground network," *Quarterly Journal of Economics* 132(4): 2019–2055.

Lehe, Lewis (2019) "Downtown congestion pricing in practice," *Transportation Research Part C: Emerging Technologies* 100: 200–223.

Vonk Noordegraaf, Diana, Jan Anne Annema and Bert van Wee (2014) "Policy implementation lessons from six road pricing cases," *Transportation Research Part A: Policy and Practice* 59: 172–191.

Vreeswijk, Jaap, Tom Thomas, Eric van Berkum and Bart van Arem (2014) "Perception bias in route choice," *Transportation* 41(6): 1305–1321.

Index

Note: Page numbers followed by "n" denote endnotes.